# The changing geography of the United Kingdom

# The changing geography of the United Kingdom

## Second edition

*Edited*
*for the*
*Institute of British Geographers*
*by*

# R. J. JOHNSTON and V. GARDINER

London and New York

Second edition first published 1991
by Routledge
11 New Fetter Lane, London EC4P 4EE

Simultaneously published in the USA and Canada
by Routledge
29 West 35th Street, New York, NY 10001

Reprinted 1992, 1995

© 1991 Institute of British Geographers

Typeset in Times by
J&L Composition Ltd, Filey, North Yorkshire
Printed and bound in Great Britain by
Biddles Ltd, Guildford and King's Lynn

*British Library Cataloguing in Publication Data*
A catalogue record for this book is available from the British Library

*Library of Congress Cataloguing in Publication Data*
A catalogue record for this book is available from the Library of Congress

ISBN 0-415-03242-3

# Contents

vi  *Contents*

# List of figures

# List of tables

# Contributors

**Mark Blacksell** is Dean of the Faculty of Social Studies and Senior Lecturer in the Department of Geography at the University of Exeter. His publications on recreation, leisure and the countryside include *The Countryside: Planning and Change* (with A. W. Gilg: Allen & Unwin 1981) and he edited the IBG's journal *Area* from 1980 to 1984.

**Ian R. Bowler** is Senior Lecturer in Geography at the University of Leicester. His publications on agricultural geography include *Government and Agriculture: A Spatial Perspective* (Longman 1978) and *Agriculture and the Common Agricultural Policy* (Manchester University Press 1985).

**Paul A. Bull** is Lecturer in Geography at Birkbeck College in the University of London.

**Keith Chapman** is Senior Lecturer in Geography at the University of Aberdeen. Among his publications on energy in the British Isles is *North Sea Oil and Gas: A Geographical Perspective* (David & Charles 1976).

**Paul A. Compton** is Professor of Geography at Queen's University, Belfast. His work on demography and population geography includes editing *Northern Ireland: A Census Atlas* (Gill and Macmillan 1978) and co-authoring, with John Coward, *Fertility and Family Planning in Northern Ireland* (Avebury 1989) and *Demographic Trends in Northern Ireland* (Northern Ireland Economic Council 1985).

**L. F. Curtis** was formerly National Park Officer for the Exmoor National Park and, before that, Reader in Geography at the University of Bristol.

**John A. Dawson** is Professor of Marketing at the University of Edinburgh. He was Honorary Secretary of the IBG from 1985 to 1988.

**Vince Gardiner** was formerly a Lecturer in Geography at the University of Leicester, and is now a civil servant. He was co-author, with R. V. Dackcombe, of *Geomorphological Field Manual* (Allen & Unwin 1982).

**D. T. Herbert** is Professor of Geography at University College, Swansea. His many publications in urban geography include, with C. J. Thomas, *Cities in Space: City as Place* (David Fulton 1990) and, coedited with David M. Smith, *Social Problems and the City* (Oxford University Press 1989).

**R. J. Johnston** is Professor of Geography at the University of Sheffield. He was Secretary of the IBG from 1982 to 1985 and President in 1990.

**David K. C. Jones** is Reader in Geography at the London School of Economics and Political Science: his publications include *The Geography of the British Isles: Southeast and Southern England* (Methuen 1981) and, with others, *Landshapes* (David & Charles 1988).

**Paul L. Knox** is Professor of Urban Affairs and Planning and Director of the Center for Urban and Regional Studies at Virginia Polytechnic Institute and State University. His publications include *The Geography of Western Europe* (Croom Helm 1984), *Urban Social Geography* (Longman 1987) and, with John Agnew, *The Geography of the World Economy* (Edward Arnold 1989).

**Malcolm J. Moseley** is Director of ACRE (Action with Communities in Rural England), the national association of England's Rural Community Councils, at Cirencester, Gloucestershire; he was formerly Reader in the School of Environmental Science at the University of East Anglia.

**Chris Park** is Principal of Furness College and Lecturer in Geography at the University of Lancaster. His publications on environmental management include *Acid Rain: Rhetoric and Reality* (Methuen 1987) and *Chernobyl: The Long Shadow* (Routledge, 1989).

**M. L. Parry** is Professor of Environmental Management at the University of Birmingham. His published land-use studies include *Climatic Change, Agriculture and Settlement* (Dawson, 1978) and *The Impact of Climatic Variations on Agriculture* (Kluwer, 1988). He has directed investigations of changes in British moorlands, published as *Surveys of Moorland and Roughland Change* (University of Birmingham, 1982).

**Peter J. Taylor** is Reader in Political Geography at the University of Newcastle upon Tyne. His recent books include *Political Geography: World-Economy, Nation-State and Locality* (Longman, 1989) and *Britain and the Cold War: 1945 as Geopolitical Transition* (Belhaven, 1990).

**B. J. Turton** is Senior Lecturer in Geography at the University of Keele; he edited *Public Issues in Transport* (1983) and coedited *Short-Sea Crossings and the Channel Tunnel* (1989), both published by the IBG's Transport Geography Study Group.

# Preface

The first edition of this book was published in 1982, as part of the celebrations marking the fiftieth anniversary of the foundation of the Institute of British Geographers. Its purpose was to summarize what geographers in the United Kingdom have learned about the changing geography of their country during those fifty years. The result was a very successful volume, which was well received, favourably reviewed, and purchased in substantial numbers.

Work on that book commenced in 1980, and most of it was written in 1981. A great deal has changed in the United Kingdom since then, reflecting both trends in the world economy over the decade and the policy directions launched by the Conservative government after its election in 1979 and sustained throughout the 1980s, following the Conservative party victories of 1983 and 1987. Much of that change is reflected in the country's geography – in, for example, spatial variations in unemployment and relative prosperity, patterns of land use, and the interrelationships between society and the physical environment. Thus by 1987 the book was clearly somewhat outdated, and needed to be replaced by a new edition rather than reprinted. With the exception of one of the editors and one of the chapter contributors, all those involved in the production of the first edition agreed to participate in the creation of a second, most of which was written in late 1988.

This entirely new book thus brings the story of *The Changing Geography of the United Kingdom* up to date. Its emphasis is on the recent past. For the first edition, contributors were constrained by its role in the celebrations of the Institute's fiftieth birthday and were required to cover the period 1932–82. That constraint was no longer important. Thus in the brief provided for this new edition, the authors were asked to retain a recent historical perspective but to focus on the last decade. This they have done, producing a detailed picture of changes in the geography of the United Kingdom during the 1980s.

As with the first edition, within the general brief the detailed organization and content for each chapter was left to the individual authors: editorial coordination has ensured a minimum of overlap. The authors have interpreted the brief according to their approaches to the relevant subject matter, and we have been more than happy to accept their interpretations. Thus there is no standard chapter format: indeed there could not be, because data availability on the various topics differs in both time and space. Unfortunately, there is still the relative paucity of data on Scotland and Northern Ireland that the editors commented on in the Preface to the first edition, so that some of the discussion is necessarily biased towards England and Wales.

In producing the book, our major debt is to the authors, who agreed to contribute, who responded to our proddings about deadlines despite their heavy workloads, and who produced such excellent material. We are extremely grateful to them. Thanks are also due to the secretaries and cartographers (especially Graham Allsopp) for the work they have done to assist in the book's production, to our publishers at Routledge (Eleanor Rivers and Tristan Palmer) for their support and assistance, and to the Officers and Council of the Institute for asking us to undertake this task on the membership's behalf and for their support during the years of toil that have resulted in this handsome volume.

Authors, editors, and publishers always hope for a wide readership, but the book is usually written for a more specific audience. Our hopes cover all those interested in the contemporary scene in the United Kingdom; our specifics are students of the country's geography. The synthesis presented here provides a valuable overview of recent changes and is a testament to the value of geographical scholarship in the quest to understand contemporary British society.

This, then, is a book about the United Kingdom (frequently referred to here, as elsewhere, as Britain, whose inhabitants are British). It is not about the country's geographers, nor about the Institute to which they belong. Its focus is the environment in which they work, and illustrates the richness and the relevance of British geographical scholarship.

R. J. Johnston                                           V. Gardiner
Sheffield                                                 Leicester

# 1 Introduction

*R. J. Johnston*

Change can be studied in two ways. The first involves establishing a baseline, a datum point against which the situation at other times (either before or after the datum) can be assessed. The second represents change as a continuous process for which baselines and the subdivision of time into distinct periods are arbitrary and artificial. If we use the first approach, therefore, we represent change as a series of steps; if we use the latter, it is presented as an unending process, though its pace may vary over both time and space.

The second of these two approaches is by far the most relevant to the study of geographical change, for major temporal discontinuities in the transformation of landscapes are rare. Certain punctuations can be recognized in the context of the present book – voting in a new government at a general election, for example – but even with these, most of the events are but landmarks in ongoing processes (changing political attitudes and affiliations in the quoted example) and their impact is often only slowly realized. Thus the basic theme in geographical studies of change must be one of continuous transformation. Unfortunately it is not always possible to achieve this ideal. Limitations in the availability of information mean that research must rely on the development of periodic snapshots only, which freeze the ongoing transformations: students of population geography, for example, rely very heavily on periodic (usually decennial) censuses, enhanced by annual surveys. If change is both continuous and unidirectional, this reliance on snapshots is constraining but unlikely to be misleading. If change is discontinuous and/or contains alterations in direction and rate, however, then cross-sectional viewing points may fail to reveal the major events or alterations. To circumvent this problem, geographers have learned to integrate the richness of information provided in the snapshots with an interpretative narrative of the ongoing transformations, as in the classic works on the historical geography of England edited by Sir Clifford Darby (1936, 1973).

No baseline has been established for the preparation of this book, therefore. Our primary focus is on the 1980s, but what occurred then cannot be understood in isolation from the events of earlier decades. Thus the various chapters are set in the context of an appreciation of preceding changes, and the present Introduction attempts no more than a very broad general background to the main concern.

## FROM RECESSION THROUGH WAR TO RECESSION ... AND OUT?

There is increasing support from social scientists of all persuasions for the identification of cyclical processes within the global capitalist economic system. Empirical studies have provided clear evidence of major cycles of about fifty-years duration each, frequently termed Kondratieff cycles after the economist who first brought them to prominence. Each cycle is characterized by a period of rapid economic expansion, as output increases and markets flourish, to be followed first by stagnation and then by recession, before the downward trend bottoms out and a new cycle is initiated. Within those long cycles, as they are also known, there are shorter cycles too, of varying length and intensity, but it is the Kondratieffs that are associated with major changes in the world economy, in the structure of national and local societies and in the practice of politics, both domestic and international.

The theory of capitalist crises, which underlies Kondratieff's work, is central to Marxian economic theory; as Peter Hall (1988: 49) expresses it:

> Capitalism does this because of its inherent logic ... Because of the accumulation of capital, by an iron arithmetic rule, the profit rate must fall. And further, since this results in substitution of capital for labour ... unemployment must rise. So capitalism must, by its own logic – its own success, in fact – come to crisis.

But what Marx failed to identify, and Kondratieff after him, according to Hall, is how capitalism recovers from those crises. This is answered, he says, by Joseph Schumpeter, whose analysis 'has the inevitable logic of Marx, but it explains why each time, capitalism overcomes its crisis'. The explanation lies in the process of innovation; as the recession at the end of a cycle deepens, entrepreneurs invest their capital in the manufacture and marketing of new products, based on inventions that have already been made. (The distinction between an invention and an innovation is crucial: an invention in this context is a scientific discovery; an innovation is the creation of a new, marketable product based on the invention – or perhaps several.) Thus recovery from recession involves entrepreneurs seizing opportunities, investing in potential profits at a time when labour and money are relatively cheap.

Recovery involves more than just the introduction of a new range of commodities to capitalist markets, however. As Hall notes, following Schumpeter, 'The key innovations are so great that they ... require enormous socio-cultural transformations' (1988: 49). Thus there is fre-quently a major geographical change in the focus of economic activity as the world economy climbs out of its fifty-year recession. To quote Hall (1988: 49–50) once more on this process of 'creative destruction':

> though the reciprocating mechanism itself has a monotonously regular rhythm, the necessary adjustments are so complex that they are far from regular or predictable. Some societies, some nations, may fail entirely to make them: their institutional structures or inherited cultures are simply too ossified. For them, Schumpeter's process of constant creative destruction may not be creative at all: the logic of capitalism has no mercy. The relentless decline in British innovative performance . . . tells its own story: this is a country that is failing to make the necessary leap from one Kondratieff to the next.

Thus some countries decline within the world economy and in their influence on international politics, while others increase both their relative prosperity and their political power. Within countries, too, some places (regions, individual towns) may decline as their local entrepreneurs fail to grasp opportunities, while others expand and prosper. The history of Kondratieff cycles is thus associated with a changing geography of economic activity, and all that goes with it, such as land use, exploitation of the environment, and social relationships in homes and communities.

The exact timing of the Kondratieff cycles is, not surprisingly, a focus of some debate among analysts, but the general pattern is agreed upon. The first after the Industrial Revolution is believed to have been initiated in 1787, and the succeeding 'bottoming out' covered the years 1825–42. The most recent complete cycle has been the fourth. The downswing of the third occurred between 1913 and 1925, and the succeeding upswing occupied the period 1935–48 (all of the dates are taken from van Duijn 1983). After a long period of decline, from 1951–74, the upswing into the fifth should have occurred during the 1980s: Peter Hall argues that 'according to Schumpeter's own chronology' (1988: 51) the nadir should have been in July 1987, with strong recovery thereafter.

As Hall and others make very clear, recovery from a long-cycle recession requires new institutional arrangements to promote the innovations. Some analysts of the fourth Kondratieff have characterized it by two main sets of arrangements: the mode of organizing production known as Fordism, with its emphasis on the mass production of consumer goods by disciplined labour forces in large factories; and the active role of the welfare state, following the dictates of Keynes's prognosis of the need for demand-led growth. Both have been replaced in order to promote the fifth, they contend: by a new 'regime of accumulation', variously termed 'flexible accumulation' and 'disorganized capitalism', whose main characteristics have been set out by Lash and Urry (1987), and by a redefinition of the role of the state, following the rejection of Keynesianism and the introduction of policies based on 'supply-side' economics, often known as 'monetarism' and promoted, *inter alia*, by Milton Friedman.

As we begin the upswing into the fifth Kondratieff in the United Kingdom, therefore, we are experiencing not just the rise of a new set of industries (both productive and service) but also the development of a wide range of new institutional structures. Nowhere is this more apparent than in the nature of the state. During the fourth cycle, the state was a major participant in the economy, as well as an increasingly important source of support for individuals, families, and entire communities; further, its participation in two major world wars did more than anything else to stimulate economic activity and extend its mechanisms of social control. That role for the state has been repudiated in the 1980s, with arguments that government controls should be relaxed, that markets should be allowed to operate much more freely, and that greater emphasis should be put on individual self-reliance, rather than the 'culture of dependency' that the welfare state had generated (Gamble 1988).

The 1980s have been a decade of major economic, social and political change, therefore, which has been firmly impressed on the United Kingdom landscape, as the chapters in this book clearly testify. We see that impress in the new organizational forms being adopted in agriculture; for example, in the patterns of land use that stem from these, and in the relationship between farming and the physical environment. Similarly, the older heavy industries, characteristic of the country's northern regions in particular, have declined very substantially, being replaced by new industries which are not only based on very different technologies and organizational structures but are also concentrated in different regions; the state has encouraged the new developments as the needed entrepreneurial response to recession, but has done very little to counter the locational shifts. Whereas during the fourth Kondratieff, governments did much to try and influence the geography of the country, in the fifth they are taking a much less assertive role and allowing market forces to rewrite the details of who does what where. Local governments, some of which still believe they can influence location patterns, attempt to attract investment to their territories, but are finding their degrees of freedom to be few and their ability to counter the general trends generally slight.

While the politicians and entrepreneurs involved may not appreciate the analysis of Kondratieff cycles – with its implication that their success will, of necessity, eventually bring about their failure – nevertheless what they are doing is clearly in line with what Marx, Kondratieff, Schumpeter and others anticipated, in general terms though not in detail. They are involved in a major restructuring of the economy, politics and social structuring of the United Kingdom, and as such they are involved in a major rewriting of the country's geography. This is thus a period of rapid and stimulating change, one which is clearly captured in the chapters of this book.

## CONCLUSION

In his classic paper on 'The changing English landscape' (1951), Sir Clifford Darby identified six themes in the creation of the present scene: clearing the woodland, draining the marsh, reclaiming the heath, the changing arable, the landscape garden, and towns and the seats of industry. Regarding the last of these, he noted that, although the greatest impact of the industrial revolution had been felt in the north and midlands, growth was now more apparent in the Home Counties. He finished with the statement that: 'He who walks abroad in the South may see on either hand the marks of this latest phase in the changing English landscape'. The present book is written by a group of geographers who have 'walked abroad' during that latest phase, and have identified its major marks.

Several of the themes that Darby identified are relevant to the period studied here; the major exceptions are the clearing of the woodland (more is now being planted) and the landscape garden (though the latter theme could be expanded to incorporate the growing interest in urban design and landscape architecture, stimulated by the Prince of Wales). Marshlands are still being drained and heathlands reclaimed, despite the protests of conservationists, and the distribution of population and economic activity is far from static. Many of these changes represent the country's economic condition. Professor Darby used the adjectives 'dreary', 'wretched' and 'satanic' to describe British industrial landscapes, for example (and was criticized by Professor East: 'I am not sure that geographers should indulge in such emotional reactions'). Whether those adjectives provide apt descriptions of what British society has done to its landscape in the last thirty years is a moot point, but much change there most certainly has been, throughout the length and breadth of the United Kingdom.

The main themes of this book are economic, political and social transformation in the United Kingdom during recent years, as they are reflected in the country's geography. They thus follow in the long tradition of writing on the country's landscapes, as set by Sir Clifford Darby, W. G. Hoskins and others. Most of those writers focus on the long view, emphasizing the many millennia of human occupance and their imprint on the country's scene. What we emphasize here, however, is that within the latest of the major periods of landscape change, covering the last two centuries only, the country's geography has been substantially rewritten several times, and it is happening again now. Coones and Patten (1988) recognize that change has been extensive in the present century and whole new landscapes are being created: they claim that study of the contemporary changes and the forces creating them would require a book in itself, but are only able to provide a brief eight-page overview. Here we take up their implicit challenge, and within the context set by our predecessors chart what is happening to the United Kingdom's geography during this period of rapid and extensive change.

## REFERENCES

Coones, P. and Patten, J. (1988) *The Penguin Guide to the Landscape of England and Wales,* London: Penguin.

Darby, H. C. (ed.) (1936) *An Historical Geography of England before* AD *1800,* Cambridge: Cambridge University Press.

Darby, H. C. (1951) 'The changing English landscape', *The Geographical Journal,* 67: 377–98.

Darby, H. C. (ed.) (1973) *A New Historical Geography of England,* Cambridge: Cambridge University Press.

Duijn, J. J. van (1983) *The Long Wave in Economic Life,* London: George Allen & Unwin.

Gamble, A. M. (1988) *The Free Economy and the Strong State,* London: Macmillan.

Hall, P. (1988) 'The intellectual history of long waves', in Young, M. and Schuller, T. (eds.) *The Rhythms of Society,* London: Routledge, pp. 37–52.

Lash, S. and Urry, J. (1987) *The End of Organized Capitalism,* Cambridge: Polity Press.

# 2 The changing use of land

*M. L. Parry*

All but a few of the 24 million ha of land in the United Kingdom are used for some purpose. Indeed, the general intensity of land use – a reflection of the limited land per head and the fact that very little land is intrinsically unusable – is a characteristic feature of the United Kingdom. Even in regions of less intensive use, such as the mountains and moorlands, the pattern is complicated by the number of competing users.

Given this complexity, it should not be surprising that our record of land use in the United Kingdom is not precise. In fact the record is somewhat fragmentary, particularly because very much more is known about land use in rural than in urban areas. This may seem curious when one considers that more than three-quarters of the population lives in towns and that a central concern of land-use planning in the United Kingdom since the Second World War has been the containment of urban types of land use. Yet until 1975, when local authorities in England and Wales were asked to record changes in urban land use, there was no mechanism by which these uses could accurately be measured. Since the mid-1980s the Department of the Environment (DOE) has conducted a trial project on monitoring land-use change, but much of the record remains incomplete and there remains doubt, as we shall see later, as to the precise extent of the UK urban area.

Part of the uncertainty stems from an imprecise definition of terms. Although, in a strict sense, the term 'land use' applies to *activity* on the land surface and not to the *appearance* of the land surface, the major sources of land-use data in the United Kingdom (the two Land Use Surveys of 1931–9 and 1961–9) were essentially concerned with mapping land *cover*. For example, they recorded the extent of heath and rough grassland (and, in the case of the Second Land Use Survey, the types of rough grassland) rather than the use being made of these areas – whether these were agricultural, recreational, or military. Land-use data in the United Kingdom can therefore more appropriately be described as a mirror of the economic and social activity on the land surface than as a specific record of that activity, and changes in the pattern of these 'land-use' data are a general surface expression of underlying changes in the economic and social geography of the country. As a pointer, then, to the changing 'look' of the land surface and to underlying trends which will be evaluated in subsequent chapters, this chapter describes the major changes in land use that have occurred in the United Kingdom over the past fifty years and particularly over the past twenty. The emphasis is on description – the explanation for many changes in land use will be found in chapters dealing with specific facets of the country's changing geography.

**SOURCES OF INFORMATION**

There are two types of land-use data for the United Kingdom. The first are data recorded either from field observation or by remote sensing. The earliest comprehensive data of this type are those from the Land Utilization Survey of the 1930s directed by L. Dudley Stamp for Great Britain and by D. A. Hill for Northern Ireland. The map sheets of the British survey were published at the 1:63,360 scale, although the manuscript 1:10,560 sheets survive in the London School of Economics. The Second Land Use Survey, directed by Alice Coleman, was completed for England and Wales in the late 1960s and sample resurveys were carried out in the 1970s. By 1989, about 1,000 of the six-inch manuscript sheets had been published at the 1:25,000 scale; the remainder can be studied in the Department of Geography at King's College, London. In addition, a survey of urban areas using 1969 aerial photography was completed by the DOE in 1978, and further surveys of landscape change from 1948 to 1980 were completed by the DOE in 1986. Over 1986–88 the DOE conducted a three-year trial estimation of changes of land use in England and Wales. These specific surveys supplement land-use data included on 1:10,000 and 1:50,000 Ordnance Survey maps which are subject to sporadic or continuous revision and which have been used to calculate changes in the urban area, and in woodland and rough grazing.

Second, there are statistical data of low resolution collected by government departments or agencies. For agricultural uses these are published annually. They are based on returns from farmers of their crop acreages and only incidentally are they therefore a source of information on land use. Information on woodland is published annually for individual conservancies, and more limited data on the recreational use of land are available for National Parks. Data on urban land uses, mineral workings and water-gathering grounds have been collected more sporadically. A comprehensive review of these data sources has been prepared by J. T. Coppock and L. F. Gebbett (1978).

In most cases these data are not compatible. They relate to different administrative units and to different periods of time, and employ different classifications of land-use type. Yet they reflect two enduring themes in the study of land use in the United Kingdom. The first of these, which has its origin in the 1930s, is that rural land is scarce and has, for some time, been under pressure from an expanding urban area. The second, and more recent, theme is that the character of the rural landscape is undergoing a radical change due to the modernization of farming practices. A result of this is a shift of concern away from the need to restrict the *quantity* of change in land use (especially of farmland transfers to urban use) towards the need to protect the *quality* of the landscape from the effects of new land uses. In fact, both themes are fuelled by a 'heady' mixture of myth and reality.

## CHANGING PATTERNS

### Pre-war patterns of land use

It is fortunate that the baseline of our period of study (1933) should be marked by a comprehensive record of land use in the UK, (the Land Utilization Surveys), but it is probably not a coincidence. The surveys, which were started in England in 1931, drew together a large number of geographers both in organizing the field work and in preparing the County Reports. It was a track on which geographers were to show their paces and was part of a phase of growing interest in the subject which included, in 1933, the establishment of the Institute of British Geographers. Before this time, the only land-use data available were for agricultural land and had been collected annually by government departments since 1866. These data were analysed and published in the 1930s as a collection of maps in agricultural atlases for England and Wales (by M. Messer 1932) and Scotland (by H. J. Wood 1931). Censuses of woodland in Great Britain had been taken in 1924 and 1939, but there was no national measure of urban land, only of land 'unaccounted for' by the agricultural returns, a figure much larger than the area not actually being farmed.

The discrepancy between the figures for Great Britain from the Land Utilization Survey and from the acreage returns from farmers reflects the fact that one was essentially a measure of land cover and the other of land use (table 2.1). Thus the survey recorded a larger area under a cover of rough pasture or heath than the area officially recorded as rough grazing, since some mountain land was not returned as agricultural land. But both sets of data indicate a broad mix of land uses in Great Britain which has not changed greatly since the 1930s (figure 2.1). One-third of the farmland is covered by rough, semi-natural vegetation used largely for extensive grazing by sheep and cattle. In the 1930s the only major transfers of use from grazing were to forestry – to new plantings by the Forestry Commission (established in 1919) and replantings of woodland felled in the 1914–18 war. In England and Wales these 'losses' from rough grazing were exceeded by gains due to the invasion of pastures by sedge and bracken and to the direct reversion of arable to rough pasture.

*Table 2.1* Land use in Great Britain, c. 1931

| | Land Utilization Survey 1931–9 | | Agricultural statistics 1931 | |
|---|---|---|---|---|
| | area (000 ha) | % | area (000 ha) | % |
| Arable (incl. orchards) | 4,990 | 21.9 | 5,113 | 22.5 |
| Permanent grass | 7,647 | 33.5 | 6,994 | 30.7 |
| Rough grazing | 7,598 | 33.3 | 5,995 | 26.4 |
| Forest and woodland | 1,303 | 5.7 ⎫ | | |
| Houses with gardens | 696 | 3.1 ⎬ | 4,643 | 20.4 |
| Land agriculturally unproductive | 566 | 2.5 ⎭ | | |
| Total area | 22,800 | | 22,744 | |

*Source:* Stamp 1962

Within the sector of improved farmland, which covered two-thirds of the agricultural area in the United Kingdom, depressed demand for agricultural products was encouraging the turnover of arable to permanent grass. In eastern England this was less marked, but elsewhere the trend seems to have been quite widespread. Arable land in the United Kingdom declined by about 8 per cent between 1931 and 1938 (figure 2.2). Moreover, the depressed agricultural land market and absence of development control, combined with an increased mobility offered by the cheap motor car, led to the rapid suburban development of farmland. Between 1936 and 1939 an average of 25,000 ha of farmland in England and Wales was transferred to urban use every year. The overall pattern of land-use change in the 1930s is indicated in figure 2.3.

**Wartime changes in land use**

The decline in the arable area continued until 1938. Thereafter, the influence of ploughing grants backed up by the compulsory powers of the County War Agricultural Executive Committees brought a reverse in the trend. The arable acreage increased by about 8 per cent in each year between 1940 and 1943 and by about half that amount in 1944. While, in national terms, this represents by far the most marked change in the fifty-year period (see figure 2.2), the effects of the war varied greatly from region to region. In the eastern counties, where almost all suitable land was already under the plough, there was little change. But in the predominantly grassland counties of the East and West Midlands the change was spectacular. In Leicestershire, for example, the extent of arable increased from 13 to about 46 per cent of the farmed area. The result was a change in the look of the land: where once the patchwork of midland arable had picked out the light or loamy soils, there was now a scatter of tillage over the whole, and the old distinctions between different types of land became less apparent.

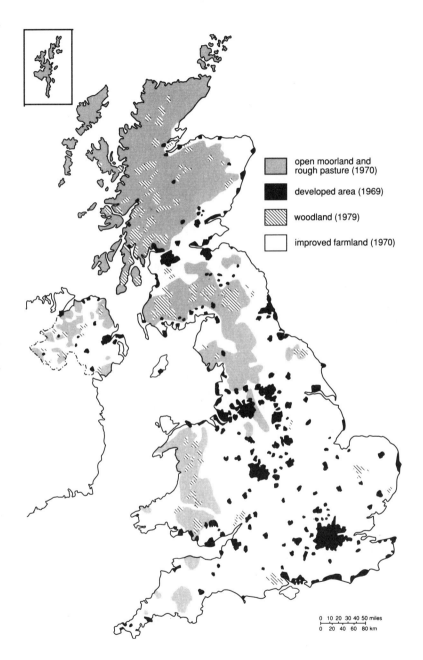

*Figure 2.1* Major land uses in the United Kingdom
*Source:* roughland – O.S. maps; woodland – Forestry Commission, *Annual Report, 1987;*
developed areas – Department of the Environment 1978

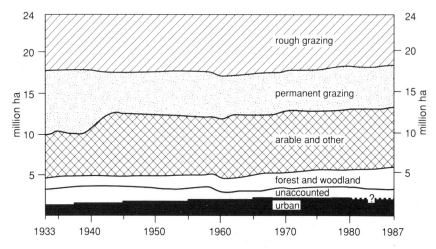

*Figure 2.2* Land-use changes in the United Kingdom, 1933–87 *Note:* In 1932 and 1959 rough grazing was redefined and, as a consequence, the amounts returned increased by 360,000 ha and 600,000 ha respectively. Annual data for agriculture and woodland, decadal estimates for urban area
*Source:* Agricultural Statistics

Here, and on the pastures of Wales, Scotland and Northern Ireland, where the inter-war years had seen a landscape neglected of farming investment, the wartime stimulus to farming promoted a rejuvenated management of the more obvious facets of the countryside – its hedges, woods and fences.

There were two other lasting changes in the national land-use pattern. First, there was the transfer of land to the Air Ministry and the War Office. Between 1939 and 1945 some 230,000 ha, representing about 1 per cent of improved farmland in England and Wales, was given over to the services. Much of this had been arable: more than 140 wartime airfields were constructed in East Anglia alone. About one-third was returned to its former use by 1954, but the remainder represented a permanent change of use (table 2.2).

Second, there was extensive felling of timber. A detailed survey by the Forestry Commission in 1946–7 revealed that a fifth of the forest and woodland in Britain had been cut over in the war years (table 2.3). Most of the felled woodland had been privately owned because nearly all the Commission's plantations were immature. The Commission itself had continued to plant on a small scale during the war, with the result that the area officially recorded as forest (a figure which includes clear-felled land) actually increased in these years (see figures 2.2 and 2.8); the extent of mature, and especially broadleaved, woodland had been greatly reduced, however.

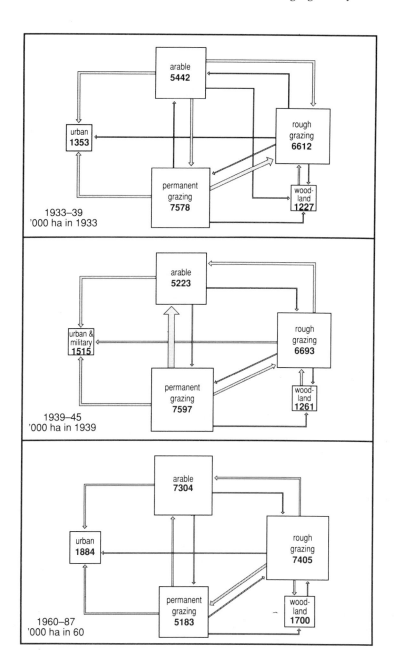

*Figure 2.3* Major land-use shifts, 1931–9, 1939–45, and 1960–87 *Note:* Arrows are a schematic, not quantitative, representation of land-use shifts
*Source:* Agricultural Statistics

*Table 2.2* Net changes in agricultural areas in England and Wales (wartime and post-war periods) (000 ha)

| | Building and general constructional development | Sports grounds | Air Ministry | War Office | Miscellaneous, mainly government departments | Total |
|---|---|---|---|---|---|---|
| 1939/40–1941/2 | 16.6 | −10.8 | 64.8 | 86.1 | 5.9 | 162.6 |
| 1942/3–1944/5 | 20.3 | −0.2 | 37.7 | 43.6 | 8.4 | 109.8 |
| 1945/6–1947/8 | 43.7 | 10.5 | −33.9 | −29.3 | 2.7 | − 6.3 |
| 1948/9–1950/1 | 34.1 | 10.0 | − | − | −16.1 | 28.0 |
| 1951/2–1953/4 | 39.2 | 4.1 | − | − | −6.9 | 36.4 |

*Source:* Stamp 1962

*Table 2.3* Forest and woodland in Great Britain, 1947 (000 ha)

| | *England* | *Wales* | *Scotland* | *Britain* |
|---|---|---|---|---|
| High forest | 417 | 75 | 232 | 724 |
| Coppice | 136 | 8 | 0.2 | 144 |
| Scrub | 81 | 16 | 104 | 201 |
| Devastated | 43 | 5 | 14 | 62 |
| Felled | 81 | 24 | 163 | 268 |
| Total | 758 | 128 | 513 | 1,399 |

*Source:* Census of woodland (1947–9) in Stamp 1962

**Agents of post-war land-use change**

The present use of land – and the resulting landscape – is the result of a myriad management decisions. In the rural sector alone there are about 271,000 separate holdings (units of management) in the United Kingdom, though fewer farmers because some operate linked holdings. About one-half of these farmers are also landowners; the remainder are tenants whose management decisions are constrained by conditions of lease from the owner. Ownership of land in the United Kingdom is thus a key to its use.

Many of the land-use decisions made by owners and tenants are, of course, a response to the market. But a particular feature of the United Kingdom since 1947 has been the increasing extent to which the array of decisions has been constrained by legislation and the increasing proportion of land controlled by non-profit-making public or semi-public institutions. We shall deal with these in turn.

The Town and Country Planning Act, 1947 (modified in 1962, 1968 and 1971) forms the basis of UK land-use planning, providing for control of urban development or changes in the use of land, and for preparation of

Structure Plans (formerly Development Plans) or Local Plans. Planning authorities thus have the power to permit, impose conditions on, or refuse applications for countryside development, except those related to agriculture and forestry.

In contrast to what is probably the most comprehensive system of land-use planning in the world, British attempts to manage and protect the rural landscape have been relatively weak. The National Parks and Access to the Countryside Act, 1949 created the National Parks but gave their Authorities few powers and insufficient resources. They were strengthened by further legislation in 1968 and 1972 but, with some exceptions, have no greater powers than those of a planning authority. There is, however, increasing use of management agreements, under which farmers are compensated for not taking certain courses of action which might damage the countryside. There is also provision under the Wildlife and Countryside Act, 1981 for grant-aid from the Ministry of Agriculture to farmers in England and Wales for assistance in landscape maintenance.

The pattern of land use since the war has also been increasingly affected by the extension of public ownership. About 11 per cent of freehold farmland and forest land and about 19 per cent of rented farmland in the UK is owned by public or semi-public institutions. The Forestry Commission, with 1,215,000 ha, is by far the largest single landowner in Britain (table 2.4). Government departments hold about 803,000 ha, the largest of these being the Ministries of Defence and Transport. Land in transport is largely exclusive of other uses, but about one-fifth of the training grounds of the armed services are also farmed. Other large owners are the National Coal Board (now British Coal: 108,500 ha, nearly two-thirds of which is farmed) and the water industry (252,000 ha, 72 per cent farmed). Local authority smallholdings cover about half a million hectares. Most of the remaining institutional land is in the hands of the National Trust, about a half of which is farmed.

Recent entrants into the farmland market have been financial institutions – insurance companies, pension funds and property unit trusts – which have bought tenanted land and leased it back to farmers. There has, however, been a growing tendency for these to buy with vacant possession and install their own managers, and there is some concern amongst the conservation lobby that this will be a growing force for brutal change in the countryside.

By contrast, those areas which have seen little change in use and are, to some extent, protected from the pressures described above, are the commons. In the lowland counties these comprise less than 2 per cent of the land surface, but in the south-west, in Wales and northern England they amount to almost 9 per cent. More than 10 per cent of rough grazings in Scotland are common pastures.

Table 2.4 Institutional ownership of rural land in Great Britain, 1971 (ha)

| | England | | Wales | | Scotland | | Great Britain | |
|---|---|---|---|---|---|---|---|---|
| | Total | Farming | Total | Farming | Total | Farming | Total | Farming |
| The Monarchy | | | | | | | | |
| Crown Estates | 84,681 | 64,186 | – | – | 35,323 | 32,375 | 120,004 | 96,561 |
| Duchy of Cornwall | 52,165 | 52,144 | – | – | – | – | 52,165 | 52,144 |
| Duchy of Lancaster | 19,466 | 15,216 | 1,700 | – | – | – | 21,166 | 15,216 |
| Sub-total | 156,312 | 131,546 | 1,700 | – | 35,323 | 32,375 | 193,335 | 163,921 |
| Forestry Commission | 307,197 | 16,800 | 159,498 | 15,800 | 748,292 | 141,198 | 1,214,987 | 173,798 |
| Government departments | | | | | | | | |
| Department of Agriculture and Fisheries for Scotland | na | – | – | – | 181,314 | 181,314 | 181,314 | 181,314 |
| Department of Health | – | – | na | – | na | – | 12,141 | – |
| Department of Trade and Industry | 537 | 249 | – | – | 2,023 | 554 | 2,560 | 803 |
| Ministry of Agriculture, Fisheries and Food | 10,181 | 9,646 | 1,731 | 1,731 | – | – | 11,912 | 11,377 |
| Ministry of Defence | 190,000 | 48,503 | 20,534 | 484 | 19,886 | 1,190 | 230,420 | 50,177 |
| Ministry of Transport | na | – | na | – | na | – | 364,221 | – |
| Sub-total | 200,718 | 58,398 | 22,265 | 2,215 | 203,223 | 183,058 | 802,568 | 243,671 |

| Nationalized industries and public services | | | | | | | | |
|---|---|---|---|---|---|---|---|---|
| British Airports Authority | 1,954 | — | | — | 497 | — | 2,451 | — |
| British Railways Board | na | — | na | — | na | — | 89,032 | — |
| British Waterways Board | na | — | na | — | na | — | 5,261 | — |
| Central Electricity Generating Board | 1,781 | 93 | 81 | — | na | na | 1,862 | 93 |
| Gas Boards | 3,586 | 134 | 187 | 2 | 343 | 12 | 4,116 | 148 |
| National Coal Board | 70,340 | 44,034 | 18,981 | 6,144 | 19,210 | 13,212 | 108,531 | 63,390 |
| Water undertakings (excl. local authorities) | 126,162 | 88,133 | 19,170 | 6,837 | 106,945 | 87,567 | 252,277 | 182,537 |
| Sub-total | 203,823 | 132,394 | 38,419 | 12,983 | 126,995 | 100,791 | 463,530 | 246,168 |
| Local authorities | 377,115 | 323,438 | 58,238 | 52,746 | 31,877 | 5,463 | 467,230 | 381,647 |
| Agricultural Research Council and other experimental farms | 2,231 | 2,231 | 448 | 448 | 4,649 | 4,749 | 7,328 | 7,328 |
| Universities and colleges | 78,070 | 72,858 | 1,299 | 546 | 4,698 | 3,828 | 84,067 | 77,232 |
| 'Conservation' authorities | 144,204 | 68,094 | 24,333 | 13,432 | 58,276 | 52,428 | 226,813 | 133,954 |
| Church land | 66,649 | 63,866 | na | — | na | — | 66,649 | 63,866 |
| Financial institutions | na | — | na | — | na | — | 40,469 | 40,469 |
| TOTAL | 1,536,319 | 869,625 | 306,200 | 98,170 | 1,213,333 | 523,790 | 3,566,976 | 1,532,054 |

*Source:* Harrison, Tranter, and Gibbs 1977

na = not available

*Table 2.5* The changing land-use structure, 1935–80 (per cent of total)

| | Rough grazings | Permanent pasture | Arable and other[a] | Woodland | Urban | Unaccounted for[b] |
|---|---|---|---|---|---|---|
| **England and Wales** | | | | | | |
| 1935 | 14.6 | 41.9 | 25.3 | 5.7 | 7.6 | 4.9 |
| 1939 | 14.9 | 42.3 | 24.1 | 6.2 | 8.6 | 3.9 |
| 1951 | 14.7 | 29.0 | 36.8 | 6.5 | 8.9 | 4.1 |
| 1961 | 13.4[c] | 29.0 | 36.7 | 6.9 | 9.9 | 4.1 |
| 1971 | 12.5 | 26.4 | 37.7 | 7.4 | 11.0 | 5.0 |
| 1980 | 11.4 | 26.4 | 36.3 | 8.0 | 11.6 | 6.3 |
| 1987 | 11.3 | 26.3 | 39.9 | nd | nd | nd |
| **% change in category 1935–61** | ,−8.0 | −31.0 | +45.0 | +21.0 | +30.0 | −16.0 |
| **% change in category 1961–87** | −15.0 | −31.0 | +10.0 | +16.0[d] | +11.0[d] | +54.0[d] |
| **Great Britain** | | | | | | |
| 1931 | 26.4 | 30.7 | 22.5 | 5.6 | 5.0 | 9.8 |
| 1961 | 30.9[c] | 20.7 | 30.4 | 7.4 | 7.4 | 3.2 |
| 1971 | 28.2 | 19.3 | 30.5 | 8.2 | 8.2 | 5.6 |
| 1980 | 26.8 | 20.0 | 29.1 | 8.9 | 8.5 | 6.7 |
| 1987 | 25.3 | 20.1 | 31.7 | 10.1 | nd | nd |
| **United Kingdom** | | | | | | |
| 1971 | 27.7 | 20.5 | 30.0 | 7.9 | 8.0 | 5.9 |
| 1980 | 25.9 | 21.3 | 29.0 | 8.7 | 8.4[e] | 6.9 |
| 1987 | 24.7 | 21.2 | 31.3 | 9.8 | nd | nd |

*Sources:* Agricultural Statistics 1935–87; data on urban area compiled by Best 1981
*Notes:*
[a] Includes fallow, temporary grass and orchards
[b] Includes unutilized rural land and land which has escaped enumeration under other headings
[c] In 1959 'rough grazing' was redefined and, as a consequence, the amount returned increased by about 600,000 ha
[d] % change in category 1961–80
[e] Data in 1979
nd: no data

## THE MODERN LAND-USE STRUCTURE

The impression given by official statistics summarized in figure 2.2 is that the present land-use structure of the United Kingdom, if not its landscape, is not substantially different from that in 1930. This impression is misleading for it is derived from aggregate figures which disguise both major changes in regional pattern and substantial internal adjustments between land-use types. The largest of these adjustments has occurred at the moorland edge, as an interchange between permanent grazing and rough grazing. But the transfers of land from agricultural to urban use, from permanent grazing to arable, and from farmland to woodland, have probably had more far-reaching impacts on the landscape (figure 2.3). Tables 2.5 and 2.6 indicate both the relative importance of these changes and the differences in the extent, which are revealed when contrasting sets of data are used. Table 2.5, compiled from data collected by R. H. Best (1981), is based upon official agricultural statistics and a study of local authority Development Plans. Table 2.6 is a comparison by A. Coleman (1977) of the two Land Use Surveys of Great Britain. Both indicate substantial increases in the urban and forested areas although, as we shall see later, the authors draw different interpretations from the data on urban growth. Moreover, the Land Use Survey data point to more substantial changes in rough pasture and arable than do the data collected from the farmer, a discrepancy due largely to differences in definition.

*Table 2.6* The changing land-use structure, from Land Use Survey data, England and Wales, 1933–63 (per cent of total area)

|          | Rough land | Permanent pasture | Arable | Woodland | Settlement | Water |
|----------|------------|-------------------|--------|----------|------------|-------|
| 1933     | 15.6       | 44.1              | 26.6   | 5.7      | 7.2        | 0.9   |
| 1963     | 12.8       | 29.2              | 38.1   | 8.0      | 10.8       | 1.1   |
| % change | −18        | −34               | +43    | +42      | +49        | +23   |

*Source:* Coleman 1977

Despite the imperfect data we can detect four major components in the pattern of changing land use: the growth of urban areas and their changing composition, changes in the agricultural sector (particularly between roughland and improved land, tillage and pasture), the extension of forest and woodland, and, finally, the growing competition for rural land from quasi-urban uses (for example, recreation and water-gathering). We shall consider these components in turn.

**The growth of urban land**

One of the dominant forces for change in post-war British land use has been the growth of the urban area. Its dual corollary has been the loss of rural land and the suburbanization of the more accessible countryside. These themes, and the extent to which planning control has 'succeeded' in reducing their impact, have been points of quite heated debate among

geographers. Much of the disagreement stems from differences in definition of terms which have led to variations in data. But even where the data
are the same there have been sufficient differences in interpretation to fuel
the argument.

The problem starts with any assessment of the extent of urban land.
Should it be defined so as to include all built-up land, including open spaces
in towns as well as the area under roads and railways in the countryside?
Such was the definition adopted by R. H. Best (1981) and A. G. Champion
(1979) in their calculations of the urban area. Should it exclude large open
spaces within the urban fence (an approach followed by R. C. Fordham
1974)? Should it include agricultural land, woodland, derelict land and
heaths where these are completely enclosed by urban uses (cf. the survey
of 'Developed Areas' by the Department of the Environment 1978)? And,
finally, how far do these assessments differ from that of settlement use,
including dispersed rural settlement (cf the Second Land Use Survey)?
These questions – and the various ways in which they have been answered
– have led to varying estimates of the extent of urban land and settlement
(table 2.7).

*Table 2.7* Estimates of urban land in England and Wales (000 ha)

| Source | Approximate date of survey | Area | % total area |
| --- | --- | --- | --- |
| R. H. Best (1981) | 1971 | 1,646 | 11.0 |
| R. H. Best (1981) | 1961 | 1,490 | 9.9 |
| A. Coleman (1977) | 1963 | 1,629[a] | 10.8 |
| R. C. Fordham (1974) | 1969 | 1,481 | 9.8 |
| Department of the Environment (1978) | 1969 | 1,485 | 9.8 |

*Note:* [a] Relates to area of settlement use, including dispersed rural settlement and rural roads

At the same time different data sources have yielded slightly different
information on the overall rate at which the urban area is growing.
Fordham's (1974) estimates, based on a sample survey of Ordnance
Survey maps, are lower than those by Best, (1981), which are based
upon a study of local authority Development Plans and which include
dispersed built-up land (table 2.8). It was intended that a more accurate
assessment of changes in land use would be possible from additions to the
Department of Environment's Survey of Developed Areas, published in
1978. This survey has been criticized, however, on the grounds that it
has only mapped developed areas which are greater than 5 ha. Small,
dispersed areas have been omitted. Moreover, subsequent checks against
independent sources of land-use data have revealed some sizeable
discrepancies.

*Table 2.8* Changing extent of urban land in Great Britain (000 ha)

| Source | 1951 | % change 1951–61 | 1961 | % change 1961–71 | 1971 |
|---|---|---|---|---|---|
| Great Britain R. H. Best (1981) | 1,529 | 9.5 | 1,689 | 9.7 | 1,871 |
| R. C. Fordham (1981) | 1,415 | 9.1 | 1,571 | 10.0 | 1,746 |
| | 1947 | % change 1947–69 | 1969 | % change 1969–80 | 1980 |
| England and Wales | 8,528 | 40.3 | 11,966 | 12.0 | 13,406 |

More recently, the DOE's Monitoring Landscape Change Project completed, in 1987, a systematic sample survey of land use from aerial photographs taken in 1947, 1969, and 1982. This analysis tends to confirm the preceding estimates of the rate of growth of the UK urban area – that this is advancing at an average rate of about 10 per cent per decade.

If this were the whole issue the debate over the threat to the countryside would probably be less fierce. But there are two other factors which cause concern. First, there are considerable regional differences in the extent of the urban area. Along the industrial axis that runs from the north-west of England through the midlands to the south-east, it exceeds one-tenth of the land – in the north-west alone it approaches one-quarter. Once again, we cannot be sure of the precise amounts because different sources give different data (table 2.9), but there is no doubt that much of these regions already have a substantially urban flavour, and that, consequently, undeveloped countryside is a particularly scarce resource.

The second cause for concern has been that in the 1950s the most rapid rates of urban growth continued to occur in the most 'urbanized' regions (for example, the East Midlands and the South-east), thus further eroding the already diminished countryside. In the 1960s, however, growth was concentrated in the less 'urbanized' regions (East Anglia, Wales and the South-west), and was *least* in the South-east. The turnabout can partly be explained by changes in the pattern of population growth, and partly by changing urban space standards. Best (1981) has illustrated this by pointing out that Lancashire and Durham, which experienced absolute decreases in population in the 1960s, had some of the highest figures for urban growth. Here the redevelopment of many industrial towns and construction of new estates on green-field sites had involved the extensive conversion of farmland.

Table 2.9 Regional pattern of urban land uses

| Economic planning region | Total urban area as % of administrative area | | | % growth of urban area | | | |
|---|---|---|---|---|---|---|---|
| | 1961 (R. C. Fordham 1974) | 1969 (Dept. of the Environment 1978) | 1970 (A. G. Champion 1974) | 1951–61 (R. C. Fordham 1974) | 1961–71 (R. C. Fordham 1974) | 1960–70 (A. G. Champion 1974) | 1969–88 (Dept. of the Environment 1986) |
| South-east | 13.0 | 17.4 | 18.7 | 10 | 11 | 7.5 | 8.1 |
| West Midlands | 12.0 | 11.8 | 13.4 | 12 | 11 | 11.8 | 10.9 |
| North-west | 22.0 | 21.8 | 25.7 | 9 | 12 | 11.7 | 16.6 |
| Northern | 7.0 | 5.7 | 6.9 | 11 | 12 | 12.7 | 14.4 |
| Yorkshire and Humberside | 10.0 | 9.9 | 11.8 | 10 | 11 | 10.3 | 12.4 |
| East Midlands | 9.0 | 9.0 | 11.2 | 18 | 16 | 10.7 | 17.1 |
| East Anglia | 4.0 | 6.8 | 6.9 | 11 | 17 | 9.9 | 13.8 |
| South-west | 7.0 | 6.1 | 7.7 | 10 | 15 | 11.9 | 8.5 |
| Wales | 3.0 | 4.2 | 6.7 | 15 | 16 | 13.3 | 27.3 |
| England and Wales | 8.9 | 9.8 | 11.4 | | | 10.4 | 11.9 |
| Scotland | 3.0 | ND | ND | 3 | 1 | | |
| Northern Ireland | 6.0 | ND | ND | 3 | 9 | | |
| United Kingdom | 6.8 | ND | ND | 11 | 11 | | |

Note: nd: no data

## The rate of loss of farmland

The rate of conversion of agricultural land to urban use has been a focus of the debate on urban growth. On the one hand, those working with data derived from the annual agricultural census have concluded that the rate of farmland loss in Britain is relatively low when compared with other developed countries, that it is being contained by the planning system, and that it should give no cause for great concern. On the other hand, those working with data from the Land Use Surveys see a disturbingly high rate of farmland loss and hold out the prospect of continued, uncontrolled erosion of the countryside, particularly of the best farmland. We shall see that this contrast in viewpoints is due as much to differences in interpretation as to differences in fact.

The only official data on changes in land use for the United Kingdom are derived from an analysis of agricultural statistics. When changes occur in the extent of individual holdings, as recorded in successive agricultural censuses, occupiers are asked to give the reason for such changes. Those which are not accounted for by transfers of agricultural land between holdings are investigated by local officers of agricultural departments who enquire into the subsequent use of such land. There are limitations to the data because some farmers may copy the last recorded acreage, but they are the only complete information on transfers of farmland to and from other uses.

The indications from these data are that there has been no sustained increase in the rate of farmland loss to urban use since 1945, although it should be noted that data are not available after 1979 owing to a change in the presentation of data culled from agricultural statistics (figure 2.4). The annual average rate of conversion over the thirty years from 1945 to 1975 was under 16,000 ha per year – less than two-thirds of the rate in the 1930s. Away from the axial belt large parts of England and Wales have a loss to urban use as low as 0.05 per cent per year and, it has been argued, most of these areas are found in the most productive agricultural regions, from Suffolk to Humberside. Moreover, these losses have been more than offset by increases in agricultural productivity: between 1966/7 and 1971/2 about 0.5 per cent of UK farmland was converted to urban use, yet agricultural gross output, net of inputs, increased by 15 per cent over the same period.

A different interpretation has been drawn by Alice Coleman (1976) from a comparison of the First and Second Land Use Surveys. This reveals a loss of about half a million hectares of farmland in England and Wales between about 1933 and 1963. Additional to this net loss was the wartime abstraction for military purposes of land which was subsequently returned to agricultural use. Those changes which were permanent have been interpreted as comprising a rate of transfer considerably greater than that implied by the official agricultural statistics. However, Best (1981) has noted that the discrepancy between the two sets of data amounts to less

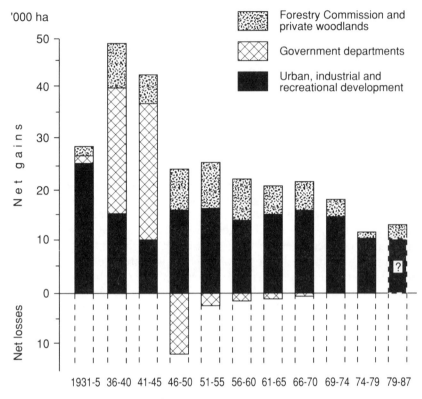

'000 ha

Forestry Commission and private woodlands

Government departments

Urban, industrial and recreational development

*Figure 2.4* Transfers of agricultural land in England and Wales to urban and other uses, 1931–87
*Source:* Agricultural Statistics

than 50,000 ha over the thirty years, which is no greater than the likely margin of error due to differences in date.

To investigate more recent changes Alice Coleman (1976) resurveyed sample areas in the 1970s in Surrey, and around Thameside and Merseyside. This indicated a continued loss of farmland at the annual rate of about 1.1 per cent and a rapid increase in the amount of urban and rural wasteland (table 2.10). In Thameside, two-thirds of the area taken out of agriculture for building between 1963 and 1972 in fact remained idle. There had also occurred both the increasing 'fragmentation' of farmland by scattered suburban development and the degeneration of improved farmland to rural waste and scrub woodland. Alice Coleman (1976) has termed the land-use patterns in these areas the 'urban fringe', a frontier zone in which there is conflict between the uses dominant in the 'townscape' and 'farmscape'.

*Table 2.10* Land-use changes, Thameside, 1961–72

| Category of use | 1962 (km²) | 1972 (km²) | Net change (km²) |
|---|---|---|---|
| Residential/commercial | 187.5 | 188.0 | +0.5 |
| Industry | 27.0 | 30.0 | +3.0 |
| Extractive industry | 21.5 | 16.5 | −5.0 |
| Derelict land | 2.5 | 7.0 | +4.5 |
| Transport | 85.5 | 93.5 | +8.0 |
| Tended open space | 72.5 | 80.0 | +7.5 |
| Total settlement | 396.5 | 415.0 | +18.5 |
| Orchards | 20.0 | 13.0 | −7.0 |
| Horticulture | 65.0 | 66.0 | +1.0 |
| Arable | 143.5 | 148.0 | +4.5 |
| Improved grass | 138.5 | 98.0 | −40.5 |
| Total improved farmland | 367.0 | 325.0 | −42.0 |
| Woodland | 23.0 | 10.0 | −4.0 |
| Scrub | 9.5 | 9.0 | −0.5 |
| Wasteland | 33.0 | 63.5 | +30.5 |
| Heath | 1.0 | 0.5 | −0.5 |
| Marsh | 10.5 | 9.0 | −1.5 |
| Water | 10.0 | 9.5 | −0.5 |
| Total cover types | 87.0 | 110.5 | +23.5 |
| Total area | 850.5 | 850.5 | − |

*Source:* Coleman 1976

The argument over the conversion of farmland to urban use has been fuelled by evidence that the 'best' farming land is being lost. A comparison of Land Classification sheets for 1933 and those more recently completed for England and Wales by the Ministry of Agriculture shows that first-class farmland has been 'urbanized' at a higher rate than lower grades (table 2.11). Alice Coleman argues that, if the planning system had succeeded, the proportion of newly urbanized 'first-class' and 'good' land should be negligible. Others reply that since first-class land is distributed in lowland areas and thus more likely to be urbanized than poor land in the uplands, the fact that its development has been kept to such low proportions is a signal achievement of the planning system.

Of course, not all land converted from agricultural use has been urbanized. More than a third as much has been converted to forestry (45,000 ha over 1946–87 in England and Wales), both in private plantings and those owned by the Forestry Commission, and, until the late 1960s, there was still some land regained for agriculture from military use (figure 2.4).

*Table 2.11* The grade of farmland transferred to urban use in England and Wales, 1933–67

| Grade (after L.D. Stamp) | National area | Newly urbanized | Settlement | Fragmented farmland | Waste land | Other |
|---|---|---|---|---|---|---|
| | % | % | % | % | % | % |
| First-class | 7.5 | 9.6 | 66.2 | 27.6 | 4.3 | 1.9 |
| Good | 37.6 | 43.5 | 63.1 | 31.1 | 2.4 | 3.4 |
| Medium | 36.5 | 37.4 | 63.2 | 28.3 | 3.9 | 4.6 |
| Poor | 18.4 | 9.5 | 68.0 | 20.2 | 3.8 | 8.0 |
| Total | 100.0 | 100.0 | 63.9 | 28.7 | 3.3 | 4.1 |

*Source:* Coleman 1977

**The component uses of urban land**

There have been several attempts to estimate the composition of urban land uses, largely from sampled town maps and from development plans, but we know little about changes in composition. The most recent comprehensive survey was that completed by the DOE in 1978, based on aerial photographs taken in 1969, and covering England and Wales only. Restricted sample surveys have been completed by the Institute of Terrestrial Ecology (ITE) for the period 1977 to 1982. In the DOE survey five types of use were distinguished although only four are illustrated in figure 2.5. The fifth use – 'educational, community, health, and indoor recreational' – accounts, on average, for only 1 per cent of the developed area. Nationally, residential uses comprise about 61 per cent of the developed area, although regionally the figure varies from 56 per cent in the north of England to as much as 69 per cent in the south-west. Conversely, industrial and commercial uses account for more than a quarter of all land in the north but only 14 per cent in the south-west. The disproportional area devoted to transport in East Anglia presumably reflects the numerous wartime airfields that survive in the region.

The survey was intended to provide a national data bank on urban land use and a base against which to measure and monitor urban land-use change in the future. In order to update the record the Department of the Environment and the Welsh Office requested local planning authorities in 1975 to provide annual data on land-use change under fifteen headings. In fact, these data have not been collected and recent changes in the composition of the urban area have not been comprehensively monitored. However, the ITE sample survey indicates that the major change over 1977–84 was the conversion of 39,000 ha to urban housing developments, 28 per cent of this area coming from vacant or derelict land and the remainder from agriculture.

In addition to land within the urban fence there are also many quasi-urban uses of land in the countryside. The most extensive of these are land worked for minerals and derelict land. As a user of land, mineral working

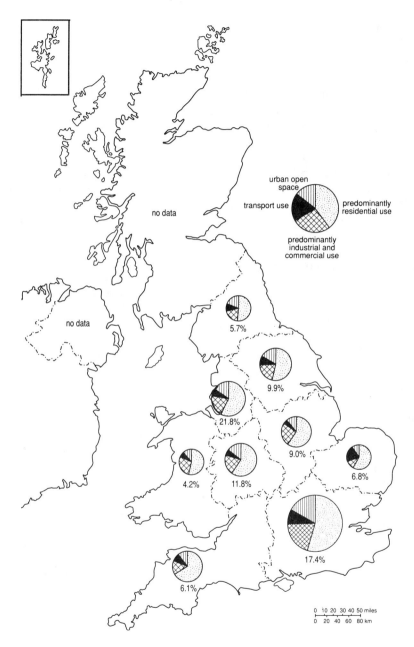

*Figure 2.5* The composition of urban land in England and Wales, 1969
*Note:* Figures indicate urban land as a proportion of all land in each region. Circles
are proportional to the area of urban land
*Source:* Department of the Environment 1978

occurs largely in the form of open pits, particularly those associated with the extraction of sand and gravel, limestone and ironstone. These cover about 49,000 ha (or 0.4 per cent of England). In spite of a threefold increase in the reclamation rate, the extent of derelict land in England increased between 1964 and 1974, and at present covers about 43,000 ha (or 0.3 per cent of the country). The DOE map of derelict land, drawn from a survey in 1974, indicates a concentration in the older industrial areas of the midlands and north, particularly in the metropolitan counties of Greater Manchester and West Yorkshire, and in Durham.

We should also consider the influences of urban life on more traditionally rural uses of land, particularly at the urban periphery. Here, urban nuisance and the anticipation of urban growth may lead to 'run-down' or 'idle' land. A survey of London's Green Belt in 1979 found that one-third of farmland exhibited signs of poor agricultural management and drew a connection between this and the fact that much of the land was in short lets and frequently occupied by part-time or spare-time farmers.

## Changes in agricultural land use

A corollary of urban growth in the United Kingdom has been the contraction of land in agricultural use. More than that, the past fifty years have seen much of the more remote countryside affected by rural depopulation with resulting changes in the economic and social structure of the countryside, as well as in its land use and landscape. We shall consider, first, the measurable changes in land use and, second, the more qualitative – but nonetheless important – changes in landscape.

There are two major components of land-use change in post-war rural Britain: changes in farmland and changes in woodland. The first of these has mirrored underlying trends in British agriculture: the intensification of farming; its increasing specialization by farm and by areas; and the increasing scale of operation. In this discussion it is convenient, simply because of their relative extent and their distinctive landscapes, to distinguish between improved farmland and rough (unimproved) land.

### Changes in the extent of tillage and grassland

Despite the loss of good quality agricultural land to urban development and poor quality upland to afforestation, total agricultural production has increased substantially since 1945. This has been the product not only of increases in yield but also of changes in the use of land. In particular, there has been a substantial increase in the area under tillage, with major regional variations of change which have served to enhance the contrast between east and west. Thus the area under crops was extended in the corn-growing counties but contracted in the west (figure 2.6). Since the mid-1980s, however, there have been indications that in eastern England this trend has slowed and possibly been slightly reversed.

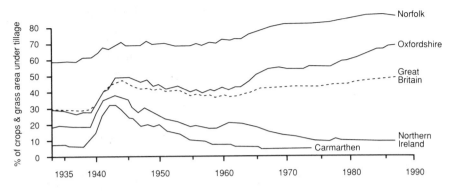

*Figure 2.6* Changes in the area under tillage in the UK and selected areas, 1933–87
*Source:* Agricultural Statistics, partly compiled by Coppock 1968

Most notable within the tillage category has been an increase in the area devoted to barley, as a feed crop for cattle, a decrease in labour-demanding root crops such as turnips and swedes, and a decline in orchards. Accompanying these changes, particularly in the east of England, has been an increase in size of enterprise, and in the degree of specialization and mechanization which has, in turn, had an impact on the farming landscape through the enlargement of fields and removal of hedgerows.

In the north and west the principal trend (though this may have been reversed in recent years) has been towards the steady increase in temporary at the expense of permanent grassland. The improvement in quality of pasture has been reflected in substantial livestock increases in the grazing counties. Changes to the farming landscape have here been less marked than in the east. A full discussion of these and other changes in agriculture will be found in chapter 4.

### Changes in the extent of rough grazing

Rough grazings cover about 6 million ha, or one-quarter of the farmland in the United Kingdom – though they contribute perhaps only 5 per cent of the nation's agricultural product by value. They are covered by a variety of semi-natural vegetation, including grasses, sedges and heather. Quite large areas have been cut by open drains and much is burned regularly to encourage new growth. In other words, these are 'managed' grazings. They are far from being a 'natural' land cover and bear no relation to the so-called 'wilderness', a North American term mistakenly adopted by some National Park planners in the United Kingdom.

Rough grazings occupy two-thirds of the agricultural area in Scotland, and one-quarter in Northern Ireland. They are also extensive in northern England and Wales. Most of them are in sole right, although about a million hectares are in common. Apart from a fringe of small enclosures along the moorland edge, most of this land is open country, unfenced and divided only by boundary walls (figure 2.1).

In the 1930s rough grazing was probably more extensive in the UK than it had been for about a century. There had been widespread reversion of marginal pasture in the 1880s and this was supplemented during the inter-war depression. However, between 1933 and 1980 about one million hectares (15 per cent of the nation's rough land) were transferred to improved farmland. In some areas reclamation was particularly extensive – on the plateau uplands of the east and south-west (the North Yorkshire Moors, Exmoor, Dartmoor, and the Brecon Beacons), where gentle slopes are no obstacle to the plough (figure 2.7); for example, about 8 per cent of rough land of the North Yorkshire Moors was ploughed in the period 1950 to 1980 (figure 2.7). Most reclamation was the re-intake of reverted fields at the moorland edge, but much is of moorland which has not been enclosed or ploughed in the past millenium. As a marked and long-term change in rural land use and landscape this is one of a number of trends which has recently attracted the attention of the conservation lobbies in the 1970s and 1980s. However there are indications from recent surveys in the mid-Wales Uplands that the rate of reclamation has diminished substantially since about 1982, following the reduction in incentives for cereal production under EC Common Agricultural Policy.

**Changes in the extent of woodland**

With about 2 million ha of woodland covering 9 per cent of the land surface, the United Kingdom is one of the least wooded countries in

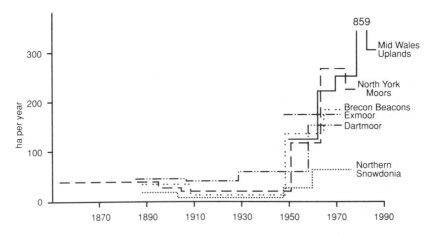

*Figure 2.7* Average annual rates of roughland reclamation for agriculture in five National Parks
*Source:* Parry, Bruce, and Harkness 1982, Parry and Sinclair 1984

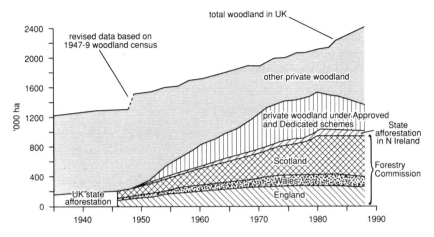

*Figure 2.8* Changes in the area under woodland in the UK, 1935–88
*Source:* Forestry Commission; Department of Agriculture (Northern Ireland)

Europe. Nevertheless, the UK area under woodland has almost doubled since the 1940s so that in several conservancies it amounts to more than a tenth of the land. Private planting, encouraged by changes in taxable status of woodland, has seen a marked increase in the 1980s (figure 2.8).

About 47 per cent of the UK woodland is owned and managed by the Forestry Commission and the Department of Agriculture (Northern Ireland), and this share has increased steadily over the past twenty-five years, in spite of a boom in private plantings in the 1960s and early 1970s, encouraged by subsidies and tax concessions. With a reduction in these concessions and the introduction of less generous grant support for Approved or Dedicated Woodlands (which in 1967 comprised two-fifths of all private woodland) the rate of private planting has declined.

The general pattern of change is shown in figure 2.8. At the time of the Land Utilization Survey in 1931–9 woodland covered about 5.7 per cent of Great Britain. By 1947 this had increased to 6.1 per cent, but less than a half of this area was high forest, the remainder being coppice, scrub, or felled woodland. Most of the high forest was immature Forestry Commission plantation which had escaped felling during the Second World War. The rate of planting by the Commission increased rapidly after 1947 to a peak in 1954 when 28,475 ha were planted. Thereafter, government policy and difficulties in acquiring land combined to reduce the rate of planting, and the Commission paid increased attention to conservation, to the provision of amenity, and to the encouragement of wood-processing industries. The Commission had been criticized in the 1960s for policies of acquisition and planting which conflicted with hill farming and, since 1974, it has adopted the objective of encouraging the integration of forestry and agriculture.

The prospects for multiple use of hill land are probably greatest in the National Parks, where authorities have experience of serving multiple rather than single interests, but it would be optimistic to expect such coordinated management elsewhere. In the long run, much will depend on the development of an EC policy towards forestry and on technical changes in the market for timber and timber products.

## The competition for land by other users

There are other uses of the countryside, some of which are exclusive (and thus more likely to be a source of conflict in the future) and some of which are capable of integration or, at least, alternation.

One of the largest groups of institutional land owners in Great Britain is the water industry, which controls about one-quarter of a million hectares, or 1.1 per cent of the land surface. About three-quarters of this land is farmed, the remainder serving only for water gathering (table 2.4). In fact, the influence of the water authorities on the use of land is most significant in the catchment areas which are leased to hill farmers. The effect on cultivation and levels of stocking of restrictions in the leases has been to encourage some hill land around reservoirs to revert from improved farmland to rough grazing. This is particularly noticeable in the southern Pennines, around the reservoirs serving Manchester, Liverpool, and West Yorkshire. The total area actually covered by water in the United Kingdom is only about 313,000 ha (1.3 per cent of the surface area) and this increasingly fulfils a dual role in providing for amenity and recreation. It remains to be seen whether the proposed privatization of the water industry in 1990 leads to changes in policy towards the use of this land.

At present more frequently criticized by farmers and conservationists is the Ministry of Defence, which owns 252,000 ha in Great Britain but which allows farming on only one-fifth of this area (table 2.4), and which severely restricts public access. On training grounds on Dartmoor, in Dorset and in South Wales, the armed services have been accused of the steady destruction of a valuable environment. Ironically, the truth may be that, by forbidding access to other users, the Ministry of Defence has preserved the countryside from a more serious fate: trampling by the holiday-maker and ploughing by the farmer.

Despite its rapid growth, outdoor recreation enjoys exclusive use of only small areas of land. Even on the urban fringe, playing fields, golf courses, and public open spaces account for less than 7 per cent of the land, and the aggregate area of all Country Parks in England and Wales (there were 130 in 1987) amounted to only 18,000 ha. Formal use of uplands as deer forests and grouse moors is still important, though not as extensive as before the break-up of the large estates. By contrast, informal types of recreation have grown rapidly since the war and have become a secondary use over large areas. During the 1970s and 1980s these showed a growth at an average annual rate of 10 to 15 per cent.

Nevertheless, land which has been designated as statutory amenity areas (National Parks and Areas of Outstanding National Beauty) now accounts for almost a fifth of the land area in England and Wales; and much of this is in the hands of conservation bodies. In the 1980s these organizations, including those such as the National Trust, Nature Conservancy Council, and the Royal Society for the Protection of Birds, owned almost a quarter of a million hectares or 1 per cent of Great Britain.

## LANDSCAPE AND LAND USE IN THE FUTURE

Each of the adjustments of land use described above has wrought changes on the landscape. Some of these can scarcely be detected, others are of increasing concern to the enthusiast of the traditional countryside. Perhaps most apparent are the new agricultural landscapes resulting from new farming practices adopted in the lowlands – landscapes of large fields and few hedgerows. Less obvious has been the reclamation of heathlands, felling of woodlands, and drainage of wetlands. Together these comprise a formidable body of changes which has provoked a rash of reaction in the 1970s and early 1980s from conservation lobbies, and a growing demand for fresh legislation to protect countryside (see chapter 17). The response to this, the Wildlife and Countryside Act 1981, in fact gave few extra powers by which the countryside may be protected. Its greatest impact was ultimately in encouraging a revision by the Ministry of Agriculture of its policy towards the grant-aid of land improvements – a revision that was long overdue.

In some regions, such as the South-east, the policy changes have come too late. In East Anglia, for example, hedgerow losses continued at the rate of 1.3 per cent per annum over 1969–85. Yet we should not exaggerate the extent of inadvertent landscape change. It has certainly been marked in the south-east of England, East Anglia and the East Midlands, but elsewhere (that is, three-quarters of the United Kingdom) the countryside has not been substantially altered. Those particular changes which have been marked in the north and west – the decline in arable, the reclamation of roughland, the increase in woodland – are changes which, with the exception of some areas of particular landscape value, have not seriously damaged the countryside.

As for the pattern of land use in the future – it (predictably) has its prophets both of deliverance and doom. There are those who believe that the planning system is failing to control development and that an already high rate of rural land loss will lead to an excessively large urban area in the United Kingdom – about 10 per cent before the end of this century. This is countered by the argument that both the rate of land loss and the proportion of land in urban use are lower in the United Kingdom than in comparable areas in the EC. In fact the argument is less about the figures themselves than about their meaning for landscape and living space in the future.

## REFERENCES

Best, R. H. (1981) *Land Use and Living Space,* London: Methuen.

Champion, A. G. (1974) 'An estimate of the changing extent and distribution of urban land in England and Wales, 1950–70', *Centre for Environmental Studies Research Papers,* 10.

Coleman, A. (1976) 'Is planning really necessary', *Geographical Journal,* 142: 411–30.

Coleman, A. (1977) 'Land-use planning: success or failure?', *Architects Journal,* 165(3): 91–134.

Coppock, J. T. and Gebbett, L. F. (1978) 'Land use, and town and country planning', in Maunder, W. F., (ed.) *Reviews of U.K. Statistical Sources,* vol. 8, Oxford: Pergamon.

Department of the Environment (1978) *Developed Areas, 1969: A Survey of England and Wales from Air Photography,* London.

Department of the Environment and Countryside Commission (1987) *Monitoring Landscape Change,* Huntings Surveys, Borehamwood.

Fordham, R. C. (1974) 'Measurement of urban land uses', *University of Cambridge, Department of Land Economy, Occasional Papers,* No. 1.

Harrison, A., Tranter, R. B., and Gibbs, R. S. (1977) 'Landownership by public and semi-public institutions in the UK', *C.A.S. Paper No. 3,* Centre for Agricultural Strategy, University of Reading.

Messer, M. (1932) *An Agricultural Atlas of England and Wales,* Southampton, Agricultural Economic Research Institute, University of Oxford.

Stamp, L. D. (1962) *The Land of Britain: Its Use and Misuse,* 3rd edn, London: Longmans.

Wood, H. J. (1931) *An Agricultural Atlas of Scotland,* London: Gill.

## FURTHER READING

Coppock, J. T. (1964) *An Agricultural Atlas of England and Wales,* London: Faber & Faber.

Coppock, J. T. (1968) 'Changes in rural land use in Great Britain', in Embleton, C., and Coppock, J. T. (eds) *Land Use and Resources: Studies in Applied Geography,* Institute of British Geographers, Special Publication No. 1.

Coppock, J. T. (1976) *An Agricultural Atlas of Scotland,* Edinburgh: John Donald.

Countryside Commission (1974) *New Agricultural Landscapes,* Cheltenham: Countryside Commission.

Parry, M. L., Bruce, A. and Harkness, C. E. (1982) *Surveys of Moorland and Roughland Change,* Department of Geography, University of Birmingham.

Parry, M. L., and Sinclair, G. (1984) *Mid Wales Uplands Study,* Cheltenham: Countryside Commission.

Symons, L. (1963) *Land Use in Northern Ireland,* London: University of London Press.

# 3 The changing population

*Paul A Compton*

Over the last fifty years the population of the United Kingdom has passed through a full cycle of growth. A low rate of natural increase during the 1930s sparked off false predictions that the population would reach a maximum and then decline. Although the 1949 Royal Commission Report on the population of Great Britain rejected this thesis, it did not anticipate the upsurge that was to follow and even its high projection of future numbers was soon to be overtaken because of the acceleration in the rate of growth which peaked in the mid-1960s. Due to this reversal of demographic trend, concern about the imminent demise of the nation in turn gave way to anxiety that the population was growing too rapidly. But this fear also proved unfounded. Since 1964 a profound drop in the birth rate has brought in its train a dramatic slow-down in growth, culminating in actual population decline between 1974 and 1978. Although modest growth has since resumed, some of the fears of the 1930s have re-emerged, especially as the lower birth rate affects future recruitment to the labour force.

Although the volatility of the birth rate was largely responsible for these abrupt reversals, this must be set against an historical background of general fertility decline coupled with rising longevity and mortality reduction. Both processes, but more so fertility decline, have profoundly affected the age composition of the population, which has acquired a decidedly older complexion. The other general trend that deserves mention is the post-war marriage boom followed by the increasing unpopularity of marriage since around 1970, which is clearly one fact associated with the fluctuating population growth rates of the recent past. While the analysis of temporal trends is largely a demographic task, the interpretation of the changing spatial patterns of population is essentially a geographical concern. More-over, the significance of the changing spatial patterns has become greater of late for, unlike previous periods, growth in some regions of the United Kingdom now means decline elsewhere since it can no longer be assumed that natural increase will offset migration loss. The emphasis in this chapter is therefore on spatio-temporal change, especially the processes of change over the last three to five decades, and includes an analysis of fertility, mortality and international migration trends.

Like many other phenomena, the geographical analysis of population is affected by spatial scale, and comparative stability at the macro-level may mask substantial variability at the micro-scale. The discussion of population distribution and the components of change is therefore most appropriately undertaken at a variety of different scales, although one is obviously tied to those groupings of areal units for which population data are readily available. Invariably these are administrative areas, which suffer from the disadvantage of not always corresponding to a functional breakdown of the population. Moreover, their boundaries do not remain constant; minor changes may be accommodated, but the major unconformity resulting from the radical restructuring of local government in 1974 is especially troublesome for spatio-temporal comparison. Indeed, the only boundaries not tampered with at that time were those between the constituent countries of the United Kingdom. A further important point is that the discussion of recent spatial change is constrained by the fact that many of the post-1981 population statistics are estimates. Unfortunately the errors inherent in such data become more of a problem as geographical complexity increases and any discussion of change since 1981 is inevitably oriented more towards the macro-scale of constituent countries and regions than towards the subregional level. Those wishing for a more detailed analysis of recent demographic developments than is contained in this chapter are referred to the OPCS 1984 review of demographic trends in Great Britain and to Compton (1986) for trends in Northern Ireland.

**NATIONAL TRENDS**

Between 1931 and 1986, the population of the United Kingdom rose from 46 to an estimated 56.8 millions; in other words, over a period of just over half a century the nation's population expanded by 23.5 per cent at an average rate of 4.2 per 1,000 per year. The trend, however, has been far from uniform and, following the low rate of increase of the 1930s, population growth accelerated quite sharply to reach a maximum of 6.4 per 1,000 per annum during the decade 1956 to 1966. Subsequently, and in unprecedented fashion, the expansion in numbers came to a halt and between mid-1974 and mid-1978 the population of the United Kingdom actually declined by 57,000, although modest growth, accelerating after 1983, has since resumed.

As demonstrated in table 3.1, natural increase (i.e. the balance of births and deaths graphed in figure 3.1 for the period 1931–86) has been the major factor contributing to this trend. In comparison, the external migration balance has been small numerically and generally negative, notwithstanding the influx of refugees from Europe immediately before and after the Second World War and the immigration of the late 1950s and early 1960s from the New Commonwealth. Although international migration has become a comparatively more significant component of population

Table 3.1 Components of population change in the UK, 1931–86 (annual averages)

| Mid-year to mid-year | Population at start of period 000s | Actual change | | Natural change | | Net migration | | Other[a] | |
|---|---|---|---|---|---|---|---|---|---|
| | | Number 000s | Rate per 1,000 | Number 000s | Rate per 1,000 | Number 000s | Rate per 1,000 | Number 000s | Rate per 1,000 |
| 1931–51[b] | 46,038 | 213 | 4.7 | 188 | 4.1 | 22 | 0.5 | 3 | 0.1 |
| 1951–6 | 50,290 | 179 | 3.6 | 214 | 4.3 | −48 | −1.0 | 13 | 0.3 |
| 1956–61 | 51,184 | 327 | 6.4 | 277 | 5.4 | 30 | 0.7 | 20 | 0.3 |
| 1961–6 | 52,807 | 339 | 6.3 | 355 | 6.6 | −8 | −0.2 | −8 | −0.2 |
| 1966–71 | 54,500 | 257 | 4.7 | 293 | 5.3 | −56 | −1.0 | 20 | 0.4 |
| 1971–6 | 55,928 | 58 | 1.0 | 96 | 1.7 | −55 | −1.0 | 16 | 0.3 |
| 1976–81 | 56,216 | 27 | 0.5 | 42 | 0.7 | −33 | −0.5 | 18 | 0.3 |
| 1981–2 | 56,352 | −46 | −0.8 | 53 | 0.9 | −86 | −1.5 | −13 | −0.2 |
| 1982–3 | 56,306 | 41 | 0.7 | 62 | 1.1 | −24 | −0.4 | 3 | 0.1 |
| 1983–4 | 56,347 | 112 | 2.0 | 66 | 1.2 | 43 | 0.8 | 4 | 0.1 |
| 1984–5 | 56,460 | 158 | 2.8 | 86 | 1.5 | 35 | 0.6 | 37 | 0.7 |
| 1985–6 | 56,618 | 145 | 2.6 | 85 | 1.5 | 75 | 1.3 | −15 | −0.3 |
| 1986–7 | 56,763 | | | | | | | | |

Source: Population Trends, 22, 46, 52

Notes:
a Changes in number of armed forces and adjustments to reconcile population change between mid-year estimates with estimates of natural change and net civilian migration
b Census enumerated population for GB, plus mid-year estimate for Northern Ireland

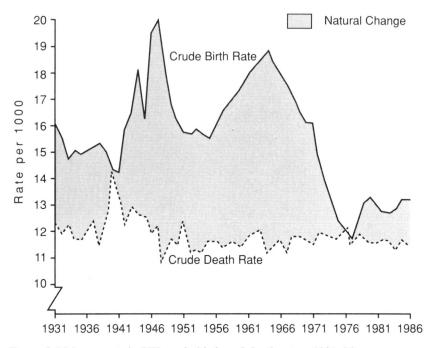

*Figure 3.1* Movements in UK crude birth and death rates, 1931–86
*Source:* Birth Statistics 1986, Annual Reports of the Registrar General for Northern Ireland;
Annual Reports of the Registrar General for Scotland

change since the mid-1970s, this has not been because of any upsurge in numbers, but rather because of the exceedingly low rate of natural change in recent years. Indeed, from the beginning of 1976 to the end of the first quarter of 1978 more deaths than births were registered in the United Kingdom, the only occasion that this has happened since civil registration began in 1837 (1863 in Northern Ireland). Furthermore, the higher growth rate since 1983 is not explained by any surge in natural increase but rather because, of late and rather exceptionally, the external balance has been positive.

Although the next few years may see some resurgence in natural increase, sustained long-term population growth at the national level seems unlikely at present unless it is to be through immigration. Fertility has been well below replacement since 1973 and seems set to remain so. Granted that period measures of replacement have proved highly fallible indicators in the past, it none the less seems likely that we have entered a phase when, although numbers may well fluctuate reflecting the relative sizes of past birth cohorts, they will do so around a stationary population mean.

## POPULATION DISTRIBUTION

The elements of the present distribution of population emerged during the last century and have remained essentially fixed since then. The continuity of urban dwelling is arguably the most salient stable element and the United Kingdom remains one of the most urbanized countries of Europe, with over one-third of its inhabitants living at high densities in the major conurbations. At the time of the reorganization of local government in 1974, around 75 per cent of the population resided in the now defunct urban districts. The most recent authoritative estimate of the rural-urban breakdown, however, comes from the Office of Population Censuses and Surveys and the Department of the Environment (see Denham 1984 and OPCS (1987) *Demographic Review 1984*) who, following the 1981 census, collaborated in the delineation of urban land in England and Wales. This exercise showed that just over 90 per cent of the population can be described as urban and is broadly consistent with the 95 per cent estimated as functioning in the urban system, viz. including those who live in the countryside but are urban-bound for their livelihoods. Northern Ireland remains the least urbanized and Scotland the most urbanized part of the United Kingdom.

The broad regional pattern of the beginning of the century is still evident today – the populous lowland south and east still contrast with the more sparsely inhabited north and west. Moreover, essential stability has also been preserved within these two major zones. In the south, for instance, the recent resurgence of East Anglia and the South-west has had little effect on the demographic dominance of the south-east:north-west axial belt running from Greater London through the midlands to West Yorkshire, Manchester and Merseyside, where over 50 per cent of the population of England and Wales reside. Equally, the north is still dominated by the four major population concentrations of Tyneside and Wearside, central Scotland and Greater Belfast, set against a backdrop of otherwise relatively sparse habitation.

That this population distribution has for long been broadly stable can be attributed in large degree to the antiquity of the built environment, the framework of which had been formed by 1850. Additionally, post-war regional policy, by encouraging the spread of employment in accordance with the existing population distribution in preference to inducing people to move to the most optimal economic locations, reinforced the status quo. Its abandonment by the 1980s governments is one factor contributing to the renewed influx of population to the south-east. Population distribution has thus achieved a broad dynamic equilibrium with internal migration functioning to maintain stability; although mobility is high and individual migration streams substantial, the net effect is largely self-cancelling.

Stability is essentially a macro-feature, however, and five separate processes generating change at lower levels of aggregation may be identified:

a concentration of population growth in the south and to a lesser extent in the midlands of England, slow growth in the older industrial centres of the north and west, continued depopulation of remote rural areas; population growth in areas of retirement migration, and centrifugal movements from the cores and inner suburbs of towns to the outer suburbs and beyond. Most of these strands have quite long antecedents and are discussed in more detail in the following sections.

## Distribution of population by constituent countries and regions

Reflecting the broad disparities that exist in wealth and prosperity, a dominant theme at the regional level continues to be the drift of population from the peripheries to the south and south-east as exemplified in the declining share of the nation's population residing in Scotland and northern England. Wales, too, saw its share diminish up to 1971 but since then has experienced a demographic revival and now accounts for 5 per cent of the UK population; Northern Ireland's proportion has also recently crept slowly upwards, although its population is still some 80,000 below the maximum recorded in 1841.

As would be expected from these changing shares, the components of population change have varied considerably between the constituent countries (table 3.2). The Scottish rate of natural increase, for instance, was generally above the national average up to the mid-1970s and Scotland's declining population share has been a function of persistent migration loss to other parts of the United Kingdom as well as overseas. Although the level of net outflow diminished substantially after 1971, natural increase fell even more rapidly and the population of Scotland is estimated to have declined by over 100,000 between then and 1986. Northern Ireland has also suffered from substantial net out-migration, for similar reasons of economic under-performance heightened by the political uncertainty of the last two decades, but high natural increase has offset migration outflow leading to a static population overall during the 1970s and renewed growth since then as, somewhat paradoxically, out-migration has declined. The province has therefore retained its share of the United Kingdom population, despite a temporary drop in numbers between 1972 and 1976.

England, as the dominant demographic component, has followed the national pattern most closely. A high rate of natural growth between 1961 and 1966 was augmented by a modest net influx of population from abroad to produce an actual growth rate in excess of 7 per 1,000 per annum. Twelve years later, however, the situation had been transformed and from mid-1973 to mid-1978 the population fell by 48,000. In turn, the 1980s have witnessed a recovery in the rate of natural increase, together with a positive migration balance since 1983 (England has invariably gained people from the rest of the United Kingdom and the Irish Republic, but,

Table 3.2 Components of population change, 1961–86

| Mid-year to mid-year | Actual change | Natural change | Net migration | | | | Other changes |
| --- | --- | --- | --- | --- | --- | --- | --- |
| | | | Total | Balance with rest of UK | Balance with Irish Republic | Balance outside British Isles | |
| England | | | | | | | |
| 1961–6 | 7.7 | 6.5 | 0.8 | 0.0 | 0.0 | 0.0 | 0.4 |
| 1966–71 | 5.0 | 5.2 | −0.4 | 0.3 | 0.2 | −0.9 | 0.2 |
| 1971–6 | 1.0 | 1.5 | −0.7 | 0.0 | −0.2 | −0.5 | 0.2 |
| 1976–81 | 0.7 | 0.7 | −0.2 | 0.1 | −0.0 | −0.3 | 0.2 |
| 1081–6 | 1.9 | 1.2 | 0.6 | 0.2 | 0.1 | 0.3 | 0.1 |
| Scotland | | | | | | | |
| 1961–6 | 0.6 | 7.4 | −7.1 | −4.2 | nd | −2.9 | 0.3 |
| 1966–71 | 1.3 | 5.8 | −5.4 | −2.2 | nd | −3.2 | 0.9 |
| 1971–6 | −0.0 | 1.9 | −2.7 | −0.8 | nd | −1.9 | 0.8 |
| 1976–81 | −2.1 | 0.4 | −3.1 | −1.3 | nd | −1.9 | 0.6 |
| 1981–6 | −2.3 | 0.4 | −2.8 | −1.4 | nd | 1.4 | 0.1 |
| Wales | | | | | | | |
| 1961–6 | 4.9 | 4.1 | 0.0 | nd | nd | nd | 0.8 |
| 1966–71 | 2.9 | 2.6 | 0.0 | 1.1 | nd | −1.1 | 0.3 |
| 1971–6 | 4.3 | 0.4 | 2.9 | 3.6 | 0.0 | −0.7 | 1.0 |
| 1976–81 | 1.1 | −0.3 | 0.7 | 1.8 | – | −0.7 | 0.7 |
| 1981–6 | 0.6 | 0.3 | 0.3 | 1.1 | – | −0.8 | – |
| Northern Ireland | | | | | | | |
| 1961–6 | 6.9 | 12.4 | −4.8 | −4.8 | nd | – | −0.7 |
| 1966–71 | 8.6 | 11.3 | −4.6 | −2.0 | nd | 2.6 | 1.9 |
| 1971–6 | −2.0 | 7.2 | −9.2 | −4.6 | nd | 4.6 | 0.0 |
| 1976–81 | 2.0 | 6.5 | −5.2 | −2.6 | nd | −2.0 | 0.7 |
| 1981–6 | 3.9 | 7.5 | −3.2 | −2.1 | nd | 1.2 | −0.4 |

Sources: *Population Trends*, 22, 46, 52. Annual Reports of Registrar General for Northern Ireland, 1961–76
Note: nd: no data

*Table 3.3* Rates of population change per 1,000 per year, 1951–86

| | 1951–61 | | | 1961–6 | | | 1966–71 | | |
|---|---|---|---|---|---|---|---|---|---|
| | Natural change | Other[a] change | Actual change | Natural change | Other[a] change | Actual change | Natural change | Other[a] change | Actual change |
| England | 4.6 | 0.9 | 5.5 | 6.5 | 0.6 | 7.1 | 5.2 | -0.8 | 4.4 |
| Scotland | 6.6 | -5.0 | 1.6 | 7.4 | -6.9 | 0.6 | 5.7 | -5.2 | 0.6 |
| Wales | 3.2 | -1.4 | 1.8 | 4.3 | 0.1 | 4.4 | 3.0 | -0.8 | 2.2 |
| Northern Ireland | 10.4 | -6.6 | 3.8 | 12.2 | -5.2 | 7.0 | 11.1 | -3.1 | 8.0 |
| **Regions of England** | | | | | | | | | |
| Northern | 6.2 | -2.4 | 3.8 | 6.2 | -5.6 | 0.8 | 4.3 | -3.6 | 0.8 |
| Yorks and Humber | 4.3 | -1.6 | 2.7 | 6.0 | -0.4 | 5.6 | 5.2 | -2.8 | 2.4 |
| North-west | 3.7 | -1.7 | 2.0 | 5.8 | -1.7 | 4.1 | 4.4 | -2.5 | 1.9 |
| West Midlands | 6.2 | 1.4 | 7.6 | 8.5 | -0.9 | 7.6 | 7.6 | -0.7 | 7.0 |
| East midlands | 5.5 | 1.8 | 7.3 | 7.2 | 2.7 | 9.8 | 6.1 | 1.6 | 7.7 |
| East Anglia | 4.7 | 2.6 | 7.3 | 5.8 | 5.7 | 11.3 | 5.1 | 8.8 | 13.7 |
| South-east | 4.4 | 3.0 | 7.4 | 6.8 | 1.2 | 7.9 | 5.3 | -2.1 | 3.3 |
| of which G. London | nd | nd | nd | 6.5 | -11.0 | -4.2 | 4.8 | -14.7 | -9.6 |
| South west | 3.2 | 2.6 | 5.8 | 4.4 | 6.7 | 11.0 | 3.1 | 5.4 | 8.4 |

| | 1971–6 | | | 1976–81 | | | 1981–6 | | |
|---|---|---|---|---|---|---|---|---|---|
| | Natural change | Other[a] change | Actual change | Natural change | Other[a] change | Actual change | Natural change | Other[a] change | Actual change |
| England | 1.5 | -0.5 | 1.0 | 0.7 | 0.0 | 0.7 | 1.2 | 0.6 | 1.9 |
| Scotland | 1.9 | -1.9 | -0.0 | 0.4 | -2.5 | -2.1 | 0.4 | -2.7 | -2.3 |
| Wales | 0.4 | 3.9 | 4.3 | -0.3 | 1.4 | 1.1 | 0.3 | 0.3 | 0.6 |
| Northern Ireland | 7.2 | -9.2 | 2.0 | 6.5 | -4.5 | 2.0 | 7.5 | -3.6 | 3.9 |
| **Regions of England** | | | | | | | | | |
| Northern | 0.8 | -1.8 | -1.0 | -0.1 | -2.1 | -2.3 | 0.4 | -2.8 | -2.4 |
| Yorks and Humb. | 1.4 | -0.4 | 1.0 | -0.1 | -0.2 | -0.3 | 0.6 | -1.4 | -0.8 |
| North-west | 1.0 | -2.5 | -1.5 | -0.4 | -2.7 | -3.1 | 0.7 | -3.3 | -2.6 |
| West Midlands | 3.3 | -1.7 | 1.7 | 1.6 | -1.3 | 0.3 | 2.2 | -2.4 | -0.2 |
| East Midlands | 2.5 | 2.9 | 5.4 | 1.2 | 3.0 | 4.2 | 1.4 | 2.0 | 3.4 |
| East Anglia | 2.5 | 11.1 | 13.5 | 1.2 | 7.6 | 8.8 | 1.1 | 9.0 | 10.1 |
| South-east | 1.7 | -2.9 | -1.2 | 1.0 | -0.6 | 0.4 | 1.8 | 1.2 | 3.0 |
| of which Gt London | 1.2 | -12.6 | -11.4 | 0.8 | -9.0 | -8.2 | 1.3 | -2.2 | -0.9 |
| South-west | -0.2 | 8.2 | 8.0 | -1.4 | 5.9 | 4.5 | -0.8 | 8.1 | 7.3 |

*Sources:* for 1951–61 Champion 1976; for 1961–6, 1966–71, and 1971–6 *Demographic Review* 1977. For 1976–81 and 1981–86 *Population Trends*, 46, 52; OPCS: Birth Statistics 1985, 1986: Birth Statistics Historical Series and Mortality Statistics

*Note:* [a] Net migration together with changes in number of armed forces and balancing adjustments

apart from the 1960s and the most recent period, has sustained an overall migration loss due to its negative balance with the rest of the world). The outcome has been a sharp increase in the growth rate, especially between 1984 and 1986 when 300,000 people were added to the population. Of the four countries, natural increase continues to be lowest in Wales, and the rise in its share of the United Kingdom population since 1971 is therefore entirely attributable to the influx of people, many on retirement, from the rest of the country. Although the early 1980s was marked by a temporary phase of stagnating numbers, like England, the Welsh rate of growth picked up strongly after 1984.

Analysis of the English standard regions highlights some other significant distributional changes that have taken place within the context of north:south division of the country (table 3.3). During the 1950s, for instance, growth was most rapid in the West Midlands and the south-east. By the 1960s, however, the focus of most rapid growth had shifted to East Anglia, the South-west and the East Midlands, where it has since remained. In part this change reflected the planned movement of people to the new and expanded towns designated to relieve congestion, especially around London, but it was also a voluntary process as people sought out more congenial environments, especially on retirement, and most recently has been reinforced by the extension of the London commuter zone, into East Anglia and the East Midlands. This factor along with a strong economy helps explain the recent resurgence of growth in the south-east outside Greater London. The 1970s witnessed yet other changes. As the national growth rate fell, so the population of the economically weaker regions of the north–Yorkshire and Humberside, the North-west and the Northern region – moved from a position of growth to one of decline and this has been maintained into the 1980s. Moreover, they were joined by the South-east for a short period in the mid-1970s, mainly because of the rapid decline of the population of Greater London, and by the West Midlands after 1981. Only three regions – East Anglia, the South-west and the East Midlands – have maintained uninterrupted growth throughout the 1970s and 1980s.

Given the modest variability in natural increase, the regional pattern of growth is largely attributable to net migration (table 3.3). For instance, the slowing down of the rate of increase in the South-east and West Midlands and the emergence of East Anglia and the South-west as the most dynamic regions has been largely due to an accelerating influx of people into East Anglia and the South-west and the transformation of the South-east and West Midlands into regions of net outflow after 1966. Similarly Yorkshire and Humberside, the North-west and the Northern region have consistently lost people to the other regions. But as well as such direct effects, migration has also had an indirect impact on regional population change because of its selective effect on age structure. Thus regions of migration gain have also tended to be regions of above average natural increase (i.e.

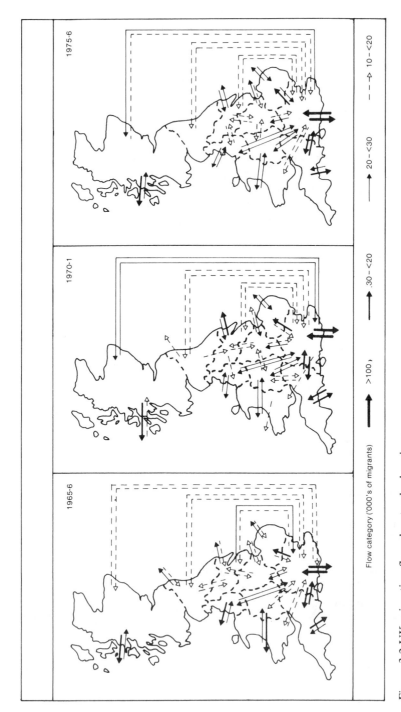

*Figure* 3.2 UK migration flows by standard regions
*Source:* Rees 1979

since 1981 East Anglia, the East Midlands and the South-east) while regions of migration loss have generally been regions of below average natural increase or decrease (i.e. the North, Yorkshire and Humberside and the North-west). The South-west and the West Midlands are exceptions, the former because much of the migrational gain is attributable to retirees among whom the death rate is high, and the latter because of the high birth rate of the ethnic minorities.

Net migration patterns are the outcome of a complex system of inter-regional migration streams which, Northern Ireland excepted, are described in figure 3.2. Although complex in delineation, these streams in fact exemplify all the regularities first discussed by Ravenstein (1885) and later embodied in the gravity model of Zipf and Stewart. Thus, given the observation that most migrations take place over comparatively short distances, the more important flows are between neighbouring regions, with both dominant and counterstreams in evidence. Again reflecting the size of its population, the largest inter-regional flows involve the South-east region. Moreover, this is the only region involved in substantial exchanges of population with non-contiguous regions, especially Scotland, Yorkshire and Humberside, the North and Wales.

Inter-regional migration streams also display distinctive patterns by age. Typically the bulk of migrants is concentrated in the age range 16 to 29; but, since this is also the section of population most likely to have young families, a comparatively high incidence of child migration also occurs; a further and more limited peak may occur around the age of retirement. But, despite these similarities, as Rees (1979) has shown, distinctive regional age patterns of net migration are none the less the outcome (figure 3.3). For instance, the economically weaker regions in particular, such as Scotland and the North-west, lose adults of prime working age presumably because of poor employment prospects. The East Midlands, East Anglia and the South-west are the principal beneficiaries, but the South-east also records substantial net gains among the 15 to 24 age group, presumably because of the attractiveness of London to people of this age for employment, educational and other reasons. Otherwise the South-east loses through migration, especially among those of retirement age, the beneficiaries again being the South-west and East Anglia, together with Wales and to a lesser extent Scotland.

Individual and household decisions, set in the context of the general socio-economic climate, form the basic components of the migration process and life-cycle stages are clearly involved in an interpretation of the age characteristics of migrants. Although inter-regional migrations only comprise a small proportion of moves in comparison with the vast majority which originate and terminate within the same region, they do tend to involve longer distances and, excepting retirement migration when residential choice is thought closely to accord with individuals' mental images of place utility, are more likely to be made for reasons of employment than are

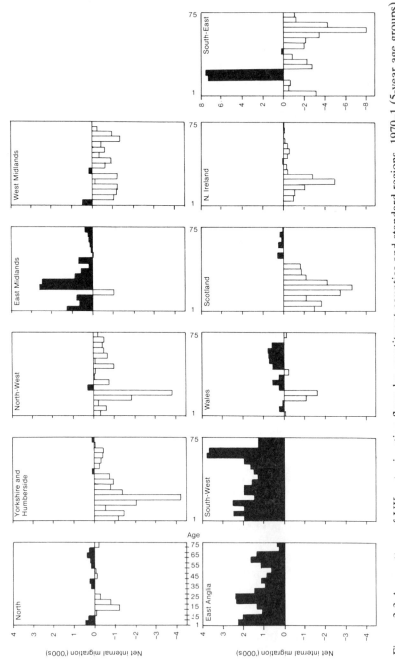

*Figure 3.3* Age pattern of UK net migration flows by constituent counties and standard regions, 1970–1 (5-year age groups)

*Source:* Rees 1979; Northern Ireland Census of Population 1971

shorter distance intra-regional moves. But the factors responsible for regional migration are varied and complex. As well as employment, housing also enters the equation. Additionally, government policies with respect to the new and expanded towns, the depressed areas and the relocation of office employment outside the Greater London area have all played significant if largely unquantifiable roles.

## URBAN POPULATION DECENTRALIZATION

Decentralization of population away from the urban centres of the country has occurred throughout this century but has accelerated noticeably since about 1960. The process first affected the largest places (for example the population of Greater London peaked at 8.6 millions in 1939) and has since spread down the urban hierarchy. It is a process made possible by an increasing level of personal mobility which, by enabling a greater separation of home and work, has had the consequence of extending urban spheres of influence. While largely spontaneous, it has at the same time been assisted by public policies concerned with the physical containment of the large cities, with urban renewal, and with the planned development of new and expanded towns specifically designed to relieve congestion in the largest population centres.

The process of decentralization is exemplified by the varying rates of population change for different administrative categories of settlement. An accelerating loss of population from the conurbations during the 1950s and 1960s was counterbalanced by substantial growth in the smaller urban centres and rural districts, and as a consequence a marked shift of population away from the cities in favour of the smaller centres occurred. Such a view of redistribution, although broadly corresponding to the physical distinction between town and country in terms of land use, is none the less deficient in the sense of not recognizing that the majority of rural residents also live an urban way of life. Nor does it take account of the fact that much of the physical expansion of towns since the Second World War has occurred in the countryside beyond the continuously built-up area. A functional division of space recognizing these realities should provide a more authentic expression of the processes of urban population change and decentralization.

It was for this reason that Hall *et al.* (1973) based their study of urban and metropolitan growth processes in England and Wales on Standard Metropolitan Labour Areas (SMLAs). According to this areal scheme, each SMLA consists of an urban core together with a metropolitan ring comprising local authority areas from which at least 15 per cent of the workers commute to the urban core, while beyond the SMLA is a more loosely associated outer commuting ring. The whole tripartite unit is termed a Metropolitan Economic Labour Area (MELA). Those parts of the country lying beyond the MELAs are considered to be outside the urban system.

A major finding of the Drewett *et al.* (1976) study of change between 1951 and 1971, which extended Hall's work, was that Great Britain has been urbanizing through an outward extension of commuter hinterlands, producing a centrifugal pattern of population change (table 3.4). During the 1950s, although the aggregate population of the urban cores increased it none the less declined relative to the rings, and by the 1960s this relative decline had turned into an absolute loss of population. In contrast, the flight of population to the metropolitan rings accelerated throughout the 1950s and 1960s; moreover the decennial growth rate of the outer commuting rings jumped sharply from 3.2 to 9.8 per cent after 1960. As Drewett *et al.* comment, the 'frontier of most active population change has moved progressively further from the urban cores', with the result that between 1951 and 1971 the proportion of Britain's population residing in the cores fell from 53.4 to 47.9 per cent while that in the metropolitan rings grew from 25.8 to 31.2 per cent and that of the outer rings from 16.0 to 16.4 per cent.

*Table 3.4* Population distribution and change by SMLAs and MELAs, 1951–71

| | *Population* | | | | | | *% change* | |
| | *1951* | | *1961* | | *1971* | | *1951–61* | *1961–71* |
| | *000s* | *%* | *000s* | *%* | *000s* | *%* | | |
|---|---|---|---|---|---|---|---|---|
| Urban cores | 26,077 | 53.4 | 26,577 | 51.8 | 25,858 | 47.9 | 1.9 | −2.7 |
| Metropolitan rings | 12,584 | 25.8 | 14,292 | 27.9 | 16,795 | 31.1 | 13.6 | 17.5 |
| SMLA total | 38,661 | 79.2 | 40,869 | 79.7 | 42,653 | 79.0 | 5.7 | 4.4 |
| Outer metropolitan rings | 7,863 | 16.0 | 8,084 | 15.8 | 8,876 | 16.4 | 3.2 | 9.8 |
| MELA total | 46,497 | 95.2 | 48,953 | 95.5 | 51,529 | 95.5 | 5.3 | 5.3 |
| Unclassified areas | 2,357 | 4.8 | 2,331 | 4.5 | 2,450 | 4.5 | −1.1 | 5.1 |
| Great Britain total | 48,854 | 100.0 | 51,284 | 100.0 | 53,979 | 100.0 | 5.0 | 5.3 |

*Source: Demographic Review* 1977, tables 6.1, 6.2

These aggregate changes suggest considerable dynamism within the urban framework of the country and this is reflected in the performance of individual SMLAs. The new and expanded towns experienced the highest rates of population growth during the 1950s and 1960s (e.g. Basingstoke, Basildon, Harlow and Milton Keynes), but in absolute terms it was certain of the large cities, immediately below the top rank, that made the greatest contribution to overall population increase (e.g. Coventry, Leicester, Bristol, Leeds and Southampton, plus some cities on the metropolitan periphery, like Plymouth and Norwich). On the other hand, many of the largest SMLAs, for instance London, Liverpool, Glasgow, Newcastle and

Manchester, moved from a position of weak growth during the 1950s to one where they were suffering the highest population losses, in both relative and absolute terms, a decade later.

As individual SMLAs have displayed different rates of aggregate population change, so the process of decentralization has also varied from city to city. During the 1950s, for instance, many places were still centralizing and absolute decentralization (i.e. the population of the urban core declining in size), a dominant process of the 1960s, was restricted to a handful of cities. London provides a good example of a city which was strongly decentralizing during both decades, for although the 1950s saw a small overall increase in the population of the SMLA this masked a net loss of 293,000 from the core and a gain of 349,000 in the metropolitan ring. By the end of the 1960s it was apparent that the process had massively accelerated, for the loss of over half a million people from the core during that decade was not compensated by a commensurate increase in the rings. Manchester, Newcastle and Glasgow experienced a similar pattern of change. By contrast, cities like Birmingham, Sheffield, Leeds and Nottingham were decentralizing only in a relative sense during the 1950s (i.e. their cores were growing at a slower pace than their rings), but by the 1960s this had been transformed into absolute decentralization when their core populations declined substantially in size. A third group is composed of some of the smaller yet rapidly growing towns of southern England, such as Bedford, Colchester, Ipswich and Peterborough, which moved from a pattern of relative centralization during the 1950s to relative decentralization during the 1960s. In summary then, the process of decentralization shows a reasonably clear association with city size, occurring earliest and developing most extensively in the largest centres and only appearing in the smaller, rapidly growing centres during the 1960s.

As in the case of regional change, internal migration has clearly been the most significant contributor to this fundamental restructuring of population both within and between MELAs for, although variation in natural increase is greater than at a regional scale, MELAs still tend to cluster close to the national average in this respect. Thus during the decade 1961–71 the net migration loss of the large cities was considerable, amounting to an outflow of almost one million people from the London MELA and up to 200,000 people each from Manchester, Liverpool and Glasgow. Moreover, whereas most MELAs in the north and west of the country either lost population or experienced a low net influx through migration, the vast majority of the MELAs recording substantial migration gains were clustered in the south-east around London and in East Anglia.

Migration was also a vital component of intra-MELA decentralization. During the 1960s the cores lost some 2.5 million people, or just under 10 per cent of their total population, due to net out-migration, while the decennial net inflow to the metropolitan rings averaged 14.7 per cent and to the outer rings 5.1 per cent. But the redistribution of population due to

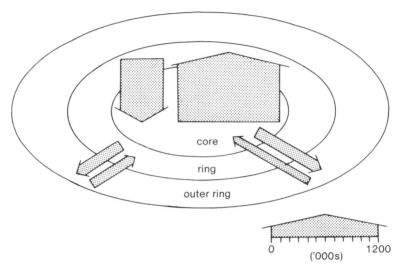

*Figure 3.4* Inter-zonal migration flows within Metropolitan Labour Areas, 1966–70
*Source:* Kennett 1977

net migration is a function of a considerably more complex system of migration streams (Kennett 1977). Thus, although the most important zonal flows were outwards from cores to rings regardless of whether the destination was within or outside a given MELA, there were also considerable counter-currents towards the centres and exchanges of population between inner and outer rings (figure 3.4).

Although the MELA-based analysis was not extended to cover Northern Ireland, it is clear that the province's population has also undergone the same process of decentralization. Despite natural increase of the order of 60,000, the Belfast Urban Area, with a population of 612,000 in 1971, grew by only 3,000 between 1966 and 1971 and out-migration was obviously occurring on a massive scale. The beneficiaries of this outflow were the new and expanded towns within a 30-mile radius of the city – Bangor, Newtownards, Ballymena, Antrim and Craigavon. Moreover, within the urban area itself, the substantial shift of population from the inner city (taken as the Belfast District Council Area) has rapidly accelerated; indeed, the population of the inner city dropped by 25 per cent from 417,000 to 340,000 between 1971 and 1981.

The evidence suggests that the process of absolute decentralization is still continuing, though not necessarily because of a further rise in centrifugal migration, and has also spread to affect areas even further from the urban cores. It is this process that produced the inverse relationship between population change and settlement size between 1971 and 1981 (table 3.5). Hence, whereas large cities with more than 200,000 inhabitants continued to decline in population over the decade, the smaller cities and towns continued to grow, the rate of gain being fastest for the smallest place. Rural areas also grew in population, but more slowly than the smaller cities and towns. Clearly, the demographic decentralization of the 1970s was mainly at the expense of the conurbations and principal cities and mostly to the advantage of the smaller cities and towns of the country, which had also been the main beneficiaries of the decentralization of employment. Rural areas in favourable locations (i.e. within commuting distance of centres of employment) also grew in population but, as the more modest overall rate of increase suggests, less accessible parts continued to lose population.

*Table 3.5* England and Wales: urban and rural population distribution and change, 1971–81

|  | Urban areas in 1981 | Population in 1981 (millions) | Per cent population change 1971–81 |
|---|---|---|---|
| Population size categories |  |  |  |
| 500,000 or more | 9 | 17.2 | 6.3 |
| 200,000–499,999 | 22 | 6.4 | −0.7 |
| 100,000–199,999 | 24 | 3.3 | 2.8 |
| 20,000–99,999 | 211 | 9.2 | 7.3 |
| 10,000–19,999 | 218 | 3.1 | 10.1 |
| Under 10,000 | 1,295 | 5.1 | 11.1 |
| All urban areas | 1,780 | 44.4 | 0.4 |
| Rural areas |  | 4.8 | 5.4 |
| All England and Wales | 1,780 | 49.2 | 1.0 |

*Source* :Adapted from *Demographic Review* 1984

It is also instructive to examine the more specific geographical characteristics of the decentralization of recent years. For instance, the populations of London and the metropolitan counties, broadly coincidental with the great conurbations, have fallen in every year since 1970, while those parts of the standard regions falling outside these areas, with the exception of the north between 1976 and 1981, have continued to grow, mainly through in-migration (table 3.6). There is, however, evidence that this outward spread of population is now beginning to moderate. Loss from Greater London peaked in 1971–6 and has since decelerated because of the slowing down of out-migration from the capital (Champion and Congdon 1988). Equally, maximum loss from the metropolitan counties peaked five years later in 1976–81 with the virtual cessation of natural growth (for the northern conurbations this was actually a period of natural decline). Moreover, although the figures post-1981 are estimates and therefore

Table 3.6 Percentage population change for metropolitan counties, Greater London, Central Clydeside and English standard regions outside these areas, 1971-6 to 1981-6

| Region | Mid-year population 1981 000s | % change 1971-6 | | | % change 1976-81 | | | % change 1981-6 | | |
|---|---|---|---|---|---|---|---|---|---|---|
| | | Natural change | Other change | Actual change | Natural change | Other change | Actual change | Natural change | Other change | Actual change |
| Tyne and Wear | 1,155 | 0.1 | -2.2 | -2.1 | -0.4 | -2.4 | -2.8 | 0.3 | -1.7 | -1.4 |
| Rest of Northern | 1,963 | 0.6 | 0.0 | 0.5 | -0.1 | -0.2 | -0.3 | 0.3 | -1.2 | 0.9 |
| South Yorkshire | 1,317 | 0.8 | -0.9 | -0.1 | -0.1 | -0.4 | -0.5 | 0.3 | -3.9 | -3.6 |
| West Yorkshire | 2,067 | 0.7 | -0.9 | -0.2 | 0.1 | -0.8 | -0.7 | 0.6 | -1.3 | -0.7 |
| Rest Y. and H. | 1,534 | 0.6 | 1.5 | 2.1 | -0.2 | 1.2 | 1.0 | 0.0 | 0.9 | 0.9 |
| Greater Man. | 2,619 | 0.7 | -2.6 | -1.8 | -0.0 | -2.2 | -2.2 | 0.6 | -2.1 | -1.5 |
| Merseyside | 1,522 | 0.5 | -5.2 | -4.6 | -0.2 | -4.0 | -3.8 | 0.3 | -3.9 | -3.6 |
| Rest North-west | 2,319 | 0.2 | 3.3 | 3.5 | -0.4 | 1.5 | 1.1 | 0.1 | 0.3 | 0.4 |
| West Mids. M.C. | 2,673 | 1.7 | -3.4 | -1.7 | 0.8 | -3.5 | -2.7 | 1.3 | -2.9 | -1.5 |
| Rest West Mids. | 2,513 | 1.6 | 2.3 | 4.0 | 0.9 | 2.5 | 3.4 | 0.8 | 0.6 | 1.4 |
| Greater Lond. | 6,806 | 0.6 | -6.1 | -5.6 | 0.4 | -4.4 | -4.0 | 1.2 | -1.7 | -0.5 |
| Rest South-east | 10,204 | | | | 0.6 | 2.6 | 3.2 | 0.7 | 2.1 | 2.8 |
| Cent. Clydeside | 1,724 | 3.7 | -6.7 | -3.0 | 0.1 | -9.4 | -9.3 | 0.8 | -7.0 | -6.2 |
| Rest Strathclyde | 665 | | | | 1.1 | -4.5 | -3.4 | 0.5 | 1.6 | 2.1 |

Sources: Demographic Review 1984; Population Trends 23, 46, 52; OPCS Birth Statistics: Birth Statistics Historical Series; Mortality Statistics

subject to a margin of error, they reveal the same pattern as for London – a substantial slowing down of metropolitan county population loss brought about by the recovery in natural increase and a somewhat reduced rate of net outflow.

Outside the great conurbations, the recent process of change has been more varied (Britton 1986). The large 'free-standing' cities, for instance Bristol, Southampton, Leicester, Cardiff and Plymouth, have followed a similar trend to the conurbations in that, while still losing population, they have been doing so at a slower rate since the mid-1970s. This contrasts markedly with smaller cities like Norwich, Exeter and Middlesbrough where population decline is still accelerating. Yet another variation is displayed by districts containing new towns (e.g. Milton Keynes and Redditch), where population is still increasing but at a decelerating rate. Different again are those districts dominated by resort and retirement settlements where the rate of growth in the 1980s has been roughly double that experienced in the second half of the 1970s.

Urban decentralization is therefore a highly complex spatio-temporal process, which may be likened to a wave that has fanned outwards from the principal cities and conurbations. The main gainers have been the districts adjacent to these conurbations and cities, but, since the peak of the wave has moved beyond these areas, they too are now experiencing sharply declining population growth and even decline. Over time, population decentralization has also spread down the urban hierarchy. Hence, the loss of population from many smaller cities is still accelerating at a time when decline in larger centres is beginning to tail off. Whether this is a harbinger of renewed population concentration in the great cities at some time in the future is, of course too early to say. Furthermore, the likely longer-term demographic future of those smaller cities and towns that are still growing rapidly is also unclear. What can be said, however, is that the re-emergence of the fashion for central urban living and the activities of urban development corporations, most spectacularly exemplified in the case of London's docklands, is leading to a revitalization of inner city areas, notwithstanding the continuing outward spread of commuter zones.

## FERTILITY

Fertility, through its bearing on natural increase, is the most important factor affecting the growth and size of the United Kingdom population. It is also a prime determinant of age structure and hence of both the ratio of active to inactive population and the proportion of females of child-bearing age. Moreover, through its impact on age structure, it also affects the demand for social services, like education and provision for the elderly.

**National characteristics**

Fertility decline began around 1870 and came to an end in the 1930s. During this period, the United Kingdom birth rate and completed family size declined by about 60 per cent but since then there has been a tendency for the cohort and period (annual) trends to diverge. On the one hand, families are now small and completed family size has ranged rather narrowly between 2.0 and 2.4 children since the war, but on the other hand period rates have been quite volatile. Thus period fertility rose rapidly from the lows of the 1930s to peak in 1947, when over one million live births were registered in the United Kingdom as a whole. A trough during the mid-1950s was in turn superseded by a sustained rise until 1964, when births again exceeded one million, but after that the number of live births fell by 35 per cent between 1964 and 1977, followed more recently by some small recovery. Moreover, whatever method is used to measure period fertility – total fertility, general fertility or crude birth rate – the essentials of this trend are preserved.

The reason for the divergence between cohort and period fertility lies in the fact that modern methods of birth control now give the majority of married couples an effective means of timing the formation of their families in response to short-term changes in socio-economic conditions, without drastically altering ultimate family size. For instance, those born in 1930 reached their peak childbearing age around 1955, when the period rate was comparatively low; the prime childbearing years of the 1940 birth cohort, by comparison, coincided with the baby boom of the mid-1960s. None the less, because the 1930 cohort went on bearing children until later in life, completed family size was approximately the same for both groups of women – 2.4 children. Moreover, the General Household Survey shows that even among women who were bearing their children during the sharp fall in the birth rate after 1964 (i.e. women born between roughly 1945 and 1960) there is an expectation of an average completed family size of around 2.2 children.

The volatility of the recent period trend can be related to a number of interconnected demographic factors. The birth rate surge between 1955 and 1964 saw a rise in the fertility of women of all ages, particularly those aged 20 to 29. The reasons for this included more couples marrying and marrying earlier, a process which had begun in the 1930s; an earlier start to childbearing and the compression of family formation into a shorter time span; and a shift away from childlessness and one child families in favour of two and three child families. By contrast, the post-1964 phase of decline saw most of these processes reversed. Marriage rates peaked in 1970 and then declined, while median age at marriage was noticeably higher in the late 1970s than at the beginning of the decade. Moreover, the interval between marriage and first birth widened, as couples deferred having children. Additionally, the proportion of third and higher order births fell markedly.

Some recovery in the birth rate around the late 1970s was anticipated, if only because the number of women of prime childbearing age was set to rise strongly as a result of the echo effect from the 1964 birth peak (the number of women aged 20 to 29 rose by 10 per cent between 1977 and 1987). But in the event, the post-1977 upturn has been a weak phenomenon. Recovery was quite strong up to 1980, affecting women of all ages but especially those over the age of 35, and represents some catching-up from the very low birth levels of previous years. Most recently, however, the recovery has tended to falter because the gain from the increase in the number of potential mothers has been offset by other factors. Hence, first marriage rates have continued to decline steeply and were roughly one third lower in 1987 than in 1977. Although more couples are now cohabiting in stable unions (almost a quarter of births were illegitimate in 1986), the fertility of such women continues to be lower than that of married couples. Moreover, increasing marital disruption – divorces now amount to one in two of all first marriages contracted in any year – also serves to depress fertility, despite a high and climbing remarriage rate. On top of this, current birth rates specific for age of mother and birth order imply increased childlessness, a renewed decline in the number of families with three or more children, and an increased proportion of women with exactly two children. In addition, the modal age for bearing children has moved firmly into the 25 to 29 age group, a clear indication that women are tending to have children later in their lives. In other words, although the birth rate may continue to edge upwards for the next few years under the pressure of more women of childbearing age, there is no suggestion of a sustained rise in fertility in the foreseeable future; if anything, the indications point to further fertility decline and a renewed fall in the birth rate once the present bulge in the 20 to 29 age group has worked itself out of the childbearing population.

There are, however, more fundamental explanations for these trends. The eminent demographer D. V. Glass (1976) interpreted the upsurge in period fertility in the immediate post-war period as a fulfilment of the family size norms which, but for the depression, would have been achieved by the marriages of the 1930s, while Eversley (1980) has explained the comparatively high fertility of the late 1950s and 1960s in terms of rapidly rising wage levels, low unemployment, and greater government involvement in the welfare of individuals. Conversely, he has associated the declining fertility of the 1970s with the worsening economic climate. In a similar economic vein, Easterlin's theory, relating fertility level to material aspirations, has also been applied with some success to the interpretation of the post-1940 period trend (Easterlin and Condran 1976). Simons (1986), by contrast, presents a socio-cultural interpretation. He sees opinion fluctuating between traditional and pragmatic views of society. When traditional views, assessed by the degree of religious conversion, are in the ascendant, as in the late 1950s and early 1960s, fertility is high, while the more pragmatic, indeed permissive, outlook of the 1970s and 1980s may be associated with low fertility.

But these aside, it is important to realize that there is no comprehensive theory to explain fertility variations or account for the values that people place upon parenthood. This makes any assessment of future fertility trends very problematical and it is no secret that in the past demographers have got their forecasts very wrong because of their inability to predict fertility. Suffice it to say that because of fertility control, every couple can now realistically weigh the satisfactions of parenthood against the costs. The changing role of women is an important factor in this connection (Ermisch 1983). As it becomes more common for married women to be gainfully employed outside the home, the financial benefits and other opportunities that would be lost by staying at home to bear and bring up children become a significant component of the cost of children. For couples used to two incomes, it can lead to a substantial reduction in living standards. Moreover, women who break their career to have children may face difficulties re-entering work and, even when this hurdle is overcome, may be disadvantaged with regard to promotion. Smaller families and the compression of childbearing into a shorter time span are the response of working mothers to this conflict between rearing a family and maintaining a career outside the home. Given these circumstances, the growing attachment of married women to the labour force makes a sustained increase in the birth rate unlikely.

Last, the means of fertility control are now more comprehensive than ever before. Not only is family planning part of the National Health Service, but legally induced abortion provides a back-up for contraceptive failure. Although no causal link necessarily exists between low fertility and methods of artificial birth control, the ready availability of contraception has none the less contributed to the decline in the birth rate by reducing the number of unwanted children in marriage and helping prevent live births outside marriage. This does not mean that no unwanted conceptions occur; that there were almost 150,000 induced abortions in England and Wales in 1986 is witness to this. It is, however, reasonable to suppose that the number of unplanned and unwanted pregnancies is substantially lower than in the past.

**Regional characteristics**

Although the national fertility trend is mirrored throughout the United Kingdom, each region exhibits certain distinctive characteristics (table 3.7). For instance in Northern Ireland fertility continues to be substantially above the national average, primarily because of the high fertility of the Catholic minority. In addition, the post-1964 decline was somewhat less pronounced than in Great Britain, with the result that by 1977 the disparity between the two areas had widened so that Northern Ireland with 2.8 per

Table 3.7 General fertility rates per 1,000 women aged 15–44, 1965–86

| | 1965 | 1977 | 1980 | 1981 | 1982 | 1983 | 1984 | 1985 | 1986 | Change % 1965–77 | Change % 1977–86 |
|---|---|---|---|---|---|---|---|---|---|---|---|
| England | 91.4 | 58.6 | 64.9 | 61.3 | 59.9 | 59.5 | 59.7 | 60.9 | 60.5 | −36.0 | 3.2 |
| Scotland | 96.3 | 59.4 | 63.8 | 63.8 | 59.8 | 58.9 | 58.4 | 59.5 | 58.5 | −38.3 | −1.5 |
| Wales | 88.7 | 59.0 | 66.7 | 63.1 | 62.3 | 61.0 | 61.3 | 62.4 | 62.1 | −38.0 | 5.3 |
| N. Ireland | 114.5 | 83.8 | 91.0 | 85.7 | 84.1 | 83.5 | 83.6 | 83.6 | 83.6 | −26.8 | −0.2 |
| *English Regions* | | | | | | | | | | | |
| Northern | 89.7 | 58.2 | 65.1 | 61.9 | 60.6 | 60.0 | 59.9 | 62.3 | 60.9 | −35.0 | 4.3 |
| York and Humb. | 92.3 | 58.4 | 65.0 | 61.7 | 60.2 | 60.8 | 60.5 | 61.5 | 61.7 | −37.0 | 5.7 |
| North-west | 94.6 | 59.3 | 65.6 | 63.7 | 62.9 | 63.1 | 62.9 | 64.5 | 63.9 | −37.0 | 7.8 |
| E. Midlands | 92.5 | 59.5 | 65.3 | 61.0 | 59.0 | 58.5 | 58.5 | 59.3 | 58.6 | −36.0 | −1.5 |
| E. Anglia | 88.5 | 59.7 | 64.4 | 60.9 | 57.5 | 57.2 | 58.1 | 58.5 | 57.3 | −33.0 | −4.0 |
| South-east | 89.6 | 59.6 | 64.7 | 60.5 | 58.7 | 58.5 | 58.8 | 60.0 | 59.9 | −33.0 | 0.5 |
| South-west | 92.4 | 55.8 | 60.8 | 57.5 | 56.6 | 55.7 | 56.2 | 57.2 | 57.0 | −40.0 | 2.2 |
| West Midlands | 93.0 | 59.5 | 67.2 | 62.3 | 62.1 | 62.0 | 62.1 | 63.1 | 62.7 | −36.0 | 5.4 |

*Sources:* OPCS Birth Statistics; Annual Reports of Registrar General for Northern Ireland; Annual Reports for Registrar General for Scotland

cent of the UK population accounted for 4 per cent of all live births compared with 3.5 per cent a decade earlier. By the same token, the post-1977 recovery has been less marked in Northern Ireland, with the result that the proportion of UK births occurring in the province had fallen back to 3.8 per cent in 1986. Somewhat different has been the Scottish experience, where fertility was traditionally higher than in England and Wales but where, in contrast to Northern Ireland, rates moved closer to the English level after 1964, and since 1975 have actually been lower than south of the border. Another contrast is that because mothers in Scotland tend to have their children earlier than elsewhere in the country, fertility rates for women under the age of 25 are still higher than in England and Wales.

Similarly, fertility in Wales and the English regions has also mirrored the national trend, but, because the rate of decline was somewhat greater in former regions of relatively high fertility, what variability there had been a decade or so earlier had largely disappeared by 1977. Hence, in eight of the nine standard regions general fertility lay within 2 per cent of the England and Wales mean and only in the South-west was it outside this range. During the post-1977 recovery, however, the trends in individual regions have again tended to diverge. The recovery has been most persistent in Wales, the West Midlands and in the northern half of England; in East Anglia and the East Midlands, by contrast, the general fertility rate has fallen sharply since the post-recovery high in 1980 and is now below the 1977 figure, i.e. in these regions, the recovery may well turn out to have been no more than a brief blip on a general downward trend post-1964. In the south-east, too, the recovery was short lived and fertility is again back at the 1977 level.

A distinctive regional fertility pattern had clearly re-emerged by the mid-1980s. In addition to the long-standing differential between Great Britain and Northern Ireland, regional fertility, leaving Scotland aside, is higher to the north of a line drawn roughly from the Wash to the Bristol Channel. North of this line more women marry and marry younger, with the consequence that the birth rates of women under the age of 25 are substantially higher than in the south of the country. In contrast, the fertility of older women is higher in the south, although this is insufficient to compensate for the lower birth rate at younger ages. An additional geographical dimension lies in the fact that the West Midlands and the northern regions also gain births because of the relatively high fertility recorded in the metropolitan counties. Hence, fertility in the West Midlands outside the Birmingham area and in Yorkshire outside the South and West Yorkshire conurbations is about the same as in the East Midlands and East Anglia. Only the non-metropolitan parts of the North-west stand out as being areas of relatively high fertility. How far these patterns are part of a more detailed rural:urban symmetry is difficult to assess. The crude birth rate variation, although suggestive, is not decisive because it is strongly influenced by the age structure of the 'at risk' population. What is clear, however, is that the crude birth rate is higher in Greater London and the metropolitan districts than in non-metropolitan districts. Moreover, within Greater London, the rate is higher in inner than outer districts; it was also higher in the principal cities than in other parts of the metropolitan counties. Of the non-metropolitan districts, resort and seaside retirement areas and remoter largely rural districts record the lowest rates, and districts with new towns and smaller cities the highest rates.

Greater variability has generally been apparent at the subregional level. In 1984–6, for instance the total period fertility rate, an age adjusted measure of fertility, deviated from the mean by more than 10 per cent in three out of every ten districts of England and Wales, whilst among the Scottish regions general fertility ranged from 15 per cent above the Scottish average in Ross and Cromarty to 20 per cent below in Aberdeen City. Moreover, at the purely local scale variations can be very substantial. Greater London is a case in point, where fertility levels tend to mirror the socio-economic and ethnic composition of the population. For instance, in 1986 the total period fertility rate was one third higher than the Greater London mean in Tower Hamlets and Newham, whose populations contain substantial ethnic minorities, and up to one third below the mean in the fashionable areas of Kensington and Chelsea, Fulham and Camden. Otherwise relatively high fertility, although associated with different types of area, is largely urban based, as in Scunthorpe, Luton, Liverpool, Ipswich, the Isles of Scilly and Rochdale; the distribution of relatively low fertility is equally disparate, for example, occurring in towns like Cambridge, Chichester and Congleton, but is also widely dispersed throughout the countryside as in the mainly rural districts of Kesteven, Broadland, Ryedale and Chiltern.

Clearly, the geographical pattern of fertility is not easily accounted for and an explanation at one scale will not necessarily apply at any other. Moreover, the pattern may vary according to the way fertility is measured and may even vary spatially by female age group. In the Northern region, Yorkshire and Humberside and the North-west, for instance, in 1986 the birth rate for women under the age of 25 was 13 per cent above the England average but 9 per cent below in the case of women aged 30 and over; whereas the reverse pattern exists within the South-east (14 per cent below the average for women under 25 and 15 per cent above for those aged 30 and over). Moreover, Coward (1987) has shown that quite marked variations exist in the regional pattern of extra-marital conceptions, which are highest in Greater London and Merseyside and lowest in East Anglia and the South-west. Whereas age composition and internal migration flows largely account for differences in crude birth rates, social class, occupational structure, the gainful employment of married women, religion, ethnic make-up, education and so on (i.e. the factors that condition attitudes to family size), are the important variables when examining 'real' fertility differences – that is, variations in marital fertility and family size. The situation in Belfast in 1971 exemplifies this point: the pattern of crude birth rates roughly varies by age of residential neighbourhood and was low in central areas with their predominantly elderly population and low ratio of childbearers, and high in the new housing areas on the outskirts where the young married adult population is largely concentrated (figure 3.5). By contrast, marital fertility and family size distributions reflect the social class and religious structure of the city and are generally higher in inner areas than in the suburbs and in the Roman Catholic west than elsewhere in the city (Compton 1978).

The comparative lack of fertility variation at the level of standard regions may therefore be interpreted as a function of their large populations and socio-economic heterogeneity with an inevitable tendency to approximate the national average. The minor differences that have existed in the recent past show some association with the pattern of migration but the correlation is not strong. At a finer level, however, the social and economic distinctiveness of individual areas emerges and generic relationships, such as the social class differential in fertility whereby the families of unskilled workers are some 25 per cent larger than those in intermediate non-manual occupations and the strong ethnic minority presence in some of the metropolitan counties, find expression on the ground. Indeed the more local the scale of analysis the greater the socio-economic homogeneity of areas and the greater the variation in fertility.

It is only through detailed area studies, therefore, that contemporary spatial patterns of fertility can be explained. Of the few geographers who have turned their attention to such work, Jones (1975) used a regression model which accounted for 85 per cent of the geographical variability in the crude birth rate in Scotland in 1971 in terms of age structure, religion, social class, and female participation in the workforce. In addition, it has been shown that the high birth rate in Northern Ireland stems from the fact that the 'Irish' and 'British' patterns of marital fertility overlap in the province. This reflects the religious composition of the population for, while the fertility of the Protestant majority is only marginally higher than that of the population of Great Britain, the Roman Catholic minority still displays one of the highest fertility rates in Europe (Compton and Coward 1989). The outcome is a fertility level roughly midway between those of Great Britain and the Irish Republic. Moreover, because the religious mix varies from one part of the province to another, there are also sharp spatial differences in fertility from low levels in the largely Protestant east to high rates in the predominantly Catholic areas of the west and along the border with the Irish Republic. These differences are also mirrored in the spatial pattern of attitudes to reproduction, e.g. attitudes to legally induced abortion (Compton, Coward and Power 1986).

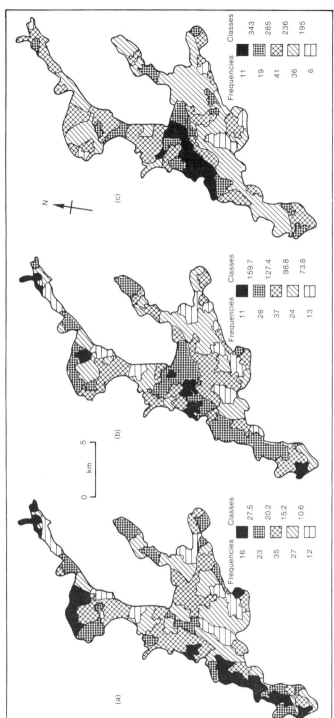

*Figure 3.5* Fertility rates in Belfast 1970/1
(a) Live births in year preceding census per 1,000 population
(b) Legitimate live births in year preceding the census per 1,000 ever–married women aged 15–49
(c) Children per 1,000 ever married women aged 50–9
*Source:* Compton 1978

## MORTALITY

The mortality rate has followed an almost uninterrupted downward path this century. Since 1945, however, although continuing to drop amongst the younger population, improvements at older ages have occurred more slowly, while amongst elderly males the position has remained virtually static over the last three decades. A further characteristic has been the more rapid decline in female mortality, with the consequence that considerable male excess mortality now exists at all ages and the gap continues to widen. As for the situation in the mid-1980s, death rates below the age of 45 are now so low that, with the exception of infant mortality, room for further reduction is severely limited. Moreover, substantial improvements at advanced ages will have to await more effective treatments for the chronic illnesses that afflict the elderly.

Declining mortality and advancing longevity have gone hand in hand. Life expectancy at birth in 1985 stood at 71.5 years for males and 77 years for females, an advance of more than one-third since 1900; more than four-fifths of this improvement had been achieved by 1950. At older ages, the gains have been less impressive. Female life expectancy at age 65 has advanced by only two years since 1950, while the improvement for males over the same period has been negligible. As a consequence, while females now enjoy something like a 10 per cent advantage in life expectancy at birth, by the age of 65 this has risen to 25 per cent and at more advanced ages is even more pronounced.

The reasons for the downward trend in mortality have been well documented and include rising living standards, improved housing, sanitation and hygiene, expanded welfare and maternity services, and advances in medical science. The decline has been accompanied by many striking changes in the relative significance of the various causes of death. For instance, the last thirty-five years have witnessed the virtual elimination of mortality from infectious diseases and, because of this, accidents are now the major cause of death during childhood and early adult life. At the same time, death rates from cancer and circulatory diseases have risen sharply, with cancer the more important cause amongst females and circulatory diseases more likely to affect males.

### Regional patterns

Within the United Kingdom, the crude death rate is lowest in Northern Ireland, followed by England, Scotland and Wales in that order. The crude death rate, however, is a poor measure of actual mortality conditions and closer investigation reveals that the low rate in Northern Ireland stems not from an inherently more healthy population but, on the contrary, reflects a youthful age structure brought about by a comparatively high birth rate. Indeed, standard mortality ratios, which eliminate any variability attributable to age composition, show that Northern Ireland experiences a comparatively high mortality level, 9 per cent above the national average for males, 5 per cent above for females in 1985, although these are exceeded in Scotland where the ratios were 11 per cent above the national average for both males and females in the same year. Otherwise the English rate is 2 per cent below the national level for both sexes, while in Wales it is 4 and 2 per cent above for males and females respectively.

Subdividing England into standard regions further clarifies the national pattern, which is one of progressive mortality increase from the south to the north of the country. Thus the south-east, East Anglia and the South-west fall well below the general level, with age standardized rates some 7 to 12 per cent under the national average; Scotland, the North and the North-west all experience mortality in excess of 10 per cent above the national average; the East Midlands is about the national average, while Wales, Northern Ireland, the West Midlands and Yorkshire and Humberside experience moderately high mortality, up to 10 per cent above the average. There is none the less considerable variability within this basic north:south division. For instance, Chilver's (1978) analysis of mortality in England and Wales between 1969 and 1973 picked out the major conurbations as areas of excess male mortality within their respective regions and, replicating the same exercise for 1983 to 1985, shows that the situation is essentially unchanged more than a decade later. The contrast is particularly striking in Yorkshire and Humberside, where the two metropolitan counties of South and West Yorkshire record male mortality levels 10 per cent above the national average, while in the remainder of the region it is marginally below average. Similarly, mortality is higher in Greater London than in the rest of the South-east, higher in the Birmingham conurbation than in the rest of the West Midlands, and so on. Outside England and Wales, the great cities of Glasgow and Belfast conform to the same pattern. Although the contrasts between the main centres of population and the rest of the country are less pronounced, female mortality tends to be similarly structured. The more detailed subregional distribution confirms the broad north:south differential and also highlights the strength of the contrast between the main population centres and the rest of the country especially outside the south-east.

As Howe (1970) has demonstrated for the United Kingdom and Gardner *et al.* (1983, 1984) more specifically for England and Wales, the distribution of overall mortality is a spatial composite of the various patterns of disease mortality. For instance, mortality for both sexes from diseases of the circulatory system as well as male mortality from respiratory diseases mirrors the north:south pattern of deaths from all causes. Cancer mortality, by contrast, is quite variable spatially; for males it is high in the North and North-west but is also at or slightly above average in the South-east, while female death rates lie everywhere close to the national average. The various causes of death can be assigned to one of four spatial groups. There are those causes, like bronchitis, pulmonary embolism, and to a lesser extent suicide, which display a higher incidence in urban than in rural areas, while others, like heart disease, are more significant in the north than in the south of the country. Yet a third group, although clearly related to area, follows no coherent regional pattern, deaths from stomach cancer being an example of this type; the last group is made up of the large number of causes that are randomly distributed spatially.

The factors that generate such distinctive geographical patterns of mortality are varied and complex, and include degree of urbanization, occupation, lifestyle, social class, relative poverty or wealth and physical environment. For instance, the high mortality rates in the northern conurbations clearly contribute to the north:south mortality division of the country, while the impact of a greater occupational hazard can be associated with the high male death rates of coal-mining areas. There is also evidence that the higher incidence of circulatory diseases in Wales, Northern Ireland, Scotland and northern England is in part a function of lifestyle, of diet, consumption of alcohol and incidence of smoking as forcefully enunciated by Mrs Edwina Currie when Junior Minister for Health in the mid–1980s, and more soberly argued in government health reports. Social class differences are yet another factor that have some bearing on the patterns (Fox 1977). Males subject to Social Class I death rates throughout their lifetime can be expected to live up to seven years longer than males subject to Social Class V rates, whilst infant mortality is some three times higher for Social Class V than Social Class I. Such social class differentials may play some role in accounting for rural/urban mortality variations and in explaining the favourable position of Greater London in comparison with the other conurbations. But that said, socio-economic composition by itself cannot explain the distinctive patterns, viz. the attractively simple notion that, since mortality varies by social class, occupation, tenure, etc., it is the way areas vary socio-economically that accounts for the spatial differences in mortality. As Fox *et al.* (1985) have shown from the OPCS Longitudinal Study there is a very wide range of mortality variations within ward clusters of similar socio-economic characteristics, such as urban council estates. Furthermore, mortality for all groups tends to be high in high mortality areas and low in low mortality areas, which may point to an independent geographical factor. As for the specific effect of the physical environment, the link between respiratory disease and air pollution has long been recognized, while stomach cancer has been variously correlated with the level of nitrates and with dissolved metals in the water supply.

Lastly it can be noted that spatial variations in longevity form a mirror image of the patterns of mortality. In the mid-1980s, for instance, male life expectancy at birth ranged from 70 years in Northern Ireland and Scotland to 73.5 years in East Anglia, a spatial range equivalent to the national improvement in life expectancy over the last twenty years and greater than the improvement that would be achieved were cancer to be eliminated as a cause of death. Although the female range is smaller, gauged in this way the regional inequalities in mortality are clearly substantial and it is surprising that they are accepted by the population with such equanimity. It is indeed ironic that health and welfare services are frequently poorest in the areas of greatest need.

## Infant mortality

Infant mortality is accepted as a reliable index of public health and social and economic well-being, and stands somewhat apart from general mortality. Although the death rate for this group has fallen substantially in recent years – it was 9.5 per 1,000 live births in 1986 – the position has stabilized of late and the United Kingdom no longer belongs to that group of countries with the lowest rates. But on the positive side, the marked spatial variation that existed before the 1980s and which mirrored the north:south pattern of all causes, has given way to one of greater uniformity, i.e. the survival chances of the newly born are now virtually the same across the country and are no longer as dependent as was once the case on the chance factor of place of birth. The cases of Northern Ireland and Scotland well exemplify this improvement; whereas ten years earlier infant mortality rates in both were substantially above the national average today they are either at or only marginally above the general norm. Similarly, the north:south divide in England is now less clear-cut, with East Anglia, for example, reporting a rate somewhat higher than in the north or the north-west. These trends would seem to run counter to what might have been expected, given the sharpening of the north:south economic divide and the presumed relationship between socio-economic well-being and infant mortality. What, however, is incontrovertible is the fact that medical treatment has made considerable advances over the last decade, especially during the crucial neonatal phase, and that conditions which would formerly have resulted in death, for instance those associated with very premature low birth weight infants, can now be treated successfully.

## INTERNATIONAL MIGRATION

The United Kingdom has a long history of exporting population to the rest of the world. The traditional destinations were the United States and the former dominions of the Old Commonwealth, but the post-war forging of new links with Europe and the emergence of restrictive immigration policies in Australia, Canada and the United States have helped to modify the traditional patterns. At the same time immigration has also been substantial; until comparatively recently citizens of the Commonwealth had the right of free entry to the United Kingdom. Additionally there has been a willingness to share responsibility for the resettlement of peoples displaced by upheavals in their own countries. Accordingly, the aftermath of the Second World War resulted in considerable resettlement in this country of people of East European origin, notably Poles and Ukrainians. Hungarians were admitted after the 1956 uprising and more recently sanctuary has been granted to Vietnamese 'boat people' and Tamils fleeing Sri Lanka.

The post-1945 period falls naturally into three distinct parts. The first phase lasted until the mid-1950s and was a period of considerable emigration. Initially, Canada and the United States were the favoured destinations but the numbers emigrating to Australia gradually increased through the policy of encouraging migration with the Assisted Passage scheme. Over the period 1946 to 1956 the net United Kingdom loss through external migration is estimated to have been of the order of 400,000 people.

The economic prosperity of the 1950s brought in its train a chronic shortage of labour and this heralded the onset of the second phase. Migrants from the Irish Republic had traditionally helped meet the labour needs of British industry but the inflow now proved insufficient, so the United Kingdom turned increasingly to the poorer countries of the Commonwealth to satisfy this demand. Initially the influx of workers was from the West Indies and Guyana, but these were soon supplemented by newcomers from the Indian sub-continent and Africa. As the rate of emigration was slackening at that time, the outcome was a sizeable net inflow of people between 1956 and 1965, amounting to approximately 200,000.

The third and most recent phase has lasted since the mid-1960s and is better, though still imperfectly, documented through the statistics collected by the International Passenger Survey. This phase has been one of slackening international movements as various pressures, both external and internal, have led countries to restrict immigration. Canada and Australia no longer follow an 'open door' policy with respect to citizens of the United Kingdom, accepting only those whose skills are demanded. Nor is there any longer the right of free entry to the United Kingdom for citizens of the Commonwealth. Restricting the entry of New Commonwealth citizens began as early as 1962 with the passage of the Commonwealth Immigrants Acts, which immediately curtailed the primary inflow from the West Indies, although dependants of immigrants already here were still admitted. The reasons for the restriction were partly economic but were also related to the problems of assimilating a large number of people not only of different culture but also of different colour. Since then the regulations governing immigration have been progressively tightened up. The 1968 Act placed limitations on the entry of New Commonwealth dependants, while the 1971 Immigration Act, by introducing the concept of patriality, made entry difficult for all those who did not have a close connection by descent with the United Kingdom, a concept reinforced in the British Nationality Act of 1981. Contrasting with these

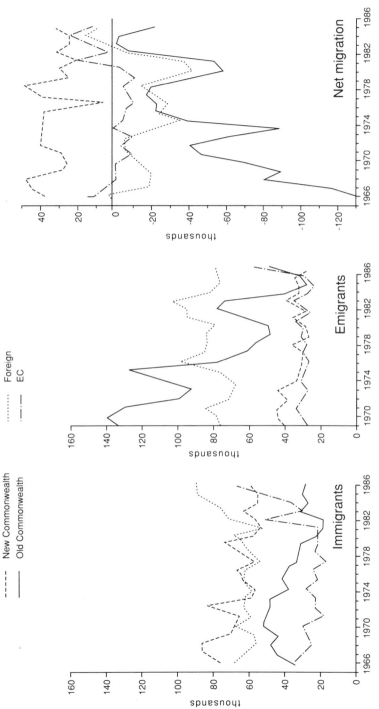

*Figure 3.6* Origins and destinations of UK external migrants, 1966–86
*Source: Demographic Review 1977, Population Trends, 22, 46, 52*

restrictive measures, which have mainly affected the Commonwealth, accession to the European Economic Community has meant accepting freedom of labour movement between the United Kingdom and other member countries.

These developments have set in train a number of important changes in the recent pattern of external migration (figure 3.6). Immigration from the New Commonwealth was on a sharply declining trend to 1974–5, interrupted by the influx of refugees from Uganda in 1972, but since then has tended to fluctuate around an average of roughly 60,000 per annum. Second, emigration to the Old Commonwealth, although subject to large fluctuations, has dropped steeply throughout the period represented. Third, given the freedom of movement within its boundaries, initially Britain's membership of the European Community had a surprisingly small effect on migration patterns up to the early 1980s. But with the accession of Greece and then Spain and Portugal, immigration from the EC has risen three-fold from just over 20,000 in 1981 to 70,000 in 1988, while emigration has also climbed substantially since 1984. Fourth, emigration to countries outside the Commonwealth and the EC has generally followed a rising, but fluctuating trend, peaking in 1975 and 1982, since when it has dropped back sharply. Much of this movement has been directed to the oil-rich states of the Middle East, whose ambitious development programmes before the latest collapse in the price of oil attracted many people from the United Kingdom, albeit on short-term contracts. It is probably a degree of synchronization in the offering of such contracts in response to business fluctuations in the Middle East that explains the distinct peaks and troughs in the trend.

The balance of migration, that is the difference between immigrants and emigrants, is sensitive to small changes in the gross flows. Hence, although showing erratic fluctuations from year to year, the decline in the number of people leaving the United Kingdom over the last two to three decades, coupled with a more stable level of inflow, has meant a turn-round in the balance and the once substantial net loss of people has been replaced by net gain since 1983. More than anything else, the drop in emigration to the Old Commonwealth has been responsible for this, but the substantial net inflow from the EC since 1984 and the even more pronounced net gain from other foreign countries since 1982, together with a continuing net influx from the New Commonwealth of around 25,000 per annum, have all contributed to this change round. However, it is important to stress that immigration is not necessarily for the purpose of permanent settlement. Many migrations are comparatively short term, involving students, employees of international companies, and so on. Moreover, the statistics of return migration of United Kingdom citizens, including those born abroad, which are calculated on a different basis to those of the International Passenger Survey show that 55,400 persons were given permission to remain indefinitely in the United Kingdom in 1985 out of a gross inflow of 232,000 (Social Trends). It is also the case that migrants now face greater occupational selection than ever before, and it is only the numbers in the professional and managerial categories that are actually rising at the present time. But that said, the greatest net gain is not of the gainfully occupied but of dependants, students, and retired persons. Otherwise, international migration continues to be highly age selective, the rate being especially high among 15 to 29 year olds; a notable change in the last few years, however, has been the emergence of a female excess among emigrants, as a consequence of a reduction in the number of young men leaving the country.

## Immigrants and foreign born

The foreign-born element of the population is regularly enumerated at the decennial census and yields, despite certain problems of definition and therefore of interpretation, useful information about immigrant groups in the United Kingdom. Between 1951 and 1981, the proportion of UK residents born overseas almost doubled from 3.4 to 6.1 per cent of the population, and at the same time underwent a marked change in composition (table 3.8). Whereas at the earlier date two-thirds of this group had been born in either the Republic of Ireland or on the continent of Europe, by 1981, reflecting the changes in the patterns of immigrant origins already described, more than one half of the foreign born were comparative newcomers from the New Commonwealth and Pakistan (NCWP). This fundamental shift in composition was largely brought about by the magnitude of the NCWP influx over the period. Hence, although declining in relative terms, the number of Old Commonwealth- and USA-born still increased in each intercensal period. However, in the case of persons born in the Irish Republic, there was a marked drop in absolute numbers after 1971 and, to a lesser extent, also in the number of continental EC-born. The post-1981 situation is, of course, difficult to assess because of the lack of concrete data. Information available from other sources, however, would suggest that the number of NCWP born has continued to rise, although at a slower rate than during the 1960s and 1970s, as has the number of persons originating from outside Europe, the Commonwealth and the USA, notably people of Middle and Far Eastern extraction. On the other hand, the decline of persons born in the Irish Republic has probably been reversed in that the brief lull in the exodus of people from the Republic during the 1970s has been followed by renewed mass emigration, much of it directed to Great Britain. In addition, recent figures from the International Passenger Survey are consistent with some increase in the number of UK-residents born in the European Community.

The geographical distribution of the foreign born within the United Kingdom provides a useful summary of migrant destinations. Characteristically, immigrant groups display a greater degree of

Table 3.8 UK distribution of foreign born, 1951, 1971, and 1981

| | 1951 | | 1971^a | | 1981^a | |
|---|---|---|---|---|---|---|
| | 000s | % | 000s | % | 000s | % |
| Irish Republic | 593 | 36.0 | 709 | 23.8 | 607 | 18.1 |
| Old C'wealth | 101 | 6.1 | 143 | 4.8 | 153 | 4.6 |
| Australia | 34 | 2.1 | 57 | 1.9 | 62 | 1.8 |
| Canada | 55 | 3.3 | 65 | 2.2 | 62 | 1.8 |
| New Zealand | 12 | 0.7 | 21 | 0.7 | 29 | 0.9 |
| New C'wealth | 221 | 13.4 | 1,151 | 38.6 | 1,513 | 45.0 |
| Africa | 17 | 1.0 | 164 | 5.5 | 267 | 7.9 |
| America | 17 | 1.0 | 304 | 10.2 | 295 | 8.8 |
| India | 120 | 7.3 | 322 | 10.8 | 392 | 11.7 |
| Bangladesh and Pakistan | 12 | 0.7 | 140 | 4.7 | 237 | 7.1 |
| Other | 55 | 3.3 | 221 | 7.4 | 322 | 9.6 |
| Europe | 482 | 29.3 | 633 | 21.2 | 625 | 18.6 |
| Eur. Commun. | – | – | – | – | 388 | 10.1 |
| USA | 69 | 4.2 | 111 | 3.7 | 118 | 3.5 |
| Other | 179 | 10.9 | 237 | 7.9 | 344 | 10.2 |
| Total | 1,645 | 100.0 | 2,984 | 100.0 | 3,360 | 100.0 |

| | 1971^b | | 1981^b | |
|---|---|---|---|---|
| | 000s | % | 000s | % |
| Irish Republic | 755 | 24.8 | 643 | 18.8 |
| Common wealth | 1,301 | 43.7 | 1,674 | 49.1 |
| Other | 989 | 32.5 | 1,095 | 32.1 |

Sources: Demographic Review 1977; Great Britain Census 1981, Country of Birth; Northern Ireland Census of Population 1951, 1971, and 1981
Notes:  ^a Great Britain
  ^b Great Britain and Northern Ireland

localization than the indigenous population. Wales and Scotland, as well as Northern Ireland (except for those born in the Irish Republic), are the least favoured places, but at the same time, because of the very heavy concentration of immigrants in the South-east, the other regions of England, with the exception of the West Midlands, also contain substantially lower proportions of foreign-born residents than would be expected from their share of the national population (table 3.9). Moreover, the degree of concentration varies from group to group. Those originating from the Old Commonwealth, and to a lesser extent the Irish Republic, that is the groups least distinguishable from the indigenous population, are comparatively widely dispersed, but against that, two-thirds of those born in the West Indies reside in the south-east, while one-fifth of those born in the USA are found in East Anglia where most American military bases are located. At the broader scale, the NCWP population, especially those from the Indian sub-continent, together with immigrants from the Irish Republic tend to favour the conurbations, whereas those from the European Community, the Old Commonwealth and the USA are more likely to be found in non-metropolitan provincial areas.

But that said, the regional scale masks the extent of localization, especially of people of NCWP ethnic origin. The expansion of the economy during the 1950s and 1960s created gaps at the lower end of the occupational and residential ladder to which coloured immigrants were drawn as a replacement population, hence their dominance in the decaying inner areas of the conurbations and industrial cities which had been vacated by the white population. Once established, communities are reinforced by further immigration and natural increase. Thus the position in 1981 was essentially the same as it had been ten and even twenty years earlier; over two-fifths of the NCWP population was still to be found in Greater London and a further 16 per cent in the West Yorkshire, West Midlands and Greater Manchester metropolitan counties. However, it must be remembered that the NCWP population is itself heterogeneous. In London, for instance, West Indians are to be found mainly in Brent, Hackney, Haringey, Hammersmith and Lambeth, whereas Indians are concentrated in West Brent, Ealing and Hounslow and Pakistanis in Newham, Tower Hamlets and Waltham Forest. Outside London, an appreciable proportion of persons born in East Africa, mainly of Indian origin, live in the Leicester area, and substantial numbers of Pakistanis and Bangladeshis are to be found in the old mill towns of Lancashire and West Yorkshire, especially Bradford. Birmingham also contains well-above average proportions of people born in India and the Caribbean. Although as yet there is little sign of any significant movement of the NCWP population into those regions of the country where the group has traditionally been under-represented, some more limited residential change did occur during the 1970s. Thus, in the case of the large centres of population, there is evidence of a

Table 3.9 Regional distribution of immigrants by place of birth, 1981 (%)

| | Distrib. of population | Irish Republic | America | Indian sub-contin. | Africa | All | Old Commonwealth | Eur. Community | Rest of Europe | USA |
|---|---|---|---|---|---|---|---|---|---|---|
| England | 85.5 | 93.3 | 98.8 | 96.3 | 95.9 | 96.1 | 87.2 | 90.9 | 92.1 | 87.8 |
| North | 5.7 | 1.3 | 0.3 | 1.5 | 1.1 | 1.3 | 2.9 | 2.8 | 2.4 | 1.3 |
| York and Humb. | 9.0 | 4.9 | 4.4 | 9.7 | 3.4 | 4.6 | 4.6 | 6.1 | 6.3 | 2.9 |
| East Midlands | 7.1 | 5.0 | 4.9 | 6.6 | 10.5 | 6.9 | 4.4 | 6.0 | 6.1 | 3.5 |
| East Anglia | 3.4 | 1.6 | 1.1 | 1.3 | 1.7 | 1.6 | 3.5 | 4.1 | 3.5 | 23.9 |
| South-east | 30.9 | 50.3 | 66.4 | 46.8 | 62.3 | 59.7 | 50.7 | 50.9 | 53.2 | 44.2 |
| South-west | 7.9 | 4.5 | 3.0 | 2.7 | 3.4 | 4.0 | 8.9 | 8.3 | 7.3 | 5.4 |
| West Midlands | 9.5 | 12.7 | 14.2 | 18.0 | 7.4 | 11.7 | 5.0 | 5.9 | 6.2 | 2.6 |
| North-west | 11.9 | 13.1 | 4.5 | 9.6 | 6.1 | 6.2 | 7.2 | 6.7 | 7.1 | 4.1 |
| Greater London | 12.3 | 32.8 | 56.7 | 32.2 | 48.7 | 44.9 | 24.3 | 24.4 | 29.2 | 18.6 |
| Metropl. C'ties | 20.8 | 24.3 | 21.0 | 31.8 | 12.9 | 18.4 | 10.2 | 11.2 | 12.4 | 5.1 |
| Remainder | 52.4 | 36.2 | 21.1 | 32.3 | 34.3 | 32.8 | 52.7 | 55.3 | 50.5 | 64.1 |
| Wales | 5.1 | 2.2 | 0.7 | 1.1 | 1.3 | 1.4 | 2.8 | 3.5 | 3.0 | 1.9 |
| Scotland | 9.4 | 4.4 | 0.5 | 2.6 | 2.8 | 2.5 | 10.0 | 5.6 | 4.9 | 10.3 |

Sources: Great Britain Census 1971 and 1981, Country of Birth

redistribution from inner city to suburban areas. London well illustrates the process; whereas in 1971, 56 per cent of the population of the capital born in the NCWP lived in the inner boroughs, by 1981 this had fallen to 47 per cent. In other words, although the size of the NCWP population continued to grow in inner London throughout the 1970s, it was in the outer boroughs like Barnet, Enfield, Harrow and Hounslow that the highest rates of increase were recorded.

Questions of race relations, assimilation and the feasibility of further immigration have prompted the authorities to monitor the size and dynamics of the population of NCWP ethnic origin. This is a complex task, not least because of the reticence about asking a direct question on ethnic/racial origin in successive censuses. The problems derived from this are clearly magnified by the rising proportion of the NCWP that has been born in the UK (estimated at 4.3 per cent of the total in 1984–5), which makes census place of birth data an increasingly unreliable estimator of the size and dynamics of this population. However, the problem is eased by the inclusion of a direct question about ethnic origin in the Labour Force Survey since 1979. This source indicates that the ethnic minorities numbered around 2.43 millions in 1984–6, or 4.5 per cent of the total population, compared with some 200,000 in 1951 and 1,371,000 in 1971 (Shaw 1988a). In other words, a more than ten-fold increase has occurred since 1951, and a doubling of the size of the group since 1971. Moreover, were it not for the fact that the ethnic minority communities are now increasing at an annual rate of between 80,000 and 90,000, the population of Great Britain would have been marginally smaller in 1986 than 1981, instead of recording a growth of just under 400,000. The most recent information about the breakdown of the group by ethnic origin (that is both overseas and UK born) is given in table 3.10.

*Table 3.10* Estimates of the size and composition of the ethnic minority population: Great Britain, 1984 (000s)

|  | All non-white persons | Non-white persons born in UK |
| --- | --- | --- |
| Total non-white | 2,361 | 980 |
| Carribean | 529 | 281 |
| Indian | 807 | 290 |
| Pakistani | 371 | 151 |
| Bangladeshi | 93 | 30 |
| African | 109 | 35 |
| Chinese | 109 | 24 |
| Arab | 63 | 5 |
| Mixed origin | 205 | 146 |
| Other | 75 | 18 |

*Source:* OPCS Population Statistics Division 1986

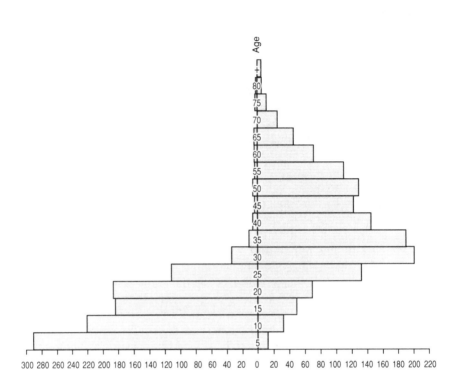

*Figure 3.7* Age structure of NCWP population in 1984–6 showing separately those born overseas and those born in the UK
*Source:* Shaw 1988

This continued rapid growth has been a function of three factors as quantified for the mid-1980s by Shaw (1988b): continued immigration, mainly of dependants including the female spouses in arranged Asian marriages (the net inflow is currently thought to be around 24,000 per annum); a low death rate (2–3 per 1,000 in the mid-1980s compared with a national rate of 11–12 per 1,000) reflecting the extraordinarily youthful age composition of the population (figure 3.7); and a high real fertility level which, again because of the young age structure, translates into an even higher crude birth rate (26–7 per 1,000 in the mid-1980s compared with around 13 in the population at large). Differencing the birth and death rates gives a current annual rate of natural increase of 23–5 per 1,000 compared with 2 per 1,000 in the UK population overall, or, leaving aside the ethnic minority component, a negligible increase within the indigenous UK white population. Over time, however, the vital statistics of the ethnic minorities may be expected increasingly to approximate those of the white population. Their death rate will most certainly rise as their age structure matures into a more normal profile. There is also evidence from many different parts of the world that immigrants and their descendants progressively acquire the same fertility behaviour as that of the communities into which they have moved, and one would clearly also expect this to occur in Britain. However, given the cultural and socio-economic heterogeneity of the ethnic minority populations, and different times of entry into the United Kingdom (e.g. the migration from the Caribbean preceded that from the Indian sub-continent), convergence is unlikely to be a uniform process but rather one specific to each individual group and this is borne out by the data for Great Britain. Thus the evidence shows that the fertility rate of women born in the Caribbean, that is of women who have on average been here longest, is already indistinguishable from that of the GB population overall (table 3.11). In addition, the rates for women born in Far Eastern and East African Commonwealth countries have dropped to within striking distance of the national average, while that of women born in India, although still moderately high, has clearly fallen substantially over the last two decades. Women born in Pakistan and Bangladesh, presumably of Moslem origin, whose total period fertility rate is still in excess of 5.5, comprise the single clear exception to this. Although women born in Britain are excluded, the total period fertility rates presented here still provide an acceptable picture of the current position within the NCWP population, because it is only in the case of the West Indian community, where fertility in any case is now at the general UK level, that there is as yet a significant number of UK-born women of childbearing age, athough this will soon begin to change in the other ethnic minority communities.

Hence, in future an increasing proportion of births among the ethnic minorities will be to parents who were themselves born in the United

*Table 3.11* Fertility by mothers' place of birth, 1981 and 1986 (total period fertility rates)

| Birthplace | 1981 | 1986 |
| --- | --- | --- |
| All | 1.80 | 1.77 |
| United Kingdom | 1.7 | 1.7 |
| New Commonwealth and Pakistan | | |
| India | 3.1 | 2.9 |
| Pakistan and Bangladesh | 6.5 | 5.6 |
| East Africa | 2.1 | 2.0 |
| Rest of Africa | 3.4 | 2.8 |
| Caribbean | 2.0 | 1.8 |
| Far East | 1.7 | 1.9 |
| Mediterranean | 2.1 | 2.1 |
| Other New Commonwealth | 2.3 | 2.3 |
| Rest of world | 2.0 | 1.9 |

*Source:* OPCS Birth Statistics 1986

Kingdom. Moreover, the number of children of mixed parentage, estimated at 9 per cent of the NCWP population in 1971, will continue to rise as inter-marriage becomes more common (Coleman 1985). Already around 1 per cent of current marriages involve one white partner and the other from an ethnic minority group. Breaking these down, around 30 per cent of West Indian husbands under the age of 45 have white wives and around 15 per cent of West Indian women in the same age range have white husbands. Additionally, a substantial number of children of such marriages (the Labour Force Survey suggests around 40 per cent) are classed as white. Although the level of inter-marriage between whites and the South Asian minority remains low and as yet shows no systematic tendency to increase, these developments, together with the uncertainty surrounding the level of immigration, make it difficult to forecast the future size of the ethnic minority population. In 1979 the Immigrant Statistics Unit of OPCS suggested that it would lie within the range 2.75 to 3.25 millions in 1991, depending mainly upon the assumptions about fertility and immigration. Now, ten years on, it looks as though this forecast will turn out to have been reasonably accurate. Taking the size of the ethnic minority population to be 2.432 millions in 1985 and projecting forward the current estimated rate of growth of around 90,000 per annum, produces a figure of 2.95–3.0 millions in 1991, which is almost precisely the mid-point of the range forecast earlier by the Immigrant Statistics Unit, approximately 5.2 per cent of the United Kingdom population. In the longer term the NCWP population may be expected to approximate the proportion of live births to ethnic minority parents, which is now 8–9 per cent of the total.

## SOME IMPLICATIONS OF SLOW GROWTH

The cessation of population growth between 1976 and 1978 is arguably the most significant demographic event of recent times in the United Kingdom. Moreover, even though growth has since resumed, the future rate of increase is expected to remain low by historical standards; for instance, the OPCS (1986) principal projection, which takes 1985 as the base year, suggests a rise of around 1.3 million people by the year 2001 when the population of the country should reach 57.7 millions. By contrast, as recently as 1964 a population of 75 millions was projected for the end of the century and the difference between this and the current expectation is a measure of the dramatic transformation of prospects generated by the fall in the birth rate between 1964 and 1977. The main assumptions behind the 1985 projection are that completed family size will stay at around 2.0 children per woman, equivalent to a small increase in the total period fertility rate, plus a modest improvement in mortality. But should completed family size fall to 1.8 children, as assumed in the lower variant of the principal projection, then numbers will remain virtually static to the end of the century. Even the higher variant of the principal projection suggests a total population of under 59 millions by 2000. While one is mindful of the rather poor track-record of earlier population forecasts, the evidence would seem to confirm that the post-war era of comparatively rapid population growth has come to an end and that we are now entering a phase when the population will remain essentially 'stationary'. Indeed population decline cannot be ruled out in the foreseeable future.

The United Kingdom is not alone in presently experiencing low growth and shares this characteristic with most other countries in Europe; some, like West Germany, Austria and Hungary, are even experiencing population decline at this moment. From the standpoint of resource and ecological conservation, the prospect of slow, if not zero growth is no doubt welcome as it is widely held that a lessening of population pressure on the natural environment is essential for long-term human survival. But in the areas of economy and society, the balance sheet is not wholly positive and disadvantages might also be expected to accrue. For instance, the fall in the birth rate after 1964 and consequent reduction in both the number and proportion of population of school age, while making it possible to reduce expenditure, has had many adverse consequences for the education system. It has already meant a dramatic contraction in primary school intake; secondary school rolls have also fallen and schools have been closed and, unless participation rates in higher education increase, the demand for places in universities and polytechnics, too, may well decline after 1990. There is also a geographical dimension to this in that the demand for educational provision has contracted more strongly in the urban cores and in certain rural areas than elsewhere, because fertility decline has been accentuated by out-migration. Moreover, the impact of the past volatility of the birth rate will be felt in the decades to come, through the 'echo' effect. Thus, the movement of the large birth cohorts of the 1960s into the prime childbearing age range is already impacting on the birth rate as evidenced by the upturn in the number of live births after 1977; but this in turn will be followed by renewed decline in the 1990s as the small generations of the 1970s reach parenthood (figure 3.8). Such a fluctuating trend makes the coherent planning of education provision difficult as periods of expansion and contraction alternate at intervals of approximately twelve years, though of diminishing amplitude. This, of course, applies to other socio-economic areas as well. Indeed, in the more interventionist systems of Eastern Europe, one aim of population policy is the maintenance of a fairly even birth rate so as to prevent the occurrence of such sharp, disruptive fluctuations in age structure.

Otherwise, between 1951 and 1981, the population of pensionable age in the United Kingdom increased by over 45 per cent, from 6.8 to 9.9 millions (almost two-thirds of whom are elderly females), and in 1987 accounted for an estimated 18.1 per cent of the total. Although a continuation of slow or near-static growth will accentuate the ageing process in the longer term, the short-term prognosis is for little change (according to the principal

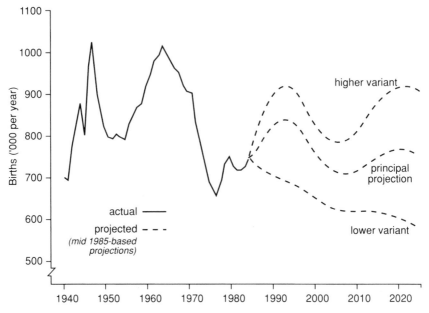

*Figure 3.8* Actual and projected live births in England and Wales to 2020 (projected live births based on 1985 base)
*Source:* OPCS 1986

projection the proportion of the UK population of pensionable age will actually fall back a little to 17.6 per cent by 2001) because those retiring between now and the end of the century will come from the small birth cohorts of the 1920s and 1930s. However, within this group both the number and proportion of the very old is expected to increase sharply, and, although the precise figure is dependent upon the rate at which mortality improves at advanced ages (the principal projection suggests that the 85 and over age group will increase by just under 50 per cent over the 15-year period 1986 to 2001), greater social and health provision for this group will clearly be needed. There is again an important geographical dimension to the national trend in that continued out-migration of younger people will ensure that the inner areas of the conurbations and major cities retain a disproportionate share of old people as will the major reception areas of retirement migration. Moreover, the likelihood that these disparities will intensify in the future is cause for concern as the burden thereby generated could well outstrip local capacity to provide the necessary support. For instance, pressure in the favoured retirement areas of the south-west has meant that planning authorities are already loath to allow any further conversion of property specifically for the residential purposes of the elderly.

Similarly, stasis or slow growth will have no immediate effect upon the population of working age. In the longer term, however, it will inevitably produce an increase in old-age dependency but this will be offset by a decline in young-age dependency. As to the immediate future, the rising birth rate between 1955 and 1964 ensured that the size of the labour force increased rapidly up to the early 1980s, a factor implicated in the rise of unemployment of past years. Since the mid-1980s, however, the number of new entrants to the labour force has started to ease back, as the effect of the post-1964 decline in the birth rate makes itself felt, and this process may be expected to accelerate into the 1990s. 'Demographically' induced pressure on employment opportunities is therefore now slackening and in future it is the problems attendant upon potential labour shortage that will become a major concern; between now and the year 2001, for instance, the number of 16 to 24 year olds will fall by over two million, that is by around one-quarter. Clearly youngsters seeking employment in the mid-1990s will find life a lot easier than those who were going through the same process in the early 1980s. By the same token, the labour force will have become markedly older by the end of the century, with attendant problems of flexibility and adaptability; for instance, the number of men aged 45 and over will rise from one in every two, to three out of every five of the male labour force between now and 2001. It is difficult to forecast the regional effects of these changes. Much depends upon technological change and the spatial and sectoral structure of employment in the future, but the trends would seem to indicate that an increasingly mobile labour force will be needed to meet regional variations in demand for labour as local supply diminishes because of low natural increase.

## CONCLUDING REMARKS

In this chapter, emphasis has been placed on the changing distribution of the population of the United Kingdom during the last three to four decades and on the fertility, mortality and migrational components of these changes. For this reason, the various aspects of population composition – age, sex, and marital status, for instance – have receded into the background and, with the exception of the ethnic minority population, have only been touched upon in an oblique fashion. At the time of writing, we are approaching the end of an intercensal period which means that the patterns and trends of population change for the 1980s depicted in this chapter have had to be based on estimated data. However, there is never an ideal moment to take stock of the demographic situation for, while the preparatory work for the 1991 census is well underway, the results will not begin to appear in print until 1992–3. In any case, the fertility and mortality components of recent population change can be fully described from the civil records of births and deaths.

Moreover, the regional patterns of United Kingdom population change during the 1980s are fairly reliably documented to the extent that migration may be established at the broad scale from information contained in the National Health Service Central Register, and these will only require minor revision in the light of the findings of the 1991 Census. These make it clear that the broad spatial processes of the 1950s, 1960s and 1970s have continued into the 1980s. Urban population decentralization remains an important process despite evidence that it is now slowing in respect of the large centres of population, while the south, notably East Anglia, the South-west and the East Midlands, are still gaining population at the expense of the north.

The most notable departure from this general theme of continuity is the emergence of the years post-1970 as a period of slow growth nationally. Because of this, regions suffering net out-migration can no longer rely upon natural increase to compensate for this loss of population and the northern regions of England together with Scotland have undergone a fairly substantial decline in numbers since around 1970. Additionally, in view of their dynamism during the 1950s, it is perhaps surprising that the South-east and West Midlands also experienced demographic decline during the 1970s, but in the case of the South-east this was accounted for entirely by the rapid contraction of Greater London and more recently growth has been resumed. None the less, because of a narrowing of net migration and natural increase differences, regional growth disparities are now less than they were in the past. Although the rate of natural increase may pick up again in the late 1980s and early 1990s because of the relatively large number of women of childbearing age in the population, it is unlikely to reach the level of earlier decades and slow growth, with its various consequences, will be with us for the forseeable future.

## REFERENCES

Britton, M. (1986) 'An analysis of the trend in population change in the 1980s in relation to the decade 1971–81, *Population Trends*, 44: 33–41.

Champion, A. G. (1976) 'Evolving patterns of population in England & Wales, 1951–71, *Transactions, Institute of British Geographers*, 1 (N.S.): 401–20.

Champion, A. G. and Congdon, P. (1988) 'Recent trends in Greater London's population', *Population Trends*, 53: 7–17.

Chilvers, C. (1978) 'Regional mortality 1969–73' *Population Trends*, 11: 16–20.

Coleman, D. (1968) 'Ethnic inter-marriage in Great Britain', *Population Trends*, 40: 10–16.

Compton, P. A. (1978) *Northern Ireland: A Census Atlas*, Dublin: Gill & Macmillan.

—— (1986) *Demographic Trends in Northern Ireland*, Northern Ireland Economic Council, Report 57, Belfast.

Compton, P. A. and Coward, J. (1989) *Fertility and Family Planning in Northern Ireland*, Aldershot: Gower.

Compton, P. A., Coward, J. and Power, J. (1986) 'Regional differences in attitude to abortion in Northern Ireland', *Irish Geography*, 19: 58–68.

Coward, J. (1987) 'Conceptions outside marriage: regional differences', *Population Trends*, 49: 24–30.

Denham, C. (1984) 'Urban Britain', *Population Trends,* 36: 10–18.

Department of Health and Social Services, Registrar General Northern Ireland (1983) 'The Northern Ireland Census 1981: Summary Report, Belfast: HMSO.

—— (various dates) 'Annual Reports', Belfast: HMSO.

Drewett, R., Goddard, J., and Spence, N (1976) 'British cities: urban population and employment trends, 1951–71', *Research Report* 10, Department of the Environment.

Easterlin, R. and Condran, G. (1976) 'A note on the recent fertility swing in Australia, Canada, England and Wales, and the United States', in Richards, H. (ed.) *Population Factor Movements and Economic Development, Studies Presented to Brinley Thomas,* Cardiff, University of Wales Press, pp. 139–51.

Ermisch, J. (1983) *The Political Economy of Demographic Change: Causes and Implications of Population Trends in Great Britain,* London: Heinemann.

Eversley, D. (1980) 'Britain's changing demographic structure: implications for social and economic policy', *Occasional Paper* 19/1, Office of Population Censuses and Surveys: 18–35.

Fox, J. C. (1977) 'Occupational mortality 1970–2', *Population Trends,* 9: 8–15.

Fox, J. C., Jones, D. and Moser, K. (1985) 'Socio-demographic differentials in mortality 1971–81', *Population Trends,* 40:10–16.

Gardner, M. J., Winter, D. D. and Barker, D. J. P. (1983) *Atlas of Cancer Mortality in England and Wales, 1968–78,* Chichester: Wiley.

—— (1984) *Atlas of Mortality from Selected Diseases in England and Wales, 1968–1978,* Chichester: Wiley.

Glass, D. V. (1976) 'Review lecture: recent and prospective trends in fertility in developed countries', *Philosophical Transactions of the Royal Society of London (B: Biological Sciences)* 277(928) 1–52.

Government of Northern Ireland (1955) 'Census of Population of Northern Ireland 1951, General Report', Belfast: HMSO.

Hall, P., Thomas, R., Gracey, H., and Drewett, R. (1973) *The containment of Urban England, vol. 1, Urban Metropolitan Growth Processes or Megalopolis Denied,* London: Allen & Unwin.

Howe, G. M. (1970) *National Atlas of Disease Mortality in the United Kingdom,* London: Nelson.

Jones, H. R. (1975) 'A spatial analysis of human fertility in Scotland', *Scottish Geographical Magazine,* 91: 102–13.

Kennett, S. (1977) 'Migration within and between the metropolitan economic labour areas of Britain, 1966–71', in Hobcraft, J. and Rees, P. (eds.) *Regional Demographic Development,* London: Croom Helm, Op. 1965–87.

Northern Ireland General Register Office (1975) 'Census of Population 1971: Summary Tables', Belfast: HMSO.

Office of Population Censuses and Surveys (OPCS) (1978) *.1977 Demographic Review,* series DR no. 1, London: HMSO.

Office of Population Censuses and Surveys (OPCS) (1981) 'Tables', *Population Trends,* 26, London: HMSO.

Office of Population Censuses and Surveys, Registrar General Scotland (1983) 'Census 1981: Country of Birth, Great Britain', London: HMSO.

Office of Population Censuses and Surveys (OPCS) (1986) 'Tables', *Population Trends,* 46, London: HMSO.

Office of Population Censuses and Surveys (1986) *Population Projections Prepared by the Government Actuary in Consultation with the Registrars General: England and Wales, Wales, Scotland, Great Britain, Northern Ireland and the United Kingdom,* London: HMSO.

Office of Population Censuses and Surveys (OPCS) (1987a) 'Birth Statistics.

Historical series of statistics from registrations of births in England and Wales, 1837–1983', Series FM1 no 13, London: HMSO.

Office of Population Censuses and Surveys (OPCS) (1987b) *1984 Demographic Review,* series DR no. 2, London: HMSO.

Office of Population Censuses and Surveys (OPCS) (1987c) 'Birth Statistics. Review of the Registrar General on birth and patterns of family building in England and Wales, 1985', Series FM1 no 14, London: HMSO.

Office of Population Censuses and Surveys (OPCS) (1988) 'Birth Statistics. Review of the Registrar General on birth and patterns of family building in England and Wales, 1986', Series FM1 no 15, London: HMSO.

Office of Population Censuses and Surveys (OPCS) (1988) 'Tables', *Population Trends,* 52, London: HMSO.

Office of Population Censuses and Surveys (OPCS) (various dates) 'Mortality Statistics' (area), series DH5, London: HMSO.

Peach, C. (1968) *West Indian Migration to Britain,* London: Oxford University Press.

Ravenstein, E. G. (1885) 'The laws of migration', *Journal of the Royal Statistical Society,* 48: 167–227.

Rees, P. H. (1979) *Migration and Settlement: 1 – United Kingdom,* Laxenburg: International Institute for Applied Systems Analysis.

Registrar General Scotland (various dates) Annual Reports, Edinburgh, HMSO.

Royal Commission on Population (1949) CMND 7695, HMSO.

Shaw, C. (1988a) 'Latest estimates of ethnic minority populations', *Population Trends,* 51: 5–8.

Shaw, C. (1988b) 'Components of growth in the ethnic minority', *Population Trends,* 52: 26–30.

Simons, J. (1986) 'Culture, economy and reproduction in contemporary Europe', in Coleman, D. and Schofield, R. (eds.) *The State of Population Theory,* Oxford: Blackwell.

# 4 The agricultural pattern

*Ian R. Bowler*

Over the last few decades the United Kingdom has shared in the same processes of transformation that have characterized agriculture in most developed economies of the world. Taken together the processes have been described variously as comprising the Second (or even Third) Agricultural Revolution, the modernization or industrialization of agriculture, and the restructuring of agriculture. There can be no doubting the deep-seated changes that have teen brought about: employment in farming has declined drastically, together with the number of independent farm businesses; farming practices have become dependent on high levels of capital expenditure and sophisticated mechanical and biological technology, and the farm sector has been absorbed into a food chain increasingly dominated by food processors and food retailers, the latter including fast-food and restaurant outlets. Yet the late 1980s have witnessed the faltering of this transformed agriculture in all developed economies: markets are in over-supply, changes in farm support policies threaten agricultural bankruptcies and pollution and degradation of the rural environment have reached critical levels.

In this chapter both the contemporary farm crisis and the preceding transformation of agriculture are examined in the context of the United Kingdom. Attention is focused on three main components of agriculture: the inputs to production, the production sector itself and the marketing of produce beyond the farm gate. The institutional context of agriculture in the United Kingdom is discussed initially for it has exercised an overriding impact on the agricultural pattern during the last few decades.

## THE INSTITUTIONAL CONTEXT OF AGRICULTURE

British agriculture has evolved within three different institutional contexts during the period under discussion. Until the end of the Second World War agriculture was subject to wartime regulations with a number of long-term consequences which are discussed below. A second context was introduced by the 1947 Agriculture Act which established the framework for national agricultural policy until the United Kingdom became a member of the

European Community (EC). During this period agriculture was largely exempt from the planning controls which moulded the built environment, but was dependent on annual consultations, verging on negotiations, between the National Farmers Union (NFU) and the Ministry of Agriculture, Fisheries and Food (MAFF) over levels of farm price support. Since 1973 agriculture has operated within the institutional context of the EC and its Common Agricultural Policy (CAP), with decision-making based in Brussels rather than London.

**Wartime regulation**

Three wartime developments can be identified as having a lasting influence on the UK pattern of agriculture. First, the requirement to produce more food from home resources, especially when the country was faced with a shipping blockade, reorientated the agricultural pattern from livestock towards crop production. The economic depression of the 1920s and early 1930s had resulted in the rundown of much of British agriculture with the widespread adoption of low-cost, mainly grassland-based livestock production – a condition captured classically by Dudley Stamp's (1962) contemporary Land Use Survey. Between 1938 and 1944, whereas numbers in most classes of livestock declined, the areas of nearly all crops increased under a 'plough up' campaign (table 4.1.). The degree of change in the agricultural pattern varied, having its greatest expression in livestock rearing areas such as northern England and the West Midlands. Crops increased in area by 2.4 million ha (5.9 million acres) with a concomitant fall of 2.7 million ha (6.7 million acres) of permanent grass. Barley, wheat, potatoes and vegetables were the crops most affected by the expansion of the tillage area. Those types of livestock production (pigs, poultry and some systems of milk production) which were previously dependent upon imported feed contracted most severely. While these classes of livestock expanded again in the post-war years, the UK agricultural pattern never reverted to its previous condition. The integration of crops and grass under ley farming systems of production became a standard practice throughout the UK, and livestock farming remained based to a greater extent than previously on domestically produced rather than imported feed. In addition, food self-sufficiency was established as a national concern.

The second long-term influence of wartime regulations was the raised tempo of technical development in agriculture in general, and the mechanization of arable farming in particular. In 1938, for example, 1.1 million horses and only 117,000 tractors operated in the United Kingdom; just seven years later the respective figures were 0.8 million and 203,000. The pace of mechanization was faster in lowland compared with upland areas, and on larger rather than smaller farms; innovations in harvesting, fertilizing and cultural equipment, such as the combine harvester and the

*Table 4.1* UK agricultural trends in selected crops and livestock, 1938–78 (crop areas or livestock numbers as per cent 1958)

| Crop or livestock | 1938 | 1944 | 1958 | 1968 | 1978 | 1988 |
|---|---|---|---|---|---|---|
| Wheat | 80 | 146 | 100 | 109 | 141 | 223 |
| Barley | 37 | 72 | 100 | 215 | 211 | 164 |
| Beef cows[a] | (80) | (90) | 100 | 136 | 186 | 158 |
| Total crops and fallow | 79 | 103 | 100 | 110 | 109 | 155 |
| Total sheep and lambs | 103 | 77 | 100 | 107 | 114 | 148 |
| Total fowls | 73 | 52 | 100 | 127 | 133 | 134 |
| Total cereals | 71 | 126 | 100 | 126 | 126 | 129 |
| Total pigs | 68 | 29 | 100 | 114 | 119 | 122 |
| Cattle under 1 year[b] | 63 | 66 | 100 | 118 | 133 | 121 |
| Sugarbeet | 79 | 98 | 100 | 106 | 118 | 114 |
| Cattle 1–2 years[b] | 70 | 66 | 100 | 96 | 123 | 103 |
| Dairy cows[a] | (80) | (90) | 100 | 102 | 103 | 96 |
| Heifers in calf (dairy and beef)[a] | (80) | (90) | 100 | 100 | 104 | 94 |
| Grass over 5 years[c] | 139 | 87 | 100 | 90 | 92 | 94 |
| Vegetables (in open) | 70 | 112 | 100 | 104 | 125 | 78 |
| Rye | 61 | 548 | 100 | 48 | 96 | 75 |
| Soft fruit | 112 | 80 | 100 | 88 | 82 | 72 |
| Grass under 5 years[c] | 65 | 76 | 100 | 94 | 82 | 67 |
| Total horticulture | 82 | 104 | 100 | 92 | 95 | 65 |
| Beans for stock feed | 150 | 320 | 100 | 254 | 101 | – |
| Hardy nursery stock | – | – | 100 | 117 | 100 | 58 |
| Cattle over 2 years[b] | 94 | 102 | 100 | 70 | 75 | 56 |
| Potatoes | 86 | 172 | 100 | 84 | 64 | 53 |
| Hops | 90 | 95 | 100 | 86 | 71 | 47 |
| Orchard fruit | 104 | 108 | 100 | 71 | 46 | 36 |
| Turnips and swedes | 140 | 161 | 100 | 53 | 51 | 33 |
| { (Rape) | 47 | 135 | 100 | 58 | 42 } | 20 |
| { (Cabbage, etc. for stock feed) | 28 | 58 | 100 | 48 | 36 } | |
| Other crops for stock feed | 136 | 238 | 100 | 18 | 25 | 20 |
| Oats | 109 | 165 | 100 | 43 | 20 | 11 |
| Mixed corn | 30 | 149 | 100 | 39 | 15 | 5 |

*Source*: MAFF *Agricultural Statistics* 1939–88, HMSO
*Notes*: [a] Before 1960, beef cows, dairy cows, and heifers in calf were collected together
[b] Dairy and beef livestock
[c] Changed census definitions in 1959 and 1975

row-crop cultivator, were accepted by the agricultural sector more readily than would otherwise have been the case.

Third, the wartime emergency introduced the state to the detailed regulation of agriculture. The rate of transformation demanded of farming was so great, and the nature of changes required so specific, that the control of agricultural production by the wartime coalition government was deemed necessary. Previous governments had become involved in agriculture during the economic depression – for example through the Agricultural

Marketing Acts of 1931 and 1933 – but the setting of national production targets, the allocation of machinery, animal feed, fertilizer and labour resources, the purchase and pricing of farm products, and the enforcement of minimum standards of husbandry were all new areas of responsibility. That these measures were put into operation at the farm level by County War Agricultural Executive Committees, composed in large part by fellow farmers, helped to ensure the acceptance by the farming community of direct intervention by the state. The net farm income of agriculture in the United Kingdom rose from £55.5 million in 1938–9 to £230.5 million in 1943–4 and, encouraged by this economic resurgence, the farming community subsequently supported the long-term involvement of the state in their industry through the Agriculture Act of 1947. Successive governments in their turn found difficulty in laying aside these new-found social and economic responsibilities, and there were also practical advantages in the food-scarce post-war years of being able to orientate agricultural production in desired directions.

## The evolution of a national agricultural policy

After 1947 agricultural policy was redirected at intervals to match the changing needs of the economy – for example, from maximum food production to efficient food production between 1953 and 1964, and again to import saving between 1965 and 1972. Price signals were provided to farmers through the manipulation of guaranteed prices and deficiency payments paid on all the main farm products. The close, if at times acrimonious, working relationship between the NFU and the MAFF, through the Annual (price) Review mechanism, was central to this process. While the system allowed consumer prices to be held near to world market levels, a heavy reliance was placed on the ability of the agricultural sector to absorb increased production costs of £30 million per year through rising efficiency. This was achieved mainly by raising the output per hectare of all the main farm products while reducing unit costs of production through the contraction of labour input. One outcome of this pressure for increased efficiency was a rising level of national agricultural self-sufficiency in many products in the decade before the United Kingdom became a member of the EC (table 4.2).

Price supports for the main agricultural products were not the only measures developed at this time. An extensive array of capital investment grants and subsidies was made available to promote an efficient agricultural industry; the measures covered items such as farm buildings, farm machinery, land drainage, fertilizers and the ploughing-out of permanent pasture and rough grazing. As we will see later, many of these grants brought the MAFF into conflict with environmental interest groups as well as those concerned more narrowly with the visual changes taking place in the rural landscape (see chapter 17). Grants to promote the more rapid reduction in

*Table 4.2* UK self-sufficiency in agricultural production, 1961–88 (production as per cent total new supply for use in United Kingdom)

| Product | 1961–4 | 1968 | 1978 | 1988[a] |
|---|---|---|---|---|
| Skimmed milk | 75 | 90 | 145 | 271 |
| Barley | 96 | 90 | 106 | 137 |
| Wheat | 42 | 42 | 68 | 113 |
| Oilseed | nd | 14 | 57 | 106 |
| Pork | 98 | 101 | 98 | 99 |
| Eggs | 94 | 99 | 102 | 98 |
| Poultrymeat | 99 | 100 | 101 | 98 |
| Butter | 11 | 12 | 39 | 96 |
| Mutton and lamb | 44 | 40 | 58 | 94 |
| Potatoes | 91 | 91 | 93 | 90 |
| Beef | 75 | 77 | 85 | 86 |
| Cauliflowers | 88 | 86 | 92 | 85 |
| Cheese | 45 | 45 | 67 | 65 |
| Sugarbeet | 28 | 33 | 41 | 58 |
| Apples | 65 | 61 | 49 | 36 |
| Pears | 45 | 52 | 50 | 34 |
| All temperate foods | nd | 59 | 68 | 73 |

*Source*: Annual Review White Papers 1961–88, HMSO
*Notes*: [a] Forecast
nd no data

the number of farms were also offered, although they met with a relatively low level of response. In general, however, the grant-aid actively encouraged both the intensification of agricultural production and the replacement of labour by purchased machinery and plant, especially on large farms. Indeed, when compared with other West European countries, United Kingdom agriculture now looks to be over-capitalized.

Guaranteed prices nevertheless failed to support farm incomes adequately in hill and upland areas. This became even more pronounced in the late 1960s when successive governments began to impose limitations on the quantity of produce eligible for price support as a means of containing costs. Consequently special grants and subsidies for upland areas were introduced at an early stage; they were paid as headage payments on hill sheep and hill cows (beef) and as more favourable rates of grant aid on capital investments.

### The EC and a supra-national agricultural policy

United Kingdom membership of the EC in 1973 brought about the end of the post-war 'cheap food' policy for consumers and, for producers, a growing competition in domestic agricultural markets from other member states. Food prices rose to a level approximately 12 per cent higher than if the United Kingdom had not entered the Community, while the nation's agricultural trade became orientated from non-EC to EC countries (table 4.3). Moreover, the broad structure of UK agriculture was subjected to further change, as revealed in table 4.1 and by the national share of EC farm output (table 4.4). Wheat, barley and potatoes, for example, expanded in relation to other members of the EC, the first product conforming to the United Kingdom government's wish for continued expansion as expressed in the 1975 policy document *Food from our own resources* (HMSO 1975). Pigmeat, mutton, eggs and poultrymeat, in contrast, have formed a declining share of EC output (note that table 4.4 has a discontinuity in the data caused by the addition of Greece to the Community from 1981).

While both the details and contradictions of the Common Agricultural Policy (CAP) are too numerous to discuss here, some of the main features must be understood in order to give perspective to changes in the UK agricultural pattern in recent years. Central to this understanding is the

*Table 4.3* UK agricultural trade with members of the EC, 1971–86

|            | % total imports from EC | % total exports to EC |
|------------|-------------------------|-----------------------|
| 1971[a]    | 14.0                    | 21.9[d]               |
| 1976[a]    | 32.7                    | 45.9                  |
| 1981[b]    | 41.1                    | 51.8                  |
| 1986[c]    | 51.6                    | 59.8                  |

*Source*: Commission of the European Communities, *The agricultural situation in the Community – Report* 1976–87, Office for Official Publications of the European Communities
*Notes*: [a] EC6
[b] EC10
[c] EC12
[d] Estimate

*Table 4.4* The UK's changing share of EC output, 1969–86 (by volume)

| Commodity   | % total 1969/70[a] | % total 1978/9[a] | % total 1986/7[b] |
|-------------|--------------------|-------------------|-------------------|
| Mutton      | 50.1               | 47.2              | 29.8              |
| Barley      | 28.3               | 27.9              | 29.7              |
| Potatoes    | 14.0               | 16.7              | 21.3              |
| Wheat       | 9.4                | 13.7              | 18.5              |
| Eggs        | 24.7               | 22.3              | 17.0              |
| Poultrymeat | 21.7               | 20.3              | 16.6              |
| Milk        | 14.2               | 15.6              | 12.3              |
| Beef        | 16.3               | 15.5              | 10.1              |
| Pigmeat     | 12.5               | 9.4               | 8.4               |
| Sugarbeet   | 9.9                | 7.9               | 8.0               |

*Source*: Eurostat *Yearbook of Agricultural Statistics* 1974–88, Statistical Office of the European Communities
*Notes*: [a] EC9
[b] EC10

way in which the full impact of modern agricultural technology was being experienced in Western Europe by the mid-1970s, such that the growth in the supply of farm products was beginning to outstrip domestic demand. The CAP, therefore, was faced with the problem of constraining and managing agricultural surpluses, whereas previous national policies, as in the UK, had been concerned mainly with managing the transition of agriculture from a position of a high to a low employer of labour. New types of agricultural policy were required for these changed circumstances, yet the CAP, through political inertia, continued with measures inherited from the original members of the Community. For example, the principle of supporting the price of farm products was maintained, even though, for the United Kingdom under the CAP, the tax-funded system of guaranteed prices was replaced by consumer-funded variable import levies. Support buying of the major farm products by EC intervention agencies even provided enhanced marketing guarantees for United Kingdom producers. Of course negotiations over these price support levels were switched from London to Brussels as far as UK farmers were concerned, and the NFU had to learn how to represent its interests through the federal organization of national farm groups (COPA-Comité des Organisations Professionnel les Agricoles) to the Council of Ministers. In the short-term, UK farmers were presented with raised levels of support prices and guaranteed markets; like their counterparts in the other member states, they responded by increasing the output of production per hectare of farmland, particularly wheat (table 4.5). But, in the longer term, as the financial burden of agricultural price support became so great as to threaten the very existence of the EC; price levels had to be reduced in real terms. In addition a variety of methods was introduced to limit expenditure on CAP price supports including co-responsibility levies, production quotas and guarantee thresholds (stabilizers); for UK farmers the products most affected were sugarbeet, milk, cereals and oilseed rape. Together these measures brought about an increase in United Kingdom aggregate net farming income from £1,264 million in 1977 to £2,061 million in 1984 but then a decrease to £1,517 million in 1987. In real terms, aggregate net farming income fell by 113 per cent between 1977 and 1987, and by 28 per cent in 1988, bringing the threat of bankruptcy to many individual farm businesses throughout the country.

Running in parallel with price policies have been EC measures designed to influence both the efficiency of farming and farm incomes in certain regions; they have continued the types of measure available in the United Kingdom since the 1950s. Regulations 17/64, 355/77 and 1932/84, for example, have offered grant-aid to improve agricultural marketing and processing, while Directives 72/159, 72/160 and 72/161, together with Regulation 1096/88, have sought to modernize individual farm businesses, pay early retirement pensions to farmers wishing to leave farming, and provide socio-economic guidance and training in occupational skills in

*Table 4.5* UK production and yield of selected crops, 1939–88

| Crop | | 1939 | 1944 | 1958 | 1968 | 1978 | 1988[a] |
|------|---|------|------|------|------|------|------|
| Wheat | P | 1,672 | 3,189 | 2,755 | 3,469 | 6,613 | 11,605 |
| | Y | 2.0 | 2.2 | 2.7 | 3.5 | 5.3 | 6.1 |
| Barley | P | 906 | 1,780 | 3,221 | 8,270 | 9,848 | 8,765 |
| | Y | 2.2 | 2.2 | 2.9 | 3.4 | 4.2 | 4.6 |
| Oats | P | 2,035 | 3,001 | 2,172 | 1,224 | 706 | 557 |
| | Y | 2.0 | 2.0 | 2.4 | 3.2 | 3.9 | 4.6 |
| Sugarbeet | P | 3,586 | 3,320 | 5,835 | 7,119 | 6,382 | 8,500 |
| | Y | 25.8 | 19.3 | 33.1 | 38.1 | 31.7 | 42.5 |
| Potatoes[b] | P | 5,302 | 9,243 | 5,646 | 6,872 | 7,331 | 6,387 |
| | Y | 18.6 | 16.1 | 17.1 | 24.6 | 34.2 | 39.3 |
| Hops | P | 14.6 | 12.9 | 15.3 | 10.1 | 9.4 | 5.2 |
| | Y | 1.9 | 1.7 | 1.8 | 1.4 | 1.6 | 1.3 |

*Source*: MAFF *Agricultural Statistics* 1939–88, HMSO
*Notes*: P: Production in 000 tonnes
Y: Yield in tonnes per hectare
[a] Forecast
[b] Maincrop

agriculture. Directive 75/268 enabled Livestock Compensatory Allowances to be paid to farmers in 'less favoured areas' of the EC; these payments have continued the UK practice of providing direct income supplements as headage subsidies on cows and sheep in the hills and uplands. The most recent development of the CAP, however, together with their implications for UK agriculture, are discussed in the conclusion.

**INPUTS TO THE AGRICULTURAL SECTOR**

The broad structure of annual expenditure by the agricultural sector is shown in table 4.6, although the depreciation of fixed capital assets, such as buildings and plant, and the appreciation in value of farmland, are not included. Livestock feed remains the largest single item of expenditure (29 per cent of the total), the rates of increase evident in the 1970s being contained by a shift from more expensive domestically produced cereals to cheaper imports of feed cake, especially soya beans and cake. The United Kingdom now imports approximately 82.5 million tonnes of compound feeding stuffs per annum, of which 36 per cent is fed to cattle (milk and beef) and the remainder mainly to pigs (33 per cent) or poultry (26 per cent).

Despite severe reductions in the number of people employed in farming (down to 671,474 in 1987 – 2.4 per cent of the employed workforce), labour remains the second most important item of farm expenditure; indeed its share of total expenditure has been rising since the late 1960s and helps explain the continuing drive for labour-saving practices in farming. In aggregate the total labour force has been falling for many years, with the

*Table 4.6* UK farm expenditure, 1950–88 (per cent total expenditure in each year)

| Item | 1950 | 1960 | 1969 | 1979 | 1988[a] |
|---|---|---|---|---|---|
| Feeding stuffs | 18.9 | 27.8 | 28.8 | 35.3 | 29.1 |
| Labour | 32.9 | 23.8 | 18.1 | 20.7 | 21.6 |
| Machinery | 15.6 | 17.0 | 15.3 | 9.5 | 10.8 |
| Fertilizers | 7.3 | 8.8 | 7.5 | 9.1 | 7.1 |
| Other: rent and | | | | | |
|    interest | 7.9 | 8.4 | 10.3 | 5.0 | 8.6 |
|    miscellaneous | | | | 11.2 | 14.4 |
|    seed | | | | 3.8 | 3.2 |
|    farm maintenance | | | | 2.6 | 3.0 |
|    livestock | 17.4 | 14.2 | 20.0 | 2.8 | 2.2 |
| Total value (£m.) | 736.5 | 1,263 | 1,876 | 5,707 | 9,758 |

*Source*: Annual Review White Papers 1950–88, HMSO
*Note*: [a] Forecast

rate of decline in the number of farm workers double that of farmers. For farm workers the rate fluctuated between 3 and 4 per cent a year in the 1960s, but fell back to 1.5 per cent during the 1980s. But these figures disguise some important changes in the structure of the workforce. For example, the number of family workers (including farmers, spouses, partners and directors) exhibits relative stability in recent years, whereas the number of full-time hired male workers has fallen, with some evidence of an accelerated rate of decline in recent years (table 4.7). As a result, family workers now provide approximately 63 per cent of the total workforce in England and Wales so that the incidence of 'family farming' is increasing. As whole-time labour has fallen, so 'intermittent' labour forms, such as part-time, seasonal and casual labour, have increased in importance to provide 52 per cent of agricultural workers. Two processes appear to be at work. First, capital has been used to purchase labour-saving plant and machinery and so substitute for full-time, hired male workers; the continuing peak demands for labour, for example at planting and harvest times, have been met by intermittent labour forms. Second, the increasing proportion of male intermittent labour, compared with the decline in full-time, hired male labour, suggests a process of substitution of one labour form by a cheaper alternative. But, even within the intermittent labour form, lower-cost female workers have become more significant, while there is also evidence that farm wives are playing an increased role in farming. Within England and Wales, the 'feminization' of the workforce is particularly evident in the West Midlands and south-eastern England in association with horticultural, vegetable and fruit farming.

Agricultural contractors supply a wide range of specialized machinery and labour for farming operations such as ploughing, fertilizing, drainage and crop spraying; they also provide an increasing proportion of the total labour input to farming. One study of small cereal farms in central

*Table 4.7* Changing types of workers employed on agricultural holdings in the UK, 1939–88 (per cent total workforce in each year)

| Type of worker | 1939 | 1944[a] | 1958 | 1968 | 1977 | 1987 |
|---|---|---|---|---|---|---|
| Total full-time | 82.5 | 77.2 | 73.5 | 72.0 | 56.4 | 47.6 |
| male | 73.7 | 63.4 | 66.7 | 65.7 | 51.0 | 42.7 |
| female | 8.8 | 13.8 | 6.8 | 6.3 | 5.4 | 4.9 |
| Total part-time[b] | 17.5 | 22.8 | 11.0 | 11.0 | 18.6 | 20.4 |
| male | 11.2 | 13.3 | 6.5 | 5.9 | 8.6 | 10.6 |
| female | 6.3 | 9.5 | 4.5 | 5.1 | 9.0 | 9.8 |
| Total seasonal and casual[b] | | | 15.5 | 17.0 | 25.0 | 32.0 |
| male | | | 9.2 | 9.3 | 14.0 | 19.2 |
| female | | | 6.3 | 7.7 | 11.0 | 12.8 |
| Total workers | 803,526 | 902,117 | 730,253 | 450,102 | 370,523 | 297,257 |

*Source*: MAFF *Agricultural Statistics* 1939–88, HMSO
*Notes*: [a] Excludes Womens Land Army and prisoners-of-war
[b] Part-time workers in Northern Ireland included with casual workers

southern England, for example, indicated that contract charges in 1985 comprised 12.4 per cent of total variable costs compared with 8.9 per cent in 1978. Just as farm labour inputs concerned with animal feed have been replaced by non-farm workers in compound feed manufacturing firms, so other labour inputs have been removed from the production sector and substituted by specialized labour and capital off the farm.

The development of capital-intensive, labour-saving agricultural industry is reflected by the rising share of national farm expenditure on machinery – nearly 11 per cent in 1988 (table 4.6). Some examples of the equipment employed by farms in the United Kingdom are shown in table 4.8. The bias towards crop as compared with livestock farming is evident, but more important is the wide range of expensive, sophisticated machinery that is now required for successful farming throughout the United Kingdom. A measure of the relative importance of modern equipment to farming in different parts of the United Kingdom can be gained by relating the data in table 4.8 to the farm-size distribution of holdings in each country (figure 4.1); for example, the difficulties experienced by producers on the small, predominantly livestock rearing farms of Northern Ireland in raising capital to buy new technology is evident. Nor are there clear signs of a reduction in the pressure to invest in modern technology. Turning to fertilizers, data for Scotland show continuing increases in purchases, especially nitrogen and potash, while fertilizers still account for 7 per cent of national farm expenditure (table 4.6).

The increased dependence on purchased inputs to farming has included buildings for housing livestock, plant to wash, grade and process vegetables and fruit, and agro-chemicals such as pesticides, herbicides and fungicides. Taken together, a new demand for capital has developed over the last two

*Table 4.8* Selected types of agricultural machinery in the UK

| Item | England | Wales | Scotland | Northern Ireland |
|---|---|---|---|---|
| Wheeled tractors (over 107 hp) | 25,500 | 1,400 | 636 | 450 |
| Tractor ploughs (reversible) | 52,000 | 1,100 | 6,679 | 1,160 |
| Spinning disc fertilizer distributors | 97,600 | 16,700 | 19,019 | 19,500 |
| Slurry tankers | 18,900 | 2,600 | 2,904 | 6,700 |
| Automatic potato planters | 8,200 | 300 | na | na |
| Field crop sprayers | 68,700 | 6,300 | 8,517 | 7,740 |
| Combine harvesters (over 134 hp) | 8,500 | 300 | na | na |
| Big bale handlers | 19,600 | 3,630 | na | na |
| Grain driers | 29,424 | 947 | 7,283 | 350 |

*Source*: MAFF *Agricultural Statistics* 1987, HMSO
*Note*: *a* England and Wales 1987; Scotland 1980; Northern Ireland 1984

decades which individual farm businesses have been unable to generate. Consequently farmers have turned to a variety of financial institutions to borrow the necessary capital, including an increased level of buying on credit from suppliers of farm requisites. Farming, therefore, has been characterized by a rising level of indebtedness during the late 1970s and 1980s, a trend stimulated by rising farmland prices and farm incomes following membership of the EC. Advances to agriculture by the London Clearing Banks, for example, rose in just four years from £2,205 million to £4,234 million between 1980 and 1984, an increase of 7.2 per cent in real terms. Relative increases in the level of indebtedness were greatest in Wales and the West Midlands, but the greatest proportion of new capital was taken up by farmers in the south-east and south-west of England. Farmers wishing to enlarge their holdings by purchasing more land also had to borrow the necessary capital in the face of rising farmland prices (see below). The Agricultural Mortgage Corporation, for example, increased its lending to farmers from £393 million in 1974 to £945 million in 1985. In 1988, United Kingdom farmers were estimated to have paid £684 million in interest charges, compared with £216 million in 1978. With the onset of falling prices under the CAP in the early 1980s, together with production quotas on milk in 1984, declining farmland prices after 1980 and increased rates of interest on borrowing, many farm businesses now face bankruptcy. The problem has been most acute for farmers who invested heavily in new buildings, plant and land in the expectation of favourable returns in the late 1970s, and those who have entered farming in the last ten years, especially young farmers. These farm businesses are now dependent on

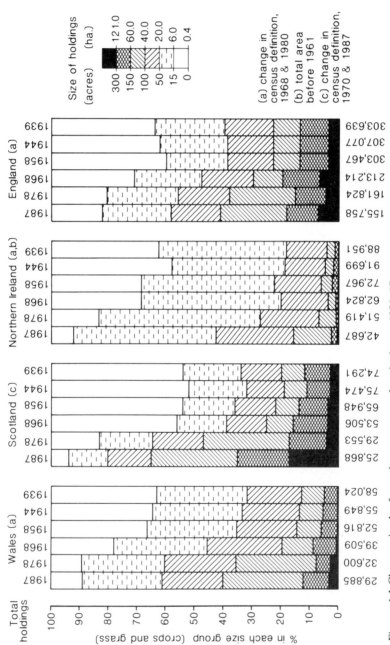

*Figure 4.1* Changes in the farm-size structure of agriculture, 1939–87
*Sources*: Agricultural Statistics, MAFF; DAFS; DANI

being able to service their loans and on the attitudes of financial institutions towards agriculture.

The capitalization of agriculture is nowhere more evident than in the value of farmland. From the end of the Second World War to the early 1980s the value of farmland increased in step with, and at times ahead of, other assets such as stocks and shares. For example, between 1970 and 1979, the farmland capital value index increased by 273 points compared with an equity price index gain of 73 points. Competition amongst farmers for access to a scarce factor of production remains the main reason for the bidding-up of farmland values; indeed this process has ensured that the favourable levels of price support under national and then EC farm policies have been capitalized into farmland values. From time to time, and notably in 1973 and 1974, financial institutions (pension funds, insurance companies and property unit trusts) have given an added impetus to rising land values as they have sought a secure investment for their finances in times of uncertainty. Thus between 1973 and 1983 the average price of farmland with vacant possession in England rose from £1,643 to £3,789 per hectare.

Considerable variations in the price of farmland are disguised by national aggregate figures. For example, the price varies with farm size, being higher per hectare on small as compared with large farms. The price of land in Wales in 1980, for example, varied from £3,489 per hectare for farms under 10 ha in size to £1,300 per hectare for farms in excess of 100 ha. The price of farmland also varies with location, reflecting expected farming profits due to the quality of the land, the ability to produce certain crops and livestock, and market opportunity near to urban areas. In 1987, for example, values varied from £3,500 per hectare in England, through £3,205 in Northern Ireland and £1,900 in Wales, to £1,485 in Scotland. Within Scotland the value of land per hectare in the 'less favoured areas' reached £1,166 in 1987 whereas other land was valued at £2,077. Within England, highest land values are found in south-central areas and East Anglia. Farmland rental values follow similar patterns by farm size, type and location. Within Wales, for example, average rents per hectare in 1986 varied from £85 in South Glamorgan, through £48 in Dyfed to only £18 in West Glamorgan.

With the economic and political tide turning against farming, the capital value of farmland in the United Kingdom has fallen in real terms every year since 1980. In England, for example, farmland with vacant possession fell in value from £3,895 to £3,500 per hectare between 1984 and 1987. Significantly, financial institutions have ceased to invest in farmland and several pension funds have sold their farmland assets. Today these institutions own only 1.6 per cent of the total crops and grass in Britain – 41 per cent under sale and leaseback and 43 per cent under direct management. Farmers who borrowed capital in the late 1970s and early 1980s for improvements to or expansion of their farm businesses now face a double financial squeeze. Not only are their farm profits falling in real terms (see below), but if they wish to sell any land to repay their debts they must do so on a falling land market. For many the result is bankruptcy.

## AGRICULTURAL PRODUCTION

The structure of aggregate national farm output (by value) has been undergoing some modification in the post-war years (table 4.9). Fatstock (cattle, sheep, pigs) still comprise the largest single product group, although their contribution to total output has been falling in recent years. In contrast farm crops, especially cereals, have increased in importance since the 1960s and now form the second most important group with 24 per cent of total output. Milk and milk products, together with eggs and poultrymeat, account for a declining share of national farm output, whereas the converse holds for horticultural products and 'other sales and receipts'. The rising value of the latter reflect the diversification of UK agriculture and the payment of direct subsidies to farming under the CAP.

*Table 4.9* National farm output, 1950–88 (per cent total United Kingdom value of gross output in each year)

| Product | 1950 | 1968 | 1978 | 1988[a] |
|---|---|---|---|---|
| Fatstock (cattle, pigs, sheep) | 22.3 | 29.5 | 31.0 | 28.9 |
| Total farm crops | 20.1 | 18.5 | 23.4 | 23.8 |
| Milk and milk products | 30.3 | 21.7 | 21.9 | 19.8 |
| Total horticultural products | 10.1 | 10.5 | 10.6 | 12.8 |
| Eggs and poultrymeat | 14.2 | 16.1 | 11.8 | 10.2 |
| Other sales and receipts | 3.0 | 3.7 | 1.3 | 4.5 |
| Gross output (£m.) | 1,030.0 | 1,939.5 | 8,163.0 | 12,525.2 |

*Source*: Annual Review White Papers 1950–88, HMSO
*Note*: [a] Forecast

### Crop and livestock trends

Individual crop and livestock trends within these aggregate figures are shown in table 4.1. Looking first at crops, the traditional east/west divide between arable and pastoral activities in both England and Scotland persists to the present day. Within England, for example, a clearly defined arable area, where over 50 per cent of agricultural land is devoted to crops, is in the eastern counties, from Essex in the south to Humberside in the north. Within this area, one notable trend within the cereals sector has been the extension of the area under wheat at the expense of barley. Stimulated by favourable price support levels under the CAP, and the introduction of higher-yielding autumn-sown varieties, such as Brigand and Avalon, the area and volume of production of wheat have increased throughout the United Kingdom. In England and Wales wheat production has been extended westwards and now occupies over 50 per cent of the

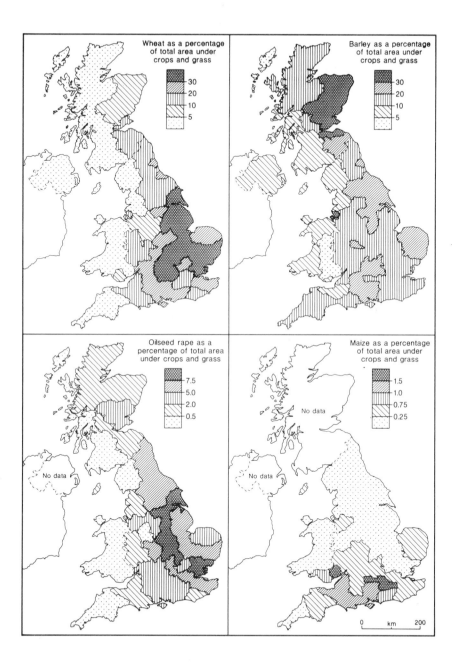

*Figure 4.2* Regional distribution of selected crops, 1986
*Sources:* Agricultural Statistics, MAFF; DAFS; DANI

tillage area in a broad region stretching from Wiltshire in the south-west to Leicestershire in the north (figure 4.2). Barley, by comparison, has been displaced as the premier cereal and now occupies a significant proportion of the tillage area only in western and northern livestock rearing areas of the United Kingdom (figure 4.2). However, the increased use of high-yielding autumn-sown varieties of barley, such as Igri and Sonja, has ensured that production has not fallen to the same extent as the crop area. Another feature of arable farming has been the extension of the area under oilseed rape, although it was first introduced into England only as a cereals break crop. Subsequently the EC gave financial encouragement to its production as a substitute for imported oils such as soyabean, cottonseed and groundnut. As a result the area under oilseed rape in England and Wales increased at an average annual rate of nearly 37 per cent between 1973 and 1986. From an initial concentration in Berkshire and Hampshire, the main production area has shifted to the eastern counties of England, especially the east midlands, as well as into arable areas of eastern Scotland (figure 4.2). While oilseed rape has increased in area, other crops have continued their long-term trend of decline; sugarbeet, potatoes and oats all fall into this category. Sugarbeet, for example, is restricted by production quotas under the CAP and is now grown under contract only in arable areas close to the remaining thirteen processing plants, mainly in eastern England. On potatoes, reductions in area have been greatest in Northern Ireland, central and west Scotland, upland Wales and central-southern England. The overall reduction in Scotland has been greater than in the rest of the United Kingdom, however, owing to the sizeable area of seed potatoes and the contraction of that crop. Only east and south-east Scotland, the Fenland, East Anglia, south-west Lancashire and South Yorkshire retain their traditional association with potato production. Other crops, such as maize and field beans, enjoy fluctuating fortunes as relatively minor elements in the arable rotation. The grain maize area, for example, peaked in the early 1970s, whereas forage maize expanded throughout southern England and Wales until 1978 since when it has declined in area (figure 4.2). However, the introduction of early maturing varieties has stimulated a revival of forage maize in the last four years.

Turning to livestock, perhaps the most significant feature has been the declining number of most types in the face of the growing importance of crop farming. Dairy cows, for example, have been declining within the United Kingdom from a maximum in 1983 and are now fewer in number than in the mid-1960s. The milk quotas imposed by the EC in 1984 have been largely responsible for this trend. Beef cows have also been declining in number since 1975 throughout the United Kingdom, but there has been an increased emphasis on younger-maturing animals fed on silage rather than cereals. High densities of cattle are now found in Staffordshire, the Borders, Dumfries and Galloway and the Northern and Western Isles. Pigs and poultry are declining in number as these farm enterprises come under competition from producers elsewhere in the EC. These enterprises are largely independent of the land, being in effect a housed system for converting animal feed, usually cereals, into poultrymeat, eggs, bacon and pork. Since there are cost savings in the transport of the main input (feed), production has become increasingly concentrated in the main cereal growing areas including Humberside, Norfolk, North Yorkshire, Suffolk, Fife, Lothian and Tayside. Only Cheshire and Lancashire, long associated with poultry production, vary significantly from this broad relationship with cereal producing areas. But even within the poultry sector there have been changes in production. An earlier emphasis on egg production has been replaced by table fowl (poultrymeat), including broilers, with production often on a contract basis with large processors and retailers. The sheep sector, in contrast, has enjoyed a revival of fortunes over the past two decades. Although a farm enterprise most associated with the hill and upland areas, sheep farming in the lowlands has increased in importance as farmers have sought alternatives to dairying and beef production.

### Changes in the structure of farm types

The previous discussion concerned individual farm enterprises such as wheat and beef cows. But agriculture is differentiated from other industries by the joint production of often disparate products, and a number of distinct farming types can be identified. There are differences in definition of farm type between the countries of the United Kingdom, as well as the minimum size of farms included in the various agricultural censuses; consequently any detailed comparison of the data should be approached with caution. However, some broad trends are evident when comparing the type of farm structure for the years 1975 and 1987 (table 4.10). Most significantly, dairying is no longer the major type of farming in the United Kingdom. The impact of EC production quotas has caused dairy farmers to diversify their businesses into cattle and sheep as well as cropping and, when taken with those leaving dairy farming altogether, the proportion of specialist dairy farms has declined throughout the United Kingdom. Cattle and sheep farms, by comparison, have increased in proportion, although there is considerable diversity of production systems ranging from the extensive hill sheep farms of Scotland to the small, pasture-based fattening farms of the English East Midlands. The number and proportion of cereal farms have also increased, particularly in England, while mixed farming shows signs of a revival, except in Northern Ireland, as farmers have sought to develop other forms of income. This trend is likely to continue as cereal farmers become the next sector to suffer restrictions on their production under the CAP. On the other hand, the numbers of horticultural and pigs/poultry farms continue their long-term decline within the overall farm-type structure.

*Table 4.10* Type of farm structure, 1987$^a$ (per cent full-time farms in each country)

| Type of farm | England | Northern Ireland | Scotland | Wales |
|---|---|---|---|---|
| Dairying | 17 (35) | 29 (36) | 18 (20) | 21 (43) |
| Cattle and sheep – less favoured areas | 6 ⎫ (18) | 42 ⎫ (24) | 34 ⎫ (53) | 31 ⎫ (48) |
| Cattle and sheep – lowland | 25 ⎭ | 10 ⎭ | 6 ⎭ | 27 ⎭ |
| Cropping | 27 (20) | 6 ( 5) | 38 (15) | 3 ( 1) |
| Horticulture | 7 (12) | 2 ( –) | 0.6 ( –) | 1 ( 2) |
| Pigs and poultry | 6 ( 8) | 2 ( 5) | 1.1 ( 6) | 3 ( 2) |
| Mixed and others | 12 ( 7) | 9 (20) | 2 ( 6) | 14 ( 4) |

*Sources*: MAFF *Agricultural Statistics United Kingdom* 1987, HMSO; DAFS *Economic Report on Scottish Agriculture* 1987; DANI *Northern Ireland Agriculture* 1987, HMSO
*Notes*: The definition of each farm type varies in detail between the countries
$^a$ 1975 in brackets

The locational dimensions of these changes in the national farm-type structure can be analysed by means of the coefficient of localization.[1] Table 4.11 presents the results of calculations using detailed data available for counties in England in 1976 and 1985, with some comparison with earlier data for England and Wales. With certain exceptions, the coefficients are relatively low, reflecting the dispersed and heterogeneous pattern of English agriculture. However, nine of the thirteen main farm types (excluding part-time) show evidence of greater locational dispersion between 1976 and 1985, especially sheep, cereals and fruit. Some consistent trends emerge if these results are compared with the 1965–73 data for England and Wales. Mainly dairy and pigs with poultry farms appear to be on a long-term trend of increasing regional localization, just as poultry, cereals and mixed farming have continued to become spatially more dispersed since 1965. In contrast, the increasing concentration of beef with sheep, general horticulture, fruit and general cropping, which was evident during the 1965–75 period, has been reversed in recent years. Taken together these results suggest that membership of the EC, with the different product price relationships that it brought, as well as production quotas on products such as sugar and milk, has had a significant effect in changing the structure of farm types in England.

Figure 4.3 shows the regional pattern of change within England of the four most numerous farm types – specialist dairy, beef with sheep, mainly cereals and general cropping. Attention is focused on the 'competitive component' from a shift and share analysis of the number of holdings of each type (sectors) in each region (counties) in England in 1976 and 1985.[2] The technique determines trends in regional performance rates by disaggregating changes in the total number of holdings in a region into three components: a national component (regional share) giving the change that would have taken place had the sectors in aggregate changed at overall

*Table 4.11* Regional localization of farm types in English counties, 1976–85

| Type of farm | Coefficient of localization | | More concentrated (C) or dispersed(D) | |
|---|---|---|---|---|
| | 1976 | 1985 | 1965–73[a] | 1976–85 |
| 1 Mainly vegetables | 0.412 | 0.445 | D | C |
| 2 Specialist dairy | 0.270 | 0.294 | D | C |
| 3 Pigs/poultry | 0.254 | 0.267 | C | C |
| 4 Mainly dairy | 0.199 | 0.235 | C | C |
| 5 Part-time | 0.044 | 0.057 | nd | C |
| 6 Mixed | 0.166 | 0.153 | D | D |
| 7 Mainly beef | 0.203 | 0.178 | C | D |
| 8 Mainly poultry | 0.198 | 0.185 | D | D |
| 9 General horticulture | 0.333 | 0.321 | C | D |
| 10 Mainly sheep | 0.386 | 0.327 | C | D |
| 11 Beef/sheep | 0.423 | 0.416 | C | D |
| 12 Mainly cereals | 0.456 | 0.420 | D | D |
| 13 General cropping | 0.442 | 0.434 | C | D |
| 14 Mainly fruit | 0.620 | 0.519 | C | D |

*Source*: Unpublished MAFF data
*Note*: [a] England and Wales
nd no data

national rates, a structural component (proportionality shift) giving the change arising from the sectoral structure of the region and trends in each sector in relation to overall national trends, and a competitive component (differential shift) giving the change that can be attributed to trends in individual sectors in the region in relation to the national trend for each sector. Using the competitive component, positive values indicate absolute increases in farm numbers or rates of decrease below the national average for that type of farm; negative values show rates of loss in excess of the national average.

In England, the total number of holdings in the agricultural census declined by 10.5 per cent between 1976 and 1985 under the dual processes of farm amalgamation and changes in the basis of enumeration. Disaggregating the competitive component by farm types (figure 4.3) reveals that specialist dairy farms are a declining structural element in agriculture in the eastern as compared with the western counties of England. The resulting spatial concentration of this farm type is serving to emphasize the historical division in British agriculture between eastern arable and western livestock producing areas. Beef with sheep farms demonstrate a more complex regional pattern, becoming more dispersed in southern and West Midland counties. Mainly cereal farms have also become more dispersed, but in south-western as well as West Midland counties at the expense of eastern counties. Last, general cropping farms have become more dispersed in eastern and south-western England at the expense of counties distributed

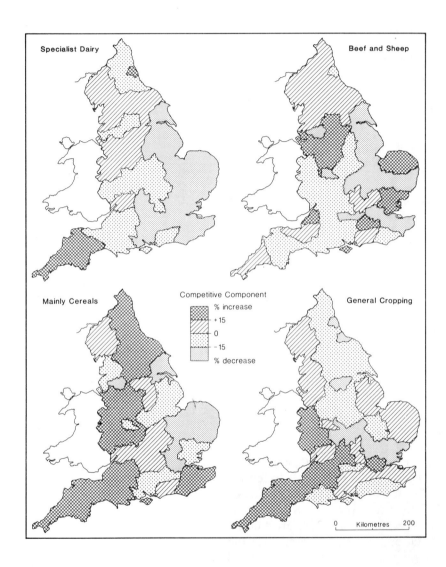

*Figure 4.3* Changes in types of farming in the English counties, 1976–85
*Source:* Unpublished MAFF data

along a north-south axis from Northumberland to Sussex. This analysis of the farm type structure strongly suggests that previous trends towards the greater regional specialization of farming have been halted; under the changing price support levels of the CAP, and competition with producers in other member states, new regional associations of farm types appear to be forming. However, further analysis using data for counties in Wales, Scotland and Northern Ireland is required before this conclusion can be extended to the United Kingdom as a whole.

## The changing structure of the farm business

The previous section has traced the rising level of purchased farm inputs throughout the post-war years, especially in animal feed, fertilizers, seed varieties, improved agro-chemicals, and plant and machinery. The result has been a rising output per hectare of almost every farm product, a trend termed 'intensification' (table 4.5). The average annual milk yield per dairy cow in Northern Ireland, for example, increased from 3,180 litres in 1964 to 4,560 litres in 1985; comparable figures for England and Wales are 3,545 and 4,930 litres. For most of the period following the Second World War, agricultural intensification has been accompanied by the greater specialization of production: individual farmers have sought economies of scale by concentrating all their productive resources, including labour and management, on one or a few agricultural products, discarding their least profitable enterprises. Thus for many years the trend towards specialization in individual farm businesses was reflected in the decline of mixed farms; the process was accompanied by the increasing regional specialization of production. However, as suggested in the previous section, the phase of development seems to be at an end for the time being: farmers are having to diversify and redirect their resources as profit levels decline in traditional types of production.

One outcome of agricultural intensification and specialization has been the greatly expanded size of surviving enterprises: the proportion of farm businesses responsible for the production of most products has tended to diminish but the average number of hectares or livestock in each farm enterprise has risen. This process, termed 'enterprise concentration', is demonstrated for dairy farming in table 4.12. The average number of cows per herd increased in the United Kingdom from forty-three to sixty-four between 1975 and 1985, while over the same period the total number of herds fell by 36 per cent. Table 4.12 also shows the varying size-structure of dairy farming; for example, in 1985 the average size of the dairy herd in Northern Ireland was thirty-six cows compared with eighty-nine in Scotland. Another way of expressing enterprise concentration is the proportion of production accounted for by the largest enterprises. Taking Scotland as an example, in 1985 54 per cent of dairy cows were found in herds of over 100 cows, but such herds accounted for only 35 per cent of all herds. However, the degree of enterprise concentration varies by product. The penetration of different farm types and enterprises by industrial farming methods and economies of scale of operation is very variable. Table 4.13 shows how the process of enterprise concentration within both Scotland and Wales is most advanced in the intensive livestock sector (pigs and poultry) where large-scale enterprises, using industrial farming techniques, are now the norm. Beef and barley production, in contrast, show only modest levels of enterprise concentration.

Changes in enterprise size have to be placed in the broader context of the farm-size structure of agriculture. Reference has been made already to the long-term decline within the United Kingdom of both employment in

*Table 4.12* Increasing enterprise concentration in the dairy sector, 1975–85

| Country | 1975 | | | 1980 | | | 1985 | | |
|---|---|---|---|---|---|---|---|---|---|
| | A | B | C | A | B | C | A | B | C |
| England and Wales | 46 | 25.7 | 7.7 | 58 | 34.5 | 13.3 | 67 | 39.3 | 16.9 |
| Scotland | 71 | 36.2 | 18.4 | 82 | 50.4 | 31.0 | 89 | 54.4 | 35.3 |
| Northern Ireland | 20 | na | na | 28 | 11.8 | 2.6 | 36 | 16.6 | 4.9 |

*Source*: The Federation of Milk Marketing Boards *Dairy facts and figures 1986*, FMMB
*Notes*: A Average number of cows per head
B Proportion of cows in herds over 100 head
C Proportion of herds over 100 head

*Table 4.13* Enterprise concentration in Scotland and Wales, 1987[a]

| Enterprise | Scotland | | Wales | |
|---|---|---|---|---|
| | A | B | A | B |
| Laying hens | 0.4 | 72.6 | 1.7 | 89.5 |
| Feeding pigs | 10.0 | 60.4 | 15.1 | 87.0 |
| Breeding pigs | 10.9 | 57.3 | 16.4 | 78.8 |
| Table fowl | 4.3 | 55.9 | 21.0 | 91.3 |
| Breeding ewes | 15.5 | 54.2 | 16.3 | 52.9 |
| Dairy cows | 29.0 | 53.7 | 21.6 | 47.5 |
| Wheat | 12.4 | 41.3 | 65.0 | 93.8 |
| Potatoes (total) | 7.4 | 41.3 | 6.3 | 51.1 |
| Feeding cattle | 9.0 | 39.3 | na | na |
| Barley (spring) | 11.8 | 38.9 | } 13.2 | } 48.2 |
| Barley (winter) | 11.5 | 37.0 | | |
| Beef cows | 13.6 | 36.5 | 9.2 | 35.4 |

*Sources*: DAFS *Economic report on Scottish agriculture* 1987; Welsh Office *Welsh Agricultural Statistics* 1988 Welsh Office
*Notes*: A Largest producers (%)
B Area or livestock numbers (%)
[a] The calculation of comparable statistics between enterprises and countries is constrained by the availability of data

agriculture and the total number of farms. Changes in the scope of the annual agricultural census make it difficult to be precise about the rate of decline, not least because occupiers of farmland make their returns according to 'holdings' rather than 'farms'. Not only are farms often comprised of several holdings, but individual occupiers have been encouraged to group their separate holdings under one census return, thus creating 'paper amalgamations'. For convenience the term 'farm' has been used interchangeably with 'holding' throughout this chapter. An annual reduction of 2 per cent in the number of farm units appears to be a reasonable estimate of the rate of decline within the United Kingdom in the post-war years, with some evidence of a gradually accelerating rate through the 1960s and early 1970s. Today there are approximately 254,300 farm holdings in the United Kingdom and an unknown number of agriculturally insignificant smallholdings.

Farm amalgamation is the process underlying the decline in farm numbers. Between 4 and 6 per cent of farms change occupiers each year, and approximately 60 per cent of the farms which fall vacant do so on the death or retirement from agriculture of the occupier. Other reasons include the movement of an occupier to another farm, a change to another form of occupation and bankruptcy. Between a third and a half of the farms changing hands are purchased by other farmers or landowners with a view to increasing the size of existing farm businesses. The main incentive for farm amalgamation, therefore, is the desire to increase income by spreading production costs over a larger enterprise; consequently the increase in business size associated with the process of enterprise concentration has been bolstered by the increase in area-size of farms.

A higher rate of farm-size change is evident amongst tenanted compared with owner-occupied farms: within certain limitations placed on security of tenure, large landowners have a relatively free hand in deciding whether to relet a farm as the tenancy falls vacant, sell the farm or take the land in hand to be managed for or farmed by the owner. Since the Second World War a large number of landed estates have had to sell tenanted farms, often to sitting tenants, in order to pay inheritance tax (estate duty, capital transfer tax) on the death of the owner. For owner-occupiers the main pressure for farm enlargement also varies with the family life cycle, but the pressure is greatest on farm families with sons and daughters who wish to remain in farming on leaving school. The farm business has to be enlarged to provide employment for the additional working members of the family. Quite complex land ownership and business arrangements are emerging based on partnerships, trusts and companies, including several individual farm businesses managed in association by an extended farm family. In addition, it is quite usual for farms to be enlarged by renting rather than owning more land; consequently a complex structure of mixed tenure has emerged within individual farm businesses. Available data show that 62 per cent of farmland is 'mainly' owned at present compared with only 38 per cent in 1950. More detailed information for Wales reveals that 27 per cent of the land is in mixed tenure with a further 58 per cent 'wholly owned'. These figures suggest that wholly rented farms are now a minor element in the contemporary agricultural pattern.

The rate of change in the number of farms is also selective by farm size. Farms below 20 ha (50 acres) have fallen in number whereas the greatest rates of increase have been in the largest farm-size categories (figure 4.1). As smaller units become marginalized, the land is purchased by those owning the larger farms; in this respect farm amalgamation reflects the reallocation of resources from economically marginal (small) to more profitable (large) production units. Up to a certain size the larger farm is able to use resources more efficiently than the smaller. But the main economies of scale are obtained in moving from small- to medium-sized farms (122 ha/300 acres) owing to the greater utilization of full-time labour (family and hired). As the scale of operation expands beyond this size the wider delegation of responsibility to subordinates, together with an increasingly fragmented pattern of land ownership, can result in less efficient management and higher unit costs of production. Although there is little evidence of decreasing returns to size on the largest holdings, the evidence of a continuing increase is sparse. Indeed the main advantage of increasing the size of farm beyond 202 ha (500 acres) appears to have more to do with taxation, capital gains and the accumulation of wealth than with farming efficiency.

Table 4.14 demonstrates how lower incomes are generated by small farms irrespective of farm type; this makes them vulnerable to marginalization and amalgamation. Nevertheless, income level also varies within the United Kingdom, suggesting that small farms of certain types are more vulnerable in some regions than others, for example, small dairy farms in Scotland and small lowland livestock farms in England. Indeed the rate of change in the number of farms has varied within the United Kingdom. Over the last four decades farm losses have been greater in Scotland and England than in Wales and Northern Ireland, but even within these countries there are detailed spatial variations. In England the trend towards larger farms began in the arable farming areas in the eastern counties in the late 1940s and spread westwards in the ensuing decades; in recent years the loss in farm numbers has been greatest in eastern counties such as Cambridgeshire, Lincolnshire, Nottinghamshire and South Yorkshire, and least in the counties of south-east England. Within Scotland the rate of amalgamation remains relatively low in the Highlands and Islands amongst crofting farms, in part because of the very small size of the holdings, but in part also because of the rigid structure of crofting as a socio-economic system.

Nevertheless, few regions demonstrate the polarization of the farm-size structure that has been reported in other countries. Except in parts of Scotland, where historically the concentration of land in large units has

*Table 4.14* Variations in net farm income, 1986–8 (£000 per farm per year)

| Farm size$^a$ and type | England | Wales | Scotland | N. Ireland |
|---|---|---|---|---|
| Dairy | | | | |
| small | 7.2 | 7.9 | 1.4 | 7.5 |
| medium | 15.0 | 15.4 | 10.4 | 18.1 |
| large | 33.3 | 35.3 | 20.6 | – |
| Upland livestock | | | | |
| small | 4.7 | 3.4 | 3.6 | 4.5 |
| medium | 11.0 | 14.7 | 7.2 | 9.9 |
| large | 22.0 | 31.4 | 17.3 | – |
| Lowland livestock | | | | |
| small | 0.2 | – | 2.0 | – |
| medium | 7.4 | – | 4.3 | – |
| large | 20.2 | – | 19.6 | – |
| Cropping | | | | |
| small | 3.6 | – | 3.3 | – |
| medium | 5.9 | – | 4.1 | – |
| large | 20.3 | – | 18.4 | – |

*Source*: MAFF *Agriculture in the United Kingdom* 1988, HMSO
*Note*: $^a$ Varies with type of farm

been particularly exaggerated (75 per cent of the land is farmed by 17 per cent of the holdings), there is little evidence of the demise of medium-sized family farms and the development of a size-structure of a few, very large farms units together with a large number of very small, usually part-time holdings. On the other hand, the exclusion of agriculturally insignificant holdings from the agricultural census may be masking this development in the structure of land holding.

## Marketing beyond the farm gate

The transformation of agriculture has involved the marketing as well as the production of farm commodities. The post-war years have witnessed a growing variety and complexity in the methods of agricultural marketing; even within the livestock sector the traditional auction market-wholesaler-retailer chain no longer predominates. In part this reflects the growing involvement of the state in agricultural marketing, but it also indicates the development of marketing alternatives by farming, processing and retailing sectors of the food chain.

An increasing proportion of farm production passes through the Intervention Board of Agricultural Produce; the Board acts as the agent of the EC within the United Kingdom and has incurred expenditure under the CAP in purchasing, storing and subsequently marketing the main farm products (table 4.15), often through subsidized exports. Cereals, beef and milk are the products most likely to pass into intervention stores from the

*Table 4.15* UK agricultural marketing of selected products through cooperatives (1982), under contracts (1982), and by CAP intervention,[a] (1987–8)

| Product | Cooperatives (%) | Contracts (%) | Intervention (£m.) |
|---------|------------------|---------------|--------------------|
| Pigmeat | 13 | 50 | −1.9 |
| Beef/veal | 10 | – | 201.4 |
| Poultrymeat | 2 | 95 | – |
| Eggs | 28 | 65 | – |
| Potatoes | – | 13 | – |
| Milk | – | – | 153.4 |
| Sugarbeet | – | 100 | 151.1 |
| Cereals | 20 | – | 229.4 |
| All fruit | 33 | – | – |
| All vegetables | 17 | 95[b] | – |

*Source*: Commission of the European Communities *The agricultural situation in the Community – 1987 Report*, Office for Official Publications of the European Communities
*Notes*: [a] Expenditure by the Intervention Board for Agricultural Produce
[b] Peas

farm or dairy, although in some years significant volumes of sugar, sheepmeat and oilseeds are also marketed in this way.

The normal channels of food distribution from the farm are shown in figure 4.4. The key role played by the food processing sector is emphasized in this diagram; indeed only a fraction of agricultural output – potatoes, fresh vegetables, fruit, some cream and eggs – now reaches the public without some industrial processing; even these products require washing, grading and packing before reaching the consumer. The bulk of farm produce, therefore, is sold to firms manufacturing food and drink, either directly or through merchants and marketing organizations. The Milk Marketing Board, for example, controls over 75 per cent of the United Kingdom manufacturing capacity for butter and 50 per cent of the capacity for hard-pressed cheese. The distribution of the manufacturing plant is displayed in figure 4.5. In common with other food manufacturing sectors, there has been considerable rationalization of capacity in recent years; the continuing concentration of dairy production in western and northern areas, for example, is reflected in the location of the dairy processing plant. Other food sectors have sought economies through vertical as well as horizontal integration and agribusinesses which produce, process and retail farm products are increasingly common. Indeed, on the employment size of processing plants, the most concentrated sectors are biscuits, margarine, starch and bread/flour confectionery; the least concentrated sectors are animal/poultry food and vegetable and animal oils/fats. Most companies hold back from direct ownership of farms but assure their supplies by placing forward contracts with individual farmers. For example, approximately 95 per cent of peas and poultrymeat, all sugarbeet and 65 per cent of eggs are produced under contract (table 4.15). In these circumstances

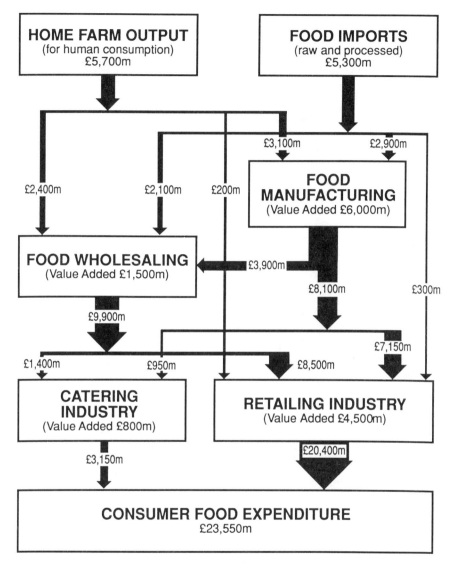

*Figure 4.4* Channels of food distribution in the UK, 1979
*Source:* J. Burns *et al.* (1983) *The food industry,* London: Heinemann

nearness to the processing factories has become a significant factor in the location of production.

Contract farming has been an important catalyst in the development of cooperative marketing amongst producers. By offering a product of assured, uniform quality and quantity, groups of farmers have been able to negotiate more favourable terms with large food processors as well as the

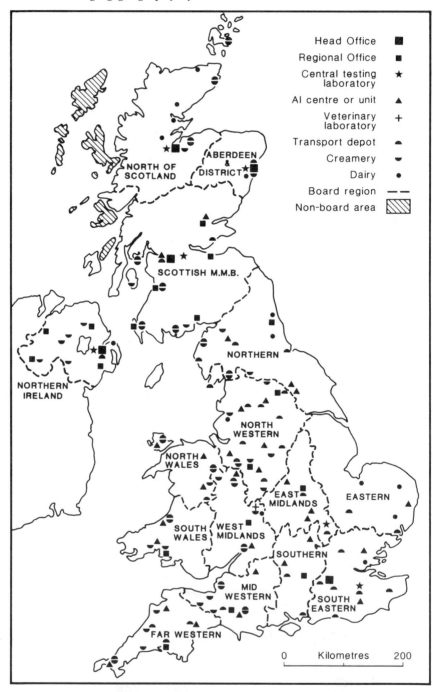

*Figure 4.5* Plant associated with the production of dairy products, 1986
*Source:* Federation of UK Milk Marketing Boards

supermarket chains. The development of marketing cooperatives has varied from product to product and, because products have regional patterns of production, there have also been variations from area to area. Fruit, eggs, cereals and vegetables are the products most associated with cooperative marketing (table 4.15).

The retailing sector, with its large multiple retailers, is increasingly able to determine the price, quantity and quality of food purchased from either the manufacturing sector or directly from larger farms. The catering industry, especially the restaurant and fast-food sectors, is also increasing its sales and becoming a significant element in the food chain. With these developments, the price of food to the consumer is determined more by the value added beyond the farm gate than on the farm itself. Consequently an increasing number of farmers is attempting to bypass the food distribution system by selling produce direct to consumers. A number of possibilities exist – farm-gate sales, roadside stalls, farm shops, and mobile shop deliveries. Crops rather than meat or livestock products tend to predominate in these forms of direct marketing. The most dynamic sector in the late 1970s, however, was 'pick-your-own' marketing (PYO), especially of soft fruit, in which customers pick and transport the crops themselves. This type of marketing has been most prevalent in south-east England and the West Midlands where traditional fruit and vegetable growing areas are near to urban consumers. However, the main growth phase of PYO appears to have passed, and in the 1980s farm shops on main transport routes or near to towns and cities have been more successful.

## CONCLUSION

The post-war transformation of agriculture, as recorded in summary form in this essay, has had an impact on farming throughout the United Kingdom. The broad trends described here have been played out in different regional contexts with varying consequences for local agricultural patterns. Unfortunately the description and explanation of such detailed regional variation must be left to another occasion. Rather, the essay concludes with a discussion of the transformation of the agricultural pattern in relation to three features – the rural environment, rural land use and rural employment.

On environment, the development of a capital-intensive, specialized and industrialized farm sector has brought contemporary agriculture into direct conflict with nature and landscape conservation. The damaging environmental consequences of modern farming are now well documented but include the ploughing of moorland and downland, the drainage of lowland marshes, the pollution of water courses by slurry effluent, silage liquor and nitrogenous fertilizers, the removal of small woods and hedgerows and the visual intrusiveness of many new farm buildings. To take just one example from the list in more detail, the Water Authorities Association has recorded an increase in the number of reported incidents of farm pollution of rivers in England and Wales from under 1,500 in 1979 to over 4,000 in 1988 (see also chapter 19). In the United Kingdom the strategy adopted to combat these problems involves education, persuasion and voluntary action by the farming community, with financial compensation available for adopting environmentally sensitive farming practices in a few selected locations – Sites of Special Scientific Interest (SSSI) and Environmentally Sensitive Areas (ESA) (see chapter 17). The latter, part-funded by the EC, are now nineteen in number but cover only 180,000 ha of the United Kingdom. Thus the agricultural interest has succeeded in extracting costly financial payments from the state for conserving the environment, and has limited the needed response to voluntary rather than mandatory action. But the industry has lost a good deal of public support in the meantime. Agriculture now finds itself increasingly isolated from that support when attempting to modify national and EC farm policies; these now aim to reduce farm support prices with the inevitable consequences of falling farm incomes.

Turning to rural land use, there is now broad acceptance of the view that either capital or land (or both) needs to be withdrawn from agricultural production; the aim is to bring the demand for and supply of farm products into equilibrium within the EC. Falling farm support prices are likely to divert capital towards other sectors of the economy, while the EC has recently put in place a Regulation (1094/88) aimed at retiring or diverting land from farm production. Approximately 10 million ha are estimated to be needed for retirement in the EC. The 'set-aside' scheme of the United Kingdom came into operation in 1988–9, but in its first year was taken up by only 2,000 farmers on 60,000 ha of land. The greatest proportion of this land was located in south-east England, especially in the counties immediately to the west and north of London, and was placed mainly in permanent fallow (the other alternatives being rotational fallow, woodland, or non-agricultural uses). Under the scheme, farmers have to retire at least 20 per cent of their arable land for a minimum of five years, but receive compensation of up to £200 per hectare for doing so. Alternative schemes apply to the extensification and conversion of production, for example to products not in surplus within the EC. Forestry appears to be the only viable, extensive and long-term alternative use for much farmland, and to this end a Farm Woodland Scheme was launched in the United Kingdom in 1988. However, the implications of the retirement or conversion of large areas of farmland for the environment and national and regional economies have yet to be examined in detail.

Finally, on rural employment, diversifying the use of farm capital and labour appears to be a further means of resolving the contemporary farm crisis. A wide range of alternatives can be identified, including both on-farm and off-farm activities, although they can be placed usefully into five groups: tourism, recreation, adding value, unconventional enterprises and ancillary buildings/resources. We cannot enter into detail here, but individual enterprises include farm holidays, horse riding, farm cheese, reindeer, farm woodland and rural crafts. The capital and skilled labour requirements of each enterprise vary in addition to their regional potential; farm tourism, for example, is probably a viable enterprise only for existing tourist areas in coastal and mountain regions, while certain types of farm recreation need an urban-fringe location for access to large numbers of participants. Moreover, experience to date suggests that each alternative enterprise offers a niche in the market for only a limited number of farmers with the appropriate entrepreneurial attitudes and skills. Consequently farm diversification is likely to proceed on a farm-by-farm basis, rather than across whole regional farm economies, and act as a supplement to, rather than total replacement of, income from traditional farm production.

## NOTES

1 Coefficient of localization for the $i$th type of farm =

$$\frac{\sum_{j} \left| \frac{e_{ij}}{\sum_{j} e_{ij}} - \frac{a_j}{\sum_{j} a_j} \right|}{2}$$

where $e_{ij}$ = number of farms of the $i$th type in the $j$th region,
$a_j$ = area of crops and grass in the $j$th region,
(0 = even distribution, 1 = concentrated distribution).

2 Regional share $(R) = E_j^o \left( \dfrac{G^1}{G^o} \right) - E_j^o$ (or national component),

proportionality shift $(P) = \sum_{i} e_{ij}^o \left( \dfrac{E_j^1}{E_j^o} - \dfrac{G^1}{G^o} \right)$ (or structural component),

differential shift $(D) = \sum_{i} \left[ e_{ij}^1 - e_{ij}^o \left( \dfrac{E_i^1}{E_i^o} \right) \right]$ (or competitive component),

where $e_{ij}$ = number of farms of the $i$th type in the $j$th region,
$E_j = \sum_i e_{ij}$, total farms in the $j$th region,

$E_i = \sum_j e_{ij}$, total farms of the $i$th type in all regions,

$G = \sum_i \sum_j e_{ij}$, total farms in all the regions,

0 = initial year of study,
1 = terminal year of study.

*Source*: Dawson, J. A. (1974) 'Analytical techniques for geographers: shift-share analysis', *Cambria*, 1: 159–62.

## REFERENCES

*Food from our own resources* (1975), CMND 6020, HMSO.
Stamp, L. D. (1962) *The land of Britain: Its Use and Misuse*, 3rd edition, London: Longmans.

## FURTHER READING

General surveys of British agricultural geography are provided in Coppock, J. T. (1976) *An Agricultural Atlas of England and Wales*, London: Faber & Faber, and (1976) *An Agricultural Atlas of Scotland*, Edinburgh: Donald; and Robinson, G. M. (1988) *Agricultural Change – Geographical Studies of British Agriculture*: Edinburgh: North British Publishing. On agricultural trends see, for example: Aitchison, J. (1980) 'The agricultural landscape of Wales', *Cambria*, 7: 43–68; Bowler, I. R. (1981) 'Regional specialization in the agricultural industry', *Journal of Agricultural Economics*, 32: 43–54; and Wrathall, J. E. (1988) 'Recent changes in arable crop production in England and Wales', *Land Use Policy*, 5: 219–31. On farm sizes and efficiency, see Britton, D. K. and Hill, B. (1975) *Size and Efficiency in Farming*, Farnborough: Saxon House; Clarke, G (1979) 'Farm amalgamation in Scotland', *Scottish Geographical Magazine*, 95: 93–107; and Edwards, C. J. W. (1977) 'The effects of changing farm size upon levels of farm fragmentation: a Somerset case study', *Journal of Agricultural Economics*, 29: 143–54. Farm labour is examined by Ball, R. M. (1987) 'Intermittent labour farms in UK agriculture: some implications for rural areas', *Journal of Rural Studies*, 3: 133–50.

Trends in marketing are discussed in Bowler, I. R. (1982) 'Direct marketing in agriculture: a British example', *Tijdschrift voor Economische en Sociale Geografie*, 73: 22–31; Hart, P. W. E. (1978) 'Geographical aspects of contract marketing', *Tijdschrift voor Economische en Sociale Geografie*, 69: 205–15; Burns, J. (1983) 'The UK food chain with particular reference to the inter-relations between manufacturers and retailers', *Journal of Agricultural Economics*, 34: 361–78; and Ilbery, B. W. (1985) 'Horticultural marketing in the Vale of Evesham', *Transactions of the Institute of British Geographers*, 11: 468–79. On land ownership and prices, see Massey, D. and Catalano, A. (1978) *Capital and Land*, London: Edward Arnold; Munton, R. J. C. (1985) 'Investment in British agriculture by the financial institutions', *Sociologia Ruralis*, 25: 155–73 and Harrison, A. (1982) 'Factors influencing ownership, tenancy, mobility and the use of farmland in the United Kingdom', *Information on Agriculture*, 74, Brussels, Commission of the European Communities. The role of the state in agriculture is discussed in Bowler, I. R. (1979) *Government and Agriculture: A Spatial Perspective*, London: Longman, and (1985) *Agriculture under the Common Agricultural Policy: A Geography*, Manchester: Manchester University Press. The restructuring of family farming is considered by Marsden, T. K., Whatmore, S. J., and Munton, R. J. (1987) 'Uneven development and the restructuring process in British agriculture; a preliminary exploration', *Journal of Rural Studies*, 3: 297–308; Gasson, R. (1988) *The Economics of Part-Time Farming*, London: Longman; and Ilbery, B. W. (1988) 'Farm diversification and the restructuring of agriculture', *Outlook on Agriculture*, 17: 35–40.

# 5 Energy production and use

*Keith Chapman*

Major changes have taken place in patterns of energy production and consumption in the United Kingdom since 1945. These changes are apparent both in the relationship between indigenous and imported sources of energy and in the relative contributions of the various fuels to total consumption. Before the Second World War, the United Kingdom's coal output made the country a significant net exporter of energy. The combined effect of inadequate investment during the war and manpower shortages resulted in a failure to meet even domestic demand when hostilities ceased and the coal industry's virtual monopoly as fuel supplier to the British economy was gradually weakened as the volume of imported oil increased. The gap between indigenous energy production and consumption widened steadily for almost twenty-five years (figure 5.1) and it was not until 1975 that any perceptible narrowing of this gap occurred. By 1980, the rapid rise in North Sea oil production had transformed the energy gap into a surplus once more.

Associated with these changes in dependence upon internal and external sources of supply have been shifts in the relative contributions of the various fuels to total energy consumption (figure 5.2). Coal consumption has been reduced not only by the substitution of imported and, more recently, domestic oil, but also by the introduction of natural gas and, to a much lesser extent, nuclear power. Thus whereas coal accounted for 95 per cent of primary energy consumption in 1950, its share had fallen to 34.4 by 1987, with oil, natural gas and nuclear power accounting for 32.4, 25.4 and 7.9 per cent respectively.[1] This chapter identifies the factors responsible for these changes in the energy situation of the United Kingdom and considers some of their spatial implications in the context of production, distribution and consumption.

## STRUCTURAL CHANGES IN THE ENERGY MARKET, 1945–80

Several inter-related factors have contributed to the structural changes in the United Kingdom energy market represented in figures 5.1 and 5.2. For the purposes of interpretation, it is convenient to distinguish between the

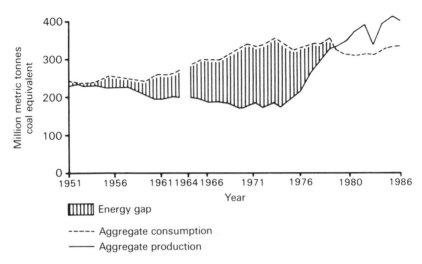

*Figure 5.1* Production and consumption of primary energy, 1951–86
*Sources:* Data for 1951–63 from United Nations Statistical papers, Series J, *World Energy Supplies;* data for 1964–86 from Department of Energy *Digest of Energy Statistics* annual

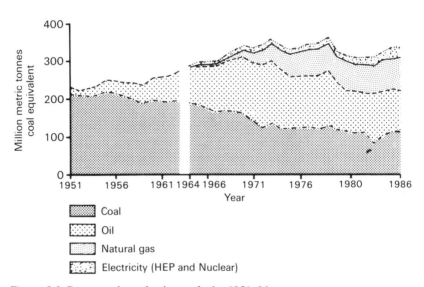

*Figure 5.2* Consumption of primary fuels, 1951–86
*Sources:* See figure 5.1

roles of: (i) costs and competition, (ii) resource availabilities, (iii) technical change, and (iv) public policy.

**Costs and competition**

Changes in the international price of oil have been the most important single influence upon the United Kingdom energy market since 1950. Producers and consumers have responded to this external influence, which has also been a major factor shaping the economic and energy policies of successive governments. Although short-term fluctuations have occurred, it is possible to identify three general phases in the evolution of oil prices. The first was a lengthy period of stability between 1950 and 1972 which saw a decline in the real price of oil relative to other commodities. This was followed by sharp and dramatic price increases between 1973 and 1981 as a consequence of the actions of the Organization of Petroleum Exporting Countries (OPEC) which saw the average f.o.b. (free on board) price of, for example, an Abu Dhabi crude rise from US $2.54 a barrel in 1972 to US $36.56 in 1981. The general trend of international oil prices has changed once again during the 1980s as OPEC has been unable to sustain its essentially political success as the countries of the developed world have reduced their dependence upon Middle East oil. Thus prices have tended to fall and the same Abu Dhabi crude was selling for US $8.45 per barrel during the slump of 1986 and most energy planning is based upon assumptions of a gradual rise towards the end of the century from a projected base level of approximately $18 per barrel at the end of the 1980s. Past experience suggests that these assumptions may prove mistaken, but the energy sector is characterized by heavy capital expenditures and long lead times and important decisions must be made on the basis of such projections. There is no doubt that the historical pattern of energy production and use within the United Kingdom has been influenced by expectations as well as by the actual cost and availability of imported oil which therefore provides an essential framework within which any inter-pretation must be set.

One of the most important effects of variations in the 'real' price of oil has been their impact upon aggregate energy consumption. This reached a peak in 1973 which had still not been surpassed by 1986. Although structural changes in the economy, such as the decline of manufacturing, are partly responsible, there have been significant improvements in the efficiency of energy use. This may be measured by calculating the ratio of energy consumption to gross domestic product. Expressed as an index relative to a base value of 100 in 1980, the corresponding values for 1967 and 1987 were 119.0 and 85.8 respectively, which amounts to a 28 per cent improvement in just twenty years. Current energy consumption is, therefore, well below the levels assumed in prudent strategic planning in the 1960s. The collective failure of both private and public sector energy industries to anticipate this fundamental change, a failure which itself reflected the prevailing stability of oil prices, has had important consequences for the subsequent development of these industries. Some of these consequences will be addressed later and it is necessary to begin with a review of the changing price relativities of coal and oil which have been the dominant primary fuels in the post-war period.

The inability of the coal industry to meet demand throughout the 1950s provided the opportunity for imported oil to increase its share of the energy market. This trend accelerated during the 1960s as a widening gap between the price of the two fuels encouraged industrial and domestic consumers to substitute oil for coal wherever possible. The average costs of producing coal in the mines of the National Coal Board (NCB) nearly doubled between 1947 and 1957, reflecting a post-war legacy of many old, inefficient and under-capitalized mines together with geological difficulties and the exhaustion of reserves in parts of such traditionally important coalfield areas as north-east England and Scotland. These problems were aggravated by the slow development of replacement capacity and by labour shortages. Meanwhile, the price of imported oil also rose during the first half of the 1950s after an initial fall between 1948 and 1950. The upward trend in oil prices was much more gradual, however, and the competitive advantage of oil increased significantly during the 1960s, despite a big improvement in the productivity of the remaining mines and a much slower inflation in the costs of producing coal.

Several factors contributed to the decline in the real price of oil throughout the 1960s. The most important was the intervention of several American-based independent oil companies in the world oil market. Successful exploration by these companies, coupled with severe restrictions on crude oil imports into the United States, encouraged them to look to Western Europe and Japan as outlets and brought them into direct competition with the established 'majors'. This competition tended to produce an over-abundance of oil, which was aggravated by the desire of the various producing countries to maintain high output levels, since their revenues were determined by the volume of production. Further pressure on crude prices resulted from the vigorous activities of state-owned oil companies and, to a lesser extent, the availability of Russian oil as a new source of supply for Western Europe.

The political risks of greater dependence upon imported energy were very much secondary to economic considerations in determining patterns of energy use. Thus the displacement of coal by oil (figure 5.2) was accompanied by an accelerated programme of pit closures (figure 5.3). The oil price shock of 1973 resulted in a rapid reappraisal of these priorities. The Plan for Coal, produced by the National Coal Board in 1974, was intended to halt the decline in output and to reduce overall costs by replacing old capacity with an approximately equivalent volume of production, by expanding suitable existing mines and creating some new ones.

*Figure 5.3* Number of collieries and employment of miners
*Source:* Data provided by National Union of Mineworkers

Although the planning horizon of the document extended only to 1985, several factors contributed to a reappearance of the industry's secular decline by the early 1980s. The economic recession triggered by the second oil price shock reduced overall energy demand. This not only increased competition between indigenous fuels within the United Kingdom, but also encouraged imports of low cost coal which was becoming available in a depressed energy market as a result of major investments in countries such as Australia and South Africa. These investments were themselves a response to the oil price shock and were just one of many strategies to reduce the power of OPEC.

Despite occasionally erratic changes in the price of oil, domestic coal has consistently struggled to compete in the United Kingdom fuel market and the 1985 output of 104 million tonnes fell far short of the projection of 135 million tonnes contained in Plan for Coal. Even during the relatively optimistic period in the immediate aftermath of the plan's publication, coal prices rose faster than the general rate of inflation. Improvements in productivity have always fallen short of expectations and an NCB prediction in 1969 that an overall output of 3.75 tonnes per man-shift could be achieved within seven years remains an elusive objective almost twenty years later. This is, perhaps, not surprising in view of the recent history of the industry and the way in which its future has become as much a political as an economic issue.

## Resource availabilities

The energy industries are not only affected by domestic political considerations, but also by international ones. Awareness of the strategic implications of dependence upon imported energy supplies is not new. Events such as the Suez crisis in 1956 and the Arab-Israeli war of 1967 provoked expressions of concern regarding Western Europe's vulnerability to the disruption of vital oil supplies from the politically unstable Middle East in, for example, various EEC and OECD (Organization for Economic Co-operation and Development) publications. These fears were accentuated with the success of the OPEC countries in harnessing their latent power as suppliers of energy to Western Europe, Japan and the United States. Although supplies were generally maintained, the first and second price shocks stimulated interest in indigenous energy sources in all the major oil-consuming countries. In the case of the EEC, this reappraisal confirmed the relatively fortunate position of the United Kingdom where the combined reserves of the conventional fossil fuels of coal, natural gas and oil exceed those of any other member country.

Volumetric estimates in 1976 suggested the existence of around 190 billion tonnes ($190 \times 10^9$) of coal-in-place in the United Kingdom. Defining the recoverable portion of this gross figure is very difficult given the many variables which determine the economics of coal production. Recovery factors are influenced not only by future economic and technical conditions, but also by present policies in the sense that colliery closures can effectively sterilize the resource. In the publicity surrounding the announcement of Plan for Coal, the NCB estimated recoverable reserves at 45 billion tonnes, which represents more than 300 years supply at present rates of consumption. Projection over such a time period is not very meaningful, but it does at least emphasize the substantial nature of the United Kingdom's coal resource base.

Although the origins of the search for oil and gas in the North Sea can be traced back to 1959 when the discovery of the massive Groningen gas field at Slochteren in the Netherlands drew attention to the possible existence of similar geological structures offshore, its accelerated development may be viewed as yet another response to the challenge of OPEC. The sharp rise in the price of imported oil in 1973 and again in 1979 effectively increased the value of the hydrocarbon resources of the North Sea both to the companies

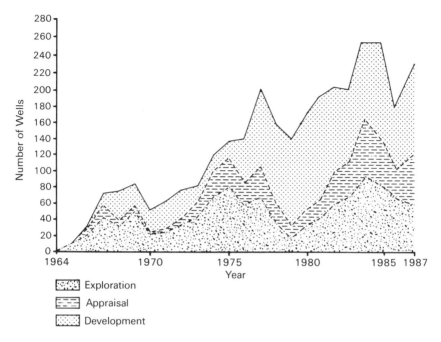

*Figure 5.4* Offshore drilling activity, 1964–87
*Source:* Data from Department of Energy, *Development of the Oil and Gas Resources of the United Kingdom* annual

involved in the search and to the country as a whole. Apart from the 1986 slump, which resulted in the postponement of development projects and a fall in drilling activity, the international oil companies have maintained their substantial commitment to the North Sea in the more stable price environment of the 1980s. More than 1,100 exploration wells had been drilled in British waters by the end of 1987 plus a very much larger number of appraisal and development wells (figure 5.4). The results of this activity have been impressive – thirty-five oilfields and fifteen gasfields were in production at the end of 1987.[2] A further nine oilfields were under development and scheduled to enter production by 1991 (figure 5.5). The ultimate number of producing oilfields is obviously speculative, but it is estimated that approximately sixty new ones will be developed by 2015.

Although most public interest has been generated by oil discoveries, it is the availability of natural gas from the North Sea which has had the most dramatic effect upon patterns of energy consumption. Early exploration off the east coast of England was very successful and five large gasfields had been discovered by the end of 1966. These fields all' reached peak production during the 1970s but the subsequent loss of output from the

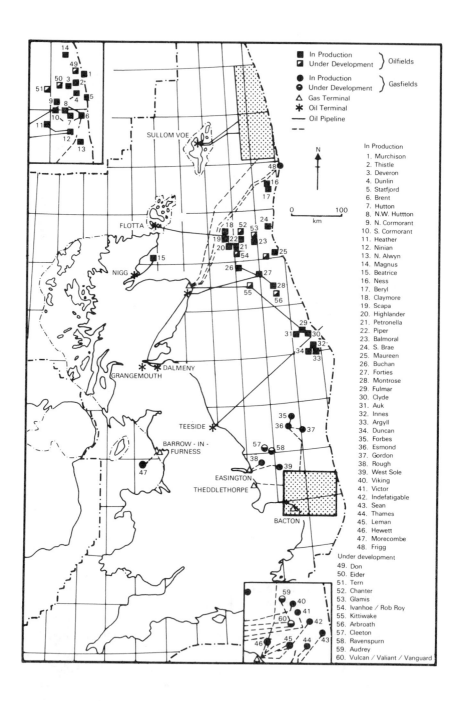

*Figure 5.5* North Sea oil and gas, 1988

southern North Sea has been more than compensated by the introduction of supplies from the Frigg field in northern waters and by the availability of increasing quantities of 'associated' gas from oilfields such as Brent. In addition to the usual geological uncertainties involved in forecasting the volume of such supplies, there is the further complication of assessing the feasibility of bringing 'associated' gas ashore. Plans to establish a coordinated gas gathering scheme were effectively scuppered by the withdrawal of government financial support in 1981 and the pipeline systems in the North Sea will continue to evolve in piecemeal fashion. Nevertheless, many are used to carry material from several fields by agreement between the various companies. Such arrangements are especially important for securing gas supplies from northern waters where two separate lines converge on the St Fergus terminal from the north-east and south-east (figure 5.5). These deliver 'associated' gas from fields in the East Shetlands area and central North Sea respectively. Although additional offshore pipelines will almost certainly be laid, access to established systems will be an important factor influencing the volume of incremental supplies from many smaller fields. Several such fields have been developed in the southern North Sea since 1985 where advantage has been taken of spare capacity in pipelines originally constructed to serve the now declining large gas fields discovered during the 1960s. British Gas is also faced with the rapid decline of production from the Frigg field which was its principal single source of supply during most of the 1980s. However, there is no shortage of gas on offer and the United Kingdom continental shelf has the capacity to meet domestic demand at least until the end of the century and, depending upon price trends, probably well beyond. This is not to deny that imports from Norway or more distant suppliers such as Algeria may be made, but these deals will be motivated by commercial factors rather than exhaustion of the indigenous resource base.

Despite the importance of natural gas, oil has been the principal objective in the exploration effort since 1970. This is apparent in the northward shift of interest in successive licensing rounds from the primarily gas-bearing areas off the English coast to the predominantly oil-producing territories off Scotland and the Shetlands. Before 1982, the oil companies were obliged to sell their gas to the British Gas Corporation. They were unhappy with this arrangement because of the monopoly power it conferred upon the state-owned corporation in purchasing negotiations. In these circumstances, it is not surprising that they concentrated their efforts on the search for oil which could be channelled through their own refining and distribution systems. The United Kingdom has been a net exporter of oil since 1980. However, output peaked in 1985 and the declining production profile is expected to converge with projected demand towards the end of the 1990s. Nevertheless, it is worth noting that the date at which self-sufficiency will end has been successively postponed in a series of official forecasts. It is generally accepted that future discoveries will be smaller, but substantial additional quantities of oil seem certain to be found. Department of Energy estimates in 1987 placed the remaining recoverable reserves within the range 1,015–4,385 million tonnes. These figures acquire greater meaning when matched to the United Kingdom's annual consumption of approximately 75 million tonnes in the same year. A combination of simple arithmetic and heroic assumptions thus makes it possible to project thirteen to fifty-eight years of self-sufficiency in oil. However, this calculation does not take account of the rapid build-up and subsequent long decline which is characteristic of the production history of any oil province, nor does it acknowledge the possibility of changes in demand. The definition of 'recoverable' adopted by the Department of Energy is also no guarantee that oil-in-place will actually be extracted under future technical and economic conditions. On the other hand, historical precedent suggests that the Department of Energy errs on the side of caution when coping with the substantial margins of error involved in making reserve estimates and some observers believe that its upper figure should be at least doubled to obtain a truer indication of the oil potential of the North Sea. The picture will only become clear when the final well runs dry, but it is probable that this resource will remain a major national asset, even if much of it is not necessarily used directly within the United Kingdom, well beyond the turn of the century.

**Technical change**

Although the decline of coal during the 1950s and 1960s was mainly due to competition with cheaper imported oil, the problems of the industry were compounded by certain technical changes which reduced the level of demand. Not only were the major coal-using industries heavily represented in the slow-growing and declining sectors of the economy, but also these large consumers were successfully developing more efficient methods of fuel use. Furthermore, several major markets were lost altogether. In 1950 the railways accounted for 7 per cent of domestic coal consumption: by 1965, the corresponding figure had fallen to 1.5 per cent as a result of the changeover to diesel and electric traction. A similar situation arose in the early 1960s as petroleum fractions replaced coal as the basic feedstock in town gas manufacture. Thus whereas over 90 per cent of the gas available to consumers in 1960 was ultimately derived from coal, this contribution had fallen to less than 10 per cent by 1970 and had become non-existent by the end of 1974. The trend was repeated in the electricity industry as oil, natural gas and nuclear power challenged the monopoly position of coal as fuel for thermal stations. In 1950, coal represented over 90 per cent of the fuel used in terms of energy content; by 1987 it accounted for 71 per cent. The decline in coal's relative share of the power-station market has been much less drastic than in other sectors and the steady growth of electricity demand to 1979 ensured that the absolute consumption of coal continued to rise. This upward trend halted during the recession of the early 1980s, but the 86.2 million tonnes of coal used for electricity generation in 1987 was more than two and a half times the amount consumed for the same purpose in 1950. Nevertheless, the fortunes of the coal industry have become increasingly dependent upon investment decisions made by the electricity generating authorities which have been steadily reducing the proportion of their capacity accounted for by coal-fired stations.

Whereas technical change has primarily influenced the demand side of the equation in the case of coal, it has been more significant in affecting the supply of certain other fuels. For example, the exploitation of the oil and gas resources of the North Sea depends upon the ability to operate in such a difficult marine environment and there is no doubt that the necessary exploration and, more especially, production technology has only become available in recent years. The relevance of technical change for energy supply can also be demonstrated by reference to the development of nuclear power. In this case, the introduction of new technology has proved difficult and the contrast between the expectations and achievements of the United Kingdom's nuclear power programme emphasizes that the uncertainties involved in energy planning are not only political and economic, but also include technical and engineering factors.

There was considerable optimism during the early 1950s regarding the future contribution of nuclear power to energy supply in the United Kingdom. This was encouraged when, in 1956, Calder Hall became the first nuclear plant in the world to supply power on a commercial rather than on an experimental basis. Similarly, the ten-year nuclear power programme announced in 1955 was the first national endorsement of this technology as a major source of energy supply. The commitment was reinforced two years later when the planned capacity of the first generation Magnox stations was trebled to twelve units with a potential output of 5,000–6,000 MW by 1965. In fact, only five were completed by the target date. If the first programme was disappointing to its supporters, the second one based on Advanced Gas-Cooled Reactors (AGR) was even more unsatisfactory. This is reflected in the discrepancy between the projected 10 per cent contribution of nuclear power to primary energy consumption by 1975, forecast in a White Paper on fuel policy in 1967, and the actual figure of less than 4 per cent. Only two of the five AGRs originally planned for completion in 1975 were operating at design capacity by 1988 when nuclear power's contribution to primary energy consumption was between 7 and 8 per cent.

The problems of the first and second nuclear power programmes are complex. Criticisms have been expressed regarding the highly centralized organization of the nuclear industry in the United Kingdom. Comparison with other countries suggests that the choice of reactor designs, particularly the AGR, was a mistake from both a technical and an economic point of view. This was implicitly acknowledged by the Central Electricity Generating

Board (CEGB) when it selected a Pressurised Water Reactor (PWR) for its Sizewell B plant in 1979. This is essentially the same technology that was rejected twenty years earlier in favour of the AGR. Construction proved much more expensive than projected in both the Magnox and, especially, the AGR programmes. Site work at Dungeness B, for example, began in 1966 and the station was still not fully operational in 1988. Such delays have been a major factor in raising serious doubts about the economics of nuclear power, which was originally justified in terms of its low cost in relation to other fuels. Concerns regarding safety and pollution were reinforced by the Chernobyl incident in 1986, but the official commitment to nuclear power, clearly expressed by the Secretary of State for Energy following the election of the first Conservative government under Mrs Thatcher in 1979, remains apparently unshaken. Projections made by the Department of Energy in 1978 and 1979 anticipate that nuclear power will meet 17 to 22 per cent of primary energy demand by the year 2000. These forecasts are based upon many dubious assumptions regarding rates of economic growth, price elasticities, and levels of conservation, but the presumed role of nuclear power rests upon the expectation of a 'policy gap' between energy demand and supply from conventional sources. Given the nature of the assumptions incorporated within the forecasting methodology and the progressive upward revision of North Sea oil and gas reserves, this 'gap' will probably not become a reality unless it is translated into a self-fulfilling prophecy by the further run-down of the coal industry. There is more than a suspicion that this is indeed the thinking behind current policy that seeks to reduce the dependence upon coal, which accounted for 75 per cent (in terms of energy equivalent) of the fuel used to generate electricity in 1985–6, as a strategic objective to limit the potential damage associated with any future disputes in the mining industry. Nevertheless, the 1978 and 1979 forecasts for the year 2000 appear to exaggerate the likely role of nuclear power in much the same way that others have done before. On the other hand, it seems that only a major disaster in the United Kingdom will modify official enthusiasm for this technology.

**Public policy**

The politics of nuclear power emphasize the way that patterns of fuel production and use may be influenced by public policy and yet government efforts to coordinate the various sectors of the energy market have been conspicuous by their absence for most of the post-war period. The Ridley Committee, set up in 1951 'to consider whether any further steps can be taken to promote the best use of our fuel and power resources', advocated a more positive role by central government through the medium of the Ministry of Fuel and Power to ensure that the conditions for 'coordination through the market were fulfilled'. These recommendations were never effectively implemented and an essentially *ad hoc* approach was adopted during the 1950s when policy measures were directed towards meeting the immediate needs of specific industries. Thus, although public ownership did provide the opportunity to adopt an overview of the energy sector, the nationalized fuel industries tended to operate as independent corporate entities.

The first steps towards the explicit formulation of a national energy policy were taken with the publication of the National Plan in 1964. Work carried out in the preparation of this document provided the basis for successive White Papers concerned with fuel policy in 1965 and 1967. These statements made it clear that the principal objective was 'to make possible the supply of energy at the lowest total cost to the community'. Policy was therefore geared towards cushioning some of the adverse consequences of changes in the fuel market, such as the social and political implications of the continued decline of the coal industry, rather than with any attempt to alter the direction of these changes fundamentally. The priorities changed after the first oil price jump in 1973, which resulted in a greater awareness of the political and economic implications of dependence upon external sources of supply. Accordingly policy statements published by the Department of Energy in 1977 and 1978 demonstrated a greater commitment to indigenous resources in the support for the expansion plans of the National Coal Board, the accelerated development of nuclear power, and the promotion of research into renewable sources of energy. Concern regarding the implications of energy shortages was also reflected in the importance attached to conservation. This included not only campaigns to encourage more efficient energy use but also restrictions upon the depletion of North Sea oil and gas.

Energy policy rests upon the premise that the market mechanism does not necessarily guarantee an outcome which is consistent with national interest, broadly conceived. The obligation upon the energy industries to consider the social and environmental consequences of their actions was exemplified by the efforts made to ameliorate the problems created by the decline of the coal industry during the 1960s. Apart from the various regional policy measures to attract new sources of employment to mining areas, several steps were taken to slow down the rate of pit closures. A tax on fuel oil introduced in 1961 as a revenue measure was subsequently maintained to assist the competitive position of coal. The Coal Industry Act of 1967 was designed to subsidize coal burning in the power stations and to discourage the electricity authorities from switching to cheaper oil. Similar measures, which recognized that the fortunes of the coal industry and, therefore, the communities associated with it, are largely dependent upon decisions taken by the CEGB and its Scottish counterparts, have been introduced more recently, but energy policy in the 1980s has been subordinated to macro-economic policy objectives.

There has been no official published statement on energy policy since 1978. This is hardly surprising in view of the contradiction between the interventionist basis of energy policy and the dominant free enterprise ethic of the 1980s. This is not to say that public policy has been unimportant. Public expenditure controls and privatization both affect the prospects of the various energy industries. The imposition of financial targets as the main performance indicator for the nationalized industries is, for example, reflected in the further decline of the coal industry after the relative stability of the 1970s (figure 5.3). Faced with the obligation to become self-financing by the early 1990s, British Coal[3] is concentrating production in low-cost areas. This effect is reinforced by similar pressures on the electricity supply industry which is seeking to reduce its own costs by increasing its consumption of cheaper imported coal, thereby further weakening the position of British Coal. It is precisely this kind of chain-reaction which energy policy has sought to limit in the past in the belief that long-term objectives, such as the survival of a substantial indigenous coal producing capacity, were more important than short-term economic considerations.

Whilst the effects of the financial policies of the Treasury upon the public sector energy industries have been immediately felt, the impact of privatization is more speculative. The assets of the British National Oil Corporation were sold-off to create Britoil in 1982 and this company was itself absorbed by British Petroleum in 1988. British Gas was privatized in 1986 and there is a commitment to repeat the process for the electricity supply industry, plus an intention that the coal industry may ultimately follow the same route. Its advocates believe that privatization will increase competition, promote the efficient allocation of resources and reduce government involvement in the operation of the economy. Such outcomes will be difficult to achieve in the gas and electricity supply industries which are natural monopolies because of the capital-intensive nature of their distribution systems. These monopolies must remain accountable and a complex formula has been devised to limit the freedom of British Gas in setting prices. Similar arrangements will be required to cope with a privatized electricity supply industry and it seems that direct government involvement in the nationalized fuel industries will be replaced by indirect systems of regulatory control. Furthermore, it is worth noting that privatization may not be consistent with other policy objectives. The commitment to nuclear power has already been mentioned, but evidence from the United States suggests that private electric utilities will be very reluctant to accept the economic risks associated with this technology.

## GEOGRAPHICAL CONSEQUENCES OF CHANGE IN THE ENERGY MARKET

The previous section was mainly concerned with the analysis of temporal changes in energy supply and demand at the national scale. However, closely associated with these changes have been significant shifts in the spatial characteristics of the energy economy and, in particular, in the sources of primary energy supply. It is convenient to consider separately the spatial implications of: (i) the decline of coal, (ii) increasing dependence upon imported oil, and (iii) the advent of North Sea oil and gas.

## Coal: the geography of decline

The overall decline in the output and relative significance of the coal industry as a contributor to national energy supply has already been noted. However, the severity of the decline has varied between the principal mining areas (table 5.1): while the proportion of total production contributed by the peripheral coalfields of Scotland, north-east England and South Wales has fallen, the focal position of the Yorkshire/Derbyshire/Nottinghamshire fields has been progressively reinforced. Several factors account for such inter-regional differences in the rate of decline. Geological circumstances have been especially important influences upon mining costs. In long-established mining areas, the NCB inherited many pits that had virtually exhausted their accessible reserves. Frequently, these were old mines exploiting relatively shallow seams. Closure of these mines has produced a characteristic spatial pattern of development within areas such as the Durham coalfield, as the zone of active working has retreated in the direction of dipping seams and output is limited to the newer, deeper mines. Exhaustion of reserves is not the only geological constraint. Severe folding and faulting make the introduction of new machinery much more difficult in areas such as South Wales as compared with the favourable conditions prevailing in Yorkshire and the East Midlands. This in turn is reflected in wide differences in productivity. For example, average output per manshift in South Wales in 1988 was 11.11 tonnes; the corresponding figure for North Yorkshire was 22.57 tonnes. Despite accelerated closures in the less productive areas these differences have, if anything, become more pronounced through time and regional disaggregation of financial results reveals that Scotland and South Wales, for example, have consistently operated at a loss whilst other areas, such as north Nottinghamshire, have generally been profitable.

Regional differences in the profitability of coalfields have been influenced by market considerations as well as cost factors. For example, the higher price commanded by the anthracite which is characteristic of South Wales has at least partly offset the greater costs of working this coalfield. The high costs of transporting coal by comparison with other primary energy sources have ensured that certain coalfields have been better placed than others to cope with a contracting market. Although distance has helped to protect Welsh and Scottish pits from the competition of the more efficient mines of Yorkshire and the East Midlands, proximity to major urban markets has reinforced the cost advantages of the latter. Another element in the chain of cumulative causation favouring these mining areas was the construction

Table 5.1 Deep-mined coal production, 1950–88

| Area | Output (m. tonnes saleable coal) | | | | | Output (% national total) | | | | |
|---|---|---|---|---|---|---|---|---|---|---|
| | 1950 | 1960 | 1970 | 1980 | 1988 | 1950 | 1960 | 1970 | 1980 | 1988 |
| Scotland | 22.9 | 17.7 | 11.4 | 8.1 | 2.6 | 13.8 | 9.6 | 8.1 | 7.4 | 3.2 |
| Northumberland/Durham | 38.4 | 33.8 | 20.5 | 14.1 | 10.2 | 19.0 | 18.4 | 14.6 | 12.9 | 12.5 |
| Yorkshire | 42.3 | 40.4 | 35.9 | 31.4 | 25.9 | 20.9 | 22.0 | 25.6 | 28.7 | 31.7 |
| Nottingham/Derby[a] | 39.9 | 43.7 | 33.5 | 28.2 | 17.6 | 19.7 | 23.8 | 23.9 | 25.8 | 21.5 |
| Warwickshire[b] | 19.1 | 15.3 | 10.3 | 8.6 | nd | 9.4 | 8.3 | 7.3 | 7.9 | nd |
| South Wales | 24.1 | 19.1 | 12.8 | 7.7 | 5.0 | 11.9 | 10.4 | 9.1 | 7.0 | 6.1 |
| Other[c] | 15.7 | 13.9 | 15.6 | 11.2 | 20.5 | 5.3 | 7.5 | 11.4 | 10.3 | 25.0 |
| United Kingdom | 202.4 | 183.9 | 140.0 | 109.3 | 81.8 | 100 | 100 | 100 | 100 | 100 |

Sources: Digests of UK Energy Statistics, NCB and British Coal Annual Reports
Notes: [a] Nottingham only in 1988
[b] Includes output from Kent coalfield. The figures for 1950 and 1960 also include output from the Staffordshire coalfield and are not directly comparable with the data for 1970 and 1980. No separate data for 1988
[c] Includes Lancashire and Cumberland coalfields plus Staffordshire coalfield in 1970, 1980, and 1988. Warwickshire and Derby included in 1988
nd: no data

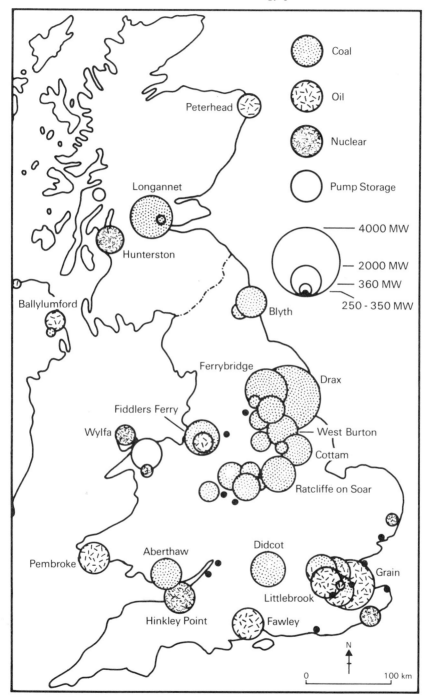

*Figure 5.6* Electricity generating stations, 1988
*Sources:* from data in CEGB *Statistical Yearbook* and annual reports of SSEB and NSHEB

during the 1950s of a series of major coal-burning power stations along the valleys of the Aire, Calder and Trent (figure 5.6). These sites offered the twin advantages of abundant cooling water and the cheapest coal available in the United Kingdom.

The progressive concentration of the coal industry's productive capacity in the Yorkshire/East Midlands area apparent in table 5.1 seems likely to continue as a result of the mutually reinforcing geographical effects of closures and new investments. An important element of Plan for Coal was the development of new mines. Although prospects were identified in Scotland and South Wales, Selby (Yorkshire) and Asfordby (Leicestershire) were the only greenfield site developments to which British Coal was firmly committed by 1988. Both of these are located in the 'core' area. By contrast, more than half the collieries closed between 1980 and 1987 were in the 'periphery' coalfields of Scotland, South Wales, Northumberland and Durham, which together accounted for just over a quarter of deep-mined production at the beginning of this period.

**Imported oil: processing and distribution patterns**

The expansion of oil-refining capacity in the United Kingdom since 1945 has transformed the country's position with regard to its supplies of petroleum products. Domestic refinery output in 1938 accounted for only 27 per cent of the total consumption of oil products but the growth in the refining industry since the Second World War has enabled it not only to keep pace with the spectacular rise in demand, but also to maintain an approximate balance between indigenous production and consumption of petroleum products. Self-sufficiency in petroleum products was first acheived in 1951 and has been maintained ever since.[4]

The development of the United Kingdom oil-refining industry may be seen as part of an international trend towards the growth of refining capacity in the major consuming areas. Before the Second World War, oil refineries were usually located on or adjacent to the oilfields and approximately 70 per cent of world refinery capacity in 1939, excluding North America and the Communist bloc, was accounted for by 'source' refineries. Many factors have encouraged this fundamental shift from 'source' to 'market' locations since 1945. Events such as the seizure in 1951 of the Anglo-Iranian Oil Company's Abadan refinery, at a time when it alone was meeting an estimated 20 per cent of the United Kingdom's refined product requirements, drew attention to the vulnerability of such investments. Political considerations favouring 'market' locations have been reinforced by developments in processing and transportation. Advances in processing technology have allowed individual refineries to achieve a closer balance between their output of the various petroleum fractions and the needs of the market they serve. Furthermore, high conversion rates of crude into usable products have virtually eliminated the weight- or process-losses which originally favoured 'source' locations. Tanker freight rates in the immediate post-war years were lower for the shipment of crude oil than for a similar quantity of refined products and this cost differential subsequently widened as the size of crude oil carriers increased. The most important stimulus to the growth of the oil-refining industry was, however, the rise in demand as fuel oils replaced coal in many markets. These general considerations encouraging investment in oil-refining capacity were reinforced by more specific factors, notably financial support from the United States under the terms of the Marshall Aid scheme.

The growth of oil refining in the United Kingdom has involved significant changes in the allocation of capacity between regions. Several small refineries were operating at widely scattered locations immediately before the Second World War. Approximately 30 per cent of total capacity was accounted for by installations on the lower Thames, and 25 per cent was situated at the seaward and inland ends of the Manchester Ship Canal, with the balance made up by three plants located at Fawley on Southampton Water, Llandarcy near Swansea and Grangemouth in Scotland. These small pre-war refineries provided a convenient basis for post-war expansion and the more than tenfold increase in throughput capacity between 1939 and 1959 involved the establishment of only two completely new sites. The largest of these added significantly to the concentration of facilities on the lower Thames which, together with Fawley, accounted for two-thirds of total United Kingdom capacity in 1959. However, the development of a succession of green-field sites during the 1960s had reduced the share of south-east England to less than one-third by 1973 and created an entirely new major refining complex, with a capacity exceeding that of lower Thameside, around the shores of Milford Haven. The relative decline of the south-east was reinforced by the creation of further new refining centres on Teesside and Humberside towards the end of the 1960s.

The expansion of refinery capacity during the 1960s was associated with the rapid displacement of coal by oil in the energy market. The new locational pattern which emerged during this period of accelerated growth was due to a combination of technical and commercial factors. The attraction of Milford Haven lay in its advantages as a deep-water harbour with the advent of the 100,000 ton oil tanker towards the end of the 1950s. These vessels offered considerable economies of scale in the movement of crude oil and Milford Haven is only one of a number of European refining complexes which owe their 1960s origins to the berthing requirements of the supertanker. The search for new sites stimulated by advances in shipping technology was also encouraged by changes in the organizational structure of the industry. In 1962, Shell, Esso and BP together controlled 94 per cent of the country's refining capacity. Several new companies entered the United Kingdom market in the late 1950s and early 1960s. Initially, these companies were content to establish a bridgehead by importing finished products from their refineries elsewhere in Western

Europe and the United States. The establishment of refining capacity in the United Kingdom was the next logical step as these companies attempted to consolidate their position at the expense of Shell, Esso and BP. By 1987, the proportion of total United Kingdom capacity controlled by the three major companies had declined to 45 per cent. Each of these only established one new site after 1960 and tended to add any incremental capacity at existing refineries. On the other hand, the new refining companies were not restricted by the location of established facilities and therefore played an important role in the emergence of Milford Haven and Humberside as major refining centres.

Many of the new refinery sites established during the 1960s were located in Development Areas. Although substantial financial incentives were available to the companies under the provisions of regional policy, this pattern of development probably reflected a fortunate coincidence of commercial advantage and political objectives rather than the result of government pressure. Environmental objections to events at Milford Haven, for example, were rejected in the face of persuasive arguments regarding the beneficial economic impact of the new refineries. In fact, the anticipated regional benefits have been limited. Oil-fired power stations have been constructed adjacent to their sources of fuel oil at Fawley and Milford Haven, for example, but, like the refineries themselves, such establishments are essentially capital-intensive and, after the construction phase, provide relatively few permanent jobs. The technical linkages between oil refining and petrochemical manufacture were used, in certain quarters, to suggest that the establishment of the latter is a logical and almost automatic consequence of the former. Casual observation of existing refineries would have demonstrated the flaws in this argument and it is no surprise to find that major petrochemical facilities and related downstream operations have failed to materialize in such a peripheral location as Milford Haven. The highly mobile nature of petroleum products ensures that delivered costs are fairly uniform. Thus the oil refineries have not exerted a locational influence comparable to the coalfields in attracting major consumers.

The spatial pattern of oil refineries in 1987 (figure 5.7) differs little from that established by 1970. The Amoco plant at Milford Haven is the only new installation and the recession prompted by the big oil price increases of the 1970s invalidated the assumptions of growth upon which the investments of the 1960s were based. Individual units and entire refineries have been shut down, especially since 1980, as the oil companies have attempted to adjust to the new circumstances and total throughput capacity in 1987 was only 60 per cent of the 1974 peak. These events not only represent a radical departure from the previously continuous post-war growth in capacity, but also emphasize that the availability of North Sea oil is no guarantee of renewed investment in refining facilities.

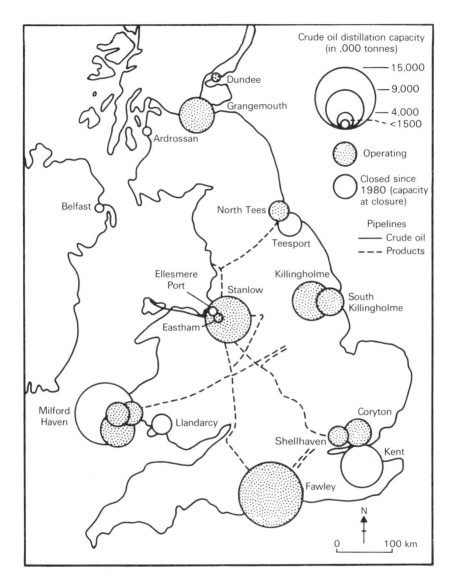

*Figure 5.7* Oil refineries, 1988
*Source:* data supplied by Institute of Petroleum

## North Sea hydro-carbons: patterns of exploitation and utilization

The significance of North Sea oil and gas has already been considered in terms of their contributions to energy supplies at the national scale. In considering the geographical, as opposed to the sectoral, impacts of these new resources it is convenient to distinguish between their exploitation and their subsequent distribution and consumption. The significance of this distinction becomes apparent when related to the different types of hydrocarbon. Whereas the restructuring of the distribution system has been the most significant explicitly spatial consequence of the discovery and use of North Sea gas, the differential impact of exploration and development activities upon regions has been the most evident geographical effect of North Sea oil.

The rapid penetration of natural gas into the energy market since the mid-1960s has already been noted. The availability of gas from the North Sea has transformed the position of the gas industry from a manufacturer and supplier of secondary energy to a distributor of primary fuel. When the industry was nationalized in 1948 the newly formed regional Gas Boards inherited a manufacturing and supply system that was geared to meeting local needs. The location of the gasworks reflected the geography of population, with concentrations of capacity in the major urban centres and a dispersed pattern of isolated plants in smaller towns. Each gasworks lay at the centre of its own distribution system and inter-regional links were virtually non-existent. The Area Boards were larger organizations than the statutory companies which they replaced and this resulted in attempts to centralize production in the bigger, more efficient works. This process necessarily involved the construction of more extensive distribution systems, although the optimal arrangement of production facilities required a careful trade-off between the lower production costs of the large works and the higher distribution costs of serving dispersed populations from fewer centres. Thus the degree of centralization was influenced by the geography of demand and small local works continued to play an important role in the Scottish, Welsh and South-western Gas Board Areas until the advent of natural gas.

The organizational structure of the gas industry created at nationalization ensured that each Area Board operated independently of its neighbours. Movement of gas across the boundaries of these areas was very limited and the contemporary national grid did not begin to emerge until the mid-1960s. It was gas from North Africa rather than the North Sea which provided the initial stimulus to a national distribution system. The Gas Council began importing liquified natural gas from Algeria in 1964; this was landed at Canvey Island on the Thames and subsequently distributed via a specially constructed transmission system to seven of the Gas Council's twelve Area Boards. The motive for the creation of this system was initially technical because the high calorific value of the Algerian gas meant that it either had to be combined with 'lean' manufactured gas or 'reformed' before being supplied to customers, but it heralded the emergence of a gas industry that was truly national in its scale of organization and pattern of distribution.

It is ironic that the first exploration wells were drilled in the United Kingdom sector of the southern North Sea in the same year that deliveries began under the terms of the Gas Council's fifteen year contract for the import of Algerian gas. The West Sole field was discovered off the east coast of England within twelve months of the allocation of exploration licences and this was followed by a series of further successes identifying reserves capable of displacing existing sources of manufactured gas. However, this could only be achieved by developing an entirely new transmission system focused on the east coast terminals of Bacton, Theddlethorpe, and Easington. Deliveries of gas from West Sole commenced in 1967 and the basic elements of the new gas grid were established by 1970, with spurs extended as far west as South Wales and Devon and as far north as central Scotland. The orientation of the network towards the English terminals was less apparent by 1980 as a result of the introduction of supplies from northern waters via St Fergus (figure 5.8) and yet another major element was added in 1985 with the first delivery from the South Morecambe field via a terminal at Barrow-in-Furness.

The transformation of the gas industry from a manufacturing to a wholesaling and distributing role was virtually complete by 1977, with an almost total switch of its consumers to natural gas. Approximately 60 per cent (by volume) of these consumers are concentrated along the London-Birmingham-Manchester axis and the principal feeders converge from the terminals into this corridor. The timing of conversion to natural gas was broadly related to distance from the terminals. In Scotland, for example, it was not until 1975 that the switch to natural gas, ultimately derived from the southern North Sea, was completed. With the commencement of production from Frigg in 1977, flow patterns within the transmission system were radically altered. As the output of fields in the southern North Sea declined and the production of those in the north increased, supplies from St Fergus penetrated further south. The system is, in fact, very flexible and future movements within it will vary with changes in the relative importance of the sources of supply to British Gas.

Since oil began flowing from the North Sea approximately ten years later than natural gas, the geographical consequences of its exploitation have been associated more with the exploration and development phases than with processing and consumption. Despite its great importance for the national economy, North Sea oil exerts little obvious effect upon existing processing and distribution patterns. Although Department of Energy policy in the 1970s was to maximize the proportion actually refined in the United Kingdom, almost two-thirds of 1987 production was exported in crude form and the pattern of oil movements reflects corporate objectives rather than any coherent government strategy. Although the availability of North Sea oil seems unlikely to exert any great impact upon the location of economic activity, the various operations involved in bringing it ashore have significantly affected patterns of regional development, especially in Scotland. An important factor in the improvement of Scotland's unemployment position *relative* to the rest of the country during the 1970s

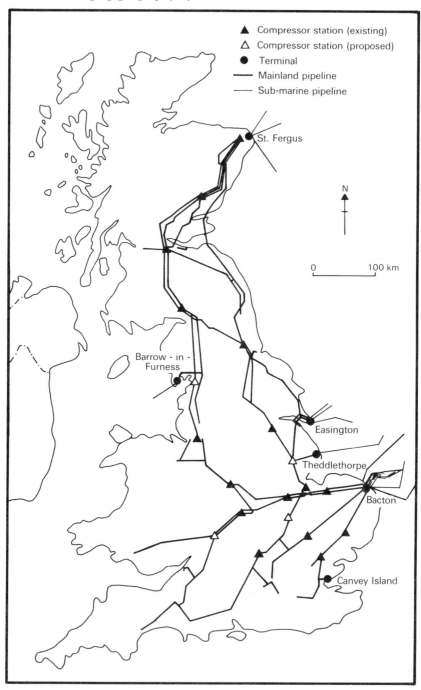

*Figure 5.8* Natural gas distribution system, 1988
*Source:* British Gas

was the creation of oil-related employment. However, these jobs are very unevenly distributed. In 1987, Grampian Region, focused on Aberdeen, accounted for approximately 80 per cent of a total of 50,830 jobs in Scotland estimated to be directly related to the North Sea oil industry. Apart from a slump related to the effect of falling oil prices upon North Sea activity in 1986, the number of such jobs in Grampian has increased in every year since 1974, when its share of the Scottish total was only 36 per cent. Although the regional contrasts are less pronounced when indirect oil-related employment is included, Grampian's overall dominance has been accentuated as the service and administration functions of the production phase have replaced the manufacturing jobs associated with the construction of capital equipment during the development stage. Thus most of the new jobs have been and will be created in areas outside the Central Belt, which has traditionally been the focus of Scotland's unemployment problem.

The fact that the impact of oil-related activities in Scotland has been greatest in areas remote from the industrial heartland of the Central Belt has had important consequences for physical and environmental as well as for economic planning. Isolated communities in the Orkneys and Shetlands and in the Highlands have been faced with major developments such as terminals and platform fabrication yards. Bitter conflicts have arisen in which local preferences have been overwhelmed, not always with good reason, by arguments couched in terms of 'the national interest'. That the national interest requires the development of North Sea oil is not in doubt, but the manner and speed of its exploitation have not been consistent with the planning horizons and resources of the local authorities responsible for monitoring and controlling associated activities at the local and regional scales. These difficulties were especially acute during the rapid development phase of the 1970s and a combination of acquired experience and the less hectic pace of the production phase promises to reduce the number of land-use conflicts associated with the exploitation of North Sea oil and gas.

## CONCLUSIONS

In 1979 UK oil production exceeded the output of coal in terms of energy equivalent for the first time, and the country became a net exporter of oil in the following year. These events underline the major changes which have taken place in the energy market since the Second World War as the country has passed from almost total dependence on indigenous coal, through a period in which imported oil became the principal fuel, to the beginning of a new era of self-sufficiency based upon a more diversified range of energy sources. These changes in the structure of the energy market have had important spatial consequences as the country's key primary energy nodes have shifted successively from the coalfields to the oil refineries to the off-shore fields and associated terminals. These shifts have in turn resulted in new distribution systems linking energy sources with their markets. Generally speaking the scale at which these systems operate has increased through time. The principal energy nodes usually served local and regional markets in the immediate post-war years. This was certainly true of the coal and gas industries and even the electricity system provided little opportunity for inter-regional transfers at the beginning of the 1950s. Despite improvements in the transportation of coal by rail, this fuel remains costly to move by comparison with other forms of energy and, because of its dependence upon the power station market, much of its output is consumed on or adjacent to the coalfields themselves. Distance is a less significant constraint upon the other fuels. National grids exist for both natural gas and electricity, while pipelines enable petroleum products to be transported in bulk from coastal refineries to regional distribution terminals serving major inland markets.

The significance of the market as the most important single influence upon the contemporary geography of the energy industries is a sharp contrast to the traditional attractions of the coalfields to certain types of manufacturing. Despite the greater mobility of petroleum products and electricity, for example, the location of both oil refineries and power stations has been strongly influenced by market considerations. The refining complexes on the Thames and Mersey estuaries are well placed to serve the intervening axial belt of population. Similarly, the distribution of power stations broadly matches the regional pattern of demand, although local concentrations of capacity are related to the proximity of fuel sources. The national grid allows complex inter-regional transfers to take place, but the fact that the first generation nuclear stations were frequently located in deficit areas exemplifies the desirability of maintaining an overall balance between supply and demand at the regional scale.

The mobility which characterizes contemporary forms of energy is, to some extent, related to the costs of the fuels themselves. Thus it might be argued that if the real costs of energy were to rise significantly in the future, attempts to minimize energy movements may be just one feature of a more conservation-oriented society. However, it is difficult to envisage any major changes in existing large-scale methods of energy production and nationwide systems of distribution except in connection with the possible development of alternative technologies such as wind and wave power which are more suited to the establishment of local supply/demand systems. Nevertheless, the great changes which have taken place on the UK energy scene during the last thirty years emphasize the risks involved in predicting future events and also account for the fail-safe approach of current policy which seeks to maximize the range of indigenous energy source options which may be available by the turn of the century.

## NOTES

1 The balance of consumption on a fuel equivalent basis was made up of 0.6 per cent
hydro-electricity and 0.5 per cent of electricity imports from France.
2 Estimates of the precise number of oil and gas fields vary. This is because of differences in the classification of individual deposits either as extensions of existing fields or as identifiable and distinct reservoirs. The problem is made even more difficult in some cases where the distinction between oil and gas deposits is ambiguous.
3 The National Coal Board adopted the title 'British Coal Corporation' in 1987.
4 The only exception was 1984 when substantial imports of fuel oil were made as a result of the miners' strike.

## FURTHER READING

Material on energy in Britain is discussed in the following: Ashworth, W (1986) *The History of the British Coal Industry: Volume 5, 1946–1982 The Nationalised Industry*, Oxford: Clarendon Press; Chapman, K. (1976) *North Sea Oil and Gas*, Newton Abbot: David & Charles; Fernie, J. (1980) *A Geography of Energy in the United Kingdom*, London: Longman; Hamilton, A. (1978) *North Sea Impact: Off-shore Oil and the British Economy*, London: International Institute for Economic Research; House of Commons Paper 165 (Session 1986–7) *The Coal Industry*, London: HMSO; House of Commons Paper 175 (Session 1986–7) *The Effect of Oil and Gas Prices on Activity in the North Sea*, London: HMSO; Manners, G. (1981) *Coal in Britain*, London: Allen & Unwin; Manners, I. R. (1982) *North Sea Oil and Environmental Planning: the United Kingdom Experience*, Austin, Texas: University of Texas Press; Openshaw, S. (1986) *Nuclear Power: Siting and Safety*, London: Routledge; Pearson, L. F. (1980) *The Organisation of the Energy Industry*, London: Macmillan; Reid, G. L., Allen, K. and Harris, D. J. (1973) *The Nationalized Fuel Industries*, London: Heinemann; Robinson, C. and Morgan, J. (1978) *North Sea Oil in the Future: Economic Analysis and Government Policy*, London: Macmillan; and Simpson, E. S. (1966) *Coal and the Power Industries in Postwar Britain*, London: Longman.

Statistics of the energy industry are available in the following two annual publications of the Department of Energy (published by HMSO, London): *Digest of United Kingdom Energy Statistics* (since 1968), and *Development of the Oil and Gas Resources of the United Kingdom* (since 1975).

# 6 Water resources

*Chris Park*

Water is one of the most valuable natural resources, and considerable efforts have been made since the last century to ensure that sufficient water of suitable quality is available at the right place and at the right time. The water industry in the United Kingdom is a capital-intensive industry with long lead times and an obligation to adapt continuously to ever-changing needs and opportunities.

This chapter focuses on water resources in the United Kingdom, with a special emphasis on developments and events during the 1980s – a decade of unprecedented change. Two themes are prominent – the changing geography of water supply and demand, and the changing structure of the water industry. The emphasis is mainly on England and Wales, because of the lack of suitable data on changing water resources in Scotland and Northern Ireland, and the different basis and structure of the water industries in those countries.

## WATER RESOURCES IN THE UNITED KINGDOM

### Supply and demand

Several caveats must be applied to the terms 'supply' and 'demand' as used in the context of water resources. First, it is difficult to distinguish clearly between supply and demand because the data available relate mainly to supply, or fulfilled demand. The terms 'supply' and 'demand' tend to be used interchangeably, rather than in the more precise traditional economic sense.

Second, definition and quantification of demand and supply are problematical. Multiple use of water resources make it difficult to evaluate the real significance of demand estimates. Water supply is also difficult to define unambiguously because of the wide diversity of sources, including the public piped supply system, direct abstractions (under licence) from rivers and aquifers, and wells. Water losses through the supply system are variable in space and time, which further complicates the picture.

Third, 'demand' as used here relates exclusively to demand for water for consumptive use (such as in industry); demand for water for non-consumptive uses (like amenity, landscaping, recreation and conservation), which continues to rise in the United Kingdom (see chapter 14), is beyond the terms of reference of this chapter.

## The geography of water supply and demand

The United Kingdom is well endowed with the ultimate source of water resources – precipitation. Most of this arrives in the form of rainfall, but snow, sleet, hail, fog and mist also provide valuable water. There is plenty of water available overall – it would only need an average annual precipitation of 30 mm across the United Kingdom to provide enough water to cater for the total demand for water in 1986 (19,888 Megalitres a day), provided that it was all available and that it fell in the right place at the right time. But supply and demand are mismatched in space and time, and so costly and elaborate schemes have been developed to ensure that enough water is available where and when it is needed.

The spatial mismatch accentuates the north:south divide, and reflects the influences on supply (figure 6.1) of climate and geology. In essence, rainfall is greatest in the uplands of the north and west where the impermeable rocks make good water collection grounds, but water is most needed in the populated and industrialized lowlands of the midlands and the south and east where rainfall is lower and permeable bedrock leaves few surface supplies. The geography of water demand mainly reflects the distribution of major centres of population and industry and variations in farming practices (see chapters 3, 4, and 8). The main areas of high demand are in central England, the Home Counties, East Anglia, the north-west and parts of north-east England. The lead-time for investment in infrastructure within the water industry is very long, and changes in population distribution, industrial location and activities and farming practices can further accentuate the spatial mismatch between supply and demand.

## Patterns and trends of water demand

Changing patterns of water use since 1945 were reviewed in the first edition of this book, so attention here is concentrated on changes through the 1970s and 1980s. Department of the Environment figures for England and Wales illustrate recent patterns and trends which reflect a complex interplay of socio-economic factors at home and abroad. Water supply in the United Kingdom as a whole rose steadily from 17,262 Megalitres (Ml) a day in 1976 to 19,888 Ml a day in 1986 (figure 6.2) – a net rise of 15 per cent. Metered supplies (mainly to industrial users) fell slightly (a net fall of 9 per cent over the period), especially since 1980. The decline was proportionally greater in Scotland (16.2 per cent) and Northern Ireland (11.6 per cent) than in England and Wales (7.5 per cent net), though much greater in

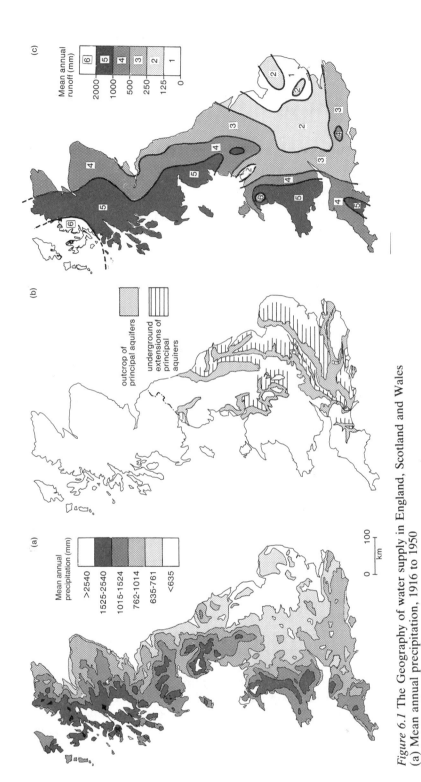

*Figure 6.1* The Geography of water supply in England, Scotland and Wales
(a) Mean annual precipitation, 1916 to 1950
(b) Distribution of the main aquifers in England and Wales
(c) Mean annual runoff
*Sources:* (a) and (b) Smith 1972; (c) Doornkamp, Gregory, and Burns 1980

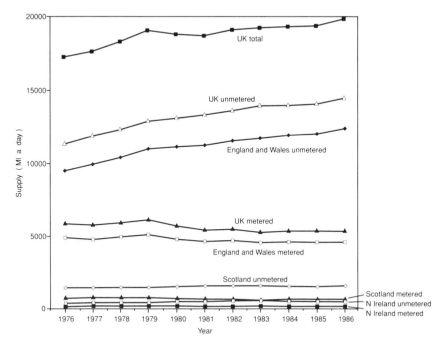

*Figure 6.2* Trends in public water supply in the UK, 1976–86

absolute terms in England and Wales (371 Ml a day compared with 127 and 22 respectively). Unmetered supplies (mainly to households, small shops, and traders) increased steadily from 11,370 Ml a day in 1976 to 14,515 Ml a day in 1986, a rise of 27 per cent overall. Most of the increase occurred in England and Wales, where unmetered supplies rose by 30 per cent from 9,502 Ml a day in 1976 to 12,411 Ml a day in 1986 (figure 6.2). The bulk of water supply in the United Kingdom overall is unmetered (73 per cent of the total supply); it accounts for 73 per cent in England and Wales, 71 per cent in Scotland and 75 per cent in Northern Ireland (1986 figures).

The last decade has seen a fairly dramatic and continuous decline in the amount of water abstracted from both groundwater and surface sources (figure 6.3). Total abstractions fell by nearly 35 per cent between 1973 and 1985, from some 42,700 Ml per day to around 31,500. The pattern of use also changed. In 1973 most (63 per cent) of the demand was industrial, with almost all the remainder (36.5 per cent) domestic. Agricultural demand was extremely small (0.5 per cent). One industrial user is dominant; the Central Electricity Generating Board (CEGB), which requires vast amounts of cooling water, accounted for over two-thirds of the total industrial demand, using 42 per cent of all the water abstracted in 1973.

By 1986 industrial demand had fallen to 50 per cent of the total, from

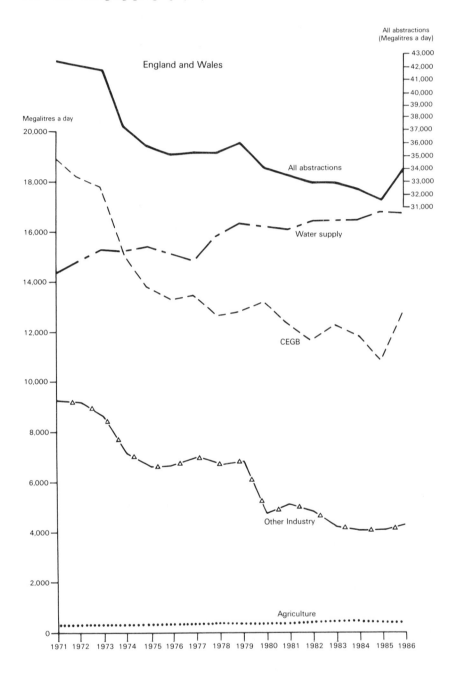

Source : Department of the Environment (1988)

*Figure 6.3* Trends in water abstraction in England and Wales, 1971–86
*Source:* Department of the Environment 1988

5,700 Ml per day to 3,600 Ml per day. Domestic use had risen to 49 per cent of the total by 1986, and agriculture was by then accounting for nearly 1 per cent. Demand from the CEGB (at 12,744 Ml per day) then amounted to 76 per cent of the total industrial demand, nearly 38 per cent of total demand. In absolute terms both agricultural and domestic demand rose between 1973 and 1983; the former by 35 per cent and the latter by 7 per cent, although in both cases fulfilled demand fell during the 1975–6 drought.

Water abstractions rose during 1986 (figure 6.3), because of an increased use of water by the CEGB for hydroelectricity in Wales. Most is accounted for by initial filling of the £450 million Dinorwig pumped storage scheme in North Wales, which uses 7,000 Ml of water to drive two turbogenerators, producing a power surge equivalent to 1,320 MW of electricity within 10 seconds. The water is recycled, however, so little further abstraction will be required.

Most of the observed fall in total demand between 1973 and 1986 (figure 6.3) was due to the decline in water use by the CEGB and other industries, from a total of 26,000 Ml per day to 16,843. The reduction of about 5,500 Ml per day in abstractions by the CEGB for cooling purposes was due mainly to the closure of old inland power stations with direct cooling, and the opening of new stations in inland and tidal areas which recirculate water. The decline in abstractions in other industries, which fell by over 52 per cent in that period, was partly a result of more efficient use of water (including recycling) but mainly due to the shrinkage of some of the traditional water-using industries such as heavy manufacturing. The 'other' industrial demand fell most markedly between 1979 and 1980, and it has continued through the 1980s as a result of economic recession and industrial restructuring (see chapter 8).

Unmetered supply, mainly to domestic and commercial users, increased steadily between 1973 (9,344 Ml per day) and 1986 (12,411 Ml per day) in England and Wales (figure 6.3). This net rise of nearly 32 per cent was only punctuated by the 1975–6 drought, when supply restrictions were imposed. Metered supply, mainly to industrial users, declined in England and Wales over that period by 17 per cent, from 5,464 Ml per day to 4,550. As a result, the balance between metered and unmetered supply (by volume) rose progressively from 63 per cent unmetered in 1973 to 73 per cent in 1986. Some commercial and domestic users have switched from unmetered to metered supplies in recent years, but these have been more than offset by the continued decline in metered industrial use. The 'unmetered' component includes water leakage from the mains and water used in fire fighting. There has been a relatively continuous increase in abstractions for water supply purposes in England and Wales, mainly by the Water Authorities and statutory water companies (figure 6.3). In recent years this has accounted for nearly half of all abstractions.

Most domestic users have unmetered supply and are charged in proportion to property rateable values, not on the basis of quantities of

*Table 6.1* Annual abstraction of water in England and Wales for different purposes, 1986 (Ml per day)

| Water authority | Agriculture | | | Industry | | Total quantity abstracted (Ml a day) | Percentage of total abstractions that were from ground water |
| | Water supply[a] | Spray irrigation[b] | Other | Central Electricity Generating Board | Other[d] | | |
| --- | --- | --- | --- | --- | --- | --- | --- |
| Anglian | 1,678 | 91 | 15 | 3 | 232 | 2,019 | 51 |
| Northumbrian | 1,032 | – | – | – | 42 | 1,074 | 10 |
| North-West | 1,794 | 2 | 5 | 163 | 1,724 | 3,688 | 12 |
| Severn-Trent | 2,105 | 37 | 7 | 3,299 | 845 | 6,293 | 19 |
| Southern | 1,237 | 7 | 11 | 5 | 111 | 1,371 | 72 |
| South-West | 535 | 3 | 31 | 250[c] | 87 | 906 | 12 |
| Thames | 3,959 | 8 | 13 | 134 | 198 | 4,312 | 41 |
| Welsh | 2,095 | 2 | 15 | 8,170[c] | 300 | 10,582 | 1 |
| Wessex | 768 | 6 | 14 | – | 117 | 905 | 48 |
| Yorkshire | 1,414 | 12 | 12 | 720 | 444 | 2,602 | 13 |
| England and Wales | 16,617 | 169 | 123 | 12,733[c] | 4,099 | 33,752 | 19 |

*Source:* Department of the Environment 1988

*Notes:* [a] Water supply (i.e. piped mains water) includes abstractions by Water Authorities, water companies, and small private abstractions
[b] Includes small amounts for non-agricultural spray irrigation
[c] Excludes tidal water but includes water used for water power (about 6,000 Ml a day in 1986)
[d] Excludes tidal water and water used for water power and fish farming

water used (which would require water metering). Domestic consumption averaged around 130 litres per person per day in 1986. Results of various water-use surveys in recent years suggest that around 32 per cent of domestic water is used in WC flushing, a further 17 per cent is used in bathing and showering, 12 per cent is used in washing machines and the remaining 39 per cent is used in a variety of ways – 1 per cent for luxury appliances (mainly dishwashers), 3 per cent outside use (like garden sprinklers), and 35 per cent miscellaneous (including hand washing, drinking, cooking and cleaning).

In England and Wales in 1986, just under half (16,617 Ml a day) of the total quantity of water abstracted from surface and groundwater sources (33,752 Ml a day) was used for water supply. Just over half (16,843 Ml a day) was used by industry, and most of this (76 per cent of the industrial, 38 per cent of the total) was used by the CEGB. Agriculture used just 0.9 per cent (292 Ml a day) overall, mostly (58 per cent) in spray irrigation.

The ten regional Water Authorities provided just over three quarters of the total water supplied throughout England and Wales in 1986–7; their 13,083 Ml a day (78 per cent) is complemented by 3,772 Ml a day (22 per cent) supplied by the twenty-nine statutory water companies. The profile of water use varies from one Water Authority to another in England and Wales (table 6.1, figure 6.4), reflecting variations in population distribution, and types and patterns of industrial and agricultural activities. The largest suppliers are the Welsh (total abstraction of 10,582 Ml a day in 1986) and Severn-Trent (6,293 Ml a day) Authorities (figure 6.4), followed by Thames (4,312 Ml a day) and North-West (3,688 Ml a day). Most (92 per cent) of Thames Water's abstractions are for piped mains water, as is Southern's (90 per cent), Anglian's (83 per cent), Northumbrian's (96 per cent) and Wessex's (85 per cent). The CEGB is the major user of water in Welsh (77 per cent of the total abstraction) and Severn-Trent (52 per cent). Other industry uses most water in the traditional industrial areas; it accounts for 1,724 Ml a day (47 per cent of the total) in North-West, and 845 Ml a day (13 per cent of the total) in Severn-Trent. Agricultural use is greatest, at 106 Ml a day (5 per cent of the total abstraction) in the Anglian Water Authority, where it is mostly (86 per cent) used for spray irrigation. Agriculture consumes 44 Ml a day (0.7 per cent of the total) in Severn Trent, again mostly (84 per cent) for spray irrigation.

Overall, 19 per cent of abstractions were from groundwater (table 6.1), but the proportion varies considerably from one Authority to another, reflecting the distribution of permeable bedrock across the country. Southern draw most (72 per cent) of their water from aquifers, Anglian (51 per cent), Wessex (48 per cent), and Thames (41 per cent) get about half; the rest use mainly surface sources (Severn-Trent 19 per cent groundwater, Yorkshire 13 per cent, South-West 12 per cent, North-West 12 per cent, Northumbrian 10 per cent, Welsh 1 per cent). Heavy reliance on surface sources can be a problem in times of drought, when supply restrictions are

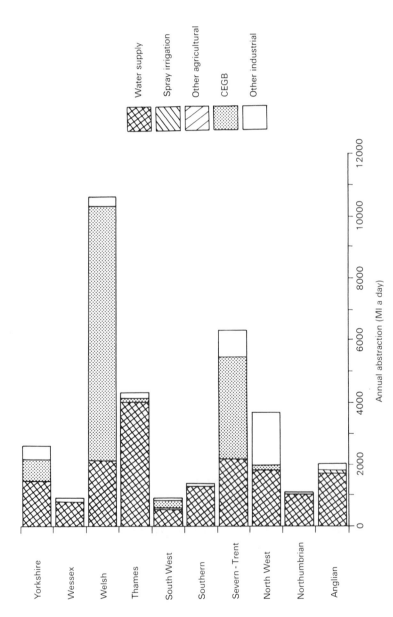

*Figure 6.4* Variations in water use between Water Authorities, 1986

imposed faster and more frequently, and often last longer, than in areas which derive significant proportions of their water from groundwater.

## WATER MANAGEMENT IN ENGLAND AND WALES SINCE 1945

The water industries have developed in different ways in England and Wales, and in Scotland. In the latter, for example, major components in the water industry are the River Purification Board (concerned with water pollution) and the Regional and Island Councils (water supply), whereas in England and Wales the basic unit is presently the multi-functional regional Water Authority.

Four important phases in the evolution of administration in England and Wales can be identified. Before 1945, water supply was not a concern of central government until widespread concern for sanitation in towns and outbreaks of cholera brought mounting pressure on Parliament, giving rise to the 1848 Public Health Act. This demanded the creation of facilities for sewage disposal and the provision of water supplies to working-class areas (by street carriers or stand-pipes), and it prompted sweeping changes in sanitation and supply provisions in major centres such as Liverpool, Birmingham, Manchester and London. A period of piecemeal public health legislation and numerous private Acts of Parliament left a legacy for the early twentieth century of numerous private water companies, municipal waterworks operating under private Acts, others operating under general Public Health Acts, and a group of joint water boards. Such a diversified and uncoordinated foundation to the water supply industry clearly demanded sweeping changes and rationalization.

Planning of water resources prior to 1945 had been piecemeal and overburdened with local constraints and conditions imposed by numerous Acts of Parliament. The water industry was clearly far from efficient, with a marked lack of coordination and standardization of practice and extreme fragmentation between the water companies, waterworks, and water boards. Three factors prompted the Water Act 1945. First, overall demands for water were increasing, and the post-war period was expected to produce rapid economic growth with even greater demands for water. Greater coordination was clearly necessary to balance available supply and predicted demands. Second, it was becoming increasingly clear that control over water abstraction (as for spray irrigation in agriculture) from private water sources was required, particularly if downstream water users were not to be seriously affected. Finally, both the water industry and public opinion were starting to demand greater (and more coordinated) control of water quality, in particular through pollution control and the introduction of strong measures to prevent discharges of harmful wastes into water courses. The Water Act sought to solve these problems by standardizing codes of practice and by aggregating small waterworks to create larger and more efficient units. River Boards were set up under the River Boards Act of 1948 to provided the basic units within the water industry, although the mosaic of boards, companies and waterworks still provided many small working units, each covering a small area. Problems of water quality were dealt with largely through a series of Rivers (Prevention of Pollution) Acts between 1951 and 1961. By the early 1960s, however, the water industry was still rather fragmented, largely unifunctional (water supply), and lacked a long-term and coordinated framework for planning future water-resource developments.

The Water Resources Act 1963 brought two main changes – the establishment of the Water Resources Board and the creation of regional River Authorities to replace existing river boards. The River Authorities' functions included the survey of existing and potential new demands for water within their areas of responsibility, preparation of plans to meet likely future demands, licensing of all abstractions of water from both surface and underground sources (the income raised from licence charges to be used in financing water-resource activities), rationalization of water use on a catchment basis, and the reduction of water pollution. These activities were to be coordinated by the Water Resources Board, which was to assume responsibility for arranging transfers of water (if required) between individual Authorities and for preparing a strategic plan for water developments throughout England and Wales up to the year 2000.

Two changes of attitude during the late 1960s undermined confidence in the 1963 Water Resources Act. First, there was mounting public concern over the preservation of land and landscape, and public opposition to planning proposals for new water-resources projects – especially new reservoirs in upland areas – was well orchestrated and formed a strong amenity/conservation lobby. Second, there was growing awareness of the inadequacies of the 1963 Act to deal with water pollution (which had increased substantially during the 1960s). Under the Act the River Authorities were empowered only to control the *output* of wastes into water-courses or aquifers. The improvement of waste treatment facilities and improved collection of wastes were beyond their remit, which raised serious questions about the extent to which it was possible to plan long-term water supplies in terms of both quantity and quality of water.

**Developments since 1970**

In 1971 the Central Advisory Water Committee found that conflicts of interest were arising between the different agencies responsible for providing water services, yet there was no adequate mechanism for resolving them (other than direct central government intervention). The industry was fragmented, with responsibilities shared between 157 water supply undertakings, 1,393 sewerage and sewage disposal authorities and twenty-nine River Authorities. This visibly hindered the effective planning, investment and management required for water services as a whole.

Responsibilities for new sources were split between River Authorities and water undertakers; there was little flexibility in the use of existing resources, little scope for proper treatment of water after use, and few opportunities to promote joint or national schemes. The time was clearly right for change in the direction of better integration of responsibilities and harmonization of objectives. The overriding goal would be to bring together the different aspects of the water cycle, which up to then had been managed by different bodies, to ensure greater coordination and a more efficient and economic use of available resources.

Major change came with the 1973 Water Act, which established ten regional Water Authorities in England and Wales (figure 6.5). There were five main objectives behind the new structure (table 6.2). The Authorities are autonomous but responsible to Parliament through the Secretary of State for the Environment and – for Welsh Water – through the Secretary of State for Wales. Integration was introduced, both functionally and spatially. The new Water Authorities were multi-functional – to meet the designated objectives – so that all aspects of the water cycle would be integrated under one management. Some of the sewerage functions (provision, maintenance and renewal of sewers) are carried out directly by the Water Authorities, but mostly by local authorities acting as agents for them. The Authorities were also delimited on the basis of river basins, so they have geographic (i.e. topographic) rather than administrative or political boundaries (figure 6.5). The difference is most evident along the border between Wales and England, where the Welsh Water Authority has control of water resources in a few small parts of England and the Severn Trent Water Authority has control over a small part of Wales. One management can thus control all aspects of the water cycle within a natural hydrological unit.

Between them the ten Water Authorities provide water services to almost every resident in England and Wales (table 6.3). In 1987 99.3 per

*Table 6.2* Main objectives behind establishment of the Water Authorities in 1973

1 To secure adequate supply of water of suitable quality to meet the rising demand from the public, industry, and agriculture (involving development of resources and water treatment, distribution and supply)

2 To provide adequate sewerage and sewage treatment and disposal facilities to meet the increasing needs of water users

3 To ensure the maintenance, and where appropriate expansion, of land drainage and flood protection in urban and agricultural areas (river management) and to oversee sea defence works

4 To enable a major clean-up of the main rivers throughout the country (pollution control)

5 To enable the broadest possible use of water space for recreation and amenity, including fishing and conservation

North
umbrian

North
West

Yorkshire

Severn Trent

Anglian

Welsh
Water

Thames

Wessex

Southern

South West

0          100          200 km

Areas in England
within Welsh Water

Areas in Wales within
Severn Trent Water

*Figure 6.5* Boundaries of the Water Authorities in England and Wales

cent of the 50 million people living within their boundaries were connected
to the public water supply (South-West Water serves the smallest proportion, at 95.8 per cent) and 95.7 per cent were connected to mains sewer
systems (South-West is again lowest, at 85.4 per cent).

The Water Authorities are also responsible for their own financial
affairs. The total turnover of the ten Authorities in 1986–7 (table 6.3) was
£2,712 million (varying from £94 million in South-West to £550 million in
Thames). Income is generated in two ways – some is borrowed, but most
comes from charges to users for water supply and environmental services.
The general public is charged for water in two ways. Most pay a 'water
rate' charge related to the rateable value of the property involved. The

Table 6.3 Profile of the Water Authorities in England and Wales, 1986–7

| Authority | Area (km²) | Population (1,000) | % connected to Public supply | % connected to Sewer | W. Authority Employees |
|---|---|---|---|---|---|
| Anglian | 26,795 | 5,208 | 99.3 | 91.6 | 5,184 |
| Northumbrian | 9,274 | 2,603 | 99.5 | 98.4 | 1,523 |
| North-West | 14,445 | 6,853 | 99.1 | 96.9 | 8,134 |
| Severn Trent | 21,600 | 8,283 | 99.6 | 96.7 | 8,493 |
| Southern | 10,552 | 3,961 | 99.6 | 95.0 | 3,160 |
| South-West | 10,884 | 1,449 | 95.8 | 85.4 | 2,003 |
| Thames | 13,100 | 11,618 | 99.9 | 97.8 | 9,152 |
| Welsh | 21,262 | 3,056 | 97.5 | 93.7 | 4,845 |
| Wessex | 9,918 | 2,415 | 98.6 | 91.3 | 1,925 |
| Yorkshire | 13,503 | 4,541 | 99.3 | 91.1 | 5,254 |

| Authority | W. Authority Supply | W. Company Supply | Total Supply | % supply from Groundwater | % supply Metered |
|---|---|---|---|---|---|
| Anglian | 1,157 | 564 | 1,721 | 47 | 31 |
| Northumbrian | 629 | 397 | 1,026 | 9 | 49 |
| North-West | 2,607 | 0 | 2,607 | 14 | 28 |
| Severn Trent | 1,942 | 415 | 2,357 | 44 | 27 |
| Southern | 673 | 582 | 1,255 | 72 | 26 |
| South-West | 467 | 0 | 467 | 11 | 23 |
| Thames | 2,719 | 1,202 | 3,921 | 41 | 20 |
| Welsh | 1,121 | 71 | 1,192 | 4 | 32 |
| Wessex | 392 | 494 | 886 | 48 | 35 |
| Yorkshire | 1,375 | 47 | 1,422 | 16 | 25 |

| Authority | Reservoirs[a] (no) | Water mains (km) | Sewers (km) | Treatment wks (no) | Capital exp. £m. | Turnover £m. | Assets £m. |
|---|---|---|---|---|---|---|---|
| Anglian | 9 | 30,700 | 24,900 | 1,090 | 144 | 332 | 3,425 |
| Northumbrian | 19 | 8,600 | 12,100 | 381 | 37 | 117 | 1,539 |
| North-West | 44 | 38,400 | 30,000 | 638 | 189 | 400 | 4,564 |
| Severn Trent | 20 | 38,200 | 3,780 | 1,071 | 156 | 428 | 4,571 |
| Southern | 5 | 11,200 | 20,100 | 433 | 74 | 193 | 2,037 |
| South-West | 13 | 14,400 | 8,300 | 600 | 42 | 94 | 1,114 |
| Thames | 20 | 28,100 | 51,400 | 408 | 148 | 550 | 4,878 |
| Welsh | 35 | 22,400 | 14,100 | 883 | 62 | 208 | 1,843 |
| Wessex | 6 | 10,100 | 11,800 | 353 | 65 | 117 | 1,175 |
| Yorkshire | 39 | 28,200 | 24,100 | 610 | 131 | 275 | 3,475 |

Source: Summarized from Water Authorities Association 1988
Note: [a] Larger than 1,000 Ml

minority who have metered supplies pay in proportion to the amount of water they use (plus a fixed charge for use of the meter). The public also pays a pollution prevention charge, which is also based on rateable values. The average household bill for water services in 1987–8 was £98.81 (£45.82 for water supply and £52.99 for sewage and environmental services). Commercial and industrial users are metered and they pay according to amounts used. They also pay for sewerage, and pay a further charge (according to amount and strength of the waste) if they discharge wastes directly into the sewer system.

The Authorities generated other income through various charges, such as for fishing licences, licences to abstract water from boreholes, rivers and lakes for industrial and some agricultural uses, and charges to occupiers of agricultural land for land drainage and flood prevention. For instance, a breakdown of a typical year's income for Anglian water is: sewerage and sewage treatment charges (50.5 per cent), water supply charges (34.4 per cent), trade effluents (2.8 per cent), environmental services (1.9 per cent), land drainage precepts (7.5 per cent) and abstraction (2.9 per cent).

There are two main items of expenditure. One is investment in capital assets, such as building treatment works and reservoirs. The net value of assets in the Water Authorities in 1986–7 (table 6.3) was £28,621 million, and capital expenditure amounted to £1,066 million (£1,005 million on water services and £61 million on land drainage). This includes a large expenditure on installing or replacing water mains and sewers (the Authorities are responsible for the upkeep of 230,000 km of water mains and 234,800 km of sewers) and maintenance of sewage treatment works (all 6,467 of them) and reservoirs (of which there are 210 with capacities in excess of 1,000 Ml, concentrated mostly in the North-West (44), Yorkshire (39) and Welsh (35) Water areas (table 6.3)). The other main item of expenditure is a target financial surplus set for each Authority by the government (DoE). For example, a breakdown of a typical year's expenditure for Anglian Water is cost depreciation and financial target (56.9 per cent), running costs (23.1 per cent), employees (15.9 per cent), agency (2.1 per cent) and other items (4.1 per cent).

Following the dissolution of the National Water Council, the Water Authorities Association was established in 1983 to represent the ten Water Authorities at a national level, and to coordinate their views when a national policy is required. The Association has played a key role in debating recent government proposals to privatize the water industry in England and Wales (see next section).

There is no doubt that the integrated river basin management made possible in the Water Authorities has increased effectiveness and decreased costs over the earlier fragmented management systems. This has happened in various ways, such as enabling optimization of investment decisions, allowing rationalization of common services and increasing flexibility in use of staff. The Authorities have also been able to develop long-term programmes through integrated resource planning. One notable example is the programme to clean up the catchment and estuary of the River Mersey (which contains much of the remaining badly polluted water in Britain). Work on the £2,000 million scheme started in 1986 and it is hoped to restore all rivers in the catchment to good quality within twenty-five years. The clean-up of the Thames in recent decades (see chapter 16) is another good example. Integrated long-term planning also made possible inter-basin water transfer schemes, such as the Yorkshire Water Grid, Anglian Water's Ely/Ouse transfer scheme and the ill-fated North-West Water's Lancashire Conjunctive Use scheme described in the first edition; this was badly damaged by the Abbeystead methane gas explosion in May 1984.

## PRIVATIZATION OF THE WATER INDUSTRY

Conservative governments have been committed through the 1980s to privatization of the major state-owned utilities (like British Telecom, British Gas, British Airways, BP and British Steel), and the water industry has not been overlooked. In February 1986 the government published a White Paper which set out eleven ways in which privatization would benefit customers, employees and the nation as a whole. The privatized water utilities envisaged would have greater freedom from government inter-ference in day-to-day management, greater protection from fluctuating political pressures, greater freedom from constraints on financing and access to private capital markets, greater incentives to determine the needs and preferences of customers, and greater motivation of employees (many of whom might become shareholders) to ensure the success of the business. They would, in short, be able to approach their task in the most cost effective manner and be free to build on their expertise in developing enterprise activities.

There are inevitable constraints on nationalized industries – such as external political influences on decisions, government interference in day-to-day management, Treasury constraints on private investment, and nationalization statutes which prevent what would otherwise be regarded as normal business practices – and the Water Authorities Association recognizes them and sees the logic of privatization. However, the industry is keen to ensure that whatever privatized water system is adopted by the government serves the present and future interests of users, investors and employees.

A number of concerns was raised within and beyond the water industry by the 1986 White Paper, and some of these were noted in the May 1987 Conservative party election manifesto and addressed in revised government proposals published in June 1987. They proposed splitting responsibilities for water management between:

(a) a new National Rivers Authority (NRA) and
(b) local privatized water utilities.

The NRA would assume responsibility for water resources, environmental quality and pollution control, land drainage and flood protection, fisheries, conservation, recreation, and navigation use of inland waters. There would be thirty-nine utilities (ten privatized water authorities and twenty-nine private water companies) which would be called Water Service PLCs (WSPLCs) and would be responsible for water supply, sewerage, sewage treatment and sewage disposal.

**Interests and concerns**

Although the government stated, in a consultative paper on the water environment (April 1986), that it was in favour of retaining the style of integrated river basin management established in 1973, many observers find it hard to see how the proposed division of responsibilities would (or even could) preserve this. The Water Authorities Association reported to the Royal Commission on Environmental Pollution in January 1987 that integrated river basin management has achieved major improvements in environmental quality, greater efficiency (through the integrated multi-functional structures), and a more economic use of scarce resources. It fears that such benefits will be lost under the privatization proposals, and the fragmentation implicit therein, and that it will be difficult to ensure that water supply, sewerage and sewage treatment and disposal continue to be provided safely, effectively and economically, with proper regard for the environment and the interests of other water users.

Reservations have also been expressed over the possible administrative structure of a privatized water industry, and the likely balance of power between the centre (NRA) and the regions (utilities). The role and powers of the proposed NRA need to be more clearly defined, along with the different roles of regulation and operational management. The industry's view is also that the number of regulating bodies responsible for charges, performance standards and environmental standards must be minimized to prevent wasteful bureaucracy and to streamline decision-making.

There is an overriding need to ensure that the regulatory framework is not so restrictive that it undermines the very purpose of privatization, which is to encourage greater freedom to manage effectively. In addition to the Director General of Water Services (DGOFWAT), the Water Service PLCs will be either controlled by, or responsible to, at least five separate government bodies – the Department of the Environment (DoE), Ministry of Agriculture, Fisheries and Food (MAFF), Her Majesty's Inspectorate of Pollution (HMIP), the Monopolies and Mergers Commission (MMC), and the National Rivers Authority (NRA). It remains to be seen how effectively the WSPLCs can operate with such dispersed accountability.

Concerns have also been expressed about the likely quality of service after privatization. The 1986 White Paper proposed that WSPLCs would be set designated standards of service which they would be required to meet. It would be for the directors of WSPLCs to decide how those standards would be achieved, and what commercial targets they would be aiming for. The White Paper stressed that 'profit is a more effective incentive than Government controls'. But the water industry has reservations over how the regulatory framework would work in practice, given the specific proposed privatization legislation and other relevant legislation such as the Control of Pollution Act and Companies Acts, and the regulation of prices and service standards by the Director General of Water Services (DGOFWAT).

Quality control should also come through competition in practice between the various water service utilities. The government expects five major competitive pressures, covering comparative competition (between neighbouring utilities), capital markets (and future prospects for takeovers between utilities), share prices (as an index of perceived corporate effectiveness), inset competition (to provide new water and sewerage supplies to 'greenfield' sites), and alternative supplies (which are sometimes available to industrial users, such as direct water abstraction). Whether these will ensure that water quality is not allowed to decline under the privatized water industry, as many commentators fear, remains to be seen.

The water industry has also been concerned about the need to minimize disruption of existing operations and organizations in the run-up to privatization. The interests of employees, in particular, need to be protected, and the Water Authorities Association has called for clear legislation to define terms of agreement for the transfer of staff and assets to the NRA, and formal confirmation of assurances to staff about the preservation of the terms of their employment contracts and of pension rights. Nearly 50,000 people were employed by the Water Authorities in 1987 (down from a peak of around 63,000 in 1979); they have a clear vested interest in such sweeping structural changes in their industry.

### Countdown to privatization

The government's proposals were, by mid-1989, being pushed forward on target. The timetable for implementation is tight. In May 1988 Public Utility Transfers and a Water Charges Act received Royal Assent, which made it legally possible for the Water Authorities to prepare for privatization; Lord Crickhowell was appointed chairman of the National Rivers Authority Advisory Committee (NRAAC) and preparations for privatization were begun. By September 1988 the members of NRAAC had been appointed, drafting of legislation was under way, and the Water Authorities were drawing up schemes of organization to separate utility from NRA functions for submission to the Secretary of State for the Environment. By

April 1989 the Water Authorities had completed restructuring in preparation for privatization (NRA and utility functions will be established as separate operational units under Water Authority management (pending flotation)).

The Privatization Bill proceeded through Parliament ready for enactment in September 1989, when the NRA was established, the Water Service PLCs created, the Director General of Water Services established, and the new regulatory framework started to operate. Flotation of the Water Service PLCs as effective, viable, and profitable concerns commenced in autumn 1989.

**Water metering and rate reform**

Since the Water Authorities were formed in 1974, they have based their charging policies to domestic users on the rating system. Users have a right to opt for charge by meter, but few – less than 1 per cent of the 19 million households (accounting for around 50 million individuals) served by Water Authorities – had in fact done so by the end of 1987.

With the government's plans to abolish the existing domestic rating system and replace it with a community charge has come a need for WSPLC to alter their domestic charging policy. The water industry favours metering as a long-term solution. But meters are costly to install and metering is unlikely to be adopted voluntarily by most water users. Water meters are now installed automatically in most new houses. But, even if a meter-installation programme were begun straight away, it would be unlikely to be completed much before the turn of the century. Pending that, the water supply utilities would need to have flexibility to adopt an appropriate method of charging for water, based on rateable value, community charge, or other suitable basis. The industry has been pressing for some years for extensive water metering trials, which would greatly help in formulating a rational metering programme. But such a move would require new legislation and financial support from the government, neither of which were forthcoming by the end of 1988.

**WATER QUALITY**

Water quality is dealt with in detail in chapter 16, but a few relevant observations are useful here. Periodic national surveys of water quality in rivers and estuaries in England and Wales have been carried out since 1958 and they show steady overall improvement in river quality from then to the early 1980s. The most recent national River Quality Survey was undertaken in 1985 and published by the Department of the Environment in 1986. It shows that river waters continue to be of high quality – 90 per cent of the lengths of river (totalling 41,390 km) and 92 per cent of estuary (total length 2,730 km) covered in the survey are of satisfactory quality (described as 'good' or 'fair'). But there still remain significant lengths of 'poor' and 'bad' quality rivers and estuaries – despite measurable improvements over the last thirty years. These are confined mainly to heavily populated and industrialized areas in the north and midlands. The dirtiest estuaries are concentrated in the north, where improvements are still being introduced in the treatment of sewage and industrial effluents.

Over a quarter of total river length had changed quality between the 1980 and 1985 national surveys – 12 per cent had increased (mainly within Anglian and Wessex Water Authority areas) and 14 per cent decreased (mainly within North-West and South-West). This does not necessarily reflect real substantive changes in water quality, because different methods were used by different Authorities and they also changed between successive surveys (e.g. nearly half of the apparent increase in length of rivers of 'poor' and 'bad' quality can be explained by the inclusion of new stretches of river in the 1985 survey).

Continued net decline is evident in more recent Water Authority measurements of water quality in rivers and canals in 1985–6 and 1986–7. But these results cannot be directly compared with earlier national surveys because the Authorities classified different reaches of river and canal for their own purposes. But the evidence suggests a slight deterioration in water quality over the period – the length of rivers and canals classed as 'good quality' fell by nearly 2 per cent (524 km) and the length classed as 'poor' or 'bad' quality rose by nearly 4 per cent (153 km).

Improvements since 1980 might reflect results of recent investments by the Water Authorities and the water industry (see previous section); deteriorations seem to reflect two main causes;

(a) discharge of poorer quality effluent from some sewage treatment works,
(b) pollution from intensive agriculture and forestry. This problem is particularly acute in terms of nitrates, which are washed from agricultural areas treated with nitrogen fertilizers. Water supplies in parts of central, eastern and southern England exceed the European Community standard of 50 parts per million (ppm). Some water supplies in the lowlands are also contaminated with pesticides, although industrial, local authority and domestic sources are also implicated (see chapter 16).

Most water supplies in Britain conform with the European Community Directive relating to the quality of water intended for human consumption (which was approved by the Council of Ministers in July 1980 for implementation in July 1985). This defines drinking water quality in terms of sixty-six parameters, describing aesthetic (taste and appearance) as well as health and safety dimensions. The appearance and taste of some British water supplies are below what customers and suppliers would wish for, because of old water mains and ageing water treatment works (which should be replaced in time as part of the industry's ongoing renovation and upgrading programme; see earlier section).

The industry argues that overall the water quality in Britain is already good and getting better. It hopes that conditions will continue to improve after privatization; legislation will be based on at least current standards and the 1974 Control of Pollution Act will be carried forward in the new legislation and other statutory provisions affecting water quality will remain in force. The National Rivers Authority will assume responsibility for safeguarding river quality after privatization. The cost of further improvements in water quality standards will probably have to be met by water users through charges for water supply and sewerage services.

## The 1974 water plan

Natural water storage in lakes and rivers (yielding an average of about 20 million $m^3.day^{-1}$) and supplementary reservoir storage (total capacity in England and Wales during the early 1970s of between 1,500 and 1,200 million $m^3$.) produce a dry-weather flow in the order of 12 million $m^3.day^{-1}$. During the early 1970s there was widespread support for proposals to expand the existing public water supply system to twice the existing output (around 28 million $m^3.day^{-1}$) to offer a sufficient basis for necessary growth, especially in industrial use of water. In 1974, however, the Water Resources Board's long-term strategic plans for water resource developments up to the year 2000 envisaged a dry-weather flow in the order of a quarter of mean flow (i.e. 45–50 million $m^3.day^{-1}$). It was thought that this target could be met by a combination of additional surface storage, improved uses of existing storage capacity, and more coordinated use of underground storage.

The Board's plan assumes that most of the expected growth in industrial use of water could be catered for from private sources – through re-use of waters carrying effluents and through intensified re-use of water within industry. New and improved storage would be required to meet the demands of an expanded domestic water supply system.

The plan (figure 6.6) has two principal foundations; the interlinking of major river systems in England and Wales (by aqueduct where necessary) into a form of water grid and the provision of an optimal pattern of reservoir storage. Structural developments would be concentrated in the wetter northern and western areas, where economic storage sites are more abundant and where storage provides overall a better return in yield than in the south and east (where evaporation and transmission losses would be somewhat greater). There are four important elements in the water plan:

(i) *River regulation and inland storage (reservoirs):* The plan recommends the development of up to ten substantial new surface storage schemes, up to half of which would be based on existing reservoir sites. Particularly

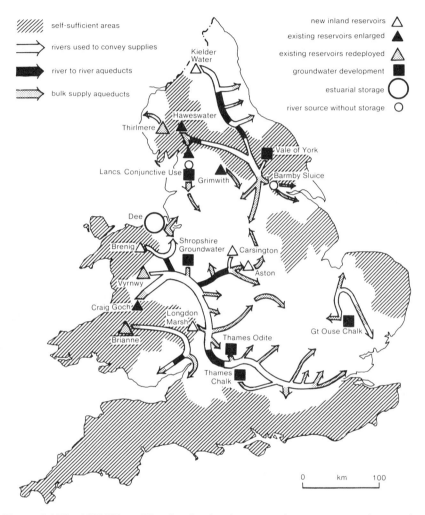

*Figure 6.6* The 1974 Water Plan for the development of new water supply capacity
*Source:* Rees, 1976

important would be new reservoirs at Kielder (Northumberland), Brenig (North Wales), and Carsington (Midlands), as well as the enlargement of Craig Goch in mid-Wales. Kielder Reservoir is designed to regulate the North Tyne and to serve the other main rivers of the north-east (this regulated river system is being linked to a Yorkshire water grid via tunnel aqueducts). The proposed enlargement of Craig Goch has raised vociferous political debate because of hostility in mid-Wales to what some local observers view as unnecessary environmental and landscape disruption there in order to provide the midlands with water at unit costs considerably below those charged to mid-Wales residents. The proposal aims to provide additional water supplies to meet rising demands in the West Midlands and South Wales, and (via inter-basin transfers) to provide water to the Rivers Thames and Dee, and to Clwyd in North Wales, in times of need. Structural requirements for the scheme include tunnel links between the Rivers Wye and the Severn, and the Severn and Thames, and the construction of aqueducts between the Wye and Usk, and the Severn and Dee.

(ii) *Groundwater:* The plan envisages that groundwater projects could conceivably provide up to a quarter of the expected growth in water supplies up to AD 2000. The total area which could be incorporated within a groundwater management scheme is very large indeed (figure 6.6) and – conveniently – the midlands and southern England are all well served with potential aquifer stores. The plan demands groundwater developments in the Vale of York, the Lancashire Fylde, Shropshire, East Anglia (the Great Ouse chalk) and the London basin (the Thames chalk and oolite). These would be based on more efficient use of the groundwater storage capacity (by pumping recharge water into the aquifers, for example), rather than an increased pumping of water from the aquifers.

(iii) *Interbasin transfers:* A key element in the plan is the provision of a suitably coordinated system of water supply links to and from the aquifers. The most convenient and economic basis for such a system is to use existing river systems, supplemented where necessary by aqueducts and tunnels. Such a system is also central to the efficient operation of the river regulation and inland storage elements of the water plan. Indeed, the cornerstone of the plan is the concept of interbasin transfers of water to allow the movement of water between areas of excess and areas of deficiency.

(iv) *Estuary storage and desalination:* The water industry has been aware for some time of the need to seek water storage capacity in the lowlands because of environmental opposition to new upland reservoir schemes and the difficulties and costs of long-distance water transfers, amongst other problems. Estuaries provide considerable potential for large-scale water storage, particularly narrow, deep, or easily dammed estuaries. Much debate and baseline research has centred on the possibilities of developing storage schemes in areas such as the Wash, the Severn Estuary, Morecambe Bay and the Dee Estuary; although options on the first three have been kept open the Water Plan specifically identified the Dee Estuary as a likely storage area for water to be supplied by aqueduct to Merseyside and North Wales.

The distillation of fresh water from sea water (desalination) provides a further option for increasing future water supplies. Experience elsewhere, however, has highlighted the massive energy requirements of the desalination process and has cast doubt on the economic viability of such schemes during the 1990s.

## CURRENT PROBLEMS AND PROSPECTS

The water industry has undergone many changes in the present century, some largely cosmetic but many of lasting importance to the evolution of a supply system geared towards meeting the needs of water users up to the year 2000. Two basic problems face those involved in water planning: how to ensure adequate supplies of water in the future and how to deal with rare situations, like the drought of 1975–6, when well-laid plans for supply provision are tested to the full.

### Supply provision

A range of policy alternatives for supply provision has been considered in recent years, based on four different premises:

(i) *Capital investment:* The traditional approach to supply provision in the United Kingdom has been to rely on capital investment to extend supply facilities in order to meet predicted demand. In the past this has centred largely on new upland reservoirs, whereas aquifer recharge and estuary storage schemes show potential for the future. The logic behind this policy has been to ensure that available dry-weather supplies are capable of meeting projected peak demands. Inevitably large safety margins are involved in water planning, and under normal weather conditions the existing public supply system includes substantial idle storage capacity. The principal arguments against increased capital investment centre around the monetary and opportunity costs involved. It has been estimated, for example, that the overall cost of implementing the Water Plan scheme would be in the order of £1,500 million (at 1972 prices). Opportunity costs include loss of agricultural land, social disturbance, and adverse impacts on the ecology and landscape of areas selected for capital investment projects.

(ii) *More efficient water use:* Alternative strategies for supply provision assume that existing supplies are adequate and that future increases in demand can be met by more efficient use of these supplies. Distribution losses account for about one-third of unmetered supplies and there seems to be ample scope for coordinated waste detection programmes. Dual quality water supplies also offer a prospect for more efficient water use – particularly because it is estimated that only perhaps 10–25 per cent of public supplies *need* to be of very high quality to satisfy the realistic demands of water users. Potable supplies of water are currently used, for example, for industrial processing, flushing of toilets, and watering of gardens, whereas lower quality water would suffice for such uses.

(iii) *Water re-use:* A third scenario is based on the re-use of water supplies, through either the direct re-use of water in homes and factories (made possible by the installation of recycling equipment) or the reclamation of sewage effluent. The second alternative would not yield potable supplies for domestic use, but it could provide water for a dual-quality system, as well as supply of suitable quality for many industrial users. Problems of gaining public acceptability for re-use schemes could be alleviated by careful public relations plans and sensitive advice and information policies, such schemes seem to stand up well to economic cost-benefit analyses.

(iv) *Demand management:*The first three approaches are based on the assumption that demand for water and the use of existing supplies are relatively fixed at any one point in time and that water is being used efficiently and without waste by consumers. Supply management thus assumes main priority in the water industry. An alternative water management strategy could be based on demand management which seeks to influence consumer behaviour. Physical methods of influencing demand might include redesigning equipment (such as flush toilets and washing machines) and the introduction of tap rewashering services, both aimed at reducing amounts of water used in normal circumstances. Alternatively, price mechanisms designed to reduce current consumption and to control rates of increase in demand would be based on charging consumers in proportion to the amounts of water used, rather than on a flat rate as is current practice. Economists point to the basic enigma underlying price mechanism controls, however. This is that, although water users probably *would* reduce their demands if forced to pay for amounts used, the extremely high cost of metering all users (domestic and others) would undoubtedly outweigh the savings to be gained (from delaying investment in new supply capacity).

## The 1975–6 drought

The attention of the water industry is generally focused on planning long-term water supplies to meet predicted future demand and rarely is the industry called upon to consider disruption or even cessation of supplies. One situation which prompted such reactions was the drought of 1975–6 which brought the most severe shortages of water ever recorded in the United Kingdom. The drought lasted from May 1975 to August 1976 and represents the driest sixteen-month period since records began in 1727. An average precipitation during summer 1975 followed by a well below average precipitation over the summer of 1976, plus a heatwave between 20 June and 6 July 1976, produced widespread problems of maintaining water supplies. Water Authorities bore many of the direct costs of the drought through large-scale losses in revenue (caused by reduced consumption) and high operating costs (such as the installation of stand-pipes and the hire of tanker trailers to supply water in areas of shortage). The National Water Council has estimated that the drought cost the water industry more than £35 million. With hindsight it is clear that many sectors of the economy adapted quite well to the stresses imposed by the water shortages and there are many cases of rapid adjustment of policies, practices and priorities in response to the drought which effectively pre-empted longer-term or more widespread changes.

Reactions within the water industry to their fluctuating fortunes changed over the sixteen month period. Little noticeable impact on water supplies was apparent throughout 1975, when shortages in precipitation could be compensated for by taking water from storage (principally in water supply reservoirs) so that the effects were not passed on directly to water consumers. In situations of possible supply shortage, calls for voluntary restrictions on consumption produced anticipated results and more direct intervention was not required. By early 1976, however, prospects for water supply were not improving and some precautionary measures were taken to protect supplies in Yorkshire, the West Midlands, the south-west, and South Wales. The National Water Council announced that the winter of 1975–6 had been one of the driest in the last 100 years and restrictions were sought to ensure preservation of existing increasingly precious stocks of water. The Council predicted that savings of between 20 and 30 per cent could be realized through banning hosepipes and encouraging voluntary savings, and that up to 40 per cent could be saved through formalized rationing of water. Early restrictions included the reduction of pressure in supply systems, checking of leakage on supply mains, and orchestrated appeals for domestic economies in water use. Although such restrictions did reduce overall consumption, reliable supplies continued to decline in the absence of rainfall.

On July 2, 1976 the government announced a bill (the Drought Act 1976) to extend the powers of the 1958 Water Resources Act; it was published on July 14, and received Royal Assent on August 6. The Drought Act specified that compensation was not payable for damage resulting from a prohibition or restriction on the use of water and it allowed for both individual consumers and different classes of consumer to be exempted from any order at the discretion of the Water Authority. The scene was set for introducing restrictions on water supplies (to affect individual householders and others, who could cope with reduced or intermittent supplies, rather than hospitals and certain industries). Thus, for example, nearly a million people in south-east Wales faced water cuts on a rota basis for between one and eleven weeks over the period July to September 1976. The scene was also set for Water Authorities to bring into operation supplementary sources of water, and to divert water from places with sufficient surplus to areas of shortage. It is a measure of the success of the adjustments facilitated by the Drought Act 1976 that in only two parts of the country – south-east Wales and parts of north Devon and north

Cornwall – did water supplies actually fail during the drought and water had to be rationed. Most Water Authorities bought in supplies of stand-pipes and drew up contingency plans for installing them if the need arose, but in few cases did installation prove absolutely necessary.

The drought had ended by late August/early September in most areas and – ironically – was immediately followed by a September which received over twice the long-term September average precipitation for England and Wales as a whole. The problems of drought were rapidly replaced by problems of flooding. The drought left behind a wide variety of legacies, such as problems of failure in building foundations related to desiccation (cracking of soils) and a boom in male babies born during August 1977 (this is believed to reflect an adjustment of sex ratios of babies related to a surge of accumulated trace elements in water consumed by the adult population nine months earlier).

Whilst the drought proved to be a costly exercise for the water industry as a whole, it did offer some valuable lessons. The crisis situation inevitably produced pressures on policy-makers to initiate further changes in administrative structures, functions and policies to prevent recurrence of operational problems which emerged during the drought period. It also encouraged water managers to consider a broader range of options in supply management (particularly in terms of recycling, groundwater development, and water rationing). In addition, some of the emergency measures introduced during the drought (such as reduced consumption self-imposed by many large industrial consumers) have since been retained on a contingency basis. Finally, some of the temporary sources introduced under the Drought Act have since been retained for regular use, and others are retained on stand-by to cater for periods of peak demand.

## CONCLUSIONS

The water industry in the United Kingdom in the 1990s will look and act very differently from how it did during the 1980s. This is a period of unprecedented change. Privatization will bring greater competition and innovation, but part of the cost of greater operating efficiency may be a decline in commitment to water quality, amenity and informal recreational use of water resources. It is ironic that such changes, related to administrative change within the industry, may come at a time of rising public interest in the water environment. Demand for water resources is also changing in response to changes in industry, agriculture and domestic lifestyle.

## FURTHER READING

Many of the themes introduced in this chapter can be explored in greater detail. The general theme of water resources is covered in Smith, K. (1972) *Water in Britain*, London: Macmillan, and in Parker, D. J. and Penning-Rowsell, E. C. (1980) *Water planning in Britain*, London: Allen & Unwin. Demand and supply are dealt with in Park, C. C. (1982) 'The supply of and demand for water', in Johnston, R. J. and Doornkamp, J. C. (eds.) *The Changing Geography of the United Kingdom*, London: Methuen, pp. 129–45, and in Park, C. C. (1986) 'Water demand forecasting and the social sciences', in Gardiner, V. and Herrington, P. (eds.) *Water Demand Forecasting*, Norwich: GeoBooks, pp. 25–35. Water resource and water quality statistics are given in Department of the Environment (1988) *Digest of Environmental Protection and Water Statistics*, London: HMSO. The water privatization debate is introduced in Cmnd 9734 (1986) *Privatisation of the Water Authorities in England and Wales*, London: HMSO, and Department of the Environment (1987) *The National Rivers Authority; The Government's Proposals for a Public Regulatory Body in a Privatised Water Industry*, London: HMSO. Water quality is dealt with in Department of the Environment (1986) *River Quality in England and Wales 1985*, London: HMSO, House of Commons Environment Committee (1987) *Pollution of Rivers and Estuaries*, London: HMSO, and Royal Commission on Environmental Pollution (1987) *Annual Report*, London: HMSO. Also recommended are: Doornkamp, J. C., Gregory, K. J., and Burns, A. S. (1980) *Atlas of Drought in Britain 1975–76*, London: Institute of British Geographers, and *Water Briefings* (free, published irregularly) and *Water Bulletin* (weekly, by subscription) – both published by the Water Authorities Association (1 Queen Anne's Gate, London SW1H 9BT).

# 7 The changing transport pattern

*B. J. Turton*

The inland transport system of the United Kingdom is a complex blend of private and public enterprise which, since the end of the Second World War, has experienced a succession of government policies and directives designed to accommodate changing economic and social conditions. In particular the period since 1980 has been marked by legislation passed to promote competition within the road passenger transport sector, representing a reversal of previous policies which were intended to secure a measure of coordination, both at the national level and within major conurbations. The dismantling of passenger transport authorities and executives in these conurbations, privatization of the National Bus Company into many smaller units and the transfer of the National Freight Corporation, the shipping interests of British Rail and the former state-owned group of seaports to the private sector all reflect the government's objective of involving the business and commercial areas of the economy much more closely in ownership and management of the principal transport modes.

Road and rail shares of passenger traffic have not altered significantly since 1980 but the division of freight between the various modes has been affected by the continuing growth in importance of pipelines, principally for crude petroleum and refined products. Planning for improvements to the transport infrastructure has been aided by comprehensive freight and passenger surveys at the local, regional and national levels and in 1977 the principal objectives of transport policy were drawn together in a White Paper which emphasized the need for an efficient system of transport to promote industrial growth and for the maintenance of a reasonable level of personal mobility by public transport in rural and urban areas. Drafted during a period when subsidization and coordination of transport services was a firmly established element of national policy, the aims of this White Paper have been strongly affected by the change in government in 1979 and by its subsequent transport legislation. Interpretation of what constitutes an acceptable road or rail system to meet the social and economic needs of the nation is inevitably a higher controversial issue and current investment plans for the motorway and trunk road networks and for British Rail are viewed by many user groups as inadequate. Throughout the decade 1980–90 development plans for the transport sector have had to take into account escalating oil prices and the effects of the economic recession, and the latter, together with a government policy favouring public expenditure reductions, have resulted in large cuts in investment in roads and railways. Continuing rises in private car ownership have created an urgent need for additional road capacity and the situation is still especially critical in major urban areas despite strenuous efforts to revitalize public transport services.

## THE RAILWAY SYSTEM

By the 1980s the railway had come to terms with its role as minority partner in the movement of passengers and freight and had largely succeeded in meeting the recommendations of the 1963 Beeching Report that the system should concentrate upon transporting those commodities and passenger traffics to which it was best suited. The process of adjustment to the growing challenge of road transport had begun in the 1930s with the withdrawal of many uneconomic passenger services and this strategy was accelerated during the first phase of state ownership in the late 1940s and early 1950s, when the British Transport Commission acquired a railway network which had suffered severe neglect during the Second World War and was in no position to offer effective resistance to the erosion of its market by an expanding road freight and passenger transport sector (table 7.1). A key element in the programme adopted to revive railway fortunes was the 1955 Modernization Plan, with its recommendations for a widespread extension of electrification from the existing Southern Region network on to major trunk routes between London, the midlands, the north-west and Scotland, and the gradual substitution of steam by the more economical diesel traction on all other parts of the network. Much of the electrification programme was finished in the early 1970s but the last element in the plan, covering the east coast main line from London to York, Newcastle, and Edinburgh, will not be completed until the early 1990s (table 7.2). The section between London and Leeds was electrified in 1989 and the new trains are capable of speeds up to 140 mph.

The 1955 plan was followed in 1962 by the dismantling of the Transport Commission and the establishment of an autonomous Railways Board, now known as British Rail, and a year later the inherited problem of declining passenger and freight traffic was tackled by the first report on the Reshaping of British Railways (the Beeching Report) with its controversial proposals for the closure of all uneconomic routes, including 8,000 kms of lines with passenger services and a large number of other loss-making passenger stations on through routes and freight depots. These proposals were an immediate response to a national survey which had revealed a grossly uneven distribution of passengers and freight flows, with concentrations of lucrative traffic on small sections of the network and with one-half

*Table 7.1* Passenger and freight traffic in Great Britain by mode of transport
(a) percentage distribution

| Year | Passengers | | | Freight | | |
|------|------|------|-----|------|------|-------------|
| | Road | Rail | Air | Road | Rail | Other modes* |
| 1965 | 89 | 11 | <1 | 57 | 21 | 22 |
| 1970 | 91 | 9 | <1 | 62 | 19 | 19 |
| 1975 | 92 | 8 | <1 | 66 | 15 | 19 |
| 1980 | 92 | 7 | 1 | 77 | 15 | 8 |
| 1985 | 92 | 7 | 1 | 79 | 12 | 9 |
| 1987 | 92 | 7 | 1 | 81 | 12 | 7 |

(b) by mode and purpose of journey 1985 (percentage)

| | Foot | Cycle/motorcycle | Car | Bus/coach/air | Rail |
|------|------|------------------|-----|---------------|------|
| Business journeys > 25 miles | – | – | 60 | 10 | 30 |
| Other journeys > 25 miles | – | – | 80 | 10 | 10 |
| Journey-to-work | 10 | 8 | 57 | 20 | 5 |

*Sources:* Transport Statistics, Great Britain; National Travel Survey 1985–6. British Road Federation
*Note:* * principally coastal shipping until after 1979 when data was excluded

*Table 7.2* Railways open for traffic in Great Britain

| Year | Total length open (km) | Length open to passenger traffic (km) | Length of route electrified (km) |
|------|------------------------|---------------------------------------|----------------------------------|
| 1965 | 24,012 | 17,516 | 2,886 |
| 1970 | 18,988 | 14,637 | 3,162 |
| 1975 | 18,118 | 14,431 | 3,655 |
| 1980 | 17,645 | 14,394 | 3,718 |
| 1985 | 16,752 | 14,310 | 3,809 |
| 1986 | 16,670 | 14,304 | 4,154 |
| 1988 | 16,629 | 14,299 | 4,205 |

*Sources*: Transport Statistics, Great Britain; Annual Reports, British Transport Commission

of the system earning insufficient revenue to meet even essential track maintenance costs.

This strategy of contraction to a viable size was to be accompanied by selective investment in those parts of the system judged best able to attract and retain revenue-earning traffic, namely the inter-city passenger routes, the commuter network around London and trunk routes with substantial bulk freight movements. A second report in 1965 identified this 'commercial railway' more precisely and the investment in new electric traction and

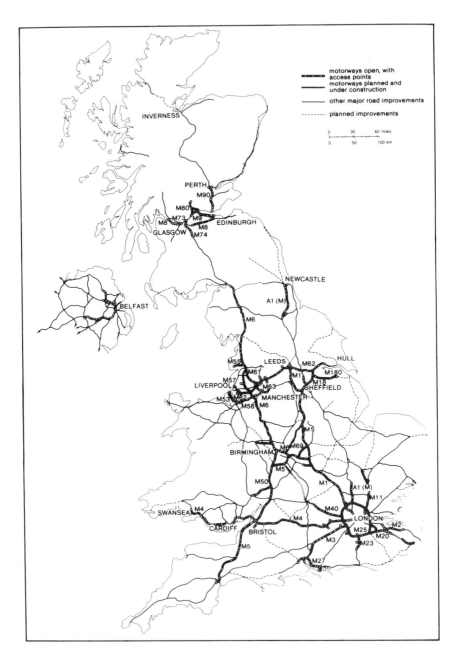

*Figure 7.1* The railway network in 1988
*Source:* B.R. timetables and maps 1980–8
*Note:* To preserve clarity closures of minor branches have been omitted and not all elements of the suburban rail networks in major conurbations are included

scheduled 'freight liner' trains and terminals continued alongside the planned service withdrawals, with 7,240 kms closed to all traffic between 1962 and 1966. Had all the closures proposed in 1963 been implemented then the network of 27,370 kms as it existed in the early 1960s would ultimately have been halved but a reprieve came in 1967 with a change in government policy based upon direct subsidization of those passenger services at risk on economic grounds but recognized to be worthy of retention on the basis of their value to the community. This approach, incorporated in the 1968 Transport Act, created the contemporary structure of British Rail with a basic framework of profitable trunk passenger routes (the Inter-City Sector), a secondary 'social railway' incorporating uneconomic cross-country services (now designated as the Provincial Sector) and the commuter network of south-east England, and a freight sector (figure 7.1).

Freight traffic, traditionally the major source of revenue on the British railway system, was overtaken in 1975 by passenger earnings and the latter have increased in importance throughout the 1980s. By 1987–8 passenger traffic was at its highest level since the formation of British Rail in 1962 although it was carried on a network 30 per cent smaller than in the latter year (table 7.3). Growth on the inter-city network has been stimulated by faster services and better timetabling and by completion of the electrification programmes joining London with Cambridge, Norwich and Leeds. These latter developments, together with extension of the electrified London-Bournemouth line westwards to Weymouth, have accelerated the growth of long-distance commuting into London and between 1985 and 1988 British Rail recorded a 15 per cent rise in its total London journey-to-work traffic. In 1987 a new Anglian Region was added to the existing British Rail regional structure to deal with the substantial increases in this commuter traffic generated by the electric services to Norwich.

*Table 7.3* Changes in rail traffic in Great Britain

| Year | Passenger journeys (m.) | Passenger-kms (m.) | Freight tonnes (m.) | Freight tonne-kms (m.) | Coal trade as percentage of total freight |
|---|---|---|---|---|---|
| 1965 | 865 | 30,116 | 232 | 25,229 | 61 |
| 1970 | 824 | 30,408 | 209 | 24,500 | 54 |
| 1975 | 730 | 30,300 | 175 | 20,900 | 55 |
| 1980 | 760 | 31,700 | 154 | 17,600 | 37 |
| 1985 | 697 | 29,700 | 122 | 15,400 | 27* |
| 1986 | 659 | 30,800 | 140 | 15,700 | 30 |
| 1988 | 764 | 34,315 | 149 | 18,100 | 55 |

*Sources*: Transport Statistics, Great Britain; British Railways Board, Annual Reports
*Note*: * Period of national coal industry dispute

These improvements in passenger carryings have also involved the reopening of closed stations and the creation of new ones, with costs shared between British Rail and local authorities wishing to secure better rail facilities. Most of these stations have been within major conurbations but there has also been experimental opening of facilities on lines serving major recreational areas, such as the Pennines. Milton Keynes Central was provided to meet the requirements of the New Town but much of its traffic now comprises London commuters. By 1989 over eighty stations closed under the Beeching proposals had been reopened and forty-six new stations have been provided.

Problems encountered by passengers travelling from the midlands and north via London rail termini to southern destinations have been considerably eased by the introduction of through trains linking Manchester and Birmingham to Gatwick Airport and the Channel ferry ports. Some of these services utilize existing cross-London routes which have been upgraded but the Thameslink line through Central London was specifically developed to give electric services from Luton and Bedford direct access to towns south of London. Designed to alleviate the growing problem of congestion on the south-eastern commuter network this Thameslink is the forerunner of a £1,375 million investment in this region to provide more reliable services.

During the early 1980s freight tonnage continued to decline and the dramatic fall in traffic in 1984 was due to the miners' strike and diversion of much coal to road haulage then. The period since 1984 has seen a revival of rail carryings and by 1987–8 total freight on the railways had risen almost to the level recorded before the coal-mining dispute. During the 1970s the railways benefited from the spread of container traffic and established terminals at major ports and inland industrial centres. It is estimated that about 40 per cent of all maritime containers are now carried to or distributed from ports by rail but there has been some reduction in traffic on shorter hauls and eight of the original freight-liner terminals have been closed. Rail-borne container traffic in general increased from 100,000 20-foot equivalent units (TEU) in the early 1970s to 450,000 units in 1986, however, with an emphasis upon routes serving deep-sea and near-sea terminals at Southampton, Tilbury and Felixstowe. Freight handling has been improved by allocating motive power, rolling stock and depots to specific traffic, with Toton yard, for example, now being concerned solely with coal haulage from the East Midlands' collieries.

There has also been a greater level of coordination between British Rail and its principal industrial customers with major investments in terminals and rolling stock for specialized commodities. Subsidies to enable private companies to install rail-connected terminals were sanctioned in the 1974 Act but initial progress was slow. By the late 1980s however about 170 depots had been installed, at a cost of £64 million, and generate about 35 million tonnes annually. The Department of Transport estimates that as a result of this investment 10,000 heavy trucks per day have been removed from the road network. Private investment in terminals and rolling stock has increased to £2.4 billion and 32 per cent of all freight wagons are now owned by industrialists, principally oil, chemical and bulk cement and aggregate firms. One limestone aggregate company also has its own locomotives and operates trains from its Mendip quarries to nine rail/road exchange depots in the south-east, with 75 per cent of its annual output being hauled over the rail network. With the exception of coal and container traffic, over 60 per cent of all freight tonne-kms was achieved in private owners' vehicles by the late 1980s.

This increased involvement of industrialists, coupled with reductions of up to one-fifth in the costs of operating trains and terminals, has led to British Rail becoming one of the most efficient and profitable freight-haulage systems in Western Europe but the reliance upon one major customer, British Coal, for much of its bulk traffic is undesirable. Privatization of the Central Electricity Generating Board and the purchase of power station coal from overseas sources could dramatically cut British Rail freight revenue in the future.

Although the railways have succeeded in making many economies in the operating sector subsidies are still essential for most passenger services outside the inter-city framework. The grants made under the 1968 Act were consolidated into a block subsidy in 1974 but since the early 1980s this has been progressively reduced and in early 1983 the Serpell report on railway financing policy contained proposals for a contraction of the network which were far more drastic than those of the Beeching report twenty years earlier. Several radical options were presented, each designed to secure improved levels of financial results by 2003. Proposals ranged from a reduction of the current network of 16,670 kms by 3.6 per cent, with the use of substitute bus services where appropriate, to a pruning to only 2,633 kms, creating what was seen as a financially viable system. If adopted, this latter option would have left Scotland with no railways north of Edinburgh and Glasgow and Wales with no services beyond Cardiff. All routes west of Bournemouth would disappear and only London would survive as a recognizable rail focus, although many commuter lines would close. Each of the options was evaluated in terms of the probable annual deficit that would be involved and although no direct action followed the Serpell report the annual subsidy continues to be steadily reduced. The British Rail Corporate Plan for 1988–93 is based upon a total subsidy of £2,900 million and the loss-making cross-country passenger services, despite the recent introduction of more efficient trains, would still require daily support of almost £1 million if they are to be maintained at current levels. Subsidies for the south-east commuter area are to be reduced from £155 million to £86 million during the Plan's period and the substantial increases in fares announced in late 1988 to counter this fall could result in changes in long-distance commuting patterns.

Much investment in the early 1990s will be concentrated upon improved routes to the Channel Tunnel. Four potential high-speed lines between London and Folkestone were outlined in 1988 and the adoption of a suitable alignment would cut the overall London-Paris journey time to two and a half hours, compared with the three hours if the Tunnel traffic used existing lines in Kent already carrying heavy commuter traffic. The final route was confirmed in March 1989 and involves new lines parallel to sections of existing railways and motorways and extensive tunnelling beneath south London to secure access to new terminal facilities at Kings Cross and Waterloo. The total construction costs of up to £1,800 million may be shared between British Rail and private investors but the new route will not be ready in time for the Tunnel's opening in 1993, and a more likely date for completion is 1996.

During the 1980s, British Rail became involved in several station redevelopment projects involving the private sector; in the Liverpool Street scheme in London, for example, track and station modernization costing £300 million will be met by the developer building offices on the site. On a national scale proposals for the transfer of British Rail to the private sector have been considered by the government with the aim of promoting competition between various rail services and ending the subsidy which in 1988 amounted to £700 million. Options could include dismantling the system into its component regions, transferring the network as a whole to the private sector or creating a statutory authority to own and maintain the track and associated equipment and premises, with services operated by private undertakings on a contract basis.

## ROADS AND ROAD TRAFFIC

The road system has been firmly established for over three decades as the nation's principal transport medium for freight and passenger traffic. Since 1970 the proportion of total personal journeys carried out by private car, bus, coach, taxi, and other vehicles has stabilized at about 90 per cent and the road-borne share of all freight (expressed as tonnes hauled) has increased from 62 per cent (1970) to 79 per cent (1986) or to 86 per cent if coastal shipping movements are discounted (table 7.1). The substantial growth in road traffic, particularly in private cars, has been met by successive programmes for new routes and road reconstruction, although when compared with the achievements of other European nations, particularly in respect of motorway provisions, the results are unimpressive. Ambitious schemes for new roads were first proposed by British motoring interests in the 1920s but actual progress prior to the Second World War was generally confined to piecemeal improvements on the more seriously overloaded sections of the network and the construction of only a limited number of arterial routes such as the East Lancashire Road and the Eastern and Western Avenues of Greater London. Urban traffic congestion at this time was usually countered by what has now become the familiar solution of the by-pass; amongst the earliest were those for Winchester, Farnham and Kingston-upon-Thames.

Proposals for a national motorway network were first embodied in the 1946 road programme, which also included plans to designate 5,932 kms of existing roads as trunk routes, to be maintained from central government funds. Many of these designated routes required upgrading to provide the capacity to deal with projected traffic densities and a series of road development plans was published during the 1950s and 1960s. Road-borne freight tonnage rose three-fold between 1945 and 1960 and commercial traffic grew to account for up to 40 per cent of total flow on many trunk routes whose inability to cope with such increases was soon apparent. Private car ownership rose by 14 per cent in the 1950s, adding to the demands for road improvements. At this time it was generally assumed by transport planners that the primary aim of the projected motorway and associated trunk road networks was to provide additional or alternative capacity on those routes which were most seriously overloaded and in this respect the primary road network of the 1960s broadly corresponded in its alignment to that of the trunk railways, linking major population concentrations.

Much of this early road planning was based upon vehicle flow data which could at best provide only a partial basis for the satisfactory interpretation of existing and the prediction of future traffic patterns. During the 1960s, comprehensive surveys of inter- and intra-regional freight flows and data on personal journey patterns from the National Travel Surveys (initiated in 1964) enabled a much more reliable geography of movement on the road system to be constructed. It became evident that, as on the railways, the use made of the roads was very uneven, with over 90 per cent of all traffic (as measured in vehicle-kms) confined to 50 per cent of the network and with an estimated 25 per cent carried on just 1 per cent, almost entirely within urban areas.

If the original motorway and trunk road plans had been carried out on schedule the 1980s would have seen the completion of a primary road network of 5,600 kms, of which 3,220 kms were to have been of motorway standard. This intended system comprised the basic elements of the original motorway plan, all of which either had been opened or were nearing completion in 1970, augmented by other routes outlined in the Roads for the Future White Paper of that year. By the mid-1980s, however, only 2,670 kms of the revised motorway network had been finished and between 1983 and 1988 only 310 kms were added. Completion of the primary road network in its entirety was also put in doubt in 1977 when two transport policy White Papers questioned the validity and effectiveness of the scale of the national road improvement programme. It was recommended that public transport services should receive more aid, at the expense of road-building, as a more effective means of combating

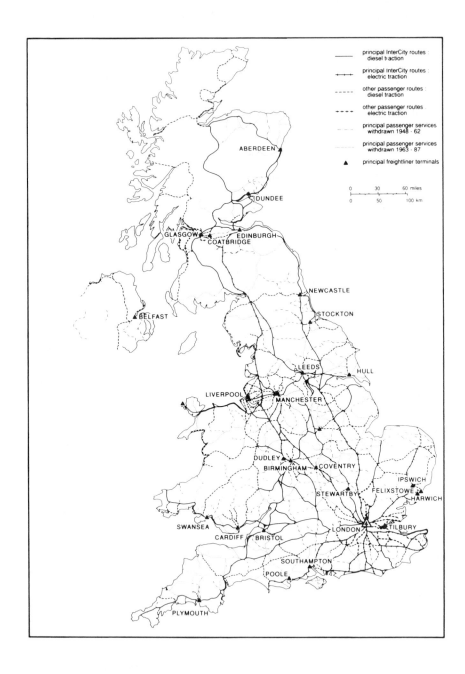

*Figure 7.2* The motorway and principal road network 1988
*Source:* Department of Transport, Transport Statistics, Great Britain 1978–88 (1989)

traffic congestion within and on the approaches to large towns and cities. The Leitch Report in turn recommended a more flexible approach to road planning, with a closer appraisal of the cost-benefit issues involved and with greater weight being given to environmental considerations. These proposals, carried forward into the current decade with its emphasis upon reductions in public sector spending, have created a situation in which the M25 London orbital motorway was the last scheme to be completed and the M40 extension between Oxford and Birmingham is the only major route now under construction (figure 7.2). A concurrent programme of conventional road improvements continues and the notorious bottlenecks on holiday traffic routes at Okehampton and Dorchester were finally relieved with by-passes in 1988, but congestion remains a major difficulty. A Civic Trust report considered that over 800 communities were in need of by-passes in the 1980s but with present building rates it is unlikely that more than half this total will gain new roads by the mid-1990s. Even the road improvements that have been completed have been severely criticized, with the inadequacies of the M25 in particular being widely publicized. This route, linking the principal radial motorways focusing upon London, became congested with both through and local traffic soon after its final completion in 1986, with particularly severe problems on the approaches to the Thames Tunnel at Dartford and in the Heathrow Airport area. Widening has already been undertaken in the worst-affected sections but the increases in traffic which will be generated when the Channel Tunnel is opened in 1993 will inevitably create further problems. Congestion on the West Midlands section of the M6, which now carries 150,000 vehicles per day through Birmingham, will eventually be countered by a 56 kms relief motorway planned to connect the M6, M54 and M42 routes to the north of the conurbation.

In May 1989 the government announced its proposals to double the current level of expenditure on roads and to invest £12,000 million up to 2000 AD in trunk road improvements and new construction. The main priorities will be the widening of overloaded sections of the M1, M4, M5, M6, M25 and M62 motorways and upgrading of parts of the Carlisle–Glasgow trunk route to motorway standard. Short sections of motorway are to be constructed to relieve congestion in outer Manchester and in Essex and many trunk roads are to be substantially improved. In total the programme involves 4,344 kms of new and upgraded roads and its main objective is to reduce congestion on inter-city routes.

Several significant changes may be identified in the nature of road traffic. Motorways now carry 15 per cent of all traffic, as compared with 10 per cent in 1975, and in consequence the proportion making use of conventional urban roads (43 per cent) has slightly fallen (table 7.4). Total traffic volume has increased over the 1975–86 period by 26 per cent but that on the motorway network has doubled. Heavy goods vehicles, including container lorries, have declined in number by 16 per cent between 1975 and 1987, but

*Table 7.4* Changes in road passenger traffic in Great Britain
(a) national data

| Year | Cars and taxis | | Buses and coaches | |
|---|---|---|---|---|
| | *000 m. vehicle-kms* | *As a percentage of all traffic* | *000 m. vehicle-kms* | *As a percentage of all traffic* |
| 1965 | 115.8 | 71 | 3.91 | 2.4 |
| 1970 | 161.3 | 78 | 3.62 | 1.7 |
| 1975 | 194.4 | 79 | 3.78 | 1.5 |
| 1980 | 197.2 | 80 | 3.06 | 1.2 |
| 1985 | 229.4 | 81 | 3.07 | 1.0 |
| 1987 | 257.9 | 81 | 3.45 | 1.0 |

(b) types of vehicle

| Vehicle | 1976 | | 1987 | | Percentage change 1975–87 |
|---|---|---|---|---|---|
| | *m.* | Percentage | *m.* | Percentage | |
| Private cars and light goods | 14.9 | 85.1 | 19.2 | 86.9 | +29 |
| Buses, coaches, taxis | 0.1 | 0.6 | 0.1 | 0.5 | – |
| Heavy goods | 0.7 | 4.0 | 0.6 | 2.7 | −16 |
| Others | 1.8 | 10.3 | 2.2 | 9.9 | +22 |
| Total | 17.5 | 100 | 22.1 | 100 | +26 |

(c) traffic distribution (percentage)

| | *1977* | *1987* | *Percentage change in absolute amount of traffic 1977–87* |
|---|---|---|---|
| Urban roads | 50.1 | 43.2 | +22 |
| Rural roads | 39.6 | 41.5 | +56 |
| Motorways | 10.3 | 15.3 | +108 |

*Source;* Transport Statistics, Great Britain

more journeys are now concentrated upon the motorways (table 7.5). The fleet of lighter commercial vehicles has risen from 700,000 to 12 million in this period and the total distance travelled by all freight trucks is also greater, reflecting increased lengths of haul caused by changing distribution patterns within the manufacturing and service sectors, and in particular by the rationalization of wholesale consumer good depots and warehouses.

Personal travel by non-public transport continues to grow at the expense of bus and coach services, a 44 per cent rise in passenger-kms accomplished by cars and taxis being accompanied by a 34 per cent fall in bus and coach

*Table 7.5* Changes in commercial road traffic in Great Britain

| Year | Heavy goods Vehicles 000 m. vehicle-kms | As percentage of all traffic | Light commercial Vehicles 000 m. vehicle-kms | As percentage of all traffic |
|------|------|------|------|------|
| 1965 | 18.20 | 11 | 18.09 | 11 |
| 1970 | 18.90 | 9 | 18.90 | 9 |
| 1975 | 19.93 | 8 | 21.20 | 8 |
| 1980 | 21.02 | 8 | 22.11 | 8 |
| 1985 | 21.48 | 8 | 23.23 | 8 |
| 1987 | 23.61 | 7 | 26.67 | 8 |

*Source:* Transport Statistics, Great Britain

traffic from 1975 to 1986. However, despite this decline there has been a resurgence of long-distance scheduled coach services as a result of the 1980 and 1985 Transport Acts which created a much greater competitive environment for such traffic. Coach travel between London, Glasgow and other cities cannot compete with rail on a time basis but fares are very much lower and a flourishing market has evolved; for journeys in excess of 25 miles almost as many people now travel by coach or bus as by rail and domestic airways combined. For business journeys, however, 60 per cent of travel is by car and 30 per cent by rail. Under the provisions of the 1985 Act the National Bus Company, first created as a state undertaking by the 1968 Act, was finally sold off in separate units by May 1988, although its National Express coach subsidiary has survived as an independent company.

Beyond this inter-city network of express coaches the future of public passenger transport on rural roads is becoming an increasingly problematic issue. With the spread of car ownership, falling patronage has resulted in a continuous erosion of conventional stage-carriage bus services since the early 1960s, and although deregulation of the bus industry in 1986 was designed to promote competition and eventually lower fare levels it was recognized that rural operators face special difficulties. A transitional rural bus grant was payable for four years to operators to guarantee some level of service but with the expiry of this subsidy the position will become critical in many areas. Greater flexibility of public transport has been achieved to some extent with the introduction of services and vehicles designed to meet more appropriately the needs of the non-car owning elements in the rural population. Multi-purpose vehicles, as typified by the postbus, social car schemes for essential journeys and community-run minibuses, often with county council financial support, are now in widespread operation although their collective contribution to rural mobility is still only very modest and the car remains the dominant medium, especially for journeys to work.

As with the railways there are indications that future road-building will involve private capital on an increasing scale. During 1988 the Department of Transport invited proposals from contractors to contribute to new road projects, based on a leasing system and toll charges. The first major scheme to be privately financed in this way is the Thames Bridge at Dartford, designed to alleviate congestion in the M25 tunnel. Construction began in 1988 and costs are being partially met by toll revenue from the Dartford Tunnel, which the bridge company has leased from the government for a twenty-year period. Proposals for increasing the capacity of the M25 with an upper road deck, for a second Severn Bridge, and for a road tunnel under the Thames from Chiswick in the west to Blackwall in the Docklands have all been advanced on the basis of private investment but none have been accepted to date.

In mid-1988, however, the House of Commons Transport Select Committee called for a fundamental review of public transport funding, with special emphasis on the need for additional trunk road capacity, a call to which the government responded in May 1989. Unless more resources are made available from the public sector it is likely that a greater involvement of private investors will be required to meet the needs for transport improvements.

## URBAN TRANSPORT

During the 1980s road traffic congestion has continued as one of the most serious problems within urban areas but many of the recent policies adopted to combat this situation represent a change from those of previous decades. Official recognition of the inability of urban road systems to cope with rapidly increasing traffic volumes came in 1963 with publication of the *Traffic in Towns* report, containing its controversial call for motorway networks in major British cities. This generated rigorous opposition on both environmental and financial grounds and although urban expressways were subsequently built in many cities construction generally has not been on the scale originally envisaged. The report's second recommendation, that transportation plans be accepted as essential elements in urban development programmes, was adopted and embodied in current legislation for county and district councils, which are now required to submit transport policy and programme documents to central government at regular intervals.

Although the percentage of all traffic using urban roads fell slightly from 1977 to 1987 (table 7.4), the absolute amount increased by 22 per cent and in major cities average speeds have not altered significantly in the last twenty years despite the massive investment in road improvements. In inner London, for example, the average speed on local roads is only 16 m.p.h in peak periods and on urban motorways and trunk roads between 20 and 22 m.p.h.

Plans to alleviate urban transport problems concentrate on the three

ated issues of general road congestion, the particular difficulties gener-
d by road-borne daily commuter traffic, and, with few exceptions, the
continued decline in patronage of public transport services.

Between the mid-1960s and 1980 expressways were built in London,
Birmingham, Glasgow, Newcastle and other major cities, with tunnelling
for estuarine crossings in Merseyside, Clydeside and Tyneside. Spiralling
land acquisition and road construction costs modified the original road
plans in these major centres and it was accepted that further encouragement
of private car usage by providing additional capacity was not always
necessarily the most logical or effective contribution towards achieving an
efficient system of urban circulation. Many authorities turned instead
towards a reappraisal of public transport facilities, with the particular
objective of attracting car-borne commuters back to bus and train services,
and an opportunity to secure these aims came in the 1970s with the
formation, under the 1968 Transport Act, of Passenger Transport Authorities (PTA) and Executives (PTE) in each of the English Metropolitan
Counties and Strathclyde. These bodies were charged with establishing and
maintaining an integrated and efficient system of all public road and rail
transport services within their boundaries, with the PTA responsible for
policy and the PTE being responsible for its execution.

Many of the recent improvements in public transport in British conurbations are due to the efforts of these organizations but their powers were
drastically reduced in 1986 with the abolition of the Metropolitan County
Councils and the privatization and deregulation of the bus industry, which
was intended to promote a competitive operating environment with lower
fares, thus attracting more patronage. Substitution of this free market
policy for that of coordination under the PTAs was also accompanied by a
withdrawal of the large subsidies payable by central government to
conurbation transport undertakings. One result of bus deregulation has
been the very rapid spread of the minibus and similar vehicles, with
capacities of sixteen to twenty-five passengers, as a noted element in urban
bus operations. These vehicles are operated at higher frequencies than
conventional buses and can penetrate housing estates and negotiate inner-
urban areas more easily. Since their introduction in Exeter in 1984,
minibus usage has spread to at least 400 urban areas in Britain and the
5,600 vehicles currently available account for about 15 per cent of the
urban bus fleet.

The achievements of the PTAs and PTEs varied according to local
authority policy and the character of existing transport infrastruture. In
conurbations where a surface rail network was available but had become
under-used because of inadequate or out-dated equipment, investments
were made in new high-speed electric trains and in schemes to integrate rail
routes more effectively with bus services, private car parks and major
shopping and employment centres (figure 7.3). The most ambitious scheme
to be completed was the Tyne and Wear Metro, incorporating 43 kms of

existing British Rail lines north and south of the Tyne and 13 kms of new track, much of it in tunnel in central Newcastle. Substantial financial aid from the government and the EEC was obtained and the system opened in 1984 with four major Metro-bus-car interchanges and park-and-ride facilities at many of the suburban stations. It is seen as a vital tool in the task of revitalizing the local economy, particularly by improving labour mobility.

Greater Glasgow also embarked upon an extensive programme of city and suburban rail modernization, including the complete re-equipment of the Underground loop, which dates from 1897, and electrification of many surface railways. A connection between the suburban networks north and south of the Clyde has been made with the electrification of the Argyle line through Glasgow Central Station, and the coastal route to Ayr and Largs, serving many commuter settlements, was electrified in 1982. The Strathclyde suburban rail system, which is the most extensive in Britain outside London, now has 330 of its 1,000 route kms electrified, with twenty major rail/bus interchanges and twenty park-and-ride stations.

On Merseyside, where Liverpool is served by several radial railways and by the Wirral peninsula system linked by tunnel to the city centre, suburban electric services to Ormskirk, Southport and other commuter towns were already established by the early 1970s. Interchanges in central Liverpool between the various rail termini were inadequate, however, and in 1977 a new loop was opened connecting the Wirral lines with the major stations. This integrated rail network was adopted by the PTA as the nucleus of its public transport system and, as in Tyneside and Strathclyde, bus interchanges and additional car parks were provided at many suburban stations.

Elsewhere there have been only limited improvements in conurbation rail networks but in London the Docklands Light Railway (DLR) represents the first introduction of light rapid transit to the capital. The DLR is an innovative addition to the established Underground and British Rail networks but its significance also lies in its role as a spearhead for economic and social revitalization of the former London dockland area under the London Docklands Development Corporation. Stage One, connecting the Tower of London with the Isle of Dogs and Stratford, was opened in 1987, a link to the Bank is under construction, and an eastward extension has been sanctioned.

Underground traffic in London rose by 60 per cent between 1983 and 1988, revealing the inadequacies of many parts of the system there, and a modernization scheme for the heavily congested Central Line has been agreed. New lines are urgently required to serve the growing commercial centres at Kings Cross and in the docklands, to improve cross-Thames services, and to cater for increased traffic at London's airports and, after 1993, at Channel Tunnel rail termini. Plans for a twenty-year improvement programme were submitted in late 1988 and these new routes will be the first since completion of the Victoria Line and the central section of the Jubilee Line in the 1970s.

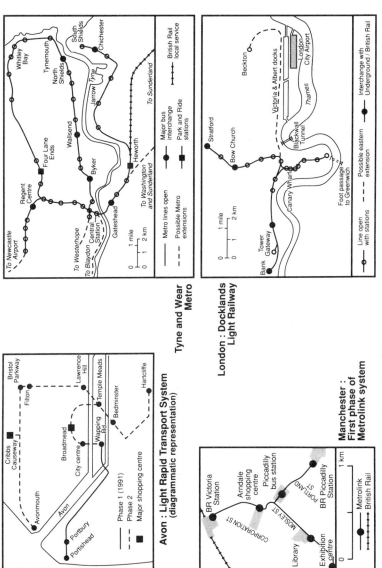

**Avon : Light Rapid Transport System**
**(diagrammatic representation)**

**Tyne and Wear**
**Metro**

**London : Docklands**
**Light Railway**

**Manchester :**
**First phase of**
**Metrolink system**

*Figure* 7.3 Light rail transport in major cities

In Greater Manchester the Metrolink, making use of existing British Rail track and roads in the city centre, is now being built as a light rapid transit system to connect the major rail stations with the Piccadilly bus station and the Arndale shopping complex, with extensions to Bury and Altrincham. The line should be open by 1991 and by that date progress on similar light rapid transit schemes in Birmingham, Sheffield and Bristol is likely to be well-advanced. Leeds, Southampton and Portsmouth also have schemes under consideration and the growth of this transport mode in Britain is in line with its already widespread adoption in European cities.

The former South Yorkshire PTA decided in 1974 to pursue a strategy based upon local subsidies designed to keep fares on public bus and rail services within its area at a low level. It was hoped that this course of action would reduce congestion caused by private cars, especially at peak periods, and increase the mobility of those without access to cars, principally members of low-income households. The subsidies survived until the 1986 abolition of the metropolitan County Councils, when fares were increased very substantially. Attempts by other authorities, notably the Greater London Council, to pursue similar actions were successfully challenged in the courts in the early 1980s, and a subsequent White Paper on public transport subsidies attempted to establish guidelines for those local authorities which considered that subsidized public transport was a more effective means of securing additional patronage than investment in new rail routes or modernization.

## AIR TRAFFIC AND AIRPORT LOCATION

By 1987 passengers on international services using British airports had increased to 90 million and those on domestic flights to 9 million, and the recent progress in airport planning and improvements may be contrasted with previous decades of inaction and indecision during a period of rising congestion at many London air terminals. During the period 1976–87 the largest rises in traffic were at Gatwick (238 per cent), Manchester (207 per cent), East Midlands (160 per cent) and Newcastle (116 per cent), although the group of London airports recorded the highest aggregate increase at 24 millions (table 7.6).

Non-scheduled flights, operated by independent airlines closely associated with the major holiday travel companies, have continued to grow in importance and in 1986 accounted for 38 per cent of all airport traffic, compared with 29 per cent in 1976. Domestic traffic doubled in the 1976–86 period but still only represents less than 1 per cent of all inland passenger travel and its proportion, at 36 per cent of all scheduled airline bookings, remains unchanged. Forecasts of between 114 and 169 million air passengers by the year 2000 have been made by the Department of Transport and it is probable that about 70 per cent of this traffic will be handled in the south-east, adding further to existing congestion despite positive moves in the 1980s to alleviate the situation.

*Table 7.6* Changes in air traffic
(a) Scheduled services operated by United Kingdom airlines

| Year | Passengers (m.) | | Freight (000 tonnes) | |
|------|-----------------------|---------------------|-----------------------|---------------------|
| | *International services* | *Domestic services* | *International services* | *Domestic services* |
| 1965 | 6  | 4  | 241 | 54 |
| 1970 | 8  | 5  | 204 | 64 |
| 1975 | 11 | 6  | 199 | 47 |
| 1980 | 15 | 7  | 264 | 31 |
| 1985 | 16 | 9  | 313 | 46 |
| 1987 | 18 | 10 | 354 | 51 |

(b) Traffic at major airports (m. arrivals and departures)

| Airport | 1976 | 1987 | Percentage increase |
|---------|------|------|---------------------|
| Heathrow | 23.2 | 34.7 | 50 |
| Gatwick | 5.7 | 19.3 | 238 |
| Manchester | 2.8 | 8.6 | 207 |
| Glasgow | 2.0 | 3.4 | 70 |
| Birmingham | 1.1 | 2.6 | 136 |
| Luton | 1.8 | 2.6 | 44 |
| Belfast | 1.1 | 2.1 | 91 |
| Edinburgh | 1.0 | 1.8 | 80 |
| Aberdeen | 0.8 | 1.5 | 87 |
| Newcastle | 0.6 | 1.3 | 116 |
| East midlands | 0.5 | 1.3 | 160 |

*Source*: Transport Statistics, Great Britain

The contemporary pattern of domestic routes is dominated by trunk services linking London, Manchester, Glasgow, Edinburgh and Belfast, with substantial traffic increases following the 1975 introduction of non-booking 'shuttle services'. Regional services between major provincial airports and routes linking those with holiday destinations such as the Channel Islands form an important secondary element, although many routes are seasonal. Finally there are localized networks, of which that serving the Scottish highlands and islands is the most important: flights are shared between British Airways and private operators, with the greatest expansion of traffic at Aberdeen and Sumburgh (Shetland) in association with North Sea oil and gas extraction.

Providing a solution to the problems created by continuing large increases in traffic at airports in the London region has proved a controversial issue since the early 1960s. Selection of the former military airfield at Stansted, 51 kms north of London, was vigorously contested then on environmental grounds and the Roskill Commission's choice in 1971 of Cublington, near Aylesbury, as an alternative site was not unanimous but accompanied by a minority report favouring Foulness on the Thames

estuary. Although the latter recommendation found government acceptance the project was abandoned in 1974 and it was not until 1983 that the
problem of securing additional capacity in the south-east was finally
resolved with confirmation of Stansted, which currently handles 0.7 million
passengers a year, as the site for London's third major airport. An eventual
maximum annual throughput there of 15 million passengers is envisaged
which, combined with facilities at Heathrow and Gatwick, will raise the
total capacity of the major London airports to 79 million by 1995.
Additional terminals have recently been provided at Heathrow (1986) and
Gatwick (1988) and Luton and Manchester have also been enlarged, with
the latter designated as Britain's major international terminal outside the
London area by the 1977 Airports White Paper. At present Manchester
Airport is only accessible by road but plans are now advanced for a rail link
to connect it with the national inter-city network. The opening in late 1987
of the London City Airport in the docklands, just 11 kms from the city,
represents a new approach to international air travel, with short take-off
and landing (STOL) aircraft on routes to Brussels and Paris. Public
transport access is limited but improvements, possibly by an extension of
the Docklands Light Railway, will be considerably cheaper than the
Paddington Station-Heathrow Airport electrified rail link which is to cost
£190 million.

## SEAPORTS AND INTERNATIONAL TRADE

Trade patterns at British seaports during the 1980s continued to reflect the
growing emphasis upon EC nations which followed the entry into the
Common Market in 1973, and by 1986 62 per cent of all exports (by
tonnage) and 36 per cent of all imports involved member-states. Furthermore, there has been a substantial increase in near- and short-sea trading
with all European markets, which in aggregate accounts for 70 per cent of
all seaport traffic and has had a substantial influence on the relative
distribution of trade between east coast and west coast ports.

One new and important trend can be traced in bulk fuel exports, which
from 1980 have grown to exceed imports and by 1987 imports of foreign
crude oil had fallen to 30 million tonnes, whereas exports of crude oil from
the United Kingdom were 77.7 million tonnes (table 7.7). This situation
has arisen through continuing exploitation of the North Sea oil supplies
and largely contributes to the fact that bulk fuel now represents two-thirds
by tonnage of all British exports, a proportion also recorded in previous
decades but then mainly as a result of coal trade rather than petroleum.
Whereas before 1979 much oil from the North Sea fields was shipped
directly from well-heads to overseas markets the pattern has changed since
1980 and supplies are now piped to British terminals for subsequent
distribution. The shift since the mid-1970s in the source of much of our
crude oil from the Middle East to the North Sea has affected many

individual ports, with a rise in traffic at east coast terminals, such as Grimsby-Immingham, Tees-Hartlepool and the Forth ports, and a decline in tonnage handled at London and the Medway ports (figure 7.4). Petroleum continues to dominate British seaborne trade, however, and is still the leading commodity by tonnage at nine out of the thirty-seven ports handling over 0.5 million tonnes in 1986. Established oil terminals at Milford Haven, on the Medway, the Clyde estuary and on Anglesey continue to flourish, although tonnages have fallen since 1976, but the major development of the 1980s has been the expansion of Sullom Voe in north Shetland. This is now the principal centre for North Sea oil distribution and in 1987 recorded a greater tonnage (50 million) than any other British port.

*Table 7.7* Changes in international trade of Great Britain
(a) Imports and exports (m. tonnes)

| Year | Imports Non-fuel | Fuel | Total | Exports Non-fuel | Fuel | Total |
|------|---------|------|-------|----------|------|-------|
| 1965 | 69.6 | 83.8 | 153.4 | 20.0 | 15.7 | 35.7 |
| 1970 | 74.3 | 121.8 | 196.1 | 24.9 | 23.1 | 48.0 |
| 1975 | 67.9 | 107.4 | 175.3 | 29.4 | 20.8 | 50.2 |
| 1980 | 67.5 | 63.7 | 131.2 | 37.3 | 79.8 | 117.1 |
| 1985 | 82.6 | 58.6 | 141.2 | 44.7 | 103.1 | 147.8 |
| 1986 | 85.7 | 61.8 | 147.5 | 48.5 | 101.9 | 150.4 |
| 1987 | 94.2 | 58.7 | 152.9 | 50.0 | 100.1 | 150.1 |

(b) Traffic composition (m. tonnes)

| Type of traffic | 1965 | 1975 | 1987 |
|-----------------|------|------|------|
| Bulk fuel | 99.55 | 128.22 | 158.92 |
| Other bulk cargo | 48.16 | 46.91 | 61.88 |
| Container and roll-on/roll-off | 2.80 | 24.96 | 57.52 |
| All other cargo | 38.60 | 25.42 | 24.75 |
| Total foreign traffic | 189.12 | 225.52 | 303.09 |

*Sources*: National Ports Council: Annual Digests of Port Statistics; British Ports Federation: Port Statistics

By 1987 foreign freight traffic at British seaports had risen to 303 million tonnes, and although exports have increased steadily since the late 1970s imports continue below the levels of the decade 1970–80. Domestic seaborne trade, at 153.6 million tonnes in 1987, has also declined since the early 1980s and bulk freight still accounts for 70 per cent of the total.

These changes are reflected in many different ways at individual ports, and of the twenty-one ports and port groups handling over 1 million tonnes in 1976 twelve recorded a lesser total in 1986. Apart from the oil terminals the list includes the general cargo ports of London, Southampton,

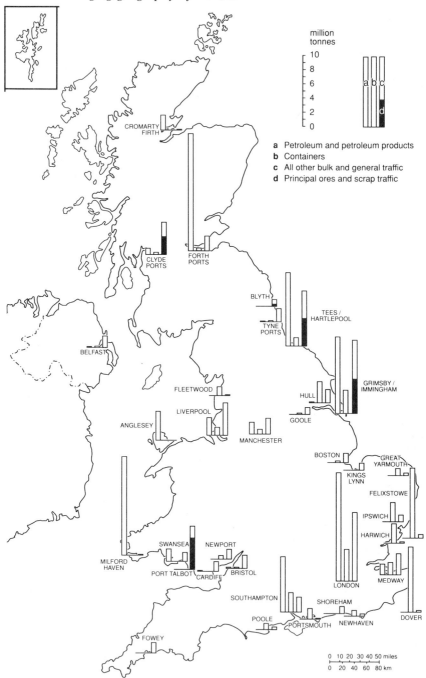

million tonnes

a  Petroleum and petroleum products
b  Containers
c  All other bulk and general traffic
d  Principal ores and scrap traffic

*Figure 7.4* Traffic at major ports 1986
*Source:* National Ports Council Report for 1986

Liverpool, Manchester, Bristol, Hull and Goole, with the greatest declines at Liverpool (60 per cent) and Manchester (48 per cent) as oceanic trade decreases.

As in the previous decade the most substantial traffic growth, and much of the investment in new facilities, has been concentrated upon ports adapted to or created for the unitized freight trade. Whereas in 1965 over 50 per cent of all general cargo was handled conventionally in small units this proportion had fallen to less than 4 per cent by 1986 as a result of the expansion of containerization. Between 1970 and 1986 container traffic, in terms of units (i.e. boxes), rose by 41 per cent but with the widespread adoption of the larger 12m container and a higher average load within each box the actual amount of freight handled by this mode more than doubled over this period and by 1987 exceeded 57 million tonnes in the foreign sector and 7.5 million tonnes on domestic coastwise routes.

Container lift-on/lift-off cranage is now available at over twenty ports and deals with one-half of all large international containers as opposed to one-quarter in 1975. Although the main impetus to containerization in Britain occurred in the 1970s some deep-sea shipping services only adopted the system in the early 1980s and as a result this long-distance traffic has increased three-fold since 1970. London (Tilbury), Southampton, Liverpool (Seaforth dock) and Hull are the principal ports to benefit from this expansion in the unitized deep-sea trade and as a group now handle one-fifth of all international container traffic by tonnage.

These increases in long-distance container traffic are however completely overshadowed by those recorded in ports whose chief concern is the Western European trade. The locational advantages enjoyed by British east and south coast ports over their western counterparts in respect of short-sea traffic have continued to be exploited in the 1980s and it is in these terminals that investment has been largely concentrated. Both roll-on/roll-off and lift-on/lift-off methods of container handling are employed and by 1986 the south-eastern ports between the Tyne and Portsmouth dealt with 84 per cent of all containers, with the larger part of this being associated with European markets. The East Anglian ports, notably Felixstowe and Harwich, now account for 28 per cent of national container traffic and increased their trade by 123 per cent in the 1976–86 decade. In 1987 Felixstowe recorded a total container throughput of almost 12 million tonnes, compared with 10.1 million at its closest rival Dover, and its pre-eminence in the unitized freight trade has been achieved almost entirely by a private harbour undertaking which specializes in short-sea container ferry services to Zeebrugge and neighbouring ports. The Trinity terminal, opened in late 1986, provided additional berths and storage facilities and further expansion is under way to cope with both roll-on/roll-off and lift-on/lift-off container trade. In contrast all container traffic at Dover is carried by road vehicles though railborne freight is still important, with completion in 1987 of a new train–ferry berth. Portsmouth also emerged in the 1980s as a leading south coast participant with a new ferry terminal for container lorries.

The dominance of road transport in hinterland movements is underlined by the fact that over forty United Kingdom ports are now equipped with roll-on/roll-off berths for conventional trucks, container lorries, new vehicle imports and exports (Southampton, Leith) and for the lucrative passenger-accompanied holiday car traffic. This latter, although still largely concentrated on the short-sea routes linking Dover and Folkestone with Boulogne and Calais, has now extended westwards to involve Portsmouth, Poole and Plymouth.

Total carryings of cars in the cross-Channel tourist sector have increased by 20 per cent since 1980 and of the 2.4 million vehicles shipped in 1987 over 60 per cent used Dover. Tourist travel by coach through Channel ports has also increased substantially since 1980 and seaborne passenger traffic to Europe, both by car and public transport, still accounts for about one-third of all travel to the continent and Mediterranean coastlands.

These developments in unitized traffic at ports with English Channel and North Sea crossings contrast with stagnation or decline at larger terminals such as Liverpool with their traditional emphasis upon deep-sea trading. Liverpool in particular has seen its share of British deep-sea tonnage fall from 25 per cent in 1966 to less than 3 per cent in 1986, with an overall decline of 60 per cent in port traffic in the 1976–86 period. Its current (1987) container trade is only 14 per cent of all trade and any substantial increase in unitized freight handling depends upon the economics of ship operation, since a diversion to Liverpool from the direct United States east coast to north-west Europe shipping route would require a guarantee of a much higher number of containers than is at present available. It is hoped, however, that Liverpool's free port status acquired in 1985 should encourage some maritime trade revival.

In recent years there has been an upturn in the fortunes of Britain's smaller ports, such as those on the rivers Ouse, Trent and Humber which have experienced a 50 per cent traffic increase since 1965. These ports, which specialize in grain, fertilizers, animal feedstuffs, timber and fuels, serve localized hinterlands and have the advantages of low terminal costs, non-dock scheme labour (prior to 1989, when the dock labour scheme was abolished for all ports) and the use of new bulk cargo vessels of up to 4.500 tonnes which, like their larger counterparts, concentrate upon the near-sea European market. Installation of roll-on/roll-off ramps is relatively cheap and smaller coastal ports such as Ramsgate, Poole and Great Yarmouth have increased trade over the 1976–86 period by up to 124 per cent. One problem which is still encountered by the majority of ports dependent upon road transport, is the inadequacy of hinterland road links and, of the major terminals, only Liverpool, Hull, Bristol and Southampton have direct access to the motorway network. Although the route through East Anglia linking Felixstowe and Harwich with the M1 has been improved and upgraded over much of its length, severe congestion is still frequently encountered on many sections.

## CONCLUSIONS

Within the transport sector the 1980s saw the completion of several development programmes, the resolution of problems dating from previous decades and also the initiation of a number of new policies whose effects cannot yet be fully evaluated. The basic motorway network is now complete with the exception of the M40 extension, electrification of the east coast trunk railway is well advanced, and the opening of light rapid transit systems in Tyne and Wear and in London's dockland represent a continuation of improvement programmes for urban public transport first promoted in the 1970s.

The dominant feature of the 1980s, however, was the introduction of policies designed to transfer much of the public sector road and rail interests to private enterprise and to encourage, as an associated objective, a much higher level of competition within the transport industry, especially in urban areas. To this end there has been a steady reduction in state financial subsidies for road and rail operations and a severe pruning of expenditure on transport infrastructure, with strong indications that future major projects will involve both private and public funding. One already apparent result of these recent economies is that much of the motorway and trunk road network is no longer capable of meeting traffic demands and the 1989 new road proposals are to be welcomed as a positive step to counter this congestion.

Completion of the London-Leeds-Edinburgh railway electrification will attract traffic now carried on domestic airways and it is likely that many regional airports will seek to acquire a greater range of international services, reducing to some extent the pressure on the London terminals. With the final resolution of the long-standing problem of selecting a location for London's Third Airport, planning for the increase in national air traffic can proceed on a firmer basis.

The introduction of a competitive element into the bus industry is designed to secure lower fares and attract car drivers who in urban areas are facing rising levels of traffic congestion. To date it is difficult to evaluate the success of the bus deregulation and privatization provisions of the 1985 Act, but in many major cities the services formerly operated by the PTEs or the National Bus Company still remain the dominant carriers and competition from new undertakings is limited.

Overshadowing these national trends and policies is the European dimension and the association of the United Kingdom by 1992 with an agreed EC transport policy which aims to minimize regulatory powers and create an efficient transport system coordinated to meet the needs of all member-states. Britain's involvement in this common policy will be greatly strengthened in 1993 with completion of the Channel Tunnel; the establishment of through rail services, coupled with a substantial reduction in transit times for road vehicles, will produce significant changes in the geography of passenger and freight movements between Britain and the continent, particularly in respect of modal shares of traffic.

The importance of transport as an agent of regional development is underlined by the analysis of the implications of these changes and by the necessity to provide improved links between the Tunnel, midland and northern Britain. There is concern that the new link will further reinforce the existing economic advantages of the south-east at the expense of peripheral Britain rather than enabling all regions to participate more fully in trade with EC members and the final outcome will depend to a large extent upon how successfully the internal transport infrastructure can be adapted to benefit from the opportunities associated with the Channel Tunnel.

## REFERENCES

Works, legislation and government White Papers cited:

Department of Transport (1955) *Plan for the Modernization of British Railways*, London: HMSO.

Department of Transport (1963, 1965) *The Re-shaping of British Railways, Parts I and II* (Beeching Report), London: HMSO.

Department of Transport (1968) *Transport Act*, London: HMSO.

Department of Transport (1969) *Roads for the Future*, London: HMSO.

Department of Transport (1971) Report of the Commission on the Third London Airport (Roskill Report), London: HMSO.

Department of Transport (1977) *Transport Policy*, London: HMSO.

Department of Transport (1977) Report of the Advisory Committee on Trunk Road Assessment (Leitch Report) London: HMSO.

Department of Transport (1978) *Airports Policy*, London: HMSO.

Department of Transport (1980) *Transport Act*, London: HMSO.

Department of Transport (1983) *Railway Finances* (the Serpell Report), London: HMSO.

Department of Transport (1984) *Buses*, London: HMSO.

Department of Transport (1985) *Transport Act*, London: HMSO.

Department of Transport (1985) *Airport Policy*, London: HMSO.

The Civic Trust (1979) *Heavy Lorries: nine years on*, London.

## FURTHER READING

Banister, D. and Hall, P. (eds.) (1981) *Transport and Public Policy Planning*, London: Mansell.

Buchanan, C. D., *Traffic in Towns* (1963) London: Penguin

Cloke P. (ed.) (1985) *Rural Accessibility and Mobility*, Lampeter.

Damesick, P. J., *et al.* (1986) 'M.25 – a new geography of development?' *Geographical Journal*, 150/2.

Fullerton, B. (1982) 'Transport', chapter 5 in House, J. W. (ed.) *The U.K. Space* Third Edition.

Hilling, D. (1984) 'The Restructuring of the Severn Estuary Ports', chapter 13 in

Hoyle, B. S. and Hilling, D. (eds.) *Seaport Systems and Spatial Change*, Chichester.

Knowles, R. (ed.) (1985) *Implications of the 1985 Transport Bill*, Transport Geography Study Group, Institute of British Geographers.

Maltby, D. and White, H. P. (1982) *Transport in the United Kingdom*, London.

Moseley, M. J. (1979) *Accessibility – the Rural Challenge*, London.

Sealey, K. R. (1976) *Airport Stategy and Planning*, London: Oxford University Press.

Tolley, R. S. and Turton, B. J. (1981) *Short-sea crossings and the Channel Tunnel* Transport Geography Study Group, Institute of British Geographers.

Turton, B. J. (ed.) (1983) *Public Issues in Transport* Transport Geography Study Group, Insititute of British Geographers.

Williams, A. F. (ed.) (1985) *Rapid Transit Systems in the UK*, Transport Geography Study Group, Institute of British Geographers.

# 8 The changing geography of manufacturing activity

*Paul A. Bull*

The manufacturing sector of the United Kingdom is a constantly evolving part of the nation's economy. Often this evolution is slow and incremental, taking many years to produce any significant change. However, such gradual long-term trends may be broken by sudden and dramatic events, when a major break with the past takes place: i.e. when, in a short period of time, new industries and new forms of business organization and control requiring new locations begin to replace what existed before. It is possible that the late 1970s and early 1980s may have been one such period of major economic transformation. An attempt to evaluate such a suggestion will form one of the important lines of argument of this chapter. However, in order to bring the events of this time into sharper relief, the last twenty-five to thirty years will also be briefly reviewed.

The late 1970s and early 1980s were characterized by a number of major economic traumas: high inflation during the 1970s, a major rise in the price of oil in 1979 following quickly on the heels of an earlier rise in 1973, and two periods of recession focused on 1974–5 and 1980–2 – the latter was the most severe since the 1930s. These events hit the manufacturing sector of the United Kingdom very hard indeed. For example, in just two years between 1979 and 1981, over 1 million industrial jobs were lost. For the first time since the Industrial Revolution the country's balance of payments in manufactured goods went into the red (from 1983). In addition the events helped to expose the uncompetitive nature of much of the UK's manufacturing activity, resulting often in firms carrying out dramatic restructuring programmes to maintain profitability. For a substantial number this necessitated extensive capacity cut-backs and the adoption of more automated forms of production. For other larger firms it necessitated investment overseas as well as rationalization at 'home'. Indeed, between 1979–86 the country's forty largest manufacturing companies reduced their employment in Britain by 415,000 while increasing employment abroad by 125,000.

At the same time, and of a more positive nature, new industries based on the manufacture and use of high technology products started to emerge and a change in the organization of production began to take place. The latter involved the use of flexible small-batch production systems, often in small firms, producing customized goods for an increasingly sophisticated and affluent clientele. Both these developments began to generate new locational patterns of industrial activity in the United Kingdom when much of the rest of the manufacturing sector was in serious decline. Furthermore, following the election of a Conservative government in 1979, which has remained in power throughout the 1980s, major policy changes took place towards the British economy in general and towards manufacturing in particular. The former marked a shift away from Keynesian demand management to an explicit supply-side monetarist stance in an attempt to control inflation. The latter had two important dimensions: first, a reduction in government financial support for industry on the alleged grounds of the inefficiency of most previous aid schemes, especially with respect to the nationalized industries and regional policy, and second, a widening of the remaining assistance to include much of the service sector as well as manufacturing.

All these changes helped to change the geography of manufacturing activity in the United Kingdom during the 1970s and 1980s. The degree to which this may be regarded as a major transformation will be assessed in the following pages. In addition, this chapter will place a great deal of emphasis on understanding the powerful forces at work shaping the changing locational distribution of manufacturing activity during this most recent of time periods, contrasting, where possible, the period of deep economic recession straddling the turn of the decade from the 1970s to the 1980s with what went before and with what followed. The chapter begins with a discussion of aggregate change in the manufacturing sector since 1950, proceeds to an analysis of locational change at the regional and subregional scales, and concludes with a review of the important organizations – namely manufacturing firms and central government – whose decisions were directly responsible for these events.

The analysis which follows is of course dependent on available empirical data. At the scale of the UK as a whole a number of different indices of change, usually of an annual nature, can be calculated from official government statistics. Unfortunately, as scale increases, data availability from these sources declines. At the regional scale only employment figures can be obtained in any temporally consistent and disaggregated form, along with some limited output information. At the subregional scale of the UK counties only employment data are regularly forthcoming, usually many years out of date by the time they eventually become publicly available when published in *Regional Trends*. This information originates from the Census of Employment, the last three of which were undertaken in 1981, 1984 and 1987. Unfortunately at the time of writing the 1987 data had not yet been published at the subregional scale. As a result, an important temporal limitation is placed on the following discussion. Industrial information for small areas may also be obtained from private, research and local authority surveys. Partly because of their expense and time-consuming nature, few have been undertaken in the United Kingdom in the post-1980 era. A further limitation of the following discussion stems from the introduction of a new Standard Industrial Classification (SIC) in 1980 to be used in all subsequent official UK statistics. This new 1980 SIC defined manufacturing activity in a slightly broader way than had hitherto been the case. In a comparative analysis of employees in employment in 1983, the 1980 SIC encompassed 3.6 per cent more jobs than the former 1968 SIC. Although total GB employment estimates for the manufacturing sector are available for the whole of this study period using the 1980 SIC, regional and subregional estimates are not; they are only available from 1981. Thus the first part of the spatial analysis in this paper uses the 1968 SIC definition of manufacturing activity and the latter part the 1980 SIC.

**AGGREGATE TRENDS**

Figure 8.1 shows trends in three important aggregate indices of the size of the manufacturing sector between 1950 and 1988. From this it can be seen than employment in manufacturing grew steadily until 1966, when a peak of over 8.5 million jobs was achieved. From then the trend is almost unrelentingly downward with a major acceleration in the rate of decline after 1979. Indeed in 1980–1 alone more than 10 per cent of all manufacturing jobs were lost. By 1986–7, however, when the number employed stood at approximately 5 million, the annual rate of decline had reduced substantially to just over 1 per cent. In the late 1970s and especially in the early 1980s, therefore, a major break with the past took place in terms of the number of people employed in manufacturing. Whether the recorded levels of employment of the 1960s will ever be achieved again is unknown. But as pointed out below there is a number of very persuasive reasons why this almost certainly will not be the case.

One of these reasons concerns recent trends in output and investment (figure 8.1). During the 1950s and 1960s, excepting occasional interruptions corresponding to minor recessions in the national economy, these were clearly upward. During the 1970s a levelling off, or slowdown, took place followed by a major downswing between 1979 and 1981. Output fell by 17 per cent and capital investment by over 30 per cent during this time, compared, with a smaller decline of 16 per cent in employment. However, unlike employment, output and investment made strong recoveries from 1982–3 onwards. Three important and closely related conclusions can be derived from these observations. First, the manufacturing sector has recently been characterized by two important phases of *jobless growth*, the first during the late 1960s and early 1970s and the second and more dramatic period after 1982. Second, although British manufacturing may be showing signs of recovery from the recession of the early 1980s in output and investment, this recovery has as yet made no net contribution to

Indices : 1980 = 100

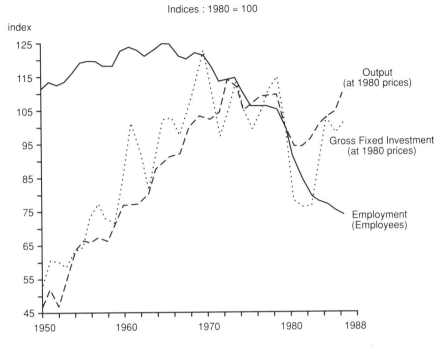

*Figure 8.1* Employment, output, and investment, in the UK manufacturing sector, 1950–87
*Source:* Martin 1988
*Note:* Employment measured at mid-year. Output and investment measured as annual totals

reducing unemployment. Third, by the last quarter of the 1980s output levels equivalent to the mid-1970s were being achieved with a significantly smaller workforce. All of these trends do not augur well for the take-up of jobs in the future, even if output and investment in the sector continue to grow. This is also strong evidence to support the view that a major change in the character of manufacturing in the United Kngdom was indeed taking place.

There are a number of possible inter-meshing reasons for these trends in employment and output. During periods of severe international economic recession, such as the late 1970s and early 1980s, one would expect a decline in national output and employment as aggregate demand for manufactured goods contracted globally. This may help to account for some of the observed decline in the manufacturing sector at the end of the 1970s. However, in this case such a trend was superimposed on an already established position of general competitive weakness and low profitability by international standards which had led to a steady loss of employment, or deindustrialization, since the mid-1960s. In addition, as we shall see below, it was coincident in time with the deflationary policies of the UK government. As a result, the impact of recession on the UK manufacturing sector in terms of output and employment loss was almost certainly magnified.

A further profoundly important factor is technological change. In a competitive market economy one of the most important ways in which firms strive to improve profitability is by reducing costs. Labour cost savings in particular became increasingly possible during the 1970s, and especially during the 1980s, for two reasons. First, technological developments resulted in the introduction of more automated production systems and efficient work practices; of particular importance here are developments in micro-electronics and information technology. These have led, on the one hand, to major changes in the way goods are manufactured in some existing industrial sectors, and on the other to entirely new high-value, knowledge-based products often necessitating flexible small-batch production systems. These developments are also leading to changes in the composition of the workforce. The demand for skilled manual labour has declined, accompanied by a rise in the need for non-manual, non-production and professional occupations. For example, between 1971 and 1981 the proportion of the manufacturing workforce in the employers, managerial and professional classes increased from 9.65 to 13.88 per cent. As a consequence manufacturing is in the middle of a period of reskilling. However, for many of the massive number of workers made redundant by a combination of technical change and recession, their experience has been one of deskilling: forced to work at a lower level of skill in either the manufacturing or service sectors in order to secure employment.

The second reason which allowed the rapid introduction of labour-saving technologies, during the 1980s in particular, relates to the problems faced by trades unions attempting to resist some of these changes in an environment of high unemployment, declining memberships, and with a government in power seemingly wholly unsympathetic to their cause. There have been some notable attempts at resistance, as in the newspaper publishing industry where the opening of a new automated press in Wapping with a single-union agreement in 1986 led to massive demonstrations. However, in general there was little effective trades union opposition, allowing British industry at this time to rapidly introduce labour-saving technologies.

Some authors have placed such explanations of the events of the 1970s and 1980s into a much broader context based on the periodization of economic and social change. One such interpretation has suggested that the decline in the importance of manufacturing employment in the workforce from, for example, over 35 per cent in 1960 to under 25 per cent by 1986 signalled a shift of the country towards a post-industrial society. In such a society machinery would replace much of the drudgery of manual factory employment, productivity would be high generating an affluent society with abundant leisure time to enjoy their wealth. Unfortunately, few of the characteristics of contemporary Britain, except for recent employment trends, can be used to support such a naive utopian thesis: jobs in services generally command lower wages than in manufacturing, income disparities have recently been increasing rather than declining, and a large minority of the population live in poverty with bad housing and limited opportunities for gainful employment.

Another view of recent change has revived the theory of long-term cycles of innovations and economic growth, suggested initially by Kondratieff in the 1920s and taken further by Schumpeter in the 1930s, whereby one dominant form of technology and its associated industries is replaced by another. For the period of this review the fourth Kondratieff upsurging which began in the 1930s and 1940s based on electrical products, motor vehicles and mass-production techniques peaked in the 1960s and is now on the wane, to be replaced by the fifth upturn based on the manufacture and use of micro-electronics, telecommunications and information processing. Although by no means dominating the industrial structure of the UK, the manufacture of high-technology goods, accounting for over 20 per cent of manufacturing employees in the early 1980s, is an important component of the industrial sector. Furthermore the use of high-tech products in all areas of manufacture is of increasing importance. Indeed it is a necessary element of the explanation of the major jobless growth phenomenon of the 1980s detailed above. The cycle of innovation approach may well have some value in an explanation of the recent transformation of industrial activity in the United Kingdom, therefore. Unfortunately it does not adequately explain why these new technologies were apparently so rapidly assimilated into British manufacturing from the mid-1970s onwards.

A final contextual explanation which offers an answer to this problem argues that the 1970s and 1980s mark a period of change in the dominant mode of production in manufacturing from Fordism to post-Fordism. Fordism is defined as a mode of production characterized by semi-automated manufacturing systems for the mass production of standardized goods, such as electrical appliances and cars, in which a clear division of labour develops. It is argued that in the 1970s a crisis for such a form of production was reached: the world market for mass-produced goods became effectively saturated while in the United Kingdom high inflation seriously undermined business profitability and competitiveness. Out of such an economic crisis it is argued that a new era of post-Fordism, or flexible accumulation, emerged, characterized by batch-production techniques for small production runs of more customized goods, fuelled by rising average incomes and enabling technologies. Large firms were able to adjust to these new conditions by using computer-aided design and manufacturing techniques and by employing subcontractors, while at the same time an increasing number of specialist niches developed to be occupied by new small firms. In addition for such a form of production organization to function effectively an increasingly flexible workforce was required, not only in the range of tasks to be carried out, but also in its willingness to accept less employment stability – shorter periods of employment in individual companies and more part-time work. The coincidental election of a Conservative government in 1979 promoting a free-enterprise business culture undoubtedly helped to accelerate such a transition in the country. However, it must be strongly emphasized that, while the introduction of more flexible and labour-saving machinery and work practices has been of recent importance in the car manufacture, clothing and electronic components industries, the degree to which manufacturing in general in the United Kingdom has embraced the new technologies and modes of business organization is as yet not at all clear. This is especially true with respect to labour flexibility. Far more empirical research is required before the post-Fordist thesis can be accepted in the case of the UK. Nevertheless on one point all the above macro-conceptions of economic change agree: since the early 1970s the manufacturing sector of the United Kingdom has been in the throes of an important reorganization. It is to an examination of the locational impacts of that reorganization that this chapter now turns.

## LOCATIONAL CHANGE

### Mid-1960s to late 1970s: gradual employment decline

In the changing locational patterns of manufacturing activity since the Second World War the mid-1960s appear to mark an important turning point. Before this time employment was becoming increasingly concentrated in the major cities. Indeed by 1959 London and its Outer Metropolitan Area, along with the conurbations of the West Midlands, Greater Manchester, West Yorkshire and Clydeside, accommodated 51 per cent of all UK manufacturing employment. However, at about the same time that aggregate employment levels in manufacturing in the country as a whole began to contract in the mid-1960s so too did employment in the nation's major cities. For example between 1966 and 1971 London lost 250,000 jobs, the West Midlands 100,000, Greater Manchester 90,000, West Yorkshire 60,000 and Clydeside 40,000. Furthermore the continuance of this decline over the period 1971 to 1978 is dramatically revealed in figure 8.2. As a result, at the scale of the eleven standard regions (table 8.1) the West Midlands, the South-east and the North-west, which include the country's biggest cities, recorded the highest rates of employment decline between 1966 and 1977. Thus the manufacturing fortunes of the core region of Britain's industrial success in the 1940s and 1950s, namely the axial belt from Manchester to London, had been severely undermined by the mid-1970s.

From figure 8.2 it can also be seen that manufacturing employment growth between 1971 and 1978 took place in areas surrounding the pockets

*Table 8.1* Regional trends in manufacturing employment, 1966–87

| | Employment manufacturing (000) 1966[a] | Employment change % 1966–77[a] | 1977–84[b] | 1984–87[c] | Employment manufacturing (000) 1987[c] |
|---|---|---|---|---|---|
| South-east | 2633 | −29.5 | −15.2 | −12.0 | 1374 |
| Greater London | — | — | −22.8 | −12.7 | 514 |
| Rose[d] | — | — | − 9.7 | −11.6 | 860 |
| East Anglia | 186 | + 9.1 | −11.8 | +16.6 | 211 |
| South-west | 402 | + 5.7 | −13.4 | − 0.0 | 367 |
| West Midlands | 1,531 | −35.2 | −28.1 | − 1.6 | 696 |
| East Midlands | 625 | − 4.6 | −17.3 | + 0.0 | 494 |
| Yorkshire and Humberside | 903 | −20.8 | −28.1 | −11.9 | 453 |
| North-west | 1,375 | −26.9 | −30.9 | −11.4 | 609 |
| North | 463 | − 6.3 | −33.2 | − 8.7 | 262 |
| Wales | 326 | − 5.2 | −31.4 | + 1.0 | 211 |
| Scotland | 755 | −18.5 | −28.1 | −10.1 | 392 |
| N.Ireland | 181 | −21.6 | −29.6 | − 6.4 | 102 |
| UK | 9,119 | −20.0 | −23.5 | − 6.8 | 5172 |

*Sources*: Keeble 1987 and *Employment Gazette* (various issues)
*Notes*: [a] 1968 SIC definition of manufacturing
[b] 1968 SIC for 1977 figures and 1980 SIC for 1984 figures
[c] 1980 SIC definition
[d] Rest of south-east

of major decline – especially to the west and south of London, as well as in areas with no major industrial cities and in the most rural and peripheral parts of Great Britain. Partly as a consequence the least urbanized standard regions of East Anglia and the South-west were the only areas to record employment growth immediately after the mid-1960s (table 8.1). Results such as these have led to the identification of a continuum of manufacturing employment change from the highest rates of decline in the most urbanized places to the highest rates of growth in the most rural areas. Evidence supporting such a phenomenon, which became known as the *urban-rural shift* of manufacturing activity, can be seen in table 8.2, with a clear gradation of rates of employment change from London to the rural areas for both 1966 to 1971 and 1971 to 1975. Interestingly this gradation increases from the latter half of the 1960s to the first half of the 1970s. Clearly an important change was beginning to take place in the locational preference of manufacturing activity in the United Kingdom after the mid-1960s, which it is tempting to suggest may well be the direct consequence of the structural changes taking place in the sector as noted above. The most persuasive theory so far developed to account for these locational trends in employment is the *constrained location theory* of Fothergill and Gudgin (1982). The theory is indeed directly dependent upon the changing characteristics of the best-practice production methods in which manufacturing industry invested during the period. Such methods

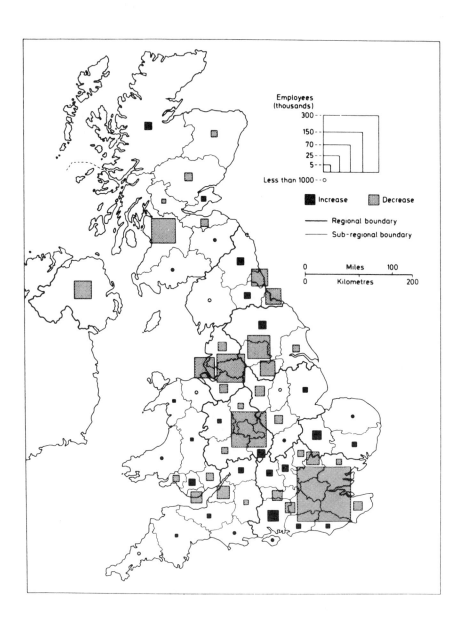

*Figure 8.2* Manufacturing employment change, 1971–8
*Source:* Keeble 1987

were becoming more space extensive per employee, as machinery replaced labour across all industries. Where this new labour-saving machinery, along with new work practices, could be adopted by existing factories jobs were, of course, lost but the factory remained in existence. Where this was not possible, as for example, in older capacity in congested urban areas, such physical constraints led to the closure of the plant and the loss of its jobs. At the same time new investment was taking place in smaller towns where space for expansion was available, resulting in the creation of new jobs in manufacturing, often where few had existed before. As a result these locations recorded absolute increases in employment, and a continuum of employment growth performance developed from the big cities where large numbers of jobs were lost to the smaller towns where small increases took place.

*Table 8.2* Manufacturing employment change by type of subregion in the UK, 1966–71, 1971–5, and 1978–81

| Type of subregion | Percentage change in employment | | |
| --- | --- | --- | --- |
| | *1966–71* | *1971–5* | *1978–81* |
| London | −3.6 | −5.1 | −15.5 |
| Other conurbations | −1.7 | −2.2 | −22.7 |
| Free-standing cities | −0.1 | −1.3 | −17.2 |
| Large towns | −0.2 | −0.5 | −16.0 |
| Small towns | +1.1 | +0.1 | −15.2 |
| Rural areas | +1.9 | +3.5 | −10.0 |

*Sources*: Fothergill and Gudgin 1982 and Fothergill, Gudgin, Kitson, and Monk 1986

An additional important element necessary to account for the changing locations of manufacturing activity at this time is regional policy. Between 1966 and 1975 such policies helped to promote almost 140,000 jobs in the five leading regions of attraction, namely Scotland, the North-west, the North, Wales, and the South-west. Indeed this must be one of the reasons why the last three of these regions recorded relatively low rates of employment loss between 1966 and 1977 (table 8.1). Unfortunately, in the case of the other two and also for Northern Ireland, the rate of in-migration of new employment was not sufficient to compensate for the rate of job loss in existing industrial activity.

## Late 1970s to early 1980s: dramatic employment loss

From table 8.1 it is clear that during the period over the turn of the decade from the 1970s to the 1980s very large numbers of jobs in the manufacturing sector were lost from all the regions of the United Kingdom, with the highest rates of regional decline in the North, Wales and the North-west.

Even the previously successful regions of East Anglia, and the South-west lost at least 10 per cent of their manufacturing jobs between 1977 and 1984. Indeed, these two regions along with the East Midlands and the South-east were the only ones to record losses of under 20 per cent for the period. All other regions were in excess of −28 per cent!

These findings reveal a substantial weakening of the scale of manufacturing activity in the north of the United Kingdom, both absolutely and relative to the south of the country. With the south-east and the West Midlands recording the two worst employment performances between 1966 and 1977 this distinction had not been so pronounced before the mid-1970s. However by the first half of the 1980s manufacturing activity had become *relatively* far more buoyant in the south. For example, between 1977 and 1984 the proportion of manufacturing employment in the four successful and contiguous regions of the south and east – East Anglia, the East Midlands, the South-east and South-west – increased from 42 to 47 per cent.

At the subregional scale the generality of employment decline was also much in evidence. From table 8.2, for example, it can be seen that, although rural areas recorded the most favourable results, all types of subregion on the urban-rural continuum recorded employment loss between 1978 and 1981. Nevertheless they do suggest a substantial weakening of the shift of manufacturing activity to more rural areas. The data for London for this time period (tables 8.1 and 8.2) reveal an interesting finding. For the first time in twenty years the capital recorded an employment change result better than the national average. For the following three years 1981–4, figure 8.3 shows that most counties were still characterized by employment decline, with substantial losses taking place as before in the major urban centres. Indeed in the eight conurbations employment declined by 30 per cent compared with 12 per cent for the United Kingdom as a whole. Employment growth took place in only six counties, of which Cambridgeshire and Buckinghamshire were the most successful. Employment growth in Clwyd (where the Shotton steelworks closed in the late 1970s) and Avon (focused on the major city of Bristol) are somewhat unexpected results.

Four possible intersecting avenues of explanation have been suggested for these trends. First, in terms of the urban-rural shift it must be remembered that this was substantially an investment-led phenomenon. During this great recession, however, fixed capital expenditure in manufacturing declined dramatically from almost £7,500 million in 1979 to only £4,619 million in 1982, and estimated excess capacity grew to more than 30 per cent by 1982. As a result, given that physical constraints have a much more significant locational impact during periods of expansion than periods of decline, the effect of preferential investment in the small towns slowed down. However, during that regime of selective capacity cut-backs generated by the recession the areas possessing the most inefficient and

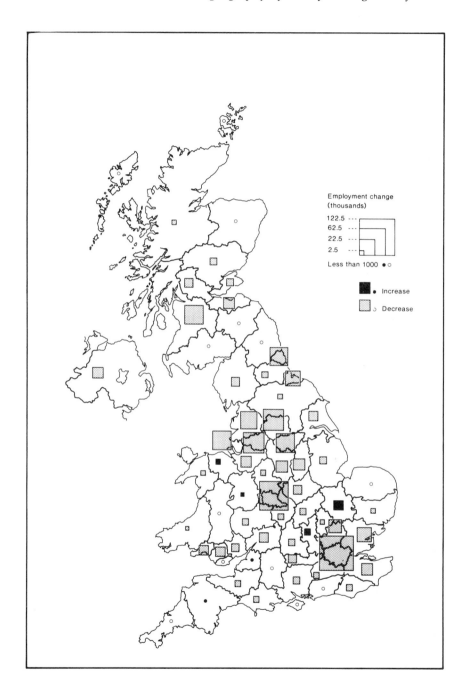

*Figure 8.3* Manufacturing employment change, 1981–4

out-moded forms of production, such as the conurbations, recorded the highest rates of employment loss. London, although registering a substantial loss of manufacturing jobs, is an exception. This may in part be a reflection of the capital's important headquarters and research and development (R&D) roles within the country's manufacturing structures at this time (see below). Such functions may be protected, initially at least, from closure and employment loss while cutbacks take place in production and distribution units elsewhere in the country.

Second, a similar investment-related line of argument may account for part of the extremely poor performance of northern Britain. Throughout the 1960s and early 1970s many parts of this area benefited from Development Area status and the in-migration of branch plants of both UK and foreign companies. However, during the recession, which was of course an international phenomenon, new branch-plant investment from any origin was extremely scarce. At the same time many multi-locational firms were forced to cut capacity. As a result branch plants in northern Britain, many of which had been set up in the 1960s and were probably nearing the end of their expected life-spans anyway, suffered disproportionately during the late 1970s (see below).

The north:south distinction in employment performance was also aggravated by the impacts of industrial structure. For example, at the end of the 1970s the north possessed an industrial structure with a disproportionate share of jobs in industries such as metal manufacture and textiles which in the wake of a declining world market brought on by the recession were losing out to foreign competition. Indeed compared with a national employment loss of 18 per cent between 1979 and 1981, metal manufacture declined by 26.6 per cent and textiles by 24.1 per cent. Interestingly during the same time period the decline of the car industry and related forms of mechanical engineering, felt most acutely in the West Midlands where the industry was heavily spatially concentrated, led not only to this area being termed the 'rust belt' of Britain but also to the suggestion that the north and its industrial problems had now moved south to include the West Midlands. Unfortunately during the late 1970s and early 1980s the north also received a disproportionately small share of employment in both the newly emerging and well-established high technology industries of electronic engineering, aerospace, telecommunications and pharmaceuticals (table 8.3); in 1981 the relatively prosperous south and east of the country had 61.4 per cent of the employment in these industries in contrast to 51 per cent of all employment in manufacturing. In addition, of the three UK regions recording employment growth in this sector between 1981 and 1984, two, East Anglia and the rest of the South-east (i.e. excluding Greater London), were in this half of the country (table 8.3). As a result by the early 1980s proportionately more new jobs had been created in the south in new industries to replace those being lost in other sectors than in the north.

*Table 8.3* The regional distribution of high-technology industry in Britain, 1981–4

|  | Percentage of employment | | Employment change |
|  | *1981* | *1984* | *1981–4 (%)* |
| --- | --- | --- | --- |
| East Anglia | 2.5 | 3.2 | +20.9 |
| Wales | 3.0 | 3.2 | +2.9 |
| Rose | 26.1 | 27.3 | +0.3 |
| Scotland | 7.1 | 7.3 | −1.9 |
| North | 3.8 | 3.7 | −5.2 |
| Greater London | 17.2 | 17.0 | −5.4 |
| East Midlands | 6.3 | 6.2 | − 5.9 |
| West Midlands | 8.5 | 8.3 | − 6.4 |
| South-west | 9.3 | 9.0 | − 8.0 |
| Yorkshire and Humberside | 4.3 | 4.0 | −11.1 |
| North-west | 11.8 | 10.9 | −11.9 |
| Great Britain | 100.00 | 100.0 | − 4.1 |

*Source*: Keeble 1988

In the recent growth of high-technology industry in the country two different types of favourable locational environment have been identified. The first is the small towns in less urbanized parts of the country, of which perhaps the best-known example is Cambridge. Many of the firms involved in these areas were relatively small, depending to a large degree on in-house high calibre R&D effort to remain at the forefront of rapidly changing market opportunities. Important locational considerations for such activity include the presence of highly qualified personnel, or at least a pleasant environment in which such individuals and their families might want to live, access to international communication networks, and in some cases proximity to government research establishments and universities not only for the supply of personnel, information and contracts, but also to provide a stimulus for new entrepreneurs to begin new firms.

The second type of environment includes areas of high unemployment such as Wales and Scotland where their respective development agencies have been particularly successful with the use of regional policy incentives in attracting large production units, often of foreign multi-national companies. Employment in high technology industry in Wales grew by almost 3.0 per cent between 1981 and 1984, for example (table 8.3). However, it would be quite wrong to stereotype these two environments too dogmatically. The reality is far more diverse. There are very large high-tech production units in the south just as there are R&D laboratories and small research-based firms in, for example, Scotland's Silicon Glen.

The final possible factor in the relative success of the south of Britain, with close links to industrial structure, is the impact of uneven regional rates of new firm formation. Unfortunately precise information is not available on this point. However, it may be possible to infer from a number of regionally specific investigations, mainly for slightly earlier periods of time, that the south possessed a rather superior rate of new manufacturing firm formation than the rest of the country. For example, Cambridgeshire (1971–81), the East Midlands (1968–75), and South Hampshire (1971–81) recorded standardized firm formation rates (formation rate divided by the number of years of the study) of 0.57, 0.42, and 0.34 respectively compared with equivalent scores of 0.08, 0.10, and 0.24 for Scotland (1968–77), Cleveland (1965–78), and Coventry (1974–82). As a result the south of Britain may have been rather better placed to weather the storms of employment loss brought by the recession than the rest of the nation.

**After the early 1980s: a return to slow employment decline**

For the post-recessional period very little empirical information is so far available except for regional employment estimates (table 8.1) which reveal a number of important findings. Following national trends all regions except Rose recorded an improvement in their rate of employment change compared with 1977–84. Partly as a result the South-east as a whole recorded the highest rate of regional employment loss of −12 per cent, signalling an end to the area's relative improvement during the previous time period. Interestingly, the rate of employment loss during these three years was almost identical in both Greater London and Rose, and not as in previous years primarily a consequence of job loss in Greater London. Relatively poor employment results were also recorded for the North-west, the North, Yorkshire and Humberside and Scotland, with a major turnround apparent in the employment fortunes of the West Midlands. Again the north of Britain, and this time excluding the West Midlands, appeared to be performing particularly badly. By contrast the most favourable employment change result of +17 per cent took place in East Anglia. Other relatively successful regions included the South-west and East Midlands with the most dramatic improvement of all taking place in Wales. Here an employment contraction of 31.4 per cent in 1977–84 changed to a 1.0 per cent expansion in 1984–7. Once again, the least urbanized regions of the country recorded the highest rates of employment growth.

Given the lack of research so far on this most recent of time periods an explanation of regional employment change is not immediately available. However, it is highly likely that some of the factors identified for earlier periods, such as the inter-regional differences in urban density, industrial structure, the rate of new firm formation, and the availability of regional aid, all had a part to play. From figure 8.1 it can be seen that the post-1984 period was characterized by jobless growth: an initial period of bringing formerly under-utilized capacity back into production followed by the continued reorganization and modernization of existing firms using labour-saving processes and work practices. As before the recession, therefore, many of the observed changes will have been investment-led. In such circumstances the constrained location theory may help to account for the apparent urban-rural shift. However, by the mid-1980s, the impact of relatively recent technological advances may be much more widespread than before, replacing not just the oldest generations of industrial activity but also much more recent ones as well. Such a scenario may help to account for the high rate of job loss in the South-east during the mid-1980s. It is also possible that this region's rate of employment loss in manufacturing may be due to development pressure on land availability and costs in one of Britain's most buoyant, yet congested, regions, forcing industrialists to search elsewhere for cheaper space for productive capacity. However, detailed empirical research is required to provide an answer to this question.

As before, the geographies of new firm formation and industrial structure will almost certainly have favoured the south of Britain. However, at the same time a significantly reduced package of regional assistance (see below) has been instrumental in attracting foreign investment to the country's problem regions. For example, a number of Japanese companies, interested in supplying the European market, have been attracted to specific locations in the north and west of the country. South Wales, for example, secured a significant number of such firms in electrical and electronic engineering. In addition the initial phase of a major new Nissan car assembly plant in 1986 was located in Washington, County Durham. However, the degree to which these various factors have helped to generate inter-regional differences in employment growth in the United Kingdom after 1984 is as yet unknown.

**Mid-1960s to mid-1980s: locational transformation?**

The evidence presented above has shown quite conclusively that a number of important changes have taken place in the location of manufacturing activity in the United Kingdom since the mid-1960s: the number of people employed in all regions except East Anglia declined dramatically over the period, and a significant shift in the preferred locations of new industrial activity away from the major conurbations to smaller towns in more rural environments has taken place. Indeed East Anglia, the least urbanized region of all, doubled its share of UK manufacturing employment between 1966 and 1987. Over the same time period the employment share of the major urban regions of the South-east, West Midlands, and North-west collectively declined by almost 9 per cent. Nevertheless it must also be noted that no major changes took place in the *relative* importance of these regions. East Anglia, despite its prodigious rate of expansion, still only accounted for 4 per cent of all UK manufacturing employment in 1987. The same sort of argument can also be applied at the subregional scale. The major urban areas have lost vast numbers of manufacturing jobs since the mid-1960s, but in 1984 the conurbations of Greater London, Greater Manchester, the West Midlands, West Yorkshire and Clydeside accommodated 32 per cent of all manufacturing jobs in the United Kingdom. These urban areas still dominated the pattern of manufacturing activity in the mid-1980s as they had done in the mid-1960s. The manufacturing sector of the United Kingdom may well be in the throes of a major structural transformation, but as yet it has not overturned the dominant geographical distribution of industrial activity in the country.

## THE DECISION-MAKERS

The changing geography of manufacturing activity in the United Kingdom is dependent upon the decisions within enterprises to open or close factories, to relocate, or to change production and work practices. So far this discussion has considered very little material at the scale of the individual firm. The concluding section will attempt to rectify this omission. In addition it will also consider the behaviour of another decision-making organization, which by virtue of its various policies has had a major impact on the locational change of manufacturing activity in the United Kingdom, namely central government.

### The corporate dimension

One of the most significant features of UK manufacturing activity during the 1970s has been its domination in both output and employment terms by a relatively small number of very large multi-plant firms, many of which organize their productive capacity not only inter-regionally within the United Kingdom but also internationally. The major phase of growth of such firms took place during the 1950s and 1960s by these firms creating new capacity and by takeovers and mergers. Indeed by 1970 the country's top 100 manufacturing companies accounted for 41 per cent of manufacturing net output, a degree of concentration much higher than in any other West European country. A further indication of their importance may be gleaned from the fact that in 1972 each of these top 100 firms on average controlled seventy-two separate establishments. The firms include major UK private sector companies such as the Imperial Chemicals Industry (ICI), Courtaulds in textiles and Guest Keen and Nettlefolds (GKN) in engineering and metal goods, along with branches and subsidiaries of large overseas companies such as Ford and Philips. Indeed, this latter group in 1977 accounted for 15 per cent of employment, 20 per cent of net output and 21 per cent of ca ital expenditure in the United Kingdom's manufacturing sector. Large firms also include major nationalized companies wholly owned by the state: in 1982 such firms, which collectively accounted for over 400,000 jobs, included British Steel, British Shipbuilders, BL, Rolls Royce, British Nuclear Fuels, Short Brothers (Belfast), the Royal Ordnance Factories, and the Royal Mint. However, by 1989 many of the these had become private companies. In addition, the government has some influence on the behaviour of a number of other important companies either directly as a major shareholder of, for example, British Petroleum and British Aerospace, accounting for almost 200,000 jobs in 1982, or more indirectly via the equity involvements of the British Technology Group and regional development agencies. For social or strategic reasons it is possible that the interests of the state and the private sector may not coincide. Therefore the locational behaviour of nationalized businesses may be quite different from privately run organizations. Historically this was certainly the case before the 1979 Conservative adminstration. However, since then state-run firms have increasingly been expected to behave like ones in the private sector, with the explicit policy of the government being their ultimate privatization. As a result, since the early 1980s state-owned businesses have begun more and more to behave like their private-sector equivalents and perhaps should not be categorized separately.

The importance of large and multi-plant firms in regional and urban economies can be shown with the use of survey evidence. In the north-west in 1975, for example, the largest fifty-four employers in the region – or 'prime-movers' – accounted for approximately 414,000 manual jobs, over 46 per cent of the region's total. When all multi-plant concerns are included they accounted for 94 per cent of manufacturing employment in Cleveland in 1965, 87 per cent in Coventry in 1982, 80 per cent in Inner Merseyside in 1975, and 63 per cent in Manchester in the same year. This gives some indication of the degree to which the activities of large multi-plant firms had penetrated the economies of most places in the United Kingdom by the mid-1970s. As a result, their investment, disinvestment and sourcing decisions have had an important impact on the size and form of manufacturing activity in the British regions.

Establishments in multi-unit firms are not necessarily dependent on their immediate spatial environments for inputs or markets; they are inter-linked in national and global production systems. As a result the United Kingdom is in competition internationally for new manufacturing investment. Cheaper labour costs in the Third World and the newly industrializing countries, especially in south-east Asia, has led to some firms shifting capacity to these areas, or firms already in these countries having significant cost advantages over the United Kingdom. In either case, be it in ship-building or silicon chip manufacture, jobs have almost certainly been lost from Britain. Similarly, and perhaps of greater importance in terms of recent overseas investment by UK firms, manufacturing capacity has been lost, or foregone, in the United Kingdom by companies which have been investing abroad for reasons of market penetration: the buying up of profitable companies, or the setting up of new capacity, in other countries to avoid their tariffs on imported goods. The United Kingdom itself has of course benefited from similar investment: indeed for many companies headquartered outside Western Europe, whose executives have some experience of the English language and culture, the United Kingdom has been seen as a suitable entry port for the entire European Community market. However, one of the interesting geographical questions for the future is how such firms may adjust the localities of their European capacity as they become more familiar with working in Europe, as the Community's markets become increasingly harmonized after 1992, and after the Channel Tunnel is opened in 1993. The United Kingdom, and even its South-east region, is not as accessible to the Community as a whole as are parts of Belgium, Holland, West Germany and northern France, which may become increasingly favoured locations in the future as the acceptable specifications for individual products become the same over the whole Community and the number of required factories for their production is reduced.

The presence of the establishments of large firms in the UK regions has clearly been of greater importance in providing employment opportunities both directly and indirectly, the latter by the employees of these firms spending their wages on the products and services of other local businesses. However, as the following discussion will suggest, their existence in regional economies, especially where a significant number are controlled from outside the region, may lead to a number of serious development problems.

An important consequence of the development and growth of large, multi-plant firms in the country has been the creation of a new spatial division of labour, not in terms of industrial sectors as before but in terms of the separate functions multi-unit firms undertake, with each function being located in the place to which it is most suited. As a result the HQ and R&D functions of manufacturing activity became concentrated in the south-east so as to benefit from close proximity to the financial services of London, the existing concentration of both public and private research establishments, a prestigious location, and the advantageous scenic and cultural environment for their high-waged, high-calibre employees. For example, of the 100 largest (by turnover) private sector manufacturing firms in the United Kingdom in 1982, 74 per cent had their head offices in the south-east. At the same time, given the good communication links throughout the United Kingdom for both freight and information, production and fabrication plants were located where their principal cost elements of labour and land could be kept to a minimum. In such circumstances the availability of large numbers of potential workers (both male and female) and industrial assistance (see below) in the traditional problem regions of the country made them popular branch-plant locations during the 1960s and early 1970s, especially for large capital-intensive projects: between 1966 and 1975 there were 940 'moves to', or branch-plant creations in, the development areas of Northern Ireland, Scotland, Wales, the North and Merseyside, for example, leading to 130,000 jobs in 1975. For many regions, therefore, the concentration of activity in multi-unit firms is not in large, functionally integrated business ventures but rather in specific parts of these businesses. In broad terms decision-making functions have become concentrated in the south-east, with production dispersed to the north and west. Given the relatively high incomes of the professional workers in the decision-making and R&D occupations, this has led to a definite regional development advantage for the south-east.

Originally there may have been an expectation in the regions in receipt of branch-plant investment that such establishments would be instrumental in leading to local self-sustaining growth through the purchase of inputs from local suppliers, technical spin-off to local firms and by staff leaving to set up their own new businesses. Unfortunately there is sufficient evidence to suggest that branch plants do not often have such positive effects, but instead truncate the local economy. Branches have their own in-house suppliers within their own companies and often do not trade with local businesses. They tend to operate with mature products and technologies and to be far too capital-intensive to permit direct imitative behaviour by potentially entrepreneurial employees. Indeed it is possible that the large size of many branch plants in which staff tasks tend to be relatively specialized does not generate a successful environment for the creation of new businessmen. In such firms individuals do not gain the experience of a variety of managerial tasks necessary for them to stand a good chance of becoming successfully self-employed. As a consequence areas with a high proportion of their employment in large plants, invariably as a result of multi-plant firm activity, such as the North (37.2 per cent), Scotland (31.1 per cent), West Midlands (30.3 per cent), and the North-west (29.8 per cent) in 1981, tend to have low rates of new firm formation.

Multi-plant firms, by virtue of their large number of establishments, have great locational flexibility, and individual companies have the ability to switch production between sites and to close premises relatively quickly without threatening their continued existence. During the late 1970s and early 1980s, under conditions of severe economic recession, multi-unit companies were forced to exercise such flexibility in major programmes of production reorganization in order to remain profitable. Such schemes, often involving the inroduction of new production technologies, resulted in large numbers of plant closures and redundancies.

It is possible to identify at least three important processes of production change which will lead to job loss:

1 *Intensification:* the reorganization of existing production by changes in work practices and layouts in order to increase productivity without major new investment or capacity closure.
2 *Investment in Technical Change:* significant investment, often at new locations, in product and process innovations to reduce labour requirements and increase productivity. The resultant employment decline is not just confined to declining industries and is a process of great importance for an understanding of employment change in the United Kingdom throughout the post–1970 period.

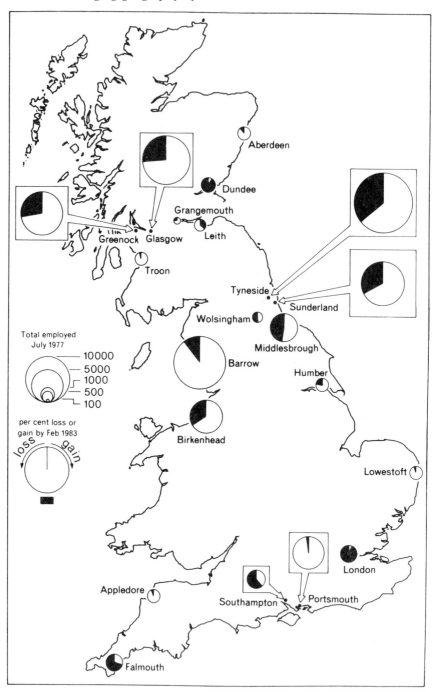

*Figure 8.4* British Shipbuilders employment change, July 1977 to February 1983
*Source:* Peck and Townsend 1984

3 *Rationalization:* the elimination of productive capacity, resulting directly in jobs being lost, due to the loss of markets.

These are, of course, stereotype images of change. In real corporate examples, the strategies adopted by large firms in the United Kingdom in response to the inter-meshed problems of economic recession, successful overseas competition and the potential of technical change were usually far more complicated. For example, the loss of almost 30 per cent of jobs, totalling over 20,000, in British Shipbuilders between 1977 and 1983 can be directly linked to world over-capacity and the uncompetitive nature of many of the UK yards. However, one can see from figure 8.4 that the impact of this decline was not felt uniformly by all shipyards. It was dependent on the type of vessel construction in which individual yards specialized. In Portsmouth and Barrow-in-Furness, where naval contracts were particularly important, job losses were relatively small, compared with yards specializing in merchant ship construction. In the rather more complicated example of Metal Box, where a 40 per cent loss of jobs (over 15,000) took place between 1976 and 1983, divisional specialization was again important for understanding the geography of change (figure 8.5). In this company factories were widely dispersed to be near their suppliers of fresh fruit and vegetables and also the manufacturers of soft drinks and beers; it was the open-can division which suffered above-average rates of employment decline. This was directly the result of two factors: first the entry into the UK in the mid-1970s of new competitors with superior production techniques and new two-piece cans, and second, the choice of locations for their new capacity, which were concentrated in the north-west, which led to over-capacity in the area and to heavy cut-backs by Metal Box. In general, however, these events forced the company to introduce, where possible, new work practices and technologies, a process accelerated by the financial pressures of the 1979–81 recession. One final example of significant corporate employment loss worthy of note concerns the Cadbury Schweppes plant at Bournville. Here major new production equipment was installed in existing premises requiring no locational change. Unfortunately in the process over 2,500 full-time job equivalents were lost, mainly among female part-time staff, resulting in a 40 per cent fall in the number employed. It is not just full-time jobs that are lost in corporate rationalization schemes.

It is clear from these few case studies that in the restructuring of British industry during the 1979–81 recession locational impacts were both dramatic and uneven. Some localities suffered major job losses. Others experienced only minor employment cutbacks. Indeed an important geographical question to ask with respect to the major corporate restructuring programmes of this era is whether some regions fared worse than others. For example, were some types of regional environments favoured locations by large multi-national firms for plant closure and redundancies? Using

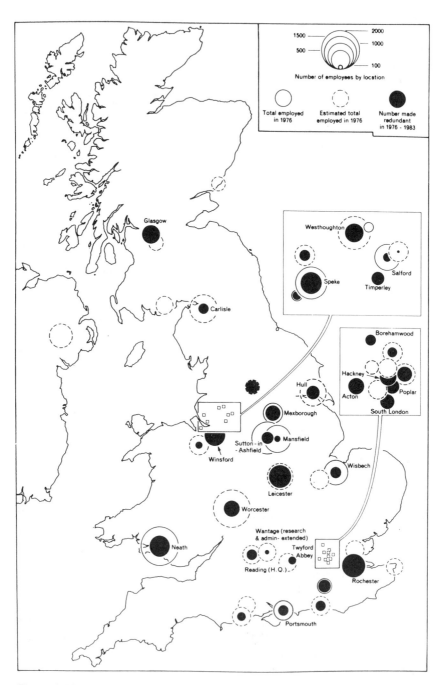

*Figure 8.5* Metal Box closures and redundancies, 1976–83
*Source:* Peck and Townsend 1984

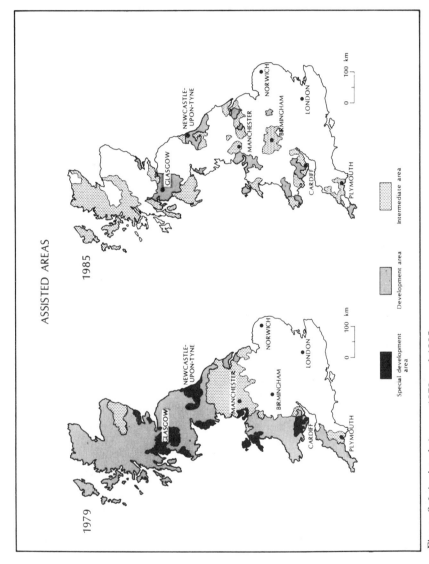

*Figure 8.6* Assisted Areas, 1979 and 1985

evidence from a major investigation by Townsend and Peck (1985) of companies issuing redundancy notices between 1978 and 1982, it is possible to investigate this issue using two different spatial frames: urban–rural differences and the performance of the development areas (figure 8.6). Interestingly both pieces of analysis add support to the explanation of the geography of industrial change presented above.

1 *Urban–rural shift* During the last few years of the 1970s plant closures in large corporations were concentrated in traditional industrial towns and coalfield areas. Indeed 86.4 per cent of all recorded closures in 1977 were in such locations. As a result corporate rationalization schemes at this time were contributing to a relative urban–rural shift. However, by 1981, the impacts of recession were being felt more widely, with only 54.4 per cent of corporate plant closures in traditional industrial areas. The evidence also indicates that this was *not* the result of individual corporations initially preferring non-urban locations, but simply that different corporations were undertaking temporally different strategies. In this case the firms, and often state-owned ones, heavily concentrated in major industrial centres, were the ones initially to be most severely hit by recession.

2 *The development areas* During the last three years of the 1970s the development areas, and especially the special development areas, recorded very high rates of job loss through closure. In 1977 94 per cent of all reported job losses through closure were in these areas. By 1981, however, the figure had fallen to 53 per cent. But in this case the evidence points to corporations, such as Plessey, GEC, Hoover and Thorn-EMI in electrical engineering, making decisions initially to close their development area capacity in favour of works in other areas. Here there is definite support for an intra-corporate hypothesis, that in this period of recession employment in the development areas was more unstable than elsewhere in the country.

The period of this analysis witnessed a substantial growth in the importance of small manufacturing firms in the United Kingdom. For example, between 1968 and 1985 firms of less than 100 workers increased their share of national employment and net output from 13.5 per cent to 23.5 per cent, and from 11.5 to 19.4 per cent, respectively. The limited empirical information on the locational patterns of new and small firms has already been discussed. However, it is worth considering here why such changes have come about. There are four sets of possible reasons, all of which are applicable, unevenly through time and over geographical space, to the UK experience: recession push, income growth, technological change, and government encouragement. *Recession push* suggests, first, that the closure of firms during an economic downturn creates market niches for new firms to exploit and, secondly, that individuals may be forced into self-employment as the only form of gainful employment open to them during a period of actual or imminent unemployment. Such a view is clearly most appropriate to the late 1970s–early 1980s period in the United Kingdom and to the regions most severely affected by the recession then; in a survey of new firms in Greater Belfast between 1970 and 1980 and still in existence in 1980 34 per cent gave redundancy as the principal reason for their creation. *Income growth* ideas bring to the fore the view that rising real household incomes in the long term have led increasingly to the demand for more individualistic, tailor-made, sophisticated and high-quality products requiring small batch-production methods more suited to small and medium-sized firms than to large ones. It has already been pointed out that major technological changes have been taking place in British industry, not only in the way goods are produced but also in the raw materials employed (e.g. plastics instead of metals) and in the actual products themselves. For many goods these changes have conspired to reduce the minimum effective scale of production, permitting small firms to flourish in markets hitherto uneconomic for them to enter. In addition they have encouraged the highly qualified 'boffin' entrepreneurs to set up specialist firms at or near the technology frontier. This type of small firm has become associated in particular with the growth of *high-technology* businesses in the south of England throughout the period of this analysis. Finally, *government encouragement* relates to the welter of legislation designed to promote the formation and growth of new firms in the country, begun before 1979 but dramatically increased by subsequent Conservative administrations as part of an attempt to create an 'enterprise culture' in the United Kingdom. These measures have included the Loan Guarantee Scheme, the creation of an Unlisted Securities Market, tax incentives for the self-employed, the Enterprise Allowance Scheme, the raising of VAT thresholds, and from 1988 financial assistance to help obtain advice on all forms of business practice from professional consultants via the Enterprise Initiative.

There have been many different claims concerning the advantages of small firms, including the promotion of competition and innovation, developing a flexible workforce and congenial working environments, diversifying the economy and the generation of new jobs. While all these points are debatable it is the role of new and small manufacturing firms in generating new employment opportunities that is probably most important in the context of regional development. In all the regions for which research evidence is available – East Anglia, East Midlands, Scotland, the north-east of England, Northern Ireland and south Hampshire – new manufacturing firms have promoted a net increase in new jobs. However, there are no examples of new firms accounting for more than 5 per cent of end-year employment in an area within a period of up to ten years. Indeed, in East Anglia, one of the most prosperous regions in the United Kingdom, new firms created during the 1970s accounted for only 4.7 per cent of the region's total manufacturing employment in 1981. Nevertheless it must be remembered that the 19,000 net new firms in the United Kingdom between

1980 and 1986 may have generated in excess of 200,000 jobs by 1986. That is twice as many manufacturing jobs as in the whole of Northern Ireland and equal to the number in the small regions of East Anglia or Wales. Unfortunately the post-1980 rates of new firm registrations were not uniformly distributed in the United Kingdom, with some of the regions most in need of new businesses such as Scotland, the north and north-west apparently representing the most 'hostile environments' in the country to their creation.

**The actions of government**

There are many different forms of government policy which have an impact on the spatial distribution of maufacturing industry in the United Kingdom. Explicitly spatial policies for the problem regions and urban areas of the country have been a traditional focus of geographical activity. But it is also clear that the government's sectoral, procurement and macro-economic policies affect regions differentially and therefore should also be included on the geographical research agenda.

Since the Callaghan Labour government of the late 1970s the Keynesian demand-management approach to the British macro-economy has been abandoned in favour of a monetarist approach. Such a view found its ultimate realization in the 'Thatcherite' economics of the post-1979 era, whose principal objective is to reduce inflation to a minimum by limiting the nation's money supply. This was achieved by raising interest rates and indirect taxes. As a result, although inflation was successfully 'controlled', the costs of borrowing and the value of the pound increased, making imports cheaper and UK exports more expensive, which is a very serious situation for a trading nation. At the same time the 'new Conservatism' was ideologically committed to the promotion of the private sector. Thus state-intervention was 'rolled back' and public expenditure cut wherever possible, releasing resources for the private sector to put profitably to work. Unfortunately, as has already been suggested, these policies were introduced as the western world plunged into a deep economic recession and helped to magnify the resultant redundancy impacts in the United Kingdom. The government at that time would not agree, but argued that these severe impacts were the result of world economic trends which etched more deeply into the fabric of UK employment than elsewhere because of the inferior efficiency, productivity and profitablility of much of Britain's manufacturing base. The new free-market order it had introduced gave the opportunity for the 'shake-out' of inefficient and over-manned businesses leading to a 'leaner and fitter' industrial sector which in the longer term will grow to reabsorb those still without jobs. Thus for the first time in the United Kingdom for many years mass redundancy became ideologically acceptable to the government of the day. However, as we have already seen, there is little evidence so far of the reabsorption of labour into manufacturing in the principal industrial cities and regions of northern Britain. Indeed, given the characteristics of modern industrial practices, it is difficult to envisage this happening for some time. Jobs, however, have been created in services in these areas. Nevertheless, as Martin (1986) has persuasively argued in 'Thatcherism and Britain's Industrial Landscape', '. . . of all forms of state policy, the free-market conservatism of the Thatcher government is the most likely to exacerbate . . .' the 'widening disparities in Britain's industrial landscape' (p. 245).

The government buys many items from private manufacturing to support its numerous activities. These range from stationery and office equipment to drugs and military hardware. Wherever government places a contract it will have a beneficial employment impact on that area. One aspect of government expenditure which has had particular significant locational impacts is defence spending. The United Kingdom spends more, in both absolute and per capita terms, than any other NATO country apart from the USA on defence, amounting to 5.3 per cent of GDP. In addition half of the government's R&D expenditure (30 per cent of the nation's total) goes on defence-related projects. Table 8.4 gives some idea of the regional geography of this expenditure in the United Kingdom. It demonstrates that the South-west in the 1970s benefited disproportionately from this type of expenditure; defence contracts were equivalent to 10 per cent of manufacturing output compared to 8 per cent in the South-east and 1.6 per cent and

*Table 8.4* Defence procurement and regional assistance by region, 1974/5–1977/8[a]

| Standard region | Net manufacturing output £m. | Regional[b] assistance £m. | Defence procurement £m. | Procurement as a percentage of output | Regional assistance as a percentage of output |
|---|---|---|---|---|---|
| North | 10,478 | 476 | 573 | 5.5 | 4.5 |
| Yorkshire and Humberside | 15,393 | 89 | 245 | 1.6 | 0.6 |
| East Midlands | 12,047 | 10[c] | 744 | 6.2 | 0.1 |
| East Anglia | 4,673 | — | 264 | 5.7 | — |
| South-east | 46,726 | — | 3,674 | 7.9 | — |
| South-west | 9,078 | 26 | 889 | 9.8 | 0.3 |
| West Midlands[c] | 20,531 | 2 | 599 | 2.9 | — |
| North-west | 23,920 | 250 | 949 | 4.0 | 1.1 |
| Wales | 7,448 | 239 | 112 | 1.5 | 3.2 |
| Scotland | 14,225 | 424 | 549 | 3.9 | 3.0 |
| Great Britain | 164,519 | 1,516 | 8,598 | 5.2 | 0.9 |

*Source*: Boddy 1987

*Notes*:
[a] Sum of totals for financial years 1974/5 to 1977/8 in current terms
[b] Regional Development Grant plus selective regional assistance
[c] Includes assistance not split between East and West Midlands

below in Wales and Yorkshire and Humberside. The South-west economy is therefore considerably defence-dependent. For the mid-1970s it has been estimated that the South-west's output share may represent up to 90,000 jobs due to Ministry of Defence contracts, much of which is concentrated in Avon, centred on Bristol. Indeed it is this industry which largely accounts for the western concentration of high-technology industry of the so-called M4 corridor.

In monetary terms defence expenditure was more important than regional assistance in the mid-1970s in all regions except Wales (table 8.4). What is more, if the two are added together they were equivalent to over 10 per cent of manufacturing output in the South-west and 8 per cent in the South-east, compared to only 2 per cent in Yorkshire and Humberside, 5 per cent in both Wales and the North-west and 7 per cent in Scotland. Only the North suffered no deficit in these terms compared to the South-west. Of course defence expenditure and regional assistance do not have equivalent economic and employment generation impacts, but this example helps to demonstrate the possible specific locational consequences of government expenditure: in this case the favouring of the South-west could be seen as an unofficial form of regional policy and assistance.

Since the mid-1930s successive UK governments have pursued different forms of explicit regional policy designed to encourage new industrial investment in areas with relatively high rates of unemployment. The areas qualifying for assistance under such schemes (figure 8.6) have consistently been concentrated in the north and west of the country in areas with declining employment opportunities in coal-mining, iron and steel production, heavy engineering, and textiles. These schemes were most successful during the 1960s and early 1970s but by the end of the 1970s were under serious assault. Regional policy during its halcyon days helped to encourage a large number of firms of both foreign and British origin to set up new, usually branch-plant, capacity in the development areas. It is possible that between 1961 and 1981 up to 604,600 new manufacturing jobs were created in the assisted areas as a result of such policies, of which 450,000 may still have been in existence by the end of 1981. For many problem regions such jobs have been fundamental in maintaining a manufacturing presence. In Northern Ireland, for example, where government financial assistance has helped to promote over 40 per cent of existing manufacturing jobs since the mid-1970s, 170,000 jobs were promoted between 1946 and 1982, amounting to over 1.4 million person-years of employment.

Unfortunately it had become clear by the late 1970s that much of the branch-plant capacity attracted to the assisted areas was not contributing in any major way to regional self-sustaining growth. Indeed upon the then conditions of economic adversity plant closures and job losses were taking place. Of greater importance, these conditions undermined the logic, central to traditional policy, of encouraging firms to move to the problem regions. Little mobile investment was available and the once-prosperous parts of the country such as the West Midlands and South-east from which branch plants had once emanated were now also suffering substantial employment losses. Other criticisms of regional policy at this time included its reliance on capital grants when the principal problem was one of too few jobs, its bias towards manufacturing – and especially the production units of such firms – and its lack of attention to the indigenous sector of problem regions to help generate growth 'from within'. In addition the Conservative government was keen both to cut public expenditure and to relax the controls on business activity.

The government's response to these points since 1979 has been the introduction of a number of major reforms. First, the regional policy budget was cut, from £700 million in 1983–4 to £400 million in 1987–8. Second, from April 1988 automatic regional development grants have been abolished and are being replaced by selective assistance for which firms have to demonstrate a need within a cost-per-job limit of £10,000. Third, the areas qualifying for assistance, shown in figure 8.6, have been reduced substantially so that available funds can be concentrated in those areas most in need. Fourth, Industrial Development Certificate controls, which attempted to limit the areas where medium to large firms could locate new establishments, were abolished in 1982. Finally in 1988 the government launched an 'Enterprise Initiative' by which it attempts to improve the quality of information and advice available to British industry. Any firm with a payroll of fewer than 500 may now receive a two-day visit from an Enterprise Counsellor, paid for by the Department of Trade and Industry (DTI), who will give impartial and confidential advice on ways of improving a firm's efficiency and will offer advice on the specialist consultants the firm should consult. The DTI will pay a proportion of the costs, up to two-thirds in the Assisted Areas and Urban Programme Areas, of such consultants (see below). It is as yet too early to evaluate the effects of these reforms.

Brief mention must also be given to urban policy and local-area initiatives of both central and local government. It has long been recognized that there are small areas of major economic and social distress in many parts of the country, especially in the large urban and older industrial areas. Following the Inner Area Studies of the mid-1970s, the Inner Urban Areas Act of 1978 defined a number of districts which were given enhanced powers and financial assistance. The most significant of these were the Partnership Authorities between the local and national governments in Liverpool, Birmingham, Lambeth, London Docklands, Manchester/Salford, Newcastle/Gateshead and Hackney/Islington, which qualified for up to a 75 per cent government grant towards approved programmes to tackle the problems of unemployment, low incomes, and bad housing in their areas. These schemes, and the plethora of similar ones which followed, were not just concerned with economic development, and even less with manufacturing industry, but had housing, social and environmental goals as well.

The additional schemes introduced during the 1980s have reflected the

Conservative government's commitment to free competition, reducing the burden of red tape on private enterprise and the encouragement of the private sector to help rejuvenate these problem localities with the aid of public money only as a 'pump-priming' device. Thus in 1981 the Urban Development Grant Programme was introduced for the provision of infrastructure and 'permanent' jobs in inner-city areas, financed by a 75 per cent central grant towards the Local Authority share of approved project costs on a one to four basis between the public and private sectors. In the same year two Urban Development Corporations, in London and Liverpool Docklands, came into being. These are independent organizations controlling the development of their own areas. They have comprehensive powers of land assembly and servicing with up to 100 per cent grant finance from the Department of the Environment for certain approved projects. By 1988 this approach to the economic revival of problem areas was extended in England and Wales to include parts of Tyneside, Teeside, Manchester, Leeds, Sheffield, Stoke-on-Trent, Cardiff and Bristol. In addition, and more specifically to promote the development of industry in problem areas, eleven Enterprise Zones were designated in 1980. The number has grown to twenty-five of which only four – Corby, Wellingborough, Isle of Dogs, and north-west Kent – are in the more prosperous regions of the south and east. Of the remainder, two are in Northern Ireland, three in Wales, three in Scotland, and the rest in north and west England (figure 8.7). In these areas firms are granted automatic planning permission, are exempted from local rates for up to ten years, and all capital investment on buildings is 100 per cent tax allowable. The success of these zones has been extremely variable; in Belfast and Gateshead new job creation has been poor, for example, whereas in Clydebank, Corby and Swansea there has been some success.

Local Authorities have also felt the need to become involved in economic development initiatives, especially in those areas most severely affected by the 1979–81 recession. This has been possible up to the legal limit set by government of up to 2p for every pound of rate income. These initiatives have varied from the provision of workshops to enterprise boards, of which the most noteworthy are those set up in the early 1980s by the Greater London Council and the West Midlands Metropolitan County Council.

Many of the above schemes have been generating new jobs in problem inner-city and industrial areas throughout the 1980s. But the important question to be asked is whether these will ever be able to generate enough jobs to arrest and reverse the massive employment losses in these areas. In terms of manufacturing jobs this has certainly not been the case and it is unlikely that it will ever be so. However, the objectives of many of these initiatives are not solely concerned with the manufacturing sector. They refer to employment in general. What many of these schemes have achieved is a transformation of employment structures in their designated

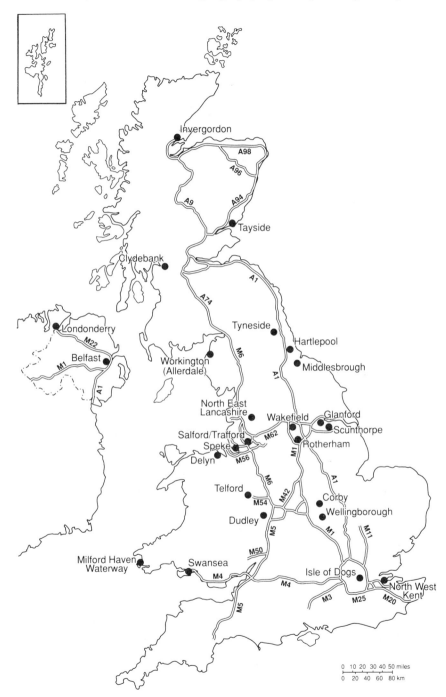

*Figure 8.7* Enterprise zones

areas away from manufacturing and into services. For example, in the London Docklands between 1981 and 1985 while total employment actually increased by 3.6 per cent, jobs in manufacturing declined by 40 per cent and jobs in services increased by the same proportion. This may result in an adverse local income effect. However, it must be assumed that new jobs in a particular locality will go to local residents; labour market adjustment mechanisms and patterns of recruitment disperse the employment effects of localized job creation. This is one of the many problems the government's policies and programmes for the inner cities and older industrial areas must now attempt to address.

## REFERENCES

Boddy, M. (1987) 'High technology industry, regional development and defence manufacture: a case study in the UK sunbelt', in Robson, B. T. (ed.) *Managing the City: The Aims and Impacts of Urban Policy*, London: Croom Helm.

Fothergill, S. and Gudgin, G. (1982) *Unequal Growth: Urban and Regional Employment Change in the UK*, London: Heinemann.

Fothergill, S., Gudgin, G., Kitson, M. and Monk, S. (1986) 'The de-industrialisation of the city', in Martin, R. and Rowthorn, B. (eds.) *The Geography of De-industrialisation*, London: Methuen.

Keeble, D. E. (1987) 'Industrial change in the United Kingdom', in Lever, W. F. (ed.) *Industrial Change in the United Kingdom*, Harlow: Longman.

Keeble, D. E. (1988) 'High technology industry and local environments in the UK', in Aydalot, P. and Keeble, D. E. (eds.) *High Technology Industry and Innovative Environments: The European experience*, London: Routledge.

Martin, R. (1986) 'Thatcherism and Britain's industrial landscape', in Martin, R. and Rowthorne, B. (eds.) *The Geography of Deindustrialization*, London: Methuen.

Martin, R. (1989) 'De-industrialisation and State intervention: Keynesianism, Thatcherism and the Regions', in Mohan, J. (ed.) *The Political Geography of Contemporary Britain*, London: Macmillan.

Peck, F. and Townsend, A. (1984) 'Contrasting experience of recession and spatial restructuring: British shipbuilders, Plessey and Metal Box', *Regional Studies*, 18: 319–38.

Townsend, A. R. and Peck, F. W. (1985) 'The geography of mass redundancy in named corporations', in Pacione, M. (ed.) *Progress in Industrial Geography*, London: Croom Helm.

## FURTHER READING

For sectoral and regional employment data see the monthly *Employment Gazette*, Department of Employment, and for subregional data see *Regional Trends*, Central Statistical Office, published annually.

On all aspects of industrial change in the UK the most important text is Lever, W. F. (1987) *Industrial Change in the UK*, London: Longman. A useful companion volume stressing the problems of particular regions is Damesick, P. and Wood, P. (1987) *Regional Problems, Problem Regions and Public Policy in the UK*, Oxford, Oxford University Press. Other recent volumes devoted to industrial change in the UK include Hoare, A. G. (1983) *Location and Industry in Britain*, Cambridge, Cambridge University Press; Massey, D. and Meegan, R. (1985)

*Politics and Method*, London: Methuen; and Massey, D. and Allen, J. (1988) *Uneven Re-development*, London: Hodder and Stoughton.

On the north:south divide see Green, A. (1988) 'The North-South divide in Great Britain: an examination of the evidence', *Transactions of the Institute of British Geographers* N,S, 13: 179–98; and Martin, R. (1988) 'The political economy of Britain's north-south divide', *Transactions of the Institute of British Geographers*, NS 13: 389–418.

On macro-conceptions of regional economic change: for post-industrialism see Lever, W. F. (1987) 'Glasgow: policy for the post-industrial city', in Robson, B. T. (ed.) *Managing the City*, London: Croom Helm.

For long-term cycles on innovation see Hall, P. (1985) 'The geography of the fifth Kondratieff', in Hall, P. and Markusen, A. (eds.) *Silicon Landscapes*, London: George Allen & Unwin.

For flexible accumulation see Cooke, P. (1988) 'Flexible integration, scope economies and strategic alliances: social and spatial mediations', *Society and Space*, 6; and Gertler, M. S. (1988) 'The limits to flexibility: comments on the post-Fordist vision of production and its geography', *Transactions of the Institute of British Geographers*, NS 13: 419–32.

On the geography of recession see Townsend, A. R. (1982) *The Impact of Recession*, Beckenham, Kent: Croom Helm; Martin, R. L. (1982) 'Job loss and the regional incidence of redundancies in the current recession', *Cambridge Journal of Economics*, 6: 375–95; Martin, R. and Rowthorn, B. (1986) *The Geography of De-industrialisation*, London; MacMillan; Danson, M. (1986) *Redundancy and Recession*, Norwich: Geo Books; and Lloyd, P. and Shutt, J. (1985) 'Recession and restructuring in the North-West region, 1974–82: the implications of recent events', in Massey, D. and Meegan, R. (eds.) *Politics and Method*, London: Methuen.

On the geography of military spending see Lovering, J. and Boddy, M. (1988) 'The geography of military industry in Britain', *Area*, 20: 41–51.

On high-technology industry see Hall, P., Breheny, M., McQuaid, R., and Hart, D. (1987) *Western Sunrise: The Genesis and Growth of Britain's Major High-tech' Corridor*, London: Allen & Unwin; Sayer, A. and Morgan, K. (1986) 'The electronics industry in regional development in Britain', in Amin, A. and Goddard, J. B. (eds.) *Technological Change, Industrial Restructuring and Regional Development*, London: Allen & Unwin; Kelly, T. (1987) *The British Computer Industry: Crisis and Development*, London: Croom Helm; Keeble, D. E. (1988) 'High-technology industry and local economic development: the case of the Cambridge phenomenon', *Environment and Planning C, Government and Policy*, 6.

The economic problems of some of Britain's most important cities are considered in the recent Inner Cities Research Programme of the Economic and Social Research Council. Publications have included Boddy, M., Lovering, J., and Bassett, K. (1986) *Sunbelt City? A Study of Economic Change in Britain's M4 Growth Corridor* on Bristol; Lever, W. F. and Moore, C. (eds.) (1987) *The City in Transition: Policies and Agencies for the Economic Regeneration of Clydeside*; Buck, N., Gordon, I., and Young, K. (1986) *The London Employment Problem*; Spencer, K., Taylor, A., Smith, B., Mawson, J., Flynn, N., and Batley, R. (1988) *Crisis in the Industrial Heartland: A Study of the West Midlands*; and Robinson, F., Goddard, J., and Wren, C. (1988) *Economic Development Policies: An Evaluative Study of the Newcastle Metropolitan Region*. All published by Oxford University Press.

On the UK's position internationally see Dicken, P. (1986) *Global Shift: Industrial Change in a Turbulent World*, London: Harper and Row.

On regional policy see Armstrong, H. and Taylor, J. (1985) *Regional Economics and*

*Policy*, Oxford: Philip Allan; Damesick, P; (1985) 'Recent debates and developments in British regional policy', *Planning Outlook*, 28: 3–7; Martin, R. L. (1985) 'Monetarism masquerading as regional policy? The government's new system of regional aid', *Regional Studies*, 19: 379–88; Martin, R. L. and Hodge, J. S. C. (1983a and b) 'The reconstruction of British regional policy', *Government and Policy*, 1: 133–2 and 317–40; and Regional Studies Association (1983) *Report of an Inquiry into Regional Problems in the UK*, Norwich; Geo Books.

On local initiatives for economic regeneration see: Donnison, D. and Middleton, A. (eds.) 1987 *Regenerating the Inner City: Glasgow's Experience*, London: Routledge & Kegan Paul; Bromley, R. D. F. and Morgan, R. H. (1985) 'The effects of enterprise zone policy: evidence from Swansea', *Regional Studies*, 19: 403–13; Boddy, M. (1984) 'Local economic and employment strategies', in Boddy, M. and Fudge, C. (eds.) *Local Socialism*, London: MacMillan-Norcliffe, G. B.; Hoare, A. G. (1982) 'Enterprise zone policy for the inner city', *Area*, 14: 265–74; and Church, A. (1988) 'Urban regeneration in London Docklands: a five year policy review', *Environment and Planning C*, 6: 187–208.

**ACKNOWLEDGEMENTS**

Acknowledgement is made to David Keeble and Longman for permission to reproduce the map in figure 8.2, to Alan Townsend, Frank Peck, and the Regional Studies Association for permission to reproduce the maps in figures 8.4 and 8.5, to Tina Buckle for the drawing of the other figures and to Shireen Karanjia and Myra Whiteson for typing the manuscript.

# 9 Market services in the United Kingdom

*John A Dawson*

There are two types of organization in the service sector. There are those that market their services and those that do not, often termed public services. This chapter is predominantly concerned with the activities of those service industries which market their services and which cover a wide range of activities, including those which provide services used by the final consumer and those which provide services to firms in the production sector or even to other firms in the service sector. Over 40 per cent of employment in the United Kingdom is accounted for by market services.

The market service sector is large and complex. Various attempts have been made to classify it in order to make analyses more manageable. One method of classification is by the three main types of consumer of the service – personal, producer industry, service activity. Thus, for example, retailing is classified as a personal service of the first type, an industrial design agency, a producer service, is of the second type, and a retail security company, a services service, would be the third type. This apparently straightforward definition, which is based on the type of customer receiving the service, is complicated in reality in two ways. First, there is interaction between the market sector and the non-market sector, each with their three types of service. Thus, for example, the National Health Service (non-market service) may buy services from a cleaning company (market service); alternatively a football club (market service) may obtain police support for crowd control (non-market service). This interaction means that substitutability between market and non-market services may occur. It thus becomes difficult to consider market services in isolation from non-market services. The second difficulty in the straightforward definition results from firms providing services to all three types of consumer. For example, Chart Services is a medium-sized distribution company which provides transport services to GEC (producer service) and British Shoe Corporation (services service), and it also provides home delivery for purchasers of electrical goods (consumer service). In addition it provides a vehicle hire service available to all three customer types and to agents in the non-market sector. The company is itself a customer for a range of specialist and more general business services provided by market and non-market sectors. Many other firms, for example British Telecom and the large banks, similarly provide services for a wide base of customers, including non-market sector activities.

Definitions of the market services sector become particularly complicated when the activities of individual firms are considered. None the less the distinction between market and non-market services is useful because it provides a framework for estimates to be calculated of the growth of the services sector. Despite the limitations this framework is used as the basis for this chapter. The remainder of this chapter is divided into five parts. First, an estimate of the size of the services sector is provided. Second, the four main structural processes underpinning contemporary change in this sector are discussed. Third, two major processes generating the spatial changes in the United Kingdom are reviewed. Fourth, short cases are presented on the financial services, wholesaling and retailing industries. Finally, consideration is given to how the sector might respond in the future to likely changes in the economic and political environment.

## SIZE OF THE SERVICES SECTOR

Since the early 1970s there has been a shift in balance in the major sectors of the British economy. Table 9.1 shows the contributions to GDP of the four main sectors in 1971 and 1986. The largest growth has been in market services, with the net loser being the production industries. Measured in terms of GDP the shift is modest, although over 40 per cent of GDP is generated by market services.

*Table 9.1* Percentage of GDP and employment by major sector

|  | GDP | | | Employment[a] | | |
|  | *1971* | *1986* | *Change* | *1971* | *1986* | *Change* |
| --- | --- | --- | --- | --- | --- | --- |
| Agriculture | 3.0 | 1.8 | −1.2 | 1.9 | 1.5 | −0.4 |
| Production industries and construction | 44.5 | 38.1 | −6.4 | 44.7 | 31.1 | −13.6 |
| Market services | 35.8 | 40.5 | +4.7 | 31.6 | 40.1 | +8.5 |
| Non-market services | 16.7 | 19.6 | +2.9 | 21.8 | 27.4 | +5.6 |

*Note*: [a] Employees in employment; self-employed are not included

In terms of employment, the shift has been more substantial. This reflects, to some extent, the relatively low pay of employees in the services in general and also the differential change in labour productivity with considerable increases in the production industries in recent years. The employment figures in table 9.1 exclude the self-employed, who are concentrated in the service sector. Between 1971 and 1986 the number of self-employed rose by 589,000 of whom 419,000 were in market services.

Employment, excluding the self-employed, in market services in 1986 was 8,577,000, which represented an increase of 1,625,000 since 1971. A considerable amount of this growth has been accounted for by the banking, finance and insurance industries which now account for almost one in six of the employed workforce. This sector has also contributed significantly to the growth in GDP in market services, but productivity growth at 2.5 per cent per annum over the period has been below the 3 per cent of the manufacturing sector, which has contributed to some shakeout in the market service sector in the late 1980s as attempts have been made to increase productivity levels. Generally there has been lower growth in labour productivity in the services compared with manufacturing. The exception to this general position is in the communications sector, where the growth in value-added per person has been considerable at 4.1 per cent per annum.

The shift in balance of GDP and the growth in employment in market services have been accompanied by an increase in the part-time workforce and a fall in the percentage of female workers, calculated on the basis of full-time equivalents. Whilst the number of female workers has risen, a large proportion are employed on a part-time basis. Table 9.2 shows that in distribution and related industry, 38 per cent of employees are part-time, 57 per cent of female employees are part-time and 48 per cent of employees are female. Whilst the first two of these figures have risen considerably since 1971, the third has fallen slightly. Thus the general increase in female participation rates in the economy has been offset in market services by the growth of part-time work. The service sector had for several decades a relatively high proportion of female employees. This proportion is now showing little change, but the use of part-time workers is still increasing rapidly and is accounting for almost all the growth in part-time labour in the economy as a whole.

The increase of the service sector during the 1980s has not been spread evenly over the United Kingdom. In non-market services (table 9.3) the large defence presence in Northern Ireland makes it the only region in which market and non-market services make similar-sized contributions to GDP at the regional level. In contrast is the South-east where, despite the presence of central government, the massive growth in market services in the financial sector makes it the only region in which services in total account for over 70 per cent of regional GDP. In this region over half of GDP is accounted for by market services. The South-east stands apart clearly from the remainder of the United Kingdom, where the regional spread of shares in market services is from 32 to 40 per cent. Whilst this differentiation has been present for many years, the high growth rate in the South-east in recent years has resulted in an increase in the degree of difference in comparison with other regions.

A final point to remember in assessing the size and growth of the market services sector in the United Kingdom is the difference between an industry-based definition of services and one based on occupation. A baker

*Table 9.2* Part-time workers and female participation in the labour force

| | *Percentage of male workers who are part-time* | | *Percentage of female workers who are part-time* | | *Percentage of all workers who are part-time* | | *Percentage of all workers who are female*[a] | |
|---|---|---|---|---|---|---|---|---|
| | *1971* | *1986* | *1971* | *1986* | *1971* | *1986* | *1971* | *1986* |
| Economy | 4.4 | 7.3 | 33.2 | 42.6 | 15.3 | 23.2 | 37.4 | 40.0 |
| Manufacturing | 1.3 | 1.4 | 19.7 | 19.2 | 6.8 | 6.7 | 27.8 | 27.8 |
| Services | 8.2 | 11.7 | 39.0 | 47.6 | 23.4 | 31.2 | 45.1 | 48.9 |
| of which: | | | | | | | | |
| Distribution, hotels, | | | | | | | | |
| repairs, catering | 11.4 | 15.5 | 42.0 | 56.7 | 27.8 | 38.0 | 49.2 | 48.2 |
| Transport | 1.6 | 3.0 | 13.4 | 22.6 | 3.1 | 6.8 | 12.4 | 17.6 |
| Communication | 2.2 | 1.4 | 22.9 | 21.0 | 7.5 | 6.2 | 23.4 | 22.5 |
| Finance | 5.3 | 6.0 | 24.7 | 26.7 | 15.3 | 16.2 | 49.2 | 46.4 |
| Public administration | | | | | | | | |
| and defence | 4.4 | 7.9 | 25.4 | 32.3 | 11.5 | 19.0 | 31.5 | 42.2 |
| Education and | | | | | | | | |
| health | 16.3 | 17.5 | 44.4 | 53.6 | 36.0 | 42.8 | 66.8 | 65.5 |

*Note*: [a] Full-time equivalent with two part-time workers being calculated as one full-time equivalent.

*Table 9.3* Percentage of GDP accounted for by services in each region, 1986

| | *Market services* | *Non-market services* |
|---|---|---|
| North | 32.4 | 21.4 |
| Yorkshire and Humberside | 37.2 | 19.0 |
| East Midlands | 32.5 | 18.2 |
| East Anglia | 39.8 | 18.2 |
| South-east | 50.3 | 19.9 |
| South-west | 40.0 | 22.0 |
| West Midlands | 35.2 | 17.4 |
| North-west | 37.7 | 18.3 |
| Wales | 32.5 | 20.7 |
| Scotland | 38.3 | 22.1 |
| Northern Ireland | 32.1 | 32.4 |

in a grocery superstore bakery will be classified as a retail worker (a market service) but the work carried out might easily be the same as a baker in a company manufacturing bread who would be defined as a production worker. In the same bread factory the wages of the baker may be calculated by a company employee (a manufacturing activity) or a wages calculation service might be bought from one of the banks (a market service). Whilst the occupation of two people may be identical, they may be quite differently classified in the industry-based statistics and hence in the tables presented so far. Whilst it would seem from the tables presented in this section that the service sector, and market services particularly, is growing, in the United Kingdom, it is far from clear how much of this growth is due to real increases and how much is due to changes in the relationship between industry and occupational specializations. In economic terms, of course, there is little if any difference between the production of goods and the production of services. Added value can come from either the transformation of materials or the transformation of behaviour, appearance, well-being or satisfaction The service sector, in exactly similar ways to the manufacturing sector, produces and delivers a set of values. The real size of market services activity is therefore very difficult to measure. None the less, a generally accepted view in the late 1980s would be that about 42 per cent of the UK economy was accounted for by market services and that this has increased in recent years and will continue to increase during the 1990s.

## STRUCTURAL CHANGES IN MARKET SERVICES

Underpinning the growth of market services in the United Kingdom, there are several structural processes at work; four are of particular importance in the context of this chapter:

the shift in social attitudes towards acceptance of the values of a post-industrial economy;
changes in corporate behaviour with a greater understanding of the implications of transaction costs;
the gradual change from a production led to a marketing led economic system; and
the steady retreat of government from intervention in the market.

It is useful to consider briefly these structural changes in the context of the service industries before looking at their spatial implications.

There has been much debate and research over the moves to a post-industrial phase in UK society. A variety of alternative terms has been used to describe a widely perceived broadly based change in social attitudes and values.

Inherent in almost all these models of social change in the United Kindom is the realization that, as society becomes more affluent, not only is it increasingly necessary to transform (in the sense of add value to) products by the addition of services but also that people demand more complex types of service in their own right. Many of these new types of service are market services based on information, which is, in Bell's terminology of post-industrialism, the dynamic which drives the change into a post-industrial phase. Thus within the UK economy there has been widespread growth of information related services. Some record information, such as market-research companies; others process it, such as accountants or market analysts in brokers' companies; others distribute it, such as commercial radio or video libraries. In all these activities there has been considerable expansion during the 1980s. Consumer spending on services has risen steadily, with for example the rise of non-residential catering such that by 1985 it contributed 1.9 per cent of GDP, more than the contribution of agriculture, and accounted for almost 25 per cent of household food expenditure. The added value in catering was over 50 per cent of its output value of £10 billion in 1985. The shift towards a more service-orientation economy has been driven by changing social values. The net result, however, is a substantial structural adjustment in the economy associated with the growth of demand for market services.

The second process causing a structural shift towards market services is a process of organizational change within companies. In recent years, managerial methods have evolved in particular ways with the gradual retreat from market-type transactions. Companies faced with decisions on whether to provide their own services or to buy them in have moved towards the purchase of services from outside groups. In these newer types of corporate organization the relationship of the company to other firms, including the providers of services, is changing. Instead of finished output (whether product or service) from a company being sold, in a market type transaction, to be used as input for another company, there is a move towards negotiation between selling and buying company in respect of various characteristics of the output process, such as product design, quality control, delivery timing, and so on. In these negotiated transactions many other variables than market price are considered, and associated with these other considerations there is often the need for market services – industrial design agencies, quality testing consultants, distribution companies and so on.

The use of the various market services creates transaction costs. As corporate behaviour has changed, so also have attitudes to these transaction costs. Whilst previously they may have been internal costs within this company, increasingly they have become externalized, partly as services have become more specialist in nature. A simple example is in the preparation of company reports – it is now commonplace to employ specialist consultants and agencies, such as Addison Design, to undertake the preparation of a company's annual report when a few years ago this activity would have been undertaken in-house by a small group within the corporate administration. This trend in corporate behaviour, associated with greater awareness of transaction costs, has generated increased demand for market services.

The third process of structural change relevant in the present context is the shift from a production-led to a marketing-led economy in the United Kingdom. This change is a long-term one and is some way from running its full course. It results from changes in production technologies, trade policies, and national wealth which have moved the economy from one of post-1945 product shortage to one of product surplus. At the same time the final consumer has become more affluent and more demanding for product variety – variety of type of product as well as variety of quality of product.

Production is now increasingly undertaken to respond to a perceived market demand as distinct from the position forty years ago when the consumer was provided with what the manufacturer produced. The emphasis within the production–distribution channel has changed, albeit not yet totally. One of many results of this structural change has been changes and expansion of consumer-related activities which sell products and services to the final consumer. For example, new sales space for retailers has been produced, often with particular retailers in mind as tenants, through a property development process which has generated a range of market services from shopping centre manager, through architects, designers, planning consultants to advisers of financial institutions providing the capital for the new shopping schemes. This contrasts with centre development in the 1960s when often local governments built what they believed the retailer should want and the consumer should have. The expansion of office-based activities in general has been associated with this overall aspect of structural change and as such it has created demand for property-related services. The transition to a marketing-led economy is far from complete and more new growth in market services is likely in this context in the coming decade.

The fourth process at work changing the structure of the economy and resulting in increased market services is the retreat of government from intervention in the market. In some ways the creation of market services by this means is a transfer of activity from the non-market to the market sector. The privatization of previously public services results in the apparent expansion of market services. The privatization of the British Airports Authority, for example, generated an increase in market services but in reality was largely a transfer from the non-market sector. In a similar way the moves to competitive tendering for support services for health, education, local government, and so on usually only result in transfers of activity rather than the creation of new service activity. Because of deregulatory activity there has been a real growth in market services, however. Within financial services a growth of market services followed deregulation; reductions in public sector support for health and education has generated new market services partly to replace those lost because of government under-funding but also partly to expand the range of services being offered; deregulation of telecommunications has allowed market expansion and new market services by Mercury and by other specialist service agencies; and the future likely deregulation of broadcasting is likely to have a similar result.

The four features of structural change described all result, to varying extent, in the growth of market services. The market services provided have been delivered by large firms which have seen strategic market opportunities. Thus there has been growth of the large accountancy firms, such as Arthur Andersen, which have moved into various types of consultancy, and by small firms which have seen tactical market opportunites in small specialist sectors, such as TMS Partnership which has become the leading specialist market research agency for the clothing sector. Structural shifts within the economy as a whole have resulted in increases in the quantity and type of market services in the United Kingdom.

## SPATIAL CHANGES IN MARKET SERVICES

Alongside the changes in structure there have also been processes operating which have changed the spatial nature of market services in the United Kingdom. Two in particular will be considered here: the use of information technology to reduce the costs of spatial separation of activities, and the growth in importance of economies of scope and spatial agglomeration.

Information technology has been an enabling agent for the establishment of various types of managerial change within the economy. These processes may have a spatial dimension because the organizations operate at different places and interact with organizations at other locations. Information technology had and continues to have implications for the management of spatially disaggregated networks of activities. By their nature many of the market service activities are widely dispersed. The networks of retailers provide facilities sometimes in many hundreds of locations: Boots is typical of many of the larger retail firms and operates through 1,026 stores. Similarly the services of hoteliers, accountants, banks, distribution companies, trade unions and other market services have to be delivered through a spatially disaggregated network throughout the United Kingdom. Although often highly dispersed, the delivery of services is by no means uniformly distributed across UK space. The importance in a spatial sense of information technology in this situation has been fourfold:

it has enabled more effective control, from a distance, of the activity at nodes in the network,
it has enabled more efficient management of flows and interactions between nodes,
it has allowed new divisions of the activities which take place at the nodes, and
it has enabled rapid expansion or contraction of the network in terms both of numbers and size of the nodes and links.

These four aspects of spatial change can be illustrated with examples in market services. The establishment of communications networks between head offices and branches in a company has allowed firms to control branch activities from head office. The growth of automatic teller machines (ATMs) is one example of a network which has been enabled by such communications links. From initial development in the mid-1960s, in January 1988 there were 12,389 ATMs in the United Kingdom, an increase of 1,500 on the previous year's total, and a similar level of growth was planned for 1988. In January 1988 the network of Lloyds/Barclays had 4,174 and the NatWest/Midland network had 3,125 outlets. Since this date the TSB network has joined the NatWest/Midland network and the new LINK network involving Building Societies has grown substantially. The activity at the ATM is controlled remotely by a central information management system. The growth of ATMs has not only reduced the constraints of space and time on the consumer's access to cash, but has also generated a support industry of market services to maintain and service the equipment. The ATM industry depends on control from the centre of activity of each node.

More efficient management of flows may be illustrated by the growth of Electronic Data Interchange (EDI) networks such as TRADANET. This EDI network links together retail head offices, shops, manufacturer head offices, factories, distributor head offices and depots. Information on transactions – purchase order, invoice, delivery order, delivery invoice, availability report, delivery confirmation, etc. – exists on the network and can be accessed, with various security controls, by the different groups. The network was tested in the early 1980s by Reckitt and Coleman, Boots, Rowntree Mackintosh and Tesco, and by 1987 was generally available. By 1988 the user group numbered 238 companies which operate through many thousands of locations. Grand Metropolitan, for example, use the service to receive invoices from the food and drink suppliers which deliver to 2,000 outlets including Chef and Brewer and Berni restaurant chains. TRADANET results in a major reduction in physical flows of paper and in the need to match and cross-check paper records. The spatial flow of product is made more efficient and is achieved at lower cost through more effective management of information.

Information technology has enabled new divisions of activities in service companies which have allowed parts of companies carrying out specific activities to be moved to locations separate from the rest of the firm. This decentralization of selected activities has been a notable aspect of the changing organizational structure of many firms in the financial services sector. Of the almost 100,000 service sector office jobs dispersed from London between 1963 and 1977, approximately half were in insurance, banking and finance. This pattern has continued through the 1980s with a number of major relocations of specific activity groups, for example the Midland Bank computer services to Sheffield, Abbey National (except finance and marketing) to Milton Keynes, and Chase Manhattan administration service to Bournemouth. Reasons for the moves vary and include labour and occupancy cost differentials and post-merger rationalizaton of activity, but the relocation is enabled by information technology (IT) and the management of information such that the physical spatial separation of activities is overcome by communications technologies. Various nodes in the technology networks have become specialist ones with the new divisions of activity enabled by the communication technology.

*Table 9.4* Store formats operated by NEXT, 1985–6

| | Retail outlets by format | | | | Floorspace in /000s sq.ft. | | | |
|---|---|---|---|---|---|---|---|---|
| | Aug. 1985 | Aug. 1986 | Nov. 1986 | Feb. 1988 | Aug. 1985 | Aug. 1986 | Nov. 1986 | Feb. 1988 |
| NEXT Too | 210 { | 112 | 117 | 97 | 284 { | 160 | 177 | 132 |
| NEXT Collection | | 109 | 114 | 115 | | 164 | 174 | 172 |
| NEXT Originals | — | — | — | 74 | — | — | — | 88 |
| NEXT for Men | 114 | 162 | 174 | 202 | 152 | 236 | 245 | 279 |
| NEXT Lingerie | — | 5 | 42 | 85 | — | 2 | 12 | 25 |
| NEXT Accessories/ Essential | — | 3 | 8 | 62 | — | 4 | 10 | 25 |
| NEXT Jewellery | — | — | — | 17 | — | — | — | 2 |
| NEXT Interior | 14 | 36 | 40 | 41 | 25 | 72 | 83 | 79 |
| NEXT BG | — | — | — | 40 | — | — | — | 40 |
| NEXT Cafe | 5 | 9 | 10 | * | 9 | 21 | 23 | * |
| NEXT Expresso Bar | 1 | 6 | 8 | * | 1 | 3 | 5 | * |
| NEXT Florist | 5 | 8 | 8 | * | 2 | 2 | 2 | * |
| NEXT Hairdressers | — | 3 | 3 | * | — | 5 | 5 | * |
| NEXT to Nothing | 2 | 15 | 23 | 121 | 5 | 44 | 57 | 195 |
| Salisburys | — | — | — | 184 | — | — | — | 168 |
| Hepworths | 84 | — | — | — | 115 | — | — | — |
| Zales | — | — | — | 127 | — | — | — | 123 |
| Dillons/Allens | — | — | — | 370 | — | — | — | 228 |
| TOTAL IN UK | 435 | 468 | 547 | 1535 | 593 | 713 | 793 | 1556 |
| Biba (West Germany) | | | | 56 | | | | 34 |

*Note*: * Included with other formats

IT has also enabled the rapid expansion of some firms in the service sector in the United Kingdom. Whether expansion is measured in terms of either number of outlets or market share, the result is the same: it is possible to see the enabling role of new technology in the spatial expansion of companies. In the retail sector for example, the rapid growth of NEXT, shown in table 9.4, was possible because of the presence of an IT network which connected stores to head office and allowed central management to control activity in the stores, and also because of the presence of management information systems in head office which could handle the plethora of information on consumer demands, products and store operations. The company in effect opened almost 1,000 new branches over a fifteen-month period between November 1986 and February 1988. The alternative form of retail growth, that of increased market share, has similarly been enabled by IT. In the retailing of groceries the market share of Tesco rose from 11 per cent to 16 per cent between 1978 and 1988, and was paralleled by enabling IT systems in store, in depot and in head office. Without IT it would have been impossble for Tesco to manage a food superstore of over

30,000 sq. ft. carrying 15,000 items with a stock-turn of 40, let alone a chain of 100 such stores spread throughout the country.

These four examples of the different aspects of the enabling nature of IT in respect of spatial change in market services all point towards a pattern of decentralization in which the cost of the spatial separation of activities is reduced. Although there are many other examples of the spread, and decentralization, of market service activity throughout the United Kingdom, there are countervailing processes at work which encourage agglomeration and centralization of market services. Of particular importance in this connection have been cost economies of scope and to a lesser extent of scale.

A major difference between the organization of production and of services is the relative importance of economies of scale – essentially a product-related concept – and economies of scope – essentially a marketing-related concept. The bringing together of different but related activities, typically services, may create economies of scope. So, for example, the large supermarkets sell ambient, frozen, chilled and fresh products and obtain cost economies in administration, in common payment, and in labour from the scope of activities they bring together at the one location. In the production of frozen chickens, however, it is cost economies of scale which are important, with bigger plants and more chickens; producing frozen chickens and frozen peas offers little opportunities for economies of scope, at least at plant level. Another example is the large accountancy companies which have attempted to benefit from economies of scope through the addition of management consultancy activities to their traditional auditing activities.

Obtaining the economies of scope can mean the spatial centralization or agglomeration of various activities. Thus the growth of food superstores has been at the expense of smaller shops with a lesser range of products. Agglomerations of shops, in shopping centres and in retail parks, has also taken place as a means to increase retail floorspace. The alternative method of increasing floorspace by the creation of many individual shops extending current high streets has not taken place. In the development of market services in the United Kingdom there are many examples of firms seeking to obtain economies of scope by bringing together different activities to a single site.

This type of agglomeration is not incompatible with the decentralization enabled by IT, discussed above. Often the group of activities from which scope economies are obtained is decentralized as a unit. The large chartered surveyor companies provide a case in point. In 1969 the largest six companies were heavily concentrated in London, particularly in Mayfair and its fringes. Although they operated a number of branch offices, sixteen in total in thirteen towns, only in Glasgow was more than one of the top six represented. Activity was heavily centralized and controlled from head office. By 1987 the same six firms had sixty-five offices in thirty-nine towns in total and the range of services offered in branch offices had extended. There had been an element of spatial spread in the provision of this market service. But, over the same period, the broadening of the scope of activities at head and branch offices had allowed the companies to obtain cost economies of scope, particularly in respect of occupancy costs and costs of administrative support, including office technologies and labour. It has been possible in the market services sector in the United Kingdom for firms to broaden their scope and at the same time decentralize activity both organizationally and spatially. The substantial growth in demand for services has provided this opportunity for spatial change which has been enabled by IT.

This contrast between agglomeration and decentralization is apparent at a national scale across the whole sector. In 1974, out of twenty-five leading centres, London contained approximately two-thirds of all employment in financial and other market services. By 1981 this had fallen to under 60 per cent and after slight growth in the early 1980s was well below 60 per cent in the late 1980s. At the same time, however, the scope of services in all the leading centres has expanded considerably and services have grouped together in the leading centres.

The spatial processes have operated alongside the structural changes outlined earlier and have together generated responses in the various parts of the broad sector of market services. It is instructive, therefore, to consider three areas of activity in market services and briefly to consider the way they have changed. The three chosen are:

consumer financial services,
wholesalers, and
retailers.

Financial services typify a rapid growth sector, wholesalers illustrate a traditional, long-established sector, and retailers exemplify a sector undergoing major structural change.

### Consumer financial services

The term 'financial services' is comparatively new and was introduced as a result of the extensions into new activities by banks, building societies, insurance companies and similar groups. Until about 1980 there were three distinct groups involved with consumer finance:

life and general insurance, which were controlled through the DTI and which traded insurance-related products,
the clearing banks, controlled through the Bank of England, and
the building societies, controlled by legislation and with their activity limited to loans for housing and the taking of deposits.

During the 1980s the various controls have been reduced, and in some cases removed, so that it has become possible for the three groups to extend into each other's traditional markets. At the same time the market expanded rapidly; for example, insurance has grown at 7.5–8.5 per cent per annum (depending on how it is measured) between 1979 and 1988 compared with 2.3 per cent for the economy as a whole. Life insurance grew by almost 10 per cent per annum over this decade.

The clearing bank sector is dominated by the Big Four – Barclays, Lloyds, Midland and National Westminster. The ceiling control on bank deposits was raised in 1981, which allowed the clearing banks to move into the new markets of investment, insurance and mortgage lending. From an 8 per cent share of the mortgage market in 1980 they had more than doubled this by 1985, since when it has stabilized or even fallen slightly as a result of competition. Credit-card lending, associated with the major banks, showed major growth during the 1980s with consequential need for investment in new technologies, organizations to manage the credit activity, and not least the creation of major office complexes with many hundreds of jobs. The credit card management services are typical of the routine service activity which have no need to be located close to the centre of strategic decision-making in the sector, namely London. Thus Access is located in Northampton, Visa in Dunfermline.

The Building Societies have grown out of the savings-based Victorian friendly societies which were concentrated in the midlands, northern England and Scotland. In the post-war housing boom and with more recent moves to higher levels of home ownership, partly associated with various governmental incentives to house buying, the Building Societies have expanded their branch network and broadened the range of services on offer. There were 151 Building Societies in the United Kingdom in 1986 with total assets over £140 billion. The level of concentration in the sector is high with the top five societies accounting for 60 per cent of activity. The competition amongst the top five has meant that each has sought to extend its branch network as quickly as possible and there was in the early 1980s the rapid appearance of branches of several Building Societies on almost all High Streets. The 1987 Building Societies Act, which had been heralded for some years, allowed them to offer unsecured loans and to take on other types of business. The branch network which had been put in place allowed delivery of these new services. The high cost of creation of this network had been accepted in anticipation of the likely future opportunities for diversification, and so the Building Societies were willing to pay high rents for prime sites at locations with high levels of customer traffic. The Financial Services legislation of 1988 reduced still further the controls over their activity in life insurance and personal pensions. The diversification of activities by the Building Societies has brought them into direct competition with the banks and in consequence similar forms of service delivery are becoming apparent, for example through networks of ATMs.

The third group of companies, the insurance and assurance companies, similarly are diversifying into new product areas as a result of deregulation and the removal of barriers to competition by the Financial Services Act of 1988. As with the other groups, the broadening of the range of products on offer has resulted in more administrative demands and the need for additional technological, clerical, and administrative support. Again, relocation of these activities has occurred. In some cases this is decentralization from London as with, for example, the 500 jobs of Sun Life of Canada from Central London to Basingstoke in 1987, 250 jobs of Confederation Life to Stevenage in 1987, 330 jobs of Commercial Insurance to Basildon in 1985, and Lloyds Life Insurance division to Peterborough in 1984. In some cases the moves anticipated the forecast changes of the Financial Services Act with the companies positioning themselves to take advantage of the new commercial opportunities. In the early 1980s a survey of business expectations of companies in financial services showed that 79 per cent of Life Assurance Companies, 56 per cent of insurance companies and 71 per cent of banks were foreseeing business expansion opportunities in the 1980s.

The majority of relocations in consumer financial services in general are from Central London to towns in the south-east, but there are other favoured cities. In Bristol the numbers employed in the insurance sector doubled during the 1970s and growth has continued such that it is now the second most important insurance centre in Britain. The experience of the early movers to the city encouraged others to follow and, as the number of insurance firms increased, so also the services for these firms became better established; for example, the facilities for taking professional examinations improved.

Alongside the three main, formerly traditional, sectors, new activity groups in consumer financial services have developed over the last decade. Most notable are those involved in retail credit cards. Marks and Spencer launched its card in 1985 and within little over two years had 2.5 million card holders. House of Fraser has over 1.4 million, and Dixons over 500,000. In these cases non-London locations for the office operations are usual and may be the result either of *ab initio* decisions, for example Marks and Spencer at Chester, or of relocations, for example Welbeck Finance to Bristol.

The convergence of telecommunications and data-processing technologies has been an important enabling factor in both the growth and in locational changes in this sector. Without the changes in technology it is inconceivable how such rapid growth could have occurred. A phased model of this technological convergence is shown in figure 9.1. This six-stage sequence begins with the establishment of a computer in the head office with manual links to branch offices. Stage two has the introduction of terminals into head office for data capture and enquiry. Stage three is the important step of the introduction of terminals in branch offices; this involves reorganization of the relationship between branch offices and head offices, for example with the printing of insurance policies on site.

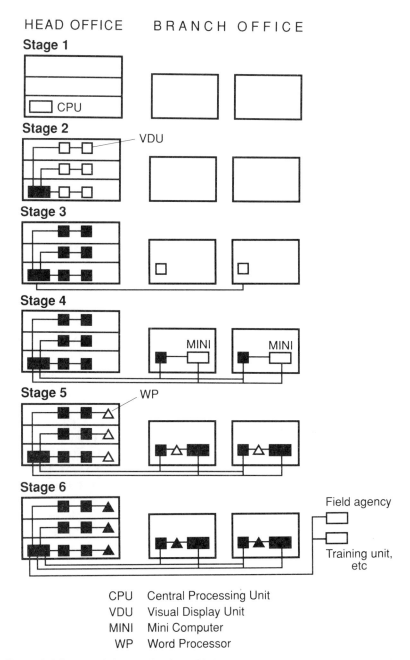

*Figure 9.1* Stages of the application of information technology in the financial services industries (based on Banking, Insurance and Financial Union, *New Technology in Banking, Insurance and Finance,* 1982)

Stage four involves a mini-computer at the branch ofice which begins to influence the managerial, rather than technical, occupations at the branch. Stage five involves the use of word processors through the network with the resultant change in work skills and the move to more flexible work patterns. Stages four and five involve the opportunity for a substantial growth in the number of branch offices as control from the centre becomes more effective. In stage six the technology extends beyond the operations office into functions such as training. A further stage may be hypothesized which involves the establishment of the electronic or paperless office with electronic mail, electronic filing, and extensive computer-to-computer links on EDI networks. This stage involves the increase of technological sophistication in the branch office at the expense of a large copy cat reinvestment in central facilities at the head office. In stage five or six there may be a move to reorganize head office with the opportunity to create factory-like processing centres for routine operations. This broad model is applicable to the consumer financial service sector in the United Kingdom during the 1970s and 1980s and has enabled the spread of branches to the High Street and the relocation of some large facilities away from head office.

**Wholesalers**

Wholesalers are unusual in being a market service which has shown only modest growth in recent years. Even in this case, however, change has occurred and it is far from straightforward. The number of wholesale businesses in the United Kingdom increased by almost 25 per cent between 1980 and 1986, from 91,000 to 112,000. The sales volume of wholesaling activity in total is volatile because of the large value component of petroleum products and recent price fluctuations in these products. Separating these items from the total sector shows a modest real growth in sales alongside the substantial increase in number of firms (table 9.5). Employment has shown little change in recent years. Consumer goods retailing accounts for over half of wholesale volumes and almost two-thirds of non-petroleum volumes. The level of penetration of the wholesale trade into various commodity areas varies from over 80 per cent of total activity in fresh meat and vegetables, newspapers, magazines and periodicals, through approximately half for furniture, toys, photographic goods, electrical goods and alcoholic drinks, to less than 25 per cent for footwear, clothing and jewellery. The level of wholesaler activity in a specific product area depends on many factors including:

1 Size of product demand. If the product has a large market there is likely to be some activity. Whilst a large market does not necessarily mean a high percentage penetration, it can mean substantial sales volume; for example, in clothing, textiles and footwear in 1986 the sales volume in

the United Kingdom was £7 billion, much of it through relatively small firms serving specialist retailers. Small wholesalers supplying small retailers with specialist ethnic clothing have increased, in recent years, in cities with large Asian populations.

2 A fragmented industry structure. If retailing or manufacturing is highly fragmented, wholesalers are likely to be involved, as with magazine distribution where retailing is highly fragmented and producers moderately so. Major wholesalers such as W. H. Smith and J. Menzies have wholesale operations which involve a two tier depot system, with small local facilities being supplied by road or rail from a regional or national depot.

3 Perishable products. These have always relied on wholesalers because of their proximity to and knowledge of the market, storage and distribution.

4 Complexity. The complexity of dealing with imports has allowed wholesalers to specialize as they have built up contacts and know-how. This has helped them sustain their position but it will be interesting to see whether this is retained after these complexities are removed, at least in Europe, in 1993.

5 Multi-markets. The ability of wholesalers to supply industrial, retailer and other service sector markets has enabled them to react to changes in the total market and cushion changes in any particular market.

Many of the traditional locational attributes of wholesalers have remained. In many cities there is a concentration of small wholesalers dealing in consumer goods on the fringe of the Central Business District (CBD). Many are operating from relatively old property. In Glasgow, for example, there is a cluster of activity on the southern fringe of the central area, but even around the rest of the fringe there is a substantial number of wholesale firms. Structural adjustment similar to other market services has occurred amongst some wholesale sectors. There is, for example, a high level of market concentration amongst food wholesalers, and particularly amongst those trading through cash and carry outlets.

*Table 9.5* Wholesale distribution in the UK

|  | 1980 | 1983 | 1986 |
|---|---|---|---|
| Number of businesses – total | 91,403 | 104,426 | 112,225 |
| of which consumer goods sector | 61,335 | 72,625 | 79,147 |
| Sales volume £b. total | 105.8 | 139.3 | 166.3 |
| excluding petroleum | 82.3 | 109.9 | 144.5 |
| of which consumer goods sector | 50.7 | 67.1 | 95.4 |

The 1960s were a period of rapid growth of cash and carry food wholesalers and depot numbers reached a peak of 632 in 1969. Since then there has been a gradual decline in numbers, associated with corporate mergers and takeovers and with increases in depot size. By 1988 the largest three companies had 60 per cent of the market and the average size of depot had increased from 12,000 square feet in 1979 to 37,000 square feet in 1985. The changes in structure have generated a spatial change with cash and carry moving out of inner city areas where it grew up in the 1960s into purpose-built single storey depots on suburban industrial estates where it has flourished in the 1980s.

The changes in wholesaler market services have taken place in a low-growth sector. It must be remembered, however, that wholesaler activity is not synonymous with wholesaling. Whilst wholesalers have seen only modest growth as a sector, wholesaling has increased substantially in parallel with the overall increase in consumption. In many cases the broad wholesaling functions of collection, storage and breaking bulk, formerly carried out by wholesalers, are now undertaken by retailers, manufacturers or very specialist distribution companies. The major retailers now operate their own depots or contract depot operation to specialist operators. More than half of major retailers have over 80 per cent of their products channelled through retailer-controlled warehouses. Safeway, for example, has a plan to reduce distribution depot numbers and to regionalize the distribution operation with almost all products passing through warehouses they control. Table 9.6 shows their plan for completion by the early 1990s. Thus the activities which 30 years ago would have been undertaken by wholesalers are now being undertaken by Safeway and specialist companies such as Glass Glover or Christian Salvesen.

*Table 9.6* Safeway's 1990s programme
Distribution division – proposed network

| Region | Location | Sq.ft. (000) | Operation | Operator | Stores serviced |
|---|---|---|---|---|---|
| Scotland | Bellshill | 500 | Composite | Christian Salvesen | 79 |
|  | Bathgate | 220 | Ambient | Glass Glover |  |
| North-east | Felling | 207 | Composite | Own Account | 37 |
|  | Stockton | 203 | Ambient | NFC |  |
| Midlands and south-west | Warrington | 340 | Composite | Own Account |  |
|  | Wolverhampton | 200 | Ambient | Third Party | 145 |
|  | Bristol | 351 | Composite | Own Account |  |
| South-east | Aylesford | 554 | Composite | Own Account |  |
|  | West London | 50 | Frozen | Third Party | 118 |
|  | Welwyn G. City | 186 | Ambient | Own Account |  |
| England and Wales | Wakefield | 206 | Ambient | Own Account |  |
|  |  |  | Common item |  | 301 |
| National | Atherstone | 20 | Speciality chill products | UCD | 380 |
| TOTAL |  | 3,037 |  |  |  |

**Retailers**

Employment by retailers accounts for approximately one-quarter of employment in market services in the United Kingdom. The share of retailing employment in market services has declined in recent years, for two main reasons. First, the number of employees in retailing has increased only slightly despite the substantial gains in output from the sector. Second, the growth in employment in other types of market service has increased employment totals. Although there have been only small changes in employment the sales volume output of retailing increased 38 per cent between 1980 and 1988 whilst shop numbers have fallen substantially. There has been structural adjustment associated with these changes, which has had several repercussions for the spatial pattern of retailing in the United Kingdom.

A major structural change has been the decrease in the number of businesses and an increase in the power of large businesses. Table 9.7 shows the scale of this change. The decrease in small firms stabilized in the 1980s, the decline becoming apparent in larger firms. Major results of this change include a decrease in the number of shops operated by large and small companies alike, more marketing-driven retailer activity resulting in a polarization of size of new store types, a change in the retailer-manufacturer (buyer-seller) relationship and adoption of formal corporate strategies by large companies and some small firms. Each of these aspects of retail sector evolution have had spatial repercussions.

The decrease in number of businesses and number of shops has been substantial but the declines have not been evenly felt either across types of retailing or through the whole country. Among small businesses the

*Table 9.7* Retailers in the UK

|  | *1950* | *1961* | *1971* | *1980* | *1986* |
|---|---|---|---|---|---|
| Number of single shop businesses (000) | 375 | 370 | 330 | 215 | 217 |
| Number of businesses with: |  |  |  |  |  |
| 50 shops and over | 362 | 430 | 330 | 300 | 220 |
| 10–49 shops | 1407 | 1470 | 940 | 960 | 636 |
| Number of establishments (000) in businesses with: |  |  |  |  |  |
| 50 shops and over | 53 | 66 | 60 | 55 | 48 |
| 10–49 shops | 28 | 30 | 19 | 19 | 12 |
| Percentage of sales in businesses with: |  |  |  |  |  |
| 50 shops and over | 24 | 31 | 36 | 45 | 52 |
| 10–49 shops | 12 | 9 | 8 | 8 | 8 |

*Note*: Precise comparisons over the 36 years are not possible due to differences in coverage and methods of the surveys. The figures are indicative of a trend rather than precisely comparable. The data are based on Censuses of Distribution and Retail Inquiry with attempts made to increase comparability

decreases have been most acute in non-specialist retailing – general food stores, general clothing stores, general hardware stores, etc. Specialization has provided the small firm with some protection from retail competitive pressures and from cost increases resulting from change in the operating environment. Specialization has allowed the small firms to emphasize the non-price aspects of their offerings and the higher margins on specialist items have provided some cushion against higher costs. Amongst large firms decreases in numbers have resulted from takeover activity which reduces company numbers and also store numbers because non-profitable branches are closed and rationalization of the store network is undertaken to remove duplicate outlets in the same market. Even in the cooperative sector, merger activity has reduced the number of societies from 216 to 85 with a fall in branches from 10,000 to 4,000 between 1979 and 1988. But amongst large firms, the increase in shop numbers which results from merger more than offsets the decrease in store numbers resulting from rationalization so a smaller number of larger firms results. Table 9.4 shows the increase in store numbers for NEXT during the mid-1980s. A substantial part of the increase was the result of takeover activity. In table 9.7 the average number of shops for the large companies shows a continued increase.

The decrease in shop numbers has been least in the central core of large city shopping areas and in the medium-sized towns such as Cheltenham, Bournemouth, York and Exeter. The decreases have been greatest, particularly associated with small firms, in inner suburban and fringe areas of central shopping districts and in small towns and rural areas. In some cases retail provision has fallen to levels at which there is now concern over access to basic services by those consumers who are unable, unwilling or cannot afford to travel some distance to purchase basic products (see also chapter 11). The reduction in the number of large firms has had spatial repercussions on major High Streets whereby there are now fewer potential firms to be represented; hence the frequently heard journalist's cry that 'All High Streets now look the same'. One implication is that large retailers may have several branches on the High Street using the same or, in many cases, different trading names. Each store format, within these large firms, is targeted at a particular consumer group. Burton has six types of shops for menswear (over 1,000 shops) and four for women's clothes (900 shops) and in addition other store types in different product sectors: British Shoe Corporation, which is owned by Sears, operates 2,500 shops through ten store formats which gave it over 20 per cent of the total UK market for shoes in 1987. Each of these shop types of major companies is targeted at serving the needs of a particular segment of consumers.

As well as engineering more uniformity on the High Street, the multi-format approach of large retailers illustrates the adoption of a marketing-driven approach. Not only the products which are sold in the shops have become targeted at particular groups of consumers but also the store types themselves have become more customer focused as the marketing approach has become used. This is one of the several reasons behind the tendency in the 1980s for a polarization of shop size in the United Kingdom. There has been investment by retailers in small shops, for example specialist shops, discount stores, convenience stores, etc, and in large units, such as superstores and department stores. The small units have been used as a method of targeting very specific consumer groups, discount stores for money-poor consumers, convenience stores for the time-pressured consumer, specialist stores for the affluent, and so on. The large stores have been used to provide a wide range of items in a broad product area to all types of consumer. There has been rapid growth of various forms of superstore, for example grocery, DIY, furniture, etc. Table 9.8 indicates the types of the over 2,000 superstores operating in 1986, when this type of retailing accounted for about 7 per cent of retail trade. The 430 food superstores accounted for almost one quarter of grocery sales at this time. The land-use planning policies, through the structure plan mechanisms (see chapter 10), were hostile initially to the superstore concept because retailers preferred locations outside existing shopping areas. Public agency intervention, however, has become less influential and permissions have been obtained for increasing numbers of these large stores, such that it seems likely that there will be at least 3,000 in operation by the end of 1990. The adoption by major retailers of a marketing-led approach has been enabled, in part, by new information technologies which have allowed collection of detailed information on actual sales made to customers. This information has then been used to help design shop layouts, to support stock control systems and to enhance the effectiveness of buying

*Table 9.8* Number of large mass merchandising shops by sector in the UK

| Sector | 1980 | 1986 | 1990/1 forecast |
|---|---|---|---|
| Food | 240 | 430 | 620 |
| DIY | 270 | 640 | 880 |
| Furniture | 150 | 340 | 480 |
| Carpets | 65 | 160 | 225 |
| Soft furnishings | 10 | 70 | 110 |
| Electricals | 125 | 200 | 270 |
| Motor accessories | | 30 | 150 |
| Garden products | 95 | 170 | 210 |
| Toys | | 10 | 100 |
| Other | | | 50 |
| TOTAL | 955 | 2050 | 3195 |
| Estimated share of all retail sales | 3% | 7% | 11% |

*Sources*: Based on company reports, sector surveys, reports of planning permissions, and extrapolations of levels of activity in recent years

products from manufacturers. The new approaches to retail marketing have encouraged the development of superstores and hence the breakdown of traditional ideas of spatial hierarchies of retail provision.

The third major result of the structural readjustment in retailing has been the new approaches to retailer-supplier relationships. The main changes here include:

1  The requirement of large firms for large quantities of product which has favoured large manufacturers over small ones.
2  A willingness of large retail firms to search nationally or internationally (rather than just regionally) from their central buying office, either for the exact products needed in their store or for manufacturers who will manufacture products according to specifications determined by the retailer.
3  The creation of retailer brands in which the retailer takes responsibility for some of the traditional manufacturer activity of product development and promotion; manufacturers then produce to the retailer's order.
4  A trend towards more stable and longer-term relationships between retailers and manufacturers, with more investment being applied in the various transactions.

The effects of these trends has been to favour big manufacturers as suppliers to big retailers with high entry barriers for manufacturers wishing to sell to the larger retailers. More widespread adoption of formal corporate strategies has occurred as firms have adjusted to economic and political change. This has been evident in the approaches of retailers to city finance and importantly to locational issues. Between April 1985 and November 1988 Tesco were able to raise £764 million, much of which was spent on new store development.

The new forms of retailing, such as superstores and targeted specialist shops, have generated demand for new types of retail property. Several strong trends in respect of retail location have emerged during the 1980s. The first, and possibly the most significant for the High Street, has been the increased attractiveness of prime sites in city centres with the small number of major retailers bidding up rent levels in their attempt to obtain prime trading locations. Prime Zone A shop rents doubled between 1980 and 1988 and in some cities growth was even stronger. In Oxford Street rent increased from approximated £200 per square foot in 1980 to £400 in 1988. In other cities comparable changes occurred: Croydon £70 to £150, Bristol £56 to £115, Cardiff £68 to £110, Glasgow £73 to £160, Manchester £50 to £115, and Oxford, where the increase has been one of the greatest, from £60 to £180. Retailer property needs have been met in part by redevelopment schemes which have been undertaken in most of the 400 or so larger retail shopping areas in the United Kingdom. Such schemes generally have provided additional space but at the same time resulted in increased rents. The scale and quality of such schemes have varied considerably and some of the earlier ones are now themselves undergoing redevelopment. Whilst the core of most shopping areas has remained strong there has been a decrease in the attractiveness of secondary sites on city centre fringes and on suburban High Streets. Physical and economic blight have afflicted some of these areas, giving rise to concern over their longer-term viability as retail districts. The decline of secondary locations and the pressure on prime sites has encouraged property developers to propose new out-of-town regional shopping centres which would create new prime shopping areas. The true economic flexibility of such projects is yet untested with the Metro-Centre at Gateshead operating within an enterprise zone which provides financial incentives for development.

A second strong locational trend in the 1980s was the establishment of groups of superstores on retail parks. The first such scheme opened in 1982 at Aylesbury, and by 1988 there were ninety in operation accounting for over 11 million square feet of floorspace. These, usually suburban or edge-of-town schemes, bring together several types of superstore which share some aspects of infrastructure, such as car parking. Most of the early schemes have involved food, DIY, electricals, and furnishings – often now termed 'bulky item superstores' – where shopping by private transport allows easier customer transport of purchases. The development of Fosse Park, near Leicester, promises to be a new type of retail park in which there are fashion retailers such as Burton and Sears present. Many retail parks are in process of development and by the early 1990s it is forecast that there are likely to be almost 250 schemes with 30 million square feet of floorspace. Development at this pace may have an impact on some of the already struggling poorer quality shopping areas on the fringes of High Streets.

The third locational trend has been towards greater variety of location. Although there has been concentration towards the core of established shopping districts and also decentralization with the proliferation of superstores either singly or in groups, there has also been fragmentation into a variety of unconventional locations to serve specific consumer needs, for example specialist impulse shops in transport termini and convenience stores associated with filling stations. This freer approach to retail location is a response both to better information about shopping behaviour being available to retailers and less rigid approaches to retail planning associated with reduced intervention in land and property markets.

The spatial and structural changes in retailing have taken place within a growth market in the 1980s. This has allowed adjustment to occur without radical conflicts emerging amongst the major participants. As the widely forecast slowing of consumer spending takes place in the early 1990s, the continued restructuring of the sector may create conflicts which could reverse the trend away from governmental intervention in market services.

## CONCLUSION

In a group of activities which constitute over 40 per cent of GDP in the United Kingdom, the diversity of activity and range of processes creating change are not surprising. The expansion in amount and variety of market services in the United Kingdom is likely to continue well into the 1990s. Not only is growth in demand expected from the home market but also there is the expectation that firms from the United Kingdom will enter foreign markets, particularly after the establishment of the Single European Market. In financial services the United Kingdom has generated large strong and commercially aggressive companies which are likely to have expansionist strategies into mainland Europe. Retailers in the United Kingdom are amongst the most profitable in Europe and have a sound base from which to launch international activity, probably through joint venture mechanisms. Precursors of international expansion are already apparent in specialist market services, such as logistics management; Christian Salvesen have established a strong trans-European presence in specialist transport and Alber Fisher have expanded by the purchase of existing fresh food distribution companies in the Netherlands and West Germany. Much more international activity is likely in the next decade.

Market services can be generally expected to show even higher levels of market concentration in the 1990s than at present. Few if any of the trends discussed in this chapter seem set to diminish in importance in the future. The underlying processes creating the growth, diversification and differentiation of market services in the United Kingdom appear resilient, which has encouraged politicians to advocate them as the basis for economic expansion in the United Kingdom in the 1990s. The next five years will reveal whether such faith is justified.

## FURTHER READING

The two most thorough analyses of the service sector are: Daniels, P. W. (1985) *Service Industries*, London: Methuen; Marshall, J. N. *et al.* (1988) *Services and Uneven Development*, Oxford: Oxford University Press.

A wider ranging review including material on the UK is presented in: Price, D. G. and Blair, A. M. (1989) *The Changing Geography of the Services Sector*, London: Belhaven.

Four specialist topical issues of *Transactions of the Institute of British Geographers, Service Industries Journal, Environment and Planning A*, and *International Journal of Retailing* since the mid-1980s have carried useful specific case studies. Amongst the most useful are: Bramley, R. D. F. and Thomas, C. J. (1988) 'Retail parks: spatial and functional integration of retail units in the Swansea Enterprise Zone', *Transactions, Institute of British Geographers*, NS 13: 4–18; Damesick, P. J. (1986) 'Service industries, employment and regional development in Britain', *Transactions of Institute of British Geographers*, NS 11; Daniels, P. W., Leyshon, A., and Thrift, N. J. (1988) 'Large accountancy firms in the UK', operational adaptation and spatial development', *Service Industries Journal*, 8(3): 317–46; Hepworth, M. E., Green, A. E., and Gillespie, A. E. (1987) 'The spatial division of information labour in GB', *Environment and Planning*, A19; Whysall, P (1989) 'Commercial change in a central area: a case study', *International Journal of Retailing*, 4(1): 45–61.

The dynamism of the sector means that more frequent magazines often carry useful illustrative material, notably *Investors Chronicle* and *Economist*.

Specific sectoral analyses have been brought together in: Smith, A. D. (1986) *Commercial Service Industries*, Aldershot: Gower; Howcroft, B. and Lavis, J. (1986) *Retail Banking*, Oxford: Basil Blackwell; Hall, M. J. B. (1987) *The City Revolution*, London: Macmillan; McKinnon, A. C. (1989) *Physical Distribution Systems*, London: Routledge.

The UK position in the development of market services in Europe is described in: Ochel, W. and Wegner, M. (1987) *Service Economies in Europe*, London: Pinter.

For the study of the concepts underpinning the growth of market services the classic analyses remain important reference works: Galbraith, J. K. (1967) *The New Industrial State*, London: Hamish Hamilton; Bell, D. (1974) *The Coming of Post-industrial Society*, London: Heinemann; Gershuny, J. and Miles, I. (1983) *The New Service Economy*, London: Pinter.

Useful reviews of approaches to defining the service sector are provided in: Rajan, A. (1987) *Services; The Second Industrial Revolution*, London: Butterworths; Elfring, T. (1988) *Service Sector Employment in Advanced Economies*. Aldershot: Gower.

# 10 The changing face of the city

*D. T. Herbert*

The forces which transformed Britain's economy from a mainly agricultural to an industrial base during the eighteenth and nineteenth centuries also brought about a major redistribution of population and the emergence of an urban nation. By the mid-nineteenth century over half of the British population could be classed as urban dwellers and by the beginning of the twentieth century this figure had reached about 75 per cent. The pattern of urban settlements which emerged was strongly guided by the pre-existing network but many settlements were added to the urban system both in the new industrial regions themselves and in those other parts of Britain which were affected by new transportation developments and the rapid expansion of trade and commerce.

Up until the 1930s, the urban growth characteristics established during the nineteenth century remained dominant; since then however, significant modifications have appeared in response to a new sequence of transformations in the economic base of British society, as older traditional industries such as coal-mining, metals manufacture and ship-building gave way to a more diversified range of manufacturing industries and these, in turn, have been replaced in significance by employment based upon new technologies and the burgeoning range of office and service activities. At the same time a changing quality-of-life assisted by a more formal planning structure has introduced new standards into places for both living and working.

Urban growth has enlarged the physical extent of British cities and improved transport facilities have considerably widened their spheres of influence for both commuting to work and the use of services. Colin Clark in 1951 argued that, ever since modern transportation technology had made decentralization possible from the middle of the nineteenth century, London and other great cities had continued to decant population at a very regular rate, decade by decade. Transport in his words was the 'maker and breaker' of cities. It was radial-concentric transport that made cities until approximately 1939; it is private car transport that has broken them since 1945 (Hall 1985: 9). As both people and enterprises moved out to suburban locations in very large numbers, there were also regional redistributions prompted by planning policies for containment on the margins of larger cities and of incentives to attract economic activity to the problem regions of the north and west. Development control in general and green belt policies in particular have been the main planning instruments for the containment of urban growth, although they have been very unevenly practised over both time and space. It is functional change, however, which is the most telling and the search for new descriptors of urban form – metropolitan area, outer metropolitan area, and local labour market areas – are but attempts to find the best geographical approximation for the modern city. The urban system is complex and dynamic and is much less easily encapsulated in a bounded area. One of the clearest outcomes of the long and continuing process of decentralization is the changing nature of the inner city. Its relative decline demographically, economically, and socially has been one of the great issues of the last part of the twentieth century. Inner-city problems have become manifest in a whole range of indicators from decaying urban fabric and services to the cumulative and interrelated forms of 'social malaise'.

The process of decentralization, which began in the largest cities, has spread to smaller centres and although there is some evidence for a slowing down of decline in inner 'cores' it is at the edges of major metropolitan areas, especially in southern England, that most rapid growth can be observed. The term 'counter-urbanization' has been widely used in developed countries to describe this kind of phenomenon whereby smaller towns and semi-rural areas beyond the traditional metropolitan ring began to act as magnets for people and activities. Gordon (1988) argues that there were two basic processes involved in counter-urbanization as it developed in Britain in the 1970s. To a large extent it was an extension of suburbanization not unlike the processes which had been evident for much longer periods of time; what was new was the pervasiveness of this process at all major spatial scales. But there was also a form of product system dispersal with small towns and extra-metropolitan locations featuring as new centres of activity. It is in southern England that modern 'counter-urbanization' effects are most evident. Hall (1985) identifies three Outer Metropolitan Area corridors – the M4 in central Berkshire, the M3 in north-east Hampshire and north-west Surrey and the M1 in south and mid-Bedfordshire and north-east Buckinghamshire – where there were substantial increases in total employment in the 1970s. Between 1971 and 1981 the total workers in employment in these three corridors increased from 484,770 to 557,970.

The most comprehensive approach to monitoring urban change in the 1970s and beyond has been that adopted by the Centre for Urban and Regional Development Studies (CURDS) at the University of Newcastle upon Tyne. Their procedure begins with the identification of urban centres as concentrations of employment and retailing and their continuous built-up areas are termed cores. To each core is attached its primary commuting field, termed a ring, from which at least 15 per cent of those employed travel to work in the core and more to that core than to any other. The core and ring form the daily urban system and to this are allocated outer areas or other districts most closely attached to them in commuting terms. Taking these definitions, the CURDS team estimated that in 1981 61.6 per cent of the British population lived in cores, 26.6 per cent in rings, 6.6 per cent in outer areas, and 5.2 per cent in rural areas. Between 1971 and 1981, cores lost 1,446,000 people, a decline of 4.2 per cent; rings gained 1,208,000, or 9.1 per cent, outer areas 327,000, or 10.1 per cent, and rural areas 228,000, or 8.8 per cent. These figures identify a massive redistribution of population during the 1970s with a decentralization from the cores which appears to have affected the more remote locations just as much as the primary commuting zones (Champion *et al*. 1987). At the head of the list of the local labour market areas (LLMAs) showing greatest absolute population declines in the 1970s (1971–81) are the traditional great cities – London, Glasgow, Manchester, Liverpool and Birmingham. The leaders on the other hand, those with greatest absolute gains, are all in the outer metropolitan fringe of southern England – Milton Keynes, Peterborough, Aldershot, Northampton, Bournemouth and Norwich. A north:south divide comes through strongly in this dichotomy of gainers and losers. Only two places south of the Severn to Lincolnshire line, London and Brighton, appear in the list of fifteen highest losers; the eight leading gainers are all south of this line. This north:south divide is even more apparent on a set of indices based on employment characteristics, composition of work force and car-ownership used to identify Britain's 'booming towns'. All top fifteen LLMAs are located in southern England; Aberdeen is ranked nineteen and is the only northern LLMA in the top twenty.

To conclude this general statement on losers and gainers in the British urban system in terms of population change since the 1970s, it is pertinent to focus on observed changes which have emerged during the 1980s and a debate which relates to the changing fortunes of London. The starting point of the debate is the observation that there are signs of population recovery in metropolitan areas and London is estimated (in the absence of full Census data) to have grown in population in the 1980s, admittedly at a slow rate of around 6,000 per year but still in sharp contrast to the annual losses of near 100,000 in the early 1970s. Tony Champion has spoken of London's 'momentous revival' and sees indicators of an end to the outflow from Central London which is related to the relative strength of the London economy, to a relaxation of planned decentralization, and to an improved housing supply. Not all would agree with this analysis. Peter Hall (1985) argues that geographical change in Britain, involving the shift of people and jobs, is really very constant and therefore predictable over long periods of time. Ian Gordon (1988) believes that London has experienced no fundamental change in the process of population deconcentration since its peak in 1964 but rather a slowing-down under the influence of macro-economic and possibly demographic fluctuations. The Greater London area was losing about 50,000 population per year in the 1950s, 110,000 in 1964–74, and around 35,000 1979–85. Gordon explains the fluctuations in terms of the vagaries of the private housing market. He argues that outward movement is likely to revive sooner rather than later, with substantial population losses re-emerging in exchange with other parts of southern England even if some gains continue to be made from the depressed regions of the north – London's revival may be momentary rather than momentous. There were new factors in the 1980s: the resurgence of interest in parts of the central city, new forces in the housing market, and the swing towards producer services, but the eventual impacts of these have yet to be realized or understood.

## THE CHANGING FORM OF BRITISH CITIES

### Economic and social processes of change

Changes in the form and spatial organization of British cities are surface manifestations of underlying economic and social processes. Decentralization has always been selective of people and activities and it is the impact upon manufacturing industry which has become more and more evident in recent decades. As Hall (1986) shows, it took over 100 years, 1851 to 1961, for technology and foreign competition to halve the numbers employed in British agriculture, but it took only fourteen years from 1971 to 1983 to cut manufacturing jobs by one-third. The impact of this devastating loss of manufacturing has fallen heavily upon the cities.

> These are striking parallels, again, between the 1880s and the 1980s. Then rural England was in the process of losing much of its traditional economic base. Now it is urban England's turn. The root cause in both was structural transformations arising from the new technologies and the changing balance of geographical advantage (Hall 1985: 10).

The impact of these changes upon British cities varies with both the type of urban situation and with regional location, but Britain is now experiencing a massive 'deindustrialization', and the decline of manufacturing employment and rise in factory closure has affected central areas of large cities in particular. Job losses in the inner city can be most clearly tied to the closure of factories which can no longer cope with the disadvantages of cramped sites and inadequate accommodation. Fothergill, Kitson and Monk (1985) show that there has been no real shift of employment from larger urban areas to smaller towns but a better employment performance of firms in smaller towns, declining inner-city firms, and an ability of land-intensive activities to expand in less urbanized areas. Within this scenario there remains the dichotomy of the north:south divide and the special position of London as a world city, a vibrant centre for producer services – insurance, banking, accountancy, advertising – geared to national and international markets. Between 1971 and 1981, producer services yielded 484,000 new jobs and one-sixth of these were in London, though other cities of southern England showed this same upsurge in professional, high-skill activities.

Economic restructuring and the redistribution of employment opportunities are critical factors in understanding the changing form of British cities. They are not the only factors, however, and in many ways they have followed rather than led the outward movement of population, which was the key feature of urban expansion. To understand this outward movement one has to consider social as well as economic factors; residential preferences, the form of the housing market, and the quality of the urban transport system are all closely involved. The three significant events which together shaped the pattern of housing development in post-war Britain can be summarized as: an increasingly favourable fiscal position for the owner-occupier, persistent inflationary trends which have meant rising building costs and land prices, and a planning system which is increasingly interventionist in character.

The favourable fiscal position of the owner-occupier can be related both to the advantageous tax position on mortgage repayment, which has made borrowing for house purchase a very desirable transaction, and to the rapid increases in house prices in some regions which have made housing a high-grade investment. Successive governments have sought to extend owner-occupation and housing policies designed towards its encouragement and maintenance remained typical of the 1980s. Since the 1920s, however, the second major role of the state in the housing market has been one of more explicit intervention with the direct provision of houses for rent by the public sector (figure 10.1). For the most part the local housing authorities have served as the initial providers and subsequent landlords of council housing; New Town Development Corporations and the Scottish Special

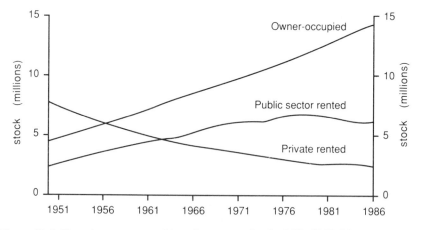

*Figure 10.1* Changing patterns of housing tenure in the UK, 1950–86
*Source:* Social Trends 1980, 1988

Housing Association have also played significant roles in some places, however.

Both the inter-war and immediate post-war periods were typified by rapid housing development in which major contributions were made in both private and public sectors. Between 1945 and 1970, some 6 million new dwellings were constructed in England and Wales, an additional increment of 37 per cent of the total housing stock. Although per capita rates of construction over this period were unexceptional compared with inter-war standards, it was the volume of new construction which was impressive. Between 1945 and 1958, public sector housing dominated with a 2:1 share of new dwellings but since then private construction has become the main component, on a 3:2 ratio. The public sector share of total housing stock rose most rapidly between 1947 and 1961 when it changed from 12 per cent to 25 per cent in England and Wales. Since that time it has grown more slowly and is now adversely affected by both public expenditure cuts and the sale of council houses which reduces its overall stock. In 1986 there were 169,000 completions in the private sector and 36,000 in the public sector. The 1980 Housing Act gave local authority tenants the right to buy, combined with generous discounts from assessed market value. Between 1979 and 1986 one million council houses were sold, two-thirds under the right to buy legislation. The sale of local authority housing has been uneven in its effects; whereas around one-quarter of local authority stock was made up of high-rise flats, this type of property only formed 4 per cent of sales, which proceed more briskly in relatively affluent estates and much more slowly in inner-city areas and problem estates. There were instances in the 1980s, at Wandsworth in London and Regent Road in Salford, of whole estates being sold off. In line with government policy, there have been transfers of ownership of local authority estates to voluntary housing associations. Alongside the selling-off of local authority housing stock is the downturn in the new building programme in this sector. Local authority house-building stood at 132,000 in 1977 and at 36,000 in 1986.

Owner-occupancy continues to grow and between 1970 and 1979 the percentage of households in Britain in this category increased from 50 to 54 per cent. Policies such as council-house sales and improvement rather than redevelopment are integral parts of this trend. As owner-occupancy has increased its share of the housing market and the public-sector housing share has stabilized following the rapid increase in the immediate post-war period, it is the private rented sector of housing which has experienced the sharpest decline, with its share of the market falling from 61 per cent in 1947 in England and Wales to 15 per cent in 1970. Private landlords became increasingly subjected to public control during this period as the general trends towards a 'protected' housing market became a major feature of British cities. One estimate suggested that over 90 per cent of British households lived in 'protected' sectors of the market of one sort or another (as owner-occupiers, local authority tenants, members of housing associations and other privately rented 'controlled' or 'regulated' properties) and less than 7 per cent in the sector in which the tenancy of the accommodation is either a short-term furnished letting or is tied to employment.

Inflation has affected all facets of the housing market, from professional fees to the price of land. There have been regional variations which can be generalized in terms of higher rates in the more prosperous regions of southern England and lowest rates in regions such as Northern Ireland, Scotland and Wales which have continuing economic problems, though there are significant differences at an intra-regional scale. House prices went through a period of very rapid increase from the late 1960s to the mid-1970s and continued to rise at a slower rate up until 1980. The early 1980s, affected by high interest rates and rising unemployment, witnessed the fall of house prices in many parts of the country but rapid increases were again widespread in the latter part of the 1980s, especially in southern England. The Nationwide Building Society's index of house prices in 1987 showed an overall annual increase of 16 per cent, with a range from 25 per cent in Greater London and East Anglia to 1 per cent in Scotland. Up to the 1960s, inflation in land prices was a major component of increases in the prices of homes (houses plus land), with the index for residential land values increasing from 100 in 1939 to 1,615 in 1963; after 1974 land values seem generally to have declined. Most parts of the country show few differences in price between new and similar old houses. The latter may lack some modern features but have the advantages of more accessible locations, larger plots, more spacious internal arrangements, and scope for improvement. Inflation is related to new housing construction, directly in terms of costs and also indirectly through its impact on fiscal policies and housing demand. Annual new housing completion rates showed a peak average of 350,000 per year in the 1960s, but were down to 250,000 in 1978 and 205,000 in 1986. As central government expenditure on housing declined, from £303 billion in 1974/5 to £190 billion in 1980/1 and £133 billion in 1987/8, the depressing effect on public sector housing in particular was considerable.

Planning has been a major factor in British urban development since the 1947 Town and Country Planning Act. Hall *et al.*'s (1973) survey recognized two main effects of post-1947 planning policy: containment, which has slowed down growth and protected some agricultural land, and constraints which have both emphasized the separation of home and workplace and pushed up land and property prices. The success of containment policies was achieved by strict applications of development control on new land use and by specific measures such as Green Belt policies around major cities. It also involved the diversion of growth into smaller towns, both new and old, creating, in Hall's words, 'a physical pattern that was a look alike of Howard's Social City'. The caveat with the 'new communities' was that they did not achieve self-containment in terms of jobs or social balance. Because the new housing was beyond green belts and metropolitan fringes, distance from home to work was actually increased. Greater London had more in-commuters in 1981 than in 1971, the Outer Metropolitan area had more out-commuters. This arises because the scale of population loss from major cities outweighs the losses in manufacturing jobs; there is an increase in long-distance commuting into London in response to its specialized producer services roles. It is a job-revolution which favours the highly skilled, and the prospects for the low-skilled pools of urban labour are less hopeful.

Containment as a planning policy has worked to maintain higher densities than were prevalent in the 1930s and has occasionally interacted with other policies to influence the type of housing under construction. Flats or apartments have never figured prominently in the private sector as the market has responded to a consistent preference for houses with gardens; in the public sector, however, many local authorities have found high-rise blocks of flats an attractive option. The amount of high-rise construction in the public sector cannot be explained in terms of consumer preferences but it can be linked to architectural fashion, encouragement from central government in the form, for example, of specific subsidies in 1930 and again in 1956, and a considerable amount of market pressure, advertising and campaigning by top firms in the construction industry during a period of high demand. The shift towards a mass housing solution was especially marked in the conurbations of Britain where, over the period 1955–70, nearly 1.5 million former occupants of sub standard inner-city housing became council tenants in high-rise flats. By yielding to commercial pressure, the local authorities became the landlords of hundreds of thousands of unpopular high-cost and lower-amenity dwellings. Although they are not limited to inner-city areas, flats have been an important component of inner-city redevelopment policy. One attraction of inner-city high-rise development is the possibility of rehousing *in situ* people displaced by urban renewal and slum clearance schemes, though more rigorous modern standards on provision of open space and local facilities do not make this wholly possible. The extensive redevelopment in Tower Hamlets (London) in the 1970s rehoused 100,000 people in a district which formerly held twice that number.

Planning attitudes towards urban renewal have changed since 1947 and the immediate post-war task of rebuilding bomb-damaged central areas. During the 1950s and 1960s urban renewal became synonymous with comprehensive redevelopment aimed at the elimination of blighted areas, and was often linked with road building. The 1969 and 1974 Housing Acts saw a shift of emphasis towards conservation and rehabilitation. The General Improvement Areas (GIAs) and Housing Action Areas (HAAs) were area policies designed to stimulate both housing and environmental improvement or rehabilitation in compact districts within British cities.

GIAs were intended for areas where sound housing, low population turnover and a majority of owner-occupiers ensured voluntary improvement through the high take-up of improvement grants; HAAs were aimed at areas of multiple deprivation. Within GIAs the householders could obtain improvement grants of the order of 60 per cent of total cost; in HAAs this proportion could rise to 75 per cent or higher. The existence of area policies did not preclude the possibilities of grant aid for individual householders living in other parts of the city but lack of funds and a decline in the level of local authority activity following some initial enthusiasm has limited the overall impact of housing-improvement policy. Industrial South Wales, for example, has extensive substandard housing but in its first HAA, in Blaenau Gwent, only one dwelling was improved in the first two and a half years. On a UK basis, 197,000 dwellings were renovated in 1971, and in the peak year of 1984 almost 500,000. In 1986 the total was 418,000, with half of these in the public sector.

Major cities have reacted in different ways. The Birmingham Housing Department revealed a changed attitude towards comprehensive rede-velopment in the 1970s; 75,000 houses in the inner city were incorporated in a ten-year programme and sixty-eight GIAs containing 60,000 dwellings were declared. Bristol, by contrast, did not pursue a strong GIA policy and by 1974 only three GIAs containing a total of 174 dwellings had been declared, of which forty-one had been improved by 1976. Although the city focused more attention on HAAs, by 1979 only four had been declared and a total of 602 dwellings improved.

The achievements of this greater emphasis upon improvement than on renewal have been patchy and generally slow. The voluntary aspect of take-up presents one problem, the funding shortages and varying attitudes of local housing authorities form others. Most evidence suggests that improvement policies do not tackle the areas of greatest housing need or the most deprived households. Decision-makers are faced with a number of trade-offs on the renewal/rehabilitation issue. Renewal is more expensive but can employ higher densities and ensure longer life for buildings; rehabilitation involves less social disruption and displacement and gives an alternative to the peripheral estate which has dominated urban development in the present century. In the 1980s, however, non-area-based policies of rehabilitation were favoured by central government, leading to a 'grants bonanza' and subsequent questioning of the whole issue of central subsidies. Criticisms are now made of the 1980s as a demand-led era which has produced large inequalities in housing investment that is both locality and social class related.

There is in the 1980s increasing evidence for an 'access crisis' with a growing number of households, especially unemployed single people and childless couples, unqualified for help under the Homeless Persons Act, and who find it impossible to gain access to formal housing markets (Kemp 1989). Homelessness increased from 53,110 in 1978 to 102,980 in 1986 and

*Figure 10.2* Urban Britain
*Source:* Based on 1981 Census with additional data from Champion *et al.* 1987

there were well over 100,000 people on supplementary benefit in board and lodgings. Problems of the urban elderly are reflected in their impact on the housing market – with the increase in sheltered homes and a range of housing alternatives. There is also evidence of deterioration in the housing stock of cities. Local authorities estimate that 84 per cent of their stock is in need of renovation at an average of £5,000 per dwelling. As Prentice (1986) argues, the problem has been compounded by the failure of government to give direction in the planning of urban research and its apparent inability either to target resources or to monitor the performance of local authorities in their private sector housing renewal policies.

**Urban outcomes: morphological change**

The economic and social processes operating in British society have significant outcomes on the changing form of urban Britain. At a regional scale, the variations over time can be illustrated by Cameron's (1980) study of the seven major conurbations which contain one-third of the total British population. The conurbations grew slowly between 1931 and 1951, hardly at all between 1951 and 1961, and lost 958,000 population from 1961 to 1971. By 1974, the conurbations had 807,000 fewer people than in 1931, following a period during which the British population as a whole increased by 10.4 million. An analysis of statistical trends for twelve other British cities in the size range 200,000 to 500,000 showed little growth up to 1971 and some downward movement afterwards: one million people migrated from larger urban areas in the 1950s and the main gainers were towns under 100,000. Figure 10.2 and table 10.1 show recent changes in eight

*Table 10.1* Population of major urban areas, 1961–81 ( ooo)

|  | 1961 | 1971 | 1981 |
|---|---|---|---|
| 1 Greater London | 7,992 | 7,452 | 6,713 |
| (inner London) | 3,493 | 3,032 | 2,498 |
| (outer London) | 4,500 | 4,420 | 4,215 |
| 2 Greater Manchester | 2,720 | 2,729 | 2,596 |
| (Manchester) | 662 | 544 | 449 |
| 3 Merseyside | 1,718 | 1,657 | 1,512 |
| (Liverpool) | 746 | 610 | 510 |
| 4 South Yorkshire | 1,303 | 1,322 | 1,304 |
| 5 West Yorkshire | 2,005 | 2,068 | 2,037 |
| 6 Tyne and Wear | 1,244 | 1,212 | 1,143 |
| (Newcastle) | 336 | 308 | 278 |
| 7 West Midlands | 2,732 | 2,793 | 2,649 |
| (Birmingham) | 1,183 | 1,098 | 1,007 |
| 8 Strathclyde | 2,584 | 2,575 | 2,405 |
| (a) All major urban areas | 22,281 | 21,808 | 20,358 |
| (b) Great Britain | 51,284 | 53,979 | 54,285 |
| (a) as % of (b) | 43.4 | 40.4 | 37.5 |

major urban areas and also identify the fifteen fastest growing and fifteen least growth urban areas (ie. highest and lowest LLMAs).

Many of the smaller towns which grew in population were aided by town expansion schemes, through which both people and jobs were moved out from larger conurbations in an attempt to ease congestion and to stimulate small town growth. This latter objective in particular achieved a great deal of success, especially in south-east England and the West Midlands in towns such as Basingstoke and Swindon. In many ways this town expansion was associated with the new towns movement which has been one of the spectacular successes of British town planning, though again the regional variations have to be acknowledged. In the immediate post-war years, new town construction occurred on an impressive scale with the initial clear objective of providing an outlet for the overcrowded inner-city populations. New Town Development Corporations were established as the agencies to achieve the new policy and in the first phase of construction thirteen new towns emerged, eight of which formed a ring around London. By 1973, twenty-eight new or expanded towns housed 1.7 million people and had provided over 200,000 new dwellings. Although the initial aim of decanting population from the conurbations has been maintained, new and expanded towns have increasingly been seen as more far-reaching components of regional policy. They have increased in both scale and in range of activities and although the 'million cities' talked of in the early 1970s are now rendered unlikely in a situation of slow population growth, new towns as growth centres remain key elements of regional planning strategy.

Britain has not created new metropolitan areas in the twentieth century, nor has it achieved any major redistribution of its economic activity; at an intra-regional scale there has been decentralization directly through the public provision of facilities, including the new and expanded town strategy, and indirectly through land-use control. In summary therefore, a major British trend for decentralization from the inner areas of the large metropolitan regions had become established by the 1980s. Whereas the rate and form of this change is modified regionally, there is no evidence for the emergence of major new urbanized areas. Indicators suggest an increasingly static population in demographic terms with little evidence of inter-regional migrations on the scale of the inter-war period. Constraints on such movements in terms of both jobs and housing are now formidable.

There are barriers of education, training, perceptions and lifestyles which are almost certainly greater in the 1980s than in the 1880s. There is a real prospect of a large urban underclass, permanently unemployed and disaffected, and the locus of worst problems may shift from inner city to older council estates, but somewhere it will remain to threaten the health of the city (Hall 1985).

**The dynamics of residential suburbanization**

The forces, such as planning control and inflation, which influence urban growth as a whole have a particular impact upon residential development. Yet the forms of residential development have been less typified by major innovations than by variations upon familiar themes. Terraced or row houses continue to dominate inner-city residential districts; in places they have been significantly modified by redevelopment and improvement schemes. Beyond the inner city there are 'rings' of suburban development which can be related to various phases of building activity and 'ages' of urban growth. These housing estates have been produced by both public and private sectors and are the main components of physical urban expansion. High-rise blocks of flats occur in both inner city and suburban locations, but are generally limited to larger cities and are much more typical of the public sector. Outside city limits, commuter residences have added new developments to many rural villages and small towns though this type of urban expansion has been subject to planning controls aimed at containment and conservation.

Housing standards have risen generally over the present century but the relative uniformity of architectural style and a general tendency to restrict design to basic utilitarian forms in privately owned suburban estates and inner terraces alike imposes a rather uninspired monotony upon many residential areas in British cities. Protection through designation of urban conservation areas has maintained and often upgraded some of the older, better-quality dwellings, and 'gentrification' has similarly restored enclaves, especially of Georgian and Edwardian terraces. For much suburban development, however, the semi-detached house became the British norm with detached houses only found in higher-status developments. Variations in the layout and in particular in the density of private housing estates reflect factors such as land costs, planning controls and consumer preferences.

Although local variations occur in the public housing sector, general factors again tend towards uniformity in design and basic structure. Main trends were established in the inter-war period. An early stage following the 1919 Addison Act was typified by housing of a high standard to meet general need – these were garden suburbs at low density. The bulk of the inter-war estates was built in times of greater financial stringency, however, and the outcome was lower quality housing, including terraces, in monotonous developments. A final ingredient of inter-war council housing was the addition of some high-rise blocks in reaction to a 1930 change in the housing subsidy. During the period which followed the Second World War there has been a virtual re-run of this sequence, though with some important modifications. Up to 1951 'idealism' returned and new neighbourhood units were developed with high quality housing; after this date, with renewed stringency, small, more economical dwelling units resulted with less attention paid to landscaping and facilities. Parker-Morris standards

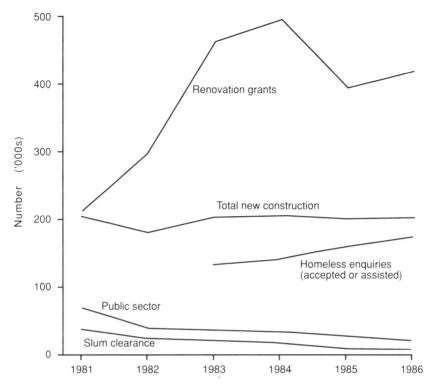

*Figure 10.3* Indicators of housing change
*Source:* Social Trends 1980, 1988

established in 1969 raised the internal quality of dwellings and it is a
curious anomaly that contemporary society can lay down relatively high
standards regarding space and fittings in the public sector whilst the private
sector, which forms approximately 65 per cent of the housing market, has
no such norms set.

Legislation and policy have affected public sector housing in other ways.
The thrust towards clearance and urban renewal in the 1960s (figure 10.3) –
Birmingham, for example, cleared 60,000 houses up to 1974 – created a
demand for new council dwellings. The 1956 subsidy encouraged many
local authorities to redevelop central areas at high densities and it was only
after 1966 that the numbers of flats under construction were sharply
reduced. This followed modification of the subsidy and also the fact
that structural defects, as evident in the collapse of a block at Ronan
Point, Newham, also highlighted the need for caution in large-scale flat
construction.

**Managers in the housing market**

Market forces and government policy strongly affect the rate and form of residential development but there are additional influences in the 'managerial' level of institutions and decision-makers at work in the housing market. Interposed between the political economy with its macro-institutions and the consumers with their varying degrees of access to 'good' housing, are the various agencies which either allocate resources or play critical entrepreneurial roles.

The powers of the many decision-makers vary significantly over time and place and in response to the conditioning effects of the social formation within which they are located. For landowners, for example, the steady growth of planning controls, state intervention and welfare imperatives has meant an accompanying diminution of power. Zoning regulations may adversely affect a landowner's potential for profit and the issue of 'betterment value' has been a consistent and difficult by-product of planning laws. Developers have the active role of injecting new housing into the system and normally respond to ways in which they perceive the market at any one time, their assessment of demand and likely profit. External sources of finance have key roles in stimulating or depressing private house-building as most builders and developers need substantial credit to finance their activity: their major costs are incurred before a dwelling is sold. One can distinguish among scales of building enterprise. Small builders operate over restricted geographical areas where they have detailed knowledge and provide for a specialized – and often expensive – market. Large builders favour the construction of mass-designed housing on large sites.

Planners have key interventionist roles in the housing market. Structure plans establish general allocations of land use and main directions for future change, and within these blueprints the details of zoning and development control assume considerable importance. In association with other local government departments, planners also play key roles in the provision of basic utilities and in the stipulation of standards and quality control. Planners are professionals who work within the rules prescribed by central government and their assessment of local needs, and they are also affected by the political complexions and aspirations of the local governments which they serve. Until the 1970s they had considerable scope to develop their own professional ideology and it was this set of values, strongly moulded by middle-class standards and in-vogue theoretical positions, which influenced their actions. During the 1970s, however, much more emphasis was placed upon public participation which, although generally concerned with modifications to rather than radical realignments of proposed policies, introduces a new dimension. Occasionally community action does build up to significant opposition to planning schemes and has achieved some notable successes. The increasing vagaries of housing policies and the complications of related fiscal legislation have added to planners' problems.

Once housing is constructed and becomes available for sale or rent on the housing market, new agents or gatekeepers are involved. In the private sector, the capital held by consumers and their creditworthiness are critical. Easiest routes to accommodation in the private sector are through rented properties where the only agents involved are the landlords, who are controlled by national legislation, local regulations and codes of practice. As the promotion of home ownership has continued, some have begun to argue that the main problem is becoming the shortage of rented housing and a housing finance system too biased towards the owner-occupier. Reports such as *Faith in the City* (1985) called for more investment in housing to rent. Since 1987 there have been government moves to deregulate the rented housing market and to reduce ownership and control of rented housing by local authorities. The aim is a pluralistic, more market-orientation approach to housing. It is difficult as yet to estimate the impact of these changes on a private rented sector which had declined from 89.8 per cent of total housing stock in 1914 to 16.1 per cent in 1975 and to under 10 per cent by 1986 (figure 10.1). Whereas there are luxury flats in the private rented sector, and rented houses or rooms may serve as 'starter' homes for new families, many people dependent on this form of tenure are now those least able to compete in the housing market. Low-income households with no access to council tenancies or owner-occupancy include large numbers of the elderly, the single and the transient. The decrease in private rented housing reflects the declining profitability of the enterprise for landlords: up to 90 per cent of properties sold in Islington in the 1970s were former rented units; students compete for tenancies with low-income households but might also be keeping property in the rented sector which would otherwise be sold off.

Other managers affect the private house buyer. Financial institutions head the list and in Britain the building societies and banks, which in 1985 provided 90 per cent of the loans for house purchase, are dominant. Building societies have a 'savings and loans' format in that they attract deposits from investors and lend to house purchasers according to their assessment of the latter's creditworthiness and security. Profiles of success-ful borrowers suggest that they typically have above average incomes and stable career prospects. Type of property is also influential. In 1976, 61 per cent of mortgages went to property built since 1945 and older, pre-1919, properties attracting mortgages were typically large and substantial. The negative practice among building society managers of 'red-lining' inner-city districts within which they do not normally lend money had been recognized and publicized in the 1970s. Even when loans were granted in such districts, usually by finance-credit companies, they were generally for a lower proportion of the buying price than is typical of suburbia. Immigrant households are often the most disadvantaged and a Small Heath,

Birmingham, study showed that Asian families were paying 5 to 10 per cent above the standard rate of interest; in Saltley, Birmingham, only 7 per cent of borrowers held mortgages at the standard rate. Local authorities have the power to lend mortgages but shortage of funds restricts their activities considerably. Even where they make loans they tend not to be directed towards households in greatest need but are similarly influenced by creditworthiness and risk.

Estate agents act as entrepreneurs in the exchange process of housing and in some cases have 'directive' roles in the housing market, often in association with the legal profession. Some estate agents have employed discriminatory practices with negative effects on immigrant housing aspirations; estate agents in Islington were central figures in the manipulated process of gentrification and there are close interconnections among estate agents, legal firms and developers.

In the public sector, significant gatekeepers are the housing managers in municipal departments who supervise the allocation of tenancies. Their decisions in a number of areas – eligibility, or who qualifies; allocation, or when and where a vacancy is offered; transfers, to match household size with dwelling size or to accommodate tenants' preferences – are highly influential on the form and content of municipal estates. It is clear, for example, that at some time or other many local authority housing managers have directed less desirable tenants to particular 'low-status' estates; the outcome is the existence of 'problem estates' in most larger cities. The rehousing of immigrant families involves these managers in decisions which help form the social geography of the British city, as do decisions affecting the level of maintenance and standards of provision applied to individual estates.

## Residential mobility

It is increasingly evident that the managerial level plays a critical part in the British housing market. Many of the managerial decisions are positive but with the discretionary powers which the managers exercise they are also discriminatory and are likely to be guided by market rather than by welfare ethics. Within the framework of constraints created by both the circumstances of individual households and the institutions who manage the housing market, consumers react in a variety of ways. For a not insignificant number of households there is no choice and these compete for private rented accommodation, which is in diminishing supply. Not far removed are the owners of low-cost terraced housing in the inner city for which improvement possibilities are limited and the environments and local services to which they have access are often of low quality. Within the public sector there is considerable variety in the quality of accommodation. Many of the earlier estates were built to low standards and have deteriorated badly. Preferences within the public sector are for newer estates with a higher quality of housing provision in favoured locations. Older, less desirable estates, often in need of major repair, are acceptable only to those either in urgent need or with low aspirations and some kind of 'self-selection' process has been identified which perpetuates the 'labels attached in the area. Recent trends in council-house sales may serve to throw further light on differentiation within the public sector as sales are higher in preferred estates where the line between municipal tenancy and owner-occupancy is blurred anyway.

The most closely studied residential mobility has been that which occurs in the private sector and involves middle- to high-income purchasers. Demand in this sector is heavily influenced by availability of mortgage funds and shows distinct temporal fluctuations, but there is variety, and pressures are greatest on younger, first-time buyers who are particularly affected by the 'geography' of house prices. Residential area status does change over time and the 'filtering' process can be observed in British cities as higher-status housing is passed down the economic hierarchy. Gentrification and improvement modify and occasionally reverse this process and there has been a general tendency for homeowners to extend or alter existing homes rather than move. Some studies suggest that individual residential moves can be generalized in terms of sectors, whereby most moves are constrained within particular segments of the city which tend to extend from the centre towards the periphery, and also in terms of neighbourhood constraints, whereby moves are short-distance and localized and seem to represent movers who change residence to obtain a larger (or sometimes smaller) dwelling but prefer to remain within the same general neighbourhood. Changing life cycle circumstances, with their consequent space needs, seem to stimulate many moves but social and career mobility are significant factors along with both general and specific access needs.

## THE CENTRAL CITIES

### Commercial functions

City centre development has been an important facet of urban change in Britain and in part has been stimulated by the need for large-scale redevelopment necessitated by war damage in cities such as London, Coventry, Plymouth, Southampton and Swansea. A more recent rash of schemes has led to projects of various scales which modify and occasionally transform city centres. There are several facets to this process of change. The continuing viability of the city centre as a retailing district has prompted a sustained flow of investment into shopping facilities – of the 155 largest city centres in Britain, 105 had developed major shopping schemes each involving over 4,600 m$^2$ of selling space in the period 1965 to 1977. Gibbs (1987) estimated that from 1965 to 1981, 88 per cent of all towns of over 100,000 population size had undertaken central area development schemes of greater than 4,644 m$^2$.

Allied with new shopping development of this kind has been a series of positive moves towards traffic control and management with the twin aims of producing pedestrianized areas and covered malls and also of improving the flow of traffic around the central city. The main projects have been labelled as in-town shopping centres, such as Nottingham's Victoria Centre and Broadmarsh and Newcastle upon Tyne's Eldon Square, designed to add to or upgrade more traditional retail provision. In addition to these in-town schemes are the smaller pedestrianized precincts and piecemeal accretions or adaptations of existing retail streets. Another related trend affecting city centres has been the more general exclusion of motor traffic from central areas. This spread of pedestrian schemes is one part of a strategy to improve the attractiveness of central areas and reduce the impact of suburbanization. A number of powerful forces operating in British cities had similar aims. These included the Chambers of Trade and Commerce, representing local retail businesses, which have consistently resisted attempts to diminish the 'monopoly' of central shopping areas, and the other commercial interest groups comprising property investors and developers whose prime concern was profit-realization from inner-city sites or projects. Both groups have considerable political influence and local government planning departments have generally also been supportive of central area shopping and have used zoning laws to stop out-of-town development; it is often argued that there is no other country in the world which exercises such stringent planning controls over the retail system particularly by resisting the market pressures for a greater amount of decentralization of trade. The maintenance of the traditional hierarchy of retail shopping centres included a clear commitment to maintain central area supremacy.

Given this level of support, large department stores have continued to invest and develop in the central city and their presence is an essential factor for the success of in-town schemes. Local authorities have also shown a willingness to improve central city environments by landscaping and traffic management schemes such as those followed in Plymouth in the late 1980s. Again, many office functions, including building societies, insurance companies and banks which have a high level of direct contact with consumers, continue to locate centrally. For financial and commercial offices of this kind face-to-face contact remains important, especially at a higher managerial level, and London's monopoly is increasing rather than diminishing. Headquarter offices do not require consumer contact but need access to London's many key facilities. Whereas many larger provincial cities such as Newcastle are losing their functional status in the control of British industry London, with 525 of the headquarter offices of the 1,000 largest UK companies in 1977, maintains its dominant position and had increased this 'share' from 420 in 1972. The telecommunications revolution is a key element in this type of increased centralization. Large-scale office developments, especially in London, have significant roles in periods of property speculation and rising land values but also bring both new employment and new consumers to central city locations, while British inner-city policies have tended to ignore retailing as an economic sector which creates jobs, despite its labour-intensive nature.

Retailing and other commercial functions in the central city have clearly been affected by the long-term process of decentralization of jobs and people and an intra-urban hierarchy has emerged. In the inter-war years the typical pattern was of a specialized central-city shopping area containing a few main streets and often extending outwards along main traffic arteries. A myriad local clusters and individual shops – usually not purpose built – served the surrounding residential areas. As the population suburbanized so there was a shift of purchasing power as well, and a more clear-cut set of shopping areas developed. These have been classified as:

1 a central area serving a population of at least 150,000;
2 regional shopping centres which have developed from the smaller central areas in conurbations;
3 district centres serving local catchments of around 30,000;
4 neighbourhood centres selling convenience goods in catchments of 10,000; and
5 local or subcentres with small clusters of stores serving 500 to 5,000 people.

Much of this framework existed in the inter-war period but was consolidated in the 1950s and greater planning control at that time added planned shopping centres to several levels of hierarchy. It has been estimated that in larger cities (over 250,000) 36.8 per cent of retail provision is found outside the centre; this proportion is inversely related to city size and is 55.3 per cent for cities in the 40,000 to 49,000 range.

Retail trade has experienced considerable structural change since 1945. There have been upheavals in the methods and organization of retailing, a blurring of the retailing/wholesaling distinction, escalation of multiples, an increase in store size, and greater bulk-buying. Several of these changes have had adverse effects on small stores and have led to a considerable decline in numbers of outlets at the bottom of the shopping hierarchy. Between 1950 and 1966 the number of general stores fell by 56.2 per cent and of grocery retailers by 16.3 per cent. In part this trend was related to the movement of population out of the inner city and the subsequent decline of the 'corner-shops'; it can also be tied to economics of scale and the changing organization of retailing. In the grocery sector by the early 1970s four organizations together operated nearly 4,500 shops and accounted for nearly 22 per cent of all grocery-store sales. There is some evidence, however, that as larger outlets concentrate upon a smaller number of locations, there may be a renewed role for small convenience stores in suburban locations. Large-scale retail organizations have sought to develop large out-of-town sites and all of these have been subject to close government scrutiny. By the late 1970s there was still only one major development in Britain – Brent Cross in north London – which could be described as an out-of-town centre though it is, in reality, contained within suburban north London.

By the late 1980s, researchers had begun to talk in terms of three 'waves' of retail decentralization. The first wave involved the emergence of superstores and hypermarkets during the period 1964 to 1975. A second wave between 1975 and 1985 was composed of retail warehouses, retail warehouse parks and retail parks; the enterprise-zones at Swansea and Dudley became characterized by this type of development. The initial sales emphasis was on DIY products, furniture, carpets and electricals but expanding later to clothing, footwear, toys and car accessories. The third wave dates from the proposal by Marks and Spencers in 1984 to open out-of-town stores. This type of decentralization has a wider variety of quality goods involving firms such as Habitat, Laura Ashley and World of Leather. Gateshead's Metro Centre, opened in an enterprise zone in 1986, is the first major example of an integrated regional shopping and leisure complex. No others have been completed but schemes such as the south-west London (M25) centre have been canvassed, and centres will soon open in Sheffield and elsewhere.

Although most of the objections to out-of-town centres stem from fears of their impact on city-centre trade, the evidence for this is ambiguous. Indications are that hypermarkets generate new and extra retail trade and their effect is spread thinly; the main impact may be on smaller branches of multiples rather than upon independent corner stores and many retailing firms retain city-centre stores whilst locating a new store in a suburban location. Social arguments against out-of-town developments involve suggestions that low income and non-car-owning groups, such as the elderly, are disadvantaged. There is some force to this but only if there are negative effects upon other shopping provision, and these are not proven. Changes in provision promote changes in consumer behaviour but also respond to them and an increase in bulk-buying associated with home freezers is one of the more significant consumer innovations.

Overall, retail provision has responded to the two basic needs of redeveloping outworn parts of the central city and adding new facilities to rapidly growing suburbs. Both of these have been paralleled by changes in the organization of retailing, shifts in consumer behaviour and a fairly consistent planning attitude towards decentralization. The central city remains a strong and viable location for commercial functions which reflects protective planning policies, continued investment, and consumer preferences but also in some ways indicates the continuing 'manageability' in scale and quality of British metropolitan areas. Having said this, there still remains a need for a comprehensive planning strategy for retail development in and around the city which reconciles the role of the centre with the continuing pressures for commercial decentralization.

## Problem residential areas

There is nothing new about inner-city problems in Britain. For much of the nineteenth and earlier twentieth centuries the problem consisted of congestion in limited space and an increasingly outmoded urban fabric; poverty areas were recognized in London in the nineteenth century. Housing and deprivation in the inner city have received most research attention. The worst 'slums' of the inner city have long since been removed and escalating levels of motor traffic have forced considerable change on the fabric of the inner city as planners have striven to accommodate late-twentieth-century traffic flows in street systems which were designed for completely different purposes. Much clearance within the inner city has been specifically for traffic schemes which now utilize considerable amounts of space and affect environmental quality.

During the 1970s awareness of British inner-city problems increased dramatically. It is unlikely that any emergence of new problems underlies this change, differences being of degree rather than of kind. Over the period from 1951 to 1981 the six largest cities in the United Kingdom lost over one-third of the population of their inner areas and almost half of their jobs; most of these came from the inner-city areas. The general situation in the 1980s was well summarized by Champion *et al.* (1987):

> Due to the greater residential mobility of the better off, the apparent attractiveness of inner urban areas for overseas immigrants and other minority groups, the political geography of council house building, the problems of renewing worn-out urban infrastructure and, above all, the large-scale collapse of their industrial base and particularly job opportunities for less skilled manual workers, the inner city areas have increasingly become the repository of people with the least economic 'clout' in our society – thereby undermining the quality of life available there by creating a situation of multiple deprivation (p.4).

Surveys in the 1970s showed the impact of population loss on inner residential areas. Between 1966 and 1976, Liverpool lost 22 per cent of its inner-city population, and Glasgow's Eastern Area population was reduced from 141,000 in 1971 to 82,000 in 1981. As the quotation indicates, the residual populations are typically composed of those least able to move – single person households, recent immigrants and transients and relatively high numbers of elderly people. Unemployment in the inner city is consistently high; Champion *et al.* (1987) showed that such rates are consistently higher in the 'cores' than in any other part of the wider urban area.

Figure 10.4 shows some of the marked differences which have emerged between inner-city populations and those of the overall urban area. In terms of housing, just over one-quarter of England's housing was built before 1919 but in inner areas the range is 40 to 60 per cent. Housing

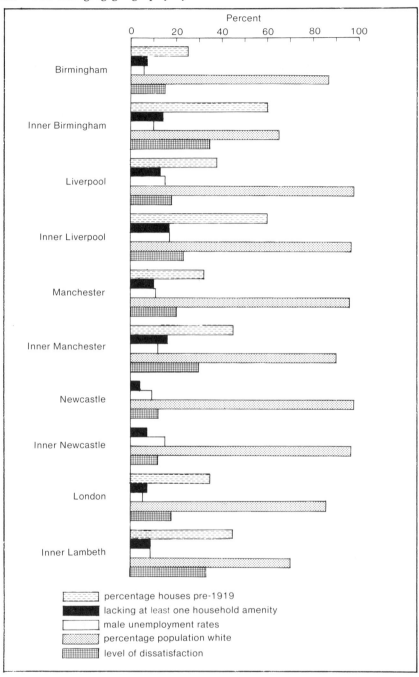

*Figure 10.4* Comparison between inner cities and overall urban areas on selected social indicators
*Source:* Allnutt and Gelardi 1980

quality is low; in inner Manchester/Salford there is less than half the total number of households in the urban area but about three-quarters of those lacking at least one basic amenity – usually an inside toilet. Accurate assessments of housing in need of repair are difficult to obtain but in 1974 the City of Liverpool estimated that 62,000 of its own properties were in need of major repair and 33,000 of these were urgent cases. Inner-city populations tend to include disproportionate shares of tenants in private rented accommodation, of unskilled manual workers, and of the unemployed. Major trends are reinforcing these characteristics; in inner Liverpool in 1974, for example, half the school leavers had no formal qualifications. Since the 1960s there have been compensating inward flows of people against the dominant decentralization movement. One of these (gentrification) is socially important but numerically insignificant; the other (the creation of ethnic residential areas) is important, both socially and numerically.

Problem residential areas are not restricted to the inner city and the problem estate has become a significant feature of the British urban scene. The Liverpool Inner Area study of 1971 spoke of people at risk of poverty in many outer council estates such as Speke and Netherley. Glasgow District Council reported from an analysis of 1981 statistics that, whereas there were some signs of improvement in inner-city conditions, the scale and intensity of deprivation in peripheral estates was increasing. The 'problem estate' is most usually defined as a phenomenon of the public housing sector. Its main features are high rates of vandalism, delinquency, and other forms of social malaise, and it is often theorized as the outcome of 'dumping' policies by local authorities who place problem tenants in the least desirable residential areas. More generally the early years of new peripheral housing developments have histories of alienation and social discontent as families are placed in unfamiliar surroundings which often lack the basic facilities and services to which they have been accustomed. Separation from friends and kinship network is often a key cause of the failure to settle into new communities. High-rise flat living engenders its own problems, especially for young families with children, and high incidence rates of neuroses are common.

### Gentrification as a return to the central city

Gentrification involves the return to the central city of professional and other higher-income groups who have tended to take over and upgrade specific districts within the inner city. Districts within which gentrification is occuring are, by and large, characterized by Georgian or Edwardian terraced housing, most commonly of three storeys; in London and most larger cities, 'gentrified' districts are of this type and are within easy access of the central city. This process was aided by provisions of the 1969 Housing Act which introduced GIAs and the more general availability of improvement grants in an attempt to raise the standard of existing housing stock. One intention of the legislation was to improve living conditions for sitting tenants, but large numbers of improved dwellings were subsequently sold for owner-occupancy at inflated prices. One outcome of gentrification has therefore been a reduction of low-cost housing and displacement of those at the bottom of the housing class hierarchy but the more positive effects represent investment in inner-city environments, upgrading of old housing stock, and attracting some middle-to-high income residents back to central areas.

The return to the central city has gathered impetus in the 1980s with major redevelopment schemes, largely funded by private investors, which are transforming old docklands from semi-derelict areas into attractive and expensive residential areas. The 'marina' or 'maritime quarter' boom has affected many cities and has fuelled an influx of investment into areas close to the inner city, though this process involves the gentrification of areas rather than of housing as most of the housing is new. The transformation of London's Docklands has had far-reaching effects, being linked both with the growth of producer-services in the city and the attractiveness of nearby waterfront residences for the new generations of financial analysts and computer-trained management consultants and also by the success of the London Docklands Development Corporation created in 1980 to induce private sector investment into an area typified by widespread dereliction, severe population loss and employment decline. The Isle of Dogs was designated as an enterprise zone in 1982 and land values there rose from £100,000 to £7 million a hectare in five years. Canary Wharf is linked physically and symbolically to the City of London by the Docklands Light Railway; this single site could offer direct employment to 40,000 people. With this scale of things, the return to the central city is assuming a new and powerful force.

**Immigrants and ethnic areas**

A far more significant movement to the inner-city areas has been that which involves overseas immigrants. Ethnic areas had been in existence in British cities for some time but generally these were of limited dimensions and had little effect upon the overall social geography of the city. London's East End had established areas of East European and Jewish colonization and similar districts could be found in other large cities and dated from the mid-nineteenth century; there were also substantial Irish communities. Most major ports had small coloured communities who were either wartime refugees or else had been formed from seafaring or dockland families. In the Stepney district of London in 1901, 55,000 out of a total population of 298,000 were foreign born, as were 6,000 out of the 15,000 in Cardiff's Bute Town district in 1940. During the 1950s and 1960s a new wave of immigration on an entirely new scale began with its main origins in

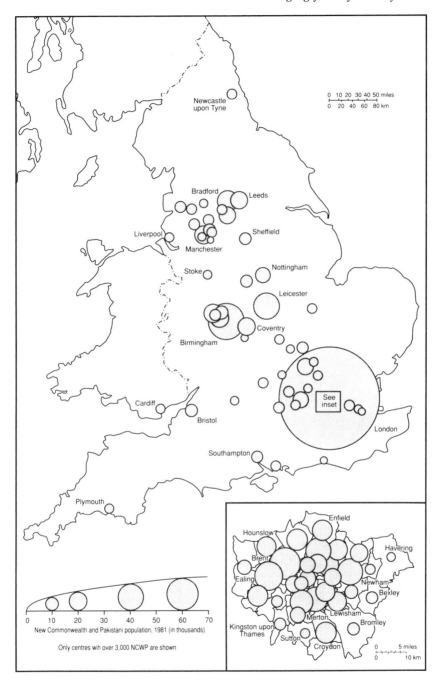

*Figure 10.5* New Commonwealth population urban distribution, 1981 (only centres with over 3,000 NCWP)
*Source:* Dr Vaughan R. Robinson

the New Commonwealth territories of the West Indies, Pakistan, India and East Africa. These population movements were stimulated by the higher standard of living and job opportunities in contemporary Britain and were fuelled by the poverty, demographic pressure and sometimes political circumstances in these source areas. The main waves of immigration occurred before restrictive legislation aimed at control in 1963–4 but some flows, of dependants and those with special skills, have continued. There were significant changes over time in the composition of the migrant streams. West Indian migration was earlier and already in decline by the early 1960s. By that stage the group had achieved some kind of age/sex demographic balance and in 1985 53 per cent of the West Indian ethnic group was UK born. By contrast the South Asian migration was still increasing in the early 1960s and controls left male-dominated communities: the male/female ratio among Pakistanis in 1961 was 538:100. Subsequent movements of dependants have allowed family reunions among Indian, Pakistani and Bangladeshi groups; in 1985 28 per cent of South Asians were UK born. During the 1960s and 1970s it became clear that these migrant flows were directed principally towards inner-city districts, replacing the out-migrating British populations. The 1985 Labour Force Survey recorded a total non-white ethnic population of 2,376,000 (see figure 10.5). The major groups were Indians 689,000, West Indians 547,000, Pakistanis 406,000, Chinese 122,000 and Bangladeshis 99,000. The average annual growth in black population by migration dropped from 80,000 in the first half of the 1970s to 53,000 in the later 1970s, and the pool of eligible dependants declined to 10,000 in the 1980s. South Asians now outnumber the West Indians on a two to one ratio but there is considerable hetero-geneity within these broad groups which is reflected in the detailed social geography of British cities. Gujaratis and Sikhs, for example, form distinctive elements within the South Asian groups. Although immigrants tend to occupy the same broad zones of housing stock within the inner city, the various groups show many signs of segregation into separate ethnic areas within these zones. A further characteristic becoming evident in the 1980s was the segregation among social classes within the ethnic group, the 'ethclass'; one example is the emerging Indian middle class.

There is clear evidence that discrimination in both employment and housing opportunities operated at an earlier phase of settlement to restrict new immigrants to a particular level within society. They mainly found employment in those types of job which, either through low pay or unpleasant working conditions, the native British worker did not want. It has also been argued that black labour was employed in those industries which were undergoing capital investment and an associated degradation of working conditions and status. Employment opportunities varied regionally and affected the distribution of immigrants. Vacancies occurred within parts of the inner city experiencing depopulation and the housing market worked in a discriminatory way, making it difficult for them to find

housing outside these districts. A 'fabric' effect was also evident by which
the residential location of immigrants was influenced by the distribution of
buildings suitable for subdivision and not yet acquired for clearance under
compulsory purchase orders. Besides these constraints, there were also
choice mechanisms in segregation which gave immigrants the opportunity
to avoid contact with the indigenous population, or 'host' society, which
was often antagonistic. Segregation also allowed them to preserve cultural
identity and traditional life styles. Choice was probably a strong factor in
Asian segregation which persisted through distinctive phases of settlement
– labelled as early pioneer, lodging house era, and family reunion.

In the early stages of New Commonwealth immigration, the new ethnic
minorities were relatively small elements of the populations in poor
environments which they shared with low-income British people and often
also with the long-established Irish communities which remain persistent
elements in larger cities. Evidence from the 1966 and 1971 censuses,
together with *ad hoc* surveys and estimates, all pointed to the fact that
levels of segregation were increasing. Birmingham has been one of the
most closely studied cities. In 1971 it had a coloured population of 92,632
which formed 9.3 per cent of the total population; by the end of the 1970s
this could be estimated as 120,000 to 140,000, which formed a larger
proportion as the overall city population had declined. By 1961, a
distribution of ethnic communities had emerged in Birmingham which
broadly conformed with a concentric zone at 1 to 1.5 km from the city
centre; within this zone immigrant densities were low but the pattern could
be related to a 'fabric effect' and a 'replacement' model. Whereas the
replacement model is general, the fabric effect will vary in its impact from
one city to another. In Birmingham, the local authority control over the
innermost housing zone 'pushed' immigrants out to a more intermediate
zone in which the larger houses were more suitable for subdivision and
multiple occupation. By 1971, the continuing combination of demographic
circumstances – outward migration of whites, overseas immigrants and
higher natural increase within the latter group – had consolidated the zonal
clusters at higher densities. During the 1970s the indications were that New
Commonwealth immigrants now formed majorities in several localized
districts and were becoming significant components of populations in many
inner-city districts. An increasing stability and introspection in ethnic areas
– particularly Asian – is suggested by the growth of specialized retailing
and business facilities catering for their particular needs.

The picture since 1971 is less clear. Whereas up to that time South Asian
segregation was increasing and West Indian segregation was either stabilizing
or decreasing, more complex patterns have now become apparent. West
Indian segregation which is now locked into council housing is very stable
but South Asian segregation varies with local circumstances from one city
to another. South Asian segregation levels increased in London between
1971 and 1981, decreased in Wolverhampton at a ward level 1961 to 1981,

and increased in Cardiff over the same period. In Blackburn the pattern was increasing up to 1974, decreasing between 1974 and 1981, and stable after 1981 though with some increases.

The emergence of ethnic areas in major British cities has stimulated spasmodic racial conflict in recent times. The causes of this conflict are multifarious and are underpinned by the economic disadvantage at which coloured minorities find themselves as well as the prejudices of sections of the white population. Several cities, including Bristol, Liverpool, Nottingham and London, have now experienced riots and violence on a major scale which have involved a certain racial dimension. These pale into insignificance, however, in comparison with the prolonged and devastating troubles of Northern Ireland. The Roman Catholic and Protestant communities have retreated into their own quarters of the cities of Belfast and Londonderry since the late 1960s. The differences between the two communities are principally ethnic rather than religious and the diametrically opposed political aspirations are one expression of this fact. Violence and murder are frequent occurrences and the impact both upon the physical structure of central Belfast and Londonderry and upon the social lives of their inhabitants is enormous.

Public sector housing policy should have provided a mechanism throughout the 1950s and 1960s whereby coloured immigrants could have been dispersed to better housing on the urban peripheries. By normal criteria of living conditions and household circumstances they qualified but their recency of residence counted against them and many local authorities, conscious of local prejudices against the rehousing of immigrants, used a series of expedients such as council-owned substandard housing for which renewal had been deferred, improved terraces, and inner-city estates, which did nothing to reduce spatial segregation. During the 1970s more open housing policies became prevalent in the public sector, largely in response to national legislation, and some dispersal, particularly of West Indians, occurred. (Asians reveal a strong preference to own houses rather than become local authority tenants.) Selectivity continues, however, not least by immigrants who prefer specific estates which are within easy reach of 'core' areas and who resist council officials' attempts to disperse them too widely. A significant trend which has become more obvious in the 1980s involves the suburbanization of elements of the South Asian population; in larger cities like Manchester this has followed a step-wise form through particular sectors of the urban area.

There is also a new phenomenon with the appearance of ethnic population growth in towns outside the traditional concentrations, such as Basingstoke, Milton Keynes and Crawley. This suburbanization and movement to new communities relates to changing patterns of social mobility. South Asians have achieved self-employment to an extent far greater than any other group in the British population. Some of the labour market constraints appear to have broken down as movement into white-collar jobs between 1971 and 1984 increased by 50 per cent for Indians and 100 per cent for Pakistanis. Among the West Indians social mobility is more limited. Some men have moved into skilled from unskilled jobs and into semi-professional jobs with local authorities who take the Race Relations Act seriously.

Although variable these shifts in social mobility have had the effect of polarizing the different ethnic groups, with the West Indians being left behind. This polarization is not reflected in spatial terms as the West Indians have been stabilized in council housing and although South Asian suburbs are appearing they are overshadowed by the continuing increases of population in the traditional clusters. Thus public sector housing and private suburbanization have some effect in redistributing ethnic groups over the wider area but the black population is often allocated to specific, and often inferior, estates and private suburbanization is limited. The black population will continue to form a significant and probably increasing component of inner-city population, and ethnic communities have all the qualities of stability and persistence.

### Jobs and the inner city

Population change is one inner-city issue in the 1980s; a second is the rapid decline of employment opportunities, especially in the manufacturing sector. Again the problem is not new as industries and businesses have been migrating out to peripheral sites, with their advantages of space and accessibility, for some decades. Closure rather than transfers and the attendant total losses of jobs has, however, become a feature. Between 1951 and 1981 the inner areas of Britain's six largest conurbations lost 45 per cent of their jobs. Many factors are involved in the loss of inner-city jobs but the general problem is that residents of the inner city occupy weak positions in competition for jobs, especially those offering security.

Between 1966 and 1973 there was an overall loss of 200,000 jobs from inner London; 140,000 of these were in manufacturing and the rest in services. In Manchester 85 per cent of the total employment decline between 1966 and 1972 was due to deaths and closures and most of these were actual closures not involving transfers or relocations. Canning Town in London and Saltley in Birmingham suffered job losses of 24 and 14 per cent respectively between 1966 and 1972. Available evidence shows a sharp downturn in the level of inner-city manufacturing and particularly high levels of vulnerability among older firms with small-size and high-cost characteristics. Among the cause of closures, inner-city redevelopment schemes which displace older firms are not insignificant. A direct result of this decline in the inner-city job market is rising unemployment; one estimate suggests that the unemployment rate in the inner city may be 3 to 5 percentage points above the city average and there are disproportionate impacts on youth and minority groups. Gordon (1989) reports that most of the inner boroughs of London had unemployment rates 50 per cent above the national average of 9.8 per cent in October 1987, and in Hackney and Tower Hamlets the rate was double that national average.

## Quality of life

The third aspect of the inner-city problem as it emerged in the 1970s can be summarized as the low quality of life which had come to be endured by most inner-city residents. On most objective criteria, such as substandard housing, educational disadvantage, ill-health and social deviance, deprivation is strongly over-represented in inner-city areas. Something of the scale and diversity of this aspect of the inner-city problem has been revealed by reports of Inner City Studies in London, Birmingham and Liverpool. Other research shows how deprivation is often clustered in inner-city areas but is not exclusive to them; on a national scale London and Glasgow in particular have high rates of inner-city deprivation. Some finer-grained analyses reveal significant variations within inner-city areas, however, and also show that much social disadvantage exists outside the inner city. Generalizations must clearly be handled with care but there is evidence that the inner city continues to hold a disproportionate share of urban problems. The proportion of inner-city residents expressing dissatisfaction with the area in which they live is two or three times higher than the figure for the country as a whole. Main concerns are deteriorating environments, dirt and litter, vandalism, poor services, lack of open space and:

> It should be remembered that the majority of people living in the inner cities are not unemployed and do not live in overcrowded houses or lack the use of basic amenities. However, they can be affected by dereliction, vandalism and petty crime; and they may well have difficulty in obtaining a mortgage, or find that their address makes it more difficult for them to get new jobs.
>
> (Allnutt and Gelardi 1980: 47)

## Urban policies

Implicit in much of the foregoing discussion has been the increasingly interventionist role of planning in British cities since the 1947 Town and Country Planning Act and the wider role of government, at both central and local levels, in the administration of urban affairs. Earlier major policies, such as containment to protect the countryside and building new towns as self-contained and balanced communities to house surplus populations from metropolitan areas, now seem less relevant to the needs of changing Britain. These were policies to deal with growth and the pressures of population expansion and will be less appropriate to a long period of no growth or at least of very slow incremental change. New towns and expanded towns are now part of the British urban system but the blueprints of the late 1960s – such as Severnside and Humberside cities – now fade into the realms of the discarded and unnecessary. Again, as recreational planning and new agricultural technologies gather force, the thrust is towards more positive use of particularly suitable space rather than extending a negative protectionist mantle over all existing non-urbanized land. The local scale objectives of promoting accessibility and environmental standards through neighbourhood planning, segregation of land use, and hierarchical transport systems are becoming of central importance.

Urban policies have shown considerable shifts over the past few decades, which in part relate to government attitudes to the issues of the time and also to the tension between policies for the regions on the one hand and for the city on the other. Stewart (1987), reviewing recent trends, argued that:

> As far as cities in general are concerned and inner areas in particular, the thrust of the main resource allocation policies of government has been to shift public resources away from cities over the last decade and indeed to limit the power and resources of local authorities to devise programmes which address local needs. In many respects inner city policy has been a charade (p. 129).

Stewart makes this statement despite the fact that between 1979 and 1987 over £2 million was spent on inner cities with partnerships, programmes, powerful new public agencies, and development corporations, on around 12,000 individual projects and involving the generation of significant private resources. Robson (1989) has a similar argument as he underlines the specific weaknesses of recent urban policy as:

> lack of national coordination with withdrawal of rate support as a key counteracting policy to urban aid schemes;
> conflict between central and local government;
> imbalance between social and economic goals of urban policy.

For the period up to 1977, several themes tended to dominate urban policy. The regional policy tension, with its tendency to favour 'regions', remained; the emphasis on the need to boost local economic development was evident. Area-based policies to deal with deprivation in its various forms existed in most large cities. For housing, area policies have a long lineage in various renewal and improvement legislation including the 1974 Housing Act. Educational deprivation was tackled with the designation of Educational Priority Areas (EPAs) following the 1967 Plowden Report; the Urban Programme included attempts to direct resources to areas of special need; and the Inner Areas Bill of 1977 established partnerships to tackle inner-city problems. Area policies are clearly ameliorative and in that role they have consistently been underfunded. Given present practice there is no assurance that the worse problems are being solved or that resources are anywhere near the kind necessary to upgrade deprived areas.

There are two main criticisms of area policies. The first suggests that they are misdirected because they channel resources into areas which may only contain a minority of individuals in need. This criticism has weight but can be accommodated by viewing area policies as part of a strategy, the other parts of which will be aimed at individuals or households in need regardless of where they live. The second criticism, which was given considerable impetus by the reports of the Community Development Projects (CDPs), is that local solutions to problems of this kind are not possible. Deprivation is an expression of inequality which finds its origins in the political economy and the allocative systems which help reproduce it; ameliorative reform is no substitute for more radical change. The relevance of this radical critique is persuasive and its influence upon the academic research community has been considerable. As British cities enter the 1980s, however, ameliorative reform, much of it exercised through area policies, continued to be the basis for urban policy. Central government policies continued to label urban problems as area issues, the responsibility of local authorities and requiring local management strategies. Finally, the fear of racial tension was a growing force in urban policy.

From 1978 to 1986 there are elements of consolidation, continuity and change in urban policy. There is continuing emphasis on economic development with several new features which include a focus on private sector involvement, a reduction of planning controls, a focus on the 'market' and a priority to new inward investment. Central government policies for urban regeneration include urban development grants, urban regeneration grants, urban development corporations, enterprise zones, and city action teams and task forces to tackle coordination: 12 per cent of the budget is now specific to the interests of ethnic minorities. A key feature of these new initiatives is the semi-autonomous nature or central accountability of the agencies created. This has led to a dilution of local authority control and a tension between central and local government.

There are many initiatives but it is in assessing their impact that opinions vary. There are regional differences of a familiar kind; private sector investment flows much more readily into southern cities and success is more apparent there. Many of the most successful schemes have capitalized on the potential of large cities as places of consumption, involving tourism or recreation (Robson 1989); exhibition complexes, waterfront developments, and maritime quarters all have this characteristic. Stewart (1987) still argues that conditions in inner cities have worsened and on the evidence of the Birmingham Partnership area, where only 17 per cent of newly created jobs went to residents of the most disadvantaged inner areas, suggests that trickle-down effects may be limited.

Relationships between central and local government will have continued significance for urban policy. Local government finance is a key factor and the moves towards a community charge or 'poll-tax' will have new and not easily predicted impacts. The major inter-governmental grant has been the Rate Support Grant (RSG) which in 1979/80 involved the transfer of £7,000 million from central to local government in England and Wales. The RSG has a domestic element which acts as a subsidy to local taxpayers, a resources element which seeks equalization of tax bases, and a needs element which seeks to compensate for high expenditure requirements. As central government funding moves towards a block grant system in the 1980s, based on clearer determinants of the need to spend on particular services, there are new implications for city governments, particularly in the context of their 'political' need to keep down the level of local taxes. Already stringent cash limits are showing their impact and the ability of local authorities to provide and maintain good services is under threat. Real fiscal problems are compounded by the uncertainty of roles: 'there is uncertainty not only about the precise role and responsibilities of central government but also following from this about how local authorities are meant to respond to many of its messages' (Central Policy Review Staff 1977: 46).

The elected governments of British cities, caught between more rigorous central governmental control over the outflow of funds and a heightening level of participation by a public to which they are directly accountable, are subject to increasing pressures, and urban policy-making has begun to take place in an atmosphere of crisis. Faced by the decline in manufacturing industry, traditionally associated with large cities, local authorities and local business consortia have used a mixture of central and local govern-ment powers to stem job loss. Local authorities have used existing legislation, particularly the powers offered by the product of a 2p rate, to develop economic initiatives. Labour councils have regarded the public sector as the necessary stimulus for change and have moved to protect indigenous industries. Central government's policy of private-sector financed, demand-led approaches to regeneration is in sharp contrast. The creation of economic development offices has become the most common form of local authority activity; these may maintain lists of available sites and information on forms of assistance and loans, ensure that relevant training programmes are in place and encourage local self-help schemes. Results are inevitably variable. Besides the criteria of locational advantage or disadvantage, research has stressed the role of leadership in advancing local regeneration. British cities in the 1980s are both manageable and habitable but the forces which create urban problems and the means of solving them lie beyond their immediate control.

## REFERENCES

Allnutt, D. and Gelardi, A. (1980) 'Inner cities in England', *Social Trends*, 10, London: HMSO, pp. 39–51.
Cameron, G. (ed.) (1980) *The Future of British Conurbations*, London: Longman.

Central Policy Review Staff (1977) *Relations between Central Government and Local Authorities*, London: HMSO.

Champion, A. G., Green, A. E., Owen, D. W., Ellin, D. J., and Coombes, M. G. (1987) *Changing Places: Britain's Demographic, Economic and Social Complexion*, Oxford: Edward Arnold.

Clark, C. (1951) 'Urban population densities', *Journal of the Royal Statistical Society*, A, 114: 490–6.

Fothergill, S., Kitson, M., and Monk, S. (1985) 'Urban industrial change: the covers of urban-rural contrast in manufacturing employment trends', *Inner Cities Research Programme, Report 11*, London: HMSO.

*Faith in the City: A Call for Action by Church and Nation* (1985), London: Church House Publishing.

Gibbs, A. (1987) 'Retail innovation and planning', *Progress in Planning*, 27: 1–67.

Gordon, I. R. (1988) *Resurrecting Counter-urbanisation: Housing Market Influences on Migration Fluctuations from London*, paper presented to IBG, Loughborough.

Gordon, I. R. (1989) 'Urban unemployment', in Herbert, D. T., and Smith, D. M. (eds.) *Social Problems and the City: New Perspectives*, Oxford: Oxford University Press.

Hall, P., Thomas, R., Gracey, H., and Drewett, R. (1973) *The Containment of Urban England*, London: Allen & Unwin.

Hall, P. (1985) 'The people: where will they go?', *The Planner*, 71: 3–12.

Hall, P. (1986) 'From the unsocial city to the social city', *The Planner*, 72: 17–24.

Kemp, P. (1989) 'The housing question', in Herbert, D. T. and Smith, D. M. (eds.) *Social Problems and the City: New Perspectives*, Oxford: Oxford University Press.

Prentice, R. C. (1986) 'Directions for a housing policy in Wales', in *Church in Wales, Housing and Homelessness in Wales*, Penarth: Church in Wales Publications.

Robson, B. T. (1989) 'Social and economic futures for the large city', in Herbert, D. T. and Smith, D. M. (eds.) *Social Problems and the City: New Perspectives*, Oxford: Oxford University Press.

Stewart, M. (1987) 'Ten years of inner city policy', *Town Planning Review*, 2: 129–45.

## FURTHER READING

The literature on British urban geography is considerable but useful general texts are:

Herbert, D. T. and Thomas, C. J. (1982) *Urban Geography: a First Approach*, Chichester: John Wiley.

Short, J. R. (1984) *An Introduction to Urban Geography*, London: Routledge.

On housing:

Dunleavy, P. (1981) *The Politics of Mass Housing in Britain 1945–1975*, Oxford: Oxford University Press.

Malpass, P. (ed.) (1986) *The Housing Crisis*, London: Croom Helm.

Smith, Neil and Williams, P. (eds.) (1986) *Gentrification of the City*, London: Allen and Unwin.

On urban morphology:
Whitehand, J. W. R. (1987) *The Changing Face of the Cities*, Oxford: Blackwell.

On retailing:
Davies, R. L. (1984) *Retail and Commercial Planning*, London: Croom Helm.

On urban problems:
Herbert, D. T. and Smith, D. M. (eds.) (1989) *Social Problems and the City: New Perspectives*, Oxford: Oxford University Press.

General:
Hausner V. A. *et al.* (ed.) *Economic Change in British Cities*, Oxford: Clarendon Press.

# 11 The rural areas

*Malcolm J. Moseley*

## A WARTIME DREAM

Writing in 1945 about the problems of the countryside, and the magnitude of the changes which he judged necessary, the agricultural economist C. S. Orwin concluded his book with a reverie about the state of rural Britain a generation later. It is worth quoting this dream at length, as a yardstick against which we can consider what actually transpired.

Let us try to reconstruct the scene which might greet the eyes of another Rip Van Winkle who had fallen asleep, say, in 1940 and awakened a generation later, after the nation, freed from its preoccupation with war, had set itself to solve some of the problems, industrial and social, of the countryside.

The landscape ... would show notable changes ... there was now a spaciousness and order which was new. The many awkward little fields ... the overgrown hedgerows and choked ditches ... all were gone. The trim hedges enclosed larger fields. There were no horses to be seen ... everywhere there was the suggestion of technical changes, all of which seemed to promote a greater activity on the land.

As he approached a homestead he found himself on a good concrete roadway ... Gone were the dilapidated old barns, gone the dark and dirty cow-sheds [and] ranges of pig hovels ... In short the homestead impressed him, just as the fields had done, with its air of order and efficiency ...

He wondered at the number of young men he saw about the place and learned that this reconstructed homestead was the headquarters of a large farming enterprise, built up from an amalgamation of several smaller farms. Only through the larger unit had it been found possible ... to give full scope to highly qualified management, to modern machinery and to skilled workers ...

The isolated cottages in the fields, remote from neighbours, public services and the amenities of village life, seemed to have disappeared ... Nearly all the men, it seemed, lived in houses in the villages, and came to their work on motor bicycles. The farming, he found, was carried on much more intensively [and] caused a considerable demand for seasonal labour ... he betook himself next to the village of his youth ... the place had grown, but not beyond recognition. New houses came out to meet him, pleasant houses, larger than those which he had known, each with a good garden and plenty of space about it ... The new houses merged almost imperceptibly into the old village without incongruity ... Most of the new houses were occupied, it seemed, by workers in a factory which had been moved out of Birmingham and set up on a site about five miles away.

Reaching the green ... the church, with its fine Norman tower, still dominated the scene, but the ugly Victorian Vicarage ... had become the Community Centre – the focus of all the social activity in the village ... The new wing ... was the Village Hall ... the rest of the house served for the health clinic, county library, clubrooms, adult education classrooms, canteen and restaurant ... and so on.

The school in which Van Winkle had been educated ... had gone and in [its] place was a new and larger building ...

A branch of the local Co-operative Society occupied the site of what had been the wheelwright's shop ... there was a new and larger general shop and a butcher's business where none had been before, but the same little post office still served ... There was no suggestion about the place of a divided community, of an old village and a new housing estate. On the contrary, Rip Van Winkle had an impression of a virile, well-knit society ... There was a vigour and activity about the place ... and he found it good.

(C. S. Orwin 1945: 105–9)

Had this dreaming farmer really awoken a half century later what would he have discovered? This chapter provides some of the answers as far as the rural population is concerned – its size, location, employment and way of life: other chapters have traced related developments in agriculture and the rural landscape. But first we must try to define 'rural Britain' and its essential characteristics.

## DEFINING RURAL BRITAIN

An attempt has been made to pull together various 1981 Census data for English and Welsh local authority districts, plus a few indications of geographical remoteness, to devise a single 'index of rurality' (Cloke and Edwards 1986). This index highlights those areas which tend to be remote from large towns, rely substantially on agricultural employment and have high levels of out-commuting, a low population density, an elderly age structure and low household occupancy rates.

It is mapped as figure 11.1 and reveals the following as 'extremely rural': most of Wales outside the principality's industrial south and north-east, most of Devon and Cornwall, a broad band of eastern England around the

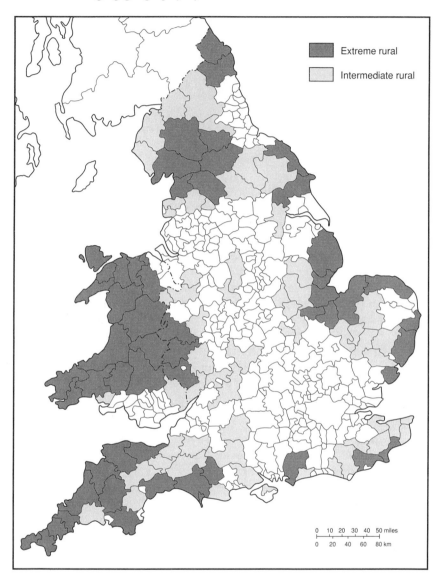

*Figure 11.1* Index of rurality, 1981

Wash, and the northern Pennines. Away from these areas, there is a gradation through what the researchers called 'intermediate rural, intermediate non-rural, and extreme non-rural'. The latter covers much of the *visually* rural south-east and the hinterlands of England's northern and midland cities, thereby clearly making the point that *socio-economically* much of Britain's countryside is essentially urban in its character.

Depending on the definition employed, about 12–15 per cent of Britain's population may be said to be 'rural'. And, if we put together 'smallness' and its 'remoteness', then a study by the Association of County Councils suggests that some 5–6 million people in Britain live in settlements which both have fewer than 5,000 inhabitants and are over five miles from a town with over 20,000 inhabitants. It is this 'hardcore' – say 10 per cent of Britain's population – for whom it is most difficult to ensure reasonable access to services and job opportunities.

*Table 11.1* Rural and urban England and Wales: some comparative data from the 1981 census

|  | *Villages(1)* | *Small towns(2)* | *All urban areas(3)* |
|---|---|---|---|
| Total population (millions) | 5.4m. | 2.4m. | 43.6m. |
| *Age structure* | % | % | % |
| Aged 0–15 | 21.7 | 22.9 | 22.3 |
| Aged over 60/5 | 18.6 | 18.1 | 17.7 |
| *Employment* |  |  |  |
| Agriculture, energy, and water | 15.9 | 7.4 | 3.9 |
| Manufacturing | 20.2 | 25.3 | 28.2 |
| Construction | 7.5 | 7.6 | 6.8 |
| Services | 59.1 | 58.8 | 59.9 |
| *Household tenure* |  |  |  |
| Owner-occupied | 62.5 | 65.5 | 57.3 |
| Local Authority rented | 17.4 | 23.0 | 30.1 |
| Private rented | 10.3 | 6.9 | 8.7 |
| *Car ownership* |  |  |  |
| No car | 21.4 | 27.7 | 40.5 |
| One car | 49.4 | 50.7 | 45.2 |
| Two + cars | 29.3 | 21.6 | 14.4 |
| *Travel to work* |  |  |  |
| By car | 59.6 | 60.1 | 49.7 |
| By bus or rail | 7.8 | 11.5 | 22.6 |
| Work at home | 11.4 | 4.9 | 2.8 |

*Notes*: (1) Settlements with under 2,000 inhabitants plus scattered dwellings
(2) Settlements with 2,000–5,000 inhabitants
(3) Includes (2)

What kind of people are we talking about? Once more using 1981 census data for England and Wales only, table 11.1 separates out the 5.4 million who live in isolated dwellings or in villages (there are about 8–10,000 villages) and the 2.4 million who live in 'small towns' (defined here as those with 2,000–5,000 inhabitants). The table shows that while the rural areas are in some ways quite distinctive from the towns (note the relatively high levels of car ownership, house ownership and the tendency to 'work at home', which can be added to the distinctive features found by Cloke and Edwards and referred to above) just as noteworthy is their *similarity* with urban Britain. Thus in rural, as in urban, areas about 60 per cent of the workforce is employed in the service sector and 20–30 per cent is in manufacturing.

## ISSUES IN RURAL BRITAIN

Change is the norm in rural Britain, and has long been so. The enclosed fields of midland England are the artificial product of an eighteenth- and nineteenth-century agrarian revolution, just as the changing social structure of villages today is the product, in part, of a contemporary transport revolution. Concern for the drift from the land, the decline of the village, and the rape of the countryside is nothing new. Going back nearly fifty years to the 1942 Scott Report on *Land Utilization in Rural Areas*, which was to be so influential in the genesis of post-war rural policies, we read of a loss of 30 per cent of the agricultural labour force in the inter-war period, and of the erosion of rural isolation as the wireless, cinema, bicycle and motorbus spread their influence. And in Orwin's description of rural Britain at much the same time, we see already the arrival of 'weekenders and retired folk' and their growing 'competition for the cottages of the local working people'. Indeed Orwin's summary of the task facing those responsible for shaping the post-war reconstruction of rural Britain has a familiar ring to it today:

> If the facts be faced, the problems of the countryside are how to bring about a regeneration of almost every condition of life within it – how to free farming from its position as a parasitic industry; how to give farm workers a comparable wage and economic opportunity; how to reintroduce industries offering employment alternative to agriculture; how to apply to rural districts the higher standards of housing and public services which are spreading rapidly in the urban areas; how to raise the standards of education, recreation, and social services and activities of all kinds, to the levels at which they are available to the rest of the nation to-day. The alternative can only be a countryside dependent upon public assistance and drained of all that is best in its human element, the young and the enterprising. (C. S. Orwin 1945: 12–13)

Nevertheless, the post-war period has undoubtedly witnessed major change. Much has stemmed from further technological developments in agriculture, industry and transport, from the greater affluence and changing values of the British people, from the expanding scope of government involvement, and from the vicissitudes of demographic change. Much of this change has originated outside the rural areas and has had to be accommodated and absorbed: it could not be totally resisted. And much has involved conflict: between those living in rural areas and those visiting, between newcomers and the indigenous, between those owning land or capital in rural areas and those without. There is also conflict between goals: between efficiency and equity, conservation and development, the protection of property rights and state intervention. Indeed Cherry has defined the central contemporary issue in rural Britain as 'competing claims on land and resources from different sectional interests ... conflict is the keynote' (Cherry 1976: 272).

Two broad themes underlie this miasma of change and conflict, and each falls fully into the established realm of geographical concern. The first concerns 'the proper use of land'. How can society reconcile the demands upon a very limited land area for agriculture, forestry, recreation, water supply, mineral working, the conservation of habitats and landscape, and residential and industrial development? The second relates to 'changing spatial relationships' – to the changing distribution of population, employment, services and the transport systems which link them. Other chapters in this book deal comprehensively with the land-use theme. What follows will relate mainly to the changing distribution within rural Britain of individuals as social and economic beings and to the problems and management issues which ensue.

## POPULATION AND EMPLOYMENT

Depopulation has *not* been the norm in post-war rural Britain. In 1951 there were 10.4 million people in the administrative rural districts of England, Wales and Northern Ireland and the county districts of Scotland: this was 20 per cent of the national total. By 1971 the corresponding figures were 12.8 million and 23 per cent. Today, if data were still collected for these old administrative units, the figures would probably be around 15 million and nearly 30 per cent. But these gross figures, which embrace some suburban as well as rural areas, conceal a number of distinctive trends which have been operating simultaneously:

1 the *depopulation* of the remotest areas, especially of younger people, generated by a marked decline in employment opportunities and, to a lesser extent, a dissatisfaction with the local social and cultural amenities;

2 *urban decentralization*, linked in part to the dispersal of employment from the inner areas of the large cities, and in part to the search for better, cheaper, and better-situated housing;

3 *retirement migration* (and the 'seasonal extension of suburbia' into second homes) in which late-middle-aged and elderly people seek cheaper housing in attractive rural areas; and

4 *local restructuring*, in which population change within rural areas is positively related to the size of villages and small towns: the larger settlements grow at the expense of their smallest neighbours.

These trends are intertwined and have served to produce a complex demographic mosaic within rural Britain. What is important is not just the numbers of people involved – whether this or that village or small area has

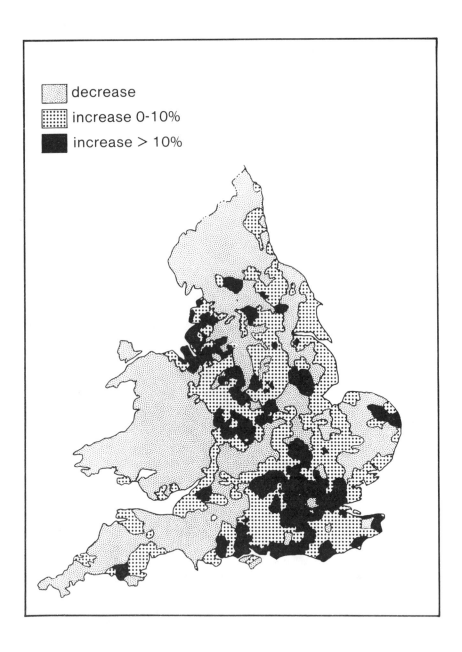

*Figure 11.2* Population change in the 1930s

been gaining or losing population – but the type of people also. We can draw a broad distinction, for example, between on the one hand the remoter areas with their ageing populations and all that that implies for local society, fecundity, and service provision, and on the other hand the commuter areas having a more balanced age-structure, thriving services, and the characteristics of 'suburbs surrounded by fields rather than by other suburbs'. As for social class, major changes have occurred not just in the commuter villages, where the middle-class newcomers tend to inhabit social worlds quite distinct from those of the indigenous working class, but also in the more favoured retirement areas such as the south-west and East Anglia, where the 'pull up the drawbridge mentality' prompts articulate newcomers to resist the notion that 'their' village should ever change.

Such trends have existed for some time, but the pace and location of change has varied over the past fifty years. Compare, for example, the map of population change in the 1930s, taken from the Scott Report, with that of the period 1971–81 (figures 11.2 and 11.3). Clearly, with the passage of time, urban decentralization and retirement migration have moved out, wave-like, to embrace most of lowland England and much of upland England and Wales. Some see this as 'counter-urbanization', or a fundamental break with the traditional advantages bestowed by urban areas upon employer and resident alike. This may be overstating the case but data assembled by Champion (1983) point in that direction. On the basis of their population density he placed the 402 districts of England and Wales into six groups of sixty-seven and calculated their rates of population change for both the 1960s and the 1970s. Table 11.2 shows that in both periods the more rural areas tended to grow; even in the 1970s, a decade of very modest growth nationally, it was the most sparsely populated sets of areas which experienced greatest population growth.

Townsend (1988) has confirmed that these trends continue, by using data for 1986. He has found that, while the population of England and Wales grew by less than 1 per cent between 1981 and 1986, that of the 'remote

*Table 11.2* Population change in six groups of local authority districts in England and Wales, ordered according to population density (after Champion)

|  | *1960s* | *1970s* |
|---|---|---|
| 1 Main towns (greatest density) | — | — |
| 2 | ++ | + |
| 3 | ++ | + |
| 4 | +++ | ++ |
| 5 | +++ | +++ |
| 6 Sparse countryside (lowest density) | ++ | ++ |

*Notes*:     − decline
         = growth (< 0.5% per annum)
         ++ growth (0.5 to 1.0% per annum)
         +++ growth (> 1.0% per annum)

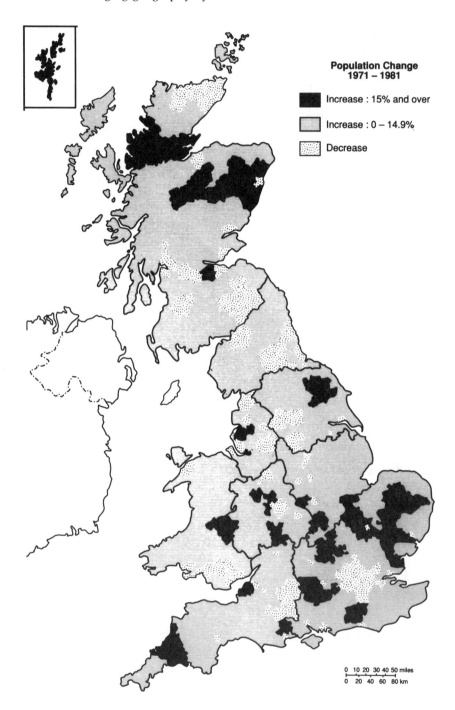

*Figure 11.3* Population change, 1971–1981

largely rural' and the 'resort and retirement' areas each grew by about 4 per cent. This was entirely due to migration (i.e. not to natural change) and, more specifically, to retirement migration, to the growth of commuting and to an increase in the number of people able to work from their home. For the single year of 1986, the 'top seven' English counties, in terms of net in-migration, were all coastal with a substantial rural population – Cornwall, Isle of Wight, Dorset, Somerset, East Sussex, Lincolnshire and Suffolk.

As for employment, the most important trend in post-war rural Britain has been the declining importance of land-based activities – notably agriculture, but also forestry and mineral-working. In agriculture a steady rise in agricultural productivity of 5 or 6 per cent per annum through much of the post-war period has found expression in a 2 per cent per annum decline in the labour force and a similar rise in output. As a result, the agricultural workforce was halved in the period 1955–77, and the decline has continued through the 1980s. Today even the most rural areas rarely have more than 15–20 per cent of their workforce in agriculture. Moreover the nature of the agricultural worker has changed. Gone is the jack-of-all-trades farm labourer. The farmer's family does more of the work than hitherto, and today most employees have defined skills and are supplemented by casual and seasonal labour. All this suggests a variety of labour market implications, some of which will be discussed later.

Some of this decline in employment has been made good by a growth in the manufacturing sector. Keeble, for example, has noted that many recent empirical studies of industrial location 'lend support to the view that . . . in developed economies, a fundamental shift in industrialists' spatial preferences has been taking place . . . with a marked current bias towards smaller settlements, including those in peripheral locations' (Keeble 1977: 308–9).

In figure 11.4, it is noteworthy that in the most peripheral regions it is the medium-sized towns, and not the villages, which are portrayed as benefiting most from the job dispersal trends. The plight of the latter has been a growing source of concern for government, both central and local, and the attempts made to promote rural industrialization by both national and regional agencies, such as the Highlands and Islands Development Board and the Rural Development Commission, and by local authorities, constitute a further major feature of the changing employment geography of rural Britain.

In 1983, for example, the Rural Development Commission designated as 'Rural Development Areas' those parts of rural England which were most disadvantaged in terms of unemployment, range of job opportunities, population decline or sparsity, net out-movement of those of working age, an age-structure biased towards the elderly and poor access to services and facilities. Most of these areas (figure 11.5) are peripheral or northern; this is where the most pronounced 'rural deprivation' is to be found (*unless* we now include the shortage of affordable housing amongst our criteria, in

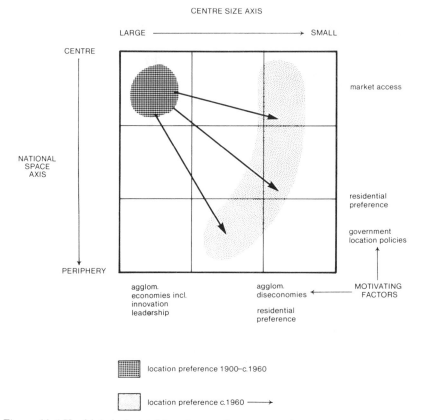

*Figure 11.4* Keeble's industrial location preference matrix

which case the rural south-east would certainly score most highly). Happily by 1987, and thanks in part to the stimulus to economic development given in these chosen areas, the average level of unemployment there had fallen to about 8 per cent, a percentage point below that of England as a whole.

But we must always remember that it is the *service* sector which provides most jobs in rural England – not agriculture or manufacturing (table 11.1). In that regard, and looking to the future, how far the *villages* develop (rather than the small- and medium-sized towns) will depend much on technology; at present many personal services (retailing, health care, etc.) seem to be moving up the urban hierarchy (as will be described below), while advances in information technology enhance the ability to work from home.

## SERVICES AND TRANSPORT

It may seem unnecessary to state it, but for the vast majority of rural residents the quality and quantity of public utilities and of public and

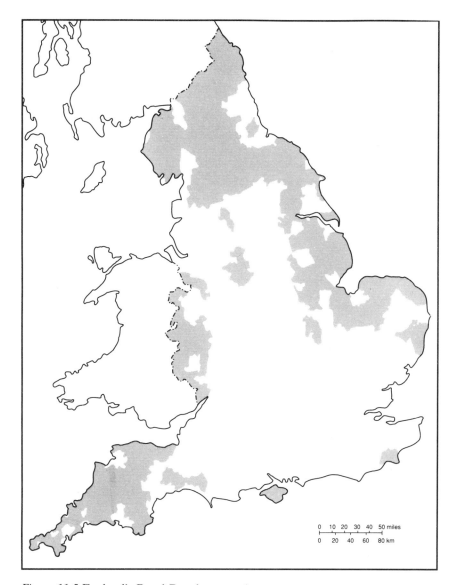

*Figure 11.5* England's Rural Development Areas

private services available to them has improved beyond measure in the post-war period. The Scott Report noted that fifty years ago one-third of all dwellings in the rural areas lacked electricity and about one-seventh lacked piped water. Amongst strictly agricultural dwellings these proportions were very much higher. By 1980, in rural England and Wales the number of people lacking basic services were:

% of settlements
with the service

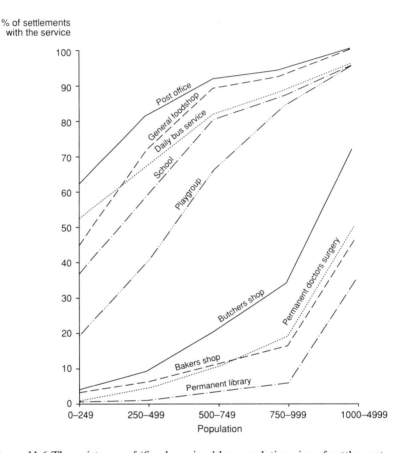

*Figure 11.6* The existence of 'fixed services' by population size of settlement

electricity: virtually zero,
mains water: 70,000,
mains sewerage: 900,000,
mains gas: 4,900,000.

Few would argue that households lacking the last two are seriously deprived if adequate alternatives are readily available.

As for service provision, the present author and John Packman carried out a survey of about 5,000 hamlets, villages and small towns in 1982 (Moseley and Packman 1983). These were widely scattered throughout Great Britain. To be included in the analysis, every settlement had *both* to have fewer than 5,000 inhabitants *and* to be at least three miles from a

% of settlements
with the service

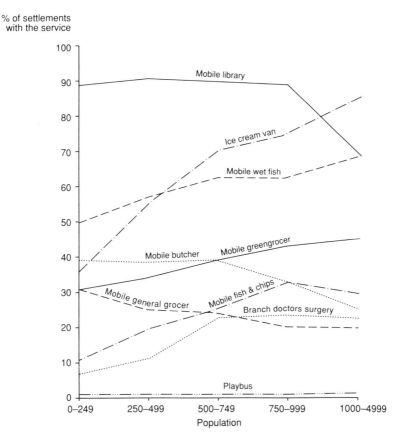

*Figure 11.7* The existence of 'mobile services' by population size of settlement

Woolworth store. We asked about three kinds of service – those occupying fixed premises, those which are mobile, and those delivered to the consumer's home.

Based on that research, the degree to which settlements of varying sizes enjoy 'fixed services' is shown in figure 11.6. Thus, of small villages (250–500 inhabitants), 80 per cent had a post office in 1982, 50 per cent a school and only 5 per cent a doctor's surgery. As far as 'mobile services' are concerned (figure 11.7), of the same group of villages 90 per cent had a mobile library, 25 per cent a mobile shop and 10 per cent a branch surgery. And, concerning 'delivery services' (figure 11.8), nearly all of these villages were visited by the 'milkman' and 'coalman', but fewer than half by 'meals on wheels'.

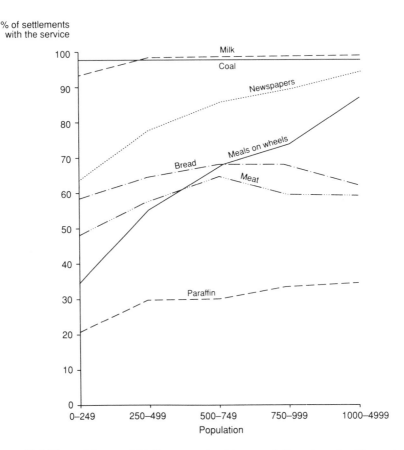

*Figure 11.8* The existence of 'delivery services' by population size of settlement

What was interesting was that by and large it was the larger villages and small towns which did best for all kinds of services; we had expected mobile and delivery services to compensate for the absence of conventional services in the smallest settlements, but this was only partially true. We did conclude, however, that the virtual ubiquity of postal and milk delivery, and of the mobile library, provided a base upon which, with ingenuity, several other services could be built. Why should the milkman not deliver medicine prescribed by the pharmacist in the neighbouring town?

It has to be said, of course, that the *majority* of rural residents are much better served than were their predecesors in terms of their access to services – because of the motor car. But village services continue to decline. Whether it is shops, post offices, pubs, surgeries or schools, a

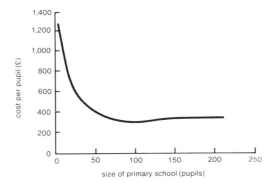

*Figure 11.9* Primary school costs by size of school

steady 1 or 2 per cent decline per annum has been in train for 30 or 40 years, and it still continues. So why has there been this steady, seemingly irrevocable decline?

Much of the answer lies with 'economies of scale' – the lower average costs of providing services in large units which permit overheads to be spread across a larger clientele. Figure 11.9 indicates how much more expensive it is to educate primary school children in schools with fewer than about fifty pupils, and counties such as Dyfed, North Yorkshire and Norfolk have over 100 schools below that size – more than Greater London and the six metropolitan counties combined. Given the falling birth rate of the late 1960s and 1970s and the growing pressures on public expenditure, it is hardly surprising that so many small rural schools have been closed in recent years.

Village shops have suffered from growing competition from their larger and generally more efficient urban counterparts following the abolition of resale price maintenance in 1963 and the general rise in personal mobility in recent years. Doctors, brewers, oil companies and the Post Office have all come in recent years to question the commercial or operating efficiency of servicing so many 'rural outlets' when most of their customers are willing and able to travel further for their product or service. Last, it has to be admitted that the thrust of strategic land-use planning policy has long been in the same direction. In the 1960s and 1970s every non-metropolitan county council produced a strategic plan which, in one guise or another, sought to guide both residential and service developments to a select group of villages and small towns, so as to reduce the inordinate cost of servicing a scattered population. Such plans proved politically difficult to implement, but they still tended to work in the same direction as the economic pressures detailed above.

As for personal transport, the rise of car ownership, so that 70 – 80 per cent of rural households now have at least one car, has led to a deterioration of public transport by reducing passengers and thereby necessitating higher fares, or a curtailed service, or both. It has generally been the smaller and more remote villages that have suffered most, so that villages without shops, post offices and schools often lack a minimal bus service as well.

The heyday of the country bus network was in the early 1950s and since then there has been a steady decline in passengers. For example, from 1965 to 1975 there was a 30 per cent fall in 'passenger-miles', but only a 10 per cent fall in 'vehicle-miles' – in other words the buses became progressively emptier and less economic to run. Since 1968, county councils have been empowered to subsidize loss-making services, and since 1986 many of the fetters of 'regulation' have been loosened to unleash, it is hoped, a more entrepreneurial approach by bus operators. Some new commercial services have resulted, and in addition community transport schemes organized and run by volunteers plug some of the gaps – but the truth is that rural England is 'excellent car country' and public transport is hard pressed to compete.

## RURAL PROBLEMS

Many of the social and economic problems that stem from the trends described above are not confined to the rural areas. A declining demand for labour, especially unskilled labour, high unemployment rates and limited opportunities for school-leavers, selective out-migration and its adverse effects upon the viability of local services and upon the 'morale' of the community – all characterize the inner cities as much as the remoter rural areas. Indeed, it is interesting that Knox and Cottam (1981) discovered from their empirical analysis of a range of economic, social and demographic indicators relating to small areas of Scotland that the worst deprivation in that country is to be found in the city of Glasgow and in the Western Isles. They conclude that

> deprivations are concentrated at the two extremes of the settlement hierarchy ... between these two extremes is a steady decrease in the incidence of deprivations with increasing levels of urbanization, so that the best-off areas are those with a fairly rural physical environment and economy but which also contain middle-order service centres ...

> (Knox and Cottam 1981: 166)

Of course, the problems of the inner-urban and outer-rural areas are not mirror-images of one another. Just as the inner cities have their own distinctive problems of physical dereliction, racial tension and overcrowding, so the rural areas have particular problems arising from their spatial structure and attractive environment. Their spatial structure underlies both the 'accessibility problem' and the problem of providing services for a scattered population; their attractive environment helps to generate conflicts in the housing market and also conflicts between recreationists and other rural land-users.

Constrained accessibility is particularly likely to afflict those on the edge of, or reluctantly outside, the rural labour market. Teenagers, women, the unskilled, and those over 55 years of age are most likely to be out of work *and* relatively immobile. Earned incomes, too, are typically low in rural areas, principally because of an adverse industrial and occupational structure with a preponderance of relatively low-paid jobs in such sectors as agriculture, footwear manufacture and timber and furniture, and a shortage of the more lucrative jobs to be found in insurance, banking and other professional services, for example.

Furthermore, gathering information about employment and training opportunities is more difficult in rural areas, especially for those without a telephone – and four-fifths of those rural households without a car also lack a telephone. This is unfortunate as recent years have witnessed a decline in such traditional local purveyors of information as the village policeman, clergyman, shopkeeper and postmistress, the withdrawal from rural areas of many local government offices and other public sector 'points of contact', and a growing sophistication in the information needed in the employment and social security fields.

What all this points to is a web of disadvantage which makes it difficult for a substantial minority of rural residents to improve their lot. But, the critics of this 'rural deprivation thesis' argue, 'do not such people live there by choice?'. Is not life in rural Britain a 'package deal' of advantages and disadvantages, with the option of moving home always available to those who dislike the particular package?

In fact this is too simplistic. Many of the rural disadvantaged have strong family or employment reasons for living where they do: to sever these would often create further problems. Many live in council housing, or the private rented sector, winter-let holiday accommodation and mobile homes which offer little basis for a move to more expensive urban accommodation. Amongst owner-occupiers, many are retired people who are effectively 'locked-in' by the house-price gradient which originally attracted them to the rural areas.

The irony is that not only is it difficult for the rural poor – especially if they have families – to move into urban accommodation, but they often experience growing insecurity in their home areas. The chief rural housing problem is no longer the squalor, overcrowding, and lack of amenities of the dwellings themselves – as it was when the Scott Report was written – but their sheer unavailability at a price people can afford. The decline of the private rented sector, the scale of council housing and the virtual absence of new-build, and the growth of competition for houses for sale from retirement migrants, commuters, and second-home buyers, all have tended to increase the insecurity of low-income rural households. Rapid house price inflation in the mid-late 1980s, and strict development control policies, linked to a variety of green belt, village envelope, key village, conservation and aesthetic objectives, have also contributed to the curtailment of the supply of moderately priced dwellings, so much so that the lack of affordable housing is now the primary social problem in rural Britain. And it is not just disadvantaged individuals who suffer, whole communities do so if district nurses, teachers and motor mechanics, say, cannot be recruited for want of affordable accommodation.

In short there are serious social and economic problems in contemporary rural Britain; a combination of public sector parsimony, reliance on the invisible hand of the market and the helping hand of the community, and a strong conservationist ethic does not ensure their resolution.

## POWER AND POLICY

In recent years, geographers with an interest in problems of either people/ environment or spatial relationships have tended to shift their attention away from the direct analysis of those relationships themselves to the decision-making processes which underlie them. Relevant decisions are taken in part by individual people, and decisions to migrate, to recreate or to shop in one place rather than another, for example, have been much researched. More recently it has become clear, however, that decisions made by powerful public and private sector agencies are at least as influential as these individual decisions in fashioning the way in which rural areas are changing.

First, statutory land-use planning, as carried out by planners employed by county and (since 1974) district councils, is relatively weak as a force for change in rural Britain. By and large it can only permit and steer development: it can neither cause it to happen nor prevent it if the momentum is too great. The patterns and processes of demographic, social and economic change that have been described above would differ only in detail if the planning machinery had been radically different, as the similarity of overseas experience confirms.

Second, and this relates to the limited effectiveness of land-use planners, the various public sector agencies with a major stake in rural Britain are both numerous and ill coordinated. A study of the promotion of economic development in a part of West Dorset, undertaken in 1980, revealed that five agencies were directly involved, financially and administratively – the Department of Industry, the Department of the Environment, the Council for Small Industries in Rural Areas, the Manpower Services Commission and the Dorset County Council. A further nine had regularly to be consulted: the Departments of Employment and Transport, the Ministry of Agriculture, the Development Commission, the National Bus Company subsidiary, the Regional Water Authority, the Dorset Community Council and the appropriate district councils and parish councils. In the subsequent decade, many of these agencies have been renamed or reformulated but the problem remains.

Moreover, this plethora of decision-makers, all with their own priorities and ways of working, not only makes it difficult to engineer effective solutions to clearly identified problems but it also bewilders the rural resident who needs to approach one or more of these bodies to get something done. Figure 11.10, for example, shows the confusing pattern of information providers relevant to residents of a small area of Lincolnshire.

A third point is that so many decisions affecting rural Britain are shaped by national bodies with national, i.e. predominantly urban, problems in mind. For example, decisions in recent years to raise petrol duty substantially, to give council house tenants a statutory right to buy, and to reduce the frequency of the payment of various pensions and allowances, respectively erode rural accessibility, the housing stock available to local people, and the viability of the sub-post office. Similarly, the policy of concentrating hospital care in large 'District General Hospitals' may be eminently sensible on medical grounds, but may not be optimal where the population is widely scattered.

In short, there is a need for geographers to learn much more about how Whitehall departments, regional quangos and local authorities reach their decisions – and to trace the effects of key decisions through to the rural environment.

## THE DREAM AND REALITY

Nearly fifty years on, if Orwin's Van Winkle were really to open his eyes today, he would find only half of his creator's dream come true. The spacious landscape, the amalgamated fields and farms, the advanced agricultural technology and the 'air of order and efficiency' – these have come about. But Van Winkle would be surprised to discover the modern farms using very little labour; he would see few young men at work and he might even have a twinge of nostalgia for the intimate and bustling landscape of his youth. The expanded villages, with their new and commodious housing, and the arrival of manufacturing firms from the cities – these also accord with the present reality. But where in Orwin's dream is the near-ubiquitous motor car? And the waking farmer would be dismayed to see many of the village services gone, with little evidence of the imagination necessary to turn redundant vicarages into multi-purpose community resources. Moreover a village sharply divided into different communities, or lacking a sense of community altogether, would be more

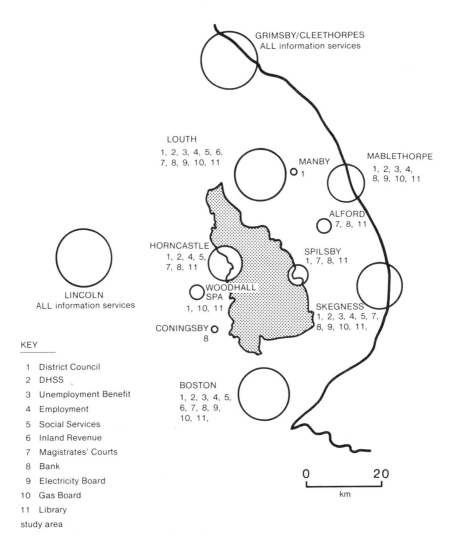

GRIMSBY/CLEETHORPES
ALL information services

LOUTH
1, 2, 3, 4, 5, 6,
7, 8, 9, 10, 11

MANBY
1

MABLETHORPE
1, 2, 3, 4,
8, 9, 10, 11

ALFORD
7, 8, 11

HORNCASTLE
1, 2, 4, 5,
7, 8, 11

SPILSBY
1, 7, 8, 11

LINCOLN
ALL information services

WOODHALL
SPA
1, 10, 11

SKEGNESS
1, 2, 3, 4, 5, 7,
8, 9, 10, 11,

CONINGSBY
8

BOSTON
1, 2, 3, 4, 5,
6, 7, 8, 9,
10, 11,

KEY

1   District Council
2   DHSS
3   Unemployment Benefit
4   Employment
5   Social Services
6   Inland Revenue
7   Magistrates' Courts
8   Bank
9   Electricity Board
10  Gas Board
11  Library
study area

0        20
km

*Figure 11.10* Sources of information for an area of central Lincolnshire

likely to greet his eyes than the 'virile well-knit society' Orwin hoped for.

In short, Orwin got it about half right, no more. But that represents a greater degree of precision than any contemporary futurologist would be able to achieve for rural Britain in 2030.

**NOTE**

[1] The first Rip Van Winkle, of course, was Washington Irving's creation who fell asleep for twenty years in eighteenth-century America.

## REFERENCES

Association of County Councils (1979) *Rural Deprivation*, London: ACC.

Champion, A. G. (1983) 'Population redistribution in the 1970s', in Goddard, J. B. and Champion, A. G. (eds.) *The Urban and Regional Transformation of Britain*, London: Methuen.

Cherry, G. E. (ed.) (1976) *Rural Planning Problems*, London: Leonard Hill.

Clark, D. and Unwin, K. I. (1980) *Information Services in Rural Areas*, Norwich: Geo Books.

Cloke, P. and Edwards, G. (1986) 'Rurality in England and Wales: a replication of the 1971 Index', *Regional Studies*, 20,4: 289–306.

Keeble, D. E. (1977) 'Industrial geography', *Progress in Human Geography*, 1: 304–12.

Knox, P. and Cottam, B. (1981) 'Rural deprivation in Scotland: a preliminary assessment', *Tijdshrift voor Economische en Sociale Geografie*, 72: 162–75.

Moseley, M. J. and Packman, J. (1983) *Mobile Services in Rural Areas*, University of East Anglia, Norwich.

Orwin, C. S. (1945) *Problems of the Countryside*, Cambridge: Cambridge University Press.

'Scott Report' (1942) *Report of the Committee on Land Utilisation in Rural Areas*, Cmnd 6378, London: HMSO.

Scottish Office Central Research Unit (1978) *Rural Indicators Study*, 2 vols.

Townsend, A. (1988) *The Outer Rural Areas* (unpublished conference paper. Dept of Geography, University of Durham).

University College, London (1980) *Decision Making for Rural Areas: West Dorset Study* (Report to Department of the Environment).

## FURTHER READING

For more recent reviews of rural social and economic problems, see three journals: *Countryside Planning Yearbook*, published annually by Geo Books, Norwich since 1980; the *Journal of Rural Studies*, published quarterly by Pergamon; and *Rural Viewpoint*, a bi-monthly magazine published by ACRE, Cirencester, Glos.

# 12 The changing political geography

*Peter J. Taylor*

## INTRODUCTION: THE WORLD ECONOMY AND 'NEW POLITICS'

The political geography of Britain has undergone many major changes over the last fifty years. Old maps, such as those of local government areas, have been thoroughly revised while new maps, such as the Treasury's Standard Regions, have been created. Relations between the four home countries have changed and been reviewed as centralization has been imposed on Northern Ireland and devolution has been proposed and withdrawn for Wales and Scotland. At the same time Britain's world role has been drastically altered from control of the world's largest empire to the perpetual maverick in the EC.

All of these political changes have occurred within the context of a relative decline of Britain in economic terms. In the 1930s Britain was still undisputed number two in the world economy after the USA. In the 1980s it is doubtful if it was still in the top twenty of the economic league table. The political decline of Britain runs parallel to this economic descent, despite the efforts of British governments, even as late as the 1960s, to pretend otherwise. The British state relies upon the British economy for its power and resources and the strength of the British economy depends upon the world economy and Britain's role within it.

In the period covered by this essay the world economy has moved out of one depression, experienced an unparalleled period of economic growth, and then descended into a second depression. British economic experience has followed this cycle, although growth has been slower and the subsequent depression more severe in the post-war era. Nevertheless the British economy, like that of other industrial countries, has followed the world economy's waves of growth and stagnation (see chapter 1). However, whereas these economic changes are global in scope, the political responses are largely restricted to the realms of the individual states. It is for this reason that state politics are a dependent variable in the world economy. Each phase of the world economy generates new problems and issues which political parties within countries respond to while they compete in their electoral politics. Hence the ups and downs of the world economy are reflected by the constant appearance of 'new politics' when old assumptions are cast off and new items are incorporated in the political agenda. Usually all major political parties accept the new agenda so that it does not itself become part of the electoral politics, which remain concerned with matters of degree and problems of implementation. Party competition thus takes place only within the agreed-upon agenda. It is for this reason that the stability of party politics is misleading as an indication of changing politics in a modern state like Britain.

In this chapter six 'new politics' are identified, each with a distinctive although obviously related agenda. They are associated with phases of the world economy as pairs of new politics. For instance the Kondratieff cycle stagnation (B) phase between the two world wars is associated with first a *politics of crisis* in the 1920s when Britain appeared at times to be ungovernable, to be followed in the 1930s by a *politics of national interest* dominated by the Conservative party in the national government. The Second World War and the ensuing period of economic growth (Kondratieff phase A) made 1930s politics disreputable and a *politics of social democratic consensus* was born which lasted through the 1950s. In the case of Britain relative economic decline during the Kondratieff A phase produced an early reaction against some of the assumptions of social democracy, producing a *technocratic politics* that dominated the 1960s. With the onset of another stagnation phase of the world economy the nature of British politics changed once more and 'ungovernability' appeared again in a new *politics of crisis* through the 1970s. Calm has once again been restored to British politics by the Conservative party in a new *politics of national interest* in the 1980s which has gone under the name of 'Thatcherism'. These six 'new politics' and their relation to Kondratieff cycles are shown in table 12.1. In the final column I have listed a series of political events that symbolize the eras identified – they provide a 'flavour' of the politics described below. The General Strike of 1926 represents a national breakdown in labour relations whereas the Jarrow March a decade later was a dignified plea for help. There is a world of difference in the politics of these two events. Similarly the National Health Service is the prime achievement of the social democratic consensus which contrasts with the futility of the Concorde project. These alternative ways of spending in the growth era again epitomize the contrast between two politics.

Finally the series of public sector strikes in 1978–9 – the 'winter of discontent' – which signalled a crisis in government–union relations and the humiliating defeat of the miners' strike in 1985 which signalled a general collapse of union power, illustrate the two very different politics in the latest stagnation phase.

The division into 'new politics' is used to organize the subsequent discussion. The first section of the chapter deals with the two politics of the first stagnation phase. The next four sections then deal with each subsequent new politics in turn. The longest discussion is about the current era

*Table 12.1* Phases of the world economy and 'new politics' in Britain

| World economy | | British state | | |
| --- | --- | --- | --- | --- |
| Period | Kondratieff cycle | Period | 'New politics' | Symbolic major events |
| 1914/18 | | 1918 | | |
| | B-phase (stagnation) | | Politics of crisis | General Strike 1926 |
| | | 1931 | | |
| | | | Politics of national interest | Jarrow March 1936 |
| 1940/5 | | 1940 | | |
| | A-phase (growth) | | Politics of the social democratic consensus | Establishment of National Health Service 1947 |
| | | 1960 | | |
| | | | Technocratic politics | Confirmation of Concorde project 1966 |
| 1967/73 | | 1972 | | |
| | B-phase (stagnation) | | Politics of crisis | 'Winter of discontent' 1978/9 |
| | | 1982 | | |
| | | | Politics of national interest | Miners strike 1984–5 |

of politics but it will be appreciated that 'Thatcherism' can only be understood in terms of what went before. Hence discussions of all the new politics are relevant to understanding the contemporary political geography of Britain.

Clearly these different politics overlap to some degree in both time and content but the broad typology is a very useful framework for considering the changing political map and form the basis for organizing the substantive discussion into the sections of this chapter. Within each section the material is arranged in the same format. In the introductions the assumptions and resulting agenda of each of the new politics are described very generally. Three particular elements of the politics are then discussed in more detail. In the first part of each section, and following on from the discussion above, the position of Britain in the world economy is set out and the political responses of government to these circumstances are described. These are vital policies because they set the framework within which domestic politics have to be pursued. These sections are termed *geopolitics* to indicate global influences upon each new politics.

In the second part of each section the *electoral geography* of the various periods is dealt with. Although governments of both major parties (Conservative and Labour) have been unable to break out of Britain's structural strait-jacket in the world economy, they have been highly effective in domestic politics. They have successfully mobilized the population behind the consecutive new politics so that they have monopolized governments for over fifty years.

Finally, each section is concluded by a discussion of *territorial policies*. It is these policies that generate the administrative geographies of Britain. However, it is not just that they reflect the changing spatial structure of the British state but also that as such they touch upon important issues of legitimation and sovereignty. This is because parts of the state's territory are treated differentially. This is obviously the case in the treatment of Northern Ireland and devolution policy but it is also true of other spatial policy which involves explicit transfer of resources between areas. Administrative maps are much more than mere spatial structures.

Geopolitics, electoral geography and the spatial structure of the state constitute three of the major areas of research in political geography. Each of these sections, therefore, provides a brief cameo of the political geography of each 'new politics' within the over-arching framework of the world economy. In a short conclusion some similarities and contrasts across the two depressions are identified.

## BRITAIN IN DEPRESSION: FROM POLITICS OF CRISIS TO POLITICS OF NATIONAL INTEREST

The 1914–18 conflict was the first war of popular mobilization. Hence the war aims came to include new domestic priorities. The prime minister, Lloyd George, promised a land fit for heroes. But the world economic situation did not provide the circumstances in which this promise could be achieved. Instead the 1920s was a period of economic crisis with continual high unemployment. The resulting politics were highly unstable, with six different governments between 1922 and 1931. The rise of the Labour movement was clear to see both electorally and industrially but there was no general settlement of how labour was to be integrated into the new politics of the state. The General Strike of 1926 was the main symptom of the uncertainty. No government seemed to have the answer to the chronic economic problems and this is the true essence of any politics of crisis.

The intensification of the worldwide depression after 1929 had profound political effects in all states. In Britain the political reaction was quite distinctive in that there was an explicit attempt to avoid conflicts by producing an all-party government of national interest in 1931. This response is quite consistent with the fundamental conservative nature of the British state described by Nairn (1977) and the related parliamentary reformism of the Labour party described by Miliband (1962). The new government had the ex-Labour leader, MacDonald, at its head, and his position in 1931 followed his earlier pronouncements as a Labour Prime Minister attempting to 'educate' his party to govern in the 'national interest'. In fact the new government was Conservative dominated, especially after Labour and Liberal resignations in 1932. In this period the Conservative party controlled Parliament to a degree never achieved in mass elections before or since.

The politics of national interest were used to blunt the rise of the Labour party and working-class aspirations generally. 'Nation' was placed before 'class' to justify sacrifices of whole communities being made in the wake of the depression. Hunger marchers received sympathy but government remained essentially non-interventionist, pursuing orthodox and frugal fiscal policies and waiting for change. For a decade that seemed to offer so much support for Marxist notions of capitalist collapse the 1930s was a profound political disappointment. The left may have believed they were winning the intellectual argument but they most clearly lost the political contest at the polls. The 1930s were undoubtedly conservative in the basic sense of accepting the inevitability of the effects of the depression (Runciman 1966). This was truly the end of an era.

### Geopolitics: towards protection and appeasement

Before the 1930s British foreign policy was based on principles developed nearly a century earlier when Britain was the hegemonic power in the world economy. Free trade and the convertibility of sterling on the gold standard facilitated world trade. After the depression of the late nineteenth century, British dominance was ended but free-trade policy continued despite attempts to overturn it in 1903 and 1923. The economic orthodoxy of the later 1920s, with free trade and the return to the gold standard in 1925, resulted in the over-pricing of British exports on world markets in a period of intense competition. This policy was particularly severe on the traditional export industries of northern England, Scotland, Wales and Northern Ireland; thus the high rates of unemployment of the 1920s were uneven in distribution, with coalfield and ship-building areas being greatly affected. The general rise in unemployment in the 1930s exacerbated these regional inequalities.

The new national government of 1931 overturned some of the tenets of this foreign policy. In 1932 protectionism finally succeeded, with the Import Duties Act and the Ottawa Agreement on 'Empire free trade'. Currency was managed by the Exchange Equalization Fund and the formation of the sterling bloc, and trading agreements were signed with seventeen countries. The effect of these policies was not to improve conditions in the depressed regions, however. In the south the depression subsided, with a boom in house-building and consumer durables production, but this left the regional balance even more unequal as a rise in demand for coal and ships had to await rearmament.

Rearmament itself was postponed by the diplomatic policy of appeasement whereby the expansionary plans of Germany were to be negotiated. This policy is symptomatic of the British state's withdrawal from its position of dominance in the world. With the failure of appeasement and arrival of a new world war Britain went back to work in a planned wartime economy in which the assumptions of the 1930s were to be swept away.

### Electoral geography: defining the Labour heartlands

The 1918 election was a very unusual one in that the wartime coalition under the Liberal, Lloyd George, agreed to fight as one 'party', issuing 'coupons' to candidates that it supported. The result was a landslide victory for the government, which in reality provided the Conservative party with a parliamentary majority. The Liberals were split between those in the coalition and those outside, leaving the small Labour party to become the official opposition. Hence this was the start of the replacement of Liberals by Labour.

In terms of geography, Labour did not simply replace the Liberals but rather it developed its own distinctive class-based distribution of support. In 1918 it was still concentrated in the coalfields and a few docklands constituencies. In the elections of the 1920s it spread its appeal to working-class areas in other cities and industrial zones. It was so successful that it was able to form minority governments in 1923 and 1929. At the same time the Conservatives were eroding rural areas of Liberal support, so that the latter party was effectively eliminated as a competitor for government by 1929. The 1920s' elections were unstable, partly because they were three-party affairs, but in hindsight they clearly represent the transition from one two-party system (Conservative–Liberal) to another (Conservative–Labour).

In 1931 the National Government won a landslide victory over Labour, giving it a majority of 468 in a parliament of 615 seats. Although this implies widespread support for the government, in fact large numbers of voters in all regions 'voted against the national interest' and for Labour in 1931. The Labour party was reduced to fifty-two seats as the electoral system rewarded a unification of its opponents under the 'national' banner. This meant that the party only won seats in 1931 where it had a *majority* (rather than a simple plurality) of the votes and hence its successes were limited to their heartlands on the coalfields and some inner-city zones. Despite the parliamentary defeat, the overall vote held up well at about its average level since 1922. In 1935 the party was able to achieve its highest ever vote proportion as it consolidated control of the heartlands but again suffered a heavy defeat. The electoral map of the 1930s can be said, therefore, to define the Labour heartlands.

Outside these 'islands' of Labour support the national government situation enabled the Conservatives to continue their erosion of Liberal support in rural areas. After 1935 the Liberals were no longer a force in rural constituencies except in a few peripheral regions, and the elections of the 1930s, while confirming first an 'anti-party' coalition and then a largely 'one-party' national government, actually provided the basis for the class-based two-party system that was to emerge after 1945. Thus the electoral map of the 1930s contains the basic distribution of party support that has come to dominate British politics. The stability of this pattern over half a century is a testament to the power of the two major parties in mobilizing their support.

### Territorial policy: towards centralization

In a non-interventionist era of politics we should not expect much territorial policy. However, there were two developments in this period which foreshadowed some important elements of later policy and both warrant some consideration.

The British state lost its most severe regional economic problem with the establishment of the Irish Free State in 1921. As we have already seen, however, British foreign policy before 1932 exacerbated the depression's effects on the export-based regions of northern Britain and the new protectionist programme served largely to protect home production in the midlands and south so that in the 1930s the government discovered it had a new regional problem on its hands. Its response was very minor in practical terms but important in theory. The 1934 Special Areas Act designated four 'special areas' of high unemployment and 'Commissioners' were appointed to carry out schemes under the Act. This is the first example of a government selecting policy regions for positive discrimination and thus tacitly admitting that the space economy is not self-adjusting.

The four special areas were on the coalfields and hence in areas which did not return 'national' MPs to Parliament in 1931 and 1935. This meant that they were often made up of local government units under Labour control. From the early 1920s Labour councils had defied central government policy and every coalfield area had its 'Little Moscow'. In London, Poplar councillors were gaoled over unemployment relief levels and 'Poplarism' spread to other areas. The government responded in 1926 by passing legislation that enabled central government to replace elected representatives by its own appointees in such disputes. This was subsequently used in Bedwellty, Chester-le-Street, West Ham, Rotherham and County Durham. This cumbersome method of controlling 'local autonomy' was replaced in 1934 by the Unemployment Act which centralized payment of relief in a national Unemployment Assistance Board. The sensitive issue of relief was thus removed from local party politics and placed in the hands of a central bureaucracy.

These examples of incipient regional policy and local government control illustrate centralizing trends that were even evident in the non-interventionist politics of national interest. The new politics of the 1940s allowed such trends to come to dominate the political map and territorial policies.

## BRITAIN IN THE INTER-DEPRESSION YEARS
## THE SOCIAL DEMOCRATIC CONSENSUS AND OPTIMISM

In many ways Labour's landslide electoral victory of 1945 represents a landmark in British political history. In terms of electoral politics it is sometimes cited as one of Britain's 'critical elections'. If we go beyond electoral politics, however, we can make a very convincing argument for starting this 'new politics' in 1940 with the formation of Churchill's wartime coalition which marked the return of the Labour party to government. This government was responsible for an elaborate system of state intervention involving socio-economic as well as military planning and it carried out detailed consideration of post-war reconstruction. In the latter case there was a series of policy statements and reports (e.g. the Beveridge Report) which were to guide post-war development of the welfare state. Therefore, despite the rhetoric of the 1945 election, much of the Labour programme had already been agreed upon by the Conservative-led coalition government, in broad principle if not in all details.

The broad continuity of policy in 1945 was repeated in 1951 with the return of the Conservatives to government. The foreign policy, welfare state and mixed economy established by Labour all survived the change in government intact. There were some changes in policy (notably steel nationalization) but the broad outlines of a basic agreement on post-war politics remained and became popularly known as 'Butskellism' (after the leading 'moderate' Conservative R. A. Butler and the 'moderate' Labour leader Hugh Gaitskell) in the 1950s: this was described by an American observer as the new 'collectivist age'.

The combination of war victory and subsequent economic growth encouraged the development of a social democratic consensus imbued with national self-confidence, in complete contrast to the 1930s. This was originally generated by Churchill through wartime policy and was maintained in support of Labour's reconstruction programme to reach its apogee in the Conservatives' 1959 electoral slogan 'You've never had it so good'. Although most discussion of the social democratic consensus emphasizes the domestic programme of welfare state and mixed economy both the consensus and the national self-confidence were most highly developed in the critical area of foreign and trade policy.

### Geopolitics: the great power illusion

The United Kingdom came out of the war as one of the 'Big Three' victors with America and Russia. Clearly Britain alone did not command equivalent potential resources to the two 'super-powers' but the illusion of great power status was maintained. Churchill postulated a special position for Britain as the lynchpin of three inter-locking circles: Commonwealth, Atlantic and European. Labour's version saw social democratic Britain in a mid-way conciliating position between communist Russia and capitalist America. Such viewpoints evaporated with the Cold War and the formation of NATO in 1949, leaving Britain militarily subservient to America. This was most clearly illustrated when Britain stepped out of line in 1956. The British–French invasion of Egypt – the Suez fiasco – did not have prior US approval and withdrawal was engineered by the Americans using economic pressure to produce a sharp decline in the value of the pound.

The link between sterling and Britain's world role was to transcend the humiliation of 1956 and in hindsight we can see that it permeated the whole geopolitics of this period.

While the Foreign Office was pursuing a military world role, the Treasury was conducting a parallel policy of attempting to maintain London as a major financial centre of world capitalism with sterling having a prime role in the new liberal economic world order. Along with the military policy this represented a financial commitment whose costs never seem to have been calculated. If the new domestic commitments of the welfare state are added to the equation then balance of payments problems would seem to be inevitable. Foreign and domestic policy soon became contradictory as Britain became locked into its infamous 'stop-go' system. Economic policy oscillated between reflationary programmes to maintain growth and full employment and deflationary programmes to curb balance of payment deficits and control sterling. In short, the domestic policy was sacrificed for the great power illusion, terminating in the failure of both sets of policies in the 1960s.

### Electoral geography: the nationalization of elections

In 1945 Labour established itself as a major political party as its vote grew from around the one-third level it had attracted between 1922 and 1935 to nearly one-half. Although the Conservatives suffered a heavy parliamentary defeat they maintained their role as the other potential governing party. As we have seen, 1945 initiated the classic era of two-party, class-based politics in Britain. In 1945 Labour had finally broken out of its heartlands in a largely two-party contest, effectively 'nationalizing' British politics outside Northern Ireland.

'Nationalization' does not mean an even distribution of support for each party across the country but rather that the same class-based issues dominated voting behaviour in all regions. This, of course, led to *local* concentrations of support as Labour did well in working-class constituencies and the Conservatives in middle-class constituencies, but every part of the country had its share of Labour and Conservative voters. There were, to be sure, differences of degree in class voting across the country, with the industrial areas of the north, Scotland, and Wales recording the highest levels of working-class support for Labour, but these were relatively minor deviations; the broad pattern overall was of a nationwide two-party system based upon social class. The only major exception was Northern Ireland where the Conservatives' Unionist tradition was translated into votes from Protestants of all social classes.

The result was that British self-confidence during this period included its electoral arrangements, which seemed to offer a self-regulating political economy with electoral politics reflecting the post-war compromise between capital and labour. The uneven spatial distribution of party support contributed to the situation by interacting with the electoral system to produce majority governments in Parliament. Furthermore, this pattern was maintained by a geographically uniform swing between parties from election to election. Many foreign observers were envious of Britain's 'ideal' electoral politics.

### Territorial politics: the birth of regionalism

The centralization trend discerned in the 1930s continued and was boosted by the wartime and Labour governments. This was most obviously represented by the nationalization programme which involved reorganization of public ownership as well as taking over private enterprise. Municipal gas and electricity holdings and local hospitals were all transferred to central control. Local authorities were compensated, as it were, by being allocated new functions, notably in land-use planning, and by the house-building programme based upon council housing. What little local/central government conflict that emerged involved central government direction of the new towns programme through appointment of the New Town Corporations. However, 'Little Moscows' were definitely a thing of the past in this optimistic era of economic growth.

In terms of political maps this period is most notable for the rise of the regional dimension in British politics. The social democratic consensus derived from wartime planning and thus involved much *de jure* spatial organization. Although regionalism had been previously proposed as popular regional devolution, the first major steps in this direction were bureaucratic. The wartime emergency led to the division of England into ten regions with the appointment of Regional Commissioners to coordinate civil defence and also to take charge in the event of a breakdown of communications from London. Part of the coordinating role led to the relevant government ministries regionalizing their administrations. After the war the Regional Commissioners disappeared but the regional organization of Ministries continued. In 1946 the Treasury devised the 'Standard Regions' to which other departments were expected to conform. In addition the new state corporations and the National Health Service were each organized into their own regional patterns.

Regionalism was much more than an administrative device, however. 'Acceptance of full employment as an objective, and of the goals of a welfare state, necessitated regional action. Discrimination against members of society can no more be accepted on a regional basis than it can on a social, racial or religious basis' (McCrone 1969: p. 13). The new Labour government devised the first major regional employment policy with the 1945 Distribution of Industry Act, which extended the old Special Areas to larger new Development Areas and designated five new areas. Positive spatial discrimination became part of the interventionist social democratic consensus.

Although the Conservative government diluted regional policy after 1951 and cut back on regional administration as part of a removal of wartime controls, these two strands of regionalism have remained part of the British political map since this time. The economic growth of the 1950s allowed for a relaxation of regional planning but as the sequence of stop-go policies became more severe a new era of politics evolved in which these initial planning experiments were to be resurrected and moved to the centre of the political stage.

## BRITAIN IN THE INTER-DEPRESSION YEARS
## TECHNOCRATIC POLITICS AND DISILLUSION

In the 1959 election campaign the Labour party had tried to introduce 'economic league tables' as an issue but it was easily defeated by a Conservative campaign of complacency. The self-confidence bubble soon burst, however, and the 1960s became an era of political concern and uncertainty over Britain's future.

The new politics to emerge from this situation were essentially technocratic, epitomized by Harold Wilson's promise of a 'white hot technological revolution' in 1964. Britain's decline had to be reversed and the means chosen were state intervention and national planning in 'the reappraisal of 1960'. This involved major reorganization of government with new departments emerging (Department of Economic Affairs and Ministry of Technology in 1964 and Department of Trade and Industry and Department of the Environment in 1970) plus the setting up of quasi-government agencies, notably the National Economic Development Council in 1962 and the Prices and Incomes Board in 1964 (a list of all of these changes is given by Broadbent 1977: pp. 68–9). Although large in number, these changes were all merely administrative reforms which could be accommodated into the traditional policies of the British state since they left intact the dominant fiscal policy axis of Treasury and Bank of England. The sterling crisis and devaluation of 1967 led to the ditching of the National Plan and the eventual abolition of the Department of Economic Affairs. This was a 'stop' phase with a vengeance: unemployment went above half a million and MacIntyre (1968) pronounced 'the strange death of social democratic Britain'. State intervention had not changed anything; Britain's relative decline actually accelerated.

Technocratic politics led to reform, biased towards large institutions, to promote 'efficiency'. This included favouring the large market offered by the EEC in foreign affairs and the production of large new local authority areas on the domestic front. Both of these examples of 'large is beautiful' are discussed below. Perhaps the two most impressive monuments to the technocratic politics of the 1960s are the supersonic Concorde financial disaster and the social disaster of the high-rise flats and concrete deck-access maisonettes that litter the modern UK townscape. Technocratic politics spawned a new disillusionment among voters, exposing the self-adjusting two-party system of the previous era to new criticism.

**Geopolitics: the European option**

Although British confidence was jolted by the Suez fiasco of 1956, the final undermining of the great power illusion was in 'the fateful year of 1960' with the abandonment of Britain's independent military deterrent in the form of the Blue Streak rocket and the collapse of the Paris summit – 'the last occasion on which a British Prime Minister attempted to play a major role at the top table of world diplomacy' (Kitzinger 1973: p. 16). The position was summed up by former US Secretary of State, Dean Acheson, in 1962 when he observed that Britain had lost an empire and not yet found a new role. In fact the British government was attempting to do just that as it turned to Europe for salvation.

The European Communities had been set up in the 1950s with Britain choosing to remain outside. In terms of economic league tables the EEC countries grew faster than Britain, which naturally attracted comment. In 1961, in a complete reversal of policy, the Conservative government applied for membership, breaking the 'three circles policy'. Already the Commonwealth was no longer the cosy white dominion club it had been and by 1961 the special relationship with the USA no longer seemed so special. Nevertheless in 1962 France vetoed British entry. The effect was further to undermine British self-confidence.

Britain's world role continued to be an issue in the politics of the 1960s. The Labour party was elected in 1964 and 1966 against campaign accusations that its government would reduce Britain's role but in fact it proved to be just as eager as its Conservative opponents to play at being a world power when in office. It was only the most severe 'stop' of 1967 that forced Britain to withdraw all but token forces from east of Suez. This retreat to Europe was accompanied by a second application to join the EEC, which suffered the same fate as the first.

And so the European haven was beyond the politicians' grasp. Nevertheless in terms of economic linkages British financial and trade interests were increasingly centred upon Europe at the expense of wider linkages. This change in City orientation made the European option compatible with the survival of the traditional international interests of the British state.

Final successful negotiation was just a few years away in 1971 and 1972, and stands as the culmination of 1960s' foreign policy.

### Electoral geography: continuity and change

The three general elections after 1959 represent a clear-cut continuity of the two-party class-based politics of the previous era. In 1964, 1966 and 1970 the two major parties dominated the voting and the reflection of the familiar social class mosaic in the voting pattern continued unabated. However, there were a few signs that things were not as stable as they seemed. For one thing the uniform swing was beginning to show variations not present before. As early as 1959 Scotland had swung *to* Labour against the overall pattern and in 1964 certain areas of the West Midlands swung *to* the Conservatives against the national swing. The latter case is particularly important since it indicated the entry of the immigration issue into British politics. Overall, however, these three general elections overwhelmingly illustrate continuity and not change in electoral politics.

What of the disillusionment of voters in the wake of the technocratic failures? Although the two main parties were adept at mobilizing their support at general elections this was not the case in by-elections. During the Conservative government of 1959–64 Liberals achieved spectacular by-election successes and at one point National Opinion Polls actually recorded them as the strongest party in the country. This potential strength evaporated in the 1964 and 1966 elections. The Labour governments of 1964–70 experienced unprecedented swings against them, including the loss of seats to Scottish and Welsh Nationalists and to Liberals as well as to the Conservatives; this may be contrasted with the 1945–51 Labour governments which maintained a proud record of not losing any by-elections. Electoral politics was showing important signs of change even if the minor parties were unable to capitalize on the disillusionment in the 1970 general election.

### Territorial politics: the search for spatial efficiency

After the slowdown in regional planning in the 1950s activity rose abruptly with the conversion of the government to national planning incorporating the notion that an efficient economy requires each region to play its part. The Conservative government published White Papers on north-east England and central Scotland in 1963 and the new Labour government continued this trend after 1964 by creating Regional Economic Councils and Planning Boards. Positive discrimination was vastly extended by the designation of large new development areas in 1966, special development areas in 1967 and intermediate areas in 1969, so that well over half the working population were now in these policy regions. All of this activity was directly related to electoral politics, particularly Labour's need to show direct concern for its areas of support, and there is some evidence that this 'vote-buying' was successful. Perhaps more significant was the overall political need to maintain national integration or what McCrone (1969: p. 27) terms the 'cohesion of the state'.

The search for efficiency was much more explicit in the plans for reorganization of administrative areas during this period. Government investigations and evaluations were implemented for Greater London and each of the four Home Counties. In each case the final report was critical of existing local government patterns as being out-of-date and larger units combining town and country were proposed as more efficient; local democracy was sacrificed. Dearlove (1979) has interpreted this new spatial arrangement as a means of ensuring middle-class leadership (either Labour or Conservative) in local government. The new areas were promoted along with new procedures of corporate planning using techniques derived from private corporations. Instead of local government, much discussion now focuses on the 'local state' where the style and practice of management is indistinguishable from 'big business'.

There was a slight hiccup for these technocratic plans with the defeat of the Labour government in 1970. Although the incoming Conservative government accepted the need for reform it used political criteria, especially in England, to plan the final map. The major result was a set of metropolitan counties that are less than metropolitan in geographical range. Functions were also arranged in a nationwide two-tier system so that where Conservatives are more likely to control counties (in non-metropolitan areas) the county is the most important unit of government but where Labour is more likely to control counties (i.e. metropolitan counties) they became largely irrelevant (except for transport) and most power resides with the districts. In the end, after a long debate about efficiency and democracy, the final solutions were very much party political.

## BRITAIN IN DEPRESSION: ANOTHER POLITICS OF CRISIS

'The comfort of the insular centralized state has ... been shattered in the past decade' according to Peele (1978: p. 2). Technocratic politics had produced administrative reforms merely aiming at greater efficiency within the existing framework: they were minor readjustments within the conservative tradition of the UK state. As the world-wide recession hit an already weak Britain the political response was to create new politics around much more basic issues. The electoral system came under fire as the electoral reform movement re-emerged as a political force after a gap of fifty years. The role of the House of Lords was revived as an issue by the left while the need for a 'Bill of Rights' became popular again on the right. This was adversary politics and the issues were constitutional. Britain was no longer the self-adjusting political economy it had seemed only two decades earlier and new means were employed to counter conflict, notably referendums over the EEC and devolution and removal of power from the Stormont Parliament in Northern Ireland. Haseler has even gone as far as to proclaim 'the death of British democracy' and has produced a list of 'milestones in the weakening of the British democratic state' with thirty-five such events identified for the period 1966 to 1975, of which twenty-two occurred in 1974 and 1975 alone!

These new politics have been those of confrontation: in 1972 trade-union pressure precipitated a U-turn in the Conservative government's economic policy and a second confrontation in the winter of 1973–4 led to the defeat of the government in the February 1974 election. This led Burnham to identify this election as 'critical', leading as it did to a partial erosion of the two-party politics that had come to dominate elections since 1931. In Northern Ireland the Protestant hegemony was challenged by continuous violence and in 1974 the Unionist strike ended the power-sharing agreement. Confrontation with the public sector unions in the winter of 1978–9 contributed to the downfall of the Labour government in 1979. This sharpened the adversary nature of the new politics as Britain entered the 1980s with a free-trade monetarist Conservative government opposed by an interventionist and protectionist Labour opposition.

### Geopolitics: the maverick of Europe

From a UK perspective, the European Community has been the major failure of the technocratic solutions proposed in the 1960s. Although accession was not finally approved by Parliament until 1972, the decision to join was by then a decade old. However, the next two governments found it necessary to renegotiate terms in 1975 and 1980. This was required because Britain's geopolitical position was unsuited to the European economic arrangements, which consisted of a compromise between German industry and French agriculture whereby the former expanded its market within a customs union while the latter obtained support through the Common Agricultural Policy. This meant that community revenues were largely from customs duties and expenditures were largely on agriculture. This resulted in Britain making large contributions to the community budget, due to its traditional high volume of world trade, while receiving little in return due to its lack of a large agricultural sector. Thus by the late 1970s Britain, as one of the poorest members of the EEC, was contributing by far the most resources to the central budget. Far from being the solution to Britain's economic problems it was becoming part of the problems.

Part of the argument used in the 'great debate' on joining Europe and in the 1975 referendum confirming membership was that Britain was no longer strong enough to stand alone in the world economy. In the most severe sterling crisis so far – in 1976 – EEC membership provided no safety net, however, and Britain had to apply to the International Monetary Fund for a loan. The terms exacted by the fund negotiators pushed the Labour government into the most severe 'stop' phase yet.

## Electoral geography: fragmentation, and polarization

The 1974 elections saw the emergence of three important minor party groups in Parliament with about a dozen seats each. The Ulster Unionists broke with the Conservative party over government policy in Northern Ireland and formed a new distinctive group. The Liberals won nearly 20 per cent of the total vote, but this was not translated into a large parliamentary representation due to the electoral system. Finally the Scottish and Welsh nationalists for the first time became electoral forces in each of their respective countries, so that in October 1974 the minor parties had thirty-seven MPs between them, by far their largest total since the 1920s. Although the electorate was obviously fragmented in these elections the two major parties still held 598 of the 635 seats in Parliament and they consolidated this position by increasing their number to 608 seats in the 1979 election. Clearly the electoral system kept the British Parliament a largely two-party affair despite some voter defections.

This decline in support for the major two parties became reflected in a diminution of class voting in Britain. Although the February 1974 election was fought on explicit class issues the electorate responded with the lowest level of class voting since the 1920s. The geographical paradox has emerged, however, that, while the class-basis of electoral politics has become diluted, the underlying electoral geography has become more polarized. The Conservatives lost support in inner-city areas, Scotland in general and of course Northern Ireland while Labour lost ground in rural areas (particularly the southern Home Counties, East Anglia and Wales) and outer suburban and resort areas. These are long-term trends that can be traced back to the 1950s but they have cumulated in additional polarization only after 1974. The result was that a decline in marginal seats meant that the electoral system no longer operated automatically to generate majority governments in Parliament. This, more than the rise of minor parties was considered likely to produce parliamentary stalemates and compromises such as the 'Lib–Lab pact' from 1977 to 1978. All of this means that the electoral politics of this crisis era were full of uncertainties.

## Territorial politics: inner cities and devolution

The territorial politics of this crisis era have emerged at two different geographical scales, concerning urban and national problems respectively.

Whereas the depression of the 1930s led to recognition of the regional problem, the current depression has led to recognition of the inner-city problem. This occurred in the wake of the entry of race as an electoral issue in the 1964 election. The economic growth of the 1950s attracted

Commonwealth immigrants from the West Indies and the Indian sub-continent. They became concentrated in the poorest private-sector housing in inner-city areas and one government response was local area-based policy. This was initially education policy (Education Priority Areas) but was subsequently the concern of the Home Office, with its responsibility for immigration and policing, and the Department of the Environment, as the planning and housing ministry. The Home Office led the way in 1968 with its Urban Programme followed by Community Development Projects and the Urban Deprivation Unit set up in 1972. In the meantime the 1969 Housing Act had initiated positive areal discrimination in its General Improvement Area policy and this was extended by the 1974 Act to Housing Action Areas. The Department of Environment commissioned the Inner Area Studies in 1972, followed by the Comprehensive Community Programme and the 1977 White Paper, and then by the partnership schemes with selected local authorities. The conversion of government to small-scale positive areal discrimination was impressive in the variety of responses if not in terms of total resources made available under the schemes.

The motives behind the proliferation of area policies are numerous but two are particularly pertinent. First, they represent a dilution of the welfare state concept of provision for all, moving away from the notion of citizens with welfare rights to problem groups and policies of control and containment. Second, the links with immigration and race should not be ignored since they account for the Home Office's involvement. It is no accident that the Urban Programme was hurriedly put together after Enoch Powell's famous 'rivers of blood' speech in 1968 and subsequent initiatives followed National Front local government electoral successes in 1976. In one sense, therefore, this urban policy was the final strand in the British state's withdrawal from empire.

Devolution policy is also interpretable as an effect of the decline of Britain as an imperial state. With the demise of the British state the advantages of membership of this political unit have lessened to such a degree that an appreciable proportion of both Welsh and Scottish citizens are promoting a new future outside the old imperial state. This was particularly the case for Scotland, where oil wealth highlighted the potential material advantages of separation.

The government reaction to nationalist pressure was, first, to institute a Royal Commission on the Constitution in 1968, which did not report until 1973 and then, after the nationalists' 1974 electoral successes, to offer devolution with a referendum in each country to ensure popular support. In neither case did the 'yes' vote reach the required threshold for acceptance of the proposals and devolution policy was shelved. There was no nationalist backlash in the 1979 election and the Scottish Nationalists lost nine of their eleven seats.

## BRITAIN IN DEPRESSION: ANOTHER POLITICS OF NATIONAL INTEREST

The 1980s have been dominated by the Conservative governments of Margaret Thatcher. In this case the changed agenda has been most explicit. It has even been given a special name by both supporters and opponents alike – 'Thatcherism'. It is a mark of the dominance of the Prime Minister that she has been given her own 'ism'. But we should not simply equate this new politics with Mrs Thatcher's term of office at 10 Downing Street. The politics of crisis continued beyond the 1979 election as the Conservative government's economic policies produced a massive rise in unemployment and the opposition Labour party split over how to combat the new government. In fact the period from 1979 to 1982 can be seen in hindsight as a time when three contrasting views of politics were competing to provide the next new politics to take Britain out of its crisis. On the right the Conservatives were offering a free market solution, on the left Labour were offering more state planning and in a rejuvenated centre a sort of half-way house, a 'social market', was being developed. The centre ground of British politics was boosted by the breakaway of the Social Democrats from Labour and their alliance with the old Liberal party. For a short period in 1981 and early 1982 this new combination achieved spectacular successes in by-elections and was easily leading in the national opinion polls. Mrs Thatcher was recording the lowest ever score in opinion polls for a British Prime Minister. The Social Democrats and Liberals claimed that they were 'breaking the mould of British politics' and it briefly seemed that the new politics would be a centre-based one. But this was not to be. Conservative fortunes began to rise in the opinion polls and then Argentina invaded the Falklands/Malvinas Islands. The whole face of British politics changed overnight. This foreign enemy proved to be a perfect foil for Mrs Thatcher's brand of nationalism. Success in the South Atlantic War – 'Mrs Thatcher's War' as it was sometimes called – consolidated the Conservative government's new found popularity. From 1982 'Thatcherism' has been the new politics of national interest that has despatched the politics of crisis back into history.

Like its counterpart in the USA under President Reagan, this 'national revival' has been built upon a 'feel good' atmosphere after military success. Like all appeals to 'national interest' it has an intolerant tendency summed up in Mrs Thatcher's claim that 'there is no alternative'. This became known as TINA and was the motif of Conservative politics in the mid-1980s. But the centre piece of Thatcherism has always been a transfer of power and resources within British society. That is why it is the defeat of the national miners strike in 1985 even more than the defeat of Argentina that symbolizes this new politics.

It is always difficult to assess a new politics while it still sets the political agenda but it does seem at this time that Thatcherism represents a break in

British politics equivalent to the emergence of the social democratic consensus in the 1940s. The latter rejected the othodox economic policies of the 1930s and replaced them with Keynesian interventionist policies, Thatcherism rejects Keynesian policies and has replaced them with monetarism or a 'return to the thirties'. It seems that 'national interest' in both the 1930s and the 1980s has been interpreted by government as favouring the rich's 'enterprise' at the expense of the poor's 'dependence'.

### Geopolitics: putting the 'Great' back into Britain

According to Tom Nairn (1983) Britain's decline symbolically ended with the victory over Argentina. There has been some debate about the importance of the South Atlantic War for the success of Thatcherism but there is no doubt about its geopolitical significance. This was the first major British military adventure since Suez in 1956. Britain was able to show that it could go it alone and still win wars on the other side of the world. In short Britain was 'Great' again and Margaret Thatcher was the true successor of Winston Churchill.

Britain's success in the South Atlantic must be seen as part of a wider role in the new geopolitics of the 1980s. In the 'Second Cold War', as Halliday (1983) calls it, Mrs Thatcher as the 'Iron Lady' combined with President Reagan in a new phase of anti-Communist rhetoric and hardening of foreign policy attitudes. This produced a rekindling of the US-UK 'special relationship' based in part upon mutual admiration between the two leaders. This enabled Britain to return briefly to the role of trusted deputy to the USA which had been cultivated after the Second World War (Taylor 1989). The mutual benefits of this arrangement were not restricted to confronting the communist foe. The USA secretly aided Britain during the South Atlantic War and Britain responded by allowing US war planes to use bases in Britain to bomb Libya in 1985. And when the 'Second Cold War' began to thaw it was Mrs Thatcher who announced that she 'could do business with' Mr Gorbachev, thus ushering in the new geopolitics of accommodation. Partly because of her time in office and partly because of her US links, Mrs Thatcher became a leading politician on the world stage, and Britain could bask in Mrs Thatcher's global stature.

Fighting wars, either hot or cold, is not the most fundamental feature of a country's geopolitics, however. In the long run the economic relations with the rest of the world are what matter (compare the current status of the defeated countries of 1945, Germany and Japan). In this context the new politics is very clear. In contrast to Labour's flirtation with protectionism, the Conservative government has applied its free market policies to external relations, abolishing restrictions on capital flows and lobbying against moves towards trade protectionism elsewhere, especially in the USA and Japan. Here the new politics of national interest contrasts with its 1930s predecessor which included protectionism within a system of imperial preferences. In contrast in the 1980s the long-term aim is to make Britain an attractive site for international investment. The main beneficiaries of this policy have been in the City of London which has been able to consolidate its role as the second financial centre in the world after New York. The degree to which this 'southern' wealth can 'spread' to other parts of the country is currently the crucial question in British politics. If this cannot be achieved then what is being created is a wealthy 'city state' supporting say 10 million people, leaving nearly 50 million people as an unnecessary appendage and increasingly a burden. This is one of the paradoxes of the politics of national interest.

The contradictory nature of the nationalism within the new geopolitics can be best seen in relation to the rest of the European Community. In this context the Conservative government has been a major supporter of producing a genuinely common market by 1992. On the other hand Mrs Thatcher has been a strident opponent of calls for a 'United States of Europe'. She has sometimes been cast as the 'new de Gaulle' with her insistence on a Europe of distinctive and separate nations. But de Gaulle's European vision was anti-American whereas Mrs Thatcher is most certainly keeping her Atlantic options open. In short she has broken the common twentieth-century link between nationalism and protectionism. This aspect of Thatcherism has a distinctive nineteenth-century national liberal hue to it.

The new politics of the 1980s has brought foreign policy back into competitive party politics. Gone are the bipartisan foreign policies of the recent past. Geopolitics is integral to the new political agenda and the Conservative party has captured the nationalist card in the debate. This has been fundamental for both the establishment of the new politics and Conservative dominance of it.

### Electoral geography: the north:south divide

The Conservative party has won three elections in succession in 1979, 1983 and 1987. This electoral dominance has been associated with a spatial polarization of party voters that has come to be commonly known as the 'north:south divide'. As such, electoral geography has become part of the political debate in Britain as the Conservatives are accused of producing 'two nations'. These two nations are shown in figure 12.1. Although this regional bias in voting returns can be traced back to earlier periods (see Curtice and Steed, 1982), the three latest elections have been marked by particularly high levels of regional differentiation. Johnston *et al.* (1988) have investigated this new geography in great detail and conclude that 'the years 1979–87 have been characterized by substantial shifts in the country's electoral geography' (p. 40). Hence the paradox that the new politics of national interest is based upon a non-national electoral geography.

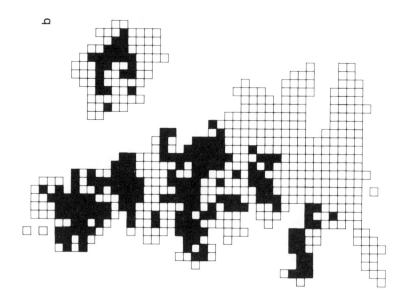

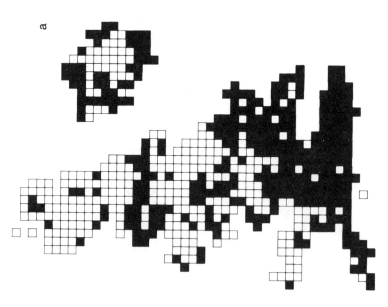

*Figure 12.1* The north:south divide
(a) Seats won by the Conservatives, 1979, 1983, and 1987
(b) Seats won by Labour, 1979, 1983 and 1987

To some extent this new electoral geography is similar to that of the 1930s when Labour was pushed back into its heartlands. There are two differences however. First, Labour has developed broader regional appeals over time so that its support has held up in larger areas and, second, some of the regional patterns are much more subtle than that produced by support for the National Government in 1931 and 1935. For instance the 1980s have produced a situation where there were different electoral contests in different parts of the country. In the north of England Labour dominated but with the Conservatives firmly in second place. In the south of England the Conservatives dominated with Labour and the centre parties competing for a poor second place. In Scotland Labour dominated and, after the collapse of the Conservatives in 1987, there were three competitors for the weak second place – Conservatives, the centre parties, and the Scottish Nationalists. Within these broad regions there were further differences. The most obvious was the rural-urban contrast with the Conservatives doing particularly well in English rural areas, even in the north, and Labour retaining some support in most southern urban areas. There were also particular regional effects such as the overwhelmingly strong support for Labour on Merseyside and the surprisingly strong showing of the Conservatives in Lancashire.

In Johnston *et al.'s* (1988) investigation of the reasons for the new spatial polarization they extend their analysis beyond class explanations of voting to incorporate the question of localities and their social contexts. They are able to show that party voting by different social classes varies immensely across the country in such a way as to accentuate a party's 'natural' strength. For instance administrators and managers are far more likely to vote Labour in the industrial areas of Scotland, Wales and northern England than elsewhere, thus accentuating Labour's dominance of those areas (Johnston *et al.* 1988: 137). Hence the resulting spatial polarization reflects more than simple class segregation of the voters. Johnston *et al.* argue for two processes behind this electoral geography. First, different localities have developed particular political cultures over time which tend to favour one party over others. Second, different parts of the country are affected differently by government policies and this is reflected in attitudes and voting. In short the 'south' rewarded Mrs Thatcher for policies that suited its economic and social structure. The two nations are much more than merely electoral artifacts.

The short-term effect of the spatial polarization was beneficial for Labour, enabling the party to win more seats than it would otherwise have done. But the long-term effects are far more serious. Part of the strength of 'Thatcherism' is in the electoral geography of the new politics. Support for the Conservative party is highest in the most populous and fastest growing regions of the country. Hence the question 'can Labour win?' does not just refer to it winning more votes, it is where the additional votes are likely to come from that matters: piling up larger Labour majorities outside the south will not remove the Conservative government. This is the reason why electoral geography is now so important in contemporary British politics.

### Territorial politics: blitzing the opposition

Political geography has appeared at the heart of the political debate in Britain in another guise – centre–local conflicts. The 1980s witnessed a revolution in centre–local relations seemingly not as an overall strategy but as a response to political challenges in local government. With the Labour party marginalized nationally but strong regionally, local government provided an opportunity to stem Conservative dominance of the political agenda. Conflict was inevitable from the time the Conservative central government obtained a mandate to cut public expenditure while Labour local councils claimed a mandate to protect and even expand local services. In Liverpool, for instance, there was growth in council house building; in Sheffield and London they developed local economic initiatives. But the way in which the British state operates has made it relatively easy for the Conservative government to defeat all these local challenges. With a parliamentary majority the government has been able to pass a huge amount of legislation that has totally changed the balance between central and local government in Britain to the advantage of the former. There is not room here to list all of these changes but we can enumerate the main strategies that have been used.

The simplest strategy is to centralize a service, that is take decisions out of local hands and transfer them to Whitehall. In education, for instance, a 'national curriculum' is being imposed on all state schools, thereby lessening local input and variety. A second strategy is to transfer functions from elected to appointed bodies. Non-elected urban development corporations have taken over land-use planning functions in several cities, for instance. Alternatively functions can be transferred completely away from the public sector. Such privatization has been completed for public bus transport. In public housing a mixture of these two strategies is being developed with estates being handed over to either non-elected housing associations or private landlords. Another strategy is to by-pass local government and appeal direct to residents who form minorities within their local authority area. In this way 'Conservative parents' will be able to vote for their school to opt out of Labour majority education authorities. Strategies for controlling local government budgets have been important involving numerous constraints and penalties as well as forcing limits on total expenditure in many cases. Finally the ultimate central state sanction against opponents in local government is abolition: all seven metropolitan counties in England, including the Greater London Council, were removed from the administrative map.

Clearly the central Conservative government has been quite ruthless in its dealings with local government, so much so that it has encountered opposition from local Conservative councillors as well as from Labour. But this revolution in centralization has been carried out with little or no delay through Parliament. It represents the practical implementation of TINA – there is no alternative.

Finally we must mention the territorial politics at the scale of the constituent countries of the United Kingdom. As we have seen the Conservative party is electorally very weak in Scotland and Wales. To some degree Scotland has been used as a laboratory for carrying out local government policies ahead of England and Wales. This has been the case with the introduction of a poll tax for instance. But the most interesting policies have been in Northern Ireland where central control of the province continues in a situation where there are no British political parties. The signing of the Anglo–Irish agreement in 1985 is remarkable in that it gives a foreign state – Ireland – a say in the running of part of the United Kingdom. This has alienated the majority Unionist community without producing any appreciable gains in terms of law and order or economic regeneration. Politically Ulster continues to be a separate 'political world' with no resolution to the conflict in sight.

## CONCLUSION: PARALLELS ACROSS TIME

What general themes traverse these six political geography cameos? Four important topics have been selected for emphasis in these concluding remarks, each of which has survived through six rounds of 'new politics'.

First, one of the most remarkable features of the period is the lack of coincidence between the emergence of a new politics and the change of governments at general elections. Although Attlee's and Wilson's first Labour governments personify social democratic and technocratic politics respectively, the origins of both were laid before these Labour governments and both survived their defeat. Similarly we have argued that the new politics associated with 'Thatcherism' was established in 1982 not 1979.

Second, this chapter has identified six 'new politics' but only one major electoral geography. This stability of party support patterns illustrates the mobilizing abilities of the two major parties, both of which emphasize the importance of general elections and hence state policies. Coupled with grass-roots stability this has tended to generate moribund local politics, with a resultant continuous growth of the state under both parties. In terms of territorial politics this has been reflected in initiatives and reforms 'from above' while little enthusiasm for change is generated from below. There has been a major trend towards centralization of government, culminating in the 1980s' Conservative government's reduction of local government autonomy to a mere political shadow. Local government is now much more like mere local administration for the central state than it has ever been.

Third, the massive difference between the politics of the two depressions resulting from this vast increase in state activity may be noted. In the 1920s and 1930s the population expected little and got little from its government. The social democratic consensus and technocratic politics have raised expectations so that the politics of the current depression are different from its predecessor. By using the same terminology for the politics of the two stagnation eras we have emphasized the similarities. That is the purpose of the method of historical analogy that has been used in this chapter. Hence it is as well to add this caveat in our conclusion. When Mrs Thatcher claims that the National Health Service is safe in her hands she is campaigning in a very different context than that of the earlier politics of national interest. Since the 1930s the 'nation's health' has been incorporated into the notion of national interest and the new politics has not been able to remove it.

Finally we can return to our premises at the beginning of the chapter concerning state politics as a dependent variable in the world economy. The new politics in Britain illustrate this process well. One of the reasons that Mrs Thatcher has such a high international reputation is that her domestic policies have been imitated in many other states. It does not seem to matter whether the state has a conservative or socialist government. Hence 'socialist' governments in France, Spain, New Zealand and Australia have aopted 'Thatcherite' economic policies. Clearly TINA operates at the world scale! What we have here is a series of governments across the world responding to similar world-economy pressures in the same manner. In an earlier period of growth, welfare states were developed in parallel across the same set of relatively rich countries. This is a good justification for my initial premise that you cannot study any state, Britain included, without understanding the world-economy context of its politics.

## REFERENCES

Beveridge Report (1942) *Social Insurance and Allied Services*, Cmnd 4606, London: HMSO.

Broadbent, T. A. (1977) *Planning and Profit in the Urban Economy*, London: Methuen.

Burnham, W. D. (1979) 'Great Britain: the death of the collectivist consensus', in Maisel, L. and Cooper, J. (eds.) *Political Parties: Development and Decay*, Beverley Hills: Sage.

Curtice, J. and Steed, M. (1982) 'Electoral choice and production of government', *British Journal of Political Science*, 12: 249–98.

Dearlove, J. (1979) *The Reorganization of British Local Government*, Cambridge: Cambridge University Press.

Halliday, F. (1983) *The Making of the Second Cold War*, London: Verso.

Haseler, S. (1976) *The Death of British Democracy*, London: Elek.

Johnston, R. J., Pattie, C. J., and Allsopp, J. G. (1988) *A Nation Dividing?*, London: Longman.

Kitzinger, U. (1973) 'Time lags in political philosophy', in Barber, J. and Reed, B. (eds.) *European Community: Vision and Reality*, London: Croom Helm.

McCrone, G. (1969) *Regional Policy in Britain*, London: Allen & Unwin.

MacIntyre,A. (1968) 'The strange death of social democratic England', *The Listener* 4 July.

Miliband, R. (1962) *Parliamentary Socialism*, London: Merlin.

Nairn, T. (1977) *The Break-up of Britain*, London: New Left Books.

Nairn, T. (1979) 'The future of Britain's crisis', *New Left Review*, 113: 43–69.

Nairn, T. (1983) 'Britain's living legacy', in Hall, S. and Jacques, M. (eds.) *The Politics of Thatcherism*, London: Lawrence & Wishart.

Peele, G. (1978) 'The developing constitution', in Cook, C. and Ramsden, J. (eds.) *Trends in British Politics since 1945*, London: Macmillan.

Taylor, P. J. (1989) 'Britain's changing role in the world-economy', in Mohan, J. (ed.) *The Political Geography of Contemporary Britain*, London: Macmillan.

## FURTHER READING

The literature on which this chapter draws is very large, and only a small proportion can be referred to here.

Important recent work includes:

Mohan, J. (ed.) (1989) *The Political Geography of Contemporary Britain*, London: Macmillan.

Johnston, R. J. *et al.* (1988) cited above.

Madgwick, P. and Rose, R. (eds.) (1982) *The Territorial Dimension in United Kingdom Politics*, London: Macmillan.

Rose, R. (1982) *Understanding the United Kingdom: The Territorial Dimension in Government*, London: Longman.

Boddy, M. and Fudge, C. (eds.) (1984) *Local Socialism? Labour Councils & New Left Alternative*, London: Macmillan.

Hall, S. and Jaques, M. (eds.) (1983) *The Politics of Thatcherism* London: Lawrence & Wishart.

For British politics in general, see Rose, R. (ed.) (1976) *Studies in British Politics: A Reader in Political Sociology* (3rd edn), London: Macmillan, and (1980) *Do Parties Make a Difference*? London: Macmillan. On the particular periods, see Peele, G. and Cook, C. (eds.) (1973) *The Politics of Reappraisal 1918–1939*, London: Macmillan; Cook, C. and Ramsden, J. (eds.) (1978) *Trends in British Politics since 1945*, London: Macmillan; and McKie, D. and Cook, C. (eds.) (1972) *The Decade of Disillusion: British Politics in the Sixties*, London: Macmillan. For a larger perspective, see Beer, S. H. (1965) *British Politics in the Collectivist Age*, New York: Knopf; see also Runciman, W. G. (1966) *Relative Deprivation and Social Justice*, London: Routledge & Kegan Paul. On the recent situation, see the items by Haseler and Nairn referred to above, plus Finer, S. E. (ed.) (1975) *Adversary Politics and Electoral Reform*, London: Anthony Wigram; and Kavanagh, D. (ed.) (1982) *The Politics of the Labour Party*, London: Allen & Unwin.

The framework for the geopolitics sections was derived from Wallerstein, I. (1979) *The Capitalist World Economy*, Cambridge: Cambridge University Press, and the British material was based on Blank, S. (1977) 'Britain: the politics of foreign economic policy, the domestic economy, and the problem of pluralist stagnation', *International Organization*, 31: 673–722 and Jessop, B. (1980) 'The transformation of the state in post-war Britain', in Scase, R. (ed.), *The State in Western Europe*, London: Croom Helm. See also Frank, A. G. (1980) *Crisis: In the World Economy*, London: Heinemann.

There is a plethora of studies of British elections and electoral geography, of which the major contributions are the Nuffield volumes (all involving Butler, D. E.) covering each general election since 1945: all are published by Macmillan (London), and are entitled *The British General Election of . . .*; recent volumes contain substantial statistical appendices and analyses. An atlas is provided in Kinnear, M. (1981) *The British Voter*, London: Batsford, and the standard texts are Butler, D. E. and Stokes, D. (1974) *Political Change in Britain* (2nd edn), London: Macmillan, and Miller, W. L. (1977) *Electoral Dynamics*, London: Macmillan. On the geography, see Taylor, P. J. and Johnston, R. J. (1979) *Geography of Elections*, London: Penguin and Gudgin, G. and Taylor, P. J. (1979) *Seats, Votes and the Spatial Organization of Elections*, London: Pion.

For territorial politics, the main texts on urban politics are Broadbent (referred to above) and Mackay, D. H. and Cox, A. W. (1979) *The Politics of Urban Change*. London: Croom Helm. On the local state, early problems are discussed in Branson, N. (1979) *Popularism, 1919–1925*, London: Lawrence & Wishart and MacIntyre, S. (1980) *Little Moscows*, London: Croom Helm; recent analyses include Bennington, J. (1976) *Local Government becomes Big Business*, London: Community Development Project and Cockburn, C. (1977) *The Local State*, London: Pluto Press.

# 13 Living in the United Kingdom

*Paul L. Knox*

Over the past fifty years the quality of life in the United Kingdom has improved dramatically. It is no longer necessary for social scientists to include the incidence of 'badly flea-bitten' children or malnourished adults as key social indicators; the infant mortality rate has been reduced to one-quarter of the 1930s level; and the ownership and consumption of everything from cars to cameras has changed from the status of luxury to that of commonplace. Underlying these changes, of course, are changes in national and international economic organization, changes in social structure, and improvements and innovations in science and technology. As previous chapters have suggested, however, these fundamental changes have been uneven in their effects on different parts of the country, with some areas benefiting more than or before others, and others experiencing a disproportionate share of the negative aspects of change. This chapter examines the cumulative and differential impact of economic and social change on the quality of life in different parts of the United Kingdom.

## THE 1930s: CASUALTIES OF PEACE

Many of the features which dominated the geography of social well-being in the 1930s can clearly be seen in present-day patterns of welfare. One legacy of the period unmistakably stamped on the political, social and physical landscape of the country is the economic depression of the old industrial heartlands of northern England, central Scotland and South Wales, where the pillars of past prosperity – coal, iron and steel, shipping and textiles – collapsed during the 'Long Weekend' between 1930 and 1935. There was, however, another face to the 1930s which is equally relevant to the condition of the United Kingdom in the 1990s. The inter-war years were also a time when a new industrial structure was being established, so that the pictures of the dole queues and the soup kitchens must be placed beside pictures of new factories and prosperous suburbs. The image of the 1930s depends very much on whether attention is focused on Jarrow or on Slough, on Merthyr Tydfil or on Oxford, on Clydebank and St. Helens or on Northampton, Bournemouth and the Home Counties.

These contrasts are reflected in the unequal distribution of the unemployed – the 'casualties of peace'. Even at the depth of the depression,
in the winter of 1932–3, the steep gradient between the regions persisted.
Moreover, there were local variations of massive proportions. In parts of
South Wales, for example, up to 80 per cent of the insured population was
unemployed. In north-east England the figure approached 70 per cent in
towns such as Jarrow; and in Scotland it approached 40 per cent in
Greenock, Motherwell and Clydebank. Meanwhile, unemployment never
rose much above 5 per cent in places such as Guildford, St. Albans and
Romford. Furthermore, recovery, when it came, affected the depressed
areas only slowly. Economic revival was concentrated in the south and the
midlands, where the patterns of employment traditionally associated with
'affluence' were forged (see chapters 8 and 9). This new prosperity also
brought the first wave of electrical domestic appliances for mass consumption, the widespread introduction of hire-purchase, and the proliferation of
shops selling cheap, mass-produced clothes and furniture. The availability
of cheap manufactured products also affected patterns of consumption in
the depressed regions and deprived neighbourhoods, producing the bizarre
situation noted by George Orwell:

> Twenty million people are underfed but literally everyone . . . has access
> to a radio. What we have lost in food we have gained in electricity.
> Whole sections of the working class are being compensated, in part, by
> cheap luxuries which mitigate the surface of life . . . It is quite likely that
> fish-and-chips, art-silk stockings, tinned salmon, cut price chocolate . . .
> the movies, the radio, strong tea and the football pools have between
> them averted revolution.
>
> (Orwell 1962: 80–1)

Meanwhile, the prosperity of the south was reflected in more tangible
ways. Fuelled by migration, the growth of the south-east and the midlands
was directly expressed in the spread of houses and factories in ribbon
developments along new arterial roads. Suburban High Streets were also
transformed as the 'retailing revolution' brought multiple chain stores; and
changing patterns of leisure and recreation brought new cinemas, dance
halls and cafes as well as new public houses with 'lounge' bars.

The contrasts between regions, neighbourhoods and classes in the 1930s
were documented in graphic detail in a welter of 'travelogue' literature
which had its academic parallel in a series of major social investigations.
Typical of the former were Priestley's *English Journey*, Orwell's *The Road
to Wigan Pier* and Greenwood's *Love on the Dole*, whilst the two most
famous and comprehensive statistical accounts of the period were the
Report of the Pilgrim Trust, *Men Without Work*, and the Carnegie
Foundation's study of South Wales, called *Disinherited Youth*. Together,
these publications lay bare the intensity of spatial inequality in every
sphere of life. Brief examples from the key life domains of health, housing

and education serve to illustrate the gap between rich and poor, which was usually expressed in the form of basic north:south contrasts: rates of infant and maternal mortality in the poorer parts of London, the industrial north, South Wales, central Scotland and Northern Ireland were roughly twice as high as in the more prosperous parts of the midlands and the south-east, and mortality from infectious diseases such as tuberculosis exhibited even sharper spatial contrasts. The system of medical care offered only a patchwork of provision, often serving to amplify differences between regions and classes. Despite the housing boom, the introduction of a slum clearance programme and the widespread introduction of local authority housing, there remained over half a million dwellings in use in the major industrial cities which had been condemned as unfit for human habitation. Manchester alone had 30,000 'back-to-back' terrace houses, many of them damp, overcrowded, infested with vermin and with only one outside toilet for every three or four families. Rural conditions were little better in many places, with dark, low dwellings having no electricity or water supply and only an earth closet. Meanwhile, towards the other end of the housing spectrum, increasing numbers of white-collar workers were enjoying the benefits of the mass-produced 'Mon Repos' typical of the affluent new suburbs of middle England. Education, like health care, was rationed by price and the whole system was weighted in a variety of ways against children from poor families. Not least among these was the 'facilitative environment' available to children in deprived neighbourhoods. In 1932 an official 'black-list' of unfit schools contained over 1,500 entries, most of which were grim Victorian fortresses located in the inner areas of industrial cities: they were ill-lit and badly ventilated, with primitive sanitary facilities and vast cold rooms shared by several classes at once.

## PATTERNS OF SOCIAL WELL-BEING IN THE WELFARE STATE

The most important single factor in shaping patterns of social well-being in the post-war period has almost certainly been the so-called 'settlement of 1945' – the creation of a welfare system under which the government undertook to guarantee for all citizens, as of right, a minimum level of living. Following the influential recommendations of the Beveridge Report (1942), this involved: (i) the protection of people against the worst distributional consequences of the market economy and the hardship associated with old age, sickness, and unemployment; (ii) an undertaking to ensure 'equality of access' to 'essential' goods, irrespective of geographical location or ability to pay; and (iii) a higher level of state intervention in economic life in order to ensure full employment and economic growth. As shown in chapter 12, these objectives led inevitably to a fourth dimension: the introduction of regional policy and spatial planning machinery in order to help manage the economy and work towards the equalization of spatial variations in welfare and opportunity.

Within ten years of the creation of the welfare state, the general public, along with politicians and social commentators, came to believe that the problems of poverty and deprivation had been more or less overcome, save for a few residual groups of people who were somehow failing to share in the 'affluent society'. By the late 1950s, under a Conservative government, some of the more radical elements of public control envisaged in the immediate post-war period were removed from the statute book, while planning became firmly established as a conservative force, channelling much of its enthusiasm into containing urban growth and creating harmonious, 'balanced' communities. The 'rediscovery' of poverty in the 1960s, however, prompted a second phase of welfare-oriented reform which brought, among other things, a more active regional policy involving a 600–700 per cent increase in the budgetary cost of aid to assisted areas, a general tightening of control over the location of offices and industry, and an extension of regional and subregional planning machinery.

For the most part, these reforms were directed towards ameliorating the effects of the trends which had begun in the pre-war period: the decline of 'traditional' industries (Lancashire, for example, lost over 500,000 jobs in the textile industry between 1945 and 1975) and the increasing congestion associated with the expansion of the south-east. Meanwhile, new trends were emerging with important implications for patterns of social well-being. Among these was the general decrease in birth and death rates which led to an ageing population and, consequently, a larger dependent population requiring higher levels of expenditure on specialized welfare services of all kinds. Moreover, because of the increasing stream of retirement migration to 'places of reward and repose' – principally the seaside resorts of the south and the villages and towns of south-west England and East Anglia – and the age-selective migration from the peripheral regions to London and the south (chapter 3), the spatial dimension of these changes became increasingly prominent. Another trend with important implications for spatial patterns of social well-being was the rationalization of services – both public and private – in response to economies of scale. The diminishing economic viability of small schools, shops and post offices, together with the increasing cost of providing health and welfare services in areas of dispersed settlement, caused serious problems in the marginal upland areas of northern England and the 'Celtic fringe' in particular, where depopulation has hastened the closure of many facilities.

What was the net effect of these changes on relative patterns of social well-being? With annual expenditure on all of the major social services in the 1970s running, in real terms, at between twice and four times the 1950 level, and with a complex and wide-ranging battery of regional policy instruments, the operation of the welfare state could reasonably be expected to have had a substantial impact on social and spatial inequality. Studies based on key social indicators such as infant mortality rates, unemployment and housing conditions have shown that the *overall* trend through the 1950s and 1960s was for the preservation of the *status quo*. Nevertheless, the position of one in every four localities had altered significantly. Particularly striking was the deterioration of the towns and cities of Lancashire and Yorkshire – especially in the textile areas – and in both the rural and urban areas of Northern Ireland. It is also worth noting that most of these areas had been eligible for regional aid from the very beginning of the welfare state, suggesting that, in these areas at least, the aid had been either insufficient or of the wrong kind, or both. On the other hand, many of the areas which made the greatest relative progress – most of them counties from the rural periphery of the United Kingdom – were also areas which had been the target of regional policy initiatives. The relationships between social policy, social process and patterns of well-being are clearly complex, and they are certainly insufficiently understood.

## RECENT TRENDS

By the 1970s, a new geographical stereotype was emerging: the decaying, impoverished inner city versus the increasing affluence of the suburbs and commuter villages. Industrial dispersion and urban decentralization were the cause of this polarization of well-being at the urban scale, and by the early 1970s the consequences had become very visible. The increasing affluence of suburbia was signposted by a proliferation of travel agents, wine bars, bathware showrooms, art galleries and delicatessens. These are not traditional suburban High Street enterprises: they are central city services gone suburban in response to decentralization. Meanwhile, as prosperity ebbed from inner-city areas, it left a tidemark of derelict land, obsolete factories and warehouses, and declining neighbourhoods. Increasingly, as urban renewal and New Town policy filtered off the young, the skilled and the vigorous, these inner-city areas became receptacles for the unskilled, the low-paid, the aged and the socially incompetent. As such problems became the subject of growing concern, the 'regional problem' was displaced as the most pressing manifestation of spatial inequality in the United Kingdom. According to a report by the Department of the Environment in 1977, almost 4 million people were living in conditions of extreme poverty and deprivation in the declining inner areas of the country's major cities; an analysis of over 87,000 enumeration districts in urban Britain, carried out by Home Office researchers, demonstrated very clearly how this 'multiple deprivation' also had a very marked spatial dimension, with inner London and urban Scotland, central Clydeside in particular, having a massively disproportionate share of deprivation.

Meanwhile, the regional problem has not gone away – even if it has changed somewhat in character. The development of a European economy has accentuated the peripherality of the peripheral regions, weakening the competitiveness of the industrial core areas in both domestic and export markets and so, eventually, eroding the quality of local life. On the other hand, the period since 1970 has seen a marked urban/rural shift in the relative distribution of manufacturing employment in response to increasing diseconomies in large industrial centres and the availability of untapped reserves of relatively cheap, less-unionized, female labour in areas such as mid-Wales, the Scottish Highlands and Islands and rural Northumberland. This, in turn, has begun to polarize the pattern of social well-being within these peripheral areas. Because the new employment opportunities tend to be concentrated in the more accessible centres, the remoter rural areas have become increasingly marginalized, leaving an ageing, indigent and dependent population to face the effects of the withdrawal of local services and the run-down of local infrastructure. It is also important to note that in this decentralization and restructuring of employment it is mainly the lower-paid and more vulnerable jobs provided by branch factories which the peripheral areas have gained: the locus of higher-paid managerial and R & D jobs, meanwhile, has moved only a short distance from central London to the Thames Valley area.

Perhaps the most important issue of the past ten years, however, has been the reformulation and retrenchment of the welfare state. Just as the deepening economic recession of the late 1970s accentuated the vulnerability of more and more people while making it increasingly difficult, in economic terms, to finance existing social welfare programmes, the Conservative party won the 1979 general election on a platform that was clearly anti welfare. The welfare state, it was asserted, had not only generated unreasonably high levels of taxation, budget deficits, disincentives to work and save, and a bloated class of unproductive workers, but had also fostered 'soft' attitudes towards 'problem' groups in society. During the next decade, the Conservative government embarked on an extensive programme of privatization in housing, health, and education, accompanied by cuts (some absolute, some relative) in higher education, in social welfare programmes for the unemployed, the disabled, the elderly, and for strikers' families, and in the regional policy budget. By the mid-1980s many recipients of Supplementary Benefits (the chief form of income support) could not afford some of the necessities of life (Mack and Lansley 1985). Among pensioners, for example, it was found that one-third could not afford a warm, waterproof coat and that one-quarter could afford only secondhand clothes. Among families, 23 per cent lived in damp houses, 25 per cent could not afford adequate heating, 28 per cent could not afford a warm waterproof coat, and 41 per cent had only one pair of all-weather shoes. Meanwhile, closer controls by the central government on local authority expenditure have precipitated corresponding cuts at the local level, particularly in economically depressed towns and cities where the incidence of need for welfare services is high but local fiscal resources are low.

**Location and real income**

Although it must be acknowledged that the changing spatial pattern of social well-being is very much a reflection of fundamental shifts in economic organization and the spatial division of labour, it has been clearly established that distance and *de jure* spatial organization exert a significant influence on such patterns. Thus, for example, while spatial variations in per capita incomes derive largely from variations in local occupational structure, they are also influenced by supply/demand relationships in local labour markets. Within the United Kingdom in 1987, average gross weekly

*Table 13.1* Average gross weekly earnings (full-time) by region, 1987 (£)

| Region | Males on adult rates, all industries | Females on adult rates, all industries | Males in manufacturing industries | Females in manufacturing industries |
|---|---|---|---|---|
| North | 206.0 | 137.0 | 214.6 | 129.7 |
| Yorkshire and Humberside | 206.8 | 135.5 | 209.1 | 119.9 |
| East Midlands | 204.2 | 132.1 | 207.8 | 119.4 |
| East Anglia | 208.9 | 137.2 | 216.8 | 129.0 |
| South-east | 254.1 | 167.6 | 249.6 | 154.9 |
| South-west | 209.3 | 137.6 | 215.4 | 130.2 |
| West Midlands | 206.7 | 136.4 | 207.3 | 124.9 |
| North-west | 212.5 | 138.0 | 214.8 | 127.1 |
| Wales | 204.3 | 137.5 | 214.8 | 127.9 |
| Scotland | 214.6 | 129.9 | 216.0 | 125.5 |
| Northern Ireland | 199.4 | 137.3 | 187.8 | 112.8 |

*Source*: *Regional Trends* 23, HMSO 1988: 40–1 and 117

*Table 13.2* Regional variations in average housing costs, (£)

| Region | Average weekly household expenditure on housing | Average cost of dwellings |
|---|---|---|
| North | 21.7 | 24,300 |
| Yorkshire and Humberside | 23.3 | 25,600 |
| East Midlands | 25.0 | 28,500 |
| East Anglia | 39.3 | 36,100 |
| South-east | 37.3 | 50,400 |
| South-west | 29.9 | 38,500 |
| West Midlands | 26.1 | 38,400 |
| North-west | 25.6 | 27,500 |
| Wales | 21.6 | 27,400 |
| Scotland | 20.4 | 38,200 |
| Northern Ireland | 21.2 | 25,700 |

*Source*: *Regional Trends* 23, HMSO 1988: 63 and 119

earnings varied by 20 per cent or more between major regions, not only for the overall male and female workforce but also for a particular industrial grouping such as manufacturing (table 13.1).

These variations must of course be seen in relation to the cost of living. Here again the existence of separate local markets leads to significant spatial variations which in many cases compound rather than compensate for differences in earnings. In the Highlands and Islands of Scotland (a low-wage area, despite the relatively high wage level for Scotland as a whole), for example, local monopoly conditions mean that the price of basic foodstuffs has been pushed to more than 20 per cent above the average for Aberdeen – itself a fairly expensive city by national standards. Housing costs are also a major contribution to spatial variations in the cost of living. As table 13.2 shows, average expenditure on housing varies by more than 80 per cent, falling steadily with distance from the South-east (over £37.00 per household per week) to Northern Ireland (£20.40). The cost of home ownership exhibits a similar (though less steep) gradient from south to north, while the gradient of price inflation exhibits an even steeper north:south gradient. Between 1981 and 1986, house prices in Greater London rose by 128 per cent, compared with an average for the United Kingdom of 94 per cent and a rise of only 57 per cent in the North-west.

Another key determinant of real incomes in a specific region, city or neighbourhood is the range of facilities which are available. Accessibility to various cultural, entertainment and sports facilities and to specialized shops and services is, for many people, a crucial factor in facilitating their preferred lifestyle. Here, of course, it is the larger metropolitan centres which offer the greatest range of opportunities. 'In the sticks', as all big-city dwellers are comforted to know, it is difficult, if not impossible, to reach first-class sports events, to attend theatres and concerts, and to find bookshops and clothes and furniture stores with more than a narrow and conservative stock. At a different spatial scale, some city neighbourhoods enjoy a wide variety of amenities while others in the same city are starved of opportunities, finding themselves, rather, as repositories for many of the noxious and unwanted features of city life: sewage works, noisy factories, and rubbish dumps. Even more important to the pattern of real incomes, however, are variations in accessibility of salutary facilities, such as hospitals and schools. Many studies of regional variations in health care provision in the United Kingdom, for example, have lent support to the idea of an 'inverse care law', whereby the availability of adequate medical care tends to vary inversely with the need of the population served. At the intra-urban scale this tends to be distorted by the inertia of facility location in relation to population changes, so that inner-city districts tend to be well served by primary medical care while outlying housing estates – both public and private – are poorly served. Such differences have implications well beyond the mere cost or inconvenience of travel, for it has been shown that the deterrent effect of distance actually affects people's willingness to seek medical care, thus leading, over a period of time, to a divergence in levels of community health.

## WHO GETS WHAT, WHERE?

This last example emphasizes the extent to which the life chances of individual citizens can be affected by the way in which public spending decisions impact on space. The expenditure patterns of local authorities are particularly important in this context. With total expenditure having more than trebled, in real terms, since 1930, and with an increasingly wide range of discretionary powers over locational issues in the crucial fields of housing, health care, education, social services, transport and environmental quality, the 'performance' of local government is a key factor in shaping and maintaining the quality of local life. In overall terms, some authorities are 'spenders' and some are 'stinters' in relation to the financial resources at their disposal. In the financial year 1980–1, for example, Dumfries, Tayside and Fife stood out as 'rich stinters', and Shetland and Orkney as 'rich spenders'; Greater Manchester, South Yorkshire, West- and Mid-Glamorgan, Tyne and Wear, Powys and the Western Isles stood out as 'impoverished spenders', with significantly high total per capita expenditures in relation to their resource potential (measured as the total rateable value per 1,000 population).

Local authorities also vary in their *pattern* of expenditure on different public services. Scottish local authorities, for example, have traditionally spent a high proportion of their budget on providing public housing, while the spending pattern of Welsh authorities tends to reflect the high priority given to education there. These emphases in spending are influenced by a wide variety of factors, including the political complexion of the local council, the size of the authority and its function in the national urban system as well as the nature and intensity of local needs for different services. Research on local authority performance in the United Kingdom suggests that there are two distinctive types of community. In the first a declining industrial base is associated with poor housing and environmental conditions, a youthful, working-class population, and Labour party control. Within their total budget they spend lower than average amounts on roads, police and parks, but higher than average amounts on health, housing, mothers and young children, and primary and special education. Their expenditure on fire services and secondary education is average or above, while that on planning tends to be below the average. In general, therefore, they spend more on socially ameliorative and redistributive services but less on 'caretaker' services. At the other end of the scale are the relatively affluent residential/commercial communities with age-ing, middle-class populations which consistently return Conservative-controlled councils. Their pattern of spending is reversed, in that they spend more than average on public goods such as roads, and less than

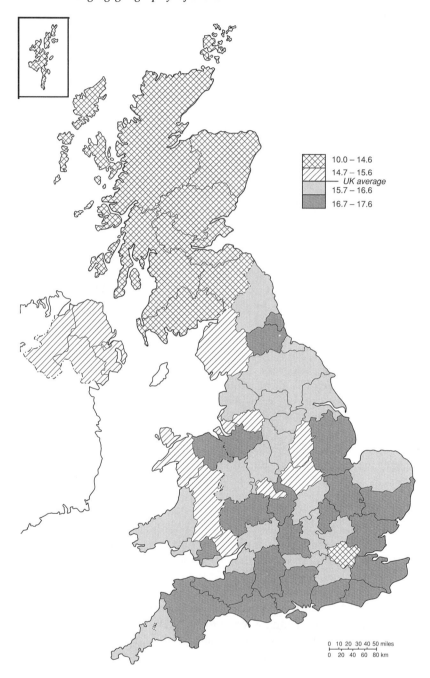

*Figure 13.1* Ratio of pupils to teachers in secondary schools 1987

average on divisible goods such as housing, health services, personal social services and education. Moreover, it is these authorities which have been most enthusiastic in cutting back on welfare-oriented expenditure under the general contraction of the welfare state which has taken place in the past decade. In short, both the size and the composition of the 'social wage' depends very much on where one lives.

The central government has had a responsibility to assist local authorities with particularly high spending needs or low resource bases, through the Rate Support Grant (RSG). For much of the post-war period, however, the operation of the RSG has tended to favour the shires at the expense of metropolitan authorities and the inner London boroughs. For a brief period (with a Labour government) between 1974–5 and 1980–1, metropolitan authorities were treated better than the shires by the RSG. More recently, however, the RSG has been used by the government as a device with which to sanction 'profligate' local authorities, with the result that the advantage has shifted back to the shires.

Local levels of living are also influenced a good deal by variations in the *quality* of service provided, and this is something which can vary within as well as between local authority areas. Educational services provide a good example. At the subregional level there were differences of up to 50 per cent in the pupil/teacher ratio in secondary schools in 1986: this ratio is a variable which is held by educationalists to be an important factor in determining the quality of the teaching environment. With this particular example, there is a broad spatial coherence, with Scottish local authorities, together with the Belfast area, emerging in the most favourable category (figure 13.1). Several of the conurbations also exhibit better-than-average levels of provision, whilst the worst-off areas are concentrated in eastern and central south-western England. Within individual local authorities, differences can be even greater, with some schools providing better teaching environments than others, not just in terms of pupil/teacher ratios but also in terms of the range and quality of teaching skills and the quality of buildings and equipment. Moreover, these differences are often accentuated by the spatial organization of catchment areas, which results in a very different social mix from one school to another. The net outcome is that some schools are much more academically successful than others.

## TWO NATIONS?

In recent years, both the Royal Commission on the Distribution of Income and Wealth and Townsend's comprehensive social survey have demonstrated that poverty and inequality are not merely the unfortunate residue of a harsh but vanishing past but, rather, a massive and structural characteristic of UK society. They have also established that, as when Disraeli first used the term 'Two Nations', it is above all the horizontal division of class which divides privilege and affluence from dependence and

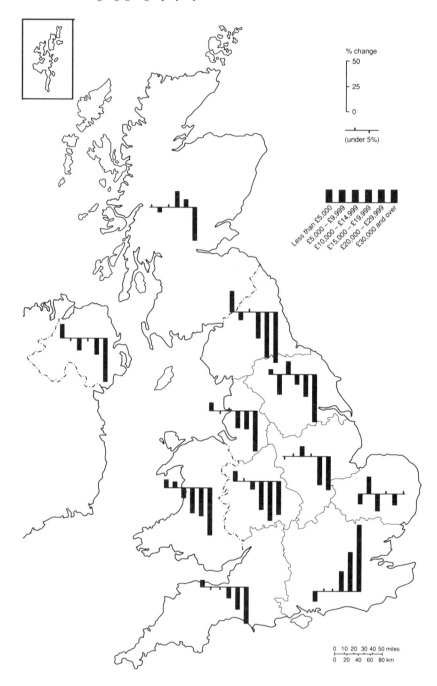

*Figure 13.2* Inter-regional deviations in income brackets 1984–5

deprivation. Nevertheless, there is clearly a spatial dimension. Because economic restructuring produces locally differentiated class and occupational structures, the fundamental class differences in economic status are reflected in the geography of welfare. In addition, as indicated here, the effects of distance and spatial organization can create, modify or reinforce these geographical patterns. Townsend's own survey showed that in areas such as north Belfast, east Salford, Shettleston (Glasgow) and Neath (West Glamorgan) there are about twice as many poor and marginally poor families as there are in the nation as a whole, and that only half of this additional poverty can be attributed to local differences in class structure. These areas also had a disproportionately high prevalence of other types of deprivation and high concentrations of 'vulnerable' households and individuals: one-parent families, the elderly, the sick and the disabled. Social commentators in general, and geographers in particular, have tended to stereotype these spatial expressions of the 'two nations' in terms of a core/periphery dichotomy: south versus north, metropolis versus the provinces, capital versus the regions, the inner city versus the suburbs (Green 1988, Martin 1987). To what extent is this a caricature of the truth?

Figures 13.2 and 13.3 provide, between them, a good indication of the geography of affluence and poverty in the United Kingdom. Figure 13.2 shows the inter-regional deviations in income brackets in 1984–5. The most striking feature of this map is the relative concentration of exceptionally high income in the south-east. In this region, less than 33 per cent of the nation's taxpayers accounted for nearly half of the personal incomes over £30,000 per annum. To the north and west there is a steady decline in incomes, so that the South-west, the North-west, Wales, Yorkshire and Humberside, the North, Scotland and, in particular, Northern Ireland are all characterized by an over-representation of low incomes and under-representation of high incomes. A major disadvantage of these income data is that they do not include those people with incomes so low that they fall below the tax base. Figure 13.3 provides a fairly sensitive picture of the incidence of poverty, however. This map shows the percentage of school children in each area receiving free school meals in 1979–80, the last point at which it was a carefully regulated and means-tested benefit which all local authorities were bound to make available to the children of needy families. Because it has been correlated significantly with many other indicators of institutionally defined poverty, this index can be regarded as diagnostic of the incidence of poverty in general. According to this criterion there is a marked concentration in just a few areas. In the greater part of the country the proportion of children receiving free school meals was less than 15 per cent, while in parts of central and eastern Scotland and in a large tract of 'Middle England' and the south-east the proportion fell below 10 per cent, reaching a low of 5.7 per cent in Surrey. Within this area, however, was the striking pocket of poverty in the inner London boroughs. Strathclyde, together with parts of south and north-west Wales,

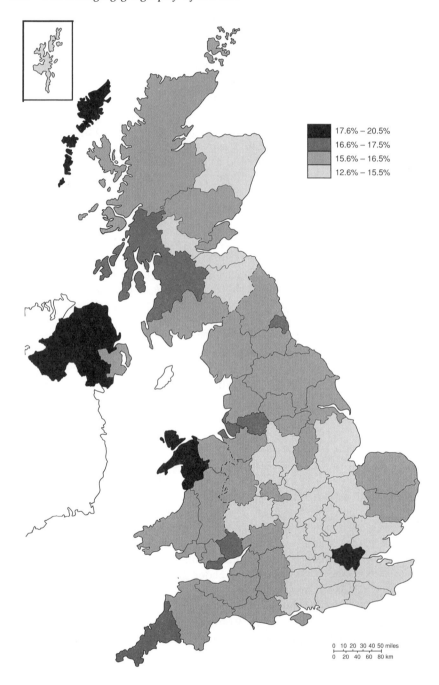

*Figure 13.3* Proportion of all schoolchildren receiving free school meals, 1979–80

and the Tyneside, Merseyside and Greater Manchester conurbations, also exhibited relatively high levels of poverty, although it was in Northern Ireland and the Western Isles that the incidence of poverty was at its highest. Once again, Northern Ireland stands out as the locus of deprivation. There may or may not be a Metropolitan Nation and a Peripheral Nation, but there certainly is an Offshore Nation which seems to be at or near the bottom of the ladder on most criteria of social well-being.

It is interesting to note that these broad patterns of affluence and deprivation are only loosely reflected in people's *sense* of well-being: something which is clearly crucial to the overall quality of a person's life. Studies of people's perceived well-being have shown that residents of Northern Ireland are strikingly – and understandably – less satisfied with life than is the 'average' UK resident; but the greatest overall levels of satisfaction are in Yorkshire and Humberside, the East Midlands, and Scotland and not in the 'objectively' more prosperous London and Southeast. In these latter areas, presumably, years of relative prosperity have led to a more highly developed sense of expectation.

These generalizations about regional patterns are clearly rather crude: regional and city-wide averages tend to obscure the substantial minorities of the deprived and disadvantaged living in 'prosperous' regions and neighbourhoods; and the same applies to the minority of relatively affluent households in poor areas. In Greater London as a whole, incomes are high, unemployment is relatively low, there are more telephones and refrigerators per head than anywhere, except the south-east, and the typical family consumes more meat and fresh fruit, less potatoes and biscuits: it is the hub of the 'golden corner'. But it is also an area of diminishing opportunity. It is rapidly losing manufacturing jobs, while the service sector is expanding at a slower rate than the national average. The trend towards decentralization has also affected the social wage. London has abnormally high costs of providing public services because of high land costs for housing, because of congestion, and high wage costs; and the loss of people and jobs has eroded the rateable values which have had to sustain a large proportion of the costs of public services. The problem is compounded by the fact that, as London loses population, the poor and needy form an increasing proportion of those left behind. In the late 1980s, thousands of families were living on incomes below the official poverty line in an environment which was not only being denuded of welfare services but which was also the inflation leader for the whole country.

## Environments of prosperity and equality

Such complexity suggests that it is more useful to think of different *kinds* of area than to think of a regionalization of the UK based on the idea of 'two nations' or on the notion of a continuum of well-being ranging simply from 'good' to 'bad'. Donnison and Soto (1980) for example, suggested that the

British urban system of 1971 could be divided into thirteen different city types: regional service centres, resorts, residential suburbs, new industrial suburbs, new towns, London, Welsh mining towns, textile towns, heavy engineering/coal towns, central Scotland, inner conurbations and two types of engineering town. At a more general level, it is suggested, there was a two-fold division between 'traditional Britain' and 'new Britain'. The significant feature about this division is that the communities of 'new Britain' – the new towns, residential suburbs, new industrial suburbs, resorts, regional service centres and London – were generally more prosperous and *equal*: for any given occupational group, opportunity and affluence tended to be greater in the urban environments of 'new Britain' than in those of 'traditional Britain' (table 13.3). Perhaps the most interesting suggestion to emerge from the analysis, however, is that there existed a type of place – the 'good city' – in which the most vulnerable members of society suffered less than they did elsewhere, even though they represented a larger proportion of the total population. These places also provided a better educational environment than most others, together with a generally high standard of public services. What is most surprising about them is that they were not part of the affluent 'new Britain'. Rather, they were part of 'Middle England': places such as Luton, Ormskirk, Peterborough and Swindon. Thus, although they provided a 'kinder' and more equal environment, they did not exhibit the imprint of elegant living or conspicuous consumption. They had few good art galleries, few buildings listed for preservation, no entry in the *Good Food Guide*, and few specialist shops catering for the tastes of the very rich.

### Environments of deprivation and disadvantage

It is also possible to distinguish different kinds of marginal areas and deprived communities. The urban stereotype is the deprived inner-city area, with its decaying nineteenth-century environments, housing concentrations of the poor, the vulnerable and the dependent. This, however, is by no means the only 'syndrome' of urban deprivation. In many industrial cities, classic inner-city 'rooming house' areas are by no means the worst off. This distinction often falls to inner-city council estates, which can have much higher levels of overcrowding, youth employment instability, long-term unemployment, pest infestation and poverty. Inner-city rooming house areas also score badly across a wide range of criteria, but they are particularly characterized by a high incidence of shared dwellings, high levels of substandard housing, and high levels of infant mortality and illness from infectious diseases. The dominant syndrome of deprivation in peripheral council estates tends to be different again, involving the straightforward association of unemployment and family poverty.

One common denominator among deprived urban neighbourhoods is the tension and stress which itself further corrodes the quality of life and

Table 13.3 Unemployment and car ownership by city type and occupational group, 1971

| | Unemployment (UK = 100) | | | | | Cars per household (UK = 100) | | | | |
|---|---|---|---|---|---|---|---|---|---|---|
| | Professional and managerial | Other non-manual | Skilled manual | Semi-skilled manual | Unskilled manual | Professional and managerial | Other non-manual | Skilled manual | Semi-skilled manual | Unskilled manual |
| *New Britain* | | | | | | | | | | |
| New industrial suburbs | 93 | 79 | 63 | 61 | 64 | 115 | 131 | 126 | 137 | 152 |
| Residential suburbs | 64 | 67 | 53 | 64 | 60 | 129 | 153 | 156 | 160 | 181 |
| London | 92 | 94 | 81 | 69 | 55 | 98 | 93 | 115 | 105 | 128 |
| New towns | 75 | 62 | 52 | 52 | 48 | 119 | 146 | 146 | 169 | 187 |
| Regional service centres | 108 | 104 | 96 | 106 | 90 | 95 | 99 | 102 | 101 | 112 |
| Resorts | 158 | 165 | 109 | 118 | 108 | 91 | 95 | 113 | 101 | 119 |
| *Traditional Britain* | | | | | | | | | | |
| Central Scotland | 157 | 161 | 210 | 209 | 228 | 79 | 65 | 55 | 50 | 43 |
| Welsh mining towns | 145 | 145 | 163 | 152 | 169 | 76 | 85 | 74 | 97 | 96 |
| Inner conurbations | 118 | 121 | 132 | 130 | 133 | 88 | 82 | 80 | 77 | 67 |
| Heavy engineering/coal | 87 | 80 | 95 | 96 | 96 | 101 | 111 | 91 | 103 | 97 |
| Textile towns | 94 | 94 | 92 | 102 | 96 | 96 | 95 | 86 | 76 | 71 |
| Engineering I | 105 | 90 | 92 | 85 | 89 | 97 | 101 | 91 | 98 | 99 |
| Engineering II | 95 | 88 | 88 | 94 | 97 | 105 | 118 | 115 | 132 | 123 |

Source: Donnison and Soto 1980: 109 and 111

which occasionally erupts in protest, disorder or conflict. The strident alienation of many inner-city residents was graphically captured by an incident during a 'fact-finding' mission by Sir Keith Joseph to Newcastle upon Tyne, when the official entourage was addressed, with apparent feeling and directness, by Beatrice, a local housewife 'Hey you! You're the f . . . Minister of Housing are you? Well then you f . . . well come in here and see what I f . . . well live in. Well . . . what do you think of that eh? I bet you don't live in a p . . . -hole like that, do you?' (Davies 1972, p. 66). Similar invitations have been issued over the past twenty years to a succession of political leaders on fact-finding tours of disadvantaged areas.

Rural problem areas are similar but different. They are *similar* to deprived urban environments in that they exhibit high levels of unemployment, low wages and restricted job opportunities stemming from local economic stagnation. They also share the consequent erosion of community morale and the associated age-selective stream of out-migration. The *differences* between urban and rural deprivation stem largely from basic contrasts in the physical and social environment. Thus, whereas the various syndromes of urban deprivation are distinguished by problems of environmental decay, overcrowding, ill-health, and stress, rural problem areas – the Highlands and Islands of Scotland, mid-Wales, and parts of the Southwest, East Anglia, Cumbria and Northern Ireland – are characterized by problems of inaccessibility, social isolation and the lack of a threshold population large enough to attract even the most basic services and facilities. The whole western coast of the Scottish Highlands between Gairloch (Wester Ross) and Bettyhill (north-west Sutherland), for example, contains no resident dentist, solicitor, estate agent or optician and no hospital, health centre, pharmacy or secondary school. As a result, there is considerable dependency on the east coast towns, involving car journeys of three hours or more for all but the most basic services. These are also the areas which suffer most from the isolation resulting from rugged topography and poor roads, which makes the provision of many social services – such as meals-on-wheels – difficult or impossible. The *quality* of rural services also tends to be poor. Small market size and local monopoly conditions make for a very restricted choice of goods in the shops, while infrequent deliveries and the low volume of sales often lead to stale bread, flaccid vegetables and over-ripe fruit – or nothing. Even in relation to highly subsidized public services, small is not necessarily beautiful. Despite very favourable pupil/teacher ratios, for example, the quality of education provided by small primary schools must be open to question because of their lack of equipment, the difficulty of providing a diversity of experience through contact with other children, and their vulnerability to the effects of a single 'bad' teacher.

# REFERENCES

Beveridge Report (1942) *Social Insurance and Allied Services*, Cmnd 4606, London: HMSO.

Carnegie, Foundation (1943) *Disinherited Youth*, Edinburgh: Carnegie Trust.

Davies, J. G. (1972) *The Evangelistic Bureaucrat*, London: Tavistock.

Donnison, D. and Soto, P. (1980) *The Good City*, London: Heinemann.

Green, A. E. (1988) 'The North-South divide in Great Britain: An examination of the evidence', *Transactions, Institute of British Geographers*, NS 13: 179–98.

Greenwood, W. (1933) *Love on the Dole*, London: Jonathan Cape.

Mack, J. and Lansley, S. (1985) *Poor Britain*, London: Allen and Unwin.

Martin, R. L. (1987) 'Mrs Thatcher's Britain: A tale of two Nations', *Environment and Planning* A, 19: 571–4.

Orwell, G. (1962) *The Road to Wigan Pier*, London: Penguin. (First published by Victor Gollancz, 1937.)

Pilgrim Trust (1938) *Men Without Work*, London: Pilgrim Trust.

Priestley, J. B. (1934) *English Journey*, London: Macmillan.

## FURTHER READING

The classic work on poverty is Townsend, P. (1979) *Poverty in the United Kingdom*, London: Penguin. For a statistical base see Royal Commission on the Distribution of Income and Wealth (1978) *Low Incomes*, Cmnd 7175, London: HMSO. See also Stevenson, J. (1977) *Social Conditions in Britain between the Wars*, London: Penguin: and Rees, G. and Rees, G. L. (eds.) (1980) *Poverty and Inequality in Wales*, London: Croom Helm.

On social indicators and their use in geography see Knox, P. L. (1975) *Social Well-Being: A Spatial Perspective*, Oxford: Oxford University Press. Applications include Holtermann, S. (1975) 'Areas of urban deprivation in Great Britain: an analysis of 1971 census data', *Social Trends*, 6: 33–47; Knox, P. L. (1979) 'Medical deprivation, area deprivation and public policy', *Social Science and Medicine*, 13D: 111–21; and Knox, P. L. (1982) 'Regional inequality and the welfare state: convergence and divergence in levels of living in the United Kingdom, 1951–71', *Social Indicators Research*, 9; and Pacione, M. (1986) 'Quality of Life in Glasgow: an applied geographical analysis', *Environment and Planning A*, 18: 1499–520. See also Newton, K. (1976) 'Community performance in Britain', *Current Sociology* 26: 49–86.

# 14 Leisure, recreation and environment

*Mark Blacksell*

One of the features of an industrial as opposed to an agrarian society is the way in which work is separated out from other parts of daily life and well-being is judged almost exclusively in terms of economic activity and output. Yet work has always taken up only a small proportion of people's time; for the most part they are at leisure – time free from work and other obligations – and much of this time is filled with recreational activities, ranging from active participation in sports to watching television or having a drink at the local pub. This chapter examines three aspects of this important but diffuse part of life in the United Kingdom: the changes that have taken place in the amount and distribution of leisure time and in leisure spending; the growing involvement of the state, at both national and local levels, in ensuring that recreational opportunities are widely available and that access is limited as little as possible by individual financial circumstances; and, finally, the impact that changing attitudes to recreation have had upon the environment.

## LEISURE TIME AND LEISURE SPENDING

Much has been made in the past of actual or expected increases in the amount of leisure time available, with talk of three or even two and a half day weeks being standard by the end of the present century and the rest of the time taken up with a frantic search for active recreations to fill the leisure time available. Certainly it is true that the average working week fell from about 70 hours in the mid-nineteenth century to 44 hours today, but most of the reduction occurred before the Second World War and before the explosion in the demand for recreation. Much more important recently have been the reorganization of time spent in work, so that holidays with pay are now standard and free weekends the norm for the majority, the enormous advances in personal mobility conferred by greater affluence and technological innovation, and the impact of demographic change.

Most workers now have at least four weeks holiday on full pay each year and well over 80 per cent only work a five-day week. At the same time average incomes have been growing, even in real terms, and a considerable proportion of the extra money has been invested in enhanced mobility, particularly the private car. In 1939 there were just under 4 million driving licences held in Great Britain; by 1986 there were over 31 million. Over the same period the number of cars in use rose from only just over 2 million to over 18 million and the change has transformed expectations and capabilities in all areas of life, not least leisure, provoking Rodgers (1969) to describe the car as the major recreational tool of our culture.

The importance of leisure has been further intensified by demographic change. The population of the United Kingdom is now 57 million, 9 per cent higher than it was a generation ago; but it is not so much the sheer force of numbers as their composition that is of significance. People are now living longer, so that there are nearly 12 million over the age of retirement, almost twice as many as in 1950, and because this section of the population has so much free time, it has a disproportionate impact on patterns of leisure and recreation. At the other end of the spectrum, the school-leaving age has now been raised to 16 and in 1986 45 per cent of those between the ages of 16 and 18 were still engaged in full-time education, altering significantly the nature of recreation demand amongst young people. Nor does the change stop there; the trend towards smaller families means that even amongst the economically active population there is more time available for non-routine tasks during leisure time.

Thus a number of factors have combined in recent years to expand the options for using leisure time. Understandably perhaps, the main concern of society has traditionally been with work, either finding people to do it or making sure that there was enough of it to go around. Although Benjamin Disraeli could say as long ago as 1872 that 'Increased means and increased leisure are the two great civilizers of man', attention focused on the former and leisure was very much a subsidiary consideration. In the 1950s and 1960s, however, this began to change. As affluence grew and spread throughout the United Kingdom, serious unemployment seemed to be a thing of the past and society began to turn its attention to other things. People sought to spend their new-found wealth on a range of novel recreations and government and private industry began increasingly to organize and exploit these new enthusiasms.

It is relatively easy to point to the general increase in the amount of leisure time available and to the growing demand for more varied outlets for the energy people wish to devote to their recreations, but it is quite another to identify them in precise and comparable terms. The huge range of activities involved makes this a complex and hazardous task, but a comprehensive attempt has been made by Martin and Mason (1980). They compiled a broad picture of patterns of expenditure on leisure from a wide variety of published sources and concluded that in 1977 just over £23 billion, almost 27 per cent of consumer spending in the United Kingdom, was devoted to leisure. Admittedly their definition of leisure spending was extremely broad and if expenditure on domestic travel and clothing was omitted the figure fell to £17.25 billion, 20 per cent of all consumer outlays.

The breakdown of consumer spending on leisure gives an interesting perspective on people's priorities. By far the largest item, accounting for 37.9 per cent of the total, was alcoholic drink, followed by holidays (11.8 per cent), television, radio and audio (10.8 per cent), and DIY and gardening (8.4 per cent). This corresponds closely with the findings of earlier studies; Sillitoe showed in 1969 that watching television was the nation's prime recreational activity.

Treating the population as a single homogeneous unit in this way has the obvious disadvantage that the variations between different groups in society and between different parts of the country are masked. Disaggregation is possible to only a limited extent, however, because in none of the standard statistical publications is there a generally accepted definition of *leisure*. Nevertheless, the government's Family Expenditure Survey contains a considerable amount of information about the habits of various sections of the British population regarding leisure expenditure. As might be expected the proportion of people's income devoted to recreation and leisure rises steadily with the overall level of their pay. On the other hand, above £150 per week, spending in the two most important categories in the Family Expenditure Survey jumps dramatically. The amount devoted to alcoholic drink rises more than 41 per cent between the two cohorts earning £125–£149 per week and £150–£174 per week, £5.20 to £7.35; and expenditure in the category 'Subscriptions and donations, hotel and holiday expenses, miscellaneous other services' rises by 28.3 per cent at the same point.

The regional pattern of expenditure for the two-year period 1985–6, based on data from the Family Expenditure Survey, reveals an uneven pattern (figure 14.1). The highest rates are in the south of England, in the south-east and the south-west regions; the lowest rates are in northern England and Northern Ireland. These extremes match closely the regional variations in overall income levels and, to that extent, are not unexpected. The intermediate patterns are less easily explained. Levels of expenditure in Scotland, Wales, Yorkshire and Humberside, and the East Midlands are relatively high; those in the North-west, the West Midlands, and East Anglia are all relatively low. The small but significant difference between the East and West Midlands is worth noting, underlining as it does how the generally better economic performance of the east has fed through into social indicators, such as expenditure on leisure.

The proportion of people's income committed to leisure has grown slowly, especially during the 1960s and early 1970s. Nevertheless, it is clear that this commitment is somewhat fickle and likely to mirror changes in economic circumstances rapidly. The difficulties which faced the United Kingdom and other western industrial nations after the sudden rise in oil prices in 1973 and the subsequent uncertainty about the future of the

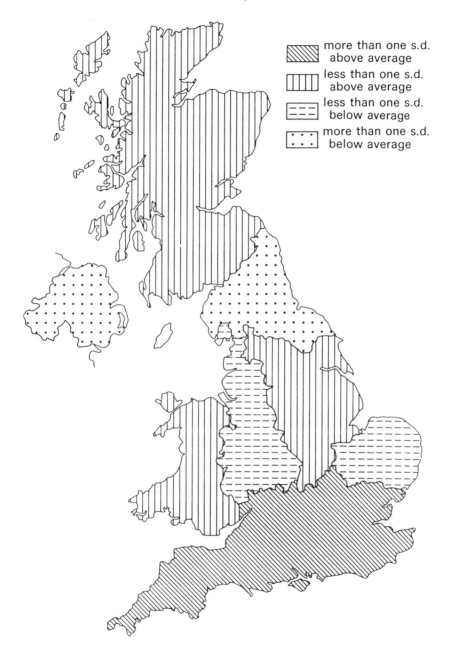

*Figure 14.1* Regional variations in the proportion of expenditure per household devoted to leisure, 1985–6 (s.d. standard deviation)
*Source:* Department of Employment (1988) *Family Expenditure Survey 1985–6,* London: HMSO

economy were paralleled by a reduction in the relative share of earnings devoted to leisure nationally. This is important corroboration of the common finding that when people are asked to rank those things that are most significant in contributing to their overall quality of life, leisure comes relatively low in the list of priorities. A survey carried out in Stoke on Trent and Sunderland by Hall and Perry for the Social Science Research Council Survey Unit between 1971 and 1975 showed consistently that people viewed health, standard of living, income, house, job, and democracy as all coming above leisure in their contribution to overall quality of life.

In the late 1980s, as prosperity gradually increased again, leisure spending also recovered. One measure of this is the numbers of holidays being taken. Over 50 million people in the United Kingdom went on holiday at least once in 1986, 17 million going abroad.

## RECREATION FOR ALL

Whatever the attitudes towards the importance of leisure, there is no doubt about the explosive and continuing growth in recreation, both in terms of the number and variety of activities that people indulge in during their free time and in the opportunities for them to do so. Demand has burgeoned in the past three decades and both informal and formal recreation are assuming an increasingly important position in the social structure, especially for the expanding middle class with more time, money and, therefore, leisure available to devote to them.

The social dimension is important for there is a widespread belief that all types of recreation offer a vital means of social contact amongst both family and friends, a function that is now usually catered for inadequately either at work or in school. This is particularly true of countryside trip-making, currently one of the most popular recreations, a major purpose of which is claimed to be the forging and sustaining of family contact and cohesion. People tend to visit remote rural or wilderness areas in the company of others and then do things such as walking or picnicking in groups. It has even been demonstrated by Burton in Cannock Chase, Staffordshire, as part of an experiment, that the majority of visitors to the countryside are little concerned by the presence of quite large numbers of other people, undermining the belief that solitude is what people are looking for when they visit the countryside.

This social function is by no means limited to informal recreation. The sports that are growing most rapidly in popularity, as Roberts (1978) and Seeley (1973) have shown, are those that do not require either peak fitness or a high level of skill in order for individuals to participate, including non-team sports which are not dependent on assembling groups before the game can be played. In essence this trend has been apparent for some time, for the popularity of swimming, a sport in which people of all ages and abilities can participate with great enjoyment, has long been recognized and it is estimated that there are about 4 million active swimmers in the United Kingdom. Although no other sport can boast such a following, it is those with similar attributes that have been growing fastest, for example golf and, more recently, tennis and squash. Conversely, it is the team games, like cricket, soccer, rugby and hockey, that have declined. Overall, however, the reduced emphasis on fitness, skill and organization has encouraged much greater participation at all levels in sport. It is also worth noting that there has been a parallel decline in spectator support for many traditional team games, in particular soccer where the top four divisions of the Football League alone attracted more than 1 million people on an average Saturday afternoon a generation ago, compared with little more than half a million today.

## Local government provision

The interest in, and demand for, sport and recreation have led to much greater public involvement in the provision of facilities and to what the Rapoports (1975) have referred to as 'the institutionalization of leisure'. The roots of this stretch back into the nineteenth century in many parts of the United Kingdom, with the provision of urban parks and public baths by local authorities. More recently, one of the driving forces behind the National Parks movement was a desire to secure open country for public recreation and enjoyment. It was in the 1970s, however, particularly in the wake of the reports of the House of Lords Select Committee on Sport and Leisure in 1973, that recreation became widely institutionalized throughout the country. The noble lords argued forcefully that recreation should be seen as an integral part of life, not just an optional extra and that, given its importance, government ought to be involved, so as to ensure that the provision of facilities was adequate. They were at pains to press for the establishment of integrated leisure and recreation departments in the new authorities that were established as a result of local government reorganization in 1974.

One of the Select Committee's chief arguments was that the public was entitled to a good time and that government had concentrated hitherto too exclusively on sport with its emphasis on competitive achievement. They suggested that instead of the 'Sport for All' programme being promoted through the Sports Council, there ought to be a broader-based policy of 'Recreation for All'. Undoubtedly the argument struck a sympathetic chord, for in August 1975 a White Paper was issued which endorsed the central importance of both sport and recreation, changed the title of the Minister of State for Sport to the Minister of State for Sport and Recreation, and proposed reconstituting the Regional Sports Councils into Regional Councils for Sport and Recreation, answerable jointly to the Sports Council and the Countryside Commission.

The more broadly based Regional Councils started work in 1976 and have played a coordinating role amongst the welter of new recreation and leisure departments set up at county and district level in the wake of local government reorganization. Unfortunately, the lack of any clear and agreed definition of what services ought to be included under the umbrella of recreation and leisure, combined with the complex and often overlapping division of responsibilities between the various levels of local government (which in any case are different in England, Wales, Scotland and Northern Ireland), produced a somewhat fragmented pattern of provision.

The major urban areas in England – Greater London, Greater Manchester, Merseyside, South Yorkshire, Tyne and Wear, the West Midlands, and West Yorkshire – are all governed by unitary metropolitan district (incorporating London borough) councils, which have responsibility for all forms of recreation provision. In some cases, such as the administration of regional parks in parts of London and some major sports centres, there is a pooling of expertise and resources between authorities, but such arrangements are entirely at the discretion of the authorities concerned.

Outside the conurbations, in the rest of England and in Wales, responsibility for recreation is divided between the County and District Councils. The upper tier of County Councils is responsible for all National Park and countryside functions and the provision and maintenance of caravan sites. They also include libraries within their remit and have a shared responsibility with the lower tier District Councils for museums and art galleries. The District Councils have sole responsibility for swimming baths, public halls, parks and open spaces, as well as sharing the management of museums and art galleries. In Wales, at the discretion of the Secretary of State, libraries are wholly managed by the District Councils in some areas.

The major problem in England and Wales is that it depends largely on where a particular recreation takes place as to which authority is responsible for its welfare. Sports like tennis and bowls, played for the most part in public parks, are almost fortuitously a District concern, whereas those located within purpose-built sports centres are usually within the County remit. A further complication is produced by the dual use of water authority, education, police and armed services' facilities, a practice that has been much extended in recent years and one that has received considerable unobtrusive encouragement from central government. Overall, however, a situation has been created in which it is very difficult to foster coordination and the development of coherent provision of facilities.

In both Scotland and Northern Ireland matters are much simpler and policies consequently clearer. The Scottish Regional and District Councils are jointly responsible for tourism, the countryside, parks, recreation, museums, art galleries and community centres. The only confusion is in respect of libraries, which are a District matter, except in the Highlands, Dumfries and Galloway and Border Regions, where they are administered regionally because of the small populations in these areas. In Northern

Ireland everything comes under the twenty-four District Councils, with the exception of libraries which are administered by five area boards.

## Inter-authority variations

The vigour with which local authorities at all levels have assumed their responsibilities for recreation and leisure under the Local Government Act 1972 is revealed in table 14.1. In England and Wales the majority at both County and District level have established specialist committees to deal with recreation and leisure. Nevertheless, given the two-tier structure outside the major conurbations, with supposedly mutually exclusive areas of responsibility, the potential for overlap mentioned above is clearly apparent. In England and Wales nearly all the County and non-metropolitan District Councils both have such committees and coordinating their activities can often prove difficult, as priorities between the two levels may differ. In Scotland, too, the division of responsibility is rather more clearly defined with the lower tier taking the lead. Only 58 per cent of the Regional and Island Councils have recreation and leisure committees, as compared to 83 per cent of the Districts. In Northern Ireland there appears to have been a collective decision not to establish separate committees for recreation and leisure at all!

*Table 14.1* Local authorities in the UK with committees dealing exclusively, or primarily with recreation and leisure

|  | *No. of authorities* | *No. of authorities with one or more relevant committees (%)* | |
|---|---|---|---|
| English and Welsh non-metropolitan counties | 47 | 37 | (79) |
| English and Welsh non-metropolitan districts | 330 | 289 | (88) |
| English metropolitan districts | 35 | 34 | (97) |
| London boroughs | 32 | 27 | (84) |
| Scottish Regional and Island Councils | 12 | 7 | (58) |
| Scottish districts | 53 | 47 | (89) |
| Northern Ireland districts | 24 | 0 | (0) |

The data in table 14.1 are but a fairly crude aggregation of a very complicated and variable administrative structure in an area over which local authorities can exercise considerable discretion. Nevertheless, they indicate the strength of the commitment nationally to leisure and recreation, although two important qualifications need to be entered. First, the fact that an authority does not have a separate committee for these purposes does not necessarily mean that it takes them any less seriously; it may simply have decided to encompass this part of its remit within another area of its committee structure. Second, the interpretation of recreation and leisure in the context of table 14.1 is itself fairly broad, including bodies with the actual title 'leisure and recreation committees' to those whose brief is amenities, and others concerned specifically with libraries, swimming baths and public parks.

The existence of committees is of course only one way of showing the depth of concern for recreation and leisure at local authority level in the United Kingdom; it gives little indication of commitment in terms of resources. To do this from an analysis of the budget is extremely difficult for reasons explained below, but a partial surrogate is provided by the number of personnel employed by authorities for these purposes. Figure 14.2 shows the variation in the numbers of principal and deputy-principal officers in relation to the total populations at County and District levels between the English, Welsh and Northern Irish counties and the Scottish regions.

The most striking feature of the map is the consistently high rating in Scotland, Northern Ireland and the north of England, as compared with the rest of England and Wales, despite the fact that in the southern half of the country there is a number of counties where tourism plays an increasingly important part in the local economy. Only two of these coastal southern counties, Dorset and West Sussex, are in the first quartile, while Norfolk, Suffolk, Kent, East Sussex, Devon and Dyfed, all of which have important coastal resorts and depend heavily on the holiday trade, languish in the third quartile. At the bottom of the league comes the midlands and the east of England, where the numbers of senior staff with responsibility for recreation and leisure is consistently low. The authorities here have relatively low levels of investment in these activities, see little prospect of their making much contribution to the local economy and, therefore, only accord them a low priority amongst the administrative responsibilities.

Another important contrast is between urban and rural areas. Most of the major conurbations are poorly staffed. Merseyside, Tyne and Wear, and South Yorkshire and West Yorkshire are all in the fourth quartile, as is the predominantly urban county of Avon. Even in Scotland, where the overall level of provision is very high, the Lothian region, which incorporates Edinburgh, stands out as the only one in the third quartile. Once again the low priority given to recreation and leisure reflects the relative importance attached to social, as opposed to economic, issues by the local authorities concerned.

Whatever the variations, there is generally a widespread and deeply entrenched commitment throughout the United Kingdom to the need for local authority provision and supervision of recreation resources. The contribution that this has made to the social fabric of the country is considerable, but it has also stored up a number of inherent problems. Resources once allocated are not always easy to move around, yet taste

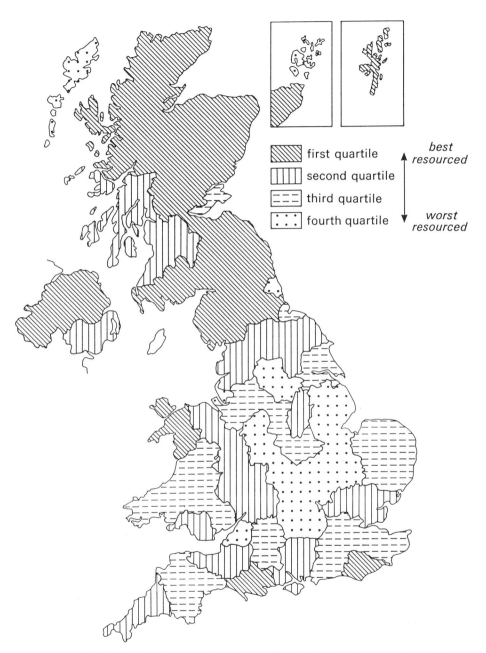

*Figure 14.2* Numbers of principal and deputy principal officers in recreation and leisure relative to population by administrative area (in England and Wales and Northern Ireland – non-metropolitan counties and erstwhile Metropolitan counties and the Greater London Council; in Scotland – Regional and Island councils)
*Source: Municipal Yearbook,* 1989

and fashion in leisure activities are notoriously fickle. Population movements can leave expensive investment in fixed assets, like sports centres
and playing fields, under-used in the wrong place. Equally heavy investment
in traditional recreations may leave little leeway for developing facilities
for new pastimes.

The problem of assessing variations in provision is seriously exacerbated
by the difficulty of separating out local authority spending on recreation
from other areas of expenditure, as Lewes and Mennell (1976) showed in
their study of Exeter City Council. This study, one of the very few to
analyse local authority expenditure on leisure and recreation in detail,
showed that in 1973–4 about £6 per head for Exeter's population of 93,000
was devoted to recreation, representing about 5 per cent of the total
budget, a percentage that had grown quite sharply since the beginning of
the decade. Nevertheless, despite its increased importance, the distribution of
moneys had stayed almost constant, with 40 per cent going to libraries 40
per cent to parks and sport, and 15 per cent to museums, leaving only a
very modest residual sum for other activities. The explanation of the
pattern and its apparent stability lay initially in the statutory requirement
on local authorities to provide libraries and parks for the public, reinforced
by the commitment to past policy and the need to honour the results of
previous decisions in terms of staff salaries and loan charges. Investment in
other types of recreation therefore depended very largely on the allocation
of new resources rather than on transfers within the leisure budget.

Lewes and Mennell's (1976) study also raised some important questions
about the value that the council was getting from its investment. Most of
the money was spent directly on facilities and services run by the authority,
where the net cost per user was generally extremely high. The charges
made for the use of sports facilities, with the exceptions of the swimming
pool and the approach golf course, met only a small part of the cost of
actually running them. Similarly, the library, with the statutory obligations
to provide a free loan service, and the museums made heavy calls on the
available resources, but generated little or no income. There are strong
arguments in favour of the local authority providing such services either
free or at only a nominal charge, of course, but the study did reveal how
disadvantaged were other, apparently equally legitimate recreations, such
as music-making and drama. In those cases where expenditure by the local
authority took the form of either leasing premises to organizations at below
the economic rent or grants of money to private bodies, the net cost per
user fell dramatically. The clear conclusion was that subsidies to private
theatre companies, orchestras and the like were a very cost-effective way
of supporting recreation in the community, yet one that was hampered by
the extent and rigidity of existing commitments.

It is of interest that these findings came as an almost total surprise to the
local authority itself. The way in which the various activities under the
general heading recreation and leisure were spread through the accounts

meant that no comparative analysis had ever been made before. With Lewes and Mennell's figures in front of them, it became clear to both officials and councillors just how expensive, in terms of cost per user, were some traditional services, although the library and sporting facilities budgets were rarely if ever challenged, compared with subsidies to theatres and orchestras – items that were invariably bitterly controversial. There is every reason for supposing that Exeter's experience is typical and it emphasizes how a lack of critical appraisal of traditional priorities can impair the quality of the service being offered. It is a problem that is hard for a local authority to tackle, not least because it is often difficult to recognize. So long as a facility is being used, it can be argued that there is a demand for it, notwithstanding the fact that the latent demand for some alternative form of provision may be many times greater.

The emphasis throughout this section has been on local authority provision of leisure and recreation services, for it is by far the most significant. Yet private industry has also played an important part, notably in promoting a few new sports such as ten-pin bowling and in providing supplementary facilities in places where demand is high, such as resort towns. There is also a number of important initiatives, some of very long standing, by private trusts. Pre-eminent amongst these is the National Trust (covering England, Wales and Northern Ireland) and the National Trust for Scotland, which in 1988 had a combined membership of well over one and a half million and owned or had covenanted over 200,000 ha of land (see chapter 17); in 1987 their properties were visited by more than 8 million people. The explosive growth of these two organizations, particularly the National Trust which has nearly trebled its membership since 1970, is an indication of people's willingness to bypass formal channels and take matters into their own hands.

In practice the distinction between public and private provision is not clear-cut; as the Trusts have grown in size and stature they have been used increasingly by government to channel and administer funds and other resources for recreation and conservation. Many of their properties were gifts, inspired by the fact that the Inland Revenue was able to allow them in lieu of Capital Transfer Tax, and Tunbridge (1981) has claimed that this more than anything else is the basis for the Trust's contribution to the country's recreational geography.

## THE DISPERSION OF DEMAND – AND SUPPLY

The new-found freedom associated with the dramatic improvements in mobility brought by motor cars, cheap air travel and high-speed trains has transformed the nature of recreation as much as, if not more than, most other spheres of life. Although less than a quarter of the UK population has exclusive use of a motor car, almost all now have access to one for at least part of the time and this has led to a very widespread dispersal of recreation demand. As recently as a generation ago the main focus of recreational movements was a string of resorts, mostly coastal. Brighton, Margate, Southend-on-Sea, Torquay and similar places were extensions of urban Britain and owed their popularity to their place on the railway network, which had wrought such fundamental change to recreation in the nineteenth and early twentieth centuries. Now *places* have largely been replaced by *areas* and people go on holiday to the south-west, Scotland and Wales, rather than to any specific town, reflecting the infinitely greater freedom of choice that car-ownership has brought. The corollary of this is that those sections of the population, such as the poor, the young, the old and the disabled, who for one reason or another are unable to make use of these new opportunities, are increasingly penalized and severely restricted in the range of recreational options open to them.

It is important to note that it is not only the motor car that has produced far-reaching changes, for cheap air travel and rapid improvements in aircraft technology have gradually brought virtually the whole globe within the recreational purview of many UK citizens. No longer is foreign travel the preserve of the privileged few. In 1980 there were nearly 17.5 million overseas visits made by UK residents, 13 per cent more than in the previous year, and in the course of their travels they spent £2,724 million, an increase of 29 per cent over 1979. The same factors have also brought the United Kingdom within easy reach of holiday-makers from elsewhere in the industrial world; in 1980 there were some 12.5 million foreign visitors, most of whom converged on London and a few other popular locations, and who between them spent £2,991 million.

Within the four countries of the United Kingdom one of the main problems caused by the dispersal of demand, coupled with the absolute growth in the volume of recreation, is that it has quite suddenly put intense pressure on areas where there is little or no provision. The countryside as a whole is now viewed by almost everyone as a potential recreational resource and the signs of strain are apparent everywhere, with overcrowded roads and inadequate facilities. The annual national survey of countryside recreation by the Countryside Commission reveals that in 1984 on an average Sunday over 15 million people visited the countryside in England and Wales alone, although more recent figures indicate that numbers may have fallen back somewhat since then in response to rather poor seasons of summer weather. Nevertheless, countryside trip-making is a well-established recreation. A 1972 study by Wall in Hull showed that over half the car-owning population of the city were likely to be away from home over the Spring Bank Holiday, mostly on day trips.

This growing imbalance between demand and supply for recreation has been investigated most thoroughly in Scotland in a whole series of surveys undertaken by the Tourism and Recreation Research Unit (TRRU) of the University of Edinburgh. Its work has attempted to specify the true nature of the recreational resource and to identify the pressures upon it. One of the most revealing studies was a roadside survey by Owen and Duffield (1971) of caravanners which showed that the most popular destinations were the Highlands and the west coast, where the infrastructure was poorest and the facilities fewest. The inevitable result was chronic over-crowding, and the survey showed that 34.1 per cent of those interviewed had camped at an unauthorized location at least once during their holiday, either because the campsites were full or because they were unable to find any. More fragmentary evidence from other parts of the country indicates that, far from being exceptional in the poverty of its resources, Scotland is probably rather better provided with camping and caravan sites than many other parts of rural Britain, notably the south-west peninsula, the Welsh coast and the Lake District.

A different facet of the dispersed demand is the growth of second home ownership in many rural areas. Estimates of their number vary and, according to Rogers (1977), the total seems to fluctuate depending on the country's economic circumstances, but including static caravans there are probably about 350,000 dwellings used solely for holiday-making. The overall figure is hardly significant as part of the nation's housing stock, but problems arise in a few remote areas where second homes account for more than 30 per cent of dwellings and it is argued that their existence is squeezing the life out of rural communities. In some areas there is a firm belief that second homes prevent local inhabitants from finding housing and in the Lake District National Park a non-statutory policy of refusing planning permission to anyone who did not work in the area was instituted in 1978, with the express intention of excluding second-home owners. However, the policy was eventually deemed unfairly discriminatory and the authority was not allowed to incorporate it into its official planning documents. Indeed, not everyone shares the Lake District view of non-locals' impact; others argue strongly that these people bring new blood to communities suffering from chronic decline, even if the dwellings are only occupied for part of the year.

The freedom that people now enjoy to pursue their recreation where they please makes it difficult to discern a consistent pattern in their behaviour, yet a great deal of research, reviewed by Elson (1979), has been devoted to trying to understand countryside trip-making in recent years. The results are by no means clear-cut, but a number of interesting conclusions have emerged. It is quite clear that the value of the car lies less in the distances it allows people to travel than in its flexibility of timing and use. The intensity with which the countryside around cities is used for recreation has increased greatly although the actual area involved has not. The popularity of the coast remains as strong as ever, but the attraction of inland lakes and reservoirs is also growing rapidly; generally calmer conditions make them ideal for activities like fishing, sailing, canoeing and water-skiing, and many are easily accessible from the main centres of population. The use of inland waters, particularly reservoirs, for recreation has been much encouraged since the Water Act 1973 required the Regional Water Authorities to realize the recreation potential of the land and water in their charge despite the fact that in some areas, like the Norfolk Broads, it can create or exacerbate existing problems of environmental management. Activities such as sailing and fishing are now standard on new reservoirs such as Rutland Water in the East Midlands and Wimbleball on the edge of Exmoor and, where appropriate, the older ones are being opened up as well. However, the Government's present plans to privatize the water authorities (see chapter 6) could seriously jeopardize access. As private companies the authorities will be under much greater pressure to dispose of unnecessary assets in order to raise capital and this could well include large parts of their land holdings which are not central to the main interests of their business. Were this to happen large areas, as in the Lake District and the Peak District National Parks, where the public presently has discretionary access, could be barred to recreation activities.

If water, either marine or inland, has acted as a magnet for all, inland sites have traditionally been the enthusiasm of the local population, but there are indications that the lure of open country is now spreading. A survey in the Dartmoor National Park in the late 1960s found that the majority of visitors were local, from the surrounding cities of Plymouth, Torbay and Exeter, but a resurvey in the mid-1970s not only revealed a sharp rise in the total number of visitors but also an increase to over 40 per cent in the proportion resident outside the immediate locality. The main reason for the change was most probably the improved accessibility resulting from the opening of the M5 motorway linking the south-west to the midlands and London.

Faced with this explosive and rapidly changing pattern in demand the providers of recreation have had to adjust what they offer to the public. In 1970 Patmore drew a crucial distinction between what he termed resource-based and user-orientated land for recreation, pointing out that with the former it was the quality of the resources irrespective of location that was important, while with the latter it was location rather than inherent quality that determined the level of utility. The initial response to the new generation of mobile recreation-seekers was to concentrate on making resource-based land available to them. The value of the countryside for these purposes was extolled on all sides and both local and central government yielded to pressure to designate tracts of countryside for recreation. Not surprisingly it was the local authorities in the Home Counties, much of which in the 1930s were being turned into suburban extensions of London, that took the first significant action. Surrey County Council was particularly active, according to Sheail (1981), promoting the Surrey County Council Act in 1931 to curb the activities of developers, and buying areas, such as Norbury Park, so that they could be preserved in their natural state for informal enjoyment and relaxation.

Gradually and somewhat chaotically public pressure, fuelled by the initiatives of individual local authorities, persuaded the government to take action, resulting eventually in the National Parks and Access to the Countryside Act 1949, which was a milestone in the history of recreation provision in the United Kingdom. Although its impact was mainly restricted to England and Wales, it led directly to the designation of the ten National Parks and thirty-three Areas of Outstanding Natural Beauty (AONBs) which now cover some 20 per cent of the two countries. In 1988, the marshes and waterways of the East Anglian Broads also became a quasi-National Park under different legislation and the New Forest in Hampshire seems likely to be designated as well in due course (see chapter 17).

Together with landscape conservation, public access for recreation was always one of the two main purposes of the National Parks, but this was not true of the AONBs. Here the chief policy objective was to preserve the traditional rural scene, but with ever growing numbers of people visiting these areas to discover for themselves the qualities that made the AONBs so exceptional, the recreation function has had to be formally recognized. In a policy statement issued in 1980, the Countryside Commission allowed for the first time that recreation should be recognized as an objective of designation when it is consistent with the conservation of natural beauty.

The more explicit recognition of recreation is symptomatic of a gradual change of emphasis from resource-based to user-orientated provision in countryside recreation which has been gathering ground since the mid-1960s in the United Kingdom. The Countryside Commissions for Scotland and for England and Wales, which replaced the National Parks Commissions in 1967 and 1968 respectively, marked a new beginning and the gradual emergence of policies for positive recreation provision, linked to demand rather than outstanding scenery. Central to these new initiatives is the country park, a rural area where the dominant land use is recreation. They are found now throughout the United Kingdom (figure 14.3) and in 1986 there were 184 managed by local authorities and non-public bodies and grant-aided by central government through the Countryside Commission. The country parks vary enormously in size from a few hectares to extensive tracts like the 1,054 hectares of Cannock Chase in Staffordshire, but most are located close to centres of population and in all the emphasis is on helping the visitor enjoy and understand the beauty of nature and the countryside. To do this needs are catered for through the provision of facilities like picnic sites and stress is laid on interpreting the immediate rural scene through published materials and displays.

Grant-aided country parks are only one facet of a mushroom-like growth in recreation provision, especially close to the major cities. A study in the London Green Belt identified nearly 500 informal recreation sites covering over 31,000 ha, 5.7 per cent of the total area, but, although there appeared to be plenty of land potentially available, much of it was relatively inaccessible and poorly located in relation to the major areas of demand emanating from the capital. If the results of this study are at all typical,

*Figure 14.3* Country parks in the UK, 1988

then sensitive planning and development will be required for the best use to be made of even such user-orientated designations.

## CONCLUSION

All the indications are that the amount of time devoted to leisure in the United Kingdom and the demand for recreations to fill that time are likely to continue to grow. As a result, recreation is placing unprecedented pressures on the environment and one of the most urgent tasks for geographers has been cited as the need to identify more precisely the ways in which the pressures are likely to develop in the future. This chapter has illustrated how both government agencies and the private sector at all levels have responded to the changing needs, tastes and, above all, capabilities of an increasingly mobile and leisured society. In terms of provision, the advent of the motor car has proved beguiling. There has been great political pressure to develop the previously untapped resources of the newly accessible countryside for recreation, whereas urban areas have tended to remain locked within a legacy of nineteenth- and early twentieth-century concepts of provision. There can be more to recreation in towns and cities than libraries, museums, parks and public baths and ways have to be found to translate this truism into freely available, novel facilities. Urban authorities have begun to make greater efforts in this direction, particularly since local government reorganization in 1974, but new initiatives have been stymied by the inadequacy of a structure which had to be revised again in 1986, with greater emphasis being placed on the need for the private sector to be more involved with the provision of recreation, and other, services through competitive tendering. Even so, much of the urban majority of the UK population, especially those living in the inner-city areas of the major conurbations, remains deprived in terms of recreation opportunity and the substantial national investment in countryside conservation in the form of National Parks and AONBs has been of little relevance to them.

## REFERENCES

Blacksell, M. (1987) 'National Parks and rural land management', in Lockhart, D. and Ilbery, B. (eds.) *The Future of the British Rural Landscape*, Norwich: Geo Books.

Burton, R. C. J. (1973) 'A new approach to perceptual capacity', *Recreation News Supplement*, 10: 31–6.

Coppock, J. T. (1983) 'The geography of recreation and tourism in the United Kingdom', in Johnson, J. H. (ed.) *Geography and Regional Planning*, Norwich: Geo Books.

Countryside Commission (1980) *Areas of Outstanding Natural Beauty: A Policy Statement*, Cheltenham: CCP 141.

Department of the Environment (1975) *Sport and Recreation*, Cmnd 6200, London: HMSO.

380 The changing geography of the UK

Elson, M. J. (1979) *Countryside Trip-Making,* London: Sports Council and SSRC.

Hall, J. and Perry, N. (1977) 'Aspects of leisure in two industrial cities', in *Leisure and the Quality of Life,* London: HMSO, pp. 445–57.

Kirby, A. (1985) 'Leisure as commodity: the role of the state in leisure provision', *Progress in Human Geography,* 9: 64–84.

Lewes, F. M. M. and Mennell, S. J. (1976) *Leisure, Culture and Local Government,* University of Exeter.

Long, J. and Hecock, R. (1984) *Leisure, Tourism and Social Change,* Centre for Leisure Research, Dunfermline College of Physical Education.

Martin, W. H. and Mason, S. (1980) *Broad Patterns of Leisure Expenditure,* London: Sports Council and SSRC.

Owens, P. L. (1984) 'Rural leisure and recreation research: a retrospective evaluation', *Progress in Human Geography,* 8: 157–88.

Patmore, J. A. (1983) *Recreation and Resources: Leisure Patterns and Leisure Places,* Oxford: Blackwell.

Pigram, J. (1983) *Outdoor Recreation and Resource Management,* Beckenham: Croom Helm.

Rapoport, R. and Rapoport, R. N. (1975) *Leisure and the Family Life Cycle,* London: Routledge & Kegan Paul.

Roberts, K. (1978) *Contemporary Society and the Growth of Leisure,* London: Longman.

Rodgers, H. B. (1969) 'Leisure and recreation', *Urban Studies,* 6: 368–84.

Rogers, A. W. (1977) 'Second homes in England and Wales: a spatial view', in Coppock, J. T. (ed.) *Second Homes: Curse or Blessing?,* Oxford: Pergamon, pp. 85–102.

Seeley, I. H. (1973) *Outdoor Recreation and the Urban Environment,* London: Macmillan.

Sheail, J. (1981) *Rural Conservation in Inter-war Britain,* Oxford: Clarendon Press.

Sillitoe, K. (1969) *Planning for Leisure,* London: HMSO.

Torkildsen, G. (1983) *Leisure and Recreation Management,* London: E. & F. N. Spon.

Travis, A. S. *et al.* (1981) *The Role of Central Government in Relation to the Provision of Leisure Services in England and Wales,* Research Memorandum No. 86, Centre for Urban and Regional Studies, University of Birmingham.

Tunbridge, J. E. (1981) 'Conservation trusts as geographic agents: their impact upon landscape, townscape and land use', *Transactions, Institute of British Geographers,* NS6: 103–25.

Wall, G. (1972) 'Socio-economic variations in pleasure trip patterns: the case of Hull car owners', *Transactions, Institute of British Geographers,* 57: 45–58.

Williams, A. and Shaw, G. (1988) *Tourism and Economic Development: Western European Experiences,* London: Belhaven Press.

## FURTHER READING

The most readable introduction to the geography of recreation and leisure in the UK by a geographer is Patmore, J. A. (1983) *Recreation and Resources: Leisure Patterns and Leisure Places,* Oxford: Blackwell, but another interesting, and rather different, sociological perspective is contained in Roberts, K. (1978) *Contemporary Society and the Growth of Leisure,* London: Longman. A somewhat dated, but surprisingly attractive, survey of the subject is to be found in the Second Report of the House of Lords Select Committee on Sport and Leisure, published in 1973. If you want to find out more about recreation management in the UK from the point of view of the local authority providers, then read Torkildsen, G. *Leisure and*

*Recreation Management,* London: E. & F. N. Spon. There are two very good reviews of the literature in Owens, P. L. (1984) 'Rural leisure and recreation research: a retrospective evaluation', *Progress in Human Geography,* 8: 157–88 and Kirby, A. (1985) 'Leisure as commodity: the role of the state in leisure provision', *Progress in Human Geography,* 9: 64–84. There is also the comprehensive series of 'state of the art' reviews of leisure and recreation published jointly by the Sports Council and the Economic and Social Research Council since 1979. For tourism, a comprehensive series of readings is contained in Williams, A. and Shaw, G. (1988) *Tourism and Economic Development: Western European Experiences,* London: Belhaven Press. Finally, the *Journal of Leisure Research* contains many articles on specific aspects of recreation and leisure in the UK.

# 15 Human occupance and the physical environment

*David K. C. Jones*

Human occupance of the United Kingdom has not been achieved without cost to society. Early, pre-industrial populations were forced to overcome often severe constraints imposed by difficult terrain conditions (steep slopes, windswept uplands, swampy flood-prone lowlands), dense forest, unpredictable weather and disease (including malaria). Although it can be argued that the constraints imposed by the physical environment on human activity have relaxed through time, because of the application of science and technology, extreme events (natural hazards) continue to impose costs on society in terms of death and injury, but more significantly as economic losses resulting from physical damage, loss of production, and the dislocation of economic activity. Indeed, it has to be recognized that increased technological ability does not necessarily make society less prone to hazard losses and in certain circumstances can result in growing vulnerability and escalating loss potentials.

It is not a one-way process, however. Ten thousand years of human occupancy have resulted in profound alterations to the physical and biological elements of the UK environment. These changes were slow and modest at first but gathered in pace and severity as the population grew, organization improved, and technology evolved. Developments in agriculture, industrialization, urbanization and the evolution of transport networks have all contributed, directly and indirectly, to modifications of landforms, atmospheric composition and behaviour, water movements, and vegetation cover, ranging in scale from the subtle to the extreme. Thus, the changes wrought in the last few decades, no matter how conspicuous and dramatic, must nevertheless be viewed in their true perspective as merely representing the most recent phase in a long history of alteration.

The best documented impacts have concerned the effects of increasing human domination on the floral and faunal components of the ecosystem. This process, sometimes referred to as the 'diminution of nature', is most obvious in the widely developed and wholly artificial urban environment or 'townscape', but it is important to recognize that virtually none of the rural landscape can be described as 'natural', except for those 'wildscapes' that survive in the remoter highlands and islands. The contemporary country-side is largely the product of culture and bears the imprint of a wide range of human activities; the varied agricultural landscapes that make up 'farmscape' have evolved through marsh drainage, forest clearance and the variable impact of the Enclosure Act. Change continues today, most particularly in the expansion of housing and the removal of copses, hedges (currently reduced by 6,400km per year) and heathland to provide larger, more efficient cultivation units. The ecology has changed as habitats have been altered (see chapter 17). Species diversification through the purpose-ful introduction of exotic trees, shrubs, plants, birds and animals (e.g. rabbits in the twelfth century), accidental releases (coypu, mink), and through the development of domesticated strains has, in part, been counteracted over the last few decades by the spread of expansive monoculture, pollution and the application of chemical fertilizers and pesticides. Although some species have adapted well to these ecosystem changes and prospered (e.g. the herring gull, house sparrow, starling, pigeon, collared dove, rabbit, fox, nettle) or have been actively encouraged (e.g. conifers in plantations), others have suffered serious decline or extinction (various raptors, Dartford Warbler, Smoothsnake, Otter, and numerous plants, butterflies, and moths). Such examples of indigenous species decline, which are frequently highlighted in calls for nature conservation measures, thus merely represent some of the most obvious repercussions of human interaction with the environment.

Anthropogenic environmental change affects all aspects of the physical environment: land, air and water. In fact, changes to any one can result in a response in the other systems. For example, the progressive changes in land use from original forest to the contemporary agricultural and urban environments have resulted in significant changes in surface conditions (roughness, water balance, thermal character) and thereby altered the micro-climate and run-off (drainage) characteristics, the most significant responses being increases in soil erosion, water pollution (suspended solids), river sedimentation and flooding. Evidence for anthropogenic induced soil erosion associated with early forest clearance, a process no doubt exacerbated by the arrival of the plough about 5,000 years ago, exists in the widespread occurrence of shallow, immature or truncated soils in upland areas, in the fact that most lowland floodplains are underlain by thick sequences of fine-grained alluvium laid-down during the last 9,000 years, and in the sedimentary sequences preserved in lakes which often reveal rapid increases in deposition at various times between 5,000 and 1,000 years ago.

Similarly, all surface changes must have altered the thermal, hydrologi-cal and dynamic properties of the overlying air, and the addition of pollutants considerably changed its composition. The most obvious reper-cussions of these changes were the creation of 'urban climates' with their distinctive 'heat islands', 'dust domes', and generally poor visibility conditions due to the prevalence of smoke fogs. Such features are of considerable antiquity. London is considered to have grown large enough to modify the local climate by the mid-thirteenth century, largely due to use of sea-coal, first in forges and then in lime kilns. John Evelyn remarked in 1661 that 'The weary traveller, at many miles distance, sooner smells than sees the city to which he repairs', an observation later supported by Gilbert White who noted the 'dingy smokey' appearance of the air in dry weather as far downwind as Selbourne, Hampshire. The characters in the novels of Charles Dickens were frequently depicted groping around the dense yellow fogs that plagued the capital, or 'London particulars' as they were known, and Byron referred to a 'huge dun cupola' over the city. Victorian London came to be affectionately known as 'The Smoke'. The industrial revolution led to particularly marked alterations, with widespread and intense air pollution in the industrialized coalfield areas, such as the Black Country, the Potteries, and South Yorkshire. What has changed during the twentieth century is that the urban areas have grown dramatically and altered in form, while at the same time pollution emissions have changed in composition (see chapter 16) with a decline in the traditional constituent (smoke) and its replacement by sulphur dioxide ($SO_2$) and motor exhaust gases. Thus, human activities have continued to modify the atmosphere with the result that urban climates, in particular, continue to evolve.

While such indirect or involuntary changes may be of great interest and significance, the impact of direct or purposeful changes to the Earth's surface are visually much more impressive. Human-made landforms of greatly differing form and antiquity are widespread. Created for an enormous variety of purposes, they range from the innumerable small pits that pock the landscape (37,000 recorded in Norfolk alone) created through the removal of a few cubic metres of material and now largely preserved as small ponds and copses, to enormous 'long-life' extraction sites where removal is measured in tens of millions of tonnes. Particularly impressive are the Norfolk Broads, a collection of twenty-five freshwater lakes created by the removal of 25.5 million cubic metres of material in peat diggings prior to 1300AD. Ancient depositional features range from the thousands of small prehistoric burial mounds (tumuli) and earthworks, to Silbury Hill (40m), Wiltshire, the tallest prehistoric mound in Europe. Equally impressive are the ridge and furrow landscapes of the English midlands which are thought to represent the survival of the medieval strip-field pattern. A survey of North Buckinghamshire in the late 1950s revealed that this patterning still covered 343km$^2$, or 28 per cent of the surface, each square kilometre of disturbance representing the movement of 62,500m$^3$ of earth. However, such legacies of past sculpturing pale into insignificance when compared with the products of the industrial revolution. The expansion of the railway network in the mid- and late-nineteenth century led to prodigious anthropogeomorphic activity, including the creation of earthworks of such magnitude that Ruskin was moved to speak of 'your railway mounds, vaster than the walls of Babylon'. Even these were to be eclipsed in scale by the thousands of colliery spoil heaps that grew to dominate the surface of the coalfields. Spoil production expanded dramatically from the middle nineteenth century as growing demand for coal led to the development of mechanical extraction techniques and exploitation of deeper and thinner seams, and the employment of mechanical tipping techniques facilitated the creation of conical heaps more than 50m high.

Human impact has not been confined to sculpturing the existing land surface. Coastal marshes and fens, as well as the lower reaches of most river valleys, were reclaimed from the sea by the construction of dykes and levées, so that hundreds of square kilometres of land could be brought under cultivation. The Somerset Levels and Romney Marsh typify a widespread phenomenon which began 800 years ago and reached its most dramatic scale in the Fens, where $153km^2$ had been reclaimed by 1241 and a further $500km^2$ added since 1640. Further modifications were achieved through the excavation of harbour basins and the dredging of channels, much of the material being used locally to extend the land area.

It is against this background of long-term and extensive environmental modification that the significance of recent and contemporary changes have to be assessed. Population growth, technological development and the changing patterns of urbanization and economic activity have ensured that human occupance has continued to exert modifying influences on the physical environment. The most important differences have been the growing appreciation of the magnitude of impacts, both past and present, and the recognition of possible adverse ramifications of such changes. This has stemmed from the growth in environmental awareness which has its roots in the 1930s, although the popular movement has only really flourished since the late 1960s. As a consequence of this interest in, and concern for, the natural environment there has been growth in environmental monitoring and some development of limited management strategies which seek to minimize the most harmful aspects of human-environment interaction. Some of these are described in the following sections. But first it is necessary to consider briefly the significance of natural hazards to the United Kingdom society and the measures that have been undertaken to minimze their impact.

## NATURAL HAZARD IMPACTS

The United Kingdom is not an environment prone to natural hazard impacts; risk assessments indicate that loss of life is much more likely to occur through industrial or transportational activity than due to so-called 'natural' events. Nevertheless, and despite technological development, natural and quasi-natural hazards continue to cause costs to society. The vast majority of cost-inducing events are either directly or indirectly due to extremes of the weather; high winds, dense fogs, intense cold, blizzards, drought, landslides and river and coastal flooding. The repeated occurrence of such impacts has resulted in management decisions ranging from no-action (loss-bearing) due to poor perception of risk, financial constraints or lack of technical knowledge, through a wide variety of adjustments which seek to limit the impact of similar events in the future. Such adjustments can be broadly subdivided into two groups; structural (engineering) solutions which seek to contain/control the hazard or to protect the threatened population and infrastructure (dams, levées, flood walls); and non-structural (planning) solutions which seek to reduce hazard impact potential by means of spatial, physical or financial adjustments (land-use zonation, forecasting, insurance, disaster relief, and so on).

Chosen responses to natural hazard impacts are variable and largely dependent on perception of risk, itself a complex function of hazard (size and character), probability of occurrence and scale of expected losses. Recent studies have shown that risk assessment by individuals and groups tends to result in risks being subdivided into two broad groups 'acceptable' or 'tolerable' risks (e.g. road accidents, lung cancer from cigarettes) and 'unacceptable' risks (e.g. radiation from nuclear power stations, depletion of the ozone shield), a perceptual subdivision often made irrespective of the statistical probabilities. Natural hazard impacts generally tend to be placed in the 'unacceptable' category by the majority of United Kingdom citizens, because of the prevailing view that accumulated technological ability in an advanced society should be sufficient to minimize (control) the impact of dynamic events in the environmental systems. This attitude partly explains why various protective measures have been adopted following recent large-scale impacts, but at the same time fails to appreciate that hazard losses are as much the result of society's vulnerability as nature's violence.

Over the last fifty years, the United Kingdom has suffered a number of costly and often visually impressive hazard impacts: severe flooding, particularly in the English West Country (1952, 1968), the Scottish Moray area (1956, 1970), and Wales (1987), as well as along the Rivers Eden, Severn, Thames and Trent; a number of severe droughts which can be ranked in terms of their agricultural impact as 1976, 1934, 1944, 1938, 1974, 1964, and 1943; blizzards and long snow-lie in the winters of 1939/40, 1941/2, 1946/7, 1950/1 (upland areas), 1954/5, 1962/3. 1969/70, 1978/9, 1985/6/7; wind damage, especially in 1950 (eastern England), 1965 (Yorkshire), 1968 (Scotland, twenty killed), and 1987 (southern England, nineteen killed); and frequent coastal storm damage. However, there have only been eight events of sufficient magnitude to qualify as natural disasters. These are the Exmoor storm and resulting Lynmouth Flood of 15 August 1952 (thirty-four killed, total cost £9 million at currently prevailing prices, including damage to ninety houses and 130 cars); the London smogs of 5–9 December 1952, 3–5 December 1957 and 3–7 December 1962, which caused the premature deaths of 12,000, 1,000, and 750 Londoners respectively; the East Coast Floods of the night of 31 January/1 February 1953, which inundated 850km$^2$, killing 307 people and causing estimated losses of £40 million, including 24,000 houses damaged; the Aberfan landslide disaster of 21 October 1966, when a spoil heap perched 150m above the South Wales colliery village suffered slope failure, the resultant enormous mudflow consuming several houses and a school, and claimed 144 lives; the drought of 1975–6 which resulted in major losses to agriculture, 584,000 outdoor fires – some of which caused widespread destruction to forest and heathland – and some £100 million damage to over 20,000 houses and buildings due to subsidence, often because of extraction of moisture by tree roots; and recently, the intense storm of 16 October 1987 when winds gusting up to 166kph blew down power-lines, telephone lines and 15 million trees, thereby virtually paralysing south-east England for twenty-four hours and causing costs in excess of £1,000 million.

These events may appear small when compared with the losses inflicted by natural hazards elsewhere in the globe (e.g. the 1988 Armenian Earthquake) or the costs sustained during wartime, or even with United Kingdom road casualty figures (5,600 killed in 1988 bringing the total to near 300,000 in the last fifty-years). Nevertheless, the scale of local devastation and/or the broader economic ramifications are more than comparable with those resulting from the most severe anthropogenic disasters such as major mining accidents, the explosions at Flixborough (1974) and Platform 'Piper Alpha' (1988), the Zeebrugge ferry tragedy (1988), Clapham rail crash (1988) and Lockerbie air disaster (1989), the 1981 inner-city riots, or the Hillsborough Stadium tragedy (1989). Thus, the shock produced by these natural disasters, reinforced by the prevailing view that natural hazards pose 'unacceptable' risks which should be minimized by an advanced technological society, stimulated investigations which resulted in management decisions of considerable environmental significance. The 1953 smog led to the establishment of the Beaver Committee whose Report (1954) identified the importance of smoke in generating toxic and persistent urban fogs and directly resulted in the Clean Air Acts of 1956 and 1968 (see chapter 16). The East Coast Floods of 1953 led to the Waverley Committee report (1954) and investment in a wide variety of coastal protection measures including the Thames Barrier Project. The Aberfan disaster provided a major stimulus for the lowering of colliery spoil heaps, thereby leading to great decreases in visual intrusiveness and spontaneous combustion. Increasing awareness of the overall importance of flooding as the main cost-inducing hazard has resulted in the widespread implementation of flood alleviation projects, albeit on a somewhat *ad hoc* and piecemeal basis.

Finally, the growing recognition of the significance of the climatic factor has resulted in improvements in the accuracy of weather forecasts and attempts to achieve better ways of communicating prognostications. The latter have involved developments in the media, the establishment of local forecasting offices, and the preparation of forecasts for specific purposes, including such hazards as adverse road conditions, severe weather, flooding and tidal surges. However, despite significant advances, forecasting accuracy is still bedevilled by difficulties stemming from the complexity of atmospheric processes and dynamics, and the fact that hazardous weather impacts can be produced by phenomena of vastly differing scale, ranging in size from a 2,500 km wide depression with frontal systems, to a small short-lived storm. Thus, the attainment of the necessary predictive precision, with respect to scale, intensity, timing and location, is a goal that is extremely difficult to achieve, and even the switch from analogue forecasting techniques (using past patterns of weather activity as a guide to the future development of synoptic situations) to quantitative computer-based numerical methods, combined with the increased employment of satellite imagery, has only recently improved the detail of short-range (24 hour) and medium range (1–7 day) forecasts. Despite the Meteorological Office's optimism that the acquisition of new and extremely powerful computers in August 1981, together with new methods of analysis, would result in dramatic improvements in forecasting accuracy, the failure to issue adequate warning of the October 1987 storm has revealed that many scientific, technical and organizational problems remain to be resolved. As a consequence, many 'weather-sensitive' industries such as transport, agriculture, and building and construction continue to suffer heavy costs through production loss, delay and the inefficient utilization of resources, while damage, destruction, injury and loss of life will still be produced by the unexpected or unanticipated occurrence of infrequent high magnitude events.

Despite technological developments in investigating, monitoring and limiting the impact of natural hazards, there is no evidence that hazard costs have declined over the past fifty years. In fact, the reverse is probably true although, as with other advanced nations, the situation is a complex one. A reduction in loss of life due to increased awareness and better warning procedures has been offset by rising economic losses, for four main reasons. First, population growth and redistribution have caused pressure on land and resulted in the siting of an ever increasing range of hazard-sensitive activities in hazard-prone zones (e.g. floodplains – see next section), despite the post-war growth of planning controls, thereby increasing the scale of potential impacts. Second, the growing complexity and interdependence of commercial and industrial activity has meant that damage and disruption at one location can have massive repercussions elsewhere. Third, technological development sometimes leads to increased vulnerability, especially in the transport sector where the significance of climatic hazards has increased with motorway construction and railway electrification. Finally, there is evidence that human activity has altered environmental conditions so as actually to increase the frequency and scale of certain hazardous events, such as smogs and floods.

# RIVER FLOODING

Despite the efforts of a succession of drainage and river management authorities, flooding continues to be a feature of both summer and winter. Prolonged precipitation and rapid snowmelt are the main causes of high winter discharges, often resulting in widespread flooding over a large region. Examples include the catastrophic snowmelt floods of March 1947 – which seriously affected much of Wales, the south-west, the midlands and the Thames Valley, and resulted in prolonged inundation of the Fenlands – the West Country and Welsh floods of 1960 and 1987, and the widespread flooding of 1968. Responses to this hazard have ranged across a variety of structural and non-structural adjustments, including the deepening, widening, straightening, and regrading of channels (e.g. the Avon through Bath), channel maintenance, and construction of levées and floodwalls along low-lying tidal reaches, the employment of floodplain zonation so that the areas most liable to repeated inundation have land uses with low loss potentials (e.g. recreation), the construction of large flood-relief channels to protect those urban areas particularly susceptible to flooding (e.g. Exeter, Spalding, Walthamstow), and the building of reservoirs. While no dams have been constructed purely for flood control purposes, there are several multi-purpose reservoirs with both water supply and floodwater storage functions. The impact of these reservoirs on flooding depends on the available storage capacity at the time of flood generation, and the volume of the flood wave. Investigations have shown that the scale of reduction of flood discharges increases with increasing reservoir size, but diminishes with increasing size of floodwave. Thus, dams may reduce the volume of frequent floods by up to 70 per cent but have little effect on infrequent high-magnitude events. The application of combinations of adjustments to rivers particularly prone to flooding, such as the Dee, Exe, Severn and Trent, have resulted in considerable modifications to both their physical and discharge characteristics.

Nevertheless, flooding continues to have a significant economic impact, despite investment in flood protection schemes. The reasons for this are complex. First, the true costs of flooding are unknown and published estimates are considered conservative. Second, structural measures have been unevenly applied across the country. Third, the cost-effectiveness of protection measures diminishes with increasing size of flood. Consequently, structures are rarely designed to protect against discharges with recurrence intervals greater than 100 years (i.e. flows likely to be equalled or exceeded *on average* once every 100 years). Thus, there will always be floods whose magnitude exceeds the capacity of the provided protection measures. Fourth, a significant proportion of floodplain inhabitants and planners still have poor perceptions of flood hazard. Last, and probably most important, pressures on space have resulted in the continued development of floodplains (e.g. the Trent at Nottingham, the Thames near

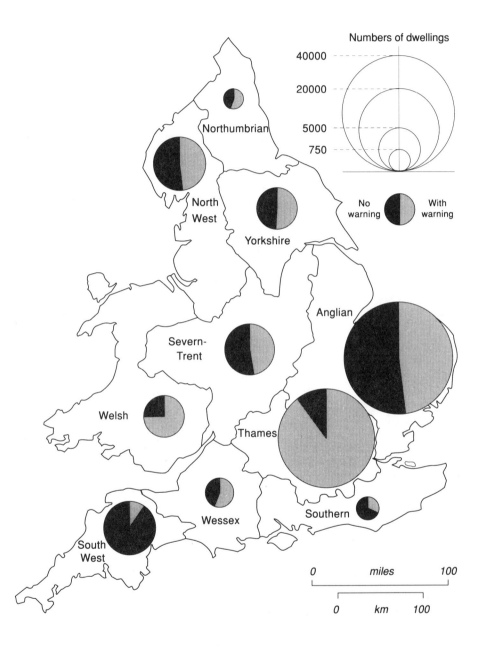

*Figure 15.1* The number of dwellings in England and Wales within zones affected by 1:50 to 1:100 year flood levels
*Source:* redrawn from Penning – Rowsell, E. C., and Handmer, J. W. (1988) 'Flood hazard management in Britain: a changing scene', *Geographical Journal,* 154: 209–220, figure 1

Maidenhead) so that zonation policies have only been poorly applied. All of these factors have tended to counterbalance the benefits stemming from improved monitoring, better warning systems, and the increasing use of predictive computer-based models. Indeed, up to 450,000 people are thought to live in areas liable to flooding with a recurrence interval of 50–100 years, many without the benefit of a flood-warning service (figure 15.1). Loss-bearing and dependence on relief funds are still common responses to floods, although the relatively recent increased use of flood insurance cover has somewhat improved the situation. It was not until 1929 that storm damage – but not flooding – was covered, and only after the widespread 1960 floods did pressure by the Ministry of Housing and Local Government and the Building Societies overcome reluctance on the part of insurance companies, and result in the encouragement of flood insurance.

The second main type of river flood, the flash flood, is the product of rapid runoff caused by intense precipitation, usually during the summer months; summer storms often result in over 100mm of rainfall in a few hours over a localized area (figure 15.2) and account for the surprising fact that August has the worst record for catastrophic floods, closely followed by July. The magnitude of the resultant flooding is dependent on a number of variables relating to precipitation (area, duration, intensity, total), antecedent moisture conditions, and drainage basin characteristics (geology, land use, network shape, topography, channel slope). Thus, the most dramatic rain storm in recent history, the Hampstead storm of 14 August 1975 (figure 15.2c) which deposited 2,000 million gallons (8 million tonnes) of water (up to 170mm of rain) over an extremely localized area of North London in under three hours, only caused local problems of surface ponding and flooding of basements, mainly because much of the water was quickly transported away by stormwater sewers. By contrast, similar storms on small impervious clay catchments can result in severe, albeit short-lived, flooding (e.g. Dorset Stour, 31 May 1979). However, the most spectacular and destructive floods occur when heavy rains fall on upland regions with short, steep catchments. The most notable recent examples include the Moray (north-east Scotland) floods of 1956 and 1970, the Mendip floods of 1931 and 1968, and the Somerset and Devonshire floods of 1952 and 1968. The last mentioned includes the catastrophic Lynmouth floods of 15–16 August 1952, when up to 300mm of rain fell on Exmoor in 24 hours (figure 15.2b), resulting in such feats of erosion by the diminutive River Lyn that fallen trees and boulders created temporary dams behind bridges, the breaching of which greatly intensified the devastating nature of the floods downstream. Such extreme floods are difficult to forecast because the storms that create them are usually the product of localized topographic or urban conditions. The short response times of the rivers (basin lag) means that warnings either cannot be given or fail to reach the entire population at risk, and emergency services are often hampered by inadequate preparation time. Planning for such events

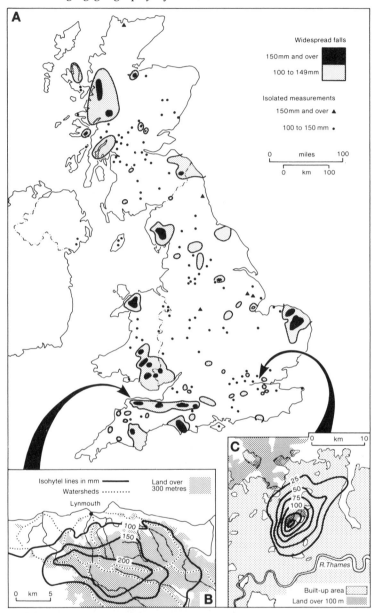

*Figure 15.2* Rainstorm hazard in the UK
(a) Distribution of daily rainfalls in excess of 100mm, 1863–1960
(b) Isohyets of Exmoor Storm, 15 August 1952
(c) Isohyets of Hampstead Storm, 14 August 1975
*Sources:*
(a) Redrawn from Newson, M. D. (1975) *Flooding and the Flood Hazard in the UK,* Oxford: Oxford University Press, figure 1
(b) From Ward, R. (1978) 'Exmoor', *Floods,* London: Macmillan, figure 2.3
(c) From Atkinson, B. W. 'Discussion', *Geographical Journal,* 142: 73

is also impracticable because their rarity (long recurrence intervals) means that there are few available comparable records to use as a guide, while the structural adjustments required to cope with potentially very high magnitude floods are prohibitively expensive and totally non-cost effective. For example, the Lynmouth floods had a calculated recurrence interval of 50,000 years, for the diminutive River Lyn had swollen to a size equivalent to the Thames in spate at Teddington and in so doing moved more than 100,000 tonnes of boulders, some weighing up to 7.5 tonnes. Such catastrophic events will continue to happen through the chance combination of factors and, as the past record of intense storms shows (figure 15.2a), could occur virtually anywhere. Thus, the only feasible loss-reduction solution is to concentrate on saving lives and minimizing damage to property by using sophisticated monitoring techniques, such as radar and interrogable rain-gauge and river-level systems, and developing efficient warning and evacuation systems.

Although the majority of floods are generated by 'natural' mechanisms, human activity has been of considerable significance in changing the discharge characteristics of rivers and, under certain circumstances, has contributed to flood generation. Urbanization has had a particularly great impact, for the sustained rapid rate of land conversion, which reached 26,000 ha per annum in the early 1970s, resulted in a wide variety of hydrological consequences (figure 15.3). Erosion during construction can cause suspended sediment concentrations to rise by factors of 2 to 10, and sometimes up to 100, the resultant sedimentation downstream choking channels thereby increasing flood risk and raising channel maintenance costs. Once completed, the urban areas provide radically different surface conditions, for buildings, roads and integrated stormwater and sewer systems cause reduced interception and infiltration to soil and ground waters, and the rapid runoff of an increased proportion of precipitation. As a consequence, even partially urbanized catchments show increased annual water yields, higher peak flows and more rapid responses to precipitation events (reduction in basin lag-times). This increase in flashiness is particularly apparent for summer floods on small catchments, which may experience up to an 11-fold increase in peak discharge, thereby contributing to the widely reported enlargement of channels downstream of urban areas. However, the urban influence is only apparent on small and medium-sized floods, for there are few indications that discharges with recurrence intervals in excess of twenty years are affected, possibly because high flows result in a 'throttling' (holding back) of water in urban stormwater sewers.

Urbanization is not merely associated with locally increased flooding, for water supply and effluent disposal can produce significant changes in river regime. Reductions in discharge result from reservoir construction, direct abstraction and the drying-up of springs due to the over-exploitation of underground aquifers. In the case of the Chalk beneath London, water table lowering amounted to as much as 60m in the period 1875–1965.

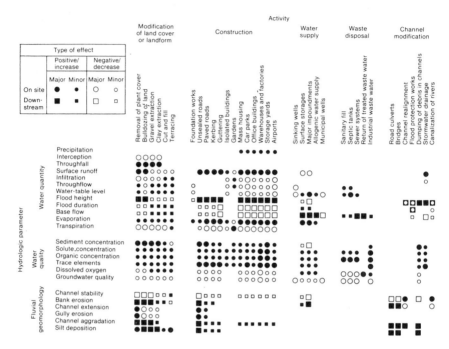

*Figure 15.3* The potential range of changes to hydrologic parameters produced by urbanization

*Source:* Redrawn from Douglas, I. (1976) 'Urban Hydrology', *Geographical Journal,* 142: 65–72, figure 1

However, growing concern about underground water resources has resulted in recent careful regulation of extraction. This, together with the employment of artificial recharge schemes (e.g. near Newbury), has halted the trend in many cases and is actually causing some water tables to rise again. Conversely, increased base-flow can result from the release of large volumes of water redistributed by piped water supply systems. The scale of such allogenic water supplies is most apparent in the case of Birmingham where water, derived from the upper Wye in Wales and piped to the midlands, is discharged into the Trent catchment after use. Many rivers appear to have a base-flow that is predominantly effluent, the River Tame being 90 per cent effluent in its 95 per cent duration flow.

Anthropogenic influences on flooding are not restricted to urbanization, for recent agricultural developments have had important hydrological consequences. The expansion of arable cultivation, the enlargement of fields by the removal of hedges and copses, the use of machinery which compacts soil thereby reducing infiltration, and the massive post-war growth in the use of tile-drains, have all contributed to the increasingly rapid transport of larger and larger proportions of precipitation from slopes into channel systems. Thus, the flashiness of most streams and small rivers in lowland Britain has been slightly increased during the last half century.

## COASTAL FLOODING

A different flood-hazard threat exists along the east coast of England. Here, progressive downwarping of the North Sea Basin, together with the global (eustatic) rise in sea-level (c.1.2 mm per annum) and changes in tidal configuration due to dredging, dumping, and coastal reclamation, have all resulted in significant rates of sea-level rise. Analysis of tide-gauge records in south-east England indicates that sea-level is currently rising at 140–340mm per 100 years. The figure is even greater along the Lower Thames because of increased tidal amplitudes and additional local subsidence. This situation of gradually rising high-water levels is exacerbated by the occurrence of storm surges generated by deep depressions over the North Sea. Sea-surface levels can be raised over 2 m through the combined effects of pressure reduction (305 mm for each 30 mb) and the piling of water against the East Coast by strong on-shore winds. Coastal defences become severely stressed when these surges coincide with particularly high (Spring) tides, and can be over-topped and breached by high waves generated by the strong winds. The risks are even greater in estuaries, for any reduction in wave-heights resulting from sheltering is more than compensated for by the raising of surge level due to funnelling, and the water surface may be dramatically raised still further if a surge coincides with a period of high river flow into the estuary. As extensive coastal tracts bordering the North Sea stand at elevations little above mean sea-level, the potential for disastrous inundations is great. The economic consequences of such an event could be enormous and include the saline contamination of agricultural land and groundwater, the swamping of residential areas, the paralysis of water-side industries, the dislocation of communications, and the severe disruption of activity in London.

Although there are documented records of local coastal flooding along the East Coast dating back to 1236, including at least seven inundations that were of disastrous proportions, the dramatic events of the night of 31 January/1 February 1953 were to have particularly great repercussions in terms of risk perception and the implementation of remedial measures. Storm-force winds generated by a deep depression (minimum 968 mb) drifting south-eastwards across the North Sea caused a surge up to 2.5m high to pass southwards down the East Coast. Fortunately, the passage of the surge did not quite coincide with the progression of only a moderately high tide and the rivers were not in spate. Nevertheless, 850 square kilometres were inundated (figure 15.4a) along nearly 500 km of coastline

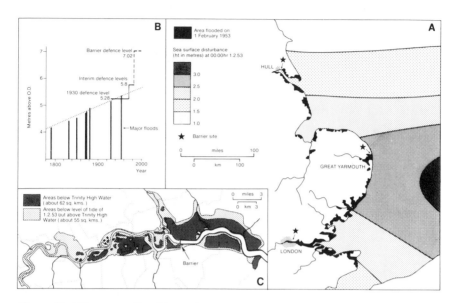

*Figure 15.4* East coast flood hazard
(a) The 1953 flood
(b) Rising surge levels and defences along the lower Thames
(c) The hazard zones in London
*Sources:*
(a) Redrawn from Ward, R. (1978) *Floods,* London: Macmillan, figure 4.4
(b) and (c) Data derived from various GLC leaflets

(the so-called Isle of Thanet reverted to a true island for a short time), 24,000 houses were swamped, cement works, factories and power-stations on Lower Thameside were inundated and brought to a standstill, and 307 people were drowned. The subsequent committee of enquiry focused attention on the factors causing flooding and stressed that the situation would get progressively more serious due to regional subsidence. The initial reaction was to strengthen and raise the level of sea-defences (levées, walls, etc.) from Yorkshire to Kent to allow them to withstand 1953 surge levels, a task that took fourteen years (1954–68) and cost £55 million. The new defences were completed none too soon, for although the initial recurrence interval calculated for the 1953 surge level was 200 years, the 1953 heights have subsequently been locally equalled or exceeded on three occasions – 29 September 1969, 3 January 1976 and 11/12 January 1978. The 1978 event involved a surge of up to 1.73 m coinciding with the highest tide of the fortnightly cycle and produced levels which were locally well in excess of those recorded in 1953. In this instance, flooding was most severe around the Wash and in Lincolnshire (King's Lynn, Wisbech and Cleethorpes), with damage estimated at £200 million but only one death. The relatively high damage costs indicate that, although the defences were

much stronger and restricted flooding, there has been minimal implementation of land-use zonation in association with the engineering works.
Thus, residential, commercial and industrial activity continues to be
located on the high-risk, low ground behind the defences, in the erroneous
belief that such areas are entirely safe because they are protected (the so-
called 'levée syndrome'). On the other hand, the low death-toll reflects the
improved forecasting and warning systems that now operate and the better
disciplined evacuation procedures that stem from greater hazard awareness
and practice. Particularly significant in this context is the Storm Tide
Warning Service established in the Meteorological Office at Bracknell,
which delivers phased warnings; an 'alert' 12 hours before expected high-
tide (on average about 100 per annum), followed by 'confirmations' (or
cancellation) at 4 hours (20 per annum) and 'danger warnings' at 1–2 hours
(5 per annum).

The protection of the coast represents a costly but technically less
difficult problem than that of defending the land flanking the Lower
Thames (figure 15.4c). No less than 61.4 km² of London lies below Trinity
High Water Mark (+3.48 m OD) and 116 km² below the 1953 flood level
(+5.48 m OD). Fortunately, the 1953 surge only affected 1,100 houses in
east London because vast volumes of water had escaped from the confines
of the Thames Estuary through the numerous breaches along the Essex
shore. A repeat of the 1953 surge, but with no such water escape, would be
catastrophic for the capital city, with a currently estimated damage
potential of over £5,000 million. Unfortunately, the area at risk is growing
steadily due to the combination of local and regional subsidence, eustatic
rise and, most importantly, changing tidal configuration. Thus, although
the medium-tide level at Tower Pier is rising at 433 ± 82 mm/100 years,
only slightly more than the outer estuary figure of 344 ± 70 mm/100 years
recorded at Southend, the high tide level at Tower Pier is rising more
rapidly (744 ± 116 mm/100 years) due to the mean tidal amplitude growing
at 344 ± 70 mm/100 years.

The management response has been to construct a flood barrier in the
Long Reach at Silvertown, near Woolwich, and to raise flood defences
downstream of this structure. Defences upstream through Central London
to Teddington Weir had already been raised to +5.28 m in 1930–5,
following the disastrous Thames Flood of 1938 (+5.15 m at London
Bridge, fourteen drowned). They were further raised to +5.80 m between
April 1971 and December 1972 as an interim protection measure (removed
in 1986), and a movable barrier constructed at Bow Creek to avoid raising
banks along the highly industrialized Lea Valley. However, the main
protection is derived from the movable drum barrier across the Thames
designed to give protection against the 1,000-year flood (+7.2 m OD). The
choice of the Long Reach site was governed by the need for firm
foundations (Chalk) and a straight section of river to ease navigation
problems, a need that has subsequently declined with the closure of the

Port of London. Work was begun in 1974 and completed in November 1983, over two years late because of technical problems and labour disputes. The cost had escalated dramatically due to inflation and spiralling labour costs, the 1960 estimate of £10 million rising to £242 million in 1978 and £500 million in 1983. The total cost of works, including the raising of downstream defences to Southend and the construction of a barrier across Dartford Creek, came to about £700 million.

Continuation of present physical trends, plus the additional rise in sea-level anticipated through carbon dioxide ($CO_2$) induced climatic warming (the Greenhouse Effect) currently estimated at between 0.5 and 2 m by 2070 AD makes it inevitable that even higher defences and more ambitious schemes will eventually be required. The Thames Barrier is currently raised less than once a year, but by 2030 AD it will be about ten times yearly and consideration will have to be given to establishing a new line of defence. Elsewhere, sea defences and river levées will have to be raised and more movable barriers constructed across inlets similar to that recently completed across the River Hull at Hull. The number of people threatened by sea-flooding, currently estimated at 200,000, will have undoubtedly increased, thereby raising the perceived need for additional defence measures. The key question is whether such measures will ever be cost effective.

## HUMAN OCCUPANCE AND CLIMATE

The interactions between human society and climate are complex and continuously evolving. As has already been mentioned, weather pheno-mena are the major cost-inducing hazard impacts that affect the United Kingdom economy. Heavy precipitation, atypical prolonged snowfall (south-east England in 1985–6 and 1986–7), unusually intense cold (−28°C, Kent, February 1985) and drought (1976) have all extracted their 'natural tax' in recent years. Rainfall is probably the most widespread problem and causes heavy costs to the agricultural and construction sectors. But the most problematic hazard is the wind. The British Isles are amongst the windiest areas on the globe and gale damage is currently estimated to affect an average of 230,000 buildings a year, resulting in costs of £15–20 million. High magnitude–low frequency winds achieve much greater impacts. The January 1953 gale blew down 5 per cent of the total standing value of coniferous timber in the United Kingdom (figure 15.5); the January 1968 gale damaged 340,000 houses in the Glasgow area; and the gale of 2 January 1976 caused widespread damage throughout England, Wales and Ireland. More recently, the storm of 16 October 1987 devastated much of south-east England and represented the most severe event since the 'greatest storm on record' (26 November 1703) which killed about 8,000 people. This time there was a mere nineteen deaths, although the damage and destruction were enormous as trees in full leaf, with root holds weakened by the saturated soil, were blown down wholesale by the violent

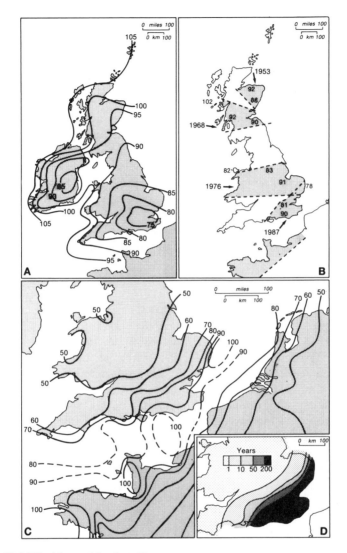

*Figure 15.5* Wind hazard in the UK
(a) gust speeds in knots with recurrence period of 50 years
(b) Regions affected by catastrophic damage to forests since 1945
(c) Highest reported gusts (knots) for storm of 16 October 1987
(d) Approximate return period (recurrence interval) of highest gusts recorded on
16 October 1987

*Sources:*
(a) Redrawn from Perry, A. H. (1981) *Environmental Hazards in the British Isles,* London:
George Allen & Unwin, figure 2.5b
(b) Redrawn from Quine, C. P. (1988) 'Damage to trees and woodlands in the storm of 15–16
October 1987', *Weather,* 43, 114–17, figure 1
(c) and (d) Redrawn from Burt, S. D. and Mansfield, D. A. (1988) 'The Great Storm of 15–16
October 1987', *Weather,* 43, 90–108, figures 10 and 11b

gusts (figure 15.5). It is fortunate that the most violent winds passed over the land during the night (2–4 am) when most people were safely in their homes.

Despite the widespread appreciation that weather events are a significant cost factor to the economy, several fundamental questions remain to be answered, even in the most general terms. First, the true cost of weather events has yet to be ascertained. The main problems here concern defining the temporal and spatial limits for impact assessment and the complexity of the various intangibles; for example, what are the full costs resulting from a one hour delay to a train due to fog, frozen points or freezing rain? Second, the extent to which costs associated with different specific weather conditions are rising or falling have yet to be evaluated. Third, the role of anthropogenic changes in increasing or decreasing vulnerability to weather-induced costs is little understood. Finally, the extent to which human activity has changed the weather is only poorly appreciated. Some of these points are developed further in the following sections.

## Local climate change

Centuries of economic activity and associated land-use changes have greatly altered the thermal, hydrological, dynamic and chemical properties of the overlying air, and consequently rainfall, temperature, visibility and windiness. Over most rural areas the increasing openness and better ground drainage have possibly resulted in slightly reduced mistiness and the accentuation of frost pockets, the latter due to greater radiation cooling at night and better air drainage. Similarly, the progressive removal of trees and hedgerows has increased near-ground windspeeds thereby raising the potential for soil erosion. In general, however, recent changes in rural micro-climates have been relatively minor and difficult to detect.

By contrast, urban-industrial environments continue to create readily observable and marked modifications to local climate, due to urban growth and expansion, changes to the physical nature of the urban fabric (buildings, streets, etc.), and variations in the volume and composition of pollutants. Although atmospheric pollutants are fully described in chapter 16, their micro-climatological significance is such that they must be described here.

Of particular significance in this context was the dense, persistent, heavily polluted fog of 5–9 December 1952 which resulted in the premature deaths of 12,000 Londoners due to bronchio-cardiac problems (4,000 during the actual period of the fog and a further 8,000 over the following three months). Although this was just one of a long succession of severely polluted London fogs (1873, 1880, 1882, 1891, 1892, 1905, 1948, 1956, 1962) whose frequency, persistence and unpleasant characteristics had led to the coining of the term 'smog' (smoke + fog) in 1905, the recognition of the economic and health consequences following the 1952 event was to have significant scientific, management and environmental ramifications.

The Beaver Committee Report (1954) identified atmospheric pollution, and smoke in particular, as the main culprit, and estimated that it was costing the nation over £300m per annum at 1954 prices. The resultant Clean Air Act of 1956 is generally considered the pioneer legislation in the management of atmospheric pollution, and the effects of this, together with the later 1968 Act, are often *claimed* to have had dramatic impact on the contemporary environmental quality of the larger cities (but see below).

The nature and variation of urban climates was revealed, first, by studies in London in the 1950s and 1960s and then in other cities including Birmingham, Manchester, Nottingham, and Leicester. The main features identified were: (i) generally higher air temperatures than surrounding rural areas; (ii) increased incidence of poor visibility; (iii) decreased average wind speeds but increased gustiness; and (iv) increased cloudiness and slight changes in precipitation characteristics. It is necessary first to examine the characteristics of urban climates as they existed in the 1950s and 1960s before looking at recent changes and assessing the true significance of the Clean Air Act.

## Urban heat-islands

Of all the changes wrought by urban areas on their atmospheric environments, the most frequently studied have been the changes to air temperatures. The development of a shallow dome of slightly warmer air above cities is a product of (i) the capacity of concrete and brick structures to absorb, store, and re-radiate energy and (ii) the heat produced by industrial, commercial and domestic activities, and by surface transport. The resultant 'heat-island' effect (figure 15.6) is variable both in time and space, for it is a function of urban size, topographic setting, urban fabric, industrial activity, atmospheric pollution load and prevailing macro-economic conditions. Large cities, especially those located in topographically sheltered positions, have the potential to show stronger thermal 'prints' than small towns, with heat-island intensity generally related to the logarithm of population size above a threshold population of about 10,000. However, land-use patterns are particularly significant, for building density appears more important in determining heat-island intensity than city size, and extensive parks (e.g. London) reduce intensity. Nevertheless, it is important to recognize that macro-climatological conditions determine whether a heat-island can form and profoundly influence its shape and intensity.

Heat-islands develop best at night under calm anticyclonic conditions characterized by low-level temperature inversions and low near-surface wind speeds (<5–6 m/sec). Under these circumstances, rural–urban temperature differences of 10°C have been recorded for both London and Birmingham. Such heat-islands are fairly shallow (<180 m), the pattern of

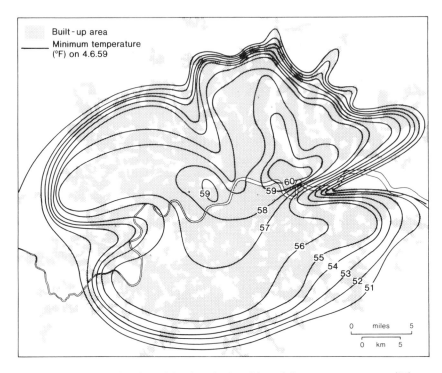

*Figure 15.6* The London heat-island as depicted by minimum temperatures (°F) on
4 June 1959
*Source:* Redrawn from Chandler, T. J. (1965) *The Climate of London,* London: Hutchinson

isotherms being gently domed over the urban area with a marked gradient
along the urban–rural boundary (figure 15.6), and form most frequently
either in early summer (May–June) or in the period September–late
January. While heat-islands may also exist by day, especially in summer,
they tend to be less intense because of higher wind speeds and greater
turbulence. Increasing wind speeds eventually result in heat-island extinction, the threshold mean velocity depending on urban size, land-use
patterns, building densities and recent thermal history. Heat-islands are
therefore transitory and repetitive rather than permanent features of the
thermal map, may be poorly developed or absent for long periods, and
may even be replaced by short-lived negative anomaly patterns. Nevertheless, their fluctuating presence traditionally resulted in city centres having
higher average temperatures than both suburbs and rural areas, the inner-
city/rural contrast being 1.02°C for nights in Birmingham (1965–74) and
1.4°C for London (1931–60) (1.9°C for minimum temperatures). As a
consequence, frosts and snowfalls were less frequent, snow-lie periods
shorter and relative humidities less, although absolute humidities were
sometimes greater, in these cities.

**Airflow**

The flow of air over urban areas is affected by the greater roughness and frequently higher temperatures of the urban fabric. The highly differenti-ated skyline exerts a powerful frictional drag on airflow and turbulence is increased. High-rise blocks generate strong eddies and air is channelled and accelerated along canyon streets, so that wind speeds and wind directions are variable and fickle. These effects are most marked in central areas and diminish outwards, indicating that the scale of wind speed modification is a function of city size and urban morphology. Small towns may, therefore, exert little or no influence on airflow.

Gustiness is a characteristic and particularly problematic aspect of airflow which becomes exacerbated in areas where surface roughness causes turbulent exchange with faster moving air at higher levels. Marked fluctuations in wind speed are a function of building form and layout, wind strength and variation with height, street widths and the relationships between wind direction and street orientation. Gustiness is usually measured by the gust ratio, the ratio of maximum gust speed in a particular period to the mean wind speed. Gust ratios vary from 1.5 at coastal sites to 1.5–2.0 over open farmland, 1.7–2.1 in well-wooded country and open suburbs, and 1.9–2.3 in the central parts of large cities. While this measure indicates the potential for increased maximum wind speeds in cities, the effect diminishes at higher wind speeds. The unpleasant conditions of sudden gusts of driving rain, blowing dust and flying litter experienced in urban areas are actually due to the increased difference between maximum and minimum speeds. This is measured by the gust factor and reaches a maximum in urban areas, largely due to weaker lulls.

**Visibility**

Published maps of reduced visibility have traditionally shown a strong correlation with urban and industrial areas, despite the reduced relative humidity due to the 'heat-island' effect. While this was certainly true for the categories of Mist/Haze (visibility of 1,000–1,990 m) and Moderate Fog (400–990 m), the patterns with respect to Fog (200–390 m), Thick Fog (41–190 m) and Dense Fog (<41 m) were more complex. In the latter cases, records show greater frequency and duration in rural areas than in city centres, but greatest of all in the suburbs (see table 15.1). Thus, the overall lowering of relative humidities due to heat-island development, which averaged 5 per cent for London but with occasional urban–rural contrasts of 20–30 per cent, actually reduced the incidence of thick and persistent fogs in central areas. The increased fogginess of suburbs, on the other hand, was caused by slightly lower air temperatures, higher relative humidities, and the greater concentration of pollution aerosols (dust, smoke, etc.) from domestic, commercial and industrial sources. The volume of the latter can be illustrated by estimated figures for particulate deposition in the United Kingdom during the early 1970s, which ranged from 70 tonnes/km$^2$ per annum in rural areas, to 132 tonnes/km$^2$ per annum in domestic suburbs and >400 tonnes/km$^2$ per annum in industrial areas. A significant proportion of these particulates formed hygroscopic condensation nuclei and thus aided in the formation of small airborne water droplets. As concentration of pollutants was greatest at times when conditions were most suitable for fog formation because (i) emissions were at maximum in generally cool/cold conditions, (ii) domestic emissions of smoke were cool and so did not disperse easily and (iii) dispersion was low because of slack winds and low-level temperature inversions, it is not surprising that fogs frequently developed. In addition, the dirtiness of suburban fogs made them more persistent because they absorbed a larger proportion of solar radiation than their rural equivalents, thereby assisting in the creation of smoke fogs, smoky fogs, smogs or 'pea-soupers'.

*Table 15.1* Fog frequencies typical of the London area in the early 1960s

| Location | *Hours per year (based on four observations per day) with visibility less than* | | | |
| --- | --- | --- | --- | --- |
| | *40m* | *200m* | *400m* | *1,000m* |
| Kingsway (Central London) | 19 | 126 | 230 | 940 |
| Kew (inner suburbs) | 79 | 213 | 365 | 633 |
| London Airport (outer suburbs) | 46 | 209 | 304 | 562 |
| South-east England (means of 7 stations) | 20 | 177 | 261 | 494 |

### Cloud cover and precipitation

Studies indicate that cloud and precipitation amounts are slightly greater over urban/industrial areas because of (i) heat-induced thermals, (ii) mechanically induced turbulence due to buildings, (iii) high absolute humidities and local concentrations of water vapour produced by industry and (iv) higher concentrations of condensation nuclei due to pollution. There is much qualitative evidence to support these assertions, such as the long lines of clouds ('streets') extending downwind of urban areas and the cloud plumes created by power station cooling towers, but few quantitative data, although satellite imagery and radar monitoring are beginning to provide valuable information on the distribution and intensity of rainfall. Evidence suggests that the cloud cover developed over large urban areas causes downwind suburbs to be significantly more cloudy than their upwind equivalents. Comparisons of observations at Kew and Heathrow, 9.7 km apart, show Kew to have 5 per cent more cloud at 1500 hours 6.2 per cent less clear days and 5.9 per cent more overcast days, with the greatest contrasts occurring in summer. However, the magnitude of the urban

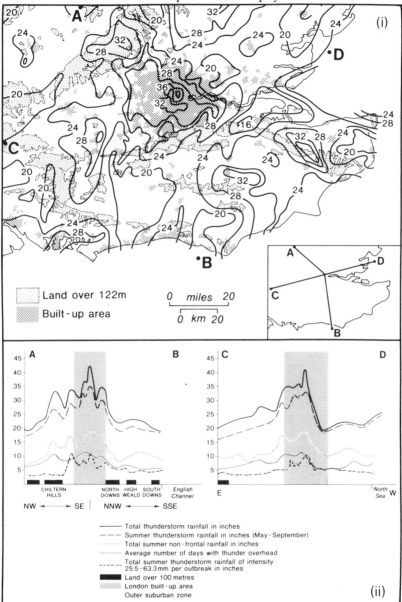

*Figure 15.7* Urban and topographical influences on thunderstorm rainfall in south-east England, 1951–60
(a) Total thunderstorm rainfall
(b) and (c) Graphical representation of urban influence on thunderstorm rainfall along transects shown in inset diagram
*Sources:*
(a) Redrawn from Atkinson, B. W. (1968) 'A preliminary examination of the possible effect of London's urban area on the distribution of thunder rainfalls, 1951–60', *Transactions of the Institute of British Geographers*, 44: 97–118, figure 6

effect is difficult to quantify, for it cannot be reliably distinguished from orographic effects and the natural variability of cloud cover.

Cloud thicknesses are known to be increased both over and downwind of large urban areas, and increases in precipitation amounts and intensities, plus thunderstorm frequency, have all been recorded. Studies have shown that mechanical and thermal turbulence generated by built-up areas as small as Reading, can re-invigorate convective storms in unstable atmospheres. The Hampstead storm of 14 August 1975 (figure 15.2c) exemplifies what can happen, although the extent to which this was an urban-induced phenomenon remains unclear. Certainly, thunderstorms have increased in frequency over London since the 1730s as the city has expanded, and thunderstorm rainfall is greater over London than elsewhere in the region (figure 15.7). However, the local significance of topographic controls must not be overlooked, for there are local peaks elsewhere which can only be partly explained by urban influences (figure 15.7). Even for London, detailed analysis suggests that urban stimulation of precipitation can only be detected in summer, and then for only six of twenty-seven possible synoptic situations.

**Recent changes**

Urban climates vary not only with the size and character of urban areas, but also with time. Thus, the continued expansion of towns and cities since 1950, despite the imposition of Green Belt girdles and other planning controls, has significantly increased the extent and intensity of the urban influence. This, together with the dramatic morphological changes resulting from the construction of high-rise blocks, and the increased insolation consequent on decreased smoke pollution, has resulted in greater mechanical and thermal instability, so that cloud cover and precipitation levels, frequencies and intensities have all been affected.

It is with respect to urban visibility that the greatest changes have occurred in recent decades. Several factors have contributed: changing patterns of pollution emissions, more efficient pollution dispersion due to increased turbulence, and processes of economic change. Particular significance has been attached to the Clean Air Acts (1956, 1968) which sought to restrict smoke emissions, particularly from domestic sources, in the belief that it was smoke that caused the heavy death tolls associated with smogs. Although subsequent research has revealed that cardio-respiratory problems were probably due to the combination of smoke with $SO_2$ and $SO_3$ (sulphur trioxide), the reduction in smoke emissions from 1.75 m tonnes in 1960 to 0.375 m tonnes in 1976 and 0.28 m tonnes in 1980 has dramatically improved urban atmospheres. This is especially true in London where over 90 per cent of domestic properties are now covered by smoke control orders, and where the mean annual values for near ground smoke have fallen from $190\mu g/m^3$ in 1955 to $55\mu g/m^3$ in 1967, $32\mu g/m^3$ in

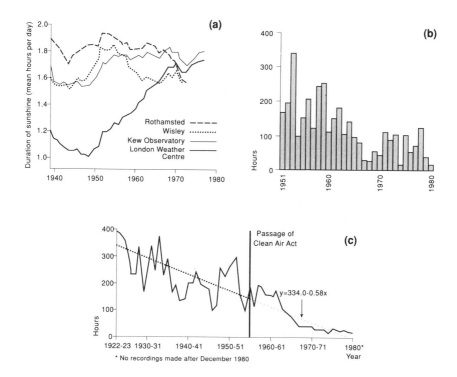

*Figure 15.8* Improvements in the urban atmospheric environment of the London area
(a) Increased winter sunshine hours in central London as compared with suburban (Kew), suburban fringe (Wisley) and rural (Rothamsted) locations; 10-year running means 1930–77
(b) Number of hours per year of thick fog (visibility <200m) at Heathrow, 1951–80
(c) Average winter smoke levels at Kew, 1921–80
*Sources:*
(a) Redrawn from Thornes, J. in Clout, H. (ed.) (1978) *Changing London,* Cambridge: University Tutorial Press, figure 13.4
(b) Redrawn from *The Climate of Great Britain: London* (1987) Meteorological Office, figure 8
(c) Redrawn from Rees, J. A. (1985) *Natural Resources* London: Methuen, figure 8.1

1976 and about $20\mu g/m^3$ in the 1980s (figure 15.8). However, some questions remain as to the actual scale of reduction because of problems with the siting of monitoring stations and the analysis techniques used, particularly as the traditional cheap 'smoke-shade test' tends to underestimate the growing contribution of motor vehicle smoke compared with the more expensive gravimetric method.

The climatological significance of domestic smoke stems from (i) its production in large quantities (2.5–5.25 per cent of coal burnt by weight passes into the atmosphere as smoke) at times favourable to the production of poor visibility and (ii) its discharge at low temperature and low elevation where the dispersion efficiency is low. In consequence domestic smoke aerosols are important in the generation of dense and persistent fogs. The fall in smoke production has therefore greatly reduced the frequency and duration of haze and fog in urban areas (table 15.2 and figure 15.8) and led to dramatic increases in recorded sunshine, especially during the winter months. Sunshine hours in Glasgow have increased by over 60 per cent since 1960, and similar changes have been recorded for Manchester, Birmingham and Leicester. Whereas urban areas received up to 30 per cent less sunshine than adjacent rural districts in the 1940s, these differences have now been eliminated (figure 15.8). Indeed, there is some evidence that the best winter visibility conditions now occur in the central parts of the larger cities.

*Table 15.2* Changing occurrence of fog in London, 1947–70

|  | Average annual number of hours of fog | | | Decrease (%) | | |
|---|---|---|---|---|---|---|
|  | 1947–54 (a) | 1955–62 (b) | 1963–70 (c) | (a–b) | (b–c) | (a–c) |
| *Thick fog (visibility <200m)* | | | | | | |
| London Weather Centre (Central London) | 68 | 52 | 17 | 24 | 68 | 75 |
| Kew Observatory (Inner suburbs) | 241 | 189 | 83 | 22 | 63 | 66 |
| Heathrow (Outer suburbs) | 202 | 177 | 67 | 12 | 62 | 69 |
| *Dense fog (visibility <50m)* | | | | | | |
| London Weather Centre | 27 | 13 | 3 | 52 | 77 | 89 |
| Kew Observatory | 95 | 73 | 20 | 23 | 73 | 79 |
| Heathrow | 57 | 54 | 10 | 5 | 82 | 82 |

Although these dramatic changes have considerably improved the appearance and amenity value of our cities, it is important to examine the possible causes. The reduction in particulate concentrations in urban/industrial areas may be partly due to better dispersion, either because of increased turbulence as urban morphology has become more accentuated, or through the employment of the 'tall stack' policy whereby industrial emissions are carried to higher elevations for better dilution.

More importantly, the significance of the Clean Air legislation has to be critically assessed, *especially as downward trends in smoke concentrations began well before 1956 and appear to be a national phenomenon irrespective of the extent to which smoke control orders have been implemented.* Although the first Clean Air Act was passed by Parliament in 1956, implementation of legislation through the creation of smokeless zones was the responsibility of local authorities. Delays were widespread for a number of reasons: shortages of smokeless fuel, civic lethargy, the impracticability of denying miners their 'perk' of free coal, and the costs involved in changing industrial processes have all been quoted as reasons for the subsequent slow spread of smoke control areas. This is well illustrated by the case of London – often claimed as the model example of the legislation's effectiveness. The City of London was covered by its own legislation from 1 October 1955, but the date of the first smoke Control Order in the wider London County Council (LCC) area was three years later on 1 October 1958, after which control spread slowly and sporadically, covering 35 per cent of the new Greater London Council (GLC) area by 1966, 60 per cent by 1970, 85 per cent by 1975 and 93 per cent by 1982. As a consequence, any improvements in air quality resulting from the legislation could not be anticipated until the late 1960s and yet smoke levels had been falling since the 1920s (figure 15.8), sunshine hours had been rising since the 1940s (figure 15.8), and the last reported smog was in December 1962. That similar trends were recorded in other cities, irrespective of whether smokeless zones had been implemented or not, shows that the legislation was in reality working in unison with strong underlying factors of economic change. While it would be incorrect to suggest that the Clean Air Acts have had no effect, for they undoubtedly speeded change and have certainly blocked any reversion associated with the contemporary fashion of open fires, it is important to recognize that the underlying causes of change were the progressive diversification from a one-fuel to a four-fuel economy, and particularly the growth in use of electricity, a process sometimes referred to as 'the electrification of society'.

Thus the improvement in environmental conditions owes much to the so-called 'flight from coal' in the 1950s when shortages of coal due to the run-down state of mines and labour disputes ('the coal gap') stimulated the search for alternative, dependable energy sources – a process subsequently enhanced by the exploitation of North Sea gas and oil supplies in 1967 and 1975. Once competition had been established, the desire for economies led to important changes in the industrial fuel-mix. For example, the dramatic reductions in smoke levels in the Potteries, and the attendant visibility improvements, are largely the product of the change from the traditional solid-fuel 'bottle ovens' to electric ovens. The growth in electricity genera-tion, coupled with the development of the 'national grid' and 'supergrid' distribution networks, resulted in the closure of numerous small inefficient urban power stations (e.g. Battersea) which had previously added gener-ously to the urban air-pollution load, and their replacement by large, modern, efficient power stations often located in rural or semi-rural locations. As a consequence, over 60 per cent of present coal production is now burned in large efficient furnaces, many fitted with particulate screening devices, so that smoke production is a minute fraction of that produced by open fires. Other important planning and economic reasons for reduced urban smoke are the decline of port functions, railway modernization and the resultant switch from steam locomotives to diesel and electric traction, urban renewal programmes, industrial relocation, decline of primary industry and changes in industrial and domestic space heating.

Two further recent climatic changes resulting from pollution are worthy of note. First, the continued high volume of $SO_2$ emissions has resulted in a gradual increase in rainfall acidity, for instead of a pH of 6.5–7.0 all areas now record less than 6.0 with some below 4.5, the minimum recorded being 2.4 at Pitlochry on 10 April 1974 (see chapter 16). Second, the uncontrolled discharge of motor vehicle exhausts has resulted in the release of growing volumes of nitrogen oxides and hydrocarbons. Oxidation in sunlight (ultra-violet radiation) can result in the production of ozone ($O_3$) and photo-chemical smog. The myth that such 'Los Angeles smogs' could not form in Britain, because of the greater turbulence and lack of sunshine, have now been disproved for weak photo-chemical smogs have been regularly reported for London during summer months since 1972. The spatial and temporal variability of photo-chemical products remains little known, but it is clear that such smogs could become increasingly widespread and common if motor exhausts remain uncontrolled. Thus, urban areas have exchanged the traditional winter smoke fog for a new, potentially equally unhealthy, summer variety.

While 'heat-islands' may be the most dramatic and well documented feature of urban climatology (see above), there is uncertainty as to how they are evolving in response to economic factors and planning changes. This is because urban climates are composed of a kaleidoscope of site micro-climates where temperatures can vary in response to very local conditions determined by a wide range of interacting influences. It seems likely that 'heat-island' intensities have reduced recently because of urban renewal programmes, improved building insulation, changes in building materials, inner-city dereliction, increased turbulence and industrial decline and restructuring. Reduction in smoke pollution and haze has increased night-time infra-red radiation, so that most urban areas have become increasingly prone to frosts, snowfalls and longer snow-lie. Motor vehicles supply growing volumes of warm exhausts containing nitric oxide ($NO_2$) which creates $O_3$ through photo-dissociation. As $NO_2$, $O_3$ and $SO_2$ (produced through oil burning) all absorb some solar radiation, it is possible that heat-islands are being strengthened during summer months but weakened in the winter.

## MORPHOLOGICAL CHANGES

Anthropogenic landform modification has significantly increased over the last fifty years. Although the most conspicuous features are the products of purposeful changes (*human-made landforms*) such as quarries, spoil heaps, motorway cuttings and embankments, there have also been widespread unintentional or 'accidental' changes consequent upon modifications to environmental conditions, either because of altered rates of operation of surface processes so as to yield *human-modified landforms,* or through the creation of *human-induced landforms* (i.e. naturally created features whose location in time and space is wholly human dependent, such as deltas in reservoirs, shingle accumulations behind groynes, gullies on tips). These 'accidental' changes, although individually small-scale, are of considerable significance in terms of work achieved. As a consequence, it is now believed that population expansion, economic growth, and technological development have combined to make human activity the most potent instigator of geomorphological change currently operating.

Urbanization has had a particularly major impact on surface form, extending far beyond the limits of urban areas. Urban development has been largely responsible for the dramatic growth in surface mineral extraction (see later), while the increased production of rubbish (refuse) yields return flows to country areas to facilitate the reclamation of derelict land. Similarly, river regime and channel form have been altered because of urban influences on discharge characteristics and increased erosion downstream of reservoirs (clear water erosion). To these must be added those changes produced by increased runoff of water and sediment from agricultural land and widespread channel modifications (enlargement, straightening, and cleaning) undertaken by management bodies to reduce flooding which, in many cases, are superimposed on the effects of canalization in the seventeenth and eighteenth centuries. No lowland river in the United Kingdom is in anything remotely like its natural state.

Changes in agricultural practices have also accelerated soil losses. The trend to expansive monoculture, the abandonment of the practice of 'claying' light soils, and the progressive switch to crops which leave much of the ground surface bare during the relatively dry early summer months (e.g. sugarbeet), have resulted in significantly increased wind-induced soil erosion. Dust storms have been increasingly recorded since the 1920s in the Fenlands, east Yorkshire, the Brecklands, and Lincolnshire, and plumes of blowing dust have recently become commonplace on the light Sherwood Sandstone soils of the midlands. On more clayey soils, erosion has often been increased because of faster runoff (overland and subsurface flows) resulting from the use of heavy machinery which destroys soil structure through compaction. As a consequence of both these processes, 7,700 km$^2$ or 44 per cent of arable soils are now considered at risk from erosion by wind and water, and maximum rates of soil removal which were estimated at 17–18 tonnes/ha per annum in the early 1970s have recently been upgraded to 50 tonnes/ha per annum. Such erosion seldom produces obvious features, except for the rills developed during severe storms. Gullies rarely develop on agricultural land in the United Kingdom, being mainly confined to spoil heaps, disturbed ground such as construction sites and deforested areas, and areas of great recreational activity (usually well-known viewpoints or sandy heathlands) where the intense use of paths results in vegetation destruction and soil compaction through trampling. However, such accelerated soil erosion is extremely significant in terms of channel sedimentation and long-term soil resource conservation. This is seen most clearly in the Fens where agriculture and land drainage since 1848 have so increased the potential for wind erosion that only 25 per cent of the original area of peat now remains.

Coastal changes have also increased. Reclamation, often using urban refuse, has resulted in useful increments of land in several areas including Belfast, Liverpool, Portsmouth and Southend. Defence works have ranged from the stabilization of eroding dune systems using wind-breaks and rapidly rooting psammophytic grasses (e.g. Braunton Burrows, Culbin Sands), via the artificial recharge of eroding beaches, to the erection of complex systems of walls and groynes to protect eroding cliff lines (e.g. east of Brighton). Coastal engineering schemes are often impressive, but they may produce unforeseen consequences, both seaward of structures (accelerated erosion) and elsewhere along the coast. Thus, the inhibition of natural longshore shingle movement by the development of Folkestone Harbour over the period 1810–1905 is thought to have contributed to the major landslides at Folkestone Warren in 1915 which moved the Folkestone to Dover railway line seawards by 50 m. Similarly, the numerous groynes on the Sussex coast and the large breakwater at Newhaven are thought to be responsible for the rapid Chalk cliff retreat at both Seaford Head and the Seven Sisters (0.91 m per annum). Further modifications include the regrading of potentially dangerous cliffs, the removal of unstable stacks (e.g. Thanet coast) and the extraction of gravel for aggregate. Shoreline or beach extraction continues in small quantities but is generally carefully controlled since the disaster at Hallsands, Devon, where the removal of 660,000 tonnes of shingle in 1887 for construction work in Plymouth Dockyards resulted in beach lowering by an average of 4 m, the abandonment of Hallsands village and cliff retreat up to 6 m in the period 1907–57. Research into sediment transport rates and nourishment status is now a prerequisite for granting extraction licences in the coastal zone. Investigations in the English Channel have revealed that submarine extraction at depths greater than 18 m below Low Water Mark should have no impact on beaches. As a consequence, submarine extraction has expanded off the coasts of Hampshire, Sussex, Essex, Suffolk, Norfolk, Lincolnshire and North Wales as well as in the Bristol Channel and Mersey Estuary, with output rising from 4.1 million tonnes in 1955, to 7.7 million tonnes in 1973 and 17.6 million tonnes in 1986 (figure 15.9).

While such modifications to surface form are significant, probably the most important recent developments have occurred through surface mineral extraction and the reclamation of derelict land.

**Mineral extraction**

Onshore mineral production has undergone major changes during this century. While the fortunes of the coal industry have waned dramatically,

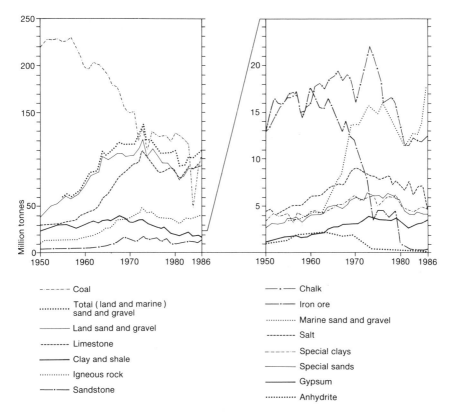

Figure 15.9 UK mineral production, 1950–86

Legend (left):
- - - - - - Coal
············ Total ( land and marine ) sand and gravel
———— Land sand and gravel
- - - - - - Limestone
———— Clay and shale
············ Igneous rock
—·— Sandstone

Legend (right):
—·— Chalk
—·— Iron ore
············ Marine sand and gravel
- - - - - - Salt
- - - - - Special clays
———— Special sands
———— Gypsum
············ Anhydrite

*Figure 15.9* UK mineral production, 1950–86

with resulting severe contraction of mining activity (see chapter 5), other categories of surface mineral extraction expanded rapidly until 1973 when affected by the economic recession (table 15.3, figure 15.9). The main impetus for this growth was provided by the post-war programmes of urban reconstruction, expansion and renewal, and the development of the motorway network, which together resulted in enormous increases in demand for 'construction' minerals, and especially those needed for making concrete. Thus, while the exploitation of clay for bricks only rose modestly after the phase of rapid increase associated with the suburban building boom of the 1930s, the growth in cement manufacture (+26.3 per cent in the decade 1960–70) stimulated increased extraction of both chalk (85 per cent used in cement production) and limestone. However, the most dramatic growth was in the production of aggregates for concrete which are, in descending order of importance, sand and gravel, crushed limestone, artificial or manufactured aggregates, and crushed sandstone. Demand for these materials grew from 20 million tonnes per annum in 1900 to 57 million tonnes in 1948, 179 million tonnes in 1964 and 276 million tonnes in

Table 15.3 Mineral production in million tonnes

| | 1930 | 1937 | 1947 | 1957 | 1967 | 1974 | 1977 | 1986 | % change 1930–83 | 1947–86 | Peak production –1986 | Peak production and year |
|---|---|---|---|---|---|---|---|---|---|---|---|---|
| Coal (deep-mined) | 247.8 | 244.3 | 190.3 | 214.0 | 170.4 | 100.0 | 107.1 | 90.4 | −63.5 | −52.4 | −69.0 | 292.0 (1913) |
| (opencast) | – | – | 10.4 | 13.8 | 7.2 | 9.3 | 13.5 | 14.3 | – | + 37.5 | −9.5 | 15.8 (1980) |
| Ironstone | 11.8 | 14.4 | 11.3 | 17.2 | 12.9 | 3.6 | 3.8 | 0.3 | −97.5 | −97.3 | −98.5 | 20.2 (1942) |
| Igneous rock | 10.2 | 11.1 | 10.2 | 14.4 | 34.2 | 41.7 | 35.6 | 41.0 | + 302.0 | +302.0 | −13.9 | 47.6 (1973) |
| Chalk | 6.8 | 10.4 | 9.7 | 16.5 | 18.3 | 20.5 | 16.3 | 12.5 | + 83.8 | + 28.9 | −43.7 | 22.2 (1973) |
| Limestone/dolomite | 15.2 | 19.3 | 18.8 | 34.4 | 77.4 | 100.9 | 86.4 | 100.5 | + 561.2 | +434.6 | −8.0 | 109.2 (1973) |
| Clay | 15.0 | 26.0 | 18.8 | 28.6 | 37.3 | 31.1 | 23.5 | 17.6 | + 17.3 | −8.0 | −53.6 | 37.9 (1968) |
| Sandstone | 3.9 | 5.2 | 3.2 | 4.7 | 9.6 | 14.4 | 9.0 | 14.0 | + 259.0 | +337.5 | −16.7 | 16.8 (1973) |
| Sand and gravel (excluding marine) | 7.0 | 20.7 | 33.4 | 57.4 | 106.3 | 105.0 | 91.8 | 94.4 | +1,248.6 | +182.6 | −21.7 | 120.5 (1973) |

Source: UK Digest of Statistics, HMSO

1973, an increase in per capita consumption from about 0.6 to about 5 tonnes per annum. This was the underlying cause of the massive expansion in surface mineral extraction from 115 million tonnes in 1938 to 192 million tonnes in 1955 and 300 million tonnes in 1967, prior to reaching a peak of 373 million tonnes in 1973 before falling back to 296 million tonnes in 1979 and 306 million tonnes in 1986. As a consequence, annual production of bulk minerals has exceeded that of coal since 1957, although coal remained the individual largest component (by weight) in the total mineral mix, until overtaken in 1984 by the combined sand and gravel production from both onshore and offshore sources. The detrimental effects of the 1984–5 miners' strike has had much to do with this change and with the increased emphasis on opencast extraction. Opencast coal extraction, which began under emergency legislation during the Second World War (1941), has ranged from 7.2–15.8 million tonnes per annum, with production running above 14 million tonnes per annum since 1980. The proportion of coal obtained by these means has steadily increased so as to exceed 10 per cent since 1977, reaching 13.7 per cent in 1986 (28.9 per cent and 17.2 per cent in the strike-affected years of 1984 and 1985).

While the post-war production trends were predominantly upward until the post-1973 recession, the same is not true for all surface minerals. Ironstone production has dramatically declined since a post-war peak in 1960 (17.35 million tonnes) due first to the closure of the Cleveland Hills and North Oxfordshire extraction areas in 1964 and 1967 on economic grounds, and subsequently to the overall contraction of the Iron and Steel Industry begun in the later 1970s, which involved the cessation of extraction in Northamptonshire in 1979. The same is true of oil shale extraction (Central Scotland) which fell from 1.4–2.0 million tonnes per annum in the 1930s to cease altogether in 1962, and indigenous production of anhydrite has also diminished to minimal proportions (figure 15.9).

Space precludes a detailed analysis of production trends and the changing spatial distribution of mineral workings, but the general consequences are as follows. Growth in surface mineral extraction has resulted in increases in the area occupied by mineral workings and their associated processing plants, storage areas and waste dumps, as well as in the rate of uptake of land, estimated at 20 square kilometres per annum in the early 1970s. Thus the potential to create disturbed and despoiled land has also increased, especially in the case of the sand and gravel industry where the shallowness and thinness of the valued mineral layer often results in rapid throughput times. Opencast coal operations are another 'land hungry' form of extraction, although the Opencast Executive of British Coal has an excellent record of rapid and high quality reclamation. In addition, the application of technology and economies of scale have dictated that workings should get larger so as to facilitate the operation of ever bigger machinery and plant. As a consequence, shallow workings have become more extensive and bluff-sites (usually amphitheatre-shaped workings cut into hillsides) have expanded, the latter to such an extent that many have become 'long life' pits (super quarries) with operational lives well in excess of twenty years.

These trends are particularly obvious in the case of aggregate production. This used to be dominated by the sand and gravel industry and characterized by scattered, small pits utilizing a wide variety of superficial deposits, but over the last four decades has moved 'downhill' and concentrated on the more extensive 'economically desirable' lowland deposits (river terraces, alluvial deposits, fluvio-glacial outwash spreads) located within reasonable distance of the main markets, for aggregates are relatively low value, high bulk goods which traditionally could only be transported economically over short distances (40–60 km). However, recent price rises and the progressive shift to bulk transport by road and rail has allowed extraction to start moving away from the urban fringes and thus away from the zones of greatest land conflicts and planning constraints. One consequence of this 'downhill' movement has been a switch from 'dry pit' to 'wet pit' workings, where the high water-table conditions result in the creation of lagoons.

Developments in crushed rock aggregate (limestone and granite) production are even more impressive and increasingly focused on a small number of super quarries (e.g. Mendip Hills) with bulk distribution by rail. The culmination of this trend is likely to see a handful of huge quarries similar to the granite quarry in north-west Scotland which began production in 1986 and is eventually destined to produce 7.5 million tonnes of crushed rock a year, all of which will be transported by ship.

Similar trends characterize the brick-making industry. In 1939 there were 1,316 brickworks served by 1,303 clay pits, one-third of the total using Coal Measure Clays brought to the surface at collieries. By 1970, a slightly larger demand for bricks was being supplied by a mere 360 brickworks and 370 pits, and the numbers have since fallen further due to the post-1973 restricted building programme, with increased concentration on the Oxford Clay belt. Similar processes of amalgamation and concentration can be seen in the cement industry and in limestone and other quarrying activities. As a result, the total number of surface mineral workings has declined from 6,500 in 1930 to 5,500 in 1945, 3,800 in 1965, and to between 3,000 and 4,000 during the 1970s, while employees have declined from 71,863 in 1950 to 42,785 in 1970, and about 40,000 today.

The changing character of mineral extraction has had significant planning implications, including the safeguarding of potentially valuable mineral reserves from sterilization by urban and industrial developments, land conflicts (e.g. mineral extraction versus agriculture or recreation), loss of amenity through dust, noise and visual intrusion, increased transport congestion, and dereliction. Such problems are widely distributed but are most clearly brought into focus where the actual or potential environmental degradation is greatest as, for example, in the cases of limestone quarrying adjacent to the Peak District National Park, the China Clay workings in

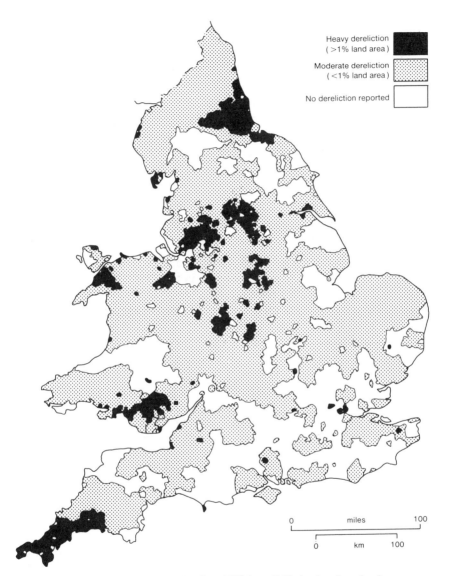

Heavy dereliction
( >1% land area )

Moderate dereliction
( <1% land area )

No dereliction reported

0       miles      100

0      km     100

*Figure 15.10* Derelict land in England and Wales, 1969, by local authority areas
*Source:* Redrawn from Wallwork, K. L. (1974) *Derelict Land,* Newton Abbot: David and
Charles

Cornwall, Potash mining on the North York Moors and the major
controversy aroused by the early 1970 proposal to extract Copper in
Snowdonia.

The contemporary surface mineral industry is therefore, the subject of controversy and competing pressures. On the one hand, there is concern over the fragmented nature of mineral resources management and the problems of maintaining assured good quality future supplies at reasonable prices. On the other, growth in environmental awareness and the increasing numbers of vocal amenity groups have resulted in pressures to restrict mineral workings in many areas, particularly those considered to be scenically attractive. The application of growing controls on mineral exploitation (no permission to mine was required prior to 1947) have been paralleled by fundamental changes in attitude towards derelict land since 1945, mainly as a result of the growth of land-use planning. While irregular disturbed terrain, often both ugly and dangerous, used to be seen as the natural consequence of mineral extraction, it has become recognized that the creation of such despoiled landscapes can be avoided and the land put to valued use.

## DERELICTION AND RECLAMATION

Studies of dereliction have been bedevilled by inadequate data, due to confusion over definitions. The government description of dereliction as 'land so damaged by industrial or other development that it is incapable of beneficial use without treatment' appears reasonable and all-embracing, but estimation of the areal extent of land so affected is difficult because many categories of unused land are excluded from local authority returns. Similarly, maps of dereliction are rare, because of the political implications, and certain local authorities have, at times, appeared unwilling to acknowledge its existence (see figure 15.10) let alone specify its location. Indeed, eight local authorities failed to respond to the most recent (1982) survey undertaken by the Department of Environment.

Derelict land can result from urban, industrial, transportation, and mineral extraction land uses. Urban changes (renewal and redevelopment) tend to produce 'short-term' dereliction, except under conditions of severe economic recession or where land is 'banked' by profit speculators awaiting future developments. By contrast, 'longer-term' or 'persistent' dereliction is usually created by changes in the other uses, and particularly mineral extraction, where the natural inclination of operators is to switch effort and resources to new operations rather than to reclaim worked-out areas that no longer yield revenue.

Interest in, and concern about, dereliction really began in the 1940s, mainly as a response to the need to evaluate and quantify the effects of wartime bomb damage. Startling maps were produced in 1946 showing the extent of derelict land in the West Midlands and Potteries. While it soon became clear that mineral extraction was the major cause, there was widespread belief that much of the dereliction was inherited, primarily from the Victorian era and the 1930s slump. It was not until the mid-1960s, particularly following the Aberfan Disaster, that the significance of

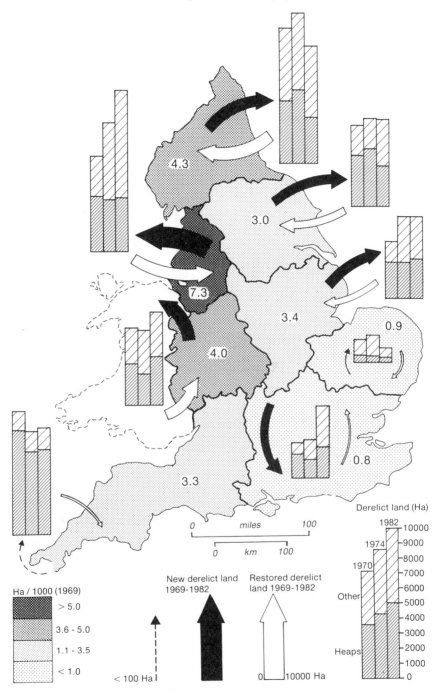

*Figure 15.11* Changing patterns of creation and restoration of derelict land in England, 1969–82

Table 15.4 Changing composition of derelict land in England by standard region 1970–82

| | Spoil heaps | | | | Excavations | | | | Military land | Aban railway land | Other | | | | Total | | |
|---|---|---|---|---|---|---|---|---|---|---|---|---|---|---|---|---|---|
| | Total | a% | b% | c% | Total | a% | b% | c% | | | Total | a% | b% | c% | Total | a% | c% |
| **Northern** | | | | | | | | | | | | | | | | | |
| 1970 | 2,438 | 17.0 | 28.9 | −2.6 | 1,490 | 15.9 | 17.6 | −2.0 | | | 4,515 | 29.3 | 53.5 | +4.1 | 8,443 | 21.6 | +1.2 |
| 1974 | 2,922 | 22.3 | 31.0 | +16.7 | 1,690 | 19.4 | 18.0 | +11.2 | 232 | 1,830 | 2,737 | 22.4 | 51.0 | +10.6 | 9,411 | 21.7 | +12.8 |
| 1982 | 1,872 | 14.0 | 25.6 | −25.2 | 1,043 | 12.2 | 14.3 | −31.4 | 168 | 1,375 | 2,849 | 18.5 | 60.1 | +1.2 | 7,307 | 16.0 | −12.4 |
| **North-west** | | | | | | | | | | | | | | | | | |
| 1970 | 2,026 | 14.1 | 33.9 | +0.8 | 1,452 | 15.5 | 24.3 | −0.3 | | | 2,498 | 16.2 | 41.8 | +5.9 | 5,975 | 15.3 | +2.6 |
| 1974 | 2,083 | 15.9 | 26.0 | +3.7 | 1,203 | 13.8 | 15.0 | −17.4 | 1,205 | 1,338 | 2,186 | 22.1 | 59.1 | +100.9 | 8,015 | 18.5 | +37.6 |
| 1982 | 2,012 | 15.1 | 20.0 | +0.1 | 1,381 | 16.1 | 13.7 | −5.2 | 398 | 1,648 | 4,603 | 28.0 | 66.2 | +181.8 | 10,045 | 22.0 | +72.4 |
| **Yorkshire and Humberside** | | | | | | | | | | | | | | | | | |
| 1970 | 1,256 | 8.7 | 25.1 | +10.7 | 1,902 | 20.4 | 37.9 | −4.2 | | | 1,875 | 12.2 | 37.4 | +16.6 | 5,012 | 12.8 | +6.0 |
| 1974 | 1,289 | 9.8 | 23.6 | +13.6 | 1,599 | 18.3 | 29.3 | −19.5 | 239 | 1,343 | 981 | 12.0 | 47.0 | +59.4 | 5,451 | 12.6 | +15.3 |
| 1982 | 1,070 | 8.0 | 19.7 | −5.7 | 1,433 | 16.7 | 26.4 | −27.8 | 385 | 1,428 | 1,115 | 12.3 | 53.9 | +82.1 | 5,431 | 11.9 | +14.9 |
| **West Midlands** | | | | | | | | | | | | | | | | | |
| 1970 | 1,861 | 12.9 | 38.5 | −5.7 | 724 | 7.7 | 15.0 | −12.9 | | | 2,246 | 14.6 | 46.5 | −6.0 | 4,830 | 12.3 | −7.0 |
| 1974 | 1,373 | 10.5 | 29.4 | −30.4 | 672 | 7.7 | 14.4 | −19.1 | 518 | 776 | 1,328 | 12.2 | 56.2 | +9.7 | 4,667 | 10.8 | −10.1 |
| 1982 | 2,174 | 16.3 | 37.6 | +10.1 | 917 | 10.7 | 15.8 | +10.3 | 330 | 875 | 1,491 | 11.3 | 46.6 | +12.8 | 5,787 | 12.7 | +11.4 |
| **East Midlands** | | | | | | | | | | | | | | | | | |
| 1970 | 989 | 6.9 | 27.8 | +4.0 | 1,155 | 12.4 | 32.5 | +4.1 | | | 1,413 | 9.2 | 39.7 | −3.3 | 3,558 | 9.1 | +1.0 |
| 1974 | 1,090 | 8.3 | 21.1 | +14.6 | 1,160 | 13.3 | 22.4 | +4.6 | 816 | 1,606 | 493 | 13.6 | 56.4 | +99.4 | 5,171 | 11.9 | +46.8 |
| 1982 | 1,225 | 9.2 | 23.6 | +28.8 | 1,258 | 14.7 | 24.2 | +13.4 | 644 | 1,339 | 732 | 11.4 | 52.2 | +85.8 | 5,198 | 11.4 | +47.6 |

|  |  |  |  |  |  |  |  |  |  |  |  |  |  |  |  |  |  |
|---|---|---|---|---|---|---|---|---|---|---|---|---|---|---|---|---|---|
| **East Anglia** | | | | | | | | | | | | | | | | | |
| 1970 | 1 | 0 | 0 | 0 | 472 | 5.1 | 35.0 | −2.2 | 513 | 875 | 249 | 5.7 | 65.0 | +2.0 | 1,349 | 3.4 | +0.6 |
| 1974 | 1 | 0 | 0 | 0 | 408 | 4.7 | 22.9 | −15.5 |  | 612 |  | 6.4 | 77.1 | +60.1 | 1,783 | 4.1 | +33.0 |
| 1982 | 15 | 0.1 | 1.9 | +1,500 | 305 | 3.6 | 37.9 | −36.8 | 251 | 170 | 63 | 2.0 | 60.2 | −43.6 | 804 | 1.8 | −40.0 |
| **South-east** | | | | | | | | | | | | | | | | | |
| 1970 | 84 | 0.6 | 3.7 | +31.3 | 1,429 | 15.3 | 63.1 | −2.9 | 113 | 752 | 396 | 4.9 | 33.2 | +26.0 | 2,264 | 5.8 | +6.2 |
| 1974 | 53 | 0.4 | 2.2 | −17.1 | 1,136 | 13.0 | 48.1 | −22.8 |  | 662 |  | 5.5 | 49.6 | +96.2 | 2,360 | 5.5 | +10.7 |
| 1982 | 102 | 0.8 | 2.3 | +59.5 | 1,821 | 21.2 | 40.7 | +23.8 | 632 | 555 | 1,369 | 10.8 | 57.1 | +328.2 | 4,479 | 9.8 | +110.1 |
| **South-west** | | | | | | | | | | | | | | | | | |
| 1970 | 5,723 | 39.8 | 74.6 | −0.3 | 743 | 8.0 | 9.7 | −2.9 | 141 | 1,234 | 184 | 8.0 | 16.1 | +7.5 | 7,670 | 19.6 | +0.2 |
| 1974 | 4,307 | 32.8 | 67.1 | −25.0 | 843 | 9.7 | 13.1 | +10.2 |  | 940 |  | 5.9 | 19.7 | +10.2 | 6,415 | 14.8 | −14.9 |
| 1982 | 4,870 | 36.5 | 73.4 | −15.1 | 420 | 4.9 | 6.3 | −45.1 | 208 | 820 | 317 | 5.7 | 20.3 | +17.2 | 6,635 | 14.5 | −13.3 |
| **TOTAL** | | | | | | | | | | | | | | | | | |
| 1970 | 14,378 | – | 36.7 | +1.0 | 9,345 | – | 23.9 | −1.5 |  | 15,408 |  | – | 39.4 | +2.6 | 39,132 | – | +1.0 |
| 1974 | 13,118 | – | 30.3 | −7.9 | 8,717 | – | 20.1 | −8.1 |  | 21,438 |  | – | 49.5 | +42.8 | 43,273 | – | +11.7 |
| 1982 | 13,340 | – | 29.2 | −6.3 | 8,578 | – | 18.8 | −9.6 |  | 23,765 | – | – | 52.0 | +58.3 | 45,683 | – | +17.9 |

*Notes:*

a% Percentage of that category of dereliction at time of survey

b% Percentage of dereliction within region

c% Percentage change in extent since 1969

contemporary processes of change in the creation of dereliction began to be appreciated. Subsequent estimates of UK derelict land in the 1970s varied from 60,000–100,000 ha with additions running at up to 1,400 ha per annum. The pattern of dereliction in England and Wales, as determined by the first country-wide survey in 1969 (figure 15.10), revealed a marked correlation with urban–industrial areas and the coalfields, although other important concentrations occurred in Cornwall (China Clay workings), and North Wales (slate). Subsequent changes have included the differential impact of reclamation schemes, particularly on traditionally despoiled lands (e.g. the Potteries, West Midlands, and East Midlands) which resulted in the treatment of 26,700 ha over the period 1968–82 (figure 15.11). However, these improvements were for the most part overwhelmed by a new wave of more widespread dereliction associated with the continuing contraction of the coal industry, the spread of sand and gravel workings, the rationalization of brick manufacture and the massive additions of abandoned land resulting from industrial 'restructuring' and changes in transport patterns (figure 15.11). As a consequence, the extent of recorded dereliction in England rose from 34,358 ha in 1964 to 38,738 ha in 1969, 39,292 ha in 1971, 43,273 ha in 1974 and 45,633 ha in 1982, although some of the increase may be due to better reporting. The changes in composition of derelict land by standard region are shown in table 15.4 and clearly reveal the trends; most noticeably the increases in 'Other Forms of Dereliction' (urban and industrial) in the South-east, East Midlands and North-west regions, expansion of excavations in the West Midlands and South-east, and the increase in abandoned spoil heaps in the West Midlands. Clearly dereliction is dynamic in both distribution and character.

Although derelict land produced by mineral extraction contains landforms of varying shape, size, origin and antiquity, an essential subdivision can be made into excavations and heaps, with the latter tending to be the main focus of attention. Well developed waste heaps covered 14,300 ha in 1971, and their visual intrusiveness and environmental impact was enormous. Their composition varied (figure 15.12), including industrial by-products such as blast furnace slag or fly-ash from power stations, as well as natural materials (spoil) of little or no economic value (e.g. overburden, mining waste, processing waste). The most dramatic examples included the elongate mounds of oil-shale waste (bings) in Lothian, the conspicuous glistening white sand cones produced by China Clay workings, and the grey colliery spoil heaps. The last mentioned have posed particularly severe problems due to their number and bulk (several thousand in 1971 covering 8,000 ha and containing in excess of 3,600 million tonnes of material), their habit of catching fire because of spontaneous combustion of iron pyrites (570 spoil heaps were aflame when the 1956 Clean Air Act was passed), and because of the rapid rate of addition (40–5 million tonnes per annum in the late 1960s).

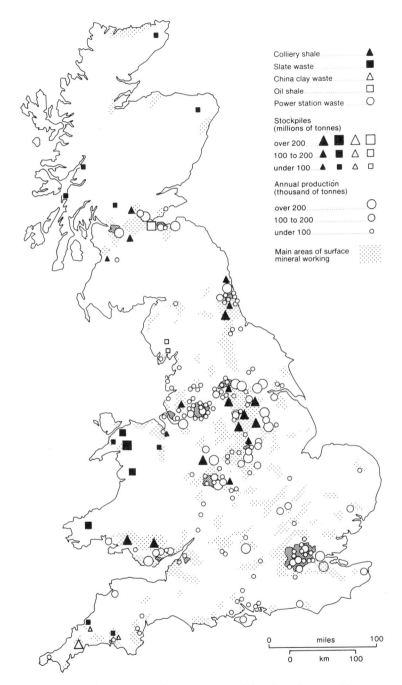

*Figure 15.12* Distribution of major waste material and surface workings
*Source:* Redrawn from *Aggregates: The Way Ahead* (1976), London: Department of the Environment, figure F2

The growing awareness of the extent of dereliction, particularly in association with the increasing pressures on land in and around cities, led to many active clearance schemes and considerable research into practicable and cost-effective reclamation methods. The problems have been both numerous and severe; legal difficulties over land ownership, lack of suitable expertise within local authorities, financial constraints, lack of suitable equipment and disinterest at local authority level have all hindered progress. Nevertheless, the need to remove the worst examples because of their negative (depressing) visual and psychological impact on community life, attitudes and aspirations, has resulted in many impressive successes, most especially the Erewash Valley, the Lower Swansea Valley and the Potteries (e.g. Hanley Park). Much credit must go to the NCB (now British Coal) for both the high quality and speed of its opencast restoration procedures and for the regrading and rehabilitation (landscaping and planning) of many large extant heaps. while the policy of keeping the height of new spoil heaps to below 15 m has considerably reduced visual intrusion and virtually eliminated spontaneous combustion, the steadfast refusal to operate underground stowage ('back-packing') of waste, for economic reasons, has resulted in spoil disposal continuing to consume some 300 ha per annum.

After a relatively slow start, the pace of reclamation in England accelerated in the late 1960s to reach about 2,300 ha in 1973 for all types (17,000 ha in the period 1974–82) with reclamation of mineral workings running at about 810 ha per annum during the mid-1970s (figure 15.11). Much of the latter was achieved through the restoration (rehabilitation) of spoil heaps, although some material was removed for use in filling holes, for making construction blocks and for the wearing courses of roads (burnt shale). The financing of nearly all reclamation operations has been partly government-assisted since the Local Government Act of 1966 empowered the Secretary of State for the Environment to make 50 per cent grants to local authorities for the restoration of derelict land. The Local Employment Act (1972) subsequently raised the proportions to 85 per cent in Development Areas and 75 per cent in Intermediate Areas and Derelict Land Clearance Areas (north midlands) and from December 1975 the proportions were raised to 100 per cent, with 75 per cent grants for National Parks and AONBs and 50 per cent elsewhere. Although local authorities have responded reasonably well – 74 per cent of the land reclaimed in 1972 was restored by local authorities – the high costs of reclamation have meant that even a proportional charge has proved prohibitive in many instances, and there was a general slowing down in the later 1970s in response to local and national economic constraints. In this context, it is important to note that the costs of reclamation have to be borne out of a fixed block grant and therefore reclamation has to compete with other calls upon finance.

While the sculpturing and rehabilitation of spoil heaps has proved relatively successful in many traditional coal-mining areas, the remaining task is large (table 15.4), costly and not without problems. Certain materials still pose difficulties for plant propagation because of the chemistry or physical character (e.g. slate waste), while in the case of the 'white alps of Cornwall' no economic market has yet been found for what is a potentially valuable sand resource. Similar problems exist in the reclamation of extraction sites, where the physical nature of dereliction depends on the ratio of overburden to extracted mineral, the nature of the overburden, the position of the water-table and the mode of extraction. The historic pattern of small 'dry-pits' posed few problems, for they could either be filled with rubble, rubbish and other waste materials, or left to be colonized by vegetation so as to blend into the landscape. In many cases, old and abandoned quarries have been used for housing, caravan parks, storage depots or industrial activities, once the side-slopes have been stabilized. However, the trend towards very large extraction sites, many of which become partially or wholly filled with water, has posed difficulties. In many cases the enormous scale of such features has made them unsuitable for alternative land uses without expensive reclamation procedures, the costs of which can be prohibitive despite government grants. The Ironstone Restoration Fund was set up under the 1951 Minerals Working Act (0.47 p/ tonne) to assist the rehabilitation of the Northamptonshire iron-workings, while in 1975 the Sand and Gravel Association set up a similar fund.

In certain cases waste from one industry was disposed in the wasteland of another, the best example being the 100 km transfer of some of the CEGB's annual 250,000 tonne production of fly-ash from the Trent-side power stations for disposal in Peterborough's brickpits. Usually, however, there is a mismatch between distribution of suitable fillers and the availability of vacant holes, with the result that about 80 million tonnes of waste material is dumped on the surface each year. This problem, was exacerbated by the post-war increase in 'wet-pit' creation, where the threat of water pollution demanded the use of inert filler materials, such as builder's rubble and fly-ash, to create reconstituted land. The situation was particularly severe in the vicinity of London, where the majority of pits are 'wet' and the largest volume of available waste material is degradable domestic rubbish. After considerable research it was found that, although domestic rubbish dumped in water decomposes to produce gases (including methane) and toxic liquids (leachate), careful disposal by 'controlling tipping' (placing rubbish in 'cells' of soil and covering within twelve hours) can result in minimal water pollution if subsurface conditions are such that the leachate can be diluted, dispersed and rendered harmless. This development not only facilitated the reclamation of numerous 'problematic' wet-pits, but also allowed the disposal of the ever-increasing volumes of domestic refuse (20 million tonnes in 1980 and growing at 0.7 per cent per head per annum). In consequence, 90 per cent of United Kingdom rubbish is still used for landfill, little being incinerated (9 per cent) and virtually none disposed by composting. While land-filling remains the most economic disposal method and successfully resolves two 'environmental' problems at the same time, there is a growing body of opinion that greater effort should be made to conserve resources by the recycling of materials, the generation of heat and power through incineration (e.g. the plants at Edmonton, North London, and Doncaster) or the conversion of organic refuse into oil or methane (e.g. the plant at Arpley, near Warrington, opened in 1988).

Arguments in favour of reducing the emphasis on landfill have been strengthened in recent years by (i) the discovery of buried toxic and hazardous wastes (including dioxin) at sites subsequently used for building, (ii) the offensive smell and leachate produced at certain sites, (iii) the occurrence of spontaneous combustion on supposedly safe reclaimed land and (iv) the potential for explosions as manifest by the destruction of a bungalow at Loscoe, Derbyshire, in 1986.

Irrespective of future trends, the post-war situation has been one in which the volume of excavations has far exceeded available filler materials. However, unfavourable groundwater conditions and limited size precluded the use of many 'wet pits' for refuse tipping, so that, in certain instances, shortage of locally available sites (e.g. Bristol and London) has resulted in longer and longer haul-distances (up to 100km by rail) to large, economic bulk-disposal locations. As a result, the rapid increase in unreclaimed 'wet pits' was a cause of concern in the 1950s and 1960s, until it was recognized that the creation of lagoons was not necessarily a blight on the landscape. In consequence, the 'fill and obliterate' doctrine was slowly replaced by a more positive approach, which recognized that former mineral working could enhance local amenity and recreation potential after landscaping and tree-planting. The Lea Valley Regional Park, the strings of lakes along the Colne and Darent Valleys, and the Holme Pierpoint National Water Sports Centre at Nottingham, are just some examples of alterations that have proved beneficial in terms of environment, nature conservation, amenity and recreation. This concept has been developed still further, for in many instances planning permission for mineral operations is now granted with conditions attached which predetermine the pattern of extraction so as to produce a pleasing landscape for ultimate use for water-based recreation (e.g. Cotswold Water Park).

**CONCLUSION**

As has been shown, the two-way interaction between human occupancy and the physical environment has become increasingly complex over the last half-century. Several reasons have been advanced: population growth and redistribution, technological development, increased mobility, and economic growth have led to changes in the urban, industrial, transportation and agricultural sectors, many of which have had important consequences in terms of local climate, geomorphology and hydrology. In addition, there has been increasing sensitivity (both apparent and real) to natural hazard impacts (especially flooding), partly due to the growing organizational complexity and inter-dependence of commercial activity, and partly because of the visual impact achieved by post-war developments in television reporting. This, in combination with the growth in environmentalism, has led to greater awareness as to the possible ramifications of human-environment interactions and some concomitant development of appraisal and monitoring programmes, including the limited use of forms of environmental impact analysis as part of development projects. Other important achievements include the establishment of limited controls on mineral operations, the appraisals of the extent and character of land dereliction and the completion of a growing number of successful reclamation schemes, all of which have been consequent upon post-war developments in land planning legislation.

Nevertheless, the power of society to create change in the physical environment continues to increase, both in scale and variety, as do the risks posed by natural hazards. While there has been some advance in understanding the nature of the physical environmental systems and their responses to changes, there remains a considerable need for further research in order to provide an adequate information base, so that adverse changes can be recognized at an early stage, and the necessary enforceable environmental legislation formulated and enacted when and where required.

## FURTHER READING

The subject of human environment interaction is a broad one and the relevant literature is both fragmented and diffuse. The general nature of anthropogenic influences on environment is outlined by Goudie, A. S. (1981) *The Human Impact,* Oxford: Blackwell, and the character and problems of natural hazards are recounted in Whittow, J. (1980) *Disasters,* Harmondsworth: Penguin. More specifically with regards to the United Kingdom, Perry, A. H. (1981) *Environmental Hazards in the British Isles,* London: Allen & Unwin focuses mainly on atmospheric hazards, but details on river flooding are available in Smith, K. and Tobin G. A. (1979) *Flooding and the Flood Hazard in the United Kingdom,* London: Longman and Penning-Rowsell, E. C. and Handmer, J. W. (1988) 'Flood hazard management in Britain: A changing scene', in *Geographical Journal,* 154: 209–20. Flooding along the East Coast and the nature of adopted defence measures are discussed in Steers, J. A. (1953) 'The east coast floods, January 31 to February 1 1953', in *Geographical Journal,* 119: 280–95; and Horner, R. W. (1979) 'The Thames Barrier project', *Geographical Journal,* 145: 242–53. For discussions of the October 1987 storm see special issues of *Weather* (March 1988) and *The Meteorological Magazine* (April 1988). The nature of urban climates is examined in Chandler, J. T. and Gregory, S. (1976) *The Climate of the British Isles,* London: Longman, pp. 307–29, while urban influences on rainfall are further discussed by Atkinson, B. W. (1981) *Man and Environmental Processes,* in Gregory, K. J., and Walling, D. E. London: Butterworths, chapter 3. For an historical review of urban atmospheric pollution see Brimblecombe, P. (1987) *The Big Smoke,* London: Methuen.

The fullest account of the UK mineral industry is to be found in Blunden, John (1975) *The Mineral Resources of Britain,* London: Hutchinson. A more detailed examination of the difficulties facing the aggregate supply industry is contained in *Aggregates: The Way Ahead,* Report of Verney Comm. HMSO, 1976, while an outline of the socio-political and environmental problems associated with mineral exploitation is to be found in Smith, J. (1975) *The Politics of Physical Resources,* Harmondsworth: Penguin. The nature, distribution and origins of land dereliction are clearly examined in Barr, J. (1969) *Derelict Britain,* Harmondsworth: Penguin and in Wallwork, K. (1974) *Derelict Land,* London: David and Charles.

# 16 Pollution of air, land, rivers, and coast

*Vince Gardiner*

We are locked into a system of 'fouling our own nest' so long as we behave only as independent, rational free-enterprisers.
(Garret Hardin (1968) 'The tragedy of the commons', *Science*, 162: 1243–8)

We are becoming a garbage dump for Europe
(Charles Secrett, Friends of the Earth)

During the past sixty years there has been a growing concern for the quality of the environment generally and an interest in pollution more specifically. This is difficult to assess in absolute terms, but figure 16.1 attempts to give some indication of growing public, or at least media, awareness of environmental pollution in Britain during the last quarter century. The number of entries in *The Times* annual index related to pollution is used as an indicator. Before the mid-1960s the space devoted to this was minimal and 'pollution' did not appear separately in the index. During the last twenty-five years there has been a very substantial and regular increase in coverage afforded to this topic, punctuated by well-marked peaks of interest associated with particular incidents, such as the Torrey Canyon oil tanker spillage, and environmental concerns, such as that of acid rain. It should be noted that the Chernobyl incident (see pp. 437–9) is not included in this tabulation, as it is not included by *The Times* indexers under pollution. However this and other major events were afforded substantial media coverage and brought environmental pollution into the public eye in a very dramatic fashion. During the earlier part of the period major incidents associated with the marine environment tended to dominate the media, whereas more recently atmospheric concerns such as the CFC crisis (see pp. 436–7) and acid rain (see pp. 434–6) have become more significant.

Growing environmental and 'ecological' awareness is also evidenced by the increasing numbers of both scientific and more popular publications devoted to such topics, by the increase in educational opportunities in environmental fields, and by the growth and acceptance of environmental pressure groups such as Friends of the Earth and Greenpeace. During the early months of 1989 such environmental groups attracted more than

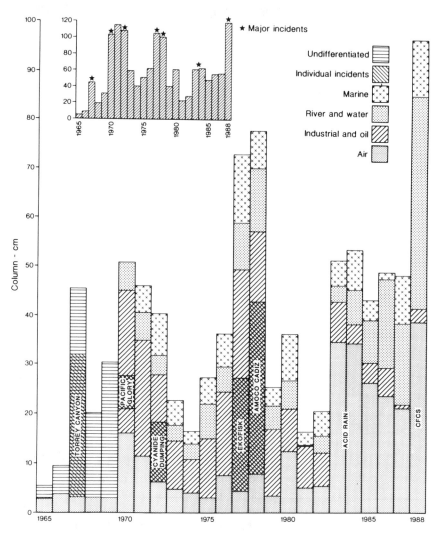

*Figure 16.1* Column-cm of *The Times* annual index devoted to pollution
*Note:* Inset shows the total coverage afforded to pollution in Britain and overseas; the main figure shows coverage afforded to specific categories in Britain

20,000 new members per month, and by mid-1989 'Green' organizations totalled 3.8 million members – almost 50 per cent of the membership of the Trade Union movement. Particularly noteworthy has been the attempt to bring 'Green' issues onto the political agenda by Mrs Thatcher in 1988, and the success, in terms of votes cast if not seats won, of the Green Party (formerly Ecology Party) in the European Community elections in 1989; the party gained 2.3 million votes, or 15 per cent of the poll.

Environmental pollution involves changes which occur in the environment, usually for the worse, as a result of human activity. This definition embraces the atmosphere, rivers, lakes, land, coasts and oceans, but excludes changes in weathering and erosion. As manufacturing and related activities increase in extent and diversity it is inevitable that the wastes produced will also increase in amount and complexity; such wastes include gases, liquids and solids, as well as heat and noise. Pollution has also been regarded as the inevitable outcome of waste disposal at the least possible cost and at the least inconvenience. Pollution is by its nature likely to be a very controversial issue, and a considerable body of British and EC legislation is devoted to its prevention and management. Pollution has also become a very fashionable issue within the media and politics within the last few decades, and some radical and superficially attractive solutions have been suggested to the apparently irreconcilable conflicts between, on the one hand, a rising standard, and hence quality, of living associated with economic development and, on the other, a desire to preserve the environment, stimulated by a deteriorating physical environment and hence quality of life.

Much of the so-called 'ecological' debate appears to have been founded on an incomplete appreciation of the reasons for this conflict. The first reason is related to the nature of the material resources upon which economic activities are founded. It is impracticable to dispose of waste materials outside the world, including the atmosphere. Pollution is therefore inevitable if resources are utilized, and all that can be done is to choose the optimum place, mode and method of coping with pollution. For example, harmful land and water pollution can be avoided by incineration of domestic waste, thereby producing relatively harmless air pollution in small amounts. This consideration is particularly appropriate to examination of the geography of pollution in the United Kingdom, where space for waste disposal of all kinds is severely restricted (see also chapter 15).

The second reason is economic. Pollution control, management and amelioration are expensive and because the costs of pollution are often borne not by the polluters but by the nation there is sometimes a reluctance to make efforts to reduce pollution. The interests of manufacturers rarely coincide with the national interest, because the latter may require them to incur extra production costs for waste treatment and disposal for which they receive no tangible return. The reconciliation of individual liberty and communal well-being is often therefore a fine balance, given the nature of British society.

Pollution has many direct and indirect implications for human activities. Almost any substance can be a pollutant, although some are obviously much more harmful than others. Some pollutants may occur in more than one medium within the environment, whereas others are restricted in occurrence. A useful distinction can be made between those pollutants with natural counterparts and those without. The former are produced by nature, but also by human activity at a rate in excess of natural production. For example carbon dioxide is produced by combustion of fossil fuels and is regarded by some as a key pollutant in understanding long-term climatic change. It is also produced by respiratory processes and its concentration in the atmosphere is stablized by a series of natural regulatory mechanisms. It is therefore reasonable to suggest that artificial generation of carbon dioxide may also be accommodated by the same mechanisms. However natural processes for degradation and regulation of synthetic pollutants are generally absent. These include chlorinated hydrocarbons (e.g. DDT) and polychlorinated biphenyls (PCBs) which may enter food chains. Because of the lack of natural mechanisms for their removal they are remarkably persistent and through biological concentration can seriously affect higher life.

Two major themes are evident in examining the recent geography of pollution in the United Kingdom. First, polluting processes are becoming increasingly complex, with ever-more sophisticated industrial processes giving rise to increasingly complex chemicals, and even simple compounds becoming involved in complicated pollutant pathways. Second, Britain is a part of a global environmental system. Pollution from Britain affects elsewhere. Concerns such as acid rain (pp. 434–6), the risk to the ozone layer because of CFCs (pp. 436–7) and the 'Greenhouse Effect' (pp. 433–4) all demonstrate how local pollutant inputs can have inadvertent and wide-spread effects on the atmosphere. In addition, Britain is affected by events elsewhere. For example, increasing industrial and economic linkages between countries have produced a deliberate international trade in pollutants, with incidents such as the saga of the Karin B (pp. 444–5) giving rise to much public concern. Both of these are recurrent themes in this chapter.

The rest of this chapter will be concerned with examining the ways in which spatial patterns of pollution within the United Kingdom have changed over the last sixty years, and will discuss some of the major influences upon this changing pattern; other aspects of the themes of pollution and conservation are dealt with in chapters 15 and 17. Here air, terrestrial water, land and marine pollution will be examined in turn. Unfortunately it is impossible to provide an even coverage of all parts of the United Kingdom, as data are not equally available for all areas, and many more data are available for the later parts of the period. Many of the general conclusions do apply uniformly, within the constraints of local factors, even if not explicitly developed for some areas. The uneven availability of data also reflects need for concern in a general sense. Very few data are available for Northern Ireland and Scotland, but it must be acknowledged that in general pollution in these countries is not as severe as in England and, to a lesser extent, Wales.

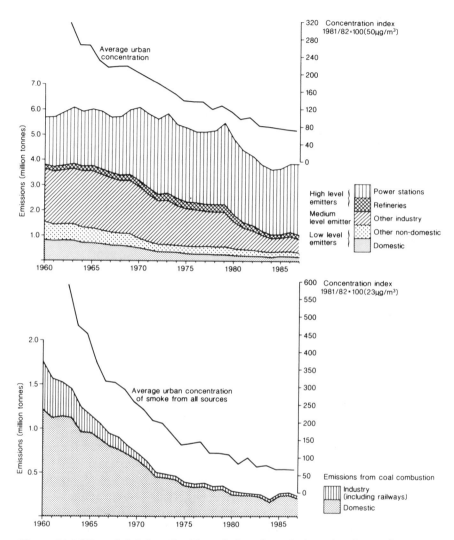

*Figure 16.2* (Upper) Sulphur dioxide emissions from fuel combustion and average urban concentrations. (Lower) Smoke emissions from coal combustion and average urban concentrations

*Source:* Department of the Environment (1988) *Digest of Environmental Protection and Water Statistics,* London: HMSO

## AIR POLLUTION

The climatological implications of air pollution have been examined in chapter 15, and attention here will be focused on the British dimension to recent global-scale air pollution issues. Two characteristics traditionally regarded as major components of air pollution are sulphur dioxide and smoke. Total sulphur dioxide emissions were relatively stable throughout the 1960s at about 6 million tonnes per year. Then emissions fell to about 5 million tonnes in 1976, and less than 4 million tonnes in 1983. Emissions declined sharply in 1984–5 because of the miners' strike, but returned to pre-strike levels in 1986 and 1987. Since 1962 average urban concentrations have fallen by almost 80 per cent, largely as a result of reduced emissions from low- and medium-level sources (figure 16.2).

A similar but even more dramatic fall in smoke emissions has also occurred (figure 16.2) with an 85 per cent reduction since 1960, largely as a result of the Clean Air Acts (see however chapter 15). Consumers have also switched from coal to cleaner and more convenient fuels in areas not covered by smoke control. The average urban concentration of smoke is now less than one-tenth of that in the early 1960s. Twenty-nine cities in Britain were granted initial exemption from the EC Smoke and Sulphur Dioxide Directive, until 1993, although seven have now complied. The remaining twenty-two are mainly in traditional mining areas in the East Midlands and north-east where subsidized coal is still burnt in open grates, along with Londonderry, where cheap imported coal with a high sulphur content is burnt.

Less visible but perhaps more insidiously dangerous than smoke and sulphur dioxide are the so-called 'Greenhouse' gases, and those responsible for acid rain. The 'Greenhouse Effect' is a natural effect resulting from the presence of certain gases in the atmosphere. The earth's surface is heated by incoming radiation from the sun; the surface in turn emits long wavelength radiation. Some gases in the atmosphere are heated by this, and therefore re-emit energy back to the earth's surface. Carbon dioxide is the most important greenhouse gas, 40 per cent of which comes from burning fossil fuels, and 10–15 per cent from cutting down forests. Ozone, chlorofluorocarbons (CFCs) – which account for 20 per cent of the total – water vapour, methane and nitrous oxide are also important. There has been increasing concern that artificial inputs of these gases might be increasing the blanketing effect, thereby increasing average temperatures. Average temperatures have been predicted to be 1.5°C higher by 2050. Other environmental effects are difficult to predict, but rising sea levels associated with melting ice caps are suggested to be quite possible, with 'Doncaster-upon-Sea' and the 'Bay of Somerset' being elements in a possible future geography of the British Isles. Improvements to sea defences necessitated by rising sea levels could cost as much as £8 billion, depending on the magnitude of sea-level rise experienced. No agreed solutions to the problem have yet been agreed, but a package of measures is being proposed, including greater emphasis upon nuclear energy, greater efficiency in energy use, and introduction of a 'carbon tax' on producers.

Both carbon dioxide and nitrogen oxide emissions have risen since the mid-1980s because of increased emissions from power stations and road transport, and since 1958 the level of carbon dioxide in the atmosphere has increased by 10 per cent. Since 1970 hydrocarbon emissions have risen by 18 per cent, and carbon monoxide by 9 per cent, despite some fluctuations in individual years (figure 16.3). Fossil fuels when burned produce about three times their weight of carbon dioxide, with the 233 million tons of carbon dioxide produced by power generating stations in Britain every year being the biggest single contributor. Environmentalists are expressing great concern over the proposed Electricity Bill which precedes privatization of the electricity industry, as this makes no provisions for reducing pollutant emissions. European legislation to reduce pollution by carbon monoxide and nitrogen oxides has focused on the compulsory introduction of catalytic converters for cars after 1993.

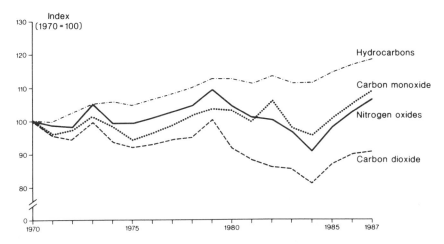

*Figure 16.3* Estimated emissions of greenhouse gases
*Source:* Department of the Environment (1988) *Digest of Environmental Protection and Water Statistics,* London: HMSO

Another Greenhouse gas is methane. This is produced from a variety of sources, including the degradation of biodegradable material in landfill sites, and the natural flatulence of cows and other animals! The former source has been estimated at about 2.2 million tonnes of methane per year, the latter at 100 million tonnes globally. Although smaller in amount than carbon dioxide, it must be noted that methane is about 25 times more effective as a Greenhouse gas.

Although rainfall is naturally slightly acidic the high and apparently increasing acidity of rainfall in parts of Europe and North America has recently been causing considerable concern. 'Acid rain' results from human-made emissions of oxides of sulphur and nitrogen when fossil fuels are burned, especially in power stations, industry and motor vehicles. In Britain most nitrogen oxides (46 per cent) come from power stations and vehicle exhausts (28 per cent). These oxides are transformed within the

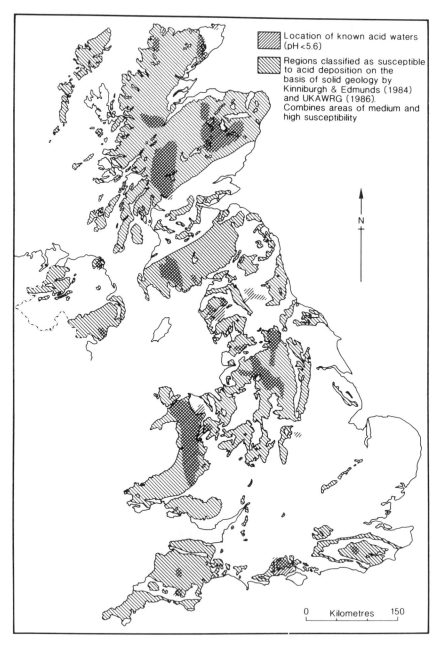

*Figure 16.4* Distribution of acid waters in the UK
*Source:* Department of the Environment (1989) Acid Waters Review Group, *Acidity in the United Kingdom 1989,* London: HMSO

atmosphere into dilute sulphuric and nitric acids and eventually deposited, perhaps hundreds of kilometres downwind, in precipitation.

The environmental effect of acid rain depends on the concentration of acid and the amount of rain. The combined effect of these two factors is a measure of the potential environmental stress resulting. Within the United Kingdom acidity deposited by rain is highest in the Scottish Highlands, south-west Scotland, North Wales, the Lake District and the Pennines. Lake sediments suggest that the downward trend in pH began about 1850. Lakes with pH values of less than 5.0 became common in only the last few decades, and are confined to the areas of high acid deposition (figure 16.4). It seems that, although major agricultural crops are unlikely to be damaged directly by current concentrations, yields of some sensitive crops in south-east England may be reduced by concentrations of ozone. There is some indication, as yet unsubstantiated, that forests and individual trees might be under some pollution-induced stress. Acid deposition is also accelerating acidification of soils, which in the longer term is likely to alter plant nutrition and the chemistry and biology of freshwaters.

More controversially, it has been suggested that acid rain deposition originating from United Kingdom sources is responsible for the decline of forests and acidification of soils and surface waters in Europe, particularly Norway and Germany. The United Kingdom government has been under considerable pressure to reduce emissions of the significant gases, but has not joined a group of over forty countries, which includes the main European countries, in agreeing to reduce emissions by at least 30 per cent by the early 1990s. Twelve major British power stations are to be fitted with pollution-limiting equipment, but this could, paradoxically, cause other environmental problems. This is because the process requires large quantities of limestone, the main source areas of which are in National Parks such as the Peak District, and also requires the disposal of large amounts of gypsum, produced as a waste product. As an alternative strategy the pro-nuclear energy lobby has used acid rain as an argument for nuclear power being more environmentally acceptable than conventional plants.

In recent years the controversy surrounding use of chlorofluorocarbons (CFCs) and the damage they are doing to the ozone layer of the atmosphere has also received a great deal of publicity. The ozone layer is part of the upper atmosphere, and screens us from 99 per cent of harmful solar ultra-violet radiation. In 1988 CFCs were used in aerosols (62 per cent), foam packaging and insulating products (18 per cent), solvents (12 per cent) and refrigerators (8 per cent), and when released into the atmosphere they have an adverse effect on ozone. Even a 1 per cent thinning of the ozone layer could result in a great increase in skin cancers. CFCs are also highly significant Greenhouse gases (see above). As a result of the complicated chemical processes involved the effects are most marked in colder parts of the globe. In 1985 British scientists discovered a 'hole' in the ozone layer above Antarctica, and in 1989 a similar one was confirmed in the northern hemisphere. The US Environmental Protection Agency has estimated the possible destruction of 50 per cent of the ozone layer by 2050 – with catastrophic effects. In September 1987 the Montreal Agreement was signed, whereby a gradual reduction of 35 per cent in use of CFCs would be made. The British government entered into this without any enthusiasm, but by 1989 the 'greening' of British politics resulted in a more enthusiastic adoption. In 1989 an international agreement was made between twenty-four countries to limit output and use of CFCs, with a 50 per cent cut by 1999. All EC governments are now committed to a complete ban by the end of the century. By 1989 public concern, largely in response to a campaign by Friends of the Earth, had been such that use of CFCs as an aerosol propellant had virtually ceased. However a 'time-bomb' effect exists, because the chlorine and bromine molecules which are oxidized by the ozone take six or seven years to rise into the ozone layer, and they can survive for up to 100 years. In addition there are many refrigerators with CFCs in insulating foam and coolants, and these will continue in use for many years to come, with CFCs being released if they are not disposed of properly. The aspirations of the developing countries to have refrigeration continue to fuel a demand for CFCs, and, although research continues on replacements for CFCs, none have as yet been fully accepted as economic alternatives.

The CFC controversy illustrates very dramatically how national pollution contributes to a global problem, which in turn has national implications. It also illustrates how changes in public attitudes and even government policy can be brought about by pressure groups and media attention.

Another atmospheric pollutant is lead. Lead emissions, largely originating from lead added to petrol as an anti-knock additive, have been reduced as a result of legislation in 1981 and 1985 which reduced the amount of lead allowed. From 1988 there has been a great increase in the availability of unleaded petrol, and recent publicity, coupled with tax differences allowing a price incentive, has been successful in persuading many motorists to convert their cars to use it. Political pressures have also resulted in many local government bodies converting public service vehicles to use lead-free fuel, and West Midlands police are even examining the feasibility of using lead-free bullets as part of an environment-friendly policy.

On April 26, 1986 there occurred what was possibly the most significant, and certainly the most emotive, pollution incident in British pollution history – an incident which again demonstrates the international dimension to the geography of British pollution. A nuclear power station at Chernobyl in the USSR suffered a major accident which resulted in a prolonged atmospheric release of large quantities of radioactive products. Variations of meteorological conditions and wind directions during the release

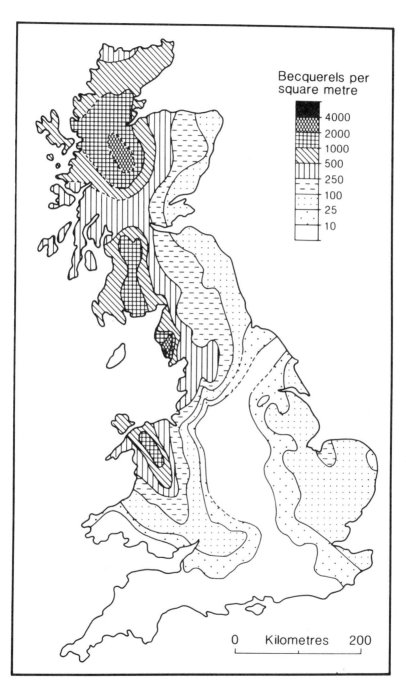

*Figure 16.5* Deposition of Caesium-137 in the UK (based upon analyses by the Institute for Terrestrial Ecology)

produced a wide-spread distribution of radioactivity throughout the northern hemisphere, and especially Europe. Although the absolute radiological impact of the incident in the United Kingdom was never critical, it caused considerable public concern, and highlighted the increasing spatial scale of pollution risk associated with the technologically more advanced society.

The distribution of Caesium-137 deposition resulting from Chernobyl is shown in figure 16.5. The highest values occurred in Snowdonia, the Lake District, south-west Scotland and the Grampians, where rainfall associated with these upland areas washed radionuclides out of the atmosphere. The immediate response of the authorities included monitoring of people from contaminated areas, control of rainwater for domestic use, restrictions on the import from overseas of many agricultural products, controls on the domestic marketing of sheep and lamb, and government compensation for agricultural losses. Longer-term reactions include the introduction of a radiation monitoring network to give early warning of any future incident, and, even three years after the event, a ban on the consumption of meat from some 70,000 Lakeland sheep.

The psychological impact of Chernobyl was even greater. The very word Chernobyl is now an emotive rallying cry to environmentalists disbelieving of official claims that the nuclear energy industry is a safe one. It is likely that this rather than any physical impact of the event will be the most significant in the long term, as governments into the twenty-first century struggle to bring about a viable energy policy in the context of falling oil reserves and rising environmental concerns. Changing attitudes to radioactive pollution are dramatically exemplified by the recent revelation that in the 1960s United States' Polaris submarines regularly dumped radioactive coolant in the Holy Loch off the Firth of Clyde.

The Conservative government of the 1980s has declared itself in favour of nuclear power generation, at least partly because it is perceived as less of a polluter than other forms of power station. However opponents argue that, irrespective of the dangers of another Chernobyl-type incident, there is the problem of disposing of the radioactive waste generated.

British Nuclear Fuels have reduced the level of waste discharged into the sea from Sellafield to a tenth of that in 1979, and further improvements are promised. The Government has approved the disposal of some 4 million tonnes of low and intermediate level radioactive waste in a single deep facility. At the time of writing test drillings are being undertaken at Sellafield in Cumbria, and Dounreay in Caithness, on land adjacent to existing nuclear installations.

Another dimension of concern over nuclear pollution is the possibility of disease, and particularly cancer, resulting from exposure to radiation associated with nuclear power stations or other nuclear plants – possibly from an airborne source. Despite government assurances that artificial radiation is less than a thousandth of that which occurs naturally, for example from radioactive minerals in granitic rocks, suspicions continue to arise. For example, incidences of childhood leukemias have been shown to be statistically higher than normal in the areas around Sellafield, Dounreay, the Atomic Weapons Research Establishment at Aldermaston, the Royal Ordnance Factory in Berkshire, and Hinkley Point nuclear power station in Somerset. No causal processes have yet been confirmed, but the suspicion of polluting radiation somehow causing these illnesses has virtually hardened into a certainty.

## INLAND WATER POLLUTION

Even in its 'natural' condition water may show marked differences in composition, and 'pure' water in nature may contain dissolved salts or peat particles and silt. In practice, therefore, no absolute definition of river pollution can be adopted, and the term is generally understood to refer to human detrimental modification of water quality.

Between 1958 and 1980 the proportion of river length classified as poor or grossly polluted fell from 13 per cent to 7 per cent, and in tidal rivers from 27 per cent to 16 per cent (figure 16.6). However this improvement in the worst category of pollution has been balanced by static or even increasing lengths of river in the doubtful or poor categories. By 1989 a downturn in British river water quality seems evident, with reports of 368 kilometres of best-quality river in the south-west being downgraded since 1986, whilst in the north-west 78 kilometres were downgraded in one year. At least 10 per cent of the 44,000 kilometres of estuaries and rivers are so polluted that they cannot support fish life. In 1988 the number of pollution incidents in England and Wales rose to a record 23,253 – double the figure for 1982 – with 1,402 regarded as serious. In 1988 manufacturing industry was responsible for 37 per cent of incidents, sewage works 20 per cent, agriculture 19 per cent and other bodies 24 per cent. The industrial areas of the midlands were the most seriously affected. However only 288 prosecutions were made. Water Authorities are being pressed to prosecute offenders more often, but a maximum fine of only £2,000 under the Control of Pollution Act 1978 is little deterrent to the major firms and even County Councils which are so often the offenders. A recent EC proposal, not yet implemented, is for polluters to pay for the costs of all clean-up operations.

Somewhat paradoxically, one of the biggest offenders is the Water Authorities themselves. For example, in 1988 the Severn-Trent was responsible for more than 900 pollution incidents. More than 700 of Britain's 4,400 sewage works do not meet EC standards concerning allowable discharges, and under the privatization legislation these will in future be liable for prosecution by the new National Rivers Authority (see chapter 6). Investment programmes of up to £1,000 million have been planned so that almost all plants should meet the standards by 1992.

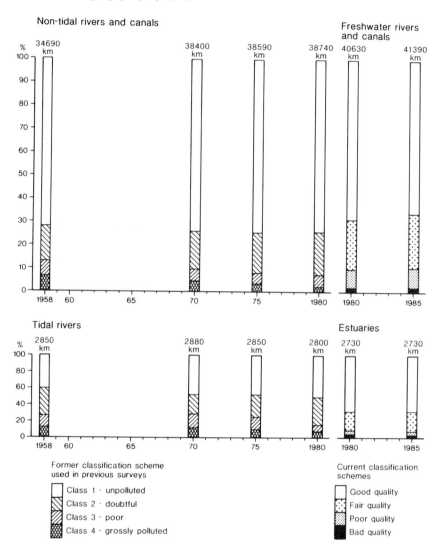

*Figure 16.6* River water quality, 1958–85
*Source:* DOE and Welsh Office (1986) *River Water Quality in England and Wales, 1985: A Report of the 1985 Survey*

Another major offender is agriculture, with over 4,000 farm pollution reports being received by the Water Authorities in 1988 – a 6 per cent increase on 1987 – although again, only 5 per cent of such reports resulted in prosecutions. In 1979 only 1,500 such incidents were reported. Slurry from intensive animal production, silage, and waste from intensive food processing plants all contribute to the problem. Silage is 200 times more potent at removing oxygen from the river than is raw sewage, and farm slurry is 100 times.

One particular cause of concern over water quality has been nitrate concentrations. The 1985 EC Directive on the Quality of Water Intended for Human Consumption set a target figure of 50mg/1, but for many sampling points in the United Kingdom, especially in the arable areas of the east where fertiliser applications are highest (see chapter 4) and rainfalls are lowest, this level is exceeded. Some authorities blame the ploughing up of grassland, whilst others blame fertilisers directly. Particularly worrying is the 'nitrate time-bomb' whereby fertilisers washed into groundwater will have their effect on nitrate values for decades after application has ceased. Computer models predicting nitrate concentrations on the assumption of no significant changes in farming practices and land use show that concentrations will continue to exceed the desired levels for the next fifty years. Possible preventative actions include the delimitation of so-called environmental protection zones within which farmers would be required to adopt less intensive farming practices. The time lag between preventative action being taken and a resulting decline in nitrate values depends on the transmission times of the aquifers, with Chalk aquifers having a delay of up to fifty years, whereas sandstone areas respond in as little as ten years. For some areas short-term curative measures such as blending or treatment will need to be taken, although it should be noted that chemical treatment to remove nitrates completely would double the cost of water treatment. The government initially hoped to be able to extend the deadline for compliance with EC drinking water standards beyond 1992, but it now looks likely that this will not be allowed by the Commissioners, and water industry privatization plans (chapter 6) are likely to be modified in the light of the investments needed.

Another agriculture-related pollutant is pesticides. A 1988 survey by Friends of the Earth found that 300 water sources in England contained pesticides at levels above the limits set by the EC, especially in the midlands.

One major pollution event which is worth brief mention, because it demonstrates how the complexity of modern pollution control methods can itself give rise to pollution if not properly managed, is that which occurred in Camelford, Cornwall, in July 1988, described as Britain's worst pollution incident. This occurred when a delivery of 20 tonnes of aluminium sulphate, a chemical used in small quantities in treating raw water destined for drinking purposes, was inadvertently dumped into the local mains supply. An estimated 5,000 people drank water containing several thousand times the EC limit for aluminium, and many suffered effects ranging from bleached hair turning green to vomiting, diarrhoea, arthritic pains and other illnesses. More than 60,000 fish were killed in local rivers, and South-West Water were obliged to pay substantial compensation claims. Even three months later complaints were being made of tap waters containing more than permitted levels of metals, leached from pipes.

Aluminium concentrations in tap water have been of particular concern more generally, because of suggested links with the occurrence of Alzheimer's disease. One survey has suggested that more than a million people in the south-west, Wales, midlands and the north are supplied with water exceeding the allowable aluminium level set by EC directive. Again, treatment to remove this metal would be prohibitively costly, and blending is the only immediate solution to the problem.

### POLLUTION OF THE LAND

Pollution of the land is in some ways less obvious than that of water and atmosphere but it is perhaps more important on the longer time-scale because, whereas air and water are in constant motion and therefore have some degree of mixing and self-cleaning, pollution on the Earth's land surface is normally resident there for long time periods. Soil may be seriously affected by this, as for example at Shipham in Somerset where anomalously high levels of cadmium in soils and stream waters were traced back to a mine waste tip. During 1972 much concern was expressed nationally in an outcry against illegal dumping of industrial wastes containing cyanide in the West Midlands, but it is feared that such exposures may represent only the tip of the illegal dumping iceberg.

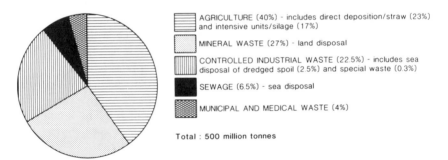

AGRICULTURE (40%) - includes direct deposition/straw (23%) and intensive units/silage (17%)

MINERAL WASTE (27%) - land disposal

CONTROLLED INDUSTRIAL WASTE (22.5%) - includes sea disposal of dredged spoil (2.5%) and special waste (0.3%)

SEWAGE (6.5%) - sea disposal

MUNICIPAL AND MEDICAL WASTE (4%)

Total : 500 million tonnes

*Figure 16.7* Estimated total annual waste arising in the UK
*Source:* Based on data in Eleventh Report of the Royal Commission on Environmental Pollution, Cmnd. 9675, December 1985

It was estimated in 1985 that the total amount of waste matter generated each year in Britain was just under 500 million tonnes, as shown in figure 16.7, and the total amount per person is increasing year by year. The composition of urban waste has changed since the 1930s, with declining amounts of coal and cinder wastes being compensated by increasing amounts of paper and plastics. Of most relevance here is that waste known as 'Controlled waste', defined as that which comes within the Control of Pollution Act, 1974. Within this, 'Special waste' is that which consists of or contains any of certain specified substances, and which is dangerous to life. The amount of special waste arising in England and Wales was estimated at

1.56 million tonnes in 1986, and some 53,000 tonnes was imported for treatment or incineration – double the amount of the previous year. In 1987–8 more than 80,000 tonnes were imported, and it is estimated that the 1989 figure will top 130,000 tonnes. Another category of waste is 'Hazardous waste', which is of a chemical nature with a recognized risk of causing damage to the environment. The amount of this is estimated to have been about 3.7 million tonnes in 1986, most of which was disposed of to landfill.

One hazard arising from landfill disposal of waste is the release of methane gas generated by decay of biodegradable waste. Buildings have been destroyed by explosions (see chapter 15), and the danger is preventing redevelopment of some landfill sites. Methane is also an important Greenhouse gas. Another hazard is the leaking of wastes into water courses and groundwater. Largely as a response to EC Directives, Water Authorities have introduced Aquifer Protection Policies with, for example in the case of Severn-Trent, four types of zone being recognized according to the importance of the aquifer and its properties. The intention is to direct waste disposers to less sensitive hydrological environments. A third hazard is the accidental inclusion of inappropriate and highly dangerous wastes which should be incinerated, such as medical refuse containing wastes from AIDS clinics in London, dumped in Lancashire in February 1989. London hospitals generate 16 million bags of clinical waste a year, most of which is incinerated at a cost of from 25p per bag.

The trend whereby the United Kingdom might be seen by other countries as the 'Dustbin of the World' has been viewed as undesirable and potentially dangerous by many environmentalists, concerned about possible contamination of ground or surface waters, or air pollution. Artificial chemicals such as PCBs can only be destroyed by high-temperature incineration, and inadequate combustion can give off carcinogenic dioxins. Leading customers for this kind of service are Holland, the Republic of Ireland, Belgium, Portugal, Canada and the United States – again demonstrating the international component in the geography of British pollution.

The saga of the Karin B in 1988, involving Italy, Nigeria, Spain, the United Kingdom, France, the Netherlands and West Germany, did much to bring this international component to the public's attention. In 1987 and 1988 five shiploads of highly poisonous chemical waste were secretly taken from Italy to Koko, a little port on the Niger Delta. Eventually 10,000 drums of a deadly poisonous chemical cocktail were stored there in the tropical sun and rain, and leakages began to occur. Under diplomatic pressure the Italian Government agreed to remove the waste, using a chartered German ship, the Karin B, with an Austrian captain. This set sail for Italy, but it was realized that no Mediterranean country had facilities for the proper disposal of the wastes. Eventually British waste disposal experts agreed to tackle the problem. An attempt to berth the ship at Neath failed because the ship was too large. A public outcry was raised; eventually the Department of the Environment banned the ship altogether, and, after being refused entry to France, the Netherlands and Spain, it returned to Italy, where the waste is still stored.

One encouraging trend to emerge is a growing pressure for recycling of waste materials of all kinds. 'Bottle banks' for the return of waste glass are becoming commonplace, and paper and metal recycling is also becoming more widespread. In 1989 Sheffield was declared Britain's first 'Recycling City', with funding from a variety of sources providing facilities for recycling of glass, plastic and metals.

## MARINE AND COASTAL POLLUTION

Three aspects of pollution of the marine environment are considered. The beaches and coastal areas of Britain are becoming increasingly polluted by solid litter, oil from shipping, and by sewage. The development of non-biodegradable materials stimulated much concern during the 1960s and 1970s, and materials such as plastics have a high potential for marine pollution because of their widespread use and inherent characteristics. They float, do not degrade and are therefore persistent. In the late 1970s a survey reported a wide variety of litter on beaches, including part of an aircraft wing, a sewing machine and a crematorium urn, as well as potentially hazardous materials such as drugs, chemicals and munitions. Most common litter was containers, including fish boxes, especially on the western coasts, and drink cans, especially near ferry routes. Little litter appears to be more than five years old, and it is thought that degradation and/or removal of the material to deeper water eventually occurs. However some marine pollutants are not so readily absorbed by the marine environment. For example in 1989 a cargo of six tons of Lindane, one of the world's most dangerous insecticides, suspected of causing cancers and other disorders, was lost in a shipwreck north-west of the Channel Islands. British and French rescue services, including mine-hunters and submarines, joined forces to avert what could have been a major disaster – six tons of Lindane would require no less than 1,500 cubic kilometres of water to dilute it to safe concentrations – a large part of the English Channel.

A second aspect of marine pollution is that concerning oil spillages. The exploration for and exploitation of North Sea oil has stimulated an increased traffic in oil in British waters, and the development of super-tankers has made the impact of individual incidents much larger than in the 1960s. Major incidents have provoked much comment (figure 16.1), but there are many other smaller incidents each year, not all accidental or traceable to individual vessels. These are concentrated around the major shipping lanes, in the North Sea oilfield area, and in the ports such as Milford Haven having oil terminals. Such pollution can have severe ecological repercussions, although it should be noted that with the benefit of hindsight and detachment it has been concluded that in some cases more damage to wildlife was caused by chemicals used to disperse oil than by the oil itself. Oil pollution can also have economic implications, when it detracts from the recreational amenity of beaches.

For the majority of coastal towns the sea provides a very convenient means of disposing of both human and industrial wastes, including colliery wastes and coal washings in the north-east of England, wastes from chemical and vegetable industries as at Teeside and the Wash, and waste from distilleries and the paper industry at Loch Linhe. More than 26 million tonnes of waste are dumped annually in the seas around Britain under licence. This is made up of dredgings (68 per cent), sewage sludge (21 per cent), solid industrial waste (10 per cent) and liquid industrial waste (1 per cent). It is estimated that over 300 million gallons of only partly treated sewage, or about 17 per cent of the total, are disposed of in British coastal waters each day. This can be washed back into beaches, resulting in medical and aesthetic problems. An investigation into sea-water bathing areas in 1986 at 391 locations around the coast of the United Kingdom revealed that only 44 per cent of the sample points reached the standard required by EC Directive 76/160. This requires the standards to be met by 1995, and, although progress has been made since 1986, a survey in 1989 showed that only 67 per cent of beaches are satisfactory. Regional differences are marked, with the south-west being best and the north-west worst. The estimated cost of restoring the rest of Britain's beaches to an acceptable standard is £600 million – a figure which has clear implications for the attractiveness or otherwise of water industry privatization plans (see chapter 6).

An incident which demonstrates the complexity of international inter-relationships which exist in marine pollution processes is the deaths of up to 20,000 of the 25,000 common seals around British coasts in 1988 and 1989. These deaths were due to a virus infection having similarities to canine distemper. One hypothesis suggested that dioxine and other pol-lutants from paper mills around Lake Baikal in the USSR, 5,000 km to the east, lowered resistance of seals to canine distemper. This strain was then carried to the North Sea by dogs and bears, where North Sea seals became infected. Their resistance was also lowered by high pollutant levels in the North Sea, especially of PCBs and mercury. Although evidence is as yet little more than circumstantial, the role of pollution in this devastation of seal populations is under great suspicion. Pollution is also suspected of being a prime culprit in the virtually complete destruction of birdlife on Steep Holm, a small island in the Bristol Channel, once the home of one of Britain's largest herring gull colonies.

## THE FUTURE

Environmental pollution in Britain first became significant in amount during the Industrial Revolution and increased until the mid-twentieth century. Since then some forms of pollution, for example atmospheric smoke, have been greatly reduced, and there is certainly now a much greater environmental awareness and collective conscience than hitherto. This has come about partly as a result of the actions of environmental pressure groups and the media, and partly as a response to the impacts of particular pollution incidents. However some kinds of pollution are becoming worse, and in addition new forms of pollution are becoming more prominent. The international and even global dimensions are becoming of increasing significance. Perhaps the single most important challenge to face civilization in the next half century will be the solution of pollution-based dilemmas, such as rising sea levels produced by the Greenhouse Effect and CFC-induced holes in the ozone layer. Britain's membership of the EC is having, and will continue to have, a beneficial effect, with the British government being required to fall into line with higher European standards in some areas.

Only a decade ago it was possible to say that pollution was not one of the major problems facing society. It is doubtful whether such a claim is now true, or whether it will be true in the foreseeable future, with governments struggling to sustain economic growth in the context of mounting global environmental problems.

## FURTHER READING

A huge literature on pollution exists, both in general and in the particular case of Britain. An excellent introduction is given by the series of Units making up the Open University course T234 (1985), *Environmental Control and Public Health*, Milton Keynes: Open University Press. A good exposition of the scientific principles necessary for a proper understanding of how pollution interacts with resource systems is given by Simmons, I. G. (1981) *The Ecology of Natural Resources* (2nd edn), London; Edward Arnold. Air pollution in Britain is considered by Chandler, T. J. (1976) 'The climate in towns', in Chandler, T. J. and Gregory S. (eds.) *The Climate of the British Isles*, London: Longman, pp. 307–30. For water pollution see McDonald, A. T. and Kay, D. (1988) *Water Resources: Issues and Strategies*, London: Longman, chapter 6. A less rigorous and now somewhat dated view of pollution in Britain is Bugler, J. (1972) *Polluting Britain*, London: Penguin, which gives a number of detailed case studies. An excellent account of the whole acid rain problem is Park, C. C. (1987) *Acid Rain: Rhetoric and Reality*, London: Methuen. For detailed factual accounts of particular incidents and for summaries of the reports of inquiries and specific investigations *The Times* newspaper is a good source.

# 17  Conservation and protection

*L. F. Curtis*

Since the early 1980s a grievous loss of habitats and landscape features has become more and more apparent. Although detailed studies by the Countryside Commission and the Nature Conservancy Council have documented this loss, the visual changes in the countryside are such that they are also noted by the general public and have given rise to concern. The landscape changes perceived by the traveller reflect equally drastic changes in the ecosystems that once gave support to a wide range of species and abundant wildlife. Landscape change is, more often than not, accompanied by a decline in both the number and diversity of plant and animal species.

The United Kingdom has a countryside richly endowed with a fascinating variety of both form and surface cover. The topographic features seen today have resulted from geomorphological processes operating upon different types of geological structure during changing climatic conditions in different geological periods. The surface cover, consisting of regosols, lithosols, rock outcrops, water bodies and vegetated zonal and intrazonal soils, is the result of an inter-play between biotic and abiotic factors. In many ways the most potent biotic factor has been the impact of human activity from the prehistoric period onwards. Thus many authors have traced the path of vegetational change as a result of human activity in the Mesolithic and Neolithic. A complex pattern of modification of the original vegetation has been created as a result of reclamation, drainage, grazing pressures, forest clearance, planting of exotic species and gaming pursuits. The resulting subseres and plagioseres comprise the vegetational bases upon which present-day conservation measures are invoked.

## TWENTIETH-CENTURY CHANGE

In the twentieth century, and particularly since the Second World War, the pace of change has increased dramatically. Humans have acquired formidable power to exploit and change both the form and the cover of the landscape. Increasingly powerful machinery is now capable of moving soil and rock at high speed. Such machinery can also operate on steep slopes and in a wide range of climatic conditions. Providing such issues as soil erosion and soil compaction are discounted as financially unimportant, machines have the power to operate over much of the year. Additional massive changes in the vegetation and animal life of an area can result from the use of pesticides and herbicides. An assessment of the probable causes of extinction and decline of the rarer British plants since 1800 was made by the Institute of Terrestrial Ecology (Perring 1970). About 50 per cent of the losses were attributed to changes in agriculture and drainage, 26 per cent were due to natural causes, 9 per cent to collecting, 8 per cent to changes in scrub and woodland management and 7 per cent to habitat destruction by building and other constructional changes. The Nature Conservancy Council considers that losses of similar proportions have taken place in more common species and has pointed to the variations in species numbers occurring on farms (table 17.1).

The changing patterns of agriculture are discussed in chapter 4 and so it is sufficient here to recall that the development of high technology farming in this country has led to larger farms, smaller labour forces in the countryside and a heavy reliance upon inputs of fertilisers and energy to achieve increased production. In large part the scale of change is due to the policy of agricultural price support which, as Marion Shoard (1981) has

*Table 17.1* Approximate number of species occurring in equivalent habitats in unmodernized and modern farms

| | *Unmodernized farms* | *Modern farms* | |
|---|---|---|---|
| Groups of animals | Habitat (a) Hedges[1] and semi-natural grass verges | Habitat (a) Wire fences with (i) sown grass | (ii) semi-natural grass verges |
| Mammals | 20 | 5 | 6 |
| Birds | 37 | 6 | 9 |
| Lepidoptera (butterflies only) | 17 | 0 | 8 |
| | (b) Permanent pasture[2] (untreated) | (b) Grass leys[2] | |
| Lepidoptera (butterflies only) | 20 | 0 | |
| | (c) Permanent ponds and ditches | (c) Temporary ditches and piped water | |
| Mammals (aquatic) | 2 | 0 | |
| Amphibia | 5 | 2 | |
| Fish | 9 | 0 | |
| Odonata (dragonflies) | 11 | 0 | |
| Mollusca (gastropods only) | 25 | 3 | |

*Souce*: Nature Conservancy Council 1977
*Notes*: [1] includes hedgerow and trees
[2] includes grasslands on chalk

pointed out, makes it 'profitable for farmers to plough up almost any kind of uncultivated land – woodland, marsh and down for example – to increase their output, even if much of it is destined for the Common Market's stockpiles of surplus produce'.

Those concerned with countryside matters will know that the individual farmer is sometimes faced by economic difficulties in an inflationary economy. Until very recently the thrust of Ministry of Agriculture advice has been in favour of increasing reclamation, increasing amalgamation of small field systems, and increased mechanization to gain the benefits of EC and national grant awards and price support systems. In essence the countryside was regarded as a factory and wildlife or landscape considerations received low priority. An unfortunate consequence of increased mechanization and large-scale farming methods has been continuing depopulation of rural areas.

For almost all parts of the country, losses of vegetation and wildlife point to a loss of amenity. For example, a review of changes in south-east Scotland over the past two decades has revealed losses of 88 per cent of lowland heath, 21 per cent of permanent grassland, 28 per cent of deciduous woodland, and 35 per cent of mixed woodland. Studies in Dorset have revealed that two-thirds of the heathland was lost between 1811 and 1860 and that only a sixth of the original area remained by 1978. Since 1865 the area of lowland bog remaining in Lancashire has been reduced by some 99 per cent.

The Nature Conservancy Council in its report on Nature Conservation in Great Britain noted 'there is justifiable alarm that economic forces and policies are increasingly pressing the managers of land and other natural resources into practices inimical to the conservation of nature'. Certainly the past story is a gloomy one if the examples of lowland heath, ancient woodland, lowland raised mires, or the grasslands, heaths and blanket bogs of the uplands are examined (figure 17.1).

In the world as a whole, some 25,000 species of plants and more than a thousand vertebrates are estimated to be threatened with extinction. The results of base-line surveys of otters in England, Wales and Scotland show that positive signs of otters occur in only 6 per cent, 20 per cent, and 73 per cent respectively of the sites investigated in these countries. The Nature Conservancy Council takes the view that even in Scotland the otter is likely to become extinct unless steps are taken for its protection. The gradual loss of species can also be exemplified by reference to the Large Blue Butterfly. Despite site management it is considered that it is now almost certainly extinct, the last known colony in Devon having produced no viable eggs in 1979.

Graphic accounts of the losses of habitats, flora and fauna have been provided by Mabey (1980) and Shoard (1981). Although there may be minor qualifications of the extent of the losses, there can be no doubting the overall magnitude of the changes which have taken place since the

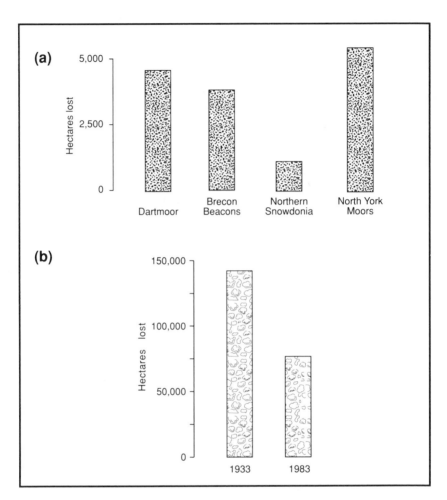

*Figure 17.1* (a) Losses of upland grasslands, heaths, and blanket bogs (b) Losses of ancient semi-natural woodland in twenty-three counties of England and Wales (hectares)
*Source: Nature Conservation in Great Britain*, Nature Conservancy Council, 1984

mid-nineteenth century. Many of the landscapes captured by painters such as Constable have gone, as have the wildscapes which formed parts of large estates in earlier times. Indeed, it is interesting to note that the continued existence of those wildscapes still remaining in Scotland is considered to be of questionable value by people who wish to see improved economies in the Highlands achieved by such measures as afforestation.

## PUBLIC RESPONSES TO CONSERVATION CONCEPTS

Human perceptions of the natural environment tend to be of two kinds. First, there is the widespread interest shown by human beings in the other living plants and animals occurring on the Earth. This is reflected in the continuing strength of the naturalist societies in this country; for example, the Royal Society for the Protection of Birds grew in membership from 92,000 to 540,000 between 1972 and 1988. Most conservation bodies are actively involved in nature conservation schemes at county or regional level and in 1988 there were some 184,000 members of County Trusts as a whole. In Somerset, the Trust for Nature Conservation's nature reserves increased from eight (68 ha) in 1971 to 48 (1,011 ha) in 1988.

The second type of perception and interest relates to the scenery rather than the animals and plants themselves. Public enjoyment of open space often consists mainly of taking in the view of hills, valleys, water, fields, moors and woodlands. The role of landscape in creating human emotions is well illustrated by generations of British poets, writers, and artists. In consequence, there are many voluntary organizations such as the National Trust and the Council for the Preservation of Rural England which voice a powerful concern for the visual beauty of an area as well as the wildlife contained therein. It is hardly surprising, therefore, that public opinion concerning the need for environmental protection has been voiced on a wide range of issues including motorway developments, siting of airports, open cast coal mining, afforestation, moorland reclamation and drainage of wetlands. Pressure groups now campaign for conservation measures at both local and national level. It is against this backcloth of sharpening protest against loss of countryside amenities that one may review existing administrative structures and policies for conservation.

The Nature Conservancy Council has emphasized that 'Government holds the scales, and ultimately it will have to decide where it wishes the balance between conservation and other sectional interests to lie. And the view taken by government in representing the people, will depend on its perception of public concern'.

## THE LEGISLATIVE STEPS TOWARDS PROTECTED LANDSCAPES

Following the deliberations of the Dower and Hobhouse Committees in 1945 and 1947, the Town and Country Planning Act of 1949 marked a major step in legislating the protection of the environment. (For a detailed account of the developments culminating in the 1949 legislation, see Sheail's (1981), review of the inter-war period.) Although this Act was concerned primarily with development control in urban areas, it set out requirements for Local Authorities to prepare development plans in which they could identify rural areas of special landscape value. At this time a further measure was the National Parks and Access to the Countryside Act

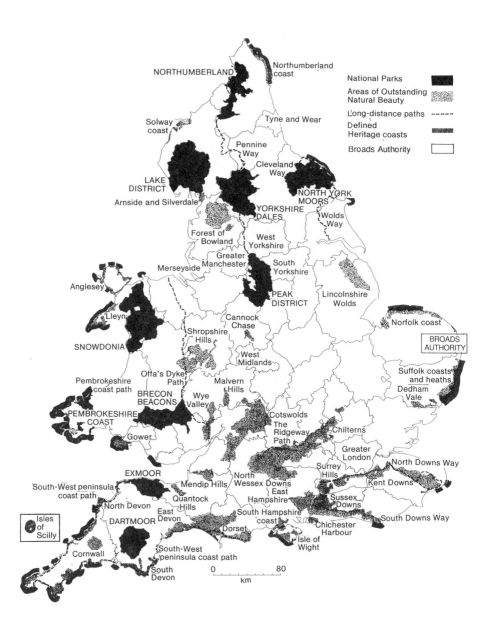

*Figure 17.2* Conservation and recreation areas in England and Wales advised or managed by the Countryside Commission

of 1949 which established a Commission empowered to designate areas of National Parks and Areas of Outstanding Natural Beauty. The designations then made placed emphasis on conservation of the visual amenity of the landscape. As a result, ten National Parks were eventually created which comprised some 9 per cent of the land area of England and Wales (figure 17.2). The National Parks were required to fulfil the following statutory objectives:

(a) the preservation and enhancement of the natural beauty of the Park,
(b) the promotion of the enjoyment of the Park by the public.

Subsequently, the Countryside Act of 1968 was introduced, which under Section 11 charged every Minister, Government Department and public body to have regard to conserving the natural beauty and amenity of the countryside. It also required Local Authorities, under the provisions of Section 14, to give due regard to the needs of agriculture and forestry, and to the economic and social interests of rural areas. Thus the stage was set for present-day inconsistencies in approaches towards landscape conservation. In particular, the Ministry of Agriculture was confronted by the difficulties of its responsibilities under Section 11 whereas the Department of the Environment struggled to reconcile its requirements under Section 14 with the broad statutory provisions for preservation and enhancement of natural beauty. Despite these emergent conflicts of purpose in the legislation, the 1968 Act was important in that it enabled Local Authorities to make provision for Country Parks and picnic sites in locations easily accessible to large urban conurbations. The concept of Country Parks was proposed in the White Paper 'Leisure in the Countryside' published in 1966, and it is estimated that some 220 Country Parks (134 in 1981) existed in 1988 (see figure 14.3).

The National Parks Commission was subsequently reorganized and became the Countryside Commission which, whilst inheriting many responsibilities for landscape protection in National Parks, became broader based with wide-ranging countryside interests. The powers of the Commission are mainly advisory rather than executive. It provides advice to Government and carries out research on landscape matters. Also, it makes recommendations for grant aid for landscape conservation and recreation projects undertaken by the private sector or Local Authorities.

In 1974 a number of important administrative changes were proposed in National Parks by a Review Committee of National Park Policy and Administration under the chairmanship of Lord Sandford. The Sandford Committee recommended that the National Parks should be run by a single executive committee instead of the former joint committees existing in many Parks. It recommended that one-third of the members should be appointed by the Secretary of State for the Environment, the remainder of the members being elected members of the constituent authorities. These recommendations did not affect the Lake District and Peak District which differ from other National Parks in that they are administered by special planning boards instead of county councils. These changes were mostly put into effect when local government reorganization took place in 1974.

Outside the National Parks, a second tier of nationally designated areas termed Areas of Outstanding Natural Beauty (AONB) was brought into being (figure 17.2). These areas include stretches of attractive countryside (e.g. Mendip Hills) which do not qualify for recognition as National Parks. The protection afforded to them is the responsibility of the Local Planning Authorities. Often there are constraints on building development and grants may be made available for tree planting schemes and the removal of eyesores. Some thirty-eight AONBs existed in 1988 having a total area of 19,287 square kilometres, forming 12.8 per cent of the area of England and Wales.

The powers contained in the National Parks and Access to the Countryside Act, 1949, did not extend to Scotland. Nevertheless, some forty National Scenic Areas have been designated in Scotland. These cover 10,173 square kilometres (12.9 per cent of the area of Scotland). Since 1981 planning authorities have had to refer planning applications for particular classes of development to the Countryside Commission for Scotland so that the national element of interest is considered. In 1989 local authorities are calling for Park status in areas like Loch Lomond. There are no National Parks in Northern Ireland, although there are powers for the designation of such areas. Nine AONBs have been designated and two others recommended. They cover about 18 per cent of the area of Northern Ireland and range in size from 2,000 to 101,000 ha. Their designation provides for planning control to limit or prevent development detrimental to scenic quality. The two proposed AONBs include part of County Fermanagh and the Slieve Croob area in County Down. In addition, five country parks have been created at Crawfordsburn and Scrabo in County Down, Roe Valley and Ness Wood in County Londonderry, and Castle Archdale in County Fermanagh.

In the United Kingdom as a whole, in addition to the initiatives taken by the Department of the Environment and the Countryside Commission in respect of National Parks, Areas of Outstanding Natural Beauty, Country Parks and picnic sites, there are substantial tracts of country (excepting in Northern Ireland) afforded some degree of protection by the Nature Conservancy Council (NCC) and the National Trust (NT). In 1973 the Nature Conservancy Council Act provided for the NCC to become an independent council responsible for the management of National Nature Reserves and for notifying Sites of Special Scientific Interest (SSSIs). On March 31, 1988, there were 224 National Nature Reserves (166 in 1980) covering 160,044 ha. There are also some 4,729 SSSIs in Great Britain which have been identified because of their flora, fauna, geological or physiographic features. These sites cover 1,517,536 ha. Planning authorities are required to notify the Nature Conservancy Council of proposed developments in SSSIs and to seek advice on their desirability in ecological terms.

Mr Ridley, then Secretary of State for the Environment, announced in 1989 that the Countryside Commission and Nature Conservancy Council will be merged together to form a new agency in Scotland and Wales. This has been seen by some as a reflection of the influence of landowners in Scotland who see the efforts of the Nature Conservancy Council to constrain afforestation as damaging to their economy. It remains to be seen whether the new administrative structure will limit the effectiveness of the Council as the agency protecting wildlife and wildlife habitats.

The National Trust was registered in 1895 as the 'National Trust for Places of Historic Interest and Natural Beauty'. Its growth has been spectacular: since 1923 its membership has increased from 825 to 1,641,246 in 1988, and the number of properties opened has increased from 102 to 297 over the same period. The main objective of the Trust has always been the conservation of the land and properties under its control but public access over much of its land is unrestricted and its leisure facilities are now extensive. It gained considerable impetus from the Act of 1937 which allowed owners to transfer the freehold, with an endowment for upkeep, to the National Trust in lieu of death duties. The owners and heirs of these properties could continue in occupancy provided they opened their premises to the public for specified periods.

It will be evident that the protection of landscape in the United Kingdom is dependent on the activities of a complex array of national government, local government, quango and voluntary organizations. In some instances, there are conflicting aims within this tangled web of administrations. As a result there are great difficulties in developing and implementing a coordinated policy for landscape protection (table 17.2).

Conservation is often viewed as an obstacle to be overcome. For the officials in the Ministry of Agriculture, Fisheries and Food, the Forestry Commission, the National Farmers' Union, and in Water Authorities and Development Boards, the issue often seems to be how much land should be set aside for conservation in order to gain acceptance of development elsewhere. Inevitably, such an approach leads to a gradual fragmentation of habitats and breakdown in the unity of forms in the landscapes. It is partly for these reasons that there has been advocacy of the 'priority area' approach as exemplified by the 'two tier' concept of the Government Inter-Departmental Countryside Review Committee (1979) and the 'heartland' approach by Porchester (1977). Such concepts of priority areas demand that there should be assessments of landscape quality and procedures for the management of such key tracts of country. The designation by government of Environmentally Sensitive Areas (ESAs) has led to a further category of protected landscape demanding such assessments.

Table 17.2 Measures to encourage conservation of protected landscapes

| | England and Wales | | | | | | Scotland | | Northern Ireland | |
|---|---|---|---|---|---|---|---|---|---|---|
| | National Parks | Broads | New Forest | AONBs | Heritage Coasts | ESAs | National Scenic Areas | ESAs | AONBs | ESAs |
| *Selected by* | CC | CC | Crown | CC | CC | CC/NCC | CCS | CCS/NCC | DOE/NI | DOE/NI |
| *Designated by* | CC | In Legislation | Historic 'perambulation' | CC | CC/LAs | MAFF/ WOAD | SO/SS | DAFS | DOE/NI | Dept Agric NI |
| Special administering authority | Yes | Yes | Yes | Optional | Optional | No | No | No | Yes DOE/NI | No |
| *Management plans* required | Yes | Yes | Yes | Optional | Yes | No | No | No | No | No |
| *Special funding* arrangements | Yes | Yes | Yes | Some grants | Some grants | Yes | No | Yes | No | Yes |

| Additional planning powers, arrangements and/or policy | Additional management powers, arrangements and/or policy | Designated staff to administer |
|---|---|---|
| Yes | Yes | Yes |
| Yes | Yes | Yes |
| No | Limited | Optional |
| Yes | Yes | Usually |
| No | Yes | No |
| No | Optional | No |
| Yes | Yes | Yes |
| No | Limited | Yes DOE/NI |

*Source*: Phillips, A. (1987) International Symposium on Protected Landscapes
*Notes*: AONBs = Areas of Outstanding Natural Beauty
ESA = Environmentally Sensitive Areas
CC = Countryside Commission
CCS = Countryside Commission for Scotland
NCC = Nature Conservancy Council
DOE/NI = Department of Environment, N. Ireland
MAFF = Ministry of Agriculture, Fisheries and Food
WOAD = Welsh Office Agriculture Department
DAFS = Department of Agriculture and Fisheries for Scotland
SO/SS = Secretary of State for Scotland

## NEW APPROACHES TOWARDS CONSERVATION OF LANDSCAPE

The two main approaches to conservation in the United Kingdom today can be exemplified by the interests and attitudes of the two principal statutory organizations most concerned with conservation. On the one hand the Nature Conservancy Council is concerned with conservation and preservation of plant and animal species whilst the Countryside Commission has devoted much effort towards the conservation of scenic qualities and the uses of landscape for recreation. Both organizations acknowledge the interdependence of nature and beauty. It is sometimes claimed, however, that advice from each organization reflects its special interests and lacks a coordinated approach to conservation (MacEwen and MacEwen 1981). Merged responsibilities in Scotland and Wales will test their effectiveness in conservation in the next few years. In its policies for *nature conservation*, the Nature Conservancy Council has adopted a list of criteria to identify 'key sites' which support the best or most unique examples of wildlife habitats and particular wild plants and flowers. The criteria were selected to examine the national scientific, economic, educational, aesthetic and recreational functions of nature conservation. In a local context they have been used to identify Sites of Special Scientific Interest (SSSI). Ratcliffe (1977) judged each site in terms of the following criteria:

1 size (extent),
2 diversity,
3 naturalness,
4 rarity,
5 typicalness,
6 fragility,
7 recorded history,
8 position in an ecological/geographical unit,
9 potential value,
10 intrinsic appeal.

Sites are graded in quality on a four point scale. Grades 1 and 2 are key sites, the former being of national or international importance, whereas the lowest grade of 4 includes sites of lesser intrinsic value. Ratcliffe does not describe the way in which the values for each of the criteria can be combined to give an overall assessment for an area. The use and importance of the criteria vary according to the purpose of the study – whether it is to identify an area of land with conservation value or whether it is to subdivide an identified area into zones of conservation importance.

A case study of the application of these criteria by Usher (1980) involved the assessment of conservation values within the large Malham-Arncliffe Site of Special Scientific Interest in North Yorkshire. He considered that the first four of Ratcliffe's criteria – size, diversity, naturalness and rarity – were particularly important in assessing parts of a large SSSI. They were the least subjective and gave the most objective interpretations. Nevertheless, in defining the categories of conservation importance in the case study area, Usher concluded that once all the data had been assembled, a considerable number of value judgements was required in order to reach a conclusion. He also warned that boundaries on the 'conservation' map should not be interpreted too literally on the ground and would give only a general indication of the categories of conservation importance.

Regarding attempts to conserve the *scenic and recreation* value of the countryside, considerable efforts have been made to develop sound techniques during the past twenty years. A detailed account of the numerous methods which have been employed is not included here, and for a comprehensive account the interested reader is directed to the reviews included in the further reading section. However, a brief summary of the types of approach applied will provide a background to consideration of the present situation. Penning-Rowsell (1981) recognizes three stages in the chronological development of landscape appraisal, characterized by different approaches to the problem. At first, intuitive methods were employed; later, statistical techniques were elaborated; and finally, there has been a growing trend favouring analyses based on preferences. British examples will be used here to illustrate the approaches.

The intuitive approach, prevalent before the 1970s, is aptly exemplified by Linton's study of landscape in Scotland. He produced a classification of landscape on the basis of two dimensions – landform character, and land use. 'Landform' landscapes were categorized according to geomorphological elements (relative relief, steepness of slope, abruptness, dissection by valleys, isolation of hill masses, views over water). 'Land use' landscapes were classified according to the predominant type of land use, such as urban, forest, farmland, moorland. (Linton's descriptions of these suggested that the categories may not be entirely mutually exclusive.) Numerical weightings were attached to these landscapes on the basis of their 'scenic interest' and 'landform' and 'land use' scores were combined to give an overall assessment. Linton's assessment was undoubtedly based on a very thorough knowledge of Scottish scenery and a deep feeling for its qualities. However, the grounds for his judgements were somewhat subjective and the attachment of numerical 'scores' to elements of the landscape in such circumstances is difficult to justify.

During the 1970s attempts were made to establish a more rigorous basis for numerical landscape assessment. The Coventry-Solihull-Warwickshire Subregional Planning Study Group (1971) obtained observer ratings for tracts of countryside and used regression procedures to establish statistical relationships between landscape quality and the incidence of certain quantifiable landscape elements, such as trees and hedgerows. This approach lacks a proper consideration of the range of factors which govern perception of landscapes. It takes no account of the significance of the arrangement of the elements, that the whole may be more than the sum of its parts, nor the influence of aspects of the landscape such as historical association, which were not observable. It was argued that the statistical relationship could be used to predict quality for other landscapes, not seen by the original observers, using information on the numbers of landscape elements. However, this is dubious since the basis for appraisal may differ from one area to another.

From 1973 onwards attempts were made to use techniques for assessing preferences and attitudes developed by social scientists in order to discover more about how various social groups perceived and valued landscape. Penning-Rowsell, Gullett, Searle and Witham (1977) conducted a household survey, collecting respondents' rating of landscapes using semantic differential scales. The reasons for the ratings were also investigated to explain sources of variation. A recent approach to coastal landscape evaluation using bipolar semantic differential tests has been subjected to multivariate analysis and offers a basis for further tests in other field areas (Gardiner *et al.* 1982).

Thus research carried out on the appraisal of landscape quality in terms of its scientific and scenic value has so far failed to produce methods which fully meet the requirements of planning authorities. An ideal system would be one which combined a sound theoretical basis with a workable technique for comparing one area with another. It seems unlikely that a single method can be produced for conservation of all types of landscape. In practice, individual authorities must work towards improved procedures in the context of specific planning problems and the plant and animal habitats that exist to give species-rich environment.

Local authorities and other organizations having duties in respect of conservation must be able to relate to precise areas of ground for which particular management is deemed desirable. A case study shows how these problems were tackled on Exmoor. In the context of what McEwen and McEwen (1987) termed the 'Exmoor Saga' the author (then National Park Officer) was charged with preparing both Porchester Map One (a map of existing Exmoor moorland) and Porchester Map Two (a policy map indicating the areas of moorland which the National Park were determined to conserve) (figure 17.3).

In drawing up criteria for Map 2 five groups were recognized – landscape, ecology, accessibility, archaeology and geomorphology. It was considered that landscape (here used in a precise sense to mean scenic and visual considerations) should be the main factor in determining Map 2 areas which were of exceptional value. Following a series of field visits, a survey procedure was adopted which assessed:

1  visual quality of vegetation and relief in terms of pattern, colour and texture;
2  enclosure or openness, impressions of bounded intimate spaces or intimate areas;

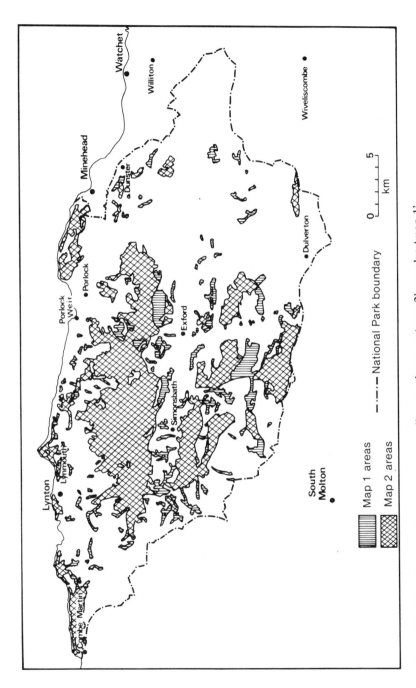

*Figure 17.3* The Exmoor 'Porchester' maps: all areas shown as 'map 2' are also 'map 1'

3 extent – real or apparent; the degree to which the landscape element predominates and fills the field of view. This criterion also involved consideration of the concepts of remoteness and wildness;
4 views and edges; different types of view experienced on the moor, visual relationship between moorland and surrounding countryside;
5 public access, rights of way and road access;
6 Landmarks and landscape features, special characteristics giving a distinctive quality to the landscape.

**Management agreements**

A management agreement is 'a formal written agreement between a public authority and an owner of an interest in land who thereby undertakes to manage the land in a specified manner in order to satisfy a particular public need, usually in return for some form of consideration' (Feist 1978). On Exmoor, a number of management agreements have been entered into by the Park Committee. These include agreements for moorland adjoining the coast at Glenthorne near Lynmouth, and at Haddon Hill, overlooking the new Wimbleball Reservoir near Dulverton. They make provision for annual payments to the owners so that moorland can be conserved. Management agreements can also be negotiated on a 'once and for all' basis. An example of this is the purchase and leaseback of land at Larkbarrow, near Exford, by the Secretary of State for the Environment. At the moment of leaseback a management agreement was signed with Exmoor National Park providing for a range of conservation measures on the land in question.

The preparation of the Exmoor Moorland maps opened the way for a rational system of treating applications for moorland reclamation (figure 17.4). Subsequently, the agreement of financial guidelines for Exmoor management agreements by the National Park Committee, National Farmers Union and the Country Landowners Association in 1981 allowed the Porchester maps to become the basis of negotiated settlements. The maps enabled the Park Committee to assess the 'threat' involved in respect of particular areas of landscape and they also aided negotiations for grants from the National Heritage Memorial Fund (e.g. in the case of purchase of heartland areas of moor at Larkbarrow and Warren Farm). The various options open to the Committee were set out by Curtis in 1983, and these remained substantially the same in 1988. Although purchase is the cheapest option, and is essentially the policy of the National Trust, annual payments are likely to be pursued for political reasons. Gradually the terms of management agreements based on annual payments on Exmoor were refined as experience was gained in their operation (figure 17.5).

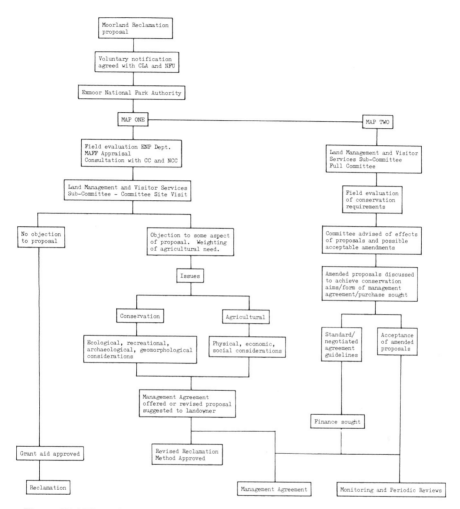

*Figure 17.4* The role of the 'Porchester' maps 1 and 2 in the negotiation of management agreements

## THE WILDLIFE AND COUNTRYSIDE ACT, 1981

The Exmoor experience, both in respect of moorland mapping and development of financial guidelines for management agreements, was used when this Act was brought into being. As a result Section 43 of the Act required all National Parks to construct moorland maps and in an Amendment (1985) such maps were extended to 'any area of mountain, moor, heath, woodland, down, cliff or foreshore (including any bank,

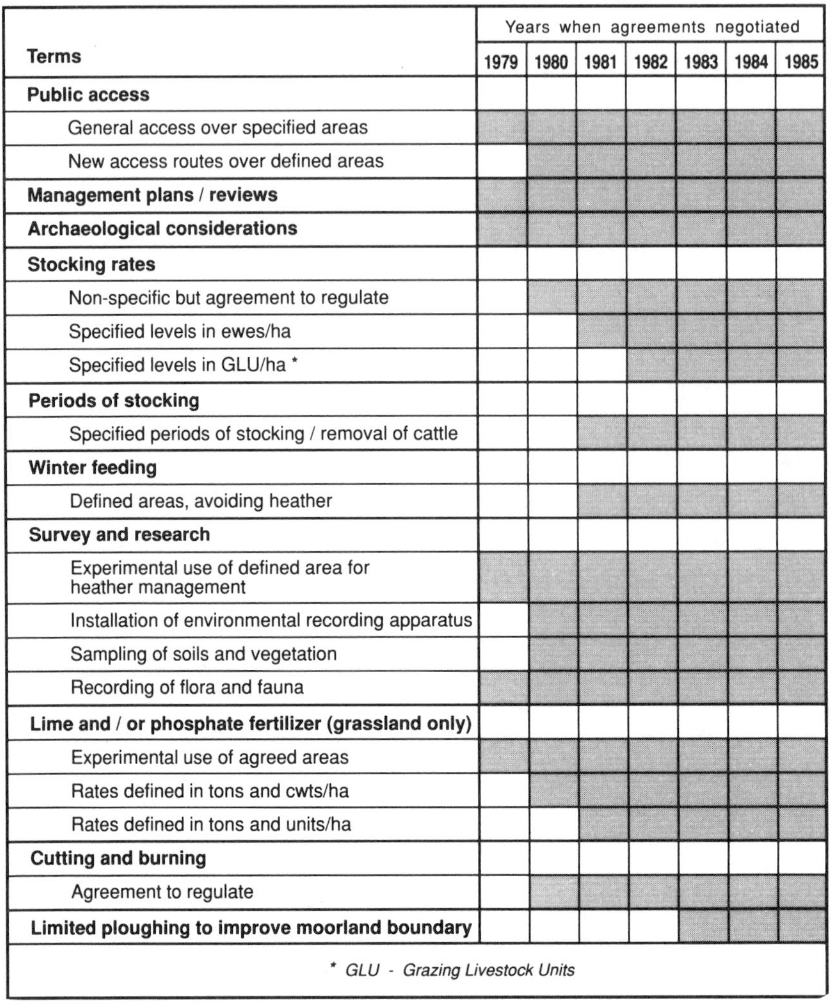

| Terms | Years when agreements negotiated | | | | | | |
|---|---|---|---|---|---|---|---|
| | 1979 | 1980 | 1981 | 1982 | 1983 | 1984 | 1985 |
| **Public access** | | | | | | | |
| General access over specified areas | ▓ | ▓ | ▓ | ▓ | ▓ | ▓ | ▓ |
| New access routes over defined areas | | ▓ | ▓ | ▓ | ▓ | ▓ | ▓ |
| **Management plans / reviews** | ▓ | ▓ | ▓ | ▓ | ▓ | ▓ | ▓ |
| **Archaeological considerations** | ▓ | ▓ | ▓ | ▓ | ▓ | ▓ | ▓ |
| **Stocking rates** | | | | | | | |
| Non-specific but agreement to regulate | | ▓ | ▓ | ▓ | ▓ | ▓ | ▓ |
| Specified levels in ewes/ha | | | | | | | |
| Specified levels in GLU/ha * | | | | | ▓ | ▓ | ▓ |
| **Periods of stocking** | | | | | | | |
| Specified periods of stocking / removal of cattle | | ▓ | ▓ | ▓ | ▓ | ▓ | ▓ |
| **Winter feeding** | | | | | | | |
| Defined areas, avoiding heather | | | | | | | |
| **Survey and research** | | | | | | | |
| Experimental use of defined area for heather management | ▓ | ▓ | ▓ | ▓ | ▓ | ▓ | ▓ |
| Installation of environmental recording apparatus | | ▓ | ▓ | ▓ | ▓ | ▓ | ▓ |
| Sampling of soils and vegetation | | ▓ | ▓ | ▓ | ▓ | ▓ | ▓ |
| Recording of flora and fauna | ▓ | ▓ | ▓ | ▓ | ▓ | ▓ | ▓ |
| **Lime and / or phosphate fertilizer (grassland only)** | | | | | | | |
| Experimental use of agreed areas | | ▓ | ▓ | ▓ | ▓ | ▓ | ▓ |
| Rates defined in tons and cwts/ha | | ▓ | ▓ | ▓ | ▓ | ▓ | ▓ |
| Rates defined in tons and units/ha | | | | ▓ | ▓ | ▓ | ▓ |
| **Cutting and burning** | | | | | | | |
| Agreement to regulate | | ▓ | ▓ | ▓ | ▓ | ▓ | ▓ |
| **Limited ploughing to improve moorland boundary** | | | | | ▓ | ▓ | ▓ |

*\* GLU - Grazing Livestock Units*

*Figure 17.5* Development of provisions within Exmoor management agreements

barrier, dune, beach, flat or other land adjacent to the foreshore)'. Also, in Section 50 of the Act, provision was made for management agreements and the financial guidelines for them were issued by the government in a circular dated 1983.

Anxieties have been expressed concerning the operation of the Act in that it might allow abuse of the goodwill on which the Exmoor voluntary system was based. This seemed a real danger because the Act, together with the methods of handling grant applications by the Ministry of Agriculture, when used according to the Government Financial Guidelines, combined to make it well nigh impossible to question the wisdom or indeed the financial soundness of a farmer's scheme for reclamation. There is, therefore, a danger that trivial and spurious claims can still be made. MacEwen and MacEwen (1987) stress that the Act transformed a voluntary system of management as practised on Exmoor into a hybrid scheme. It made agreements obligatory on the NCC and the National Parks but voluntary for the farmer and landowner. Also, it was pointed out that the publication of Section 43 (later Section 3) maps of open country may trigger off demands for compensation. A report to government suggested that:

> potentially the 1981 Act together with the Financial Guidelines place a price on virtually all the destructible features of scientific or landscape interest, which the owner may claim on threat of destroying it ... it is impossible to test the genuineness of an individual's intention without putting the site at risk.

The Parliamentary phase of the Wildlife and Countryside Act is described by Lowe, *et al.* (1986). The failure to embody sufficient power to protect landscape is still commented upon but one thing is certain – the true cost of conservation as determined by the Act will be revealed gradually in the payments provided for in the Act. The public will soon be in a position to judge whether they wish to support farmers through conservation grants rather than by the traditional agricultural grants which have led to unacceptable surpluses and all the costs involved in their storage and disposal.

In recent years a number of books have appeared advocating changes in price support mechanisms and the introduction of some degree of planning control over farm operations. So far as moorland and hedgerows are concerned the withdrawal of MAFF grant aid for moorland reclamation and grubbing out of hedgerows marked a recent advance. However the maintenance of income from land remains a major concern for organizations such as the Country Landowners Association. The Gretton report of 1985 outlines opportunities and suggests that income from further public funding of extensive grazing regimes and farm woodland schemes could be investigated. The Farm Woodland Scheme introduced by the government in 1987 may provide some additional woodland but the immediate response does not suggest that the decline in broadleaved woodland will be arrested quickly. The extent of loss is considerable; in Somerset, for example, loss of ancient semi-natural woodland has been estimated at 45 per cent since 1930. The Nature Conservancy Council expressed concern that the proposals may be damaging to conservation in that planting in marginal livestock-rearing land may threaten semi-natural vegetation.

There is little doubt that a sea change has occurred in attitudes towards agricultural subsidy. Laurence Gould Consultants have estimated that 9,000–12,000 square kilometres of agricultural land in the UK will potentially be surplus to requirments by 1990 and 24,000–29,000 square kilometres by the year 2000. This prospect of over-production within the EC may afford the opportunity to allow some land to revert to moorland, fen and downland. Trials are already taking place on National Trust land at Ballard Down near Studland in which arable land is being (a) left fallow (b) sown to 'conservation' mixes of chalkland species.

## FUTURE PROSPECTS

The scale of the changes in the landscapes of the United Kingdom is now so great that many organizations and individuals are looking for better ways of protecting the remaining areas of wild and beautiful countryside. The Countryside Review Committee has suggested that National Parks and AONBs should be abolished and replaced with a new two-tier system based on the wilderness concept used in Europe and the USA. Many critics of this suggestion have pointed out that it would only give protection to very small areas and for many areas of ecological or scenic interest there would be less protection than at present. Shoard (1981) stated 'the truth is that AONBs have failed, but the National Parks have succeeded. The proposed new system would neatly duck the challenge which the National Parks have been meeting'. She also concluded that the solution must lie in new measures affecting agricultural grants and subsidies.

The potential importance of the Ministry of Agriculture, Fisheries and Food was foreseen by the 1978 Strutt Report entitled 'Agriculture and the Countryside'. This report recommended that MAFF should take on greater responsibility for wildlife and landscape conservation and that conservation criteria should be included in the grant-aided schemes which it administers. The Tourism and Recreation Research Unit in their 1981 study of the economy of rural communities in National Parks have also recommended that MAFF play a synthesizing role in relation to agriculture, conservation and socio-economic welfare. However, many will avow that, desirable though these objectives may be, the Ministry of Agriculture does not at present have the staff or the will for conservation which would solve present problems.

The Broads Grazing Marshes Conservation Scheme set up in 1985 may prove to be a test case. A small unit at MAFF Headquarters in Norwich with Countryside Commission leadership has been responsible for payments of about £50 per acre in the Halvergate Marshes within a budget of £1.7 million over three years.

The designation of Environmentally Sensitive Areas (ESA) has put some responsibility on MAFF to become aware of the environmental needs of particular landscapes. At present the government is unwilling to designate further ESAs until their effectiveness is proven. Present indications suggest that independent examination of 'the ability of ESAs to improve the conservation status of an area are necessary. The evidence of the 1986 study 'Monitoring of Landscape Change' undertaken by the Department of the Environment and the Countryside Commission revealed large losses of hedgerows (about 25 per cent) in the period 1947–80, together with decline in moorland, decline in broadleaved woodland, and heavy losses of Chalk and Jurassic grasslands. Thus, the problem of conservation is not just one of maintaining the status quo but one of remedying some of the land cover losses in significant areas.

The proposals for 'set aside' in which some agricultural land will be taken out of production in order to reduce surpluses gives an opportunity to recreate some habitats which have been lost. They could also enable particular problems such as nitrate pollution (see chapter 16) to be countered. In 1957 MAFF recommended the addition of 75–90 kg of nitrate per hectare for arable cropping. By 1985 farmers were adding 190 kg/ha in their search for higher and higher productivity. Of this it is estimated that some 50–70 kg/ha is leached out into the ground water thereby creating potential health hazards and development of algal blooms and weeds in water courses. Reduction of nitrate levels is clearly necessary, but the rate of leaching could be further reduced by reducing the amount of ploughland and reintroducing grassland.

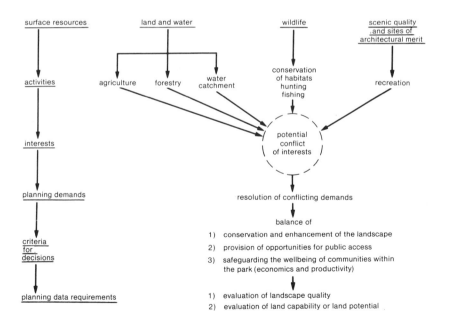

*Figure 17.6* The management requirements for a National Park Committee

The introduction of the Farm Land and Development Bill in 1987 has been accompanied by publications by the Development Commission (Rural Enterprise and Development, 1987) and the Countryside Commission (New Opportunities for the Countryside, 1987). The latter emphasizes integration of farming and environmental conservation. Many alternative uses of land are now under examination and it seems clear that planning control will become an important issue where sites of conservation importance adjoin areas of developable land.

The roles of geographers in the protection of important habitats and exceptional landscapes are likely to be twofold. First, a traditional role exists as gatherers of information concerning surface features and earth processes. The rapid development of remote sensing techniques described by Curtis (1986) has led to the use of remotely sensed data in studies of National Parks and other protected landscapes. These data are now being combined with those from other sources in geographic information systems, in an approach which promises to yield valuable results in elucidating the conflicting demands upon surface resources (figure 17.6).

Second, in the field of regional and economic planning the geographer will be required to play a role in assessing the environmental cost of existing and new developments. Present indications are that government is moving towards the view that the polluter pays. In this event the consumer costs of pollution may well be highlighted in any analyses of developments.

The changes which affected the landscapes in the past only rarely obliterated previous environments. Mostly the changes were such that the early, ancient landscapes were merely modified so that they remain important conservation issues in their own right. The English landscape, as described by Hoskins and others, was a true 'palimpsest' – a plate which when held up and examined closely yielded the secrets of its long and varied history. All is now changing in the face of twentieth-century technology. The plate is now experiencing a complete resurfacing, degraded by the power of modern machinery. The question facing the people of the United Kingdom is where and how should the impact of such changes be reduced or eliminated.

## REFERENCES

Countryside Review Committee (1979) *Conservation and the Countryside Heritage: A Discussion Paper*, London: HMSO.
Coventry City Council. (1971) *Coventry – Solihull – Warwickshire: A Strategy for the Sub-region*, Supplementary Report No. 5, Coventry City Council.
Curtis, L. F. (1983) 'Reflections on management agreements for conservation of Exmoor moorland', *Journal of Agricultural Economics*, 34: 397–406.
Curtis, L. F. (1986) 'Remote sensing for environmental management of National Parks with special reference to Exmoor', *Journal of the British Interplanetary Society*, 39.
Department of the Environment and Countryside Commission (1986), *Monitoring Landscape Change*, Report by Hunting Surveys and Consultants.

Feist, M. J. (1978) *A Study of Management Agreements*, UK, Countryside Commission.

Gardiner, V., Matthews, H., and Richards, K. (1982), 'An approach to coastal landscape evaluation', in Grant, E. and Newby, P. *Landscape and Industry*, pp. 81–92.

Gretton Report (1985), *Maintaining Income from Land*, Country Landowners Association.

Hoskins, W. G. (1955) *Making of the English Landscape*, London: Hodder and Stoughton.

Linton, D. L. (1968) 'The assessment of scenery as a natural resource', *Scottish Geographical Magazine*, 84: 219–38.

Lowe, P., Cox, G., MacEwen, M., O'Riordan, T., and Winter, M. (1986) *Countryside Conflicts*, Gower/Maurice Temple Smith.

Mabey, R. (1980) *The Common Ground*, London: Hutchinson.

MacEwen, A. and MacEwen, M. (1981) 'Why the great divide?' *Ecos*, 2,2.

MacEwen, A. and MacEwen, M. (1987), *Greenprints for the Countryside?* London: Allen & Unwin.

Nature Conservancy Council (1987) *Nature Conservation in Great Britain* London: HMSO.

Penning-Powell, E., Gullet, G., Searle, G., and Witham, S. (1977) *Public Evaluation of Landscape Quality*, Middlesex Polytechnic Planning Research Group Report, 13.

Perring, F. H. (ed.) (1970) *The Flora of a Changing Britain*, Report of the Botanical Society of the British Isles, No. 11

Porchester, Lord, KBE (1977) *A Study of Exmoor*, London: HMSO.

Ratcliffe, D. (ed.) (1977) *A Nature Conservation Review*, NCC and NERC Cambridge: Cambridge University Press.

Sheail, J. (1981) *Rural Conservation in Inter-War Britain* Oxford: Oxford University Press.

Shoard, M. (1981) *The Theft of the Countryside*, London: Temple Smith.

Usher, M. B. (1980) 'An assessment of conservation values', *Field Studies*, 5.

**FURTHER READING**

On vegetational change see:

Dimbleby, G. W. (1962) *The Development of British Heathlands and their Soils*, Oxf. For. Mem. 23

Godwin, H. (1956) *The History of the British Flora*, Cambridge, Cambridge University Press.

Moore, P. D. and Chater, E. H. (1969) 'Studies in the vegetational history of Mid-Wales. 1 The post-glacial period in Cardiganshire', *New Phytologist*, 68: 183–96.

For the Exmoor Studies see:

Exmoor National Park Committee (1977) *Exmoor National Park Plan*, Exmoor National Park Department, Exmoor House, Dulverton, Somerset.

Exmoor National Park Committee (1987) *Financial Guidelines for Management Agreements*, Exmoor National Park Department, Exmoor House, Dulverton, Somerset.

Exmoor National Park Committee (2nd Edn) (1979) *Porchester Map One, Explanatory Notes*, Exmoor National Park Department, Exmoor House, Dulverton, Somerset.

Exmoor National Park Department (1982), *Moorland Conservation on Exmoor, Porchester Map Two*.

On National Parks see:

Dower, J. (1945) *National Parks in England and Wales*, Cmnd. 6628, London: HMSO.

Hobhouse, Sir A. (1947) *Report of the National Parks Committee*, England and Wales: HMSO.

Sandford, The Rev. Rt. Hon., Lord (1974) *Report of the National Parks Policies Review Committee*, London: HMSO.

On the conflicts between various land uses see, *inter alia*:

Body, R. (1982) *Agriculture: The Triumph and the Shame*, London: Gower/ Maurice Temple Smith.

Body, R. (1984) *Farming in the Clouds*, London: Gower/Maurice Temple Smith.

Bowers, J. and Cheshire, P. (1983) *Agriculture, the Countryside and Land Use; An Economic Critique*, London: Methuen.

Countryside Commission (1987), *New Opportunities for the Countryside*.

Hebblethwaite, R. L. (1968) *East Hampshire A. O. N. B.: A Study in Countryside Conservation*, Winchester: Hampshire County Council.

MacEwen, M. and Sinclair, G. (1983), *New Life for the Hills*, Council for National Parks.

O'Riordan, T. (1983) *Putting Trust in the Countryside*, in The Conservation and Development Programme for the UK, London: Kogan Page.

Parry, M., Bruce, A., and Harkness, C. (1981) 'The plight of British moorlands', *New Scientist*, 90 (1255): 550–1.

Strutt, , Sir Nigel (Chairman), Advisory Council for Agriculture and Horticulture In England and Wales (1978) *Agriculture and the Countryside*, Ministry of Agriculture, Fisheries and Food.

Tourism and Recreation Research Unit (1981) *Economy of Rural Communities in National Parks*. Department of Geography, Edinburgh University, Edinburgh.

On landscape classification see:

Fines, K. P. (1968) 'Landscape evaluation: A research project in East Sussex', *Regional Studies*, 2: 41–55.

Lowenthal, D. and Prince, H. (1965) 'English landscape tastes', *The Geographical Review*, 55: 186–222.

Penning-Rowsell, E. C. (1981) 'Fluctuating fortunes in gauging landscape' *Progress in Human Geography*, 5: 25–41.

Robinson, D. G. (ed.) (1976) *Landscape Evaluation Research Project*, University of Manchester and Countryside Commission.

Welsh Office (1980) *A Landscape Classification of Wales*, Cardiff, Planning Services, Welsh Office.

Acts of Parliament referred to in text:

Town and Country Planning Act (1949)

National Parks and Access to the Countryside Act (1949)

Countryside (Scotland) Act (1967)

Countryside Act (1968)

Nature Conservancy Council Act (1973)

Wildlife and Countryside Act (1981)

Farm Land and Development Bill (1987) Consultation Paper, HMSO.

Command Papers:

Leisure in the Countryside (1966) Cmnd. 2928

# 18 And the future?

*R. J. Johnston*

What will be the future geography of the United Kingdom, as the trends of recent years set out in this book continue, as major changes already set in motion (such as the Single European Market, scheduled for inauguration in 1992, and the opening of the Channel Tunnel in the following year) come about, and as the unexpected events of local, national and international economic, social and political affairs stimulate responses from individuals, corporate bodies, and governments? The answer is far from clear, for it is in the nature of human activity that the future is unknowable. We can but speculate, using our understanding of the past and the present to paint a general picture of what the next decades will probably be like.

## TWO BASIC THEMES

As the basis for the scenario to be presented, two basic themes are identified, carrying forward what has happened in the 1980s. These are further economic restructuring, with the associated social changes, and the continued momentum of the political trends of the last decade.

### Economic restructuring

The world is becoming increasingly integrated into a single economic unit, a truly global world economy (incorporating the countries of the second as well as the first and third worlds) in which the fortunes of the various parts are more and more interdependent and at the same time those various parts (notably the separate nation-states) are competing harder for standing within the system. The contest is between the people in the different states, but involves them competing for sources of wealth that are controlled by non-state organizations. Thus, for example, the people of the United Kingdom compete against their compatriots in the other eleven countries of the European Community for investment by multi-national corporations, for jobs in the production of goods and services, to be marketed widely across the earth, which will stimulate wealth-creation locally even if the profits from the ventures are largely accumulated elsewhere.

There are two basic quests in economic transformation: for greater efficiency in the production of goods and services, and for the development of new products. With regard to the first, greater efficiency is sought through increases in productivity, to allow UK producers to compete in the increasingly open home and overseas markets. If such increases are not forthcoming, and the competitive position of British production weakens, then investment will be withdrawn: it may be transferred to similar production facilities in other countries, where the profit potential is higher; it may be switched to other forms of production, for similar reasons, either within the United Kingdom or elsewhere; or it may no longer be invested in the wealth-creation process. With local UK capital, the switch to overseas investment (whether in the same sector of production or not) may continue to generate profits for British investors, with some positive impacts on the country's economy, but the multiplier processes will be less than if the investment were in local production, and the overall impact on employment and levels of living in Britain thereby deleterious. With foreign capital, the multiplier process associated with the repatriation of profits is totally lost, and the impacts on British economy and society are more profound. Similarly, if capital is removed from investment in job-creation altogether, the likely consequence is a run-down in the British economy.

How, then, can the United Kingdom compete successfully for investment in job and wealth creation? How can productivity increases be promoted, recalling that those gains must be relative as well as absolute: if productivity improvements are higher in other countries, whatever the rate in the United Kingdom, then investors will be attracted elsewhere because the more efficiently produced goods and services will capture the markets and offer the largest profits. There are two main ways of increasing productivity – the value of a unit of production relative to the costs of inputs (of which by far the major element, indirectly if not directly, is labour). The first is to improve the productive process, which almost invariably means investment in new machines and methods and in training people to develop and to use them. (Those machines and methods may be in 'service' industries, every bit as much as they may be in 'productive' industries, for, as chapter 9 has shown, the drive for greater efficiency and greater profits is as demanding in both.) Thus people must be willing to invest, which means that they must be confident in the outcome – that the UK labour force will deliver the higher levels of productivity by using the new processes effectively and efficiently. Second, wages can be held down relative to prices, which again focuses on the more efficient use of labour.

Ultimately, investment in production facilities for goods and services is investment in labour, for no production facility is entirely automated, nor is it likely to be so in the near future. (In any case, even if the day-to-day running of a facility demands little labour, apart from that involved in its oversight and maintenance, the costs of creating such a facility involve very high labour costs – as seen, for example, in the very high costs for building nuclear power stations to exacting technical specifications.) So what are the characteristics of a labour force which make it attractive to investors? Cheapness is clearly one, but this is a relative and not an absolute criterion, for well-paid workers may be more efficient than poorly paid ones; the better-paid they are, the more productive they must be. To be more productive they must be either more skilled, which means that they must be either or both well-trained and well-disciplined, willing to work to exacting demands (often at repetitive and unskilled tasks). Further, they must be flexible, for as changes in production methods occur more frequently so workers must be prepared to do different things, to work in different ways, and to be retrained often. Some argue that this has been one of the major problems of the UK economy in recent decades, that the labour force, mobilized through trades unions, has been too inflexible and has thereby discouraged investment in the British economy. The result, it is said, is a country with much obsolescent (if not obsolete) fixed capital and a workforce with a reputation for blocking changes.

Although increasing productivity in existing activities is necessary for continued relative success in the world economy it is insufficient by itself; as well as getting better at the things it already does, a country which aspires to economic success must also develop successful new activities. This calls for investment too, in the research and development processes that lead to new, saleable products. Again, such investment is only likely to be forthcoming if those with the capital are confident of the returns. It is, of course, more of a gamble to invest in research and development than in improved production facilities, because the outcomes are less certain. So what investors are looking for are not only people who can have the ideas that will lead to new products but also those who can then ensure that those products can be both produced efficiently and marketed successfully. Again, expertise is needed, alongside entrepreneurship and flair. Without it, the investment in the new will occur elsewhere, and the United Kingdom can then at best hope to attract facilities for the manufacture and/ or assembly of the new products developed elsewhere, to be sold on the British market; it would become a branch-plant economy.

These economic imperatives are associated with social demands, there-fore, calling for a population which is prepared to accept the dictates of a competitive market system. Ensuring such acceptance involves the promo-tion of a certain set of attitudes within the country, a task that involves the participation of the state and leads to the second of the two themes.

### Political trends

The 1980s have witnessed major political changes in the United Kingdom, with repercussions for all aspects of economic and social life, and for all areas of the country. Those changes are sometimes summarized by phrases such as 'rolling back the frontiers of the state' and 'ridding the country of socialism'; less prosaically, they involve the collapse of what is often termed the post-war consensus, with its emphases on the role of the state as the guarantor as far as possible of full employment, and on the importance of the welfare state for the provision of a wide range of goods and services. Since the election of the first Conservative government led by Margaret Thatcher in May 1979, the role of the state in contemporary capitalism has been substantially redefined and the nature of the welfare state has come under very close scrutiny.

The nature of 'Thatcherism', as it is so frequently called, is the focus of much debate among political scientists and commentators, for there is no authoritative single statement of its fundamental ideology and there have been substantial shifts in several major policy directions over the decade. According to Gamble (1988), the basic principles on which the Thatcher governments have operated are 'the free economy' and 'the strong state'. Market mechanisms are clearly perceived as the best for determining what should be produced, in what volumes and at what price, and certainly as much superior to centralized planning. Thus the role of the state is presented as being that of guarantor of a milieu within which market operations can flourish, and by far its most important role is seen as ensuring 'sound money' by ensuring that inflation is kept low. With low inflation, investment is encouraged because returns are less uncertain than when it is high. But to ensure that investment is undertaken an 'enterprise culture' has to be promoted which encourages and rewards entrepreneurial characteristics, hence the emphasis on low rates of income tax. Promoting the entrepreneurial culture is very much an ideological as well as a fiscal task, hence the stress on changes at all levels of the country's educational system and the desire to ensure that people are trained for the new working environments. Similarly, investment will only be forthcoming if the labour force has not only the desired skills but also the requisite attitudes, hence the drive against the perceived restrictive practices and inflexibilities of trades unions.

According to 'Thatcherism', therefore, a strong state is one that sustains and promotes a free economy, which plays as little part as possible in the decisions about production and price and leaves the shape of the country's economy, and thus the contours of its geography, to the operation of market forces. Elements of the welfare state have thus been either 'privatized' (i.e. sold to private buyers) or required to operate in the same ways (i.e. to make profits) as private sector organizations. The state defends the interests of the private sector, and those of the individual within it, but interferes as little as possible in the day-to-day operations of the market places that are central to the capitalist dynamic.

But will this situation continue, might it not be that 'Thatcherism' will be defeated in the not too distant future, since public opinion poll evidence indicates that 'Thatcherite' values are supported by a minority of the electorate only (Crewe 1989)? (It must be noted, of course, that the

Conservative party under Margaret Thatcher won only 43.9, 42.4 and 42.3 per cent of the votes cast at the 1979, 1983 and 1987 general elections respectively. Given that turnout at those elections was 76.0, 72.7 and 75.3 per cent of the registered electorate, this means the party never achieved a mandate from more than one-third of the electorate.) The nature of the British electoral system and of the current electoral geography of Great Britain is such, however, that the main opposition party (Labour) is very seriously disadvantaged in its attempts to defeat the incumbent government (as discussed in detail in Johnston, Pattie and Allsopp 1988). The proportion of marginal seats is small and declining (Curtice and Steed 1986), in part because of the polarization of the country which has resulted from the geography of the economic recession and later recovery of the 1980s; although there is some evidence that the electorate is more volatile than in the past, and more prepared to shift its allegiance, at least temporarily, by the late 1980s the prosperous south offers few hopes to any opposition party, other than gains either if there is a major recession there before the next election or if there is a major decline in confidence in the government on other grounds.

It may be, of course, that the Conservative party will lose power early in the 1990s, probably to the Labour party. But even if this were to happen, it is far from clear that it would result in major shifts from the 'free market' and 'strong state' policies of the 1980s. In reassessing its policies following its third defeat in a row in 1987, the Labour party sought to present itself as much more 'social democrat' and much less 'socialist'. It had analysed trends in both the socio-economic structure of the electorate and voters' attitudes, and concluded that it needed to appeal more widely across the 'class spectrum', with a political message that sees it as a sympathetic manager of capitalist markets (promoting equality and justice within their operation) rather than as an opponent of capitalism; central planning now has a subordinate position in its draft manifesto (on the strategies open to Labour, see Crewe 1986).

Further evidence that the general poltical trends of the 1980s are likely to continue through the next decade is given by the international context. Although there are certain aspects of 'Thatcherism' which are unique to the United Kingdom, its general ethos is shared with a large number of countries, whose governments have a wide range of political complexions. There is little difference between the Conservative capitalism of Mrs Thatcher's governments and the policies of, for example, the Republican capitalism of 'Reaganism' in the United States, and the 'socialist' capitalism of 'Rogernomics' in New Zealand. Furthermore, the late 1980s have seen major shifts away from centralized planning of all aspects of the economy in many of the socialist states of Eastern Europe: *glasnost* and *perestroika* are bringing about the opening-up of markets and the expansion of individual freedoms there too. To some commentators, these shifts towards greater freedom for market mechanisms and revised roles for the state reflect changes in the nature of capitalism itself, and while they may not be necessary responses to the era of 'flexible accumulation' (Lash and Urry 1987) they have certainly been identified by some as the best. There are many who disagree, of course, and many more who contest the details of current policies, but the main trend seems to be firmly established. New issues will undoubtedly be added to the political agenda – as with the 'green politics' of the late 1980s – and others may decline in importance in response to contemporary events, but it is unlikely that we will return to the level of centralized planning which characterized the United Kingdom in the period 1945–79.

## THE EMERGING GEOGRAPHY

Given these basic trends in the nature of British society, what are the likely geographical consequences? Few British geographers have been prepared to speculate on this, preferring to analyse the recent past and to enlarge on its pathologies rather than to suggest blueprints for the future. The scenario painted here is little more than vague guesswork, therefore.

### Employment and the regional pattern

Fundamental to the emerging geography of the country will be the geography of employment, because this underpins wealth creation and patterns of consumption. If some areas of the United Kingdom are likely to be more prosperous than others, because they are more attractive to the investors who provide jobs, then the country is likely to be divided into a core and a periphery, just as many analysts portray the world economy of which it is a part.

One geographer who has been prepared to speculate on the future geography of employment is Peter Hall, who has related the changing industrial geography of the United Kingdom to a periodization of its manufacturing structure. Drawing on the works of economic analysts such as Kondratieff and Schumpeter (see Hall 1988), he has identified five main long cycles in the economic history of the British economy since the Industrial Revolution. Each cycle is associated with a burst of investment in new industrial processes. After two or three decades of prosperity, these industries start to falter, economic growth slackens, and general levels of prosperity are threatened. This comes about because profits start to fall (since markets are saturated, further productivity increases are difficult to achieve, and competitors are able to produce more cheaply); investment declines, unemployment rises with the multiplier effects, and a recession is initiated. Recovery comes about through an industrial transformation, with investment attracted to new product lines for which large potential markets have been identified.

Each cycle is thus characterized by a new set of industries, while those that were the key to previous periods of prosperity become less important, both relatively and absolutely. Few of them entirely disappear, but technological changes reduce their importance to the economy, especially in terms of employment. The first of the cycles was characterized by the dominance of two industries – the smelting of iron with coal and the machine production of textiles in factories. It was followed by a steel and railways era (c. 1842–97), whereas in the third the foundations of prosperity were provided by the chemical and vehicle industries and the new sources of power – electricity and oil. The decades from 1940 on formed the fourth cycle; its key industries have been those based on electronics and aerospace. It will be followed, from the mid-1990s in all probability, by a fifth, in which industries based on biotechnology and information technology will prevail. Hall's particular contribution to the study of these cycles lies in his association of them with separate geographies. Each set of industries characteristic of a cycle has its particular location pattern, so that the fifth cycle inherits an industrial landscape which is a palimpsest, a series of layers representing the geography of each of the previous cycles, with the older the layer the weaker its contribution to the present geography of production (see also the analogy drawn by Massey 1984). Thus the boom areas of the first cycle were the coalfields, especially those with exposed seams and those where textile industries flourished – notably on the flanks of the southern Pennines; for the third cycle, the vehicle industries were clustered in the West Midlands and the electronics industries of the fourth are prevalent in the south of the country, notably the so-called M4 corridor stretching west from London through Reading and Swindon to Bristol.

According to Hall, a new geography is one of the characteristic features of a new cycle, and if the growth that the cycle offers is going to occur, that new geography must be allowed to evolve. Thus in writing about the geography of the fifth Kondratieff cycle, he argues that (Hall 1981: p. 537):

> The new industries are not going to be born in Port Talbot or Consett. They might just be born again in Glasgow or Manchester and Birmingham, or any other British city with a prestigious university . . . But most likely they will originate in the south . . . the innovating firms are overwhelmingly in the south-east . . . this region has the right climate of innovation . . . tomorrow's industries are not going to be born in yesterday's regions . . . [so] the aim of government should be to start planning for a massive move of people from the old areas and cities to the new. Britain's future, if it has one, is in that broad belt that runs from Oxford and Winchester through the Thames Valley and Milton Keynes to Cambridge.

The events of the 1980s have proved Hall right, for it was the 'old industrial regions' of the north of England, central Scotland, South Wales, and eastern Northern Ireland which suffered most in the recession of the mid-1980s and recovered slowest at the end of the decade. Figure 18.1a shows

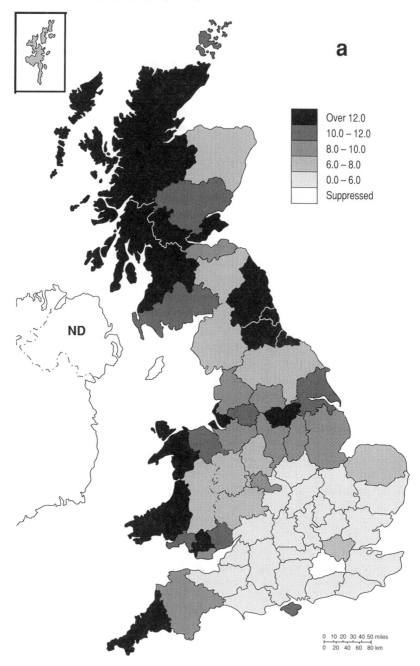

*Figure 18.1* (a) Unemployment, as a percentage of the registered workforce, in January 1989, by county in England and Wales and by region in Scotland

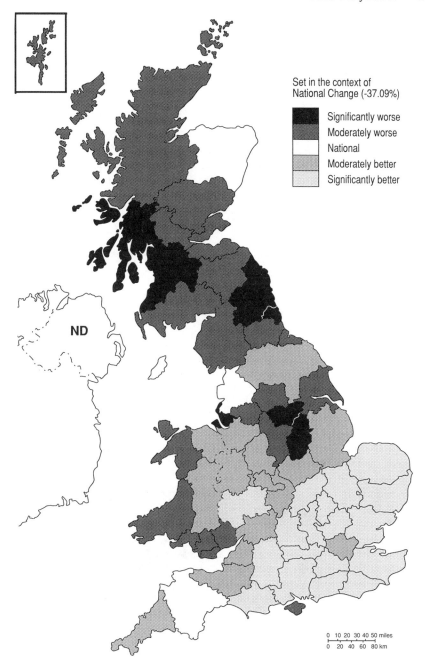

Set in the context of
National Change (-37.09%)

Significantly worse
Moderately worse
National
Moderately better
Significantly better

ND

0  10  20  30  40  50 miles
0   20   40   60   80 km

(b) Change in unemployment, relative to the national (Great Britain) rate, January
1987–January 1989
*Source:* The data are taken from the Department of Employment statistics base at the
University of Durham – NOMIS – and were provided by Mr A. Townsend

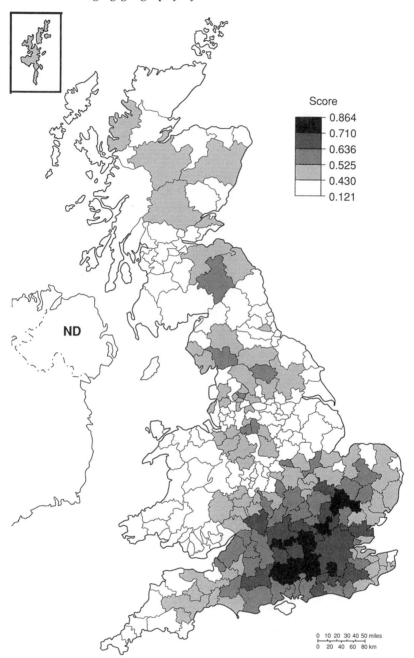

*Figure 18.2* Champion and Green's *static index* showing variations in local prosperity, by Local Labour Market Area (LLMA), in the mid-1980s. (a) shows the LLMAs with index values above the median for Great Britain. Those shaded black have the highest prosperity levels

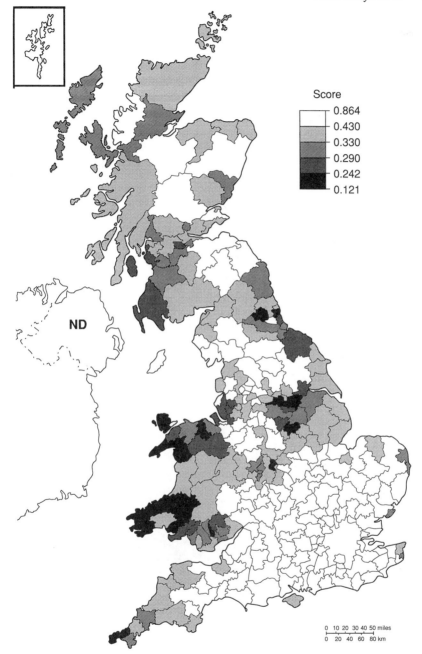

(b) shows the LLMAs below the median. Those shaded black have the lowest values

*Source:* Champion and Green 1989: 76–7; reproduced with permission from Paul Chapman Publishing

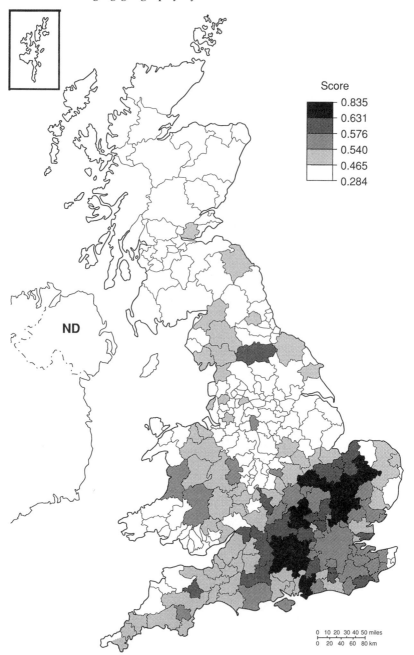

Score

| | |
|---|---|
| | 0.835 |
| | 0.631 |
| | 0.576 |
| | 0.540 |
| | 0.465 |
| | 0.284 |

ND

0  10  20  30  40  50 miles
0    20   40   60   80 km

*Figure 18.3* Champion and Green's *change index* showing changes in local prosperity by LLMA during the 1980s. (a) shows LLMAs whose rate of change exceeded the median, so that those with the darkest shading experienced the greatest rate of prosperity growth

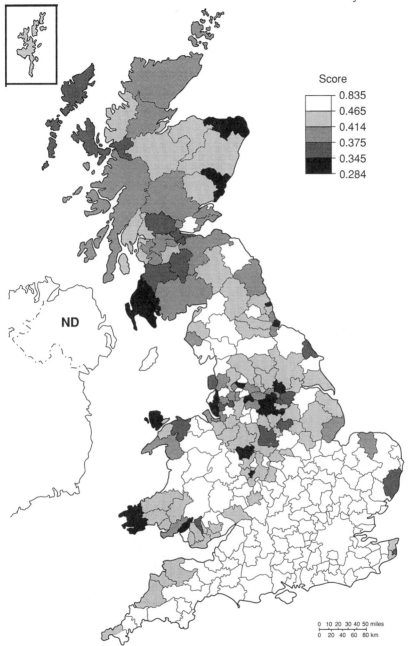

Score
0.835
0.465
0.414
0.375
0.345
0.284

ND

0  10 20  30 40 50 miles
0    20   40   60  80 km

(b) shows LLMAs whose rate of change was less than the median, so that those with the darkest shading had the lowest rate of change
*Source:* Champion and Green 1989: 82–3; reproduced with permission from Paul Chapman Publishing

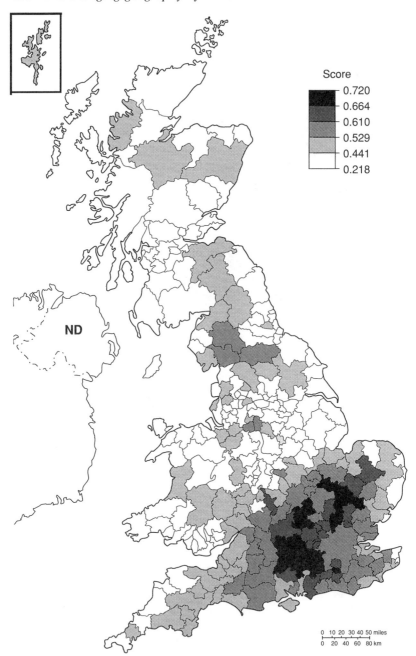

*Figure 18.4* Champion and Green's *amalgamated index* of local prosperity and changes in local prosperity by LLMA. (a) shows LLMAs with index values above the median, so that those with the darkest shading had the highest levels of prosperity and the greatest relative increase

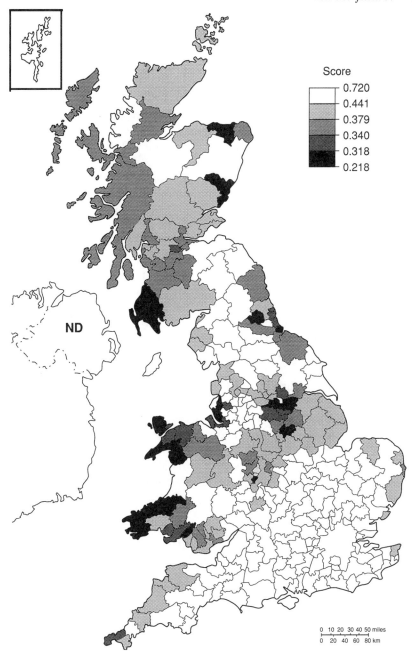

(b) shows the LLMAs with values below the median, so that those with the darkest
shading had the lowest levels and the worst performance on the change index
*Source:* Champion and Green 1989: 88–9; reproduced with permission from Paul Chapman
Publishing

the unemployment rate in January 1989, by county in England and Wales and by region in Scotland (unfortunately, the data source does not cover Northern Ireland), and figure 18.1b shows changes over the two previous years. Thus in the south-east of England, virtually every county had a rate below 6.0 per cent (that for Surrey was suppressed because there was virtually full employment); only in Greater London and in the Isle of Wight were as many as one in seventeen of the labour force out of work (as defined for government statistics), compared with one in eight or more in much of Scotland and Wales, on Teeside, Tyneside and Wearside, in South Yorkshire, and in Cornwall. Furthermore, between January 1987 and January 1989 the national number of unemployed fell by just over 37 per cent. Set in the context of that figure, most of the south-east performed even better (i.e. unemployment fell by more than 37 per cent, significantly so throughout the Home Counties), whereas all of the 'old industrial regions' except the West Midlands performed worse than the country as a whole.

One interpretation of the patterns shown in figure 18.1 identifies a clear north:south divide within the United Kingdom, a view which has attracted a great deal of support from geographers and others during the 1980s (see, for example, the essays in Lewis and Townsend 1989). According to this argument, the country is becoming increasingly polarized – between the 'haves' and the 'have-nots', who are spatially concentrated in the 'have' and the 'have-not' regions. To illustrate this, Tony Champion and Anne Green (1989) have produced two indices of local prosperity. The first, the *static index*, shows spatial variations in conditions in the mid-1980s (figure 18.2: the index is a composite of five variables, as described in their essay): the concentration of the more prosperous local labour market areas (LLMAs), with above median index values, in the south-east of England is clear, as is that of the least prosperous (with below median values) in Cornwall, almost all of Wales, the 'old industrial areas' of the West Midlands, Lancashire, Yorkshire, and north-east England, and much of Scotland (unfortunately their data do not cover Northern Ireland). Their second, *change index*, focuses on changes in prosperity during the 1980s (figure 18.3); the patterns are almost exactly the same as those in figure 18.2, with the greatest increases in prosperity in the areas that were already the most prosperous. Thus when they amalgamate the two indices, the north:south divide remains the salient feature of the maps (figure 18.4). The patterns just described could be presented as a likely permanent feature of the United Kindom's geography over the next decade, representing as they do the culmination of trends that are now nearly 200 years old. Expanding manufacturing industries are attracted to the south-eastern regions of England because they offer the most attractive environments: the population is more innovative and entrepreneurial; wage labour is more disciplined and flexible; the prestigious research universities are nearby; and the expanding, increasingly accessible markets of the EC are near to hand. Furthermore, the main focus of growth in the service industries – in the burgeoning financial sector based on the City of London and its increasing role in the circulation of finance capital around the world – is in the same region.

But is it necessarily always going to be so? It could be argued that, if prosperity is sustained over several decades, and full or near-full employment results, then the regional differences will be reduced. As the south-east becomes 'saturated', so wages will rise (especially if the government succeeds in reducing, if not removing, national wage bargaining as part of its freeing of the market), congestion will increase, property values will become prohibitive, and investors will look for more attractive propositions elsewhere. Evidence to support this argument will be found in the end of the property-price boom in the south-east in 1989, while prices elsewhere continued to increase, and in the willingness of workers in the older industrial regions to accept new working practices (as with the single-union factories such as those established by Nissan at Sunderland and by Toyota at Derby, and the grudging acceptance of six-day coal-cutting by miners in some regions). But, as studies of the United Kingdom's declining industrial regions have shown (see, for example, Hausner 1988), the number of new jobs needed in areas like Clydeside and Merseyside is very large, and it is unlikely that they will be forthcoming. Places in those areas are competing for new investment (against a background of reduced regional aid: chapter 6), but although some (like Scunthorpe and Corby) claim substantial success, the problems in many areas remain very large.

**Big city and small town**

The examples of Corby and Scunthorpe are probably exceptions, for two reasons: first, they are on the fringes of the 'old industrial regions' only; and second, they are relatively small, free-standing towns and not parts of the nineteenth-century conurbations. They are more typical of a second geographical trend which has paralleled that of the north:south divide, the relative growth of smaller towns and the decline of the large cities.

As demonstrated by Paul Compton (chapter 3) and David Herbert (chapter 10), there has been a process of population decentralization in the United Kingdom throughout the present century, and probably much longer. Until relatively recently this was basically a process of suburbanization, as developers capitalized first on public transport systems and then on the growing use of the motor car to promote new residential developments from which people commuted to the traditional employment areas of the central cities. After the First World War, suburban employment areas began to mushroom (as, for example, at Wembley in north-west London), a trend that was accentuated later in the century. More importantly, after the Second World War the introduction of strict growth controls around the large conurbations, notably by the creation of Green Belts, and the

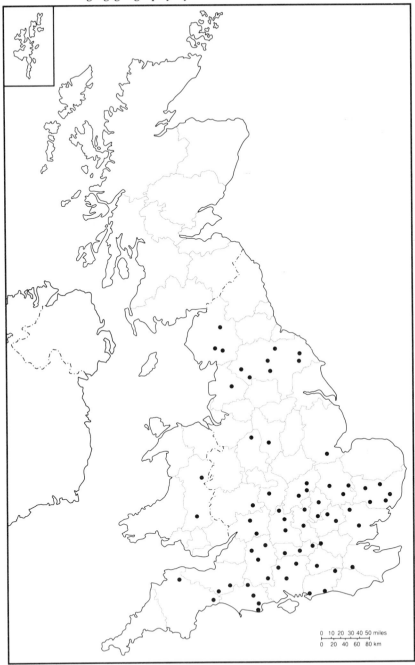

*Figure 18.5* The sixty-six towns identified by the Department of Employment as having full employment in November 1989

*Source:* Data published by the Department and reported in *The Sunday Times,* 12 November 1989

promotion of New Towns and Expanded Towns, encouraged a wider spread of people and jobs, especially in south-east England. Inner-city decline was now countered not only by suburban expansion but also by exurban growth.

This trend has continued through to the late 1980s, so that the ten highest-rated LLMAs on Champion and Green's change index were not the cities of the south (places like Bristol and Portsmouth, Southampton and Norwich) but the larger towns: Milton Keynes led, followed by Huntingdon, Newbury, Thetford, Hertford and Ware, Corby, Basingstoke, Cambridge, Reading and Aylesbury. Some of these, like Milton Keynes (and also Peterborough and Northampton) benefited from the growth impulses provided by the New Town legislation, whereas others (such as Thetford and Basingstoke) were beneficiaries of the Expanded Towns programme. But others grew 'naturally', because the social, economic, political and physical environments that they offered were attractive to investors. Like Swindon, they were accessible to all other parts of the country via the motorway network, the modern industries that they attracted did not produce bulky items which were costly to move to their customers, they had no traditions of militant trades unions, land and buildings were relatively cheap, and their political leaders in local govern-ment were favourably disposed to the 'enterprise culture'. So those places prospered, as did similar towns in the 'old industrial regions' – places like Harrogate and Ripon – where unemployment also fell rapidly in the late 1980s. Meanwhile, the large cities continued to languish, especially their inner, working-class areas. The result is what is often presented as an urban:rural (more exactly a large city:medium-sized town) divide within the north:south pattern.

Figure 18.5 illustrates this point very clearly. It shows the sixty-six towns listed by the Department of Employment in November 1989 (the list was published in *The Sunday Times* for 12 November 1989) which were recognized as having full employment (defined as an unemployment rate below 3 per cent). The majority of them were in the south of England, with none in either Scotland or Northern Ireland and only two in Wales. Of the sixty-four in England, there were ten in the northern regions. None of those – Clitheroe, Harrogate, Kendal, Malton, Northallerton, Penrith, Pickering and Helmsley, Ripon, Settle, and Skipton – is in the major urban-industrial conurbations of those regions; all, indeed, are some distance from those major centres of population. They represent the large city:medium sized town divide within the north, in which the latter are the most prosperous parts of the region. Similarly, of the towns in the southern regions on the list, few (like Cambridge, Oxford, Reading and Swindon) are large; the majority are affluent country towns outside the immediate environs of the main urban agglomerations.

The existence of these two divides is hinted strongly in government data on disposable income per head in households in 1987 (figure 18.6); the

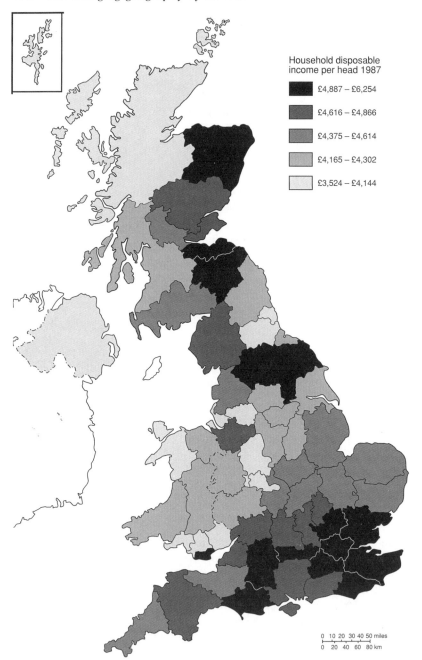

*Figure 18.6* Household disposal income per head, 1987, by county in England and Wales and by region in Scotland
*Source:* Data produced by the Central Statistical Office and initially mapped in *The Independent,* 16 August 1989

county/regional averages ranged from £3,524 to £6,254. Within England, the highest averages were in the south-east, plus the rural counties of North Yorkshire, Cumbria and Cheshire, which contain substantial concentrations of suburbanites from major conurbations (notably in Cheshire), of wealthy retired people (especially in Cumbria), and of prosperous small towns in fertile areas (North Yorkshire). In Wales, the only county with its average income in the highest bracket is South Glamorgan, adjacent to the industrial counties of Mid and West Glamorgan and Gwent, which are in the lowest bracket (and which probably provide a substantial proportion of the incomes being 'consumed' in South Glamorgan). Scotland has two areas of high incomes, one comprising the region focused on Edinburgh, and the other in the Aberdeen region, sustained by the high incomes paid in the oil-related industries. Elsewhere in the country, average incomes are below the national figure, as they are throughout Northern Ireland.

Increasingly during the 1970s and, especially, the 1980s the decentralization of people and jobs from the large cities was accompanied by a further decentralization of people that was not linked to the outward movement of employment. Two main elements can be identified within this trend. The first is the growth of long-distance commuting, particularly to London, encouraged by improvements in the road network, the provision of high-speed trains on the main routes (notably those extending north-east and west), the property price inflation in the country's core, and the congestion on local traffic arteries in the capital and its immediate surroundings. A growing number of people were prepared to travel 100 miles or more each way, each day, from places such as Grantham and Swindon, finding that the costs were substantially countered not only by cheaper properties but also by the more pleasant physical environments. Thus many of the towns and their surrounding villages along the main rail routes (even as far north as York) have become attractive 'dormitory settlements'.

The second element is the growth of retirement migration, which again has favoured the smaller settlements with the more attractive physical environments and the lower property values. With an ageing, healthier population, a growing number of people taking early retirement (in their fifties) on substantial pensions, and the ability of many households to capitalize on their expensive properties in the large cities, an increasing number of people are moving away from the places where they worked. For many of them, the area within which they will search for a retirement home is much wider than that for the long-distance commuters, for accessibility is much less salient to them, lower property prices in the more remote areas are attractive to many, and the nostalgia for small towns and villages (in some cases, those in which they grew up) pulls them into more remote areas. Thus, while the traditional resorts and spas continue to attract large numbers of retirees (Eastbourne and Bournemouth, Cheltenham and Harrogate), a large number of other places are now expanding, with consequences for property markets there and the housing chances of local residents, especially those in relatively lowly paid occupations and lacking the capital to make large down-payments. Those lowly paid locals (many of them old, and many of them relatively immobile) suffer too because the new residents rarely attract new services to the villages that they find fit their view of the rural idyll. They can use their cars to travel to the towns, while the locals have to rely on increasingly infrequent buses to get to the nearest shops.

### The population and employment patterns of the future?

What, then, is the likely outcome of these trends? Is it of a United Kingdom increasingly divided between both north and south and city and countryside? All of the evidence suggests yes.

With regard to the inter-regional differentials, there is little at present to suggest that sufficient investment will be attracted to the northern regions to replace the very large number of jobs lost from manufacturing industries in the last two decades. The new manufacturing industries are not attracted to the northern regions, for a variety of reasons, and the burgeoning service industries (other than those directly servicing prosperous customers) certainly are not. As the southern regions become 'saturated' and congested, so some investment may shift to the more attractive northern towns (though probably not to the large cities there), but with increased integration with the EC economy, and the link provided by the Channel Tunnel, the southern regions, especially those on its eastern rim, have a strong comparative advantage. Although there are schemes to have trains using the Tunnel proceeding directly to termini outside the south-east (at Rugby, perhaps, or Doncaster), and resistance to growth pressures in the south-east is substantial, there is little to suggest a substantial renaissance for the north, especially since government commitment to regional aid and directing investment to the 'depressed areas' is low. (There are three partial exceptions to this, for the separate Development Agencies in Scotland, Wales and Northern Ireland offer much more support than is available in comparable English areas, which may mean that in the long run the latter are the major sufferers from continued relative deprivation.) Indeed, the commitment to the free economy is likely to exacerbate the problems of some of the northern regions. For example, the privatization of the electricity generation industry has broken the link between two massive formerly nationalized concerns – the Central Electricity Generating Board and the National Coal Board. The two new power generation companies must compete for coal and other raw materials in the international market, making substantial difficulties for British Coal in its attempts to obtain markets for its relatively expensive products. The closures of many pits foreseen by the National Union of Mineworkers' leaders at the time of their 1984–5 strike are now more than being fulfilled, with consequences not only for the many mining communities without their local employment base (even in the prosperous Nottinghamshire and South Yorkshire fields) but also for the country's balance of payments.

The likely situation with regard to the urban:rural divide is a little less clear. The process known as counterurbanization, of large city decline countered by growth in smaller places, has slowed recently, according to some commentators. In part, this reflects the substantial efforts made to revive the larger places, especially their inner-city areas characterized by industrial dereliction and residential squalor. The problems of the inner cities were recognized by the Prime Minister immediately after the 1987 general election, in part at least because they posed the greatest potential threat to the legitimation of her government, not only in terms of votes but also in the violence that occasionally erupts out of alienation. Policies of inner-city revival have thus been given a high profile (see Robson 1988, for an excellent review), and many schemes involving public and private sector cooperation (but in some cases excluding local governments) have been launched. Whereas most are able to produce environmental improvements, few it seems offer long-term jobs in productive activities: Sheffield, for example, has pinned hopes for a revival (after the literal decimation of the steel industries on which its economy was based for more than a century) on the investment of over £100 million in the facilities for the 1991 Universiade (World Student Games), but whether these can provide permanent replacement employment for tens of thousands of displaced workers in heavy industries remains to be seen. It may be, therefore, that part of the counterurbanization trend associated with the decentralization of people and jobs will be countered by inner-city policies, at least to the extent of halting the flood of commuters away from the cities: new fare-fixing policies by British Rail in the late 1980s will probably assist in this, for the costs to commuters, especially long-distance commuters, have risen much more rapidly than those for other travellers. But it is unlikely that the flow of people away from the cities to their retirement homes in the country will be stemmed. Thus the result is likely to be a growing polarization, at several levels. At the macro-scale, the cities will become increasingly the homes of the relatively deprived; locally within them, the segregation associated with prosperity and housing tenure (and exacerbated by the construction of housing aimed mainly at affluent 'yuppies' in the inner-city redevelopments, such as London's Docklands) will confine them to inner-city and suburban council estate ghettos: the social and political problems for the next decades will almost certainly be in 'those inner cities', where they may well be exacerbated by growing tensions among different ethnic groups, and especially between those groups and the host population from which they feel increasingly alienated.

## AND THE ENVIRONMENT

These continuing trends in the distribution of population and economic activity have considerable environmental implications. The decaying inner cities and depressed industrial regions are characterized by many hectares of derelict land and abandoned properties, many of them sporting hopeful 'For Sale' or 'To Rent' signs. They are the 'empty spaces' of the British economy, places that nobody wants. Elsewhere, however, space is at a premium, as developers press to be allowed to erect new factories and residential properties on 'green field' sites, and the landowners want to realize the immense capital gains that the accidents of location have brought them. Thus, the Kondratieff cycles that characterize the economic fortunes of the country and its constituent regions have a visible impact on the landscape; the areas that prospered under previous cycles are now the areas of dereliction and visual pollution.

The recent developments in agriculture and land use, as described by Martin Parry (chapter 2) and Ian Bowler (chapter 4), add to the environmental issues facing the United Kingdom. The substantial increases in the productivity of land over recent decades, and in the ability of British agriculture to provide food for the local population, mean that a considerable proportion of farmland is now not needed; there is no market for what it produces. How, then, should it be used? Is it sensible to respond to the pressures for converting more and more to urban uses, especially in the booming southern regions?

The sensible answer to the second question might at first glance seem to be yes; if land is not needed for food production any more, it may as well be converted to desirable and attractive low density housing, to golf courses and other leisure facilities, and so forth. But there are arguments to the contrary, with two major, inter-related strands. The first concerns the protection of the landscape for aesthetic reasons, conserving the visual features of both the physical environment and the built environment. There are protests, for example, against the removal of hedgerows and other field boundaries to allow more intensive use of machinery in arable farming, because it removes much of the variety from the 'traditional' British countryside. Similarly, there are protests against the expansion of small towns and villages, because the new developments destroy the 'character' of existing settlements. There is a strong desire to maintain the status quo, especially in the countryside, to preserve the model of the British rural landscape.

Alongside this desire, and increasingly powerful in the society as a whole, is the growth of what is known as the environmental movement and the associated 'green politics'. There is growing evidence that the many centuries of human abuse of the physical environment have led to a situation wherein the future ability of much of that environment to sustain human life (at least in the numbers now present) is in doubt. At the global scale this is manifested in the concerns over the ozone layer and the greenhouse effect. Within Britain it is shown in the issue of nuclear power generation and the disposal of hazardous wastes, as well as in the concerns over the short- and long-term impacts of various measures used to improve land productivity (as with the application of fertilisers): success in increasing the country's food production has brought with it problems in sustaining the environment on which that success is based. That success can bring problems in its train has been appreciated often in the past, and has led to government action to remove the problems, in the wider public interest. The air pollution in large industrial cities resulting from the burning of large volumes of coal was shown to have serious health effects, thereby reducing the efficiency of the working population, and a series of Clean Air Acts was passed to reduce very substantially, if not eliminate, the source of the problem. Today, however, the extent of the problems has been shown to be much wider, and the late 1980s witnessed a rise in the environmental consciousness of the population. 'Green' issues were firmly placed on the political agenda: they were recognized by politicians of all parties, who were prepared to address them in their manifestoes, and they were reminded of their importance to a substantial proportion of the British population (especially in the more affluent regions) when the Green Party won 15 per cent of the votes cast (admittedly, the turnout was only 35 per cent) at the elections for the European Parliament in June 1989.

In tackling both the landscape preservation and the environmental protection issues, governments face major problems, because many of the policies they apparently need to adopt to satisfy the demands (and, some would argue, to ensure a future for humankind on earth) run counter to policies designed to promote economic growth: as pointed out at the beginning of this chapter, if economic growth is not promoted then the country's prosperity declines (and hence its ability to tackle the environmental problems!). This leads to arguments for policies of sustainable development, for adopting policies that will promote economic growth without diminishing the stock of environmental resources available to future generations. As yet, such policies do not seem to be available. It is possible for the government to pay farmers not to use all of their land productively all of the time (the 'set-aside' policies described by Ian Bowler, for example), but only because the land that remains under production is being used more intensively, with potential deleterious consequences. Similarly, farmers can be paid not to use such intensive methods in environmentally sensitive and visually attractive areas such as the Norfolk Broads, but only because those methods are being used elsewhere: one could argue that the protection of the Broads is being bought by the rapid removal of the Fenland soils. And there is an international dimension to the problem, too, for the protection of the British environment is, according to some, being bought by the rape of the countryside elsewhere, especially in the 'Third World'.

The pressures for environmental policies posed a particular threat to the British governments of the 1980s, because they wished to withdraw from the control of land use via public sector planning and to rely much more on the market mechanisms to determine what use would be made of what land: in the terms of the twin ideology of 'the free market' and 'the strong state' they wished to place land use and environmental protection firmly into the former category. (Hence, for example, proposals to privatize nature conservation; if people wanted certain areas conserved, they would pay for it.) The extent of the pressure for 'green politics' in the late 1980s and the realization of the scientific message regarding the increasing fragility of the planet's environment required a re-evaluation, as to whether environmental protection should not be one of the tasks of the strong state (just as national defence is): this was illustrated by the Prime Minister's statement at the Conservative party conference in 1988 that we have only a full-repair lease on the nation's environment. But whether it is possible to enact environmental policies that will fulfil the terms of that lease while not damaging economic growth, presumably through the use of market mechanisms, remains to be seen. Certain changes can be readily achieved with popular support, such as reduced use of aerosol sprays, but these do not tackle the fundamental problem. After all, when CFC gases which power those sprays were first introduced they were believed to be 'environmentally friendly'; can we know whether their replacement will be? Similarly, the greater use of nuclear power is promoted by some because it is 'environmentally clean', despite the evidence of the consequences of human error at Chernobyl and Three Mile Island and the unsolved problem of the safe disposal of hazardous waste with very long life.

Conflict over the environment will undoubtedly continue at the two levels, therefore. Within the United Kingdom, the pattern of land use will remain a source of concern, as interested groups seek to protect their treasured environments and governments wrestle with the degree to which landscape conservation should be allowed to triumph over market forces. More generally, concern about environmental futures will almost certanly mount, raising the issue of sustainable development to a major political theme, internationally as well as nationally. Whether it can be achieved will depend to a great deal on international collaboration, and a willingness of the 'developed' countries in particular to subordinate their desires for ever-increasing wealth and material possessions to the concerns of Third World populations and governments whose lands continue to be systematically raped. The evidence to date does not favour an optimistic view, for international accord on the uses of the oceanic deeps and the Antarctic continent has not been achieved (see Johnston 1989), and it may be that realization that cooperation is essential will come too late.

## IN SUMMARY

The geography of the United Kingdom has been rewritten several times, and is being rewritten again now, every bit as radically as it was in the nineteenth century; the successors to H. C. Darby and W. G. Hoskins who continue their task of charting the changing British scene will add a further chapter, focused on the late twentieth century. In it, they will recognize that the emerging landscape is the product of conflict, probably more so in many ways than was the case with previous chapters. Within the country there are the conflicts between the various regions and their towns and cities for the bases of prosperity – jobs – but those conflicts will in part be resolved in the context of wider international trends, as the United Kingdom competes with other countries for continued prosperity in an increasingly interdependent and volatile situation. There will be conflicts, too, over the use of land and the protection of the environment, both for the enjoyment of the present generations and the life chances of those to come; again, these conflicts will be set in the context of wider international developments, over which Britain has relatively little control.

As these conflicts are fought out and resolved, there will be substantial related debate over the role of the state in the creation of new geographies. In the nineteenth century, while the state was an agent of geographical change and influenced some of the details of the new topography (through its decisions on Acts of Parliament for the enclosure of open fields and the construction of railways, for example), the state's role was relatively small, and free market forces dominated. For much of the twentieth century, and especially in the three decades after the end of the Second World War, the state was much more active in the processes of geographical change, producing blueprints for the country's future spatial structuring (even if many of them were at best only partial successes). In the 1980s, successive governments have sought to reduce state involvement again, and to reinstate the importance of market forces as determinants of the country's geography. But where the boundary between the 'free economy' and the 'strong state' should lie is determined pragmatically, in response to circumstances, rather than theoretically. The conflicts between regions, between inner-city deprived populations and suburban and exurban prosperous groups, over the use of land and sustaining the environment, and between nation-states may, individually or together, bring about a reconsideration and a shift back towards a greater state involvement in geographical change. As yet, there is little evidence that this is forthcoming, except in the environmental field, but it may be that the conflicts which free markets stimulate will bring about yet another chapter when people write of the changing UK landscape in the early twenty-first century.

## REFERENCES

Champion, A. G. and Green, A. E. (1989) 'Local economic differentials and the 'north-south divide' in Lewis, J. and Townsend, A. (eds.) *The North-South Divide: Regional Change in Britain in the 1980s*, London: Paul Chapman Publishing, pp. 61–96.

Crewe, I. (1986) 'On the death and resurrection of class voting', *Political Studies*, 34: 620–38.

Crewe, I. (1989) 'Has the electorate become Thatcherite?' in Skidelsky, R. (ed.) *Thatcherism*, London: Chatto and Windus, pp. 25–49.

Curtice, J. and Steed, M. (1986) 'Proportionality and exaggeration in the British electoral system', *Electoral Studies*, 5: 209–28.

Gamble, A. M. (1988) *The Free Economy and the Strong State*, London: Macmillan.

Hall, P. (1981) 'The geography of the fifth Kondratiev cycle', *New Society*, 55 (958) 535–7.

Hall, P. (1988) 'The intellectual history of long waves', in Young, M. and Schuller, T. (eds.) *The Rhythms of Society*, London: Routledge, pp. 37–52.

Hausner, V. (ed.) (1988) *Urban Economic Change: Five City Studies*, Oxford: Clarendon Press.

Johnston, R. J. (1989) *Environmental Problems: Nature, Economy and the State*, London: Belhaven Press.

Johnston, R. J., Pattie, C. J. and Allsop, J. G. (1988) *A Nation Dividing? The Electoral Map of Great Britain 1979–1987*, London: Longman.

Lash, S. and Urry, J. (1987) *The End of Organized Capitalism*, Cambridge: Polity Press.

Lewis, J. and Townsend, A. (eds.) (1989) *The North-South Divide: Regional Change in Britain in the 1980s*, London: Paul Chapman Publishing.

Massey, D. (1984) *Spatial Divisions of Labour*, London: Macmillan.

Robson, B. T. (1988) *Those Inner Cities*, Oxford: Clarendon Press.

## FURTHER READING

As well as the works quoted above, three recent books focus on the trends identified in this chapter:

Ball, M., Gray, F., and McDowell, L. (1989) *The Transformation of Britain: Contemporary Social and Economic Change*, London: Fontana Press.

Hudson, R. and Williams, A. M. (1989) *Divided Britain*, London: Belhaven Press.

Smith, D. (1989) *North and South: Britain's Economic, Social and Political Divide*, London: Penguin.

# Index